An Introduction
to Philosophical
Inquiry

An Introduction to Philosophical Inquiry

Contemporary and Classical Sources

Second Edition

Edited by Joseph Margolis

Temple University

Alfred A. Knopf   New York

THIS IS A BORZOI BOOK
PUBLISHED BY ALFRED A. KNOPF, INC.

Second Edition

987654321

Library of Congress Cataloging in Publication Data

Margolis, Joseph Zalman, 1924–   comp.
    An introduction to philosophical inquiry.

    Includes bibliographies and index.
    1. Philosophy—Introductions.   2.   Philosophy—
Addresses, essays, lectures.   I.   Title.
BD21.M26   1978   108   77–14352
ISBN 0–394–31274–0

Manufactured in the United States of America

For the larger family

Preface to the Second Edition

It is now nearly ten years since the first edition of *An Introduction to Philosophical Inquiry* was issued. In the interim, a good many currents of educational taste have come and gone—some, of a rather dubious sort. In those ten years, introductory readers in philosophy had been surprisingly responsive to such fashions. In the search for what was loosely called relevance, some sampled the views of then currently influential men and movements, displacing sounder if less adventurous selections.

Philosophical education now seems to have returned to an emphasis on what is fully pertinent to the discipline. But the earlier tendency did yield several favorable developments. For one thing, it has enlarged the range of professional philosophy in areas of social concern, adding a measure of vigor that an earlier practice could not claim. For another thing, it has obliged us to trace the continuity of the central tradition into our own day more pointedly than is usually thought necessary.

Under the pressure of making effective use of space, and recognizing the impossibility of providing in one book a satisfactory selection from all fields of philosophy, I have reduced coverage in an effort to increase depth and to show how the central pursuits of philosophy have fared in our own time. I still insist on the features of the first edition—the provision of a historical sense of the principal questions and an introduction to characteristic contemporary views and methods of analysis. Also, I still favor a selection of papers that are eminently readable for students and yet of enduring interest to professional philosophers. I believe the present collection satisfies these objectives even more successfully than the first edition did.

The organization of the book has been considerably altered; and the introductions have all been rewritten and enlarged. Several rather recent currents have been sampled—for instance, the new rationalism associated with linguistic studies, the refinement of the theory of meaning, and the problem of personal identity.

I have dropped the sections on the philosophy of religion and on ethics and political philosophy: the first, because its puzzles do not seem tellingly central to the professional tradition; the other, because no sampling seems to promise a sufficiently useful selection within the intended scope of the book. Correspondingly, the short section introducing philosophy in general has been dropped—partly, because what philosophy is is amply illustrated in all its variety by the range of selections included; partly, because a general introductory statement has been provided in its place.

The result, I very much hope, is a fresh collection, bolder than most, more responsive to recent professional work, yet at the same time selected so as to be relatively free of arbitrary choice. The *Instructor's Manual to An Introduction* has been duly recast as well.

I have added headnotes on all the authors represented. For authors represented by several entries, the headnotes are with the first selection. Inevitably, in the effort to give a fair sense of their work and a brief word about their lives, a great many issues are mentioned that could not be developed within the span of an introductory reader. To have omitted them altogether would have been indefensible; to have included them is to have risked a certain measure of incomprehension. It is to be hoped that instructors will flesh out these résumés more congenially.

I have received advice from a number of colleagues—the best of it anonymous. And I have been encouraged by many in the belief that *An Introduction* may well be the best reader in the field. If it was not that in the first edition, I hope it may be so judged in the revision. I must single out Professor Richard Nagel of North Carolina State University and Ms. Jane Cullen of Random House for interest in the revision and for their sustaining enthusiasm, as well as several anonymous readers for Random House who have helped me considerably. Also, thanks are due to Ms. Ruth Bray, who prepared the manuscript.

J. M.

Philadelphia, Pennsylvania
August 1977

Contents

III

PERCEPTION AND THOUGHT   309

Perception

V

EXPLANATORY CONTEXTS: HUMAN BEHAVIOR AND PHYSICAL PHENOMENA 548

An Introduction
to Philosophical
Inquiry

General Introduction

In a book of readings in philosophy, one must expect to face the question of their proper use and, with it, the question of the nature of philosophy. It is not especially helpful to answer that philosophy is the pursuit of the truth about certain matters and then to enumerate those matters—for instance, whether time is real, whether physical objects are perceived by the senses, whether we can distinguish between dreaming and waking, whether we can know that something continues to exist when it is not perceived, whether what happens happens of necessity, whether something can be in two places at once, whether the future can be known, whether we can have knowledge of other minds, whether a private language is possible. Such a list is bewildering, however accurate it may be in some sense. To offer it as a helpful catalogue— perhaps with the intention of distinguishing philosophy from psychology or grammar or physics—is either disingenuous or silly.

The most difficult question for the beginner is how to construe and resolve questions of the sort enumerated. With this in mind, it is helpful to consider philosophy as a studio art—that is, to consider how philosophers actually work on problems. In a sense, a collection of philosophical essays—this collection, for instance—is a set of studio specimens of philosophers at work. The trouble is that it is often extremely difficult, without trained guidance, to formulate what might be called the studio problem that a set of philosophical artists have posed for themselves.

Philosophical questions are oddly remote and familiar. Classic answers have an air of being at once authoritative, impregnable, and bafflingly divergent. Philosophical texts move in a noticeably assured way, as if the procedures, the strategies, the tactics of professional debate were familiar to and agreed upon by all would-be contributors, and as if every reader could be expected to understand what issues were being contested. But the uninformed reader who begins his philosophical inquiries informally is bound to be puzzled about what Schopenhauer or Spinoza or Locke or Kant is attempting to do, quite as much as he is by what would justify their apparent claims. Furthermore, it is notoriously difficult to move from one philosophical exposition to another that is nominally concerned with the same or related issues, then judge with any assurance which is the sounder account.

Pedagogically, the situation both requires and invites the instructor's ingenuity. What the instructor must do is to locate, to expose, to appraise, to compare with others how a particular philosopher conceives his question and works to answer it. Without doubt, there is a large family of related methods of work that could be called philosophical analysis. But generalizations about these are bound to obscure the precision and finesse of each philosopher's program of inquiry.

Philosophy is itself the collection of inventions about how to investigate

1

conceptual matters. What a conceptual question is is itself a central question of philosophy. But as a first pass at an answer we may say this: In sorting conceptual questions, philosophers are attempting to analyze the meaning of fundamental notions—truth, knowledge, physical body, mind, meaning, identity —in such a way as to illuminate the entire set of distinctions that we use in discourse about anything and, in particular, to illuminate how each bears on other concepts systematically linked with that concept. For instance, the meaning of *truth* and the meaning of *knowledge* must be closely linked in order to make sense of the fact that we explain (provide a kind of knowledge about) how things actually work (about which, that is, certain truths may be stated).

No single method of philosophical work is more or less supported by the profession at large, and no straightforward canons are published anywhere that a budding philosopher could master in order to contribute to the developing corpus of philosophical science. True, philosophers suppose that their findings are testable, open to confirmation and disconfirmation. Here the studio image may be somewhat misleading, and one is tempted to substitute the image of the experimental laboratory.

But it is difficult to show that a theory of what is real, or of the nature of a person, or of what truth itself is, or of knowledge, is testable in the sense that the less profound issues of the empirical sciences can be tested. For example, it seems preposterous to suppose that a physicist or a chemist could determine, by means of any laboratory procedure, that a hypothesis about the nature of truth is true. Any of *his* truths already presuppose that the concept of truth is sufficiently settled to permit him to detail particular truths about freely falling bodies or the melting point of gold without fear of being challenged about the meaning of truth itself. And yet we have good reason to think that the questions of science lead directly and continuously to the questions of philosophy.

In a sense, genuinely memorable philosophers provide us with paradigms for investigating selected conceptual issues. Their ingenuity lies as much with exhibiting a convincing or plausible way of illuminating a conceptual puzzle as with the solutions they actually supply. There is hardly any sense in asking without further qualification whether Bertrand Russell's deservedly famous analysis of denoting phrases and of such sentences as "The present King of France is bald" (in Part IV) is valid. To some extent the point of the exercise lies in Russell's formulation of the original question to be resolved and in his reliance on a certain implicit model of adequacy—and congruent method of analysis. But to an equal extent the point lies in the proffered solution.

Those who disagree with Russell—P. F. Strawson, for instance (in Part IV also)—do not do so by showing an internal flaw in Russell's argument or by appealing to more accurate evidence of the sort Russell considers. Instead, they recast the question, reshape our sense of the relevant considerations, and thus subtly and implicitly revise the process of philosophical method itself. What the reader gains is a developing appreciation of the dynamics of philosophical inquiry, the very way in which related modes of investigation evolve, with the give-and-take of competing views.

It may be that from time to time powerful solutions to well-established puzzles are provided, in which there is hardly any noticeable shift or deviation from a familiar, almost canonical, way of working. By and large, such contributions are likelier in the context of philosophy wherever purely formal logic is adequate. But most of the movement of philosophy is bound up with the gradual elaboration of an inventive—often quite individual though by no means idiosyncratic—way of constructing a philosophical argument.

It is difficult, for instance, to find anyone who had the keenness of ear for the nuances of English that J. L. Austin exhibited in developing his unusual method of exploring the tenability of so-called sense-data theories (in Part III). The power of his account clearly depends on applying the distinctive method he himself first introduced. Other investigators are as likely to reject his procedures as his findings.

There are no discoveries here that can be entered in a handbook of solutions in the manner in which the specific gravity of physical elements can be collected and made increasingly accurate. To say this is to orient students correctly with respect to the philosophical tradition, but it is also to engender a sense of disorder, a sense of a lack of method and rigor, and even possibly a disposition to treat philosophy as ultimately pointless.

Nevertheless, it is the easiest thing in the world to persuade attentive students that there could not be any fixed way of investigating the characteristic questions of philosophy and that the questions remain important and unavoidable. Imagine asking *anyone* to say straight off *how* to determine what we mean when we say that given words and sentences have meaning, are meaningful, or how to decide *what* it is they mean (see Part IV). Clearly, with questions of such a sort, what we want are precise proposals about how to pursue the investigation fruitfully. Generalize the need and the game and you have a picture of the nature and the distinctive way of proceeding of philosophy itself.

What many students seem wedded to, *before* they study philosophy, is a conviction that all "objective" issues are cut and dried and that whatever cannot be made to conform to that conviction (roughly based on presumptions regarding the physical sciences) must be "subjective," a matter of "opinion," not of "fact," and beneath discussion in the context of discovering "the truth." It seems to take an enormous wrenching for students to grasp that the most settled matters rest on assumptions open to radical challenge as well as that there must be varied forms of investigative rigor that cannot be ranked along one simple scale.

Not only can we not ask (paraphrasing Aristotle) for more rigor than a given inquiry will allow; we cannot impose one kind of rigor on an inquiry to which it is not suited. If we speak of physics and chemistry as enlarging our knowledge of the physical world, what analogue of physics and chemistry would yield a true account of the nature of knowledge itself? Clearly, the inquiries of physics and chemistry *presuppose* a solution to the question of knowledge (see Part II); they are themselves incompetent to answer the question; and there is no familiar procedure (leaving aside mere intuitions) by which to resolve it. So we see that conceptual or philosophical issues cannot be eliminated.

Yet, paradoxically, the puzzle remains. How should we draw the essential distinctions on which our relatively confident science depends?

The point of an introductory course in philosophy, then, is to orient students to the most promising ways of organizing and illuminating the deepest conceptual issues generated by our familiar achievements—in science, in ordinary perceptual situations, in effective speech, in deliberate activity, in thinking, experiencing, intending, deciding, making. What we drive toward here, it seems, is a coherent and comprehensive account of the categories or concepts in terms of which those achievements are best understood.

In the context of a potential dispute about alternative ways of understanding smallish sectors of a presumably unified world, a great deal of philosophical work is occupied with presenting the reasons for favoring one conceptual line rather than another. It lies with the instructor's professional skill and with the acquired skill of newly oriented students to weave a skein of plausible argument by which to show the relevance of apparently isolated pieces written over the lifetime of Western civilization, in many idioms, with divergent interests and convictions, and with incomplete hints about the power of favored themes of unification. To do this is to risk a philosophical sketch of one's own—of what the central puzzles are, of how they should be viewed, and of which among the available accounts are the weaker or more promising proposals and analyses. There is no way to set this out abstractly that could be instructive to students who have not yet tried their hands at assessing the set pieces of a sampler of some sort.

All this suggests the importance of a careful selection of texts. The initial philosophy anthology, after all, traces for the student the approximate channels of thought for what is supposed to be the most effective orientation to the entire discipline. Probably, such a collection cannot fail to be partisan—not in the sense of favoring one author rather than another, but in the more profound sense of favoring one rather than another family of lines of investigation.

That particular papers are replaceable may be easily granted. What is arguable is whether certain lines of investigation are properly weighted and linked in a reasonable way with other supposedly important developments. The present anthology, therefore, has not merely selected specimens from the most important classical and modern authors. A great many of the most important authors are sampled, of course. But the point of the selections has in all instances been to provide a basis for mapping the development of a set of central issues in each of the principal areas of philosophical inquiry. Thus students may grasp the continuity that is peculiar to the history of philosophy as well as the most powerful or most promising or most revealing lines of exploration that have led to our present understanding of these issues.

This is not an easy undertaking. Philosophers are talkers and writers; in more than two thousand years the tradition has cluttered its attic with paper. No one has command of the entire literature, and apparently no one cares to have. But the introductory reader can serve forth at least one viable and plausible way of construing the central movement of the philosophical tradition. In this sense, it is an instrument for shaping that movement. Though superseded by more detailed study as well as by later samplers, it tends to confirm in its time that certain issues are most strategically related to the preparation of students for entry into the philosophical lists at whatever level of skill they may exhibit.

For example, before the appearance of Russell's paper "On Denoting" (Part IV), the problem of referring to and denoting things that admittedly do not exist could hardly have been considered central to an adequate philosophy. Russell's account has the force it does because he and Alfred North Whitehead also prepared a system of formal logic, which made it possible in terms of the logical particles or quantifiers "all" and "some" to account for the structure of sentences purporting to be about what does not exist. "Whatever there is is what exists" is a maxim that captures one of the deepest convictions of the most influential tradition in Anglo-American philosophy since the advent of Russell's paper in the first decade of the twentieth century.

Still, there seems to be a difference between referring to Pegasus, who is understood to be mythical, and referring to the present king of France as if to an existing king; so there is room for quarrel. And we seem to have many ways of referring to things. For instance, we refer to things we are already familiar with and intend to say something about, or we refer to something that satisfies a certain description even if we are not familiar with anything of that sort. We also seem to have difficulty in understanding how we first identify the thing we successfully refer to. Furthermore, there is a question about how much change is possible in what we purport to refer to before it becomes indefensible to say that the thing actually exists or continues to exist.

These questions—a number of which are canvassed in Parts II and IV—gain their significance from the original force of Russell's contribution. In a sense, therefore, it is no longer necessary that Russell's position be upheld. Whether it is or is not is undoubtedly decisive for certain currents in contemporary philosophy. But larger issues concerned with the application of Whitehead's and Russell's system of logic have already replaced the initial paper in importance. For example, logic is used to paraphrase certain critical sentences of natural languages so as to exhibit their logical structure explicitly. The question arises whether that use captures the import of the maxim, "Whatever there is is what exists."

The full force of the provisional adoption of Russell's and Whitehead's achievement, in order to entertain newer questions that it makes possible and that threaten to undermine the adoption itself, can hardly be appreciated apart from a close reading of the papers. But we may gain an inkling of the kind of quarrel generated by considering the point of such a question as the following. Is it false that Pegasus flies, because Pegasus doesn't exist; or is it true that there "was" a flying horse in spite of the fact that Pegasus never existed?

The issue is posed by Quine's account (Part IV) and is viewed there in a way that favors the maxim. We need only note here that the tradition has moved *through* the contributions of intervening papers since Russell's to view in a changing light the entire question of what there is, of what exists, of what can be denoted, of what can be referred to, of what we might mean by talking of possible and actual entities, of what constraints are imposed on what actually exists. More important, there is every reason to think the development of this particular line of inquiry down to our own day is central to a grasp of Anglo-

American philosophy. And yet a good many anthologies provide no papers on the issue. This illustrates that a volume of readings is a partisan selection favoring a certain understanding of the movement of philosophy.

In fact, this entire anthology has been constructed with that sense of strategy. Its distinction lies in its *not* having attempted to give a hearing to every current of thought, every philosopher of importance. In other words, it has resisted the philosophical scatter sometimes offered in the name of introducing the major authors or the major topics without heeding the lines of conceptual debate that now dominate the professional tradition. In each Part of the collection are essays that stand at the beginning of a current of investigation, now being pursued because it bears on other currents that are thought to be essential to formulating a comprehensive and viable philosophy. And in each Part is a selection of contemporary authors who are recognized as having contributed classic papers or who have suggested new lines of investigation of what remains unsolved.

Arbitrariness is inevitable as we approach our contemporaries. There is no escape; and there is no point in hedging, once we adopt the studio conception of philosophy. An essential element of the venture is to prophesy the direction of the strongest future currents. There is no doubt, for instance, that some contemporary papers that were selected for the first edition of this anthology have already lost their seemingly strong connection with the main directions. There is nothing to do but sort the entries again. At the same time, it would be manifestly unfair to skew a reader in such a direction as to favor developments that are untested in terms of the consensus of the profession. The issue is rather like that of Rousseau's famous General Will: It need not be the majority who decides, but a single voice must still search for the "spirit" of the profession.

The brief Introductions to the various Parts provide the rationale for the organization of the book, yielding at least one network of philosophical continuity. The preponderance of the papers would be ranked high by most professionals working within the Anglo-American tradition. The selection escapes arbitrariness to that extent, but it also blunts the division between a merely serviceable reader and the preferred materials of the most active professionals.

So it is quite likely that there are many ways of organizing the sequence of selections. What must be remembered is that these attempts at providing a unified picture of a set of philosophical selections, like the one in effect sketched by the Introductions, are themselves implicit accounts of how we are to understand a certain set of conceptual issues. They are in effect the schemata of further papers. Hence the problem of tact in introducing well-established contributions to well-established issues. Presumably, one wants the student to train his own sense of how to manage the conceptual questions raised in these papers: He needs a certain amount of guidance, but he must also be led to understand that there is no single correct way to assess the import of these papers.

In fact, one supposes the tyro to be an incipient philosopher. Particularly with regard to more recent entries, it is entirely likely that a clever student will on occasion bowl over a knowledgeable instructor with a sudden insight about a rich line of argument that has theretofore been overlooked or slighted. Students are sometimes unnerved by the prospect, because they hesitate to concede that an important professional discipline can claim a high measure of rigor and at one and the same time permit the insights of the relatively inexperienced to command professional respect. But that is what they must learn, and that is just what an anthology encouraging a studio conception and favoring the contemporary phase of the literature makes possible in a dramatic way.

In the same spirit, it needs to be emphasized that the papers collected here include a number of those chiefly debated by the profession at the present time. The student therefore ought to know that they stand reasonably close to the frontier of philosophy in pondering the collection. Hence their position is utterly unlike that of students who are regularly introduced, as in chemistry and physics, to what the profession frankly regards as an indefensible model of the structure of the physical world. The usual defense of the practice supposes that the model will stimulate inquiry and is open to suitable correction if or when the student pursues the subject further.

The position of the young philosopher is also unlike that of students in history and the social sciences. They are regularly introduced to the conclusions of selected authorities, without knowing how to inquire into the given issue by way of what are conceded to be the basic data or relatively less overinterpreted materials.

It is clearly difficult to characterize philosophy in an altogether neutral way. Every specification, however implicit, is a commitment to a particular way of exploring questions—even when it is intended in the most strictly neutral spirit. But this very fact highlights the particular sort of objectivity and advance that the tradition sustains. However partisan philosophers may be, serious students of any persuasion can, within limits, grasp one another's formulations as well as the alternative procedures by which the posited questions are presumed to be resolved.

Reverting to the productive literature that has followed the appearance of Russell's denoting paper, it is on the face of it equally reasonable to insist that everything there is, exists and that there are things (such as things we can refer to) that do not exist. It may seem impossible to reject either of these convictions or intuitions by a mere appeal to what we would ordinarily say. Yet it should be noted that this does not lead to an impasse. Partisans of either maxim are bound to try to show the systematic advantages of their own preference, the prospects of anomalies in either thesis, and the simplicity or naturalness or elegance of competing systems relative to supposedly neutral intuitions about cases to be accommodated.

The objectivity of philosophy, then, lies in the articulation of such competing systems, of the price of shifting from one to the other, and of the relative arbitrariness of disqualifying alternatives that may be incompatible with one another. Once we enter the debates of the papers provided, we cannot fail to see the incredible rigor of the enterprise: It is under the pressure of a dawning discovery of a new discipline that one comes to appreciate the warning of Aristotle already mentioned.

What ultimately links all the diverse elements of philosophical inquiry and assures some measure of common commitment is the acknowledgment of a shared world. Furthermore, philosophy has a strong historical sense, so the emergence of newer philosophical methods generally depends on reaction against the alleged limitations of earlier methods. As contemporary journals will confirm, the result is that disputes about philosophical issues tend to cut across philosophical persuasions: Advocates of quite different procedures often share common views about the testing of particular doctrines.

In contrast to the sciences (where the sense of authoritative, prevalent practice is much more dominant), the philosophical tradition preserves significant achievements in the form of questions that have been answered in accordance with this or that method. The philosophical tradition thus includes alternative ways of construing particular issues as well as alternative ways of resolving them. One hallmark of philosophical novelty is the provision of a new way of construing an old problem. Such novelty becomes increasingly difficult to exhibit and its achievement is correspondingly prized, if only because the tradition is then seen to preserve all relevant constructions, thereby taxing the ingenuity and insight of would-be contributors.

In the main, the questions to which philosophers address themselves are focused on items, often homely ones, that disputants through the ages have recognized as central. The bent stick in water, the melted piece of wax, the front surface of a tomato, the raising of an arm, the sun's rising tomorrow, the cat on the mat, and a thousand other examples testify to the resolve of philosophers to provide an analysis of common questions. In that sense, the alternative and subtly modified interpretations of what appear to be the same questions form a family of ways to view an issue. In one sense, philosophical progress is occupied with attaining a critical grasp of these developing families of possible ways of dealing with questions. Responsible partisans are those who, for reasons defended in the arena of exchange, are persuaded that one way of posing and answering a question is superior to all alternatives.

Thus there is a sense of the preservation of alternatives and of the comparative power of such alternatives. For one thing, there is always the need to avoid extravagant paradox, self-defeating solutions, contradictions, and extreme and unjustifiable departures from relatively neutral insights. Moreover, in a sense all philosophical questions are linked conceptually, and the power of partial solutions is gauged in terms of their compatibility with related solutions, as well as in terms of the scope and detail made possible through the methods by which they are generated.

Sometimes famous puzzles are associated with established areas of inquiry—how to justify induction, what we mean by the unity of the self, whether freedom and causality are compatible, whether we have evidence for the existence of the entities of microphysics, whether the mind and body interact. By these we gauge the comparative force and standing of particular theories in particular philosophical domains. A great deal of philosophical work is in fact conditional. We pursue the implications of a particular way of proceeding or of particular assumptions until they yield consequences that are relatively terminal, in the sense that we are provisionally committed to these implications or assumptions.

One result is that to a very great extent the history of philosophy has been a history of impressive failures, of large conceptions whose deficiencies have been laid bare for all to behold. These efforts are distinct from the historical respect appropriate in the presence of the cumulative achievement of the physical sciences. The seriousness and importance of the efforts lie in this: Try as we may, our own attempts to propose solutions for the puzzles that are part of the philosophical tradition cannot help imitating the solutions that have already left their mark on the tradition. This is emphatically not true in the usual work of the physical sciences.

That is why reading in philosophy ranges comfortably, and without any sense of inappropriate juxtaposition, from the statements of ancient Greek writers to those of our own age. For example, Plato's classic exploration, in *Thaeatetus* (see Part III), of the definition of knowledge has been recast (not simply revived) by Roderick Chisholm in our own time and has spawned a considerable and exciting debate (see Part II). With this reawakened interest come new prospects regarding certainty and the foundations of knowledge. But what is remarkable is that after more than two thousand years there is no incongruity when the original is compared with the speculations of contemporary discussants. This hardly signifies the hopelessness of the philosophical venture. What it indicates, rather, is the classic nature of certain ways of viewing the world.

In attempting to do philosophy, we are attracted by the possibility of formulating a coherent and comprehensive account of our fundamental concepts and categories—that is, the basic distinctions in terms of which we classify the things and features of the world. There is an impressive agreement about the concepts and categories that must be considered by philosophers: physical object, person, cause, intention, truth, meaning, statement, action, choice, perception, memory, concept, thought, value, knowledge, fact, certainty, necessity, possibility, God, history, science, art, existence, reality, and so on.

Much of philosophy, particularly in the grand tradition but increasingly in contemporary work, exhibits its power by way of its systematic command of important sets of concepts, each linked to the clusters of particular puzzles that the tradition has collected. The neophyte who confronts Leibniz's monads for the first time, or Plato's Forms, or Spinoza's God, cannot be expected to see the justification for positing such entities. It is only as one grasps the usefulness of these constructions in solving philosophical puzzles that the power and elegance of such projects can be appreciated. It is only through a familiarity with alternatives that the genius of particular solutions to these puzzles can be gauged. Hence even the discovery of an apparent stalemate between opposing philosophical systems or of the difficulty of comparing seemingly related alternatives enlarges our sense of the coherence of conceptual analysis.

Philosophy is thus a discipline primarily concerned with conceptual crisis. Given any sector of our investigations and findings about the world, we ask ourselves for an analysis of those concepts that are particularly relevant or fundamental, for an account of whether they are significantly alterable, for a sketch of what conceivable alternatives may be constructed, for an argument that demonstrates the superiority of preferred ways of answering questions.

Normally, although not always, methods for testing claims are reasonably settled in the empirical disciplines. When one answers a bona fide question there, one is not also bound to answer an implied and apparently deeper question about the relative power and admissibility of one's way of answering. Periodically, such issues do arise in the sciences, and we then absorb the disputes into the body of philosophy. But although there are always loyal adherents to particular ways of doing philosophy, there is never the sense in philosophy, as there is in science, of a prevailing way of working, to which professionals everywhere are more or less committed. Every prominent philosophical method has arisen in a field of perpetually changing contenders, each with its important champions and a fair number that may be regarded as peers.

The endlessly fascinating feature of all this exchange is that what may on first glance seem to lead to chaos and possibly to intellectual despair, in fact provides a powerful command over our conceptual endeavors. What we gain is the recognition of the limits of our conceptual framework, as well as the extent to which concepts and relations between concepts can be altered and with what consequences. Must time be directional? Can sensations be known in a public way? Can a language be constructed that would preserve certain fundamental functions of natural languages and yet omit singular terms? What are the minimal entities that we can admit to exist, compatibly with a given range of true statements? What are the consequences of denying that mental events have causal consequences? Is there any way to prove the existence of God?

What we seek to isolate are (1) the points in our conceptual scheme at which viable options are available, (2) the adjustments required in other critically affected portions of the scheme, and (3) the points at which changes are markedly difficult, if not impossible, to undertake systematically. The result, which develops with the tradition, is an understanding of the very conditions of intelligible discourse.

Generally speaking, we inquire into our concepts by reflecting on the languages in which they are expressed. In effect, then, philosophy is the exploration of those properties of our language or of any language with which, as by assertion and directive, we relate ourselves in various ways to the things of the world. As has been seen, we can describe the venture only in a general way; for each formula is designed either to prepare us for a particular enterprise, for use in a particular paper, or to help us collect, in summary form, a sense of the purpose of entire sets of detailed philosophical contributions. And these, after all, are the principal things.

I

MINDS AND
PERSONS

The central questions of philosophy concern the nature of humans and of the human mind. Even the characterization of the real world apart from people presupposes human cognition. Hence we are moved to reflect on our own nature —at least in order to account for supposed achievements. This draws us on to explore certain of the salient features of man. For one thing, only man appears to reflect on his nature, his accomplishments, his own mental states. For another, he alone has a sense of history, a mastery of language, a changing cultural experience. Reflecting on these features, we mark differences between mental and physical attributes as well as between human and other forms of animate and inanimate nature. These distinctions are central to what has come to be called the philosophy of mind, or philosophical psychology.

What mind and body are is a question that took its modern form in the inquiries of René Descartes (I:1).* He construed human beings in terms of thought and extension—the two being taken to be such different substances that interaction between mind and body was a mystery. One theme needs to be remembered in searching for a solution to Descartes's problem: that personal and mental attributes do seem quite different from those of things and those we call physical.

The contrast between attributes is much more compelling than the Cartesian division between substances. It is clear that having a certain weight and having a certain image or thought are different. It is less clear that stones and persons must be composed of different kinds of substance—say, matter and something immaterial such as spirit or thought. Nevertheless, it was probably Descartes's perception of the contrast between attributes that led him to formulate the division between substances. The question remains whether the attributes can be plausibly analyzed and related.

The Cartesian problem has haunted philosophy to this day in forms that are not much altered from their classic formulation. Thus the interaction between substances of apparently radically different sorts is central to the accounts of C. D. Broad (I:2) and Gilbert Ryle (I:3)—who, incidentally, reach quite incompatible conclusions.

In the accounts of Broad and Ryle there are inevitable metaphysical implications—that is, implications about the ultimate nature of reality. But their attention is focused primarily on the admissibility of causal interaction. Broad is inclined to dismiss assertions about radical differences in nature as too vague to be relevant. Ryle tends to substitute categorical questions for metaphysical questions. The sense of what Ryle views as a categorical question will be clear in the context of his paper. His idea is that distinctions regarding the mental and the physical cannot be jointly used in a meaningful way where causal interaction between the mental and the physical is intended.

But the Cartesian puzzle is not merely about causality. It also concerns the ultimate characterization of the nature of mind and body. In particular, Ryle

---

* Part I, paper 1. Designations like this are used in the introductions to show where pertinent papers are to be found.

12

questions the adequacy of interpreting mental phenomena in terms of behavior. Yet in stressing conceptual differences between mental and physical discourse, Ryle himself is opposed to viewing the mental as merely behavior or the tendency to behave in some particular way. Reference to the mental has another use for him, closely linked with the *reasons* for behaving in one way or another.

The distinctiveness of the Cartesian solution lies in the fact that Descartes's two fundamental substances are intelligible solely in terms of exclusive properties. They are, in fact, mental and physical properties raised to the status of being the ultimate stuff out of which things are composed. This alone suggests an economy. Some properties or attributes are not mental or physical and nevertheless do not threaten any causal relationships among things or the admission of things that do exhibit mental and/or physical properties. For instance, things are said to have numerical properties or the property of being different from other things. Such properties are neither mental nor physical, but they may be attributed to things that have mental or physical properties.

Descartes considered "thinking" and "extended substance" to be mutually exclusive. At the same time he held that human beings exhibit attributes of both sorts. Yet we need not refuse to ascribe mental and physical attributes to the same entity (see P. F. Strawson [I:7]). Similarly and perhaps more compellingly—since difference and numerical properties are rather different from the usual properties by which we describe things—things are said to have functional properties that may be manifested in alternative ways involving the mental and the physical (see Hilary Putnam [I:5]).

Suppose a variety of systems—machines, animals, humans, angels—are all ascribed the same functional property of preferring one thing to another. (Think of preference as an ordering of elements of some sort.) Preference could not be said to obtain except in ways appropriate to the systems that are said to exhibit preference. The movements and states of a machine need not resemble the movements and states of an angel in order to say that a certain robot and a certain angel both prefer one thing to another. In fact, in Putnam's view, mental attributes are functional attributes. Hence they cannot be analyzed solely in physical terms, since they may be realized or manifested in a variety of physical ways. We may not even be able to say what the limits of such realization are, and we need not, even in principle, preclude nonphysical forms of realization.

Two puzzles begin to emerge here, both grounded in Descartes's work. The first concerns the distinction between mental and physical attributes. The second concerns the distinction between entities that have minds (or, as in the tradition of Aristotle and St. Thomas Aquinas, entities that have souls) and entities that do not. Descartes tends to blend the two issues.

The modern version of the first distinction between mental and physical attributes dates from Franz Brentano's thesis (I:11), that the *intentional* is the mark of the mental. The intentional (or intentionality) is a technical notion of great power, the proper analysis of which is open to considerable disagreement. The original thesis has been much disputed and much refined. Yet in one form or another it remains at the center of current debates about the relationship between the mental and the physical. Brentano introduced certain criteria of intentionality that have since been sorted more clearly.

Despite the variety of ways in which intentionality has been explored, two issues have proved of paramount importance. The first issue is the feature of *directedness* or *aboutness,* regarding which some phenomena may be assigned "objects" that do not exist (as in hunting for unicorns). The second issue is the feature of intensionality, in which relevant sentences do not preserve truth values when other (so-called codesignative) terms are substituted (as in its being true that Tom believes that Cicero denounced Cataline, but false that Tom believes that Tully denounced Cataline, even though Cicero and Tully are the same man).

One may gain a sense of the scope of the intentional by considering that it ranges over such phenomena as remembering a dream, worrying about a lost object, imagining a trip to Cairo, calculating a sum, musing about an odd incident, wishing it were tomorrow. As James Cornman shows (I:12), not all intentional phenomena (or the sentences about them) behave intensionally. The distinction of the mental, then, proves to be particularly elusive.

Also, since mental and physical phenomena are ascribed properties that cannot be ascribed to one another, the question arises whether the mental can be reduced to the physical or at least conceded to obtain in a way that does not threaten the thesis that whatever is real is, ultimately, physical (see J. J. C. Smart [I:4]). In short, the movement of science since the Renaissance has been inclined to favor some form of materialism or physicalism; that is, that (materialism) everything there is is composed of matter or that (physicalism) everything there is is composed of matter and has none but physical properties.

The irony is that the one being responsible both for the achievement of the physical sciences and for their interpretation in favor of materialism is confronted with the puzzle of his own distinction—as well as the prospect that his own properties may not be analyzable in terms adequate to the physical sciences themselves. This is the persistent theme of Descartes's dualism as well as of the empiricist endeavors of David Hume (I:6). The thesis of empiricism is that all knowledge depends on what is originally discriminated in sensory impression. Wherever empiricism is pursued, the result is an impossible caricature of the knowing mind or self: witness Hume's conception of it as a "bundle of ideas." (But Hume always gives us a richer suggestion about our commonsense notions of the mind, that his own system cannot accommodate.) Precisely here, the issue regarding mental and physical attributes gives way to the issue regarding entities having and not having minds.

The tradition of Aristotle and Aquinas views the mind or soul as the form of the body of (animate) things. The issue of whether the soul is separable provides an additional interest in the career of Cartesian dualism. But the central reasons for the mind–body puzzle concern the difference between animate entities and persons and the conditions on which we may both individuate particular entities of each sort and reidentify each such entity through temporal and qualitative changes. John Locke's criterion of memory generates a muddle (see Anthony Quinton [I:8]); Hume's solution loses the prospect of self-identity. Nevertheless, both the Cartesian and empiricist traditions respected, even emphasized, the distinctive attributes of persons. An adequate account must do justice to both issues.

The signal attempt in the Anglo-American tradition came late in the twentieth century. It is the theory advanced by P. F. Strawson (I:7). His is an account of persons designed to accommodate the problem of ascribing mental and physical properties to the same entity. Strawson's solution is anti-dualistic about entities or substances but dualistic about attributes. That is, Strawson rejects Descartes's view that things are composed of two entirely different substances (extended substance and thinking substance) but agrees that mental and physical attributes are different.

Strawson never fully explains the relationship between persons and physical bodies or even the essential distinction between mental and physical properties. So the question persists as to the necessary and sufficient conditions for identifying and reidentifying persons—in particular, the role of memory and of the identity of a physical body (see Anthony Quinton [I:8]).

Strawson refused to identify persons with physical bodies, and Quinton explores the prospects of dualism. Their reflections suggest the issue of one's knowledge of one's own mental states—which stems from Descartes's original reflections.

In trying to distinguish the mental and the physical, Descartes sought to provide a foundation for the certainty of science (see Part II). More recently we have come to recognize certain asymmetries between one's knowledge of one's own mental states and one's knowledge of another's—in particular, differences regarding certainty and doubt about, and even the accessibility of, given mental states. J. J. C. Smart favors identifying the mind and the body, yet he denies that a physical paraphrase of mental descriptions can be given. The identity thesis would seem to preclude asymmetries. Strawson resists the identity but concedes the asymmetry, at least to the extent that one does not have to rely on behavioral criteria in order to come to know one's own mental states, whereas one *does* have to rely on public or behavioral criteria in order to know that another is in a certain mental state. But what the relationship is between persons and bodies, Strawson does not say.

The deeper puzzle on which these disputes rest concerns the question of how we come to have knowledge at all of other minds. The classical empiricist position (see Bertrand Russell [I:11]) relies on *induction* from analogy. For instance, when I am in pain I wince or behave in similar ways. By analogy, I conclude that when another winces or behaves similarly, he too is in pain.

According to the view of Ludwig Wittgenstein and his followers (see Norman Malcolm [I:11]), the argument from analogy is inherently defective and itself generates the puzzle. Malcolm's solution requires a public language for private mental states. It was in virtue of this that Strawson conceded an asymmetry between knowledge of one's own mental states and knowledge of another's. In effect, Malcolm denies that there is any first-person knowledge of mental states and reinterprets first-person reports as a form of newly learned behavior.

The result is somewhat paradoxical, since first-person knowledge of one's own mental states seems so intimate and familiar. What is more, it is not clear that Malcolm's thesis captures Wittgenstein's intention. In any event, the question of the privacy of mental states and of privileged access to them—not to mention the possibility of a private language—seems to threaten the plausibility of Smart's identity thesis (that the mental is identical with the physical) and of similar doctrines.

The analysis of minds and persons thus is a thicket of puzzles. The principal lines of inquiry intersect. To pursue any one of them is to generate the puzzles associated with another. It is perhaps the appreciation of just this feature of the puzzles known as the mind–body problem that distinguishes Descartes's original account. The strands may be sorted thus:

1. Whether mental and physical attributes are uniformly similar among themselves and uniformly different from one another; and, if they are, in what respect they differ.
2. How any entity can be ascribed both mental and physical attributes; or what, in this sense, it means to say that an entity (creature, person, machine, angel) has a mind or soul.
3. Whether there is a difference between physical bodies and animate creatures or persons; and, if there is, whether the difference entails fundamentally different substances.
4. How persons are distinguished under conditions of change.
5. Under what conditions, if any, we come to know something of other minds; and whether we can be said to know something of our own minds.

The complexity and interrelatedness of these issues are reasonably clear. The last topic, in fact, is often explored separately in the context of the nature and varieties of knowledge. Thus in a sense philosophical inquiry is seamless. More narrowly construed, the resolution of the worries of the last topic concerns the avoidance of skepticism (doubts about the very prospect of knowledge) and solipsism (confinement to knowledge of one's own mental states).

On Malcolm's view, for instance, the accounts of John Stuart Mill and, implicitly, Bertrand Russell insure that we cannot be said to have knowledge of the mental states of others. Also, Malcolm holds, the traditional thesis that one is directly aware of one's own mental states threatens us with the conclusion that one knows only the content of one's own mind and cannot know anything about another's. Hence the importance of a public language for both Strawson and Malcolm, regardless of their different assessments of the possibility of first-person knowledge.

Before Wittgenstein's argument, the basis for our knowledge of other minds (in particular, of the pains, feelings, and thoughts of others) was cast in terms of the argument from analogy. This argument admits that we do have independent knowledge of our own sensations and that our knowledge of another's sensations entails terms first used for private experience. But as Malcolm interprets Wittgenstein's challenge, not only is the theory of a private language unintelligible but the doctrine of knowledge of one's own sensations is misleading if not untenable.

Others allow for the relevant sorts of knowledge of one's own mind without subscribing to the argument from analogy. Nevertheless, *if* knowledge of one's own mental states is conceded, then one is tempted, because of the peculiarity of our awareness of pains, thoughts, intentions, mental images, and the like, to speak of *certain* knowledge. This is the master theme of Descartes's philosophy, of course. And *if* knowledge of pains, images, thoughts, and the like is conceded, then the attraction of Cartesian dualism, whatever its faults and extravagances, remains impressive.

The Mind–Body Problem

1

René Descartes

The Human Mind and the Human Body

René Descartes (1596–1650) was possibly the greatest of the founders of modern philosophy and modern thought. His influence is as vigorous today as it has been through the whole course of modern Western philosophy—as much in the Anglo-American tradition as in the Continental, though with rather different emphasis. He seems to have been so worried by the church's condemnation of Galileo's defense of the Copernican thesis that he suppressed one book (Le Monde) *on that account. What is more, the formulation of what he later published appears to have been adjusted so as to make his more controversial views less objectionable to the authorities. This has, of course, complicated the explication of his doctrines, notably with regard to the treatment of the mind–body problem and his grounds for relying on the so-called method of doubt.*

Descartes's earliest work, Rules for the Direction of the Mind, *written about the age of 30 but never completed, indicates his original preoccupation with methodological aspects of rational and scientific inquiry. His contemporary reputation was assured with the publication of several essays including the famous* Discourse on Method *(1637), or* Discourse on the Method, *since he had definite rules in mind by which to pursue any inquiry. The* Discourse *and the* Meditations on First Philosophy—*including the objections of the leading philosophers of the day and his replies—are probably his best-known and most influential statements. But his output was extensive. Even at the end of his life, cut short by the rigors of the Swedish winter after he had reluctantly agreed to travel to Stockholm and instruct Queen Christina, he was engaged in important research.*

Descartes's most familiar doctrines include his dualism and his method. By dualism, we may understand his insistence that the essence of the mind is to think, which is different from the essence of the body. By the method, we may understand his conviction that by reflecting on its own content, the mind is capable of immediately discerning certain indubitable truths.

These are cautious and minimal formulations of Descartes's admittedly controversial and much-debated doctrines. But the developing quarrels about these

From "Meditations on First Philosophy," in *The Philosophical Works of Descartes,* E. S. Haldane and G. R. T. Ross, trans. (Cambridge: Cambridge University Press, 1931), Meditation VI, pp. 187–198. Reprinted by permission of the publisher.

issues, linked to the interpretation of Descartes's texts, constitute the central motivation of much of later Western philosophy.

Meditation VI

Of the Existence of Material Things, and of the Real Distinction Between the Soul and Body of Man

. . .

. . . I shall recall to my memory those matters which I hitherto held to be true, as having perceived them through the senses, and the foundations on which my belief has rested; in the next place I shall examine the reasons which have since obliged me to place them in doubt; in the last place I shall consider which of them I must now believe.

First of all, then, I perceived that I had a head, hands, feet, and all other members of which this body—which I considered as a part, or possibly even as the whole, of myself—is composed. Further I was sensible that this body was placed amidst many others, from which it was capable of being affected in many different ways, beneficial and hurtful, and I remarked that a certain feeling of pleasure accompanied those that were beneficial, and pain those which were harmful. And in addition to this pleasure and pain, I also experienced hunger, thirst, and other similar appetites, as also certain corporeal inclinations towards joy, sadness, anger, and other similar passions. And outside myself, in addition to extension, figure, and motions of bodies, I remarked in them hardness, heat, and all other tactile qualities, and, further, light and colour, and scents and sounds, the variety of which gave me the means of distinguishing the sky, the earth, the sea, and generally all the other bodies, one from the other. And certainly, considering the ideas of all these qualities which presented themselves to my mind, and which alone I perceived properly or immediately, it was not without reason that I believed myself to perceive objects quite different from my thought, to wit, bodies from which those ideas proceeded; for I found by experience that these ideas presented themselves to me without my consent being requisite, so that I could not perceive any object, however desirous I might be, unless it were present to the organs of sense; and it was not in my power not to perceive it, when it was present. And because the ideas which I received through the senses were much more lively, more clear, and even, in their own way, more distinct than any of those which I could of myself frame in meditation, or than those I found impressed on my memory, it appeared as though they could not have proceeded from my mind, so that they must necessarily have been produced in me by some other things. And having no knowledge of those objects excepting the knowledge which the ideas themselves gave me, nothing was more likely to occur to my mind than that the objects were similar to the ideas which were caused. And because I likewise remembered that I had formerly made use of my senses rather than my reason, and recognised that the ideas which I formed of myself were not so distinct as those which I perceived through the senses, and that they were most frequently even composed of portions of these last, I persuaded myself easily that I had no idea in my mind which had not formerly come to me through the senses. Nor was it without some reason that I believed that this body (which by a certain special right I call my own) belonged to me more properly and more strictly than any other; for in fact I could never be separated from it as from other bodies; I experienced in it and on account of it all my appetites and affections, and finally I was touched by the feeling of pain and the titillation of pleasure in its parts, and not in the parts of other bodies which were separated from it. But when I inquired, why, from some, I know not what, painful sensation, there follows sadness of mind, and from the pleasurable sensation there arises joy, or why this mysterious pinching of the stomach which I call hunger causes me to desire to eat, and dryness of throat causes a desire to drink, and so on, I could give no reason excepting that nature taught me so; for there is certainly no affinity (that I at least can understand) between the craving of the stomach and the desire to eat, any more than between the perception of whatever causes pain and the thought of sadness which arises from this perception. And in the same way it appeared to me that I had learned from nature all the other judgments which I formed regarding the objects of my senses, since I remarked that these judgments were formed in me before I had the leisure to weigh and consider any reasons which might oblige me to make them.

But afterwards many experiences little by little destroyed all the faith which I had rested in my senses; for I from time to time observed that those towers which from afar appeared to me to be round, more closely observed seemed square, and that colossal statues raised on the summit of these towers, appeared as quite tiny statues when viewed from the bottom; and so in an infinitude of other cases I found error in judgments founded on the external senses. And not only in those founded on the external senses, but even in those founded on the internal as well; for is there anything more intimate or more internal than pain? And yet I have learned from some persons whose arms or legs have been cut off, that they sometimes seemed to feel pain in the part which had been amputated, which made me think that I could not be quite certain that it was a certain member which pained me, even although I felt pain in it. And to those grounds of doubt I have lately added two others, which are very general; the first is that I never have believed myself to feel anything in waking moments which I cannot also sometimes believe myself to feel when I sleep, and as I do not think that these things which I seem to feel in sleep, proceed from objects outside of me, I do not see any reason why I should have this belief regarding objects which I seem to perceive while awake. The other was that being still ignorant, or rather supposing myself to be ignorant, of the author of my being, I saw nothing to prevent me from having been so constituted by nature that I might be deceived even in matters which seemed to me to be most certain. And as to the grounds on which I was formerly persuaded of the truth of sensible objects, I had not much trouble in replying to them. For since nature seemed to cause me to lean towards many things from which reason repelled me, I did not believe that I should trust much to the teachings of nature. And although the ideas which I receive by the senses do not depend on my will, I did not think that one should for that reason conclude that they proceeded from things different from myself, since possibly some faculty might be discovered in me—though hitherto unknown to me—which produced them.

But now that I begin to know myself better, and to discover more clearly the author of my being, I do not in truth think that I should rashly admit all the matters which the senses seem to teach us, but, on the other hand, I do not think that I should doubt them all universally.

And first of all, because I know that all things which I apprehend clearly and distinctly can be created by God as I apprehend them, it suffices that I am able to apprehend one thing apart from another clearly and distinctly in order to be certain that the one is different from the other, since they may be made to exist in separation at least by the omnipotence of God; and it does not signify by what power this separation is made in order to compel me to judge them to be different: and, therefore, just because I know certainly that I exist, and that meanwhile I do not remark that any other thing necessarily pertains to my nature or essence, excepting that I am a thinking thing, I rightly conclude that my essence consists solely in the fact that I am a thinking thing [or a substance whose whole essence or nature is to think]. And although possibly (or rather certainly, as I shall say in a moment) I possess a body with which I am very intimately conjoined, yet because, on the one side, I have a clear and distinct idea of myself inasmuch as I am only a thinking and unextended thing, and as, on the other, I possess a distinct idea of body, inasmuch as it is only an extended and unthinking thing, it is certain that this I [that is to say, my soul by which I am what I am], is entirely and absolutely distinct from my body, and can exist without it.

I further find in myself faculties employing modes of thinking peculiar to themselves, to wit, the faculties of imagination and feeling, without which I can easily conceive myself clearly and distinctly as a complete being; while, on the other hand, they cannot be so conceived apart from me, that is without an intelligent substance in which they reside, for [in the notion we have of these faculties, or, to use the language of the Schools] in their formal concept, some kind of intellection is comprised, from which I infer that they are distinct from me as its modes are from a thing. I observe also in me some other faculties such as that of change of position, the assumption of different figures and such like, which cannot be conceived, any more than can the preceding, apart from some substance to which they are attached, and consequently cannot exist without it; but it is very clear that these faculties, if it be true that they exist, must be attached to some corporeal or extended substance, and not to an intelligent substance, since in the clear and distinct conception of these there is some sort of extension found to be present, but no intellection at all. There is certainly further in me a certain passive faculty of perception, that is, of receiving and recognising the ideas of sensible things, but this would be useless to me [and I could in no way avail myself of it], if there were not either in me or in some other thing another active faculty capable of forming and producing these ideas. But this active faculty cannot exist in me [inasmuch as I am a thing that thinks] seeing that it does not presuppose thought, and also that those ideas are often produced in me without my contributing in any way to the same, and often even against my will; it is thus necessarily the case that the faculty resides in some substance different from me in which all the reality which is objectively in the ideas that are produced by this faculty is formally or eminently contained, as I remarked before. And this substance is either a body, that is, a corporeal nature in which there is contained formally [and really] all that which is objectively [and by representation] in those ideas, or it is God Himself, or some other creature more noble than body in which that same is contained eminently. But, since God is no deceiver, it is very manifest that He does not communicate to me these ideas immediately and by Himself, nor yet by the intervention of some creature in which their reality is not formally, but only eminently, contained. For since He has given me no faculty to recognise that this is the case, but, on the other hand, a very great inclination to believe [that they are sent to me or] that they are conveyed to me by corporeal objects, I do not see how He could be defended from the accusation of deceit if these ideas were produced by causes other than corporeal objects. Hence we must allow that corporeal things exist. However, they are perhaps not exactly what we perceive by the senses, since this comprehension by the senses is in many instances very obscure and confused; but we must at least admit that all things which I conceive in them clearly and distinctly, that is to say, all things which, speaking generally, are comprehended in the object of pure mathematics, are truly to be recognised as external objects.

As to other things, however, which are either particular only, as, for example, that the sun is of such and such a figure, etc., or which are less clearly and distinctly conceived, such as light, sound, pain and the like, it is certain that although they are very dubious and uncertain, yet on the sole ground that God is not a deceiver, and that consequently He has not permitted any falsity to exist in my opinion which He has not likewise given me the faculty of correcting, I may assuredly hope to conclude that I have within me the means of arriving at the truth even here. And first of all there is no doubt that in all things which nature teaches me there is some truth contained; for by nature, considered in general, I now understand no other thing than either God Himself or else the order and disposition which God has established in created things; and by my nature in particular I understand no other thing than the complexus of all the things which God has given me.

But there is nothing which this nature teaches me more expressly [nor more sensibly] than that I have a body which is adversely affected when I feel pain, which has need of food or drink when I experience the feelings of hunger and thirst, and so on; nor can I doubt there being some truth in all this.

Nature also teaches me by these sensations of pain, hunger, thirst, etc., that I am not only lodged in my body as a pilot in a vessel, but that I am very closely united to it, and so to speak so intermingled with it that I seem to compose with it one whole. For if that were not the case, when my body is hurt, I, who am merely a thinking thing, should not feel pain, for I should perceive this wound by the understanding only, just as the sailor perceives by sight when something is damaged in his vessel; and when my body has need of drink or food, I should clearly understand the fact without being warned of it by confused feelings of hunger and thirst. For all these sensations of hunger, thirst, pain, etc.

are in truth none other than certain confused modes of thought which are produced by the union and apparent intermingling of mind and body.

Moreover, nature teaches me that many other bodies exist around mine, of which some are to be avoided, and others sought after. And certainly from the fact that I am sensible of different sorts of colours, sounds, scents, tastes, heat, hardness, etc., I very easily conclude that there are in the bodies from which all these diverse sense-perceptions proceed certain variations which answer to them, although possibly these are not really at all similar to them. And also from the fact that amongst these different sense-perceptions some are very agreeable to me and others disagreeable, it is quite certain that my body (or rather myself in my entirety, inasmuch as I am formed of body and soul) may receive different impressions agreeable and disagreeable from the other bodies which surround it.

But there are many other things which nature seems to have taught me, but which at the same time I have never really received from her, but which have been brought about in my mind by a certain habit which I have of forming inconsiderate judgments on things; and thus it may easily happen that these judgments contain some error. Take, for example, the opinion which I hold that all space in which there is nothing that affects [or makes an impression on] my senses is void; that in a body which is warm there is something entirely similar to the idea of heat which is in me; that in a white or green body there is the same whiteness or greenness that I perceive; that in a bitter or sweet body there is the same taste, and so on in other instances; that the stars, the towers, and all other distant bodies are of the same figure and size as they appear from far off to our eyes, etc. But in order that in this there should be nothing which I do not conceive distinctly, I should define exactly what I really understand when I say that I am taught somewhat by nature. For here I take nature in a more limited signification than when I term it the sum of all the things given me by God, since in this sum many things are comprehended which only pertain to mind (and to these I do not refer in speaking of nature) such as the notion which I have of the fact that what has once been done cannot ever be undone and an infinitude of such things which I know by the light of nature [without the help of the body]; and seeing that it comprehends many other matters besides which only pertain to body, and are no longer here contained under the name of nature, such as the quality of weight which it possesses and the like, with which I also do not deal; for in talking of nature I only treat of those things given by God to me as a being composed of mind and body. But the nature here described truly teaches me to flee from things which cause the sensation of pain, and seek after the things which communicate to me the sentiment of pleasure and so forth; but I do not see that beyond this it teaches me that from those diverse sense-perceptions we should ever form any conclusion regarding things outside of us, without having [carefully and maturely] mentally examined them beforehand. For it seems to me that it is mind alone, and not mind and body in conjunction, that is requisite to a knowledge of the truth in regard to such things. Thus, although a star makes no larger an impression on my eye than the flame of a little candle there is yet in me no real or positive propensity impelling me to believe that it is not greater than that flame;

but I have judged it to be so from my earliest years, without any rational foundation. And although in approaching fire I feel heat, and in approaching it a little too near I even feel pain, there is at the same time no reason in this which could persuade me that there is in the fire something resembling this heat any more than there is in it something resembling the pain; all that I have any reason to believe from this is, that there is something in it, whatever it may be, which excites in me these sensations of heat or of pain. So also, although there are spaces in which I find nothing which excites my senses, I must not from that conclude that these spaces contain no body; for I see in this, as in other similar things, that I have been in the habit of perverting the order of nature, because these perceptions of sense having been placed within me by nature merely for the purpose of signifying to my mind what things are beneficial or hurtful to the composite whole of which it forms a part, and being up to that point sufficiently clear and distinct, I yet avail myself of them as though they were absolute rules by which I might immediately determine the essence of the bodies which are outside me, as to which, in fact, they can teach me nothing but what is most obscure and confused.

But I have already sufficiently considered how, notwithstanding the supreme goodness of God, falsity enters into the judgments I make. Only here a new difficulty is presented—one respecting those things the pursuit or avoidance of which is taught me by nature, and also respecting the internal sensations which I possess, and in which I seem to have sometimes detected error [and thus to be directly deceived by my own nature]. To take an example, the agreeable taste of some food in which poison has been intermingled may induce me to partake of the poison, and thus deceive me. It is true, at the same time, that in this case nature may be excused, for it only induces me to desire food in which I find a pleasant taste, and not to desire the poison which is unknown to it; and thus I can infer nothing from this fact, except that my nature is not omniscient, at which there is certainly no reason to be astonished, since man, being finite in nature, can only have knowledge the perfectness of which is limited.

But we not unfrequently deceive ourselves even in those things to which we are directly impelled by nature, as happens with those who when they are sick desire to drink or eat things hurtful to them. It will perhaps be said here that the cause of their deceptiveness is that their nature is corrupt, but that does not remove the difficulty, because a sick man is none the less truly God's creature than he who is in health; and it is therefore as repugnant to God's goodness for the one to have a deceitful nature as it is for the other. And as a clock composed of wheels and counter-weights no less exactly observes the laws of nature when it is badly made, and does not show the time properly, than when it entirely satisfies the wishes of its maker, and as, if I consider the body of a man as being a sort of machine so built up and composed of nerves, muscles, veins, blood and skin, that though there were no mind in it at all, it would not cease to have the same motions as at present, exception being made of those movements which are due to the direction of the will, and in consequence depend upon the mind [as opposed to those which operate by the disposition of its organs], I easily recognise that it would be as natural to this body, supposing it to be, for example, dropsical, to suffer the parchedness of the throat which usually signifies to the mind the feeling of thirst, and to be disposed by this parched feeling to move the nerves and other parts in the way requisite for drinking, and thus to augment its malady and do harm to itself, as it is natural to it, when it has no indisposition, to be impelled to drink for its good by a similar cause. And although, considering the use to which the clock has been destined by its maker, I may say that it deflects from the order of its nature when it does not indicate the hours correctly; and as, in the same way, considering the machine of the human body as having been formed by God in order to have in itself all the movements usually manifested there, I have reason for thinking that it does not follow the order of nature when, if the throat is dry, drinking does harm to the conservation of health, nevertheless I recognise at the same time that this last mode of explaining nature is very different from the other. For this is but a purely verbal characterisation depending entirely on my thought, which compares a sick man and a badly constructed clock with the idea which I have of a healthy man and a well made clock, and it is hence extrinsic to the things to which it is applied; but according to the other interpretation of the term nature I understand something which is truly found in things and which is therefore not without some truth.

But certainly although in regard to the dropsical body it is only so to speak to apply an extrinsic term when we say that its nature is corrupted, inasmuch as apart from the need to drink, the throat is parched; yet in regard to the composite whole, that is to say, to the mind or soul united to this body, it is not a purely verbal predicate, but a real error of nature, for it to have thirst when drinking would be hurtful to it. And thus it still remains to inquire how the goodness of God does not prevent the nature of man so regarded from being fallacious.

In order to begin this examination, then, I here say, in the first place, that there is a great difference between mind and body, inasmuch as body is by nature always divisible, and the mind is entirely indivisible. For, as a matter of fact, when I consider the mind, that is to say, myself inasmuch as I am only a thinking thing, I cannot distinguish in myself any parts, but apprehend myself to be clearly one and entire; and although the whole mind seems to be united to the whole body, yet if a foot, or an arm, or some other part, is separated from my body, I am aware that nothing has been taken away from my mind. And the faculties of willing, feeling, conceiving, etc. cannot be properly speaking said to be its parts, for it is one and the same mind which employs itself in willing and in feeling and understanding. But it is quite otherwise with corporeal or extended objects, for there is not one of these imaginable by me which my mind cannot easily divide into parts, and which consequently I do not recognise as being divisible; this would be sufficient to teach me that the mind or soul of man is entirely different from the body, if I had not already learned it from other sources.

I further notice that the mind does not receive the impressions from all parts of the body immediately, but only from the brain, or perhaps even from one of its smallest parts, to wit, from that in which the common sense[3] is said to reside, which, whenever it is disposed in the same particular way, conveys the same thing to the mind, although meanwhile the other portions of the body may be differently disposed, as is testified by innumerable experiments which it is unnecessary here to recount.

I notice, also, that the nature of body is such that none of its parts can be moved by another part a little way off which cannot also be moved in the same way by each one of the parts which are between the two, although this more remote part does not act at all. As, for example, in the cord ABCD [which is in tension] if we pull the last part D, the first part A will not be moved in any way differently from what would be the case if one of the intervening parts B or C were pulled, and the last part D were to remain unmoved. And in the same way, when I feel pain in my foot, my knowledge of physics teaches me that this sensation is communicated by means of nerves dispersed through the foot, which, being extended like cords from there to the brain, when they are contracted in the foot, at the same time contract the inmost portions of the brain which is their extremity and place of origin, and then excite a certain movement which nature has established in order to cause the mind to be affected by a sensation of pain represented as existing in the foot. But because these nerves must pass through the tibia, the thigh, the loins, the back and the neck, in order to reach from the leg to the brain, it may happen that although their extremities which are in the foot are not affected, but only certain ones of their intervening parts [which pass by the loins or the neck], this action will excite the same movement in the brain that might have been excited there by a hurt received in the foot, in consequence of which the mind will necessarily feel in the foot the same pain as if it had received a hurt. And the same holds good of all the other perceptions of our senses.

I notice finally that since each of the movements which are in the portion of the brain by which the mind is immediately affected brings about one particular sensation only, we cannot under the circumstances imagine anything more likely than that this movement, amongst all the sensations which it is capable of impressing on it, causes mind to be affected by that one which is best fitted and most generally useful for the conservation of the human body when it is in health. But experience makes us aware that all the feelings with which nature inspires us are such as I have just spoken of; and there is therefore nothing in them which does not give testimony to the power and goodness of the God [who has produced them]. Thus, for example, when the nerves which are in the feet are violently or more than usually moved, their movement, passing through the medulla of the spine to the inmost parts of the brain, gives a sign to the mind which makes it feel somewhat, to wit, pain, as though in the foot, by which the mind is excited to do its utmost to remove the cause of the evil as dangerous and hurtful to the foot. It is true that God could have constituted the nature of man in such a way that this same movement in the brain would have conveyed something quite different to the mind; for example,

---

[3] *Sensus communis.*

it might have produced consciousness of itself either in so far as it is in the brain, or as it is in the foot, or as it is in some other place between the foot and the brain, or it might finally have produced consciousness of anything else whatsoever; but none of all this would have contributed so well to the conservation of the body. Similarly, when we desire to drink, a certain dryness of the throat is produced which moves its nerves, and by their means the internal portions of the brain; and this movement causes in the mind the sensation of thirst, because in this case there is nothing more useful to us than to become aware that we have need to drink for the conservation of our health; and the same holds good in other instances.

From this it is quite clear that, notwithstanding the supreme goodness of God, the nature of man, inasmuch as it is composed of mind and body, cannot be otherwise than sometimes a source of deception. For if there is any cause which excites, not in the foot but in some part of the nerves which are extended between the foot and the brain, or even in the brain itself, the same movement which usually is produced when the foot is detrimentally affected, pain will be experienced as though it were in the foot, and the sense will thus naturally be deceived; for since the same movement in the brain is capable of causing but one sensation in the mind, and this sensation is much more frequently excited by a cause which hurts the foot than by another existing in some other quarter, it is reasonable that it should convey to the mind pain in the foot rather than in any other part of the body. And although the parchedness of the throat does not always proceed, as it usually does, from the fact that drinking is necessary for the health of the body, but sometimes comes from quite a different cause, as is the case with dropsical patients, it is yet much better that it should mislead on this occasion than if, on the other hand, it were always to deceive us when the body is in good health; and so on in similar cases.

·   ·   ·

2

C. D. Broad

The Traditional Problem
of Body and Mind

C. D. Broad, who was Knightbridge Professor of Moral Philosophy at Cambridge University until his retirement in 1953, was one of the most prolific and wide-ranging English philosophers of the twentieth century. His output is almost unmatched. It ranges over nearly every important philosophical issue of his time, with characteristic precision and accuracy. His work is an inescapable reference more than an imaginative influence among later philosophers. Unlike his somewhat older contemporaries, G. E. Moore and Bertrand Russell, he is notably without followers. His best-known works are The Mind and Its Place in Nature *(1925) and various papers exploring in a sympathetic way the familiar problems about sense data. His own muted dualistic tendencies he was inclined to pursue, much as with the puzzles about sense data, in an empirical manner, with the certainty that at least some forms of mind–body interaction were reasonably well confirmed. His distinction between bodies and "sensa" (the immediate contents of sensory awareness) led also to a strong empirical interest in psychical phenomena* (Lectures on Psychical Research, 1963).

. . . There is a question which has been argued about for some centuries now under the name of "Interaction"; this is the question whether minds really do act on the organisms which they animate, and whether organisms really do act on the minds which animate them. (I must point out at once that I imply no particular theory of mind or body by the word "to animate". I use it as a perfectly neutral name to express the fact that a certain mind is connected in some peculiarly intimate way with a certain body and under normal conditions with no other body. This is a fact even on a purely behaviouristic theory of mind; on such a view to say that the mind M animates the body B would mean that the body B, in so far as it behaves in certain ways, *is* the mind M. A body which did not act in these ways would be said not to be animated by a mind. And a different Body B′, which acted in the same general way as B, would be said to be animated by a different mind M′.)

The problem of Interaction is generally discussed at the level of enlightened common-sense; where it is assumed that we know pretty well what we mean by "mind", by "matter" and by "causation". Obviously no solution which is reached at that level can claim to be ultimate. If what we call "matter" should turn out to be a collection of spirits of low intelligence, as Leibniz thought, the argument that mind and body are so unlike that their interaction is impossible would

From C. D. Broad, *The Mind and Its Place in Nature* (London: 1925), Chap. III, pp. 95–103. Reprinted by permission of Routledge & Kegan Paul Ltd. and Humanities Press, Inc., New Jersey.

become irrelevant. Again, if causation be nothing but regular sequence and concomitance, as some philosophers have held, it is ridiculous to regard psycho-neural parallelism and interaction as mutually exclusive alternatives. For inter-action will mean no more than parallelism, and parallelism will mean no less than interaction. Nevertheless I am going to discuss the arguments here at the common-sense level, because they are so incredibly bad and yet have imposed upon so many learned men.

We start then by assuming a developed mind and a developed organism as two distinct things, and by admitting that the two are now intimately con-nected in some way or other which I express by saying that "this mind *animates* this organism". We assume that bodies are very much as enlightened common-sense believes them to be; and that, even if we cannot define "causation", we have some means of recognising when it is present and when it is absent. The question then is: "Does a mind ever act on the body which it animates, and does a body ever act on the mind which animates it?" The answer which common-sense would give to both questions is: "Yes, certainly." On the face of it my body acts on my mind whenever a pin is stuck into the former and a painful sensation thereupon arises in the latter. And, on the face of it, my mind acts on my body whenever a desire to move my arm arises in the former and is followed by this movement in the latter. Let us call this common-sense view "Two-sided Interaction". Although it seems so obvious it has been denied by probably a majority of philosophers and a majority of physiologists. So the question is: "Why should so many distinguished men, who have studied the subject, have denied the apparently obvious fact of Two-sided Interaction?"

The arguments against Two-sided Interaction fall into two sets:—Philosoph-ical and Scientific. We will take the philosophical arguments . . . ; for . . . the professedly scientific arguments come back in the end to the principles or prejudices which are made explicit in the philosophical arguments.

Philosophical Arguments Against Two-sided Interaction

No one can deny that there is a close correlation between certain bodily events and certain mental events, and conversely. Therefore anyone who denies that there is action of mind on body and of body on mind must presumably hold (*a*) that concomitant variation is not an adequate criterion of causal con-nexion, and (*b*) that the other feature which is essential for causal connexion is absent in the case of body and mind. Now the common philosophical argu-ment is that minds and mental states are so extremely unlike bodies and bodily states that it is inconceivable that the two should be causally connected. It is certainly true that, if minds and mental events are just what they seem to be to introspection and nothing more, and if bodies and bodily events are just what en-lightened common-sense thinks them to be and nothing more, the two *are* extremely unlike. And this fact is supposed to show that, however closely cor-related certain pairs of events in mind and body respectively may be, they cannot be causally connected.

Evidently the assumption at the back of this argument is that concomitant variation, together with a high enough degree of likeness, is an adequate test for causation; but that no amount of concomitant variation can establish causation in the absence of a high enough degree of likeness. Now I am inclined to admit part of this assumption. I think it is practically certain that causation does not simply *mean* concomitant variation. (And, if it did, *cadit quæstio* [the matter would be resolved—Ed.].) Hence the existence of the latter is not *ipso facto* a proof of the presence of the former. Again, I think it is almost certain that concomitant variation between A and B is not in fact a sufficient sign of the presence of a *direct* causal relation between the two. (I think it may perhaps be a sufficient sign of *either* a direct causal relation between A and B *or* of several causal relations which indirectly unite A and B through the medium of other terms C, D, etc.) So far I agree with the assumptions of the argument. But I cannot see the least reason to think that the other characteristic, which must be added to concomitant variation before we can be sure that A and B are causally connected, is a high degree of likeness between the two. One would like to know just how unlike two events may be before it becomes impossible to admit the existence of a causal relation between them. No one hesitates to hold that draughts and colds in the head are causally connected, although the two are extremely unlike each other. If the unlikeness of draughts and colds in the head does not prevent one from admitting a causal connexion between the two, why should the unlikeness of volitions and voluntary movements prevent one from holding that they are causally connected? To sum up. I am willing to admit that an adequate criterion of causal connexion needs some other relation between a pair of events beside concomitant variation; but I do not believe for a moment that this other relation is that of qualitative likeness.

This brings us to a rather more refined form of the argument against Interaction. It is said that, whenever we admit the existence of a causal relation between two events, these two events (to put it crudely) must also form parts of a single substantial whole. E.g., all physical events are spatially related and form one great extended whole. And the mental events which would commonly be admitted to be causally connected are always events in a single mind. A mind is a substantial whole of a peculiar kind too. Now it is said that between bodily events and mental events there are no relations such as those which unite physical events in different parts of the same Space or mental events in the history of the same mind. In the absence of such relations, binding mind and body into a single substantial whole, we cannot admit that bodily and mental events can be causally connected with each other, no matter how closely correlated their variations may be.

This is a much better argument than the argument about qualitative likeness and unlikeness. If we accept the premise that causal relations can subsist only between terms which form parts of a single substantial whole must we deny that mental and bodily events can be causally connected? I do not think that we need. (i) It is of course perfectly true that an organism and the mind which animates it do not form a physical whole, and that they do not form a mental whole; and these, no doubt, are the two kinds of substantial whole with which we are most familiar. But it does not follow that a mind and its organism do not form a substantial whole of *some* kind. There, plainly, is the extraordinarily intimate union between the two which I have called "animation" of the one by the other. Even if the mind be just what it seems to introspection, and the body be just what it seems to perception aided by the more precise methods of science, this seems to me to be enough to make a mind and its body a substantial whole. Even so extreme a dualist about Mind and Matter as Descartes occasionally suggests that a mind and its body together form a quasi-substance; and, although we may quarrel with the language of the very numerous philosophers who have said that the mind is "the form" of its body, we must admit that such language would never have seemed plausible unless a mind and its body together had formed something very much like a single substantial whole.

(ii) We must, moreover, admit the possibility that minds and mental events have properties and relations which do not reveal themselves to introspection, and that bodies and bodily events may have properties and relations which do not reveal themselves to perception or to physical and chemical experiment. In virtue of these properties and relations the two together may well form a single substantial whole of the kind which is alleged to be needed for causal interaction. Thus, if we accept the premise of the argument, we have no right to assert that mind and body *cannot* interact; but only the much more modest proposition that introspection and perception do not suffice to assure us that mind and body are so interrelated that they *can* interact.

(iii) We must further remember that the Two-sided Interactionist is under no obligation to hold that the *complete* conditions of any mental event are bodily or that the complete conditions of any bodily event are mental. He needs only to assert that some mental events include certain bodily events among their necessary conditions, and that some bodily events include certain mental events among their necessary conditions. If I am paralysed my volition may not move my arm; and, if I am hypnotised or intensely interested or frightened, a wound may not produce a painful sensation. Now, if the complete cause and the complete effect in all interaction include both a bodily and a mental factor, the two wholes will be related by the fact that the mental constituents belong to a single mind, that the bodily constituents belong to a single body, and that this mind animates this body. This amount of connexion should surely be enough to allow of causal interaction.

This will be the most appropriate place to deal with the contention that, in voluntary action, and there only, we are immediately acquainted with an instance of causal connexion. If this be true the controversy is of course settled at once in favour of the Interactionist. It is generally supposed that this view was refuted once and for all by Mr Hume in his *Enquiry concerning Human Understanding* (Sect. VII, Part I). I should not care to assert that the doctrine in question is true; but I do think that it is plausible, and I am quite sure that Mr Hume's arguments do not refute it. Mr Hume uses three closely connected arguments. (1) The connexion between a successful volition and the resulting bodily movement is as mysterious and as little self-evident as the connexion between any other event and its effect. (2) We have to learn from experience which of our volitions will be effective and which will not. E.g., we do not know, until we have tried, that we can voluntarily move our arms and cannot voluntarily move our livers. And again, if a man were suddenly paralysed, he would still expect to be able to move his arm voluntarily, and would be surprised when he found that it kept still in spite of his volition. (3) We have discovered that the immediate consequence of a volition is a change in our nerves and muscles, which most people know nothing about; and is not the movement of a limb, which most people believe to be its immediate and necessary consequence.

The second and third arguments are valid only against the contention that we know immediately that a volition to make a certain movement is the *sufficient* condition for the happening of that movement. They are quite irrelevant to the contention that we know immediately that the volition is a *necessary* condition for the happening of just that movement at just that time. No doubt many other conditions are also necessary, *e.g.*, that our nerves and muscles shall be in the right state; and these other necessary conditions can be discovered only by special investigation. Since our volitions to move our limbs are in fact followed in the vast majority of cases by the willed movement, and since the other necessary conditions are not very obvious, it is natural enough that we should think that we know immediately that our volition is the *sufficient* condition of the movement of our limbs. If we think so, we are certainly wrong; and Mr Hume's arguments prove that we are. But they prove nothing else. It does not follow that we are wrong in thinking that we know, without having to wait for the result, that the volition is a *necessary* condition of the movement.

It remains to consider the first argument. Is the connexion between cause and effect as mysterious and as little self-evident in the case of the voluntary production of bodily movement as in all other cases? If so, we must hold that the first time a baby wills to move its hand it is just as much surprised to find its hand moving as it would be to find its leg moving or its nurse bursting into flames. I do not profess to know anything about the infant mind; but it seems to me that this is a wildly paradoxical consequence, for which there is no evidence or likelihood. But there is no need to leave the matter there. It is perfectly plain that, in the case of volition and voluntary movement, there *is* a connexion between the cause and the effect which is not present in other cases of causation, and which does make it plausible to hold that in this one case the nature of the effect can be foreseen by merely reflecting on the nature of the cause. The peculiarity of a volition as a cause-factor is that it involves as an essential part of it the idea of the effect. To say that a person has a volition to move his arm involves saying that he has an idea of his arm (and not of his leg or his liver) and an idea of the position in which he wants his arm to be. It is simply silly in view of this fact to say that there is no closer connexion between the desire to move my arm and the movement of my arm than there is between this desire and the movement of my leg or my liver. We cannot detect any analogous connexion between cause and effect in causal transactions which we view wholly from outside, such as the movement of a billiard-ball by a cue. It is therefore by no means unreasonable to suggest that, in the one case of our own voluntary movements, we can see without waiting for the result that such and such a volition is a necessary condition of such and such a bodily movement.

It seems to me then that Mr Hume's arguments on this point are absolutely irrelevant, and that it may very well be true that in volition we positively know that our desire for such and such a bodily movement is a necessary (though not a sufficient) condition of the happening of just that movement at just that time. On the whole then I conclude that the philosophical arguments certainly do not disprove Two-sided Interaction, and that they do not even raise any strong presumption against it. And, while I am not prepared definitely to commit myself to the view that, in voluntary movement, we positively *know* that the mind acts on the body, I do think that this opinion is quite plausible when properly stated and that the arguments which have been brought against it are worthless. . . .

3

Gilbert Ryle
Descartes' Myth

Gilbert Ryle was until his death Waynflete Professor of Metaphysical Philosophy at Oxford. He had for many years been editor of Mind, *the leading English philosophical journal, and was noticeably hospitable to the work of new authors. His most famous work was* The Concept of Mind (1949), *for a time the most influential volume on the mind–body problem in Anglo-American philosophy. The key to* The Concept of Mind *has usually been taken to be Ryle's effort to refute Cartesianism, to exorcise "the ghost in the machine"—that is, to expose as a category mistake the treatment of mental phenomena as "ghostly" analogues of physical phenomena. The theme appeared earlier in his "Systematically Misleading Expressions" (1931–1932).*

Although there is some question about the extent of Ryle's indebtedness to Wittgenstein, there is a noticeable convergence in their conception of philosophical work. Ryle posed the need to investigate the category mistake but never quite provided sufficient grounds for ascertaining when a thing is classified in a category other than the one to which it belongs. The matter is important because Ryle believed that certain linguistic tendencies involved category mistakes, but many of his critics deny that they actually do.

The Concept of Mind is often judged to be behavioristic in spirit; that is, to define the mental entirely in terms of behavior. Actually, behaviorism is curiously

From pages 11–23 in "Descartes' Myth," *The Concept of Mind,* by Gilbert Ryle, by permission of Barnes & Noble Books (Div. of Harper & Row, Publishers, Inc.). Copyright 1949, by Gilbert Ryle. Reprinted also by permission of Hutchinson Publishing Group Ltd.

akin to Ryle's thesis but incompatible with it. Had he been a behaviorist, he would not have maintained that the ghost in the machine was a category mistake, or a mistake about intelligible discourse. It would instead have been seen as an empirical mistake, or a mistake about the facts.

The Official Doctrine

There is a doctrine about the nature and place of minds which is so prevalent among theorists and even among laymen that it deserves to be described as the official theory. Most philosophers, psychologists and religious teachers subscribe, with minor reservations, to its main articles and, although they admit certain theoretical difficulties in it, they tend to assume that these can be overcome without serious modifications being made to the architecture of the theory. It will be argued here that the central principles of the doctrine are unsound and conflict with the whole body of what we know about minds when we are not speculating about them.

The official doctrine, which hails chiefly from Descartes, is something like this. With the doubtful exceptions of idiots and infants in arms every human being has both a body and a mind. Some would prefer to say that every human being is both a body and a mind. His body and his mind are ordinarily harnessed together, but after the death of the body his mind may continue to exist and function.

Human bodies are in space and are subject to the mechanical laws which govern all other bodies in space. Bodily processes and states can be inspected by external observers. So a man's bodily life is as much a public affair as are the lives of animals and reptiles and even as the careers of trees, crystals and planets.

But minds are not in space, nor are their operations subject to mechanical laws. The workings of one mind are not witnessable by other observers; its career is private. Only I can take direct cognisance of the states and processes of my own mind. A person therefore lives through two collateral histories, one consisting of what happens in and to his body, the other consisting of what happens in and to his mind. The first is public, the second private. The events in the first history are events in the physical world, those in the second are events in the mental world.

It has been disputed whether a person does or can directly monitor all or only some of the episodes of his own private history; but, according to the official doctrine, of at least some of these episodes he has direct and unchallengeable cognisance. In consciousness, self-consciousness and introspection he is directly and authentically apprised of the present states and operations of his mind. He may have great or small uncertainties about concurrent and adjacent episodes in the physical world, but he can have none about at least part of what is momentarily occupying his mind.

It is customary to express this bifurcation of his two lives and of his two worlds by saying that the things and events which belong to the physical world, including his own body, are external, while the workings of his own mind are internal. This antithesis of outer and inner is of course meant to be construed as a metaphor, since minds, not being in space, could not be described as being spatially inside anything else, or as having things going on spatially inside themselves. But relapses from this good intention are common and theorists are found speculating how stimuli, the physical sources of which are yards or miles outside a person's skin, can generate mental responses inside his skull, or how decisions framed inside his cranium can set going movements of his extremities.

Even when 'inner' and 'outer' are construed as metaphors, the problem how a person's mind and body influence one another is notoriously charged with theoretical difficulties. What the mind wills, the legs, arms and the tongue execute; what affects the ear and the eye has something to do with what the mind perceives; grimaces and smiles betray the mind's moods and bodily castigations lead, it is hoped, to moral improvement. But the actual transactions between the episodes of the private history and those of the public history remain mysterious, since by definition they can belong to neither series. They could not be reported among the happenings described in a person's autobiography of his inner life, but nor could they be reported among those described in some one else's biography of that person's overt career. They can be inspected neither by introspection nor by laboratory experiment. They are theoretical shuttlecocks which are forever being bandied from the physiologist back to the psychologist and from the psychologist back to the physiologist.

Underlying this partly metaphorical representation of the bifurcation of a person's two lives there is a seemingly more profound and philosophical assumption. It is assumed that there are two different kinds of existence or status. What exists or happens may have the status of physical existence, or it may have the status of mental existence. Somewhat as the faces of coins are either heads or tails, or somewhat as living creatures are either male or female, so, it is supposed, some existing is physical existing, other existing is mental existing. It is a necessary feature of what has physical existence that it is in space and time; it is a necessary feature of what has mental existence that it is in time but not in space. What has physical existence is composed of matter, or else is a function of matter; what has mental existence consists of consciousness, or else is a function of consciousness.

There is thus a polar opposition between mind and matter, an opposition which is often brought out as follows. Material objects are situated in a common field, known as 'space', and what happens to one body in one part of space is mechanically connected with what happens to other bodies in other parts of space. But mental happenings occur in insulated fields, known as 'minds', and there is, apart maybe from telepathy, no direct causal connection between what happens in one mind and what happens in another. Only through the medium of the public physical world can the mind of one person make a difference to the mind of another. The mind is its own place and in his inner life each of us lives the life of a ghostly Robinson Crusoe. People can see, hear and jolt one another's bodies, but they are irremediably blind and deaf to the workings of one another's minds and inoperative upon them.

What sort of knowledge can be secured of the workings of a mind? On the one side, according to the official theory, a person has direct knowledge of the

best imaginable kind of the workings of his own mind. Mental states and processes are (or are normally) conscious states and processes, and the consciousness
which irradiates them can engender no illusions and leaves the door open for
no doubts. A person's present thinkings, feelings and willings, his perceivings,
rememberings and imaginings are intrinsically 'phosphorescent'; their existence
and their nature are inevitably betrayed to their owner. The inner life is a stream
of consciousness of such a sort that it would be absurd to suggest that the mind
whose life is that stream might be unaware of what is passing down it.

True, the evidence adduced recently by Freud seems to show that there
exist channels tributary to this stream, which run hidden from their owner.
People are actuated by impulses the existence of which they vigorously disavow;
some of their thoughts differ from the thoughts which they acknowledge; and
some of the actions which they think they will to perform they do not really will.
They are thoroughly gulled by some of their own hypocrisies and they successfully ignore facts about their mental lives which on the official theory ought to
be patent to them. Holders of the official theory tend, however, to maintain that
anyhow in normal circumstances a person must be directly and authentically
seized of the present state and workings of his own mind.

Besides being currently supplied with these alleged immediate data of consciousness, a person is also generally supposed to be able to exercise from time
to time a special kind of perception, namely inner perception, or introspection.
He can take a (non-optical) 'look' at what is passing in his mind. Not only can
he view and scrutinize a flower through his sense of sight and listen to and discriminate the notes of a bell through his sense of hearing; he can also reflec-
tively or introspectively watch, without any bodily organ of sense, the current
episodes of his inner life. This self-observation is also commonly supposed to
be immune from illusion, confusion or doubt. A mind's reports of its own
affairs have a certainty superior to the best that is possessed by its reports of
matters in the physical world. Sense-perceptions can, but consciousness and
introspection cannot, be mistaken or confused.

On the other side, one person has no direct access of any sort to the events
of the inner life of another. He cannot do better than make problematic inferences from the observed behaviour of the other person's body to the states of
mind which, by analogy from his own conduct, he supposes to be signalised by
that behaviour. Direct access to the workings of a mind is the privilege of that
mind itself; in default of such privileged access, the workings of one mind are
inevitably occult to everyone else. For the supposed arguments from bodily movements similar to their own to mental workings similar to their own would lack
any possibility of observational corroboration. Not unnaturally, therefore, an
adherent of the official theory finds it difficult to resist this consequence of his
premises, that he has no good reason to believe that there do exist minds other
than his own. Even if he prefers to believe that to other human bodies there
are harnessed minds not unlike his own, he cannot claim to be able to discover
their individual characteristics, or the particular things that they undergo and
do. Absolute solitude is on this showing the ineluctable destiny of the soul. Only
our bodies can meet.

As a necessary corollary of this general scheme there is implicitly prescribed a special way of construing our ordinary concepts of mental powers and operations. The verbs, nouns and adjectives, with which in ordinary life we describe the wits, characters and higher-grade performances of the people with whom we have to do, are required to be construed as signifying special episodes in their secret histories, or else as signifying tendencies for such episodes to occur. When someone is described as knowing, believing or guessing something, as hoping, dreading, intending or shirking something, as designing this or being amused at that, these verbs are supposed to denote the occurrence of specific modifications in his (to us) occult stream of consciousness. Only his own privileged access to this stream in direct awareness and introspection could provide authentic testimony that these mental-conduct verbs were correctly or incorrectly applied. The onlooker, be he teacher, critic, biographer or friend, can never assure himself that his comments have any vestige of truth. Yet it was just because we do in fact all know how to make such comments, make them with general correctness and correct them when they turn out to be confused or mistaken, that philosophers found it necessary to construct their theories of the nature and place of minds. Finding mental-conduct concepts being regularly and effectively used, they properly sought to fix their logical geography. But the logical geography officially recommended would entail that there could be no regular or effective use of these mental-conduct concepts in our descriptions of, and prescriptions for, other people's minds.

The Absurdity of the Official Doctrine

Such in outline is the official theory. I shall often speak of it, with deliberate abusiveness, as 'the dogma of the Ghost in the Machine'. I hope to prove that it is entirely false, and false not in detail but in principle. It is not merely an assemblage of particular mistakes. It is one big mistake and a mistake of a special kind. It is, namely, a category-mistake. It represents the facts of mental life as if they belonged to one logical type or category (or range of types or categories), when they actually belong to another. The dogma is therefore a philosopher's myth. In attempting to explode the myth I shall probably be taken to be denying well-known facts about the mental life of human beings, and my plea that I aim at doing nothing more than rectifying the logic of mental-conduct concepts will probably be disallowed as mere subterfuge.

I must first indicate what is meant by the phrase 'Category-mistake'. This I do in a series of illustrations.

A foreigner visiting Oxford or Cambridge for the first time is shown a number of colleges, libraries, playing fields, museums, scientific departments and administrative offices. He then asks 'But where is the University? I have seen where the members of the Colleges live, where the Registrar works, where the scientists experiment and the rest. But I have not yet seen the University in which reside and work the members of your University.' It has then to be explained to him that the University is not another collateral institution, some ulterior counterpart to the colleges, laboratories and offices which he has seen. The University is just the way in which all that he has already seen is organized.

When they are seen and when their co-ordination is understood, the University has been seen. His mistake lay in his innocent assumption that it was correct to speak of Christ Church, the Bodleian Library, the Ashmolean Museum *and* the University, to speak, that is, as if 'the University' stood for an extra member of the class of which these other units are members. He was mistakenly allocating the University to the same category as that to which the other institutions belong.

The same mistake would be made by a child witnessing the march-past of a division, who, having had pointed out to him such and such battalions, batteries, squadrons, etc., asked when the division was going to appear. He would be supposing that a division was a counterpart to the units already seen, partly similar to them and partly unlike them. He would be shown his mistake by being told that in watching the battalions, batteries and squadrons marching past he had been watching the division marching past. The march-past was not a parade of battalions, batteries and squadrons *and* a division; it was a parade of the battalions, batteries, and squadrons *of* a division.

One more illustration. A foreigner watching his first game of cricket learns what are the functions of the bowlers, the batsmen, the fielders, the umpires and the scorers. He then says 'But there is no one left on the field to contribute the famous element of team-spirit. I see who does the bowling, the batting and the wicket-keeping; but I do not see whose role it is to exercise *esprit de corps*.' Once more, it would have to be explained that he was looking for the wrong type of thing. Team-spirit is not another cricketing-operation supplementary to all of the other special tasks. It is, roughly, the keenness with which each of the special tasks is performed, and performing a task keenly is not performing two tasks. Certainly exhibiting team-spirit is not the same thing as bowling or catching, but nor is it a third thing such that we can say that the bowler bowls *and* then exhibits team-spirit or that a fielder is at a given moment *either* catching *or* displaying *esprit de corps*.

These illustrations of category-mistakes have a common feature which must be noticed. The mistakes were made by people who did not know how to wield the concepts *University, division* and *team-spirit*. Their puzzles arose from inability to use certain items in the English vocabulary.

The theoretically interesting category-mistakes are those made by people who are perfectly competent to apply concepts, at least in the situations with which they are familiar, but are still liable in their abstract thinking to allocate those concepts to logical types to which they do not belong. An instance of a mistake of this sort would be the following story. A student of politics has learned the main differences between the British, the French and the American Constitutions, and has learned also the differences and connections between the Cabinet, Parliament, the various Ministries, the Judicature and the Church of England. But he still becomes embarrassed when asked questions about the connections between the Church of England, the Home Office and the British Constitution. For while the Church and the Home Office are institutions, the British Constitution is not another institution in the same sense of that noun. So inter-institutional relations which can be asserted or denied to hold between the Church and the Home Office cannot be asserted or denied to hold between either of them and the British Constitution. 'The British Constitution' is not a term of the same logical type as 'the Home Office' and 'the Church of England'. In a partially similar way, John Doe may be a relative, a friend, an enemy or a stranger to Richard Roe; but he cannot be any of these things to the Average Taxpayer. He knows how to talk sense in certain sorts of discussions about the Average Taxpayer, but he is baffled to say why he could not come across him in the street as he can come across Richard Roe.

It is pertinent to our main subject to notice that, so long as the student of politics continues to think of the British Constitution as a counterpart to the other institutions, he will tend to describe it as a mysteriously occult institution; and so long as John Doe continues to think of the Average Taxpayer as a fellow-citizen, he will tend to think of him as an elusive insubstantial man, a ghost who is everywhere yet nowhere.

My destructive purpose is to show that a family of radical category-mistakes is the source of the double-life theory. The representation of a person as a ghost mysteriously ensconced in a machine derives from this argument. Because, as is true, a person's thinking, feeling and purposive doing cannot be described solely in the idioms of physics, chemistry and physiology, therefore they must be described in counterpart idioms. As the human body is a complex organised unit, so the human mind must be another complex organised unit, though one made of a different sort of stuff and with a different sort of structure. Or, again, as the human body, like any other parcel of matter, is a field of causes and effects, so the mind must be another field of causes and effects, though not (Heaven be praised) mechanical causes and effects.

The Origin of the Category-Mistake

One of the chief intellectual origins of what I have yet to prove to be the Cartesian category-mistake seems to be this. When Galileo showed that his methods of scientific discovery were competent to provide a mechanical theory which should cover every occupant of space, Descartes found in himself two conflicting motives. As a man of scientific genius he could not but endorse the claims of mechanics, yet as a religious and moral man he could not accept, as Hobbes accepted, the discouraging rider to those claims, namely that human nature differs only in degree of complexity from clockwork. The mental could not be just a variety of the mechanical.

He and subsequent philosophers naturally but erroneously availed themselves of the following escape-route. Since mental-conduct words are not to be construed as signifying the occurrence of mechanical processes, they must be construed as signifying the occurrence of non-mechanical processes; since mechanical laws explain movements in space as the effects of other movements in space, other laws must explain some of the non-spatial workings of minds as the effects of other non-spatial workings of minds. The difference between the human behaviours which we describe as intelligent and those which we describe as unintelligent must be a difference in their causation; so, while some movements of human tongues and limbs are the effects of mechanical causes, others must be the effects of non-mechanical causes, i.e. some issue from movements of particles of matter, others from workings of the mind.

The differences between the physical and the mental were thus represented as differences inside the common framework of the categories of 'thing', 'stuff', 'attribute', 'state', 'process', 'change', 'cause' and 'effect'. Minds are things, but different sorts of things from bodies; mental processes are causes and effects, but different sorts of causes and effects from bodily movements. And so on. Somewhat as the foreigner expected the University to be an extra edifice, rather like a college but also considerably different, so the repudiators of mechanism represented minds as extra centres of causal processes, rather like machines but also considerably different from them. Their theory was a para-mechanical hypothesis.

That this assumption was at the heart of the doctrine is shown by the fact that there was from the beginning felt to be a major theoretical difficulty in explaining how minds can influence and be influenced by bodies. How can a mental process, such as willing, cause spatial movements like the movements of the tongue? How can a physical change in the optic nerve have among its effects a mind's perception of a flash of light? This notorious crux by itself shows the logical mould into which Descartes pressed his theory of the mind. It was the self-same mould into which he and Galileo set their mechanics. Still unwittingly adhering to the grammar of mechanics, he tried to avert disaster by describing minds in what was merely an obverse vocabulary. The workings of minds had to be described by the mere negatives of the specific descriptions given to bodies; they are not in space, they are not motions, they are not modifications of matter, they are not accessible to public observation. Minds are not bits of clockwork, they are just bits of not-clockwork.

As thus represented, minds are not merely ghosts harnessed to machines, they are themselves just spectral machines. Though the human body is an engine, it is not quite an ordinary engine, since some of its workings are governed by another engine inside it—this interior governor-engine being one of a very special sort. It is invisible, inaudible and it has no size or weight. It cannot be taken to bits and the laws it obeys are not those known to ordinary engineers. Nothing is known of how it governs the bodily engine.

A second major crux points the same moral. Since, according to the doctrine, minds belong to the same category as bodies and since bodies are rigidly governed by mechanical laws, it seemed to many theorists to follow that minds must be similarly governed by rigid non-mechanical laws. The physical world is a deterministic system, so the mental world must be a deterministic system. Bodies cannot help the modifications that they undergo, so minds cannot help pursuing the careers fixed for them. *Responsibility, choice, merit,* and *demerit* are therefore inapplicable concepts—unless the compromise solution is adopted of saying that the laws governing mental processes, unlike those governing physical processes, have the congenial attribute of being only rather rigid. The problem of the Freedom of the Will was the problem how to reconcile the hypothesis that minds are to be described in terms drawn from the categories of mechanics with the knowledge that higher-grade human conduct is not of a piece with the behaviour of machines.

It is an historical curiosity that it was not noticed that the entire argument was broken-backed. Theorists correctly assumed that any sane man could already recognise the differences between, say, rational and non-rational utterances or between purposive and automatic behaviour. Else there would have been nothing requiring to be salved from mechanism. Yet the explanation given presupposed that one person could in principle never recognise the difference between the rational and the irrational utterances issuing from other human bodies, since he could never get access to the postulated immaterial causes of some of their utterances. Save for the doubtful exception of himself, he could never tell the difference between a man and a Robot. It would have to be conceded, for example, that, for all that we can tell, the inner lives of persons who are classed as idiots or lunatics are as rational as those of anyone else. Perhaps only their overt behaviour is disappointing; that is to say, perhaps 'idiots' are not really idiotic, or 'lunatics' lunatic. Perhaps, too, some of those who are classed as sane are really idiots. According to the theory, external observers could never know how the overt behaviour of others is correlated with their mental powers and processes and so they could never know or even plausibly conjecture whether their applications of mental-conduct concepts to these other people were correct or incorrect. It would then be hazardous or impossible for a man to claim sanity or logical consistency even for himself, since he would be debarred from comparing his own performances with those of others. In short, our characterisations of persons and their performances as intelligent, prudent and virtuous or as stupid, hypocritical and cowardly could never have been made, so the problem of providing a special causal hypothesis to serve as the basis of such diagnoses would never have arisen. The question, 'How do persons differ from machines?' arose just because everyone already knew how to apply mental-conduct concepts before the new causal hypothesis was introduced. This causal hypothesis could not therefore be the source of the criteria used in those applications. Nor, of course, has the causal hypothesis in any degree improved our handling of those criteria. We still distinguish good from bad arithmetic, politic from impolitic conduct and fertile from infertile imaginations in the ways in which Descartes himself distinguished them before and after he speculated how the applicability of these criteria was compatible with the principle of mechanical causation.

He had mistaken the logic of his problem. Instead of asking by what criteria intelligent behaviour is actually distinguished from non-intelligent behaviour, he asked 'Given that the principle of mechanical causation does not tell us the difference, what other causal principle will tell it us?' He realised that the problem was not one of mechanics and assumed that it must therefore be one of some counterpart to mechanics. Not unnaturally psychology is often cast for just this role.

When two terms belong to the same category, it is proper to construct conjunctive propositions embodying them. Thus a purchaser may say that he bought a left-hand glove and a right-hand glove, but not that he bought a left-hand glove, a right-hand glove and a pair of gloves. 'She came home in a flood of tears and a sedan-chair' is a well-known joke based on the absurdity of conjoining terms of different types. It would have been equally ridiculous to construct the disjunction 'She came home either in a flood of tears or else in a sedan-chair'. Now the dogma of the Ghost in the Machine does just this. It maintains that there exist both bodies and minds; that there occur physical processes and mental processes; that there are mechanical causes of corporeal movements and mental causes of corporeal movements. I shall argue that these and other analogous conjunctions are absurd; but, it must be noticed, the argument will not show that either of the illegitimately conjoined propositions is absurd in itself. I am not, for example, denying that there occur mental processes. Doing long division is a mental process and so is making a joke. But I am saying that the phrase 'there occur mental processes' does not mean the same sort of thing as 'there occur physical processes', and, therefore, that it makes no sense to conjoin or disjoin the two.

If my argument is successful, there will follow some interesting consequences. First, the hallowed contrast between Mind and Matter will be dissipated, but dissipated not by either of the equally hallowed absorptions of Mind by Matter or of Matter by Mind, but in quite a different way. For the seeming contrast of the two will be shown to be as illegitimate as would be the contrast of 'she came home in a flood of tears' and 'she came home in a sedan-chair'. The belief that there is a polar opposition between Mind and Matter is the belief that they are terms of the same logical type.

It will also follow that both Idealism and Materialism are answers to an improper question. The 'reduction' of the material world to mental states and processes, as well as the 'reduction' of mental states and processes to physical states and processes, presuppose the legitimacy of the disjunction 'Either there exist minds or there exist bodies (but not both)'. It would be like saying, 'Either she bought a left-hand and a right-hand glove or she bought a pair of gloves (but not both)'.

It is perfectly proper to say, in one logical tone of voice, that there exist minds and to say, in another logical tone of voice, that there exist bodies. But these expressions do not indicate two different species of existence, for 'existence' is not a generic word like 'coloured' or 'sexed'. They indicate two different senses of 'exist', somewhat as 'rising' has different senses in 'the tide is rising', 'hopes are rising', and 'the average age of death is rising'. A man would be thought to be making a poor joke who said that three things are now rising, namely the tide, hopes and the average age of death. It would be just as good or bad a joke to say that there exist prime numbers and Wednesdays and public opinions and navies; or that there exist both minds and bodies. In the succeeding chapters I try to prove that the official theory does rest on a batch of category-mistakes by showing that logically absurd corollaries follow from it. The exhibition of these absurdities will have the constructive effect of bringing out part of the correct logic of mental-conduct concepts.

4

J. J. C. Smart

Sensations and Brain Processes

J. J. C. Smart is Hughes Professor of Philosophy at the University of Adelaide, Australia. His most famous paper is "Sensations and Brain Processes" (1959, 1962 rev.). At the time of its appearance, it may well have been the most discussed paper of the day on the mind–body problem. It offers an uncompromising materialism, with its dual emphasis on the identity of mental and physical phenomena and the irreducibility of mental language to physical language. Subsequent versions of materialism have treated Smart's paper as the touchstone. Smart has attempted a thoroughgoing materialistic system (Philosophy and Scientific Realism, 1963) *based on his identity thesis. He has also published* Between Science and Philosophy (1968) *and an exchange with Bernard Williams titled* Utilitarianism: For and Against (1973).

This paper[1] takes its departure from arguments to be found in U. T. Place's "Is Consciousness a Brain Process?"[2] I have had the benefit of discussing Place's thesis in a good many universities in the United States and Australia, and I hope that the present paper answers objections to his thesis which Place has not considered and that it presents his thesis in a more nearly unobjectionable form. This paper is meant also to supplement the paper "The 'Mental' and the 'Physical,'" by H. Feigl,[3] which in part argues for a similar thesis to Place's.

Suppose that I report that I have at this moment a roundish, blurry-edged after-image which is yellowish towards its edge and is orange towards its center. What is it that I am reporting? One answer to this question might be that I am not reporting anything, that when I say that it looks to me as though there is a roundish yellow-orange patch of light on the wall I am expressing some sort of *temptation*, the temptation to say that there *is* a roundish yellow-orange patch on the wall (though I may know that there is not such a patch on the

J. J. C. Smart, "Sensations and Brain Processes," in *The Philosophy of Mind*, V. C. Chappell, ed., © 1962. Reprinted by permission of Prentice-Hall, Inc., Englewood Cliffs, New Jersey; *The Philosophical Review*; and the author, who has authorized the revisions adopted.

---

[1] This is a very slightly revised version of a paper which was first published in the *Philosophical Review*, LXVIII (1959), 141–56. Since that date there have been criticisms of my paper by J. T. Stevenson, *Philosophical Review*, LXIX (1960), 505–10, to which I have replied in *Philosophical Review*, LXX (1961), 406–7, and by G. Pitcher and by W. D. Joske, *Australasian Journal of Philosophy*, XXXVIII (1960), 150–60, to which I have replied in the same volume of that journal, pp. 252–54.

[2] *British Journal of Psychology*, XLVII (1956), 44–50.

[3] *Minnesota Studies in the Philosophy of Science*, Vol. II (Minneapolis: University of Minnesota Press, 1958), pp. 370–497.

wall). This is perhaps [Ludwig—Ed.] Wittgenstein's view in the *Philosophical Investigations* (see §§367, 370). Similarly, when I "report" a pain, I am not really reporting anything (or, if you like, I am reporting in a queer sense of "reporting"), but am doing a sophisticated sort of wince. (See §244: "The verbal expression of pain replaces crying and does not describe it." Nor does it describe anything else?)[4] I prefer most of the time to discuss an after-image rather than a pain, because the word "pain" brings in something which is irrelevant to my purpose: the notion of "distress." I think that "he is in pain" entails "he is in distress," that is, that he is in a certain agitation-condition.[5] Similarly, to say "I am in pain" may be to do more than "replace pain behavior": it may be partly to report something, though this something is quite non-mysterious, being an agitation-condition, and so susceptible of behavioristic analysis. The suggestion I wish if possible to avoid is a different one, namely that "I am in pain" is a genuine report, and that what it reports is an irreducibly psychical something. And similarly the suggestion I wish to resist is also that to say "I have a yellowish-orange after-image" is to report something irreducibly psychical.

Why do I wish to resist this suggestion? Mainly because of Occam's razor. It seems to me that science is increasingly giving us a viewpoint whereby organisms are able to be seen as physicochemical mechanisms:[6] it seems that even the behavior of man himself will one day be explicable in mechanistic terms. There does seem to be, so far as science is concerned, nothing in the world but increasingly complex arrangements of physical constituents. All except for one place: in consciousness. That is, for a full description of what is going on in a man you would have to mention not only the physical processes in his tissues, glands, nervous system, and so forth, but also his states of consciousness: his visual, auditory, and tactual sensations, his aches and pains. That these should be *correlated* with brain processes does not help, for to say that they are *correlated* is to say that they are something "over and above." You cannot correlate something with itself. You correlate footprints with burglars, but not Bill Sikes the burglar with Bill Sikes the burglar. So sensations, states of consciousness, do seem to be the one sort of thing left outside the physicalist picture, and for various reasons I just cannot believe that this can be so. That everything should be explicable in terms of physics (together of course with descriptions of the ways in which the parts are put together—roughly, biology

---

[4] Some philosophers of my acquaintance, who have the advantage over me in having known Wittgenstein, would say that this interpretation of him is too behavioristic. However, it seems to me a very natural interpretation of his printed words, and whether or not it is Wittgenstein's real view it is certainly an interesting and important one. I wish to consider it here as a possible rival both to the "brain-process" thesis and to straight-out old-fashioned dualism.

[5] See Ryle, *The Concept of Mind* (London: Hutchinson's University Library, 1949), p. 93.

[6] On this point see Paul Oppenheim and Hilary Putnam, "Unity of Science as a Working Hypothesis," in *Minnesota Studies in the Philosophy of Science*, Vol. II (Minneapolis: University of Minnesota Press, 1958), pp. 3–36.

is to physics as radio-engineering is to electromagnetism) except the occurrence of sensations seems to me to be frankly unbelievable. Such sensations would be "nomological danglers," to use Feigl's expression.[7] It is not often realized how odd would be the laws whereby these nomological danglers would dangle. It is sometimes asked, "Why can't there be psychophysical laws which are of a novel sort, just as the laws of electricity and magnetism were novelties from the standpoint of Newtonian mechanics?" Certainly we are pretty sure in the future to come across new ultimate laws of a novel type, but I expect them to relate simple constituents: for example, whatever ultimate particles are then in vogue. I cannot believe that ultimate laws of nature could relate simple constituents to configurations consisting of perhaps billions of neurons (and goodness knows how many billion billions of ultimate particles) all put together for all the world as though their main purpose in life was to be a negative feedback mechanism of a complicated sort. Such ultimate laws would be like nothing so far known in science. They have a queer "smell" to them. I am just unable to believe in the nomological danglers themselves, or in the laws whereby they would dangle. If any philosophical arguments seemed to compel us to believe in such things, I would suspect a catch in the argument. In any case it is the object of this paper to show that there are no philosophical arguments which compel us to be dualists.

The above is largely a confession of faith, but it explains why I find Wittgenstein's position (as I construe it) so congenial. For on this view there are, in a sense, no sensations. A man is a vast arrangement of physical particles, but there are not, over and above this, sensations or states of consciousness. There are just behavioral facts about this vast mechanism, such as that it expresses a temptation (behavior disposition) to say "there is a yellowish-red patch on the wall" or that it goes through a sophisticated sort of wince, that is, says "I am in pain." Admittedly Wittgenstein says that though the sensation "is not a something," it is nevertheless "not a nothing either" (§304), but this need only mean that the word "ache" has a use. An ache is a thing, but only in the innocuous sense in which the plain man, in the first paragraph of [Gottlob— Ed.] Frege's *Foundations of Arithmetic*, answers the question "What is the number one?" by "a thing." It should be noted that when I assert that to say "I have a yellowish-orange after-image" is to express a temptation to assert the physical-object statement "There is a yellowish-orange patch on the wall," I mean that saying "I have a yellowish-orange after-image" is (partly) the exercise of the disposition[8] which is the temptation. It is not to *report* that I have the

---

[7] Feigl, *op. cit.*, p. 428. Feigl uses the expression "nomological danglers" for the laws whereby the entities dangle: I have used the expression to refer to the dangling entities themselves.

[8] Wittgenstein did not like the word "disposition." I am using it to put in a nutshell (and perhaps inaccurately) the view which I am attributing to Wittgenstein. I should like to repeat that I do not wish to claim that my interpretation of Wittgenstein is correct. Some of those who knew him do not interpret him in this way. It is merely a view which I find myself extracting from his printed words and which I think is important and worth discussing for its own sake.

temptation, any more than is "I love you" normally a report that I love someone. Saying "I love you" is just part of the behavior which is the exercise of the disposition of loving someone.

Though for the reasons given above, I am very receptive to the above "expressive" account of sensation statements, I do not feel that it will quite do the trick. Maybe this is because I have not thought it out sufficiently, but it does seem to me as though, when a person says "I have an after-image," he *is* making a genuine report, and that when he says "I have a pain," he *is* doing more than "replace pain-behavior," and that "this more" is not just to say that he is in distress. I am not so sure, however, that to admit this is to admit that there are nonphysical correlates of brain processes. Why should not sensations just be brain processes of a certain sort? There are, of course, well-known (as well as lesser-known) philosophical objections to the view that reports of sensations are reports of brain-processes, but I shall try to argue that these arguments are by no means as cogent as is commonly thought to be the case.

Let me first try to state more accurately the thesis that sensations are brain processes. It is not the thesis that, for example, "after-image" or "ache" means the same as "brain process of sort X" (where "X" is replaced by a description of a certain sort of brain process). It is that, in so far as "after-image" or "ache" is a report of a process, it is a report of a process that *happens to be* a brain process. It follows that the thesis does not claim that sensation statements can be *translated* into statements about brain processes.[9] Nor does it claim that the logic of a sensation statement is the same as that of a brain-process statement. All it claims is that in so far as a sensation statement is a report of something, that something is in fact a brain process. Sensations are nothing over and above brain processes. Nations are nothing "over and above" citizens, but this does not prevent the logic of nation statements being very different from the logic of citizen statements, nor does it insure the translatability of nation statements into citizen statements. (I do not, however, wish to assert that the relation of sensation statements to brain-process statements is very like that of nation statements to citizen statements. Nations do not just *happen* to be nothing over and above citizens, for example. I bring in the "nations" example merely to make a negative point: that the fact that the logic of A-statements is different from that of B-statements does not insure that A's are anything over and above B's.)

Remarks on Identity

When I say that a sensation is a brain process or that lightning is an electric discharge, I am using "is" in the sense of strict identity. (Just as in the—in this case necessary—proposition "7 is identical with the smallest prime number greater than 5.") When I say that a sensation is a brain process or that lightning is an electric discharge I do not mean just that the sensation is somehow spatially or temporally continuous with the brain process or that the lightning

---

[9] See Place, *loc cit.*, and Feigl, *op. cit.*, p. 390, near top.

is just spatially or temporally continuous with the discharge. When on the other hand I say that the successful general is the same person as the small boy who stole the apples I mean only that the successful general I see before me is a time slice[10] of the same four-dimensional object of which the small boy stealing apples is an earlier time slice. However, the four-dimensional object which has the general-I-see-before-me for its late time slice is identical in the strict sense with the four-dimensional object which has the small-boy-stealing-apples for an early time slice. I distinguish these two senses of "is identical with" because I wish to make it clear that the brain-process doctrine asserts identity in the *strict* sense.

I shall now discuss various possible objections to the view that the processes reported in sensation statements are in fact processes in the brain. Most of us have met some of these objections in our first year as philosophy students. All the more reason to take a good look at them. Others of the objections will be more recondite and subtle.

OBJECTION 1. Any illiterate peasant can talk perfectly well about his after-images, or how things look or feel to him, or about his aches and pains, and yet he may know nothing whatever about neurophysiology. A man may, like Aristotle, believe that the brain is an organ for cooling the body without any impairment of his ability to make true statements about his sensations. Hence the things we are talking about when we describe our sensations cannot be processes in the brain.

REPLY. You might as well say that a nation of slugabeds, who never saw the Morning Star or knew of its existence, or who had never thought of the expression "the Morning Star," but who used the expression "the Evening Star" perfectly well, could not use this expression to refer to the same entity as we refer to (and describe as) "the Morning Star."[11]

You may object that the Morning Star is in a sense not the very same thing as the Evening Star, but only something spatiotemporally continuous with it. That is, you may say that the Morning Star is not the Evening Star in the strict sense of "identity" that I distinguished earlier.

There is, however, a more plausible example. Consider lightning.[12] Modern physical science tells us that lightning is a certain kind of electrical discharge due to ionization of clouds of water vapor in the atmosphere. This, it is now believed, is what the true nature of lightning is. Note that there are not two things: a flash of lightning and an electrical discharge. There is one thing, a flash of lightning, which is described scientifically as an electrical discharge to the earth from a cloud of ionized water molecules. The case is not at all like that of explaining a footprint by reference to a burglar. We say that what light-

---

[10] See J. H. Woodger, *Theory Construction*, International Encyclopedia of Unified Science, II, No. 5 (Chicago: University of Chicago Press, 1939), 38. I here permit myself to speak loosely. For warnings against possible ways of going wrong with this sort of talk, see my note "Spatialising Time," *Mind*, LXIV (1955), 239–41.

[11] Cf. Feigl, *op. cit.*, p. 439.

[12] See Place, *loc. cit.*; also Feigl, *op. cit.*, p. 438.

ning really is, what its true nature as revealed by science is, is an electrical discharge. (It is not the true nature of a footprint to be a burglar.)

To forestall irrelevant objections, I should like to make it clear that by "lightning" I mean the publicly observable physical object, lightning, not a visual sense-datum of lightning. I say that the publicly observable physical object lightning is in fact the electrical discharge, not just a correlate of it. The sense-datum, or rather the having of the sense-datum, the "look" of lightning, may well in my view be a correlate of the electrical discharge. For in my view it is a brain state *caused* by the lightning. But we should no more confuse sensations of lightning with lightning than we confuse sensations of a table with the table.

In short, the reply to Objection 1 is that there can be contingent statements of the form "A is identical with B," and a person may well know that something is an A without knowing that it is a B. An illiterate peasant might well be able to talk about his sensations without knowing about his brain processes, just as he can talk about lightning though he knows nothing of electricity.

OBJECTION 2. It is only a contingent fact (if it is a fact) that when we have a certain kind of sensation there is a certain kind of process in our brain. Indeed it is possible, though perhaps in the highest degree unlikely, that our present physiological theories will be as out of date as the ancient theory connecting mental processes with goings on in the heart. It follows that when we report a sensation we are not reporting a brain process.

REPLY. The objection certainly proves that when we say "I have an after-image" we cannot *mean* something of the form "I have such and such a brain process." But this does not show that what we report (having an after-image) is not *in fact* a brain process. "I see lightning" does not *mean* "I see an electrical discharge." Indeed, it is logically possible (though highly unlikely) that the electrical discharge account of lightning might one day be given up. Again, "I see the Evening Star" does not *mean* the same as "I see the Morning Star," and yet "The Evening Star and the Morning Star are one and the same thing" is a contingent proposition. Possibly Objection 2 derives some of its apparent strength from a "Fido"–Fido theory of meaning. If the meaning of an expression were what the expression named, then of course it *would* follow from the fact that "sensation" and "brain process" have different meanings that they cannot name one and the same thing.

OBJECTION 3.[13] Even if Objections 1 and 2 do not prove that sensations are something over and above brain processes, they do prove that the qualities of sensations are something over and above the qualities of brain processes. That is, it may be possible to get out of asserting the existence of irreducibly psychic processes, but not out of asserting the existence of irreducibly psychic *properties*. For suppose we identify the Morning Star with the Evening Star. Then there

---

[13] I think this objection was first put to me by Professor Max Black. I think it is the most subtle of any of those I have considered, and the one which I am least confident of having satisfactorily met.

must be some properties which logically imply that of being the Morning Star, and quite distinct properties which entail that of being the Evening Star. Again, there must be some properties (for example, that of being a yellow flash) which are logically distinct from those in the physicalist story.

Indeed, it might be thought that the objection succeeds at one jump. For consider the property of "being a yellow flash." It might seem that this property lies inevitably outside the physicalist framework within which I am trying to work (either by "yellow" being an objective emergent property of physical objects, or else by being a power to produce yellow sense-data, where "yellow," in this second instantiation of the word, refers to a purely phenomenal or intro-spectible quality). I must therefore digress for a moment and indicate how I deal with secondary qualities. I shall concentrate on color.

First of all, let me introduce the concept of a normal percipient. One person is more a normal percipient than another if he can make color discriminations that the other cannot. For example, if A can pick a lettuce leaf out of a heap of cabbage leaves, whereas B cannot though he can pick a lettuce leaf out of a heap of beetroot leaves, then A is more normal than B. (I am assuming that A and B are not given time to distinguish the leaves by their slight difference in shape, and so forth.) From the concept of "more normal than" it is easy to see how we can introduce the concept of "normal." Of course, Eskimos may make the finest discriminations at the blue end of the spectrum, Hottentots at the red end. In this case the concept of a normal percipient is a slightly idealized one, rather like that of "the mean sun" in astronomical chronology. There is no need to go into such subtleties now. I say that "This is red" means some-thing roughly like "A normal percipient would not easily pick this out of a clump of geranium petals though he would pick it out of a clump of lettuce leaves." Of course it does not exactly mean this: a person might know the meaning of "red" without knowing anything about geraniums, or even about normal percipients. But the point is that a person can be *trained* to say "This is red" of objects which would not easily be picked out of geranium petals by a normal percipient, and so on. (Note that even a color-blind person can reasonably assert that some-thing is red, though of course he needs to use another human being, not just himself, as his "color meter.") This account of secondary qualities explains their unimportance in physics. For obviously the discriminations and lack of discriminations made by a very complex neurophysiological mechanism are hardly likely to correspond to simple and non-arbitrary distinctions in nature.

I therefore elucidate colors as powers, in Locke's sense, to evoke certain sorts of discriminatory responses in human beings. They are also, of course, powers to cause sensations in human beings (an account still nearer Locke's). But these sensations, I am arguing, are identifiable with brain processes.

Now how do I get over the objection that a sensation can be identified with a brain process only if it has some phenomenal property, not possessed by brain processes, whereby one-half of the identification may be, so to speak, pinned down?

REPLY. My suggestion is as follows. When a person says, "I see a yellowish-orange after-image," he is saying something like this: *"There is something going on which is like what is going on when* I have my eyes open, am awake, and there is an orange illuminated in good light in front of me, that is, when I really see an orange." (And there is no reason why a person should not say the same thing when he is having a veridical sense-datum, so long as we construe "like" in the last sentence in such a sense that something can be like itself.) Notice that the italicized words, namely "there is something going on which is like what is going on when," are all quasi-logical or topic-neutral words. This explains why the ancient Greek peasant's reports about his sensations can be neutral between dualistic metaphysics or my materialistic metaphysics. It explains how sensations can be brain processes and yet how a man who reports them need know nothing about brain processes. For he reports them only very abstractly as "something going on which is like what is going on when. . . ." Similarly, a person may say "someone is in the room," thus reporting truly that the doctor is in the room, even though he has never heard of doctors. (There are not two people in the room: "someone" *and* the doctor.) This account of sensation statements also explains the singular elusiveness of "raw feels"—why no one seems to be able to pin any properties on them.[14] Raw feels, in my view, are colorless for the very same reason that *something* is colorless. This does not mean that sensations do not have plenty of properties, for if they are brain processes they certainly have lots of neurological properties. It only means that in speaking of them as being like or unlike one another we need not know or mention these properties.

This, then, is how I would reply to Objection 3. The strength of my reply depends on the possibility of our being able to report that one thing is like another without being able to state the respect in which it is like. I do not see why this should not be so. If we think cybernetically about the nervous system we can envisage it as able to respond to certain likenesses of its internal processes without being able to do more. It would be easier to build a machine which would tell us, say on a punched tape, whether or not two objects were similar, than it would be to build a machine which would report wherein the similarities consisted.

OBJECTION 4. The after-image is not in physical space. The brain process is. So the after-image is not a brain process.

REPLY. This is an *ignoratio elenchi* [irrelevant conclusion—Ed.]. I am not arguing that the after-image is a brain process, but that the experience of having an after-image is a brain process. It is the *experience* which is reported in the introspective report. Similarly, if it is objected that the after-image is yellowy-orange, my reply is that it is the experience of seeing yellowy-orange that is being described, and this experience is not a yellowy-orange something. So to say that a brain process cannot be yellowy-orange is not to say that a brain process cannot in fact be the experience of having a yellowy-orange after-image. There is, in a sense, no such thing as an after-image or a sense-datum, though there is such a thing as the experience of having an image, and this experience is

---

[14] See B. A. Farrell, "Experience," *Mind*, LIX (1950), 170–98.

described indirectly in material object language, not in phenomenal language, for there is no such thing.[15] We describe the experience by saying, in effect, that it is like the experience we have when, for example, we really see a yellowy-orange patch on the wall. Trees and wallpaper can be green, but not the experience of seeing or imagining a tree or wallpaper. (Or if they are described as green or yellow this can only be in a derived sense.)

OBJECTION 5.   It would make sense to say of a molecular movement in the brain that it is swift or slow, straight or circular, but it makes no sense to say this of the experience of seeing something yellow.

REPLY.   So far we have not given sense to talk of experiences as swift or slow, straight or circular. But I am not claiming that "experience" and "brain process" mean the same or even that they have the same logic. "Somebody" and "the doctor" do not have the same logic, but this does not lead us to suppose that talking about somebody telephoning is talking about someone over and above, say, the doctor. The ordinary man when he reports an experience is reporting that something is going on, but he leaves it open as to what sort of thing is going on, whether in a material solid medium or perhaps in some sort of gaseous medium, or even perhaps in some sort of nonspatial medium (if this makes sense). All that I am saying is that "experience" and "brain process" may in fact refer to the same thing, and if so we may easily adopt a convention (which is not a change in our present rules for the use of experience words but an addition to them) whereby it would make sense to talk of an experience in terms appropriate to physical processes.

OBJECTION 6.   Sensations are private, brain processes are *public*. If I sincerely say, "I see a yellowish-orange after-image," and I am not making a verbal mistake, then I cannot be wrong. But I can be wrong about a brain process. The scientist looking into my brain might be having an illusion. Moreover, it makes sense to say that two or more people are observing the same brain process but not that two or more people are reporting the same inner experience.

REPLY.   This shows that the language of introspective reports has a different logic from the language of material processes. It is obvious that until the brain-process theory is much improved and widely accepted there will be no *criteria* for saying "Smith has an experience of such-and-such a sort" *except* Smith's introspective reports. So we have adopted a rule of language that (normally) what Smith says goes.

---

[15] Dr. J. R. Smythies claims that a sense-datum language could be taught independently of the material object language ("A Note on the Fallacy of the 'Phenomenological Fallacy,' " *British Journal of Psychology*, XLVIII [1957], 141–44). I am not so sure of this: there must be some public criteria for a person having got a rule wrong before we can teach him the rule. I suppose someone might *accidentally* learn color words by Dr. Smythies' procedure. I am not, of course, denying that we can learn a sense-datum language in the sense that we can learn to report our experience. Nor would Place deny it.

OBJECTION 7.   I can imagine myself turned to stone and yet having images, aches, pains, and so on.

REPLY.   I can imagine that the electrical theory of lightning is false, that lightning is some sort of purely optical phenomenon. I can imagine that lightning is not an electrical discharge. I can imagine that the Evening Star is not the Morning Star. But it is. All the objection shows is that "experience" and "brain process" do not have the same meaning. It does not show that an experience is not in fact a brain process.

This objection is perhaps much the same as one which can be summed up by the slogan: "What can be composed of nothing cannot be composed of anything."[16] The argument goes as follows: on the brain-process thesis the identity between the brain process and the experience is a contingent one. So it is logically possible that there should be no brain process, and no process of any other sort either (no heart process, no kidney process, no liver process). There would be the experience but no "corresponding" physiological process with which we might be able to identify it empirically.

I suspect that the objector is thinking of the experience as a ghostly entity. So it is composed of something, not of nothing, after all. On his view it is composed of ghost stuff, and on mine it is composed of brain stuff. Perhaps the counter-reply will be[17] that the experience is simple and uncompounded, and so it is not composed of anything after all. This seems to be a quibble, for, if it were taken seriously, the remark "What can be composed of nothing cannot be composed of anything" could be recast as an a priori argument against Democritus and atomism and for Descartes and infinite divisibility. And it seems odd that a question of this sort could be settled a priori. We must therefore construe the word "composed" in a very weak sense, which would allow us to say that even an indivisible atom is composed of something (namely, itself). The dualist cannot really say that an experience can be composed of nothing. For he holds that experiences are something over and above material processes, that is, that they are a sort of ghost stuff. (Or perhaps ripples in an underlying ghost stuff.) I say that the dualist's hypothesis is a perfectly intelligible one. But I say that experiences are not to be identified with ghost stuff but with brain stuff. This is another hypothesis, and in my view a very plausible one. The present argument cannot knock it down a priori.

OBJECTION 8.   The "beetle in the box" objection (see Wittgenstein, *Philosophical Investigations*, §293). How could descriptions of experiences, if these are genuine reports, get a foothold in language? For any rule of language must have public criteria for its correct application.

REPLY.   The change from describing how things are to describing how we feel is just a change from uninhibitedly saying "this is so" to saying "this looks so." That is, when the naïve person might be tempted to say, "There is a patch

---

[16] I owe this objection to Dr. C. B. Martin. I gather that he no longer wishes to maintain this objection, at any rate in its present form.

[17] Martin did not make this reply, but one of his students did.

of light on the wall which moves whenever I move my eyes" or "A pin is being stuck into me," we have learned how to resist this temptation and say "It *looks as though* there is a patch of light on the wallpaper" or "It *feels as though* someone were sticking a pin into me." The introspective account tells us about the individual's state of consciousness in the same way as does "I see a patch of light" or "I feel a pin being stuck into me": it differs from the corresponding perception statement in so far as it withdraws any claim about what is actually going on in the external world. From the point of view of the psychologist, the change from talking about the environment to talking about one's perceptual sensations is simply a matter of disinhibiting certain reactions. These are reactions which one normally suppresses because one has learned that in the prevailing circumstances they are unlikely to provide a good indication of the state of the environment.[18] To say that something looks green to me is simply to say that my experience is like the experience I get when I see something that really is green. In my reply to Objection 3, I pointed out the extreme openness or generality of statements which report experiences. This explains why there is no language of private qualities. (Just as "someone," unlike "the doctor," is a colorless word.)[19]

If it is asked what is the difference between those brain processes which, in my view, are experiences and those brain processes which are not, I can only reply that it is at present unknown. I have been tempted to conjecture that the difference may in part be that between perception and reception (in D. M. MacKay's terminology) and that the type of brain process which is an experience might be identifiable with MacKay's active "matching response."[20] This, however, cannot be the whole story, because sometimes I can perceive something unconsciously, as when I take a handkerchief out of a drawer without being aware that I am doing so. But at the very least, we can classify the brain processes which are experiences as those brain processes which are, or might have been, causal conditions of those pieces of verbal behavior which we call reports of immediate experience.

I have now considered a number of objections to the brain-process thesis. I wish now to conclude with some remarks on the logical status of the thesis itself. U. T. Place seems to hold that it is a straight-out scientific hypothesis.[21] If so, he is partly right and partly wrong. If the issue is between (say) a brain-process thesis and a heart thesis, or a liver thesis, or a kidney thesis, then the issue is a

---

[18] I owe this point to Place, in correspondence.

[19] The "beetle in the box" objection is, *if it is sound,* an objection to *any* view, and in particular the Cartesian one, that introspective reports are genuine reports. So it is no objection to a weaker thesis that I would be concerned to uphold, namely, that if introspective reports of "experiences" are genuinely reports, then the things they are reports of are in fact brain processes.

[20] See his article "Towards an Information-Flow Model of Human Behaviour," *British Journal of Psychology,* XLVII (1956), 30–43.

[21] *Op. cit.* For a further discussion of this, in reply to the original version of the present paper, see Place's note "Materialism as a Scientific Hypothesis," *Philosophical Review,* LXIX (1960), 101–4.

purely empirical one, and the verdict is overwhelmingly in favor of the brain. The right sorts of things don't go on in the heart, liver, or kidney, nor do these organs possess the right sort of complexity of structure. On the other hand, if the issue is between a brain-or-liver-or-kidney thesis (that is, some form of materialism) on the one hand and epiphenomenalism on the other hand, then the issue is not an empirical one. For there is no conceivable experiment which could decide between materialism and epiphenomenalism. This latter issue is not like the average straight-out empirical issue in science, but like the issue between the nineteenth-century English naturalist Philip Gosse[22] and the orthodox geologists and paleontologists of his day. According to Gosse, the earth was created about 4000 B.C. exactly as described in *Genesis*, with twisted rock strata "evidence" of erosion, and so forth, and all sorts of fossils, all in their appropriate strata, just as if the usual evolutionist story had been true. Clearly this theory is in a sense irrefutable: no evidence can possibly tell against it. Let us ignore the theological setting in which Philip Gosse's hypothesis had been placed, thus ruling out objections of a theological kind, such as "what a queer God who would go to such elaborate lengths to deceive us." Let us suppose that it is held that the universe just *began* in 4004 B.C. with the initial conditions everywhere just as they were in 4004 B.C., and in particular that our own planet began with sediment in the rivers, eroded cliffs, fossils in the rocks, and so on. No scientist would ever entertain this as a serious hypothesis, consistent though it is with all possible evidence. The hypothesis offends against the principles of parsimony and simplicity. There would be far too many brute and inexplicable facts. Why are pterodactyl bones just as they are? No explanation in terms of the evolution of pterodactyls from earlier forms of life would any longer be possible. We would have millions of facts about the world as it was in 4004 B.C. that just have to be *accepted*.

The issue between the brain-process theory and epiphenomenalism seems to be of the above sort. (Assuming that a behavioristic reduction of introspective reports is not possible.) If it be agreed that there are no cogent philosophical arguments which force us into accepting dualism, and if the brain-process theory and dualism are equally consistent with the facts, then the principles of parsimony and simplicity seem to me to decide overwhelmingly in favor of the brain-process theory. As I pointed out earlier, dualism involves a large number of irreducible psychophysical laws (whereby the "nomological danglers" dangle) of a queer sort, that just have to be taken on trust, and are just as difficult to swallow as the irreducible facts about the paleontology of the earth with which we are faced on Philip Gosse's theory.

---

[22] See the entertaining account of Gosse's book *Omphalos* by Martin Gardner in *Fads and Fallacies in the Name of Science*, 2nd ed. (New York: Dover, 1957), pp. 124–27.

5

Hilary Putnam
Minds and Machines

Hilary Putnam has been Professor of Philosophy at Harvard University since 1965. His Philosophical Papers (2 vols., 1975) collects most of his articles. His interests are not merely wide-ranging but strategically centered on the current issues regarding the theory of meaning and the nature of scientific theory and explanation. He studied with Hans Reichenbach and W. V. Quine and has worked extensively in the philosophy of mathematics. He has also been extremely active in social and political affairs, chiefly associated with the criticism of the Vietnam war.

Putnam has contributed instructively to a variety of fields. For example, he has argued, against the extreme views of Paul Feyerabend and J. J. C. Smart, that changes in theory are not tantamount to changes in the meaning of the terms that the theories employ ("How Not to Talk About Meaning," 1963). In a series of papers he has developed a distinctive theory of meaning that introduces the notions of "core facts" and "stereotypic" specimens (for instance, "Is Semantics Possible?" 1970). In the article that follows, he argues that the mind–body problem is the analogue of the structural–logical–state contrast with respect to machines.

The various issues and puzzles that make up the traditional mind-body problem are wholly linguistic and logical in character: whatever few empirical "facts" there may be in this area support one view as much as another. I do not hope to establish this contention in this paper, but I hope to do something toward rendering it more plausible. Specifically, I shall try to show that all of the issues arise in connection with any computing system capable of answering questions about its own structure, and have thus nothing to do with the unique nature (if it *is* unique) of human subjective experience.

To illustrate the sort of thing that is meant, one kind of puzzle that is sometimes discussed in connection with the "mind-body problem" is the puzzle of *privacy*. The question "How do I know I have a pain?" is a *deviant*[1] ("logically odd") question. The question "How do I know Smith has a pain?" is not at all deviant. The difference can also be mirrored in impersonal questions: "How does anyone ever know he himself has a pain?" is deviant; "How does anyone ever know that someone else is in pain?" is non-deviant. I shall show that the difference in status between the last two questions is mirrored in the case of machines: if T is any *Turing machine* (see below), the question "How does T ascertain

Reprinted by permission of New York University Press from *Dimensions of Mind: A Symposium*, edited by Sidney Hook, pp. 138–64, © 1960 by New York University.

---

[1] By a "deviant" utterance is here meant one that deviates from a semantical regularity (in the appropriate natural language). The term is taken from (14).

that it is in state A?" is, as we shall see, "logically odd" with a vengeance; but if T is capable of investigating its neighbor machine T' (say, T has electronic "sense-organs" which "scan" T'), the question "How does T ascertain that T' is in state A?" is not at all odd.

Another question connected with the "mind-body problem" is the question whether or not it is ever permissible to identify mental events and physical events. Of course, I do not claim that this question arises for Turing machines, but I do claim that it is possible to construct a logical analogue for this question that does arise, and that all of the arguments on both sides of the question of "mind-body identity" can be mirrored in terms of the analogue.

To obtain such an analogue, let us identify a scientific theory with a "partially-interpreted calculus" in the sense of Carnap.[2] Then we can perfectly well imagine a Turing machine which generates theories, tests them (assuming that it is possible to "mechanize" inductive logic to some degree), and "accepts" theories which satisfy certain criteria (e.g., predictive success). In particular, if the machine has electronic "sense organs" which enable it to "scan" itself while it is in operation, it may formulate theories concerning its own structure and subject them to test. Suppose the machine is in a given state (say, "state A") when, and only when, flip-flop 36 is on. Then this statement: "I am in state A when, and only when, flip-flop 36 is on," may be one of the theoretical principles concerning its own structure accepted by the machine. Here "I am in state A" is, of course, "observation language" for the machine, while "flip-flop 36 is on" is a "theoretical expression" which is partially interpreted in terms of "observables" (if the machine's "sense organs" report by printing symbols on the machine's input tape, the "observables" in terms of which the machine would give a partial operational definition of "flip-flop 36 being on" would be of the form "symbol # so-and-so appearing on the input tape"). Now all of the usual considerations for and against mind-body identification can be paralleled by considerations for and against saying that state A is in fact *identical* with flip-flop 36 being on.

Corresponding to Occamist arguments for "identity" in the one case are Occamist arguments for identity in the other. And the usual argument for dualism in the mind-body case can be paralleled in the other as follows: for the machine, "state A" is directly observable; on the other hand, "flip-flops" are something it knows about only via highly-sophisticated inferences—How *could* two things so different *possibly* be the same?

This last argument can be put into a form which makes it appear somewhat stronger. The proposition:

(1) I am in state A if, and only if, flip-flop 36 is on,

is clearly a "synthetic" proposition for the machine. For instance, the machine might be in state A and its sense organs might report that flip-flop 36 was *not* on.

---

[2] Cf. (1), (2). This model of a scientific theory is too oversimplified to be of much general utility, in my opinion: however, the oversimplifications do not affect the present argument.

In such a case the machine would have to make a methodological "choice"—namely, to give up (1) or to conclude that it had made an "observational error" (just as a human scientist would be confronted with similar methodological choices in studying his own psychophysical correlations). And just as philosophers have argued from the synthetic nature of the proposition:

(2) I am in pain if, and only if, my C-fibers are stimulated,

to the conclusion that the *properties* (or "states" or "events") being in pain, and having C-fibers stimulated, cannot possibly be the same [otherwise (2) would be analytic, or so the argument runs]; so one should be able to conclude from the fact that (1) is synthetic that the two properties (or "states" or "events")—being in state A and having flip-flop 36 on—cannot possibly be the same!

It is instructive to note that the traditional argument for dualism is not at all a conclusion from "the raw data of direct experience" (as is shown by the fact that it applies just as well to non-sentient machines), but a highly complicated bit of reasoning which depends on (A) the reification of universals[3] (e.g., "properties," "states," "events"); and on (B) a sharp analytic-synthetic distinction.

I may be accused of advocating a "mechanistic" world-view in pressing the present analogy. If this means that I am supposed to hold that machines think,[4] on the one hand, or that human beings are machines, on the other, the charge is false. If there is some version of mechanism sophisticated enough to avoid these errors, very likely the considerations in this paper support it.[5]

1. Turing Machines

The present paper will require the notion of a *Turing machine*[6] which will now be explained.

Briefly, a Turing machine is a device with a finite number of internal configurations, each of which involves the machine's being in one of a finite number of *states*,[7] and the machine's scanning a tape on which certain symbols appear.

The machine's tape is divided into separate squares, thus:

---

[3] This point was made by Quine in (9).

[4] Cf. Ziff's paper (13) and the reply (10) by Smart. Ziff has informed me that by a "robot" he did not have in mind a "learning machine" of the kind envisaged by Smart, and he would agree that the considerations brought forward in his paper would not necessarily apply to such a machine (if it can properly be classed as a "machine" at all). On the question of whether "this machine thinks (feels, etc.)" is *deviant* or not, it is necessary to keep in mind both the point raised by Ziff (that the important question is not whether or not the utterance is deviant, but whether or not it is deviant for non-trivial reasons), and also the "diachronic-synchronic" distinction discussed in section 5 of the present paper.

[5] In particular, I am sympathetic with the general standpoint taken by Smart in (11) and (12). However, see the linguistic considerations in section 5.

[6] For further details, cf. (4) and (6).

[7] This terminology is taken from (6) and differs from that of Davis and Turing.

on each of which a symbol (from a fixed finite alphabet) may be printed. Also the machine has a "scanner" which "scans" one square of the tape at a time. Finally, the machine has a *printing mechanism* which may (A) *erase* the symbol which appears on the square being scanned, and (B) print some other symbol (from the machine's alphabet) on that square.

Any Turing machine is completely described by a *machine table*, which is constructed as follows: the rows of the table correspond to letters of the alphabet (including the "null" letter, i.e., blank space), while the columns correspond to states A,B,C, etc. In each square there appears an "instruction," e.g., "s_5L A", "s_7C B", "s_3R C". These instructions are read as follows: "s_5L A" means "print the symbol s_5 on the square you are now scanning (after erasing whatever symbol it now contains), and proceed to scan the square immediately to the left of the one you have just been scanning; also, shift into state A." The other instructions are similarly interpreted ("R" means "scan the square immediately to the *right*," while "C" means "center," i.e., continue scanning the *same* square). The following is a sample machine table:

		A	B	C	D
(s_1)	1	s_1RA	s_1LB	s_3LD	s_1CD
(s_2)	+	s_1LB	s_2CD	s_2LD	s_2CD
	blank				
(s_3)	space	s_3CD	s_3RC	s_3LD	s_3CD

The machine described by this table is intended to function as follows: the machine is started in state A. On the tape there appears a "sum" (in unary notation) to be "worked out," e.g., "11 + 111."

The machine is initially scanning the first "1." The machine proceeds to "work out" the sum (essentially by replacing the plus sign by a 1, and then going back and erasing the first 1). Thus if the "input" was 1111 + 11111 the machine would "print out" 111111111, and then go into the "rest state" (state D).

A "machine table" *describes* a machine if the machine has internal states corresponding to the columns of the table, and if it "obeys" the instructions in the table in the following sense: when it is scanning a square on which a symbol s_1 appears and it is in, say, state B, that it carries out the "instruction" in the appropriate row and column of the table (in this case, column B and row s_1). Any machine that is described by a machine table of the sort just exemplified is a Turing machine.

The notion of a Turing machine is also subject to generalization[8] in various ways—for example, one may suppose that the machine has a second tape (an "input tape") on which additional information may be printed by an operator

---

[8] This generalization is made in (4), where it is employed in defining relative recursiveness.

in the course of a computation. In the sequel we shall make use of this generalization (with electronic "sense organs" taking the place of the "operator").

It should be remarked that Turing machines are able in principle to do anything that any computing machine (of whichever kind) can do.[9]

It has sometimes been contended (e.g., by [Ernest—Ed.] Nagel and [James R.—Ed.] Newman in their book *Gödel's Proof*) that "the theorem (i.e., [Kurt—Ed.] Gödel's theorem) does indicate that the structure and power of the human mind are far more complex and subtle than any non-living machine yet envisaged" (p. 10), and hence that a Turing machine cannot serve as a model for the human mind, but this is simply a mistake.

Let T be a Turing machine which "represents" me in the sense that T can prove just the mathematical statements I can prove. Then the argument (Nagel and Newman give no argument, but I assume they must have this one in mind) is that by using Gödel's technique I can discover a proposition that T cannot prove, and moreover *I* can prove this proposition. This refutes the assumption that T "represents" me, hence I am not a Turing machine. The fallacy is a misapplication of Gödel's theorem, pure and simple. Given an arbitrary machine T, all I can do is find a proposition U such that *I* can prove:

(3) If T is consistent, U is true,

where U is undecidable by T if T is in fact consistent. However, T can perfectly well prove (3) too! And the statement U, which T *cannot* prove (assuming consistency), *I* cannot prove either (unless I can prove that T is consistent, which is unlikely if T is very complicated)!

2. *Privacy*

Let us suppose that a Turing machine T is constructed to do the following. A number, say "3000," is printed on T's tape and T is started in T's "initial state." Thereupon T computes the 3000th (or whatever the given number was) digit in the decimal expansion of π, prints this digit on its tape, and goes into the "rest state," (i.e., turns itself off). Clearly the question "How does T 'ascertain' (or 'compute,' or 'work out') the 3000th digit in the decimal expansion of π?" is a sensible question. And the answer might well be a complicated one. In fact, an answer would probably involve three distinguishable constituents:

(i) A description of the sequence of states through which T passed in arriving at the answer, and of the appearance of the tape at each stage in the computation.

(ii) A description of the *rules* under which T operated (these are given by the "machine table" for T).

(iii) An explanation of the *rationale* of the entire procedure.

---

[9] This statement is a form of *Church's thesis* (that recursiveness equals effective computability).

Now let us suppose that someone voices the following objection: "In order to perform the computation just described, T must pass through states A,B,C, etc. But how can T ascertain that it is in states A,B,C, etc.?"

It is clear that this is a silly objection. But what makes it silly? For one thing, the "logical description" (machine table) of the machine describes the states only in terms of their *relations* to each other and to what appears on the tape. The "physical realization" of the machine is immaterial, so long as there *are* distinct states A,B,C, etc., and they succeed each other as specified in the machine table. Thus one can answer a question such as "How does T ascertain that X?" (or "compute X," etc.) only in the sense of describing the *sequence of states* through which T must pass in ascertaining that X (computing X, etc.), the rules obeyed, etc. But there is no "sequence of states" through which T must pass to be in a single state!

Indeed, suppose there were—suppose T could not *be* in state A without first *ascertaining* that it was in state A (by first passing through a sequence of other states). Clearly a vicious regress would be involved. And one "breaks" the regress simply by noting that the machine, in ascertaining the 3000th digit in π, *passes through* its states—but it need not in any significant sense "ascertain" that it is passing through them.

> Note the analogy to a fallacy in traditional epistemology: the fallacy of supposing that to know that p (where p is any proposition) one must first know that q_1, q_2, etc. (where q_1, q_2 etc., are appropriate *other* propositions). This leads either to an "infinite regress" or to the dubious move of inventing a special class of "protocol" propositions.
>
> The resolution of the fallacy is also analogous to the machine case. Suppose that on the basis of sense experiences E_1 E_2, etc., I know that there is a chair in the room. It does not follow that I verbalized (or even *could* have verbalized) E_1, E_2, etc., nor that I remember E_1, E_2, etc., nor even that I "mentally classified" ("attended to," etc.) sense experiences E_1, E_2, etc., when I had them. In short, it is necessary to *have* sense experiences, but not to *know* (or even *notice*) what sense experiences one is having, in order to have certain kinds of knowledge.

Let us modify our case, however, by supposing that whenever the machine is in one particular state (say, "state A") it prints the words "I am in state A." Then someone might grant that the machine does not in general ascertain what state it is in, but might say in the case of state A (after the machine printed "I am in state A"): "The machine ascertained that it was in state A."

Let us study this case a little more closely. First of all, we want to suppose that when it is in state A the machine prints "I am in state A" without first passing through any other states. That is, in every row of the column of the table headed "state A" there appears the instruction: *print*[10] "*I am in State A.*" Secondly, by way of comparison, let us consider a human being, Jones, who says "I am in pain" (or "Ouch!", or "Something hurts") whenever he is in pain. To make the comparison as close as possible, we will have to suppose that Jones'

---

[10] Here it is necessary to suppose that the entire sentence "I am in state A" counts as a single symbol in the machine's alphabet.

linguistic conditioning is such that he simply says "I am in pain" "without thinking," i.e., without passing through any introspectible mental states other than the
pain itself. In [Ludwig—Ed.] Wittgenstein's terminology, Jones simply *evinces*
his pain by saying "I am in pain"—he does not first reflect on it (or heed it, or
note it, etc.) and then consciously describe it. (Note that this simple possibility
of uttering the "proposition," "I am in pain" without first performing any mental
"act of judgment" was overlooked by traditional epistemologists from [David—
Ed.] Hume to [Bertrand—Ed.] Russell!) Now we may consider the parallel questions "Does the machine 'ascertain' that it is in state A?" and "Does Jones 'know'
that he is in pain?" and their consequences.

Philosophers interested in semantical questions have, as one might expect,
paid a good deal of attention to the verb "know." Traditionally, three elements
have been distinguished: (1) "X knows that p" implies that p is *true* (we may
call this the *truth* element); (2) "X knows that p" implies that X believes that p
(philosophers have quarreled about the word, some contending that it should be
'X is *confident* that p,' or 'X *is in a position to assert* that p'; I shall call this
element the *confidence* element); (3) "X knows that p" implies that X has
evidence that p (here I think the word "evidence" is definitely wrong,[11] but it
will not matter for present purposes; I shall call this the *evidential* element).
Moreover, it is part of the meaning of the word "evidence" that nothing can be
literally evidence for itself: if X is evidence for Y, then X and Y must be different
things.

In view of such analyses, disputes have arisen over the propriety of saying
(in cases like the one we are considering) "Jones knows that he is in pain." On
the one hand, philosophers who take the common-sense view ("When I have a
pain I *know* I have a pain") argue somewhat as follows: It would be clearly
false to say Jones does *not* know he has a pain; but either Jones knows or he does
not; hence, Jones knows he has a pain. Against these philosophers, one might
argue as follows: "Jones does not know X" implies Jones is not in a position to
assert that X; hence, it is certainly wrong to say "Jones does not know he has a
pain." But the above use of the Law of the Excluded Middle was fallacious:
words in English have *significance ranges*, and what is contended is that it is not
semantically correct to say *either* "Jones knows that he has a pain" *or* "Jones
does not know he has a pain" (although the former sentence is certainly less misleading than the latter, since *one* at least of the conditions involved in knowing
is met—Jones is in a position to assert he has a pain). (In fact the *truth* and *confidence* elements are both present; it is the evidential element that occasions the
difficulty.)

I do not wish to argue this question here;[12] the present concern is rather

---

[11] For example, I know that the sun is 93 million miles from the earth, but I have no
evidence that this is so. In fact, I do not even remember where I learned this.

[12] In fact, it would be impossible to decide whether "Jones knows he has a pain" is
deviant or not without first reformulating the evidential condition so as to avoid the objection
in note 11 (if it can be reformulated so as to save anything of the condition at all). However,
the discussion above will indicate, I believe, why one might *want* to find that this sentence is
deviant.

with the similarities between our two questions. For example, one might decide to accept (as "non-deviant," "logically in order," "nonselfcontradictory," etc.) the two statements:

(a) The machine ascertained that it was in state A,
(b) Jones knew that he had a pain,

or one might reject both. If one rejects (a) and (b), then one can find alternative formulations which are certainly semantically acceptable: e.g., [for (a)] "The machine was in state A, and this caused it to print: 'I am in state A;' " [for (b)] "Jones was in pain, and this caused him to say 'I am in pain' " (or, "Jones was in pain, and he evinced this by saying 'I am in pain' ").

On the other hand, if one accepts (a) and (b), then one must face the questions (a¹) "*How* did the machine ascertain that it was in state A?", and (b¹) "*How* did Jones know that he had a pain?"

And if one regards these questions as having answers at all, then they will be degenerate answers—e.g., "By being in state A" and "By having the pain."

At this point it is, I believe, very clear that the difficulty has in both cases the same cause. Namely, the difficulty is occasioned by the fact that the "verbal report" ("I am in state A," or "I am in pain") issues directly from the state it "reports": no "computation" or additional "evidence" is needed to arrive at the "answer." And the philosophic disagreements over "how to talk" are at bottom concerned with finding a terminology for describing cognitive processes in general that is not misleading in this particular case. [Note that the traditional epistemological answer to (b¹)—namely, "by introspection"—is false to the facts of this case, since it clearly implies the occurrence of a mental event (the "act" of introspection) distinct from the feeling of pain.]

Finally, let us suppose that the machine is equipped to "scan" its neighbor machine T¹. Then we can see that the question "How does T ascertain that T¹ is in state A?" may be a perfectly sensible question, as much so as "How does T ascertain that the 3000th digit of π is so-and-so?" In both cases the answer will involve describing a whole "program" (plus explaining the *rationale* of the program, if necessary). Moreover, it will be necessary to say something about the physical context linking T and T¹ (arrangement of sense organs, etc.), and not just to describe the internal states of T: this is so because T is now answering an *empirical* and not a mathematical question. In the same way "How did Sherlock Holmes know that Jones was in pain?" may be a perfectly sensible question, and may have quite a complicated answer.

3. "Mental" States and "Logical" States

Consider the two questions:

(1) How does Jones know he has a pain?
(2) How does Jones know he has a fever?

The first question is, as we saw in the preceding section, a somewhat peculiar one. The second question may be quite sensible. In fact, if Jones says "I have a pain" no one will retort "You are mistaken." (One *might* retort "You have made a slip of the tongue" or "You are lying," but not "You are *mistaken*.") On the other hand, if Jones says "I have a fever," the doctor who has just taken Jones' temperature may quite conceivably retort "You are mistaken." And the doctor need not mean that Jones made a linguistic error, or was lying, or confused.

It might be thought that, whereas the difference between statements about one's own state and statements about the state of others has an analogue in the case of machines, the difference, just touched upon, between statements about one's "mental" state and statements about one's "physical" state, in traditional parlance, does not have any analogue. But this is not so. Just what the analogue is will now be developed.

First of all, we have to go back to the notion of a Turing machine. When a Turing machine is described by means of a "machine table," it is described as something having a tape, a printing device, a "scanning" device (this may be no more than a point of the machine which at any given time is aligned with just one square of the tape), and a finite set (A,B,C, etc.) of "states." (In what follows, these will be referred to at times as *logical states* to distinguish them from certain other states to be introduced shortly.) Beyond this it is described only by giving the deterministic rules which determine the order in which the states succeed each other and what is printed when.

In particular, the "logical description" of a Turing machine does not include any specification of the *physical nature* of these "states"—or indeed, of the physical nature of the whole machine. (Shall it consist of electronic relays, of cardboard, of human clerks sitting at desks, or what?) In other words, a given "Turing machine" is an *abstract* machine which may be physically realized in an almost infinite number of different ways.

As soon as a Turing machine is physically realized, however, something interesting happens. Although the machine has from the logician's point of view only the states A,B,C, etc., it has from the engineer's point of view an almost infinite number of additional "states" (though not in the same sense of "state"—we shall call these *structural states*). For instance, if the machine consists of vacuum tubes, one of the things that may happen is that one of its vacuum tubes may fail—this puts the machine in what is from the physicist's if not the logician's point of view a different "state." Again, if the machine is a manually operated one built of cardboard, one of its possible "non-logical" or "structural" states is obviously that its cardboard may buckle. And so on.

A physically realized Turing machine may have no way of ascertaining its own structural state, just as a human being may have no way of ascertaining the condition of his appendix at a given time. However, it is extremely convenient to give a machine electronic "sense organs" which enable it to scan itself and to detect minor malfunctions. These "sense organs" may be visualized as causing certain symbols to be printed on an "input tape" which the machine "examines" from time to time. (One minor difficulty is that the "report" of a sense organ might occupy a number of squares of tape, whereas the machine only "scans" one square at a time—however this is unimportant, since it is well known that the effect of "reading" any finite number of squares can be obtained using a program which only requires one square to be scanned at a time.)

(By way of a digression, let me remark that the first actually constructed digital computers did not have any devices of the kind just envisaged. On the other hand, they *did* have over 3000 vacuum tubes, some of which were failing at any given time! The need for "routines" for self-checking therefore quickly became evident.) [13]

A machine which is able to detect at least some of its own structural states is in a position very analogous to that of a human being, who can detect some but not all of the malfunctions of his own body, and with varying degrees of reliability. Thus, suppose the machine "prints out": "Vacuum tube 312 has failed." The question "How did the machine ascertain that vacuum tube 312 failed?" is a perfectly sensible question. And the answer may involve a reference to both the physical structure of the machine ("sense organs," etc.) and the "logical structure" (program for "reading" and "interpreting" the input tape).

If the machine prints: "Vacuum tube 312 has failed" when vacuum tube 312 is in fact functioning, the mistake may be due to a miscomputation (in the course of "reading" and "interpreting" the input tape) or to an incorrect signal from a sense organ. On the other hand, if the machine prints: "I am in state A," and it does this simply because its machine table contains the instruction: *Print:* "*I am in state* A *when in state* A," then the question of a miscomputation cannot arise. Even if some accident causes the printing mechanism to print: "I am in state A" when the machine is *not* in state A, there was not a "miscomputation" (only, so to speak, a "verbal slip").

It is interesting to note that just as there are two possible descriptions of the behavior of a Turing machine—the engineer's structural blueprint and the logician's "machine table"—so there are two possible descriptions of human psychology. The "behavioristic" approach (including in this category theories which employ "hypothetical constructs," including "constructs" taken from physiology) aims at eventually providing a complete physicalistic[14] description of human behavior, in terms which link up with chemistry and physics. This corresponds to the engineer's or physicist's description of a physically realized Turing machine. But it would also be possible to seek a more abstract description of human mental processes, in terms of "mental states" (physical realization, if any, unspecified) and "impressions" (these play the role of symbols on the machine's tapes)—a description which would specify the laws controlling the order in which the states succeeded one another, and the relation to verbalization (or, at any rate, verbalized thought). This description, which would be the analogue of a "machine table," it was in fact the program of classical psychology to provide! Classical psychology is often thought to have failed for *methodological* reasons; I would suggest, in the light of this analogy, that it failed rather for empirical reasons—the mental states and "impressions"

---

[13] Actually, it was not necessary to add any "sense organs"; existing computers check themselves by "performing crucial experiments with themselves" (i.e., carrying out certain test computations and comparing the results with the correct results which have been given).

[14] In the sense of (7); not in the "epistemological" sense associated with Carnap's writings on "physicalism."

of human beings do not form a causally closed system to the extent to which the "configurations" of a Turing machine do.

The analogy which has been presented between logical states of a Turing machine and mental states of a human being, on the one hand, and structural states of a Turing machine and physical states of a human being, on the other, is one that I find very suggestive. In particular, further exploration of this analogy may make it possible to further clarify the notion of a "mental state" that we have been discussing. This "further exploration" has not yet been undertaken, at any rate by me, but I should like to put down, for those who may be interested, a few of the features that seem to distinguish logical and mental states respectively from structural and physical ones:

(1) The functional organization (problem solving, thinking) of the human being or machine can be described in terms of the sequences of mental or logical states respectively (and the accompanying verbalizations), without reference to the nature of the "physical realization" of these states.
(2) The states seem intimately connected with *verbalization*.
(3) In the case of rational thought (or computing), the "program" which determines which states follow which, etc., is open to rational criticism.

4. Mind-Body "Identity"

The last area in which we have to compare human beings and machines involves the question of *identifying* mental states with the corresponding physical states (or logical states with the corresponding structural states). As indicated at the beginning of this paper, all of the arguments for and against such identification can perfectly well be discussed in terms of Turing machines.

For example, in the 1930's Wittgenstein used the following argument: If I observe an after-image, and observe at the same time my brain state (with the aid of a suitable instrument) I observe *two* things, not one. (Presumably this is one argument *against* identification.) But we can perfectly well imagine a "clever" Turing machine "reasoning" as follows: "When I print 'I am in state A,' I do not have to use my 'sense organs.' When I do use my 'sense organs' and compare the occasions upon which I am in state A with the occasions upon which flip-flop 36 is on, I am comparing *two* things and not one." And I do not think that we would find the argument of this mechanical Wittgenstein very convincing!

By contrast, Russell once carried the "identity" view to the absurd extreme of maintaining that all we ever *see* is portions of our own brains. Analogously, a mechanical Russell might "argue" that "all I ever observe is my own vacuum tubes." Both "Russells" are wrong—the human being observes events in the outside world, and the process of "observation" involves events in his brain. But we are not therefore forced to say that he "really" observes his brain. Similarly, the machine T may "observe," say, cans of tomato soup (if the machine's job is sorting cans of soup), and the process of "observation" involves the functioning of vacuum tubes. But we are not forced to say that the machine "really" observes its own vacuum tubes.

But let us consider more serious arguments on this topic. At the beginning of this paper, I pointed out that the *synthetic* character of the statement (1) "I am in pain if, and only if, my C-fibers are stimulated" has been used as an argument for the view that the "properties" (or "events" or "states") "having C-fibers stimulated" and "being in pain" cannot be the same. There are at least two reasons why this is not a very good argument: (A) the "analytic-synthetic" distinction is not as sharp as that, especially where scientific laws are concerned; and (B) the criterion employed here for identifying "properties" (or "events" or "states") is a very questionable one.

With respect to point (A): I have argued elsewhere[15] that fundamental scientific laws cannot be happily classified as either "analytic" or "synthetic." Consider, for example, the kind of conceptual shift that was involved in the transition from Euclidean to non-Euclidean geometry, or that would be involved if the law of the conservation of energy were to be abandoned. It is a distortion to say that the laws of Euclidean geometry (during their tenure of office) were "analytic," and that Einstein merely "changed the meaning of the words." Indeed, it was precisely because Einstein did *not* change the meaning of the words, because he was really talking about shortest paths in the space in which we live and move and have our being, that General Relativity seemed so incomprehensible when it was first proposed. To be told that one could come back to the same place by moving in one direction on a straight line! Adopting General Relativity was indeed adopting a whole new system of concepts—but that is not to say "adopting a new system of verbal labels."

But if it is a distortion to assimilate the revision of fundamental scientific laws to the adoption of new linguistic conventions, it is equally a mistake to follow conventional philosophers of science, and assimilate the conceptual change that Einstein inaugurated to the kind of change that arises when we discover a black swan (whereas we had previously assumed all swans to be white)! Fundamental laws are like principles of pure mathematics (as Quine has emphasized), in that they cannot be overthrown by isolated experiments: we can always hold on to the laws, and explain the experiments in various more or less *ad hoc* ways. And—in spite of the pejorative flavor of "ad hoc"—it is even *rational* to do this, in the case of important scientific theories, *as long as no acceptable alternative theory exists.* This is why it took a century of concept formation—and not just some experiments—to overthrow Euclidean geometry. And similarly, this is why we cannot today describe *any* experiments which would *by themselves* overthrow the law of the conservation of energy—although that law is not "analytic," and might be abandoned if a new Einstein were to suggest good *theoretical* reasons for abandoning it, plus supporting experiments.

As Hanson has put it,[16] our concepts have theories "built into" them—thus, to abandon a major scientific theory without providing an alternative would be to "let our concepts crumble." By contrast, although we *could* have held on to "all swans are white" in the face of conflicting evidence, there would have been

---

[15] In (8).
[16] In (5).

no *point* in doing so—the concepts involved did not *rest* on the acceptance of this or some rival principle in the way that geometrical concepts rest on the acceptance, not necessarily of Euclidean geometry, but of *some* geometry.

I do not deny that *today* any newly-discovered "correlation" of the form: "One is in mental state ψ if, and only if, one is in brain state Φ" would *at first* be a *mere* correlation, a pure "empirical generalization." But I maintain that the interesting case is the case that would arise if we had a worked out and theoretically elaborated *system* of such "correlations." In such a case, scientific talk would be very different. Scientists would begin to say: "It is impossible *in principle* to be in mental state ψ without being in brain state Φ." And it could very well be that the "impossibility in principle" would amount to what Hanson rightly calls a *conceptual*[17] impossibility: scientists could not *conceive* (barring a new Einstein) of someone's being in mental state ψ without being in brain state Φ. In particular, no experiment could *by itself* overthrow psychophysical laws which had acquired this kind of status.[18] Is it clear that in this kind of scientific situation it would not be correct to say that Φ and ψ are the *same* state?

Moreover, the criteria for identifying "events" or "states" or "properties" are by no means so clear. An example of a law with the sort of status we have been discussing is the following: Light passes through an aperture if, and only if, electromagnetic radiation (of such-and-such wavelengths) passes through the aperture.

This law is quite clearly *not* an "analytic" statement. Yet it would be perfectly good scientific parlance to say that: (i) light passing through an aperture and (ii) electromagnetic radiation (of such-and-such wavelengths) passing through an aperture are two descriptions of the same event. (Indeed, in "ordinary language" not only are descriptions of the same event not required to be equivalent: one may even speak of *incompatible* descriptions of the same event!)

It might be held, however, that *properties* (as opposed to events) cannot be described by different nonequivalent descriptions. Indeed, [Gottlob—Ed.] Frege, [C. I.—Ed.] Lewis, and Carnap have *identified* properties and "meanings" (so that *by definition* if two expressions have different meanings then they "signify" different properties). This seems to me very dubious. But suppose it were correct. What would follow? One would have to admit that, e.g., being in pain and having C-fibers stimulated were different properties. But, in the language of the "theory-constructing" Turing machine described at the beginning of this paper, one would equally have to admit that "being in state A" and "having flip-flop 36 on" were different properties. Indeed the sentences (i) "I am in state A" and (ii) "Flip-flop 36 is on" are clearly nonsynonymous in the machine's language by any test (they have different syntactical properties and also different "conditions of utterance"—e.g., the machine has to use different "methods of verification"). Anyone who wishes, then, to argue on this basis for the existence of the soul will have to be prepared to hug the souls of Turing machines to his philosophic bosom!

---

[17] Cf. (5).
[18] Cf. the discussion of geometry in (8).

5. A "Linguistic" Argument

The last argument I shall consider on the subject of mind-body identity is a widely used "linguistic" argument—it was, for example, used by Max Black against Herbert Feigl . . . Consider the sentence:

(1) Pain *is identical with* stimulation of C-fibers.

The sentence is deviant (so the argument runs, though not in this terminology): there is no statement that it could be used to make in a normal context. Therefore, if a philosopher advances it as a thesis he must be giving the words a new meaning, rather than expressing any sort of discovery. For example (Max Black argued) one might begin to say "I have stimulated C-fibers" instead of "I have a pain," etc. But then one would *merely* be giving the expression "has stimulated C-fibers" the new meaning "is in pain." The contention is that as long as the words keep their present meanings, (1) is unintelligible.

I agree that the sentence (1) is a "deviant" sentence in present-day English. I do *not* agree that (1) can never become a normal, non-deviant sentence unless the words change their present meanings.

The point, in a nutshell, is that what is "deviant" depends very much upon context, including the state of our knowledge, and with the development of new scientific theories it is constantly occurring that sentences that did not previously "have a use," that were previously "deviant," acquire a use—not because the words acquire *new* meanings, but because the old meanings as fixed by the core of stock uses, *determine* a new use given the new context.

There is nothing wrong with trying to bring linguistic theory to bear on this issue, but one must have a sufficiently sophisticated linguistic theory to bring to bear. The real question is not a question in *synchronic* linguistics but one in *diachronic*[19] linguistics, not "Is (1) *now* a deviant sentence?", but "If a change in scientific knowledge (e.g., the development of an integrated network of psychophysical laws of high "priority" in our overall scientific world view) were to lead to (1)'s becoming a *non*-deviant sentence, would a change in the meaning of a word necessarily have taken place?"—and this is not so simple a question.

Although this is not the time or the place to attempt the job of elaborating a semantical theory,[20] I should like to risk a few remarks on this question.

In the first place, it is easy to show that the mere uttering of a sentence which no one has ever uttered before does not necessarily constitute the introduction of a "new use." If I say "There is a purple Gila monster on this desk," I am very likely uttering a sentence that no English-speaker has uttered before me: but I am not in any way changing the meaning of any word.

In the second place, even if a sentence which was formerly deviant begins to

---

[19] Diachronic linguistics studies the language as it changes through time; synchronic linguistics seeks only to describe the language at one particular time.

[20] For a detailed discussion, cf. (14). I am extremely indebted to Ziff, both for making this work available to me and for personal communications on these matters. Section 5 of the present paper represents partly Ziff's influence (especially the use of the "synchronic-diachronic" distinction), and partly the application of some of the ideas of (8) to the present topic.

acquire a standard use, no change in the *meaning* of any word need have taken place. Thus the sentence "I am a thousand miles away from you," or its translation into ancient Greek, was undoubtedly a deviant sentence prior to the invention of *writing*, but acquired (was not "given," but *acquired*) a normal use with the invention of writing and the ensuing possibility of long-distance interpersonal address.

Note the reasons that we would not say that any word (e.g., "I," "you," "thousand") in this sentence changed its meaning: (A) the new use was not *arbitrary*, was not the product of *stipulation*, but represented an automatic projection[21] from the existing stock uses of the several words making up the sentence, given the new context; (B) the meaning of a sentence is in general a function of the meanings of the individual words making it up (in fact this principle underlies the whole notion of word meaning)—thus, if we said that the *sentence* had changed its meaning, we should have to face the question "*Which word* changed its meaning?" But this would pretty clearly be an embarrassing question in this case.

The case just described was one in which the new context was the product of new technology, but new theoretical knowledge may have a similar impact on the language. (For example, "He went all the way around the world" would be a deviant sentence in a culture which did not know that the earth was round!) A case of this kind was discussed by [Norman—Ed.] Malcolm: We are beginning to have the means available for telling, on the basis of various physiological indicators (electroencephalograms, eye movements during sleep, blood pressure disturbances, etc.), when dreams begin and end. The sentence "He is halfway through his dream" may, therefore, someday acquire a standard use. Malcolm's comment on this was that the words would in that case have been *given* a use. Malcolm is clearly mistaken, I believe; this case, in which a sentence acquires a use *because* of what the words mean is poles apart from the case in which words are literally *given* a use (i.e., in which meanings are stipulated for expressions). The "realistic" account of this case is, I think, obviously correct: the sentence did not previously have a use because we had no way of telling when dreams start and stop. Now we are beginning to have ways of telling, and so we are beginning to find occasions upon which it is natural to employ this sentence. (Note that in Malcolm's account there is no explanation of the fact that we give *this* sentence *this* use.)

Now, someone may grant that change in meaning should not be confused with change in distribution,[22] and that scientific and technological advances frequently produce changes in the latter that are not properly regarded as changes in the former. But one might argue that whereas one could have envisaged beforehand the circumstances under which the sentence "He went all the way around the world" would become non-deviant, one cannot now envisage any circumstances under which[23] "mental state ψ is identical with brain state Φ"

---

[21] The term is taken from (14).

[22] The *distribution* of a word = the set of sentences in which it occurs.

[23] Here "Mental state ψ is identical with brain state Φ" is used as a surrogate for such sentences as "Pain is identical with stimulation of C-fibers."

would be non-deviant. But this is not a very good objection. In the first place, it might very well have been impossible for primitive people to envisage a spherical earth (the people on the "underside" would obviously fall off). Even forty years ago, it might have been difficult if not impossible to envisage circumstances under which "he is halfway through his dream" would be non-deviant. And in the second place, I believe that one *can* describe in general terms circumstances under which "mental state ψ is identical with brain state Φ" would become non-deviant.

In order to do this, it is necessary to talk about one important kind of "is" —the *"is" of theoretical identification*. The use of "is" in question is exemplified in the following sentences:

(2) Light is electromagnetic radiation (of such-and-such wavelengths).
(3) Water is H_2O.

What was involved in the scientific acceptance of, for instance, (2) was very roughly this: prior to the identification there were two distinct bodies of theory— optical theory (whose character [Stephen—Ed.] Toulmin has very well described in his book on philosophy of science), and electromagnetic theory (as represented by Maxwell's equations). The decision to *define* light as "electromagnetic radiation of such-and-such wavelengths" was scientifically justified by the following sorts of considerations (as has often been pointed out):

(1) It made possible the *derivation* of the laws of optics (up to first approximation) from more "basic" physical laws. Thus, even if it had accomplished nothing else, this theoretical identification would have been a move toward simplifying the structure of scientific laws.
(2) It made possible the derivation of *new* predictions in the "reduced" discipline (i.e., optics). In particular, it was now possible to predict that in certain cases the laws of geometrical optics would *not* hold. (Cf. [Pierre —Ed.] Duhem's famous comments on the reduction of Kepler's laws to Newton's.)

Now let us try to envisage the circumstances under which a theoretical identification of mental states with physiological states might be in accordance with good scientific procedure. In general terms, what is necessary is that we should have not *mere* "correlates" for subjective states, but something much more elaborate—e.g., that we should know of physical states (say micro-states of the central processes) on the basis of which we could not merely *predict* human behavior, but causally explain it.

In order to avoid "category mistakes," it is necessary to restrict this notion, "explain human behavior," very carefully. Suppose a man says "I feel bad." His behavior, described in one set of categories, is: "stating that he feels bad." And the explanation may be "He said that he felt bad because he was hungry and had a headache." I do not wish to suggest that the event "Jones *stating* that he feels bad" can be explained in terms of the laws of *physics*. But there is *another* event which is very relevant, namely "Jones' body producing such-and-such sound waves." From one point of view this is a "different event" from Jones' stating that he feels bad. But (to adapt a remark of Hanson's) there would be no point in remarking that these are different events if there were not a sense in which they were the *same* event. And it is the sense in which these are the "same event" and not the sense in which these are "different events" that is relevant here.

In fine, all I mean when I speak of "causally explaining human behavior" is: causally explaining certain physical events (motions of bodies, productions of sound waves, etc.) which are in the sense just referred to the "same" as the events which make up human behavior. And no amount of "Ryle-ism" can succeed in arguing away[24] what is obviously a possibility: that physical science might succeed in doing this much.

If this much were a reality, then theoretically identifying "mental states" with their "correlates" would have the following two advantages:

(1) It would be possible (again up to "first approximation") to derive from physical theory the classical laws (or low-level generalizations) of common-sense "mentalistic" psychology, such as: "People tend to avoid things with which they have had painful experiences."

(2) It would be possible to predict the cases (and they are legion) in which common-sense "mentalistic" psychology fails.

Advantage (2) could, of course, be obtained without "identification" (by using correlation laws). But advantage (2) could equally have been obtained in the case of optics without identification (by assuming that light *accompanies* electromagnetic radiation, but is not *identical* with it). But the *combined* effect of eliminating certain laws altogether (in favor of theoretical definitions) *and* increasing the explanatory power of the theory could not be obtained in any other way in either case. The point worth noticing is that *every* argument for *and against* identification would apply equally in the mind-body case and in the light-electromagnetism case. (Even the "ordinary language" argument could have been advanced against the identification of light with electromagnetic radiation.)

Two small points: (i) When I call "light is electromagnetic radiation (of such-and-such wavelengths)" a definition, I do not mean that the statement is "analytic." But then "definitions," *properly so called*, in theoretical science virtually *never* are analytic.[25] (Quine remarked once that he could think of at least nine good senses of "definition," none of which had anything to do with analyticity.) Of course a philosopher might then object to the whole *rationale* of theoretical identification on the ground that it is no gain to eliminate "laws" in favor of "definitions" if both are *synthetic* statements. The fact that the scientist does not feel at all the same way is another illustration of how unhelpful it is to look at science from the standpoint of the question "Analytic or synthetic?" (ii) Accepting a theoretical identification, e.g., "Pain *is* stimulation of C-fibers," does not commit one to *interchanging* the terms "pain" and "stimulation of C-fibers" in idiomatic talk, as Black suggested. For instance, the identification of "water" with "H_2O" is by now a very well-known one, but no one says "Bring me a glass of H_2O," except as a joke.

---

[24] As one young philosopher attempted to do in a recent article in the *British Journal for the Philosophy of Science*.

[25] This is argued in (8).

I believe that the account just presented is able (a) to explain the fact that sentences such as "Mental state ψ is identical with brain state Φ" are deviant in present-day English, while (b) making it clear how these same sentences might become *non-deviant* given a suitable increase in our scientific insight into the physical nature and causes of human behavior. The sentences in question cannot today be used to express a theoretical identification, because no such identification has been made. The act of theoretical identification is not an act that can be performed "at will"; there are *preconditions* for its performance, as there are for many acts, and these preconditions are not satisfied today. On the other hand, if the sort of scientific theory described above should materialize, then the preconditions for theoretical identification would be met, as they were met in the light-electromagnetism case, and sentences of the type in question would then *automatically* require a use—namely, to express the appropriate theoretical identifications. Once again, what makes this way of *acquiring* a use different from being *given* a use (and from "change of meaning" properly so called) is that the "new use" is an automatic *projection* from existing uses, and does not involve arbitrary stipulation (except insofar as some element of "stipulation" may be present in the acceptance of *any* scientific hypothesis, including "The earth is round").

So far we have considered only sentences of the form[26] "mental state ψ is identical with brain state Φ." But what of the sentence:

(3) Mental states are micro-states of the brain?

This sentence does not, so to speak, "give" any *particular* theoretical identification: it only says that unspecified theoretical identifications are possible. This is the sort of assertion that Feigl might make. And Black[27] might reply that in uttering (3) Feigl had uttered an odd set of words (i.e., a deviant sentence). It is possible that Black is right. Perhaps (3) is deviant in present-day English. But it is also possible that our descendants in two or three hundred years will feel that Feigl was making perfectly good sense, and that the linguistic objections to (3) were quite silly. And they too may be right.

6. Machine Linguistics

Let us consider the linguistic question that we have just discussed from the standpoint of the analogy between man and Turing machine that we have been presenting in this paper. It will be seen that our Turing machine will probably not be able, if it lacks suitable "sense organs," to construct a correct theory of its own constitution. On the other hand "I am in state A" will be a sentence with a definite pattern of occurrence in the machine's "language." If the machine's "language" is sufficiently complex, it may be possible to analyze it

---

[26] By sentences of this *form* I do not literally mean *substitution instances* of "mental state ψ is identical with brain state Φ." Cf. note 23.

[27] I have, with hesitation, ascribed this position to Black on the basis of his remarks at the Conference. But, of course, I realize that he cannot justly be held responsible for remarks made on the spur of the moment.

syntactically in terms of a finite set of basic building blocks (morphemes) and rules for constructing a potentially infinite set of "sentences" from these. In particular, it will be possible to distinguish *grammatical*[28] from *ungrammatical sentences* in the machine's "language." Similarly, it may be possible to associate regularities with sentence occurrences (or, "describe sentence uses," in the Oxford jargon), and to assign "meanings" to the finite set of morphemes and the finite set of forms of composition in such a way that the "uses" of the various sentences can be effectively projected from the meanings of the individual morphemes and forms of composition. In this case, one could distinguish not only "grammatical" and "ungrammatical" sentences in the "machine language," but also "deviant" and "non-deviant" ones.

[Roderick—Ed.] Chisholm would insist that it is improper to speak of machines as employing a language, and I agree. This is the reason for my occasionally enclosing the words "language," "meaning," etc., in "raised-eyebrow" quotes—to emphasize, where necessary, that these words are being used in an extended sense. On the other hand, it is important to recognize that machine performances may be wholly *analogous* to language, so much so that the whole of linguistic theory can be applied to them. If the reader wishes to check this, he may go through a work like Chomsky's *Syntactic Structures* carefully, and note that *at no place is the assumption employed that the corpus of utterances studied by the linguist was produced by a conscious organism.* Then he may turn to such pioneer work in empirical semantics as Ziff's *Semantical Analysis* and observe that the same thing holds true for *semantical* theory.

Two further remarks in this connection: (i) Since I am contending that the mind-body problem is *strictly analogous* to the problem of the relation between structural and logical states, not that the two problems are *identical*, a suitable *analogy* between machine "language" and human language is all that is needed here. (ii) Chisholm might contend that a "behavioristic" semantics of the kind attempted by Ziff (i.e., one that does not take "intentionality" as a private notion) is impossible. But even if this were true, it would not be relevant. For if *any* semantical theory can fit human language, it has to be shown why a completely *analogous* theory would not fit the language of a suitable machine. For instance, if "intentionality" plays a role as a primitive notion in a *scientific* explanation of human language, then a theoretical construct with similar *formal* relations to the corresponding "observables" will have the *same* explanatory power in the case of machine "language."

Of course, the objection to "behavioristic" linguistics might *really* be an objection to all attempts at *scientific* linguistics. But this possibility I feel justified in dismissing.

Now suppose we equip our "theory-constructing" Turing machine with "sense organs" so that it can obtain the empirical data necessary for the construction of a theory of its own nature.

Then it may introduce into its "theoretical language" noun phrases that can be "translated" by the English expression "flip-flop 36," and sentences that

---

[28] This term is used in the sense of (3), not in the traditional sense.

can be translated by "Flip-flop 36 is on." These expressions will have a meaning and use quite distinct from the meaning and use of "I am in state A" in the machine language.

If any "linguistic" argument really shows that the sentence "Pain is identical with stimulation of C-fibers" is deviant, in English, the same argument must show that "State A is identical with flip-flop 36 being on" is deviant in the machine language. If any argument shows that "Pain is identical with stimulation of C-fibers" could not become non-deviant (viewing English now *diachronically*) unless the words first altered their meanings, the same argument, applied to the "diachronic linguistics of machine language," would show that the sentence "State A is identical with flip-flop 36 being on" could not become non-deviant in machine language unless the words first changed their meanings. In short, every philosophic argument that has ever been employed in connection with the mind-body problem, from the oldest and most naïve (e.g., "states of consciousness can just be *seen* to be different from physical states") to the most sophisticated, has its exact counterpart in the case of the "problem" of logical states and structural states in Turing machines.

7. Conclusion

The moral, I believe, is quite clear: It is no longer possible to believe that the mind-body problem is a genuine theoretical problem, or that a "solution" to it would shed the slightest light on the world in which we live. For it is quite clear that no grown man in his right mind would take the problem of the "identity" or "non-identity" of logical and structural states in a machine at all seriously—not because the answer is obvious, but because it is obviously of no importance *what* the answer is. But if the so-called "mind-body problem" is nothing but a different realization of the same set of logical and linguistic issues, then it must be just as empty and just as verbal.

It is often an important insight that two problems with distinct subject matter are the same in all their logical and methodological aspects. In this case, the insight carries in its train the realization that any conclusion that might be reached in the case of the mind-body problem would have to be reached, *and for the same reasons,* in the Turing machine case. But if it is clear (as it obviously is) that, for example, the conclusion that the logical states of Turing machines are hopelessly different from their structural states, even if correct, could represent only a purely *verbal* discovery, then the same conclusion *reached by the same arguments* in the human case must likewise represent a purely verbal discovery. To put it differently, if the mind-body problem is identified with any problem of more than purely conceptual interest (e.g., with the question of whether or not human beings have "souls"), then *either* it must be that (a) no argument *ever* used by a philosopher sheds the *slightest* light on it (and this independently of the way the argument tends), or (b) that some philosophic argument for mechanism is correct, or (c) that some dualistic argument does show that *both* human beings *and* Turing machines have souls! I leave it to the reader to decide which of the three alternatives is at all plausible.

Bibliography

(1) CARNAP, RUDOLF. "The Interpretation of Physics." Reprinted in H. Feigl and M. Brodbeck, *Readings in the Philosophy of Science*. New York: Appleton-Century-Crofts, 1953, pp. 309–18.

(2) ————. "The Methodological Character of Theoretical Concepts," in *Minnesota Studies in the Philosophy of Science*, I, 38–76. Minneapolis: University of Minnesota, 1956.

(3) CHOMSKY, NOAM. *Syntactic Structures*. The Hague: Mouton & Co., 1957.

(4) DAVIS, MARTIN. *Computability and Unsolvability*. New York: McGraw-Hill Book Co., 1958.

(5) HANSON, NORWOOD RUSSELL. *Patterns of Discovery*. Cambridge: Cambridge University Press, 1958.

(6) KLEENE, STEPHEN COLE. *Introduction to Metamathematics*. New York: Van Nostrand, 1952.

(7) OPPENHEIM, PAUL, and PUTNAM, HILARY. "Unity of Science as a Working Hypothesis," in H. Feigl, G. Maxwell, and M. Scriven (eds.), *Concepts, Theories, and the Mind–Body Problem* (Minnesota Studies in the Philosophy of Science, Vol. II). Minneapolis: University of Minnesota, 1958.

(8) PUTNAM, HILARY. "The Analytic and the Synthetic," in *Minnesota Studies in the Philosophy of Science*, III. Minneapolis: University of Minnesota, 1960.

(9) QUINE, WILLARD VAN ORMAN. "The Scope and Language of Science," *British Journal for the Philosophy of Science*, VIII (1957).

(10) SMART, J. J. C. "Professor Ziff on Robots," *Analysis*, XIX (1959), 117–18.

(11) ————. "Incompatible Colors," *Philosophical Studies*, X (1959), 39–42.

(12) ————. "Sensations and Brain Processes," *Philosophical Review*, LXVIII (1959), 141–56.

(13) ZIFF, PAUL. "The Feelings of Robots," *Analysis*, XIX (1959), 64–68.

(14) ————. *Semantic Analysis*. Ithaca: Cornell University Press, 1960.

Personal Identity

6

David Hume

Of Personal Identity

David Hume (1711–1776), the great Scottish philosopher of the Newtonian era, is one of the most popular and influential philosophers of all time. It is therefore particularly instructive to know that his A Treatise on Human Nature, *which he published anonymously at the age of twenty-eight, largely on the basis of his own intensive studies before he was twenty, was essentially ignored by the learned. Some ten years later he published* An Enquiry Concerning the Principles of Morals *and what came to be retitled* An Enquiry Concerning the Human Understanding. *He was actually better known as a historian of Great Britain and as a man of letters and affairs, and he held several governmental posts. But the original* Treatise *already showed a capacity for sustaining a complete philosophical system, though Hume himself wished to have the two* Enquiries *taken to contain his principal philosophical work. He is often said to be the ironist of philosophy. Hume is uncompromising in the application of his method of skepticism, which is the analogue of Descartes's method of doubt. At the same time he recommends that we follow our natural inclinations in every way appropriate to "common life," which seems at variance with his philosophical findings. His skepticism is occupied with linking our assessment of the certainty and scope of our knowledge to a close study of our cognitive capacities. Characteristically, Hume finds that we are only psychologically disposed to make the inductive leap and to treat what is correlated as if it were connected; hence nature inclines us to favor that practice in our ordinary life.*

Hume offers a comparable but rather notorious account of our idea of a unified self. On reflection, he holds, we see that there is no separably discoverable self but only particular perceptions. Personal identity is an irresistible fiction attached to a "bundle of ideas"—that is, quite separate ideas somehow in the same vicinity. He maintains that all perception or experience divides into impressions (primary sensations and the like) and ideas (representations of sensations and the like, as in memory and imagination). This empiricist orientation led him to solve most of the puzzles of philosophy by appealing to the psychological habits of the mind. Abstract ideas, for instance, are explained by the association of concrete ideas; the meaning of terms is explained by reference to associated ideas.

From David Hume, A *Treatise of Human Nature*, L. A. Selby-Bigge, ed. (Oxford: The Clarendon Press, 1888), Book I, Part IV, Sec. 6, pp. 251–263.

There are some philosophers, who imagine we are every moment intimately conscious of what we call our SELF; that we feel its existence and its continuance in existence; and are certain, beyond the evidence of a demonstration, both of its perfect identity and simplicity. The strongest sensation, the most violent passion, say they, instead of distracting us from this view, only fix it the more intensely, and make us consider their influence on *self* either by their pain or pleasure. To attempt a farther proof of this were to weaken its evidence; since no proof can be deriv'd from any fact, of which we are so intimately conscious; nor is there any thing, of which we can be certain, if we doubt of this.

Unluckily all these positive assertions are contrary to that very experience, which is pleaded for them, nor have we any idea of *self*, after the manner it is here explain'd. For from what impression cou'd this idea be deriv'd? This question 'tis impossible to answer without a manifest contradiction and absurdity; and yet 'tis a question, which must necessarily be answer'd, if we wou'd have the idea of self pass for clear and intelligible. It must be some one impression, that gives rise to every real idea. But self or person is not any one impression, but that to which our several impressions and ideas are suppos'd to have a reference. If any impression gives rise to the idea of self, that impression must continue invariably the same, thro' the whole course of our lives; since self is suppos'd to exist after that manner. But there is no impression constant and invariable. Pain and pleasure, grief and joy, passions and sensations succeed each other, and never all exist at the same time. It cannot, therefore, be from any of these impressions, or from any other, that the idea of self is deriv'd; and consequently there is no such idea.

But farther, what must become of all our particular perceptions upon this hypothesis? All these are different, and distinguishable, and separable from each other, and may be separately consider'd, and may exist separately, and have no need of any thing to support their existence. After what manner, therefore, do they belong to self; and how are they connected with it? For my part, when I enter most intimately into what I call *myself*, I always stumble on some particular perception or other, of heat or cold, light or shade, love or hatred, pain or pleasure. I never can catch *myself* at any time without a perception, and never can observe any thing but the perception. When my perceptions are remov'd for any time, as by sound sleep; so long am I insensible of *myself*, and may truly be said not to exist. And were all my perceptions remov'd by death, and cou'd I neither think, nor feel, nor see, nor love, nor hate after the dissolution of my body, I shou'd be entirely annihilated, nor do I conceive what is farther requisite to make me a perfect non-entity. If any one upon serious and unprejudic'd reflexion, thinks he has a different notion of *himself*, I must confess I can reason no longer with him. All I can allow him is, that he may be in the right as well as I, and that we are essentially different in this particular. He may, perhaps, perceive something simple and continu'd, which he calls *himself*; tho' I am certain there is no such principle in me.

But setting aside some metaphysicians of this kind, I may venture to affirm of the rest of mankind, that they are nothing but a bundle or collection of different perceptions, which succeed each other with an inconceivable rapidity, and are in a perpetual flux and movement. Our eyes cannot turn in their sockets without varying our perceptions. Our thought is still more variable than our sight; and all our other senses and faculties contribute to this change; nor is there any single power of the soul, which remains unalterably the same, perhaps for one moment. The mind is a kind of theatre, where several perceptions successively make their appearance; pass, re-pass, glide away, and mingle in an infinite variety of postures and situations. There is properly no *simplicity* in it at one time, nor *identity* in different; whatever natural propension we may have to imagine that simplicity and identity. The comparison of the theatre must not mislead us. They are the successive perceptions only, that constitute the mind; nor have we the most distant notion of the place, where these scenes are represented, or of the materials, of which it is compos'd.

What then gives us so great a propension to ascribe an identity to these successive perceptions, and to suppose ourselves possest of an invariable and uninterrupted existence thro' the whole course of our lives? In order to answer this question, we must distinguish betwixt personal identity, as it regards our thought or imagination, and as it regards our passions or the concern we take in ourselves. The first is our present subject; and to explain it perfectly we must take the matter pretty deep, and account for that identity, which we attribute to plants and animals; there being a great analogy betwixt it, and the identity of a self or person.

We have a distinct idea of an object, that remains invariable and uninterrupted thro' a suppos'd variation of time; and this idea we call that of *identity* or *sameness*. We have also a distinct idea of several different objects existing in succession, and connected together by a close relation; and this to an accurate view affords as perfect a notion of *diversity*, as if there was no manner of relation among the objects. But tho' these two ideas of identity, and a succession of related objects be in themselves perfectly distinct, and even contrary, yet 'tis certain, that in our common way of thinking they are generally confounded with each other. That action of the imagination, by which we consider the uninterrupted and invariable object, and that by which we reflect on the succession of related objects, are almost the same to the feeling, nor is there much more effort of thought requir'd in the latter case than in the former. The relation facilitates the transition of the mind from one object to another, and renders its passage as smooth as if it contemplated one continu'd object. This resemblance is the cause of the confusion and mistake, and makes us substitute the notion of identity, instead of that of related objects. However at one instant we may consider the related succession as variable or interrupted, we are sure the next to ascribe to it a perfect identity, and regard it as invariable and uninterrupted. Our propensity to this mistake is so great from the resemblance above-mention'd, that we fall into it before we are aware; and tho' we incessantly correct ourselves by reflexion, and return to a more accurate method of thinking, yet we cannot long sustain our philosophy, or take off this biass from the imagination. Our last resource is to yield to it, and boldly assert that these different related objects are in effect the same, however interrupted and variable. In order to justify to ourselves this absurdity, we often feign some new and unintelligible principle, that connects the objects together, and prevents their interruption or variation. Thus we feign the continu'd existence of the perceptions of our senses, to remove the interruption; and run into the notion of a *soul,* and *self,* and *substance,* to disguise the variation. But we may farther observe, that where we do not give rise to such a fiction, our propension to confound identity with relation is so great, that we are apt to imagine[1] something unknown and mysterious, connecting the parts, beside their relation; and this I take to be the case with regard to the identity we ascribe to plants and vegetables. And even when this does not take place, we still feel a propensity to confound these ideas, tho' we are not able fully to satisfy ourselves in that particular, nor find any thing invariable and uninterrupted to justify our notion of identity.

Thus the controversy concerning identity is not merely a dispute of words. For when we attribute identity, in an improper sense, to variable or interrupted objects, our mistake is not confin'd to the expression, but is commonly attended with a fiction, either of something invariable and uninterrupted, or of something mysterious and inexplicable, or at least with a propensity to such fictions. What will suffice to prove this hypothesis to the satisfaction of every fair enquirer, is to shew from daily experience and observation, that the objects, which are variable or interrupted, and yet are suppos'd to continue the same, are such only as consist of a succession of parts, connected together by resemblance, contiguity, or causation. For as such a succession answers evidently to our notion of diversity, it can only be by mistake we ascribe to it an identity; and as the relation of parts, which leads us into this mistake, is really nothing but a quality, which produces an association of ideas, and an easy transition of the imagination from one to another, it can only be from the resemblance, which this act of the mind bears to that, by which we contemplate one continu'd object, that the error arises. Our chief business, then, must be to prove, that all objects, to which we ascribe identity, without observing their invariableness and uninterruptedness, are such as consist of a succession of related objects.

In order to this, suppose any mass of matter, of which the parts are contiguous and connected, to be plac'd before us; 'tis plain we must attribute a perfect identity to this mass, provided all the parts continue uninterruptedly and invariably the same, whatever motion or change of place we may observe either in the whole or in any of the parts. But supposing some very *small* or *inconsiderable* part to be added to the mass, or subtracted from it; tho' this absolutely destroys the identity of the whole, strictly speaking; yet as we seldom think so accurately, we scruple not to pronounce a mass of matter the same, where we find so trivial an alteration. The passage of the thought from the object before the change to the object after it, is so smooth and easy, that we scarce perceive the transition, and are apt to imagine, that 'tis nothing but a continu'd survey of the same object.

---

[1] If the reader is desirous to see how a great genius may be influenc'd by these seemingly trivial principles of the imagination, as well as the mere vulgar, let him read my Lord *Shaftsbury*'s reasonings concerning the uniting principle of the universe, and the identity of plants and animals. See his *Moralists; or, Philosophical rhapsody.*

There is a very remarkable circumstance, that attends this experiment; which is, that tho' the change of any considerable part in a mass of matter destroys the identity of the whole, yet we must measure the greatness of the part, not absolutely, but by its *proportion* to the whole. The addition or diminution of a mountain wou'd not be sufficient to produce a diversity in a planet; tho' the change of a very few inches wou'd be able to destroy the identity of some bodies. 'Twill be impossible to account for this, but by reflecting that objects operate upon the mind, and break or interrupt the continuity of its actions not according to their real greatness, but according to their proportion to each other: And therefore, since this interruption makes an object cease to appear the same, it must be the uninterrupted progress of the thought, which constitutes the [perfect] identity.

This may be confirm'd by another phænomenon. A change in any considerable part of a body destroys its identity; but 'tis remarkable, that where the change is produc'd *gradually* and *insensibly* we are less apt to ascribe to it the same effect. The reason can plainly be no other, than that the mind, in following the successive changes of the body, feels an easy passage from the surveying its condition in one moment to the viewing of it in another, and at no particular time perceives any interruption in its actions. From which continu'd perception, it ascribes a continu'd existence and identity to the object.

But whatever precaution we may use in introducing the changes gradually, and making them proportionable to the whole, 'tis certain, that where the changes are at last observ'd to become considerable, we make a scruple of ascribing identity to such different objects. There is, however, another artifice by which we may induce the imagination to advance a step farther; and that is, by producing a reference of the parts to each other, and a combination to some *common end* or purpose. A ship, of which a considerable part has been chang'd by frequent reparations, is still consider'd as the same; nor does the difference of the materials hinder us from ascribing an identity to it. The common end, in which the parts conspire, is the same under all their variations, and affords an easy transition of the imagination from one situation of the body to another.

But this is still more remarkable, when we add a *sympathy* of parts to their *common end*, and suppose that they bear to each other, the reciprocal relation of cause and effect in all their actions and operations. This is the case with all animals and vegetables; where not only the several parts have a reference to some general purpose, but also a mutual dependance on, and connexion with each other. The effect of so strong a relation is, that tho' every one must allow, that in a very few years both vegetables and animals endure a *total* change, yet we still attribute identity to them, while their form, size, and substance are entirely alter'd. An oak, that grows from a small plant to a large tree, is still the same oak; tho' there be not one particle of matter, or figure of its parts the same. An infant becomes a man, and is sometimes fat, sometimes lean, without any change in his identity.

We may also consider the two following phænomena, which are remarkable in their kind. The first is, that tho' we commonly be able to distinguish pretty exactly betwixt numerical and specific identity, yet it sometimes happens, that we confound them, and in our thinking and reasoning employ the one for the other. Thus a man, who hears a noise, that is frequently interrupted and renew'd, says, it is still the same noise; tho' 'tis evident the sounds have only a specific identity or resemblance, and there is nothing numerically the same, but the cause, which produc'd them. In like manner it may be said without breach of the propriety of language, that such a church, which was formerly of brick, fell to ruin, and that the parish rebuilt the same church of free-stone, and according to modern architecture. Here neither the form nor materials are the same, nor is there any thing common to the two objects, but their relation to the inhabitants of the parish; and yet this alone is sufficient to make us denominate them the same. But we must observe, that in these cases the first object is in a manner annihilated before the second comes into existence; by which means, we are never presented in any one point of time with the idea of difference and multiplicity; and for that reason are less scrupulous in calling them the same.

Secondly, We may remark, that tho' in a succession of related objects, it be in a manner requisite, that the change of parts be not sudden nor entire, in order to preserve the identity, yet where the objects are in their nature changeable and inconstant, we admit of a more sudden transition, than wou'd otherwise be consistent with that relation. Thus as the nature of a river consists in the motion and change of parts; tho' in less than four and twenty hours these be totally alter'd; this hinders not the river from continuing the same during several ages. What is natural and essential to any thing is, in a manner, expected; and what is expected makes less impression, and appears of less moment, than what is unusual and extraordinary. A considerable change of the former kind seems really less to the imagination, than the most trivial alteration of the latter; and by breaking less the continuity of the thought, has less influence in destroying the identity.

We now proceed to explain the nature of *personal identity*, which has become so great a question in philosophy, especially of late years in *England*, where all the abstruser sciences are study'd with a peculiar ardour and application. And here 'tis evident, the same method of reasoning must be continu'd, which has so successfully explain'd the identity of plants, and animals, and ships, and houses, and of all the compounded and changeable productions either of art or nature. The identity, which we ascribe to the mind of man, is only a fictitious one, and of a like kind with that which we ascribe to vegetables and animal bodies. It cannot, therefore, have a different origin, but must proceed from a like operation of the imagination upon like objects.

But lest this argument shou'd not convince the reader; tho' in my opinion perfectly decisive; let him weigh the following reasoning, which is still closer and more immediate. 'Tis evident, that the identity, which we attribute to the human mind, however perfect we may imagine it to be, is not able to run the several different perceptions into one, and make them lose their characters of distinction and difference, which are essential to them. 'Tis still true, that every distinct perception, which enters into the composition of the mind, is a distinct existence, and is different, and distinguishable, and separable from every other perception, either contemporary or successive. But, as, notwithstanding this distinction and separability, we suppose the whole train of perceptions to be united by identity, a question naturally arises concerning this relation of identity; whether it be something that really binds our several perceptions together, or only associates their ideas in the imagination. That is, in other words, whether in pronouncing concerning the identity of a person, we observe some real bond among his perceptions, or only feel one among the ideas we form of them. This question we might easily decide, if we wou'd recollect what has been already prov'd at large, that the understanding never observes any real connexion among objects, and that even the union of cause and effect, when strictly examin'd, resolves itself into a customary association of ideas. For from thence it evidently follows, that identity is nothing really belonging to these different perceptions, and uniting them together; but is merely a quality, which we attribute to them, because of the union of their ideas in the imagination, when we reflect upon them. Now the only qualities, which can give ideas an union in the imagination, are these three relations above-mention'd. These are the uniting principles in the ideal world, and without them every distinct object is separable by the mind, and may be separately consider'd, and appears not to have any more connexion with any other object, than if disjoin'd by the greatest difference and remoteness. 'Tis, therefore, on some of these three relations of resemblance, contiguity and causation, that identity depends; and as the very essence of these relations consists in their producing an easy transition of ideas; it follows, that our notions of personal identity, proceed entirely from the smooth and uninterrupted progress of the thought along a train of connected ideas, according to the principles above-explain'd.

The only question, therefore, which remains, is, by what relations this uninterrupted progress of our thought is produc'd, when we consider the successive existence of a mind or thinking person. And here 'tis evident we must confine ourselves to resemblance and causation, and must drop contiguity, which has little or no influence in the present case.

To begin with *resemblance*; suppose we cou'd see clearly into the breast of another, and observe that succession of perceptions, which constitutes his mind or thinking principle, and suppose that he always preserves the memory of a considerable part of past perceptions; 'tis evident that nothing cou'd more contribute to the bestowing a relation on this succession amidst all its variations. For what is the memory but a faculty, by which we raise up the images of past perceptions? And as an image necessarily resembles its object, must not the frequent placing of these resembling perceptions in the chain of thought, convey the imagination more easily from one link to another, and make the whole seem like the continuance of one object? In this particular, then, the memory not only discovers the identity, but also contributes to its production, by producing the relation of resemblance among the perceptions. The case is the same whether we consider ourselves or others.

As to *causation*; we may observe, that the true idea of the human mind, is to consider it as a system of different perceptions or different existences, which are link'd together by the relation of cause and effect, and mutually produce, destroy, influence, and modify each other. Our impressions give rise to their correspondent ideas; and these ideas in their turn produce other impressions. One thought chases another, and draws after it a third, by which it is expell'd in its turn. In this respect, I cannot compare the soul more properly to any thing than to a republic or commonwealth, in which the several members are united by the reciprocal ties of government and subordination, and give rise to other persons, who propagate the same republic in the incessant changes of its parts. And as the same individual republic may not only change its members, but also its laws and constitutions; in like manner the same person may vary his character and disposition, as well as his impressions and ideas, without losing his identity. Whatever changes he endures, his several parts are still connected by the relation of causation. And in this view our identity with regard to the passions serves to corroborate that with regard to the imagination, by the making our distant perceptions influence each other, and by giving us a present concern for our past or future pains or pleasures.

As memory alone acquaints us with the continuance and extent of this succession of perceptions, 'tis to be consider'd, upon that account chiefly, as the source of personal identity. Had we no memory, we never shou'd have any notion of causation, nor consequently of that chain of causes and effects, which constitute our self or person. But having once acquir'd this notion of causation from the memory, we can extend the same chain of causes, and consequently the identity of our persons beyond our memory, and can comprehend times, and circumstances, and actions, which we have entirely forgot, but suppose in general to have existed. For how few of our past actions are there, of which we have any memory? Who can tell me, for instance, what were his thoughts and actions on the first of *January* 1715, the 11th of *March* 1719, and the 3d of *August* 1733? Or will he affirm, because he has entirely forgot the incidents of these days, that the present self is not the same person with the self of that time; and by that means overturn all the most establish'd notions of personal identity? In this view, therefore, memory does not so much *produce* as *discover* personal identity, by shewing us the relation of cause and effect among our different perceptions. 'Twill be incumbent on those, who affirm that memory produces entirely our personal identity, to give a reason why we can thus extend our identity beyond our memory.

The whole of this doctrine leads us to a conclusion, which is of great importance in the present affair, *viz.* that all the nice and subtile questions concerning personal identity can never possibly be decided, and are to be regarded rather as grammatical than as philosophical difficulties. Identity depends on the relations of ideas; and these relations produce identity, by means of that easy transition they occasion. But as the relations, and the easiness of the transition may diminish by insensible degrees, we have no just standard, by which we can decide any dispute concerning the time, when they acquire or lose a title to the name of identity. All the disputes concerning the identity of connected objects are merely verbal, except so far as the relation of parts gives rise to some fiction or imaginary principle of union, as we have already observ'd.

What I have said concerning the first origin and uncertainty of our notion of identity, as apply'd to the human mind, may be extended with little or no variation to that of *simplicity*. An object, whose different co-existent parts are bound together by a close relation, operates upon the imagination after much the same manner as one perfectly simple and indivisible, and requires not a much greater stretch of thought in order to its conception. From this similarity of operation we attribute a simplicity to it, and feign a principle of union as the support of this simplicity, and the center of all the different parts and qualities of the object.

.   .   .

7

P. F. Strawson

Persons

P. F. Strawson is Waynflete Professor of Metaphysical Philosophy at Oxford, having succeeded Gilbert Ryle. He is the most influential British philosopher since the period of Russell, Moore, and Wittgenstein. He has written extensively, but he is best known for an early article, "On Referring" (1950), and for his much-discussed book, Individuals *(1959). He has also published* An Introduction to Logical Theory *(1952), which in part attempts to show the limited success with which formal logic captures the logical features of ordinary language. His more recent book,* The Bounds of Sense *(1966), attempts to convict Kant of having violated his own constraints on the limits of intelligible discourse and thus to vindicate those constraints.*

Individuals *provides a scheme for the identification and reidentification of physical bodies and persons within a unified spatio-temporal world. In the central chapter on persons it fails to explain the relationship between persons and bodies. But Strawson does suggest strong reasons for resisting the identification of persons and bodies. His concern is whether psychological attributes can be ascribed to physical bodies or only to persons.*

The second part of the book is occupied with the conditions for distinguishing subjects and predicates, a topic Strawson has pursued in later papers. He insists on an asymmetry here. In particular, his characterization of the way a subject term introduces a particular is closely linked to his account in "On Referring" (IV:9). In

P. F. Strawson, "Persons," in *Minnesota Studies in the Philosophy of Science*, Vol. II (Minneapolis: University of Minnesota Press), pp. 330–353. © Copyright 1958 by the University of Minnesota. Reprinted by permission of the publisher.

*that well-known paper, Strawson criticizes Russell's account of denoting, for having
confused sentences and expressions and the uses of either. He stresses that
where terms denote, sentences are used to refer. Hence, in making an appropriate
assertion, one presupposes that something is denoted by a given referring expression.
Should there be nothing to be referred to by the expression, the utterance fails in that
the assertion can be neither true nor false.*

Strawson thus introduces so-called truth–value gaps. The connection with
Individuals *lies in the fact that Strawson does not admit purely referential
expressions in identifying contexts; relevant expressions involve the presentation of
empirical facts about the referent itself.*

Strawson has also edited Philosophical Logic *(1967) and published a short
collection of his essays, in particular* Freedom and Resentment *(1974) and an
extended essay,* Subject and Predicate in Logic and Grammar *(1974). The latter takes
up the topic of Part Two of* Individuals *and deliberately adheres to the analysis of
ordinary, nonformalized languages. In particular, Strawson pursues the
question of "singular predication"—that is, predication in ordinary contexts in
which the devices of quantification ("some" and "all") are not, and need not be,
called into play.*

I

In the *Tractatus* (5.631–5.641) [Ludwig—Ed.] Wittgenstein writes of the I
which occurs in philosophy, of the philosophical idea of the subject of experiences. He says first: "The thinking, presenting subject—there is no such thing."
Then, a little later: "*In an important sense* there is no subject." This is followed
by: "The subject does not belong to the world, but is a limit of the world." And
a little later comes the following paragraph: "There is [therefore] really a sense
in which in philosophy we can talk non-psychologically of the I. The I occurs
in philosophy through the fact that the 'world is my world.' The philosophical
I is not the man, not the human body, or the human soul of which psychology
treats, but the metaphysical subject, the limit—not a part of the world." These
remarks are impressive, but also puzzling and obscure. Reading them, one might
think: Well, let's settle for the human body and the human soul of which
psychology treats, and which is a part of the world, and let the metaphysical
subject go. But again we might think: No, when I talk of myself, I do after
all talk of that which has all of my experiences, I do talk of the subject of my
experiences—and yet also of something that is part of the world in that it, but
not the world, comes to an end when I die. The limit of *my* world is not—and
is not so thought of by me—the limit of *the* world. It may be difficult to explain
the idea of something which is both a subject of experiences and a part of the
world. But it is an idea we have: it should be an idea we can explain.

Let us think of some of the ways in which we ordinarily talk of ourselves,
of some of the things which we ordinarily ascribe to ourselves. They are of
many kinds. We ascribe to ourselves *actions and intentions* (I am doing, did,
shall do this); *sensations* (I am warm, in pain); *thoughts and feelings* (I think,
wonder, want this, am angry, disappointed, contented); *perceptions and
memories* (I see this, hear the other, remember that). We ascribe to ourselves,

in two senses, position: *location* (I am on the sofa) and *attitude* (I am lying down). And of course we ascribe to ourselves not only temporary conditions, states, and situations, like most of these, but also enduring characteristics, including such physical characteristics as height, coloring, shape, and weight. That is to say, among the things we ascribe to ourselves are things of a kind that we also ascribe to material bodies to which we would not dream of ascribing others of the things that we ascribe to ourselves. Now there seems nothing needing explanation in the fact that the particular height, coloring, and physical position which we ascribe to ourselves, should be ascribed to *something or other*; for that which one calls one's body is, at least, a body, a material thing. It can be picked out from others, identified by ordinary physical criteria and described in ordinary physical terms. But it can seem, and has seemed, to need explanation that one's states of consciousness, one's thoughts and sensations, are ascribed *to the very same thing* as that to which these physical characteristics, this physical situation, is ascribed. Why are one's states of consciousness ascribed to the very same thing as certain corporeal characteristics, a certain physical situation, etc.? And once this question is raised, another question follows it, viz.: Why are one's states of consciousness ascribed to (said to be of, or to belong to) anything at all? It is not to be supposed that the answers to these questions will be independent of one another.

It might indeed be thought that an answer to both of them could be found in the unique role which each person's body plays in his experience, particularly his perceptual experience. All philosophers who have concerned themselves with these questions have referred to the uniqueness of this role. (Descartes was well enough aware of its uniqueness: "I am *not* lodged in my body like a pilot in a vessel.") In what does this uniqueness consist? Well, of course, in a great many facts. We may summarize some of these facts by saying that for each person there is one body which occupies a certain *causal* position in relation to that person's perceptual experience, a causal position which is in various ways unique in relation to each of the various kinds of perceptual experience he has; and—as a further consequence—that this body is also unique for him as an *object* of the various kinds of perceptual experience which he has. This complex uniqueness of the single body appears, moreover, to be a contingent matter, or rather a cluster of contingent matters; we can, or it seems that we can, imagine many peculiar combinations of dependence and independence of aspects of our perceptual experience on the physical states or situation of more than one body.

Now I must say, straightaway, that this cluster of apparently contingent facts about the unique role which each person's body plays in his experience does not seem to me to provide, *by itself*, an answer to our questions. Of course these facts explain *something*. They provide a very good reason why a subject of experience should have a *very special regard* for just one body, why he should think of it as unique and perhaps more important than any other. They explain —if I may be permitted to put it so—why I feel *peculiarly attached* to what in fact I call my own body; they even might be said to explain why, granted that I am going to speak of one body as *mine*, I should speak of this body (the body that I do speak of as mine) as mine. But they do not explain why I should have the concept of *myself* at all, why I should ascribe my thoughts and experiences to *anything*. Moreover, even if we were satisfied with some other explanation of why one's states of consciousness (thoughts and feelings and perceptions) were ascribed to *something*, and satisfied that the facts in question sufficed to explain why the "possession" of a particular body should be ascribed to the *same* thing (i.e., to explain why a particular body should be spoken of as standing in some special relation, called "being possessed by" to that thing), yet the facts in question still do not explain why we should, as we do, ascribe certain corporeal characteristics not simply to the body standing in this special relation to the thing to which we ascribe thoughts, feelings, etc., but to the thing itself to which we ascribe those thoughts and feelings. (For we say "I am bald" as well as "I am cold," "I am lying on the hearthrug" as well as "I see a spider on the ceiling.") Briefly, the facts in question explain why a subject of experience should pick out one body from others, give it, perhaps, an honored name and ascribe to it whatever characteristics it has; but they do not explain why the experiences should be ascribed to any subject at all; and they do not explain why, if the experiences are to be ascribed to something, they *and* the corporeal characteristics which might be truly ascribed to the favored body, should be ascribed to the same thing. So the facts in question do not explain the use that we make of the word "I," or how any word has the use that word has. They do not explain the concept we have of a person.

II

A possible reaction at this point is to say that the concept we have is wrong or confused, or, if we make it a rule not to say that the concepts we have are confused, that the usage we have, whereby we ascribe, or seem to ascribe, such different kinds of predicate to one and the same thing, is confusing, that it conceals the true nature of the concepts involved, or something of this sort. This reaction can be found in two very important types of view about these matters. The first type of view is Cartesian, the view of Descartes and of others who think like him. Over the attribution of the second type of view I am more hesitant; but there is some evidence that it was held, at one period, by Wittgenstein and possibly also by [Moritz—Ed.] Schlick. On both of these views, one of the questions we are considering, namely "Why do we ascribe our states of consciousness to the very same thing as certain corporeal characteristics, etc.?" is a question which does not arise; for on both views it is only a linguistic illusion that both kinds of predicate are properly ascribed to one and the same thing, that there is a common owner, or subject, of both types of predicate. And on the second of these views, the other question we are considering, namely "Why do we ascribe our states of consciousness to anything at all?" is also a question which does not arise; for on this view, it is only a linguistic illusion that one ascribes one's states of consciousness at all, that there is any proper subject of these apparent ascriptions, that states of consciousness belong to, or are states of, anything.

That Descartes held the first of these views is well enough known. When we speak of a person, we are really referring to one or both of two distinct substances (two substances of different types), each of which has its own appropriate type of states and properties; and none of the properties or states of either can be a property or state of the other. States of consciousness belong to one of these substances, and not to the other. I shall say no more about the Cartesian view at the moment—what I have to say about it will emerge later on—except to note again that while it escapes one of our questions, it does not escape, but indeed invites, the other: "Why are one's states of consciousness *ascribed* at all, to *any* subject?"

The second of these views I shall call the "no-ownership" or "no-subject" doctrine of the self. Whether or not anyone has explicitly held this view, it is worth reconstructing, or constructing, in outline.[1] For the errors into which it falls are instructive. The "no-ownership" theorist may be presumed to start his explanations with facts of the sort which illustrate the unique causal position of a certain material body in a person's experience. The theorist maintains that the uniqueness of this body is sufficient to give rise to the idea that one's experiences can be ascribed to some particular individual thing, can be said to be possessed by, or owned by, that thing. This idea, he thinks, though infelicitously and misleadingly expressed in terms of ownership, would have some validity, would make some sort of sense, so long as we thought of this individual thing, the possessor of the experiences, as the body itself. So long as we thought in this way, then to ascribe a particular state of consciousness to this body, this individual thing, would at least be to say something contingent, something that might be, or might have been, false. It might have been a misascription; for the

---

[1] The evidence that Wittgenstein at one time held such a view is to be found in the third of [G. E.—Ed.] Moore's articles in *Mind* on "Wittgenstein's Lectures in 1930–33" (*Mind*, 1955, especially pp. 13–14). He is reported to have held that the use of "I" was utterly different in the case of "I have a tooth-ache" or "I see a red patch" from its use in the case of "I've got a bad tooth" or "I've got a matchbox." He thought that there were two uses of "I" and that in one of them "I" was replaceable by "this body." So far the view might be Cartesian. But he also said that in the other use (the use exemplified by "I have a tooth-ache" as opposed to "I have a bad tooth"), the "I" *does not denote a possessor*, and that no ego is involved in thinking or in having tooth-ache; and referred with apparent approval to Lichtenberg's dictum that, instead of saying "I think," we (or Descartes!) ought to say "There is a thought" (i.e., "Es denkt").

The attribution of such a view to Schlick would have to rest on his article "Meaning and Verification," Pt. V (*Readings in Philosophical Analysis*, H. Feigl and W. Sellars, eds.). Like Wittgenstein, Schlick quotes Lichtenberg, and then goes on to say: "Thus we see that unless we choose to call our body the owner or bearer of the data [the data of immediate experience]—which seems to be a rather misleading expression—we have to say that the data have no owner or bearer." The full import of Schlick's article is, however, obscure to me, and it is quite likely that a false impression is given by the quotation of a single sentence. I shall say merely that I have drawn on Schlick's article in constructing the case of my hypothetical "no-subject" theorist; but shall not claim to be representing his views.

[Georg—Ed.] Lichtenberg's anti-Cartesian dictum is, as the subsequent argument will show, one that I endorse, if properly used. But it seems to have been repeated, without being understood, by many of Descartes' critics.

The evidence that Wittgenstein and Schlick ever held a "no-subject" view seems indecisive, since it is possible that the relevant remarks are intended as criticisms of a Cartesian view rather than as expositions of the true view.

experience in question might be, or might have been, causally dependent on the state of some other body; in the present admissible, though infelicitous, sense of "belong," it might have belonged to some other individual thing. But now, the theorist suggests, one becomes confused: one slides from this admissible, though infelicitous, sense in which one's experiences may be said to belong to, or be possessed by, some particular thing, to a wholly inadmissible and empty sense of these expressions; and in this new and inadmissible sense, the particular thing which is supposed to possess the experiences is not thought of as a body, but as something else, say an ego.

Suppose we call the first type of possession, which is really a certain kind of causal dependence, "having$_1$," and the second type of possession, "having$_2$"; and call the individual of the first type "B" and the supposed individual of the second type "E." Then the difference is that while it is genuinely a contingent matter that *all my experiences are had$_1$ by B*, it appears as a necessary truth that *all my experiences are had$_2$ by E*. But the belief in E and in having$_2$ is an illusion. Only those things whose ownership is logically transferable can be owned at all. So experiences are not owned by anything except in the dubious sense of being causally dependent on the state of a particular body. This is at least a genuine relationship to a thing, in that they might have stood in it to another thing. Since the whole function of E was to own experiences in a logically non-transferable sense of "own," and since experiences are not owned by anything in this sense, for there is no such sense of "own," E must be eliminated from the picture altogether. It only came in because of a confusion.

I think it must be clear that this account of the matter, though it contains *some* of the facts, is not coherent. It is not coherent, in that one who holds it is forced to make use of that sense of possession of which he denies the existence, in presenting his case for the denial. When he tries to state the contingent fact, which he thinks gives rise to the illusion of the "ego," he has to state it in some such form as "All *my* experiences are had$_1$ by (uniquely dependent on the state of) body B." For any attempt to eliminate the "my," or some other expression with a similar possessive force, would yield something that was not a contingent fact at all. The proposition that *all* experiences are causally dependent on the state of a single body B, for example, is just false. The theorist means to speak of all the experiences *had by a certain person* being contingently so dependent. And the theorist cannot consistently argue that "all the experiences of person P" *means the same thing* as "all experiences contingently dependent on a certain body B"; for then his proposition would not be contingent, as his theory requires, but analytic. He must mean to be speaking of some class of experiences of the members of which it is in fact contingently true that they are all dependent on body B. And the defining characteristic of this class is in fact that they are "*my* experiences" or "the experiences *of* some person," where the sense of "possession" is the one he calls into question.

This internal incoherence is a serious matter when it is a question of denying what prima facie is the case: that is, that one does genuinely ascribe one's states of consciousness to something, viz., oneself, and that this kind of ascription is precisely such as the theorist finds unsatisfactory, i.e., is such that it does not seem to make sense to suggest, for example, that the identical pain which was in fact one's own might have been another's. We do not have to seek far in order to understand the place of this logically non-transferable kind of ownership in our general scheme of thought. For if we think of the requirements of identifying reference, in speech, to *particular* states of consciousness, or private experiences, we see that such particulars cannot be thus identifyingly referred to except as the states or experiences *of* some identified *person*. States, or experiences, one might say, *owe* their identity as particulars to the identity of the person whose states or experiences they are. And from this it follows immediately that if they can be identified as particular states or experiences at all, they must be possessed or ascribable in just that way which the no-ownership theorist ridicules, i.e., in such a way that it is logically impossible that a particular state or experience in fact possessed by someone should have been possessed by anyone else. The requirements of identity rule out logical transferability of ownership. So the theorist could maintain his position only by denying that we could ever refer to particular states or experiences at all. And *this* position is ridiculous.

We may notice, even now, a possible connection between the no-ownership doctrine and the Cartesian position. The latter is, straightforwardly enough, a dualism of two subjects (two types of subject). The former could, a little paradoxically, be called a dualism too: a dualism of one subject (the body) and one non-subject. We might surmise that the second dualism, paradoxically so called, arises out of the first dualism, nonparadoxically so called; in other words, that if we try to think of that to which one's states of consciousness are ascribed as something utterly different from that to which certain corporeal characteristics are ascribed, then indeed it becomes difficult to see why states of consciousness should be ascribed, thought of as belonging to, anything at all. And when we think of this possibility, we may also think of another: viz., that both the Cartesian and the no-ownership theorist are profoundly wrong in holding, as each must, that there are two uses of "I" in one of which it denotes something which it does not denote in the other.

III

The no-ownership theorist fails to take account of all the facts. He takes account of some of them. He implies, correctly, that the unique position or role of a single body in one's experience is not a sufficient explanation of the fact that one's experiences, or states of consciousness, are ascribed to something which *has* them, with that peculiar non-transferable kind of possession which is here in question. It may be a necessary part of the explanation, but it is not, by itself, a sufficient explanation. The theorist, as we have seen, goes on to suggest that it is perhaps a sufficient explanation of something else: viz., of our confusedly and mistakenly *thinking* that states of consciousness are to be ascribed to something in this special way. And this suggestion, as we have seen, is incoherent: for it involves the denial that someone's states of consciousness are anyone's. We avoid the incoherence of this denial, while agreeing that the special role of a single body in someone's experience does not suffice to explain why that experience should be ascribed to anybody. The fact that there is this special role does not, by itself, give a sufficient reason why what we think of as a subject of experience should have any use for the conception of himself as such a subject.

When I say that the no-ownership theorist's account fails through not reckoning with all the facts, I have in mind a very simple but, in this question, a very central, thought: viz., that it is a necessary condition of one's ascribing states of consciousness, experiences, to oneself, in the way one does, that one should also ascribe them (or be prepared to ascribe them) to others who are not oneself.[2] This means not less than it says. It means, for example, that the ascribing phrases should be used in just the same sense when the subject is another, as when the subject is oneself. Of course the thought that this is so gives no trouble to the non-philosopher: the thought, for example, that "in pain" means the same whether one says "I am in pain" or "He is in pain." The dictionaries do not give two sets of meanings for every expression which describes a state of consciousness: a first-person meaning, and a second- and third-person meaning. But to the philosopher this thought has given trouble; indeed it has. How could the sense be the same when the method of verification was so different in the two cases—or, rather, when there *was* a method of verification in the one case (the case of others) and not, properly speaking, in the other case (the case of oneself)? Or, again, how can it be right to talk of *ascribing* in the case of oneself? For surely there can be a question of ascribing only if there is or could be a question of identifying that to which the ascription is made? And though there may be a question of identifying the one who is in pain when that one is another, how can there be such a question when that one is oneself? But this last query answers itself as soon as we remember that we speak primarily to others, for the information of others. In one sense, indeed, there is no question of my having to *tell who it is* who is in pain, when I am. In another sense I may have to *tell who it is*, i.e., to let others know who it is.

---

[2] I can imagine an objection to the unqualified form of this statement, an objection which might be put as follows. Surely the idea of a uniquely applicable predicate (a predicate which *in fact* belongs to only one individual) is not absurd. And, if it is not, then surely the most that can be claimed is that a necessary condition of one's ascribing predicates of a certain class to one individual (oneself) is that one should be prepared, or ready, on appropriate occasions, to ascribe them to other individuals, and hence that one should have a conception of what those appropriate occasions for ascribing them would be; but not, necessarily, that one should actually do so on any occasion.

The shortest way with the objection is to admit it, or at least to refrain from disputing it; for the lesser claim is all that the argument strictly requires, though it is slightly simpler to conduct it on the basis of the larger claim. But it is well to point out further that we are not speaking of a single predicate, or merely of some group or other of predicates, but of the whole of an enormous class of predicates such that the applicability of those predicates or their negations determines a major logical type or category of individuals. To insist, at this level, on the distinction between the lesser and the larger claims is to carry the distinction over from a level at which it is clearly correct to a level at which it may well appear idle or, possibly, senseless.

The main point here is a purely logical one: the idea of a predicate is correlative with that of a range of distinguishable individuals of which the predicate can be significantly, though not necessarily truly, affirmed.

What I have just said explains, perhaps, how one may properly be said to ascribe states of consciousness to oneself, given that one ascribes them to others. But how is it that one can ascribe them to others? Well, one thing is certain: that *if* the things one ascribes states of consciousness to, in ascribing them to others, are thought of as a set of Cartesian egos to which *only* private experiences can, in correct logical grammar, be ascribed, *then* this question is unanswerable and this problem insoluble. If, in identifying the things to which states of consciousness are to be ascribed, private experiences are to be all one has to go on, then, just for the very same reason as that for which there is, from one's own point of view, no question of telling that a private experience is one's own, there is also no question of telling that a private experience is another's. All private experiences, all states of consciousness, will be mine, i.e., no one's. To put it briefly: one can ascribe states of consciousness to oneself only if one can ascribe them to others; one can ascribe them to others only if one can identify other subjects of experience; and one cannot identify others if one can identify them *only* as subjects of experience, possessors of states of consciousness.

It might be objected that this way with Cartesianism is too short. After all, there is no difficulty about distinguishing bodies from one another, no difficulty about identifying bodies. And does not this give us an indirect way of identifying subjects of experience, while preserving the Cartesian mode? Can we not identify such a subject as, for example, "the subject that stands to that body in the same special relation as I stand to this one"; or, in other words, "the subject of those experiences which stand in the same unique causal relation to body N as *my* experiences stand to body M"? But this suggestion is useless. It requires me to have noted that *my* experiences stand in a special relation to body M, when it is just the right to speak of *my* experiences at all that is in question. (It requires me to have noted that *my* experiences stand in a special relation to body M; but it requires me to have noted this as a condition of being able to identify other subjects of experience, i.e., as a condition of having the idea of myself as a subject of experience, i.e., as a condition of thinking of any experience as *mine*.) So long as we persist in talking, in the mode of this explanation, of experiences on the one hand, and bodies on the other, the most I may be allowed to have noted is that experiences, *all* experiences, stand in a special relation to body M, that body M is unique in just this way, that this is what makes body M unique among bodies. (This "most" is, perhaps, too much— because of the presence of the word "experiences.") The proffered explanation runs: "Another subject of experience is distinguished and identified as the subject of those experiences which stand in the same unique causal relationship to body N as *my* experiences stand to body M." And the objection is: "But what is the word 'my' doing in this explanation? (It could not get on without it.)"

What we have to acknowledge, in order to begin to free ourselves from these difficulties, is the *primitiveness* of the concept of a person. What I mean by the concept of a person is the concept of a type of entity such that *both* predicates ascribing states of consciousness *and* predicates ascribing corporeal characteristics, a physical situation, etc. are equally applicable to a single individual of that single type. And what I mean by saying that this concept is primitive can be put in a number of ways. One way is to return to those two questions I asked earlier: viz., (1) why are states of consciousness ascribed to anything at all? and (2) why are they ascribed to the very same thing as certain corporeal characteristics, a certain physical situation, etc.? I remarked at the beginning that it was not to be supposed that the answers to these questions were independent of each other. And now I shall say that they are connected in this way: that a necessary condition of states of consciousness being ascribed at all is that they should be ascribed to the *very same things* as certain corporeal characteristics, a certain physical situation, etc. That is to say, states of consciousness could not be ascribed at all, *unless* they were ascribed to persons, in the sense I have claimed for this word. We are tempted to think of a person as a sort of compound of two kinds of subject—a subject of experiences (a pure consciousness, an ego), on the one hand, and a subject of corporeal attributes on the other.

Many questions arise when we think in this way. But, in particular, when we ask ourselves how we come to frame, to get a use for, the concept of this compound of two subjects, the picture—if we are honest and careful—is apt to change from the picture of two subjects to the picture of one subject and one non-subject. For it becomes impossible to see how we could come by the idea of different, distinguishable, identifiable subjects of experiences—different consciousnesses—*if this idea is thought of as logically primitive*, as a logical ingredient in the compound idea of a person, the latter being composed of two subjects. For there could never be any question of assigning an experience, as such, to any subject other than oneself; and therefore never any question of assigning it to oneself either, never any question of ascribing it to a subject at all. So the concept of the pure individual consciousness—the pure ego—is a concept that cannot exist; or, at least, cannot exist as a primary concept in terms of which the concept of a person can be explained or analyzed. It can only exist, if at all, as a secondary, nonprimitive concept, which itself is to be explained, analyzed, in terms of the concept of a person. It was the entity corresponding to this illusory primary concept of the pure consciousness, the ego-substance, for which Hume was seeking, or ironically pretending to seek, when he looked into himself, and complained that he could never discover himself without a perception and could never discover anything but the perception. More seriously—and this time there was no irony, but a confusion, a Nemesis of confusion for Hume—it was this entity of which Hume vainly sought for the principle of unity, confessing himself perplexed and defeated; sought vainly because there is no principle of unity where there is no principle of differentiation. It was this, too, to which Kant, more perspicacious here than Hume, accorded a purely formal ("analytic") unity: the unity of the "I think" that accompanies all my perceptions and therefore might just as well accompany none. And finally it is this, perhaps, of which Wittgenstein spoke when he said of the subject, first, that there is no such thing, and, second, that it is not a part of the world, but its limit.

So, then the word "I" never refers to this, the pure subject. But this does not mean, as the no-ownership theorist must think and as Wittgenstein, at least at one period, seemed to think, that "I" in some cases does not refer at all. It refers, because I am a person among others. And the predicates which would, *per impossibile*, belong to the pure subject if it could be referred to, belong properly to the person to which "I" does refer.

The concept of a person is logically prior to that of an individual consciousness. The concept of a person is not to be analyzed as that of an animated body or of an embodied anima. This is not to say that the concept of a pure individual consciousness might not have a logically secondary existence, if one thinks, or finds, it desirable. We speak of a dead person—a body—and in the same secondary way we might at least think of a disembodied person, retaining the logical benefit of individuality from having been a person.[3]

IV

It is important to realize the full extent of the acknowledgment one is making in acknowledging the logical primitiveness of the concept of a person. Let me rehearse briefly the stages of the argument. There would be no question of ascribing one's own states of consciousness, or experiences, to anything, unless one also ascribed states of consciousness, or experiences, to other individual entities of the same logical type as that thing to which one ascribes one's own states of consciousness. The condition of reckoning oneself as a subject of such predicates is that one should also reckon others as subjects of such predicates. The condition, in turn, of this being possible, is that one should be able to distinguish from one another (pick out, identify) different subjects of such predicates, i.e., different individuals of the type concerned. And the condition, in turn, of this being possible is that the individuals concerned, including oneself, should be of a certain unique type: of a type, namely, such that to each individual of that type there *must* be ascribed, or ascribable, *both* states of consciousness *and* corporeal characteristics. But this characterization of the type is still very opaque and does not at all clearly bring out what is involved. To bring this out, I must make a rough division, into two, of the kinds of predicates properly applied to individuals of this type. The first kind of predicate consists of those which are also properly applied to material bodies to which we would not dream of applying predicates ascribing states of consciousness. I will call this first kind M-predicates: and they include things like "weighs 10 stone," "is in the drawing room," and so on. The second kind consists of all the other predicates we apply to persons. These I shall call P-predicates. And P-predicates, of course, will be very various. They will include things like "is smiling," "is going for a walk," as well as things like "is in pain," "is thinking hard," "believes in God," and so on.

So far I have said that the concept of a person is to be understood as the concept of a type of entity such that *both* predicates ascribing states of consciousness *and* predicates ascribing corporeal characteristics, a physical situation,

---

[3] A little further thought will show how limited this concession is. But I shall not discuss the question now.

etc. are equally applicable to an individual entity of that type. And all I have said about the meaning of saying that this concept is primitive is that it is not to be analyzed in a certain way or ways. We are not, for example, to think of it as a secondary kind of entity in relation to two primary kinds, viz., a particular consciousness and a particular human body. I implied also that the Cartesian error is just a special case of a more general error, present in a different form in theories of the no-ownership type, of thinking of the designations, or apparent designations, of persons as *not* denoting precisely the same thing, or entity, for all kinds of predicate ascribed to the entity designated. That is, if we are to avoid the general form of this error we must *not* think of "I" or "Smith" as suffering from type-ambiguity. (If we want to locate type-ambiguity somewhere, we would do better to locate it in certain predicates like "is in the drawing room," "was hit by a stone," etc., and say they mean one thing when applied to material objects and another when applied to persons.)

This is all I have so far said or implied about the meaning of saying that the concept of a person is primitive. What has to be brought out further is what the implications of saying this are as regards the logical character of those predicates in which we ascribe states of consciousness. And for this purpose we may well consider P-predicates in general. For though not all P-predicates are what we should call "predicates ascribing states of consciousness" (for example, "going for a walk" is not), they may be said to have this in common, that they imply the possession of consciousness on the part of that to which they are ascribed.

What then are the consequences of this view as regards the character of P-predicates? I think they are these. Clearly there is no sense in talking of identifiable individuals of a special type, a type, namely, such that they possess both M-predicates and P-predicates, unless there is in principle some way of telling, with regard to any individual of that type, and any P-predicate, whether that individual possesses that P-predicate. And, in the case of at least some P-predicates, the ways of telling must constitute in some sense logically adequate kinds of criteria for the ascription of the P-predicate. For suppose in no case did these ways of telling constitute logically adequate kinds of criteria. Then we should have to think of the relation between the ways of telling and what the P-predicate ascribes (or a part of what it ascribes) always in the following way: we should have to think of the ways of telling as *signs* of the presence, in the individual concerned, of this different thing (the state of consciousness). But then we could only know that the way of telling was a sign of the presence of the different thing ascribed by the P-predicate, by the observation of correlations between the two. But this observation we could each make only in one case, namely, our own. And now we are back in the position of the defender of Cartesianism, who thought our way with it was too short. For what, now, does "our own case" mean? There is no sense in the idea of ascribing states of consciousness to oneself, or at all, unless the ascriber already knows how to ascribe at least some states of consciousness to others. So he cannot (or cannot generally) argue "from his own case" to conclusions about how to do this; for unless he already knows how to do this, he has no conception of *his own case*, or any *case* (i.e., any subject of experiences). Instead, he just has evidence that pain, etc. may be expected when a certain body is affected in certain ways and not when others are.

The conclusion here is, of course, not new. What I have said is that one ascribes P-predicates to others on the strength of observation of their behavior; and that the behavior criteria one goes on are not just signs of the presence of what is meant by the P-predicate, but are criteria of a logically adequate kind for the ascription of the P-predicate. On behalf of this conclusion, however, I am claiming that it follows from a consideration of the conditions necessary for any ascription of states of consciousness to anything. The point is not that we must accept this conclusion in order to avoid skepticism, but that we must accept it in order to explain the existence of the conceptual scheme in terms of which the skeptical problem is stated. But once the conclusion is accepted, the skeptical problem does not arise. (And so with the generality of skeptical problems: their statement involves the pretended acceptance of a conceptual scheme and at the same time the silent repudiation of one of the conditions of its existence. This is why they are, in the terms in which they are stated, in-soluble.) But this is only half the picture about P-predicates.

Now let us turn to the other half. For of course it is true, at least of some important classes of P-predicates, that when one ascribes them to oneself, one does not do so on the strength of observation of those behavior criteria on the strength of which one ascribes them to others. This is not true of all P-predicates. It is not, in general, true of those which carry assessments of character and capability: these, when self-ascribed, are in general ascribed on the same kind of basis as that on which they are ascribed to others. And of those P-predicates of which it is true that one does not generally ascribe them to oneself on the basis of the criteria on the strength of which one ascribes them to others, there are many of which it is also true that their ascription is liable to correction by the self-ascriber on this basis. But there remain many cases in which one has an entirely adequate basis for ascribing a P-predicate to oneself, and yet in which this basis is quite distinct from those on which one ascribes the predicate to another. (Thus one says, reporting a present state of mind or feeling: "I feel tired, am depressed, am in pain.") How can this fact be reconciled with the doctrine that the criteria on the strength of which one ascribes P-predicates to others are criteria of a logically adequate kind for this ascription?

The apparent difficulty of bringing about this reconciliation may tempt us in many directions. It may tempt us, for example, to deny that these self-ascriptions are really ascriptions at all; to *assimilate* first-person ascriptions of states of consciousness to those other forms of behavior which constitute criteria on the basis of which one person ascribes P-predicates to another. This device seems to avoid the difficulty; it is not, in all cases, entirely inappropriate. But it obscures the facts, and is needless. It is merely a sophisticated form of failure to recognize the special character of P-predicates (or at least of a crucial class of P-predicates). For just as there is not (in general) one primary process of learning to apply such predicates to others on the strength of behavior criteria, and then another process of acquiring the secondary technique of exhibiting a new form of behavior, viz., first-person P-utterances. Both these pictures are refusals to acknowledge the unique logical character of the predicates concerned.

Suppose we write 'Px' as the general form of propositional function of such a predicate. Then according to the first picture, the expression which primarily replaces "x" in this form is "I," the first-person singular pronoun; its uses with other replacements are secondary, derivative, and shaky. According to the second picture, on the other hand, the primary replacements of "x" in this form are "he," "that person," etc., and its use with "I" is secondary, peculiar, not a true ascriptive use. But it is essential to the character of these predicates that they have both first- and third-person ascriptive uses, that they are both self-ascribable otherwise than on the basis of observation of the behavior of the subject of them, and other-ascribable on the basis of behavior criteria. To learn their use is to learn both aspects of their use. In order to *have* this type of concept, one must be both a self-ascriber and an other-ascriber of such predicates, and must see every other as a self-ascriber. And in order to *understand* this type of concept, one must acknowledge that there is a kind of predicate which is unambiguously and adequately ascribable *both* on the basis of observation of the subject of the predicate *and* not on this basis (independently of observation of the subject): the second case is the case where the ascriber is also the subject. If there were no concepts answering to the characterization I have just given, we should indeed have no philosophical problem about the soul; but equally we should not have *our* concept of a person.

To put the point—with a certain unavoidable crudity—in terms of one particular concept of this class, say, that of depression, we speak of behaving in a depressed way (of depressed behavior) and also of feeling depressed (of a feeling of depression). One is inclined to argue that feelings can be felt, but not observed, and behavior can be observed, but not felt, and that therefore there must be room here to drive in a logical wedge. But the concept of depression spans the place where one wants to drive it in. We might say, in order for there to be such a concept as that of X's depression, the depression which X has, the concept must cover both what is felt, but not observed, by X and what may be observed, but not felt, by others than X (for all values of X). But it is perhaps better to say: X's depression *is* something, one and the same thing, which is felt but not observed by X and observed but not felt by others than X. (And, of course, what can be observed can also be faked or disguised.) To refuse to accept this is to refuse to accept the structure of the language in which we talk about depression. That is, in a sense, all right. One might give up talking; or devise, perhaps, a different structure in terms of which to soliloquize. What is not all right is simultaneously to pretend to accept that structure and to refuse to accept it; i.e., to couch one's rejection in the language of that structure.

It is in this light that we must see some of the familiar philosophical difficulties in the topic of the mind. For some of them spring from just such a failure to admit, or fully appreciate, the character which I have been claiming for at least some P-predicates. It is not seen that these predicates could not have either aspect of their use (the self-ascriptive and the non-self-ascriptive) without having the other aspect. Instead, one aspect of their use is taken as self-sufficient, which it could not be, and then the other aspect appears as problematical. And so we oscillate between philosophical skepticism and philosophical behaviorism. When we take the self-ascriptive aspect of the use of some P-predicate (say, "depressed") as primary, then a logical gap seems to open between the criteria on the strength of which we say that another is depressed, and the actual state of depression. What we do not realize is that if this logical gap is allowed to open, then it swallows not only his depression, but our depression as well. For if the logical gap exists, then depressed behavior, however much there is of it, is no more than a sign of depression. And it can become a sign of depression only because of an observed correlation between it and depression. But whose depression? Only mine, one is tempted to say. But if *only* mine, then *not* mine at all. The skeptical position customarily represents the crossing of the logical gap as at best a shaky inference. But the point is that not even the syntax of the premises of the inference exists if the gap exists.

If, on the other hand, we take the other-ascriptive uses of these predicates as self-sufficient, we may come to think that all there is in the meaning of these predicates, as predicates, is the criteria on the strength of which we ascribe them to others. Does this not follow from the denial of the logical gap? It does not follow. To think that it does is to forget the self-ascriptive use of these predicates, to forget that we have to do with a class of predicates to the meaning of which it is essential that they should be both self-ascribable and other-ascribable to the same individual, when self-ascriptions are not made on the observational basis on which other-ascriptions are made, but on another basis. It is not that these predicates have two kinds of meaning. Rather, it is essential to the single kind of meaning that they do have that both ways of ascribing them should be perfectly in order.

If one is playing a game of cards, the distinctive markings of a certain card constitute a logically adequate criterion for calling it, say, the Queen of Hearts; but, in calling it this, in the context of the game, one is also ascribing to it properties over and above the possession of those markings. The predicate gets its meaning from the whole structure of the game. So it is with the language which ascribes P-predicates. To say that the criteria on the strength of which we ascribe P-predicates to others are of a logically adequate kind for this ascription is not to say that all there is to the ascriptive meaning of these predicates is these criteria. To say this is to forget that they are P-predicates, to forget the rest of the language-structure to which they belong.

V

Now our perplexities may take a different form, the form of the question "But how can one ascribe to oneself, not on the basis of observation, *the very same thing* that others may have, on the basis of observation, a logically adequate reason for ascribing to one?" And this question may be absorbed in a wider one, which might be phrased: "How are P-predicates possible?" or "How is the concept of a person possible?" This is the question by which we replace those two earlier questions, viz.: "Why are states of consciousness ascribed at all, ascribed to anything?" and "Why are they ascribed to the very same thing as certain corporeal characteristics, etc.?" For the answer to these two initial questions is to be found nowhere else but in the admission of the primitiveness of the concept of a person, and hence of the unique character of P-predicates. So residual perplexities have to frame themselves in this new way. For when we have acknowledged the primitiveness of the concept of a person and, with it, the unique character of P-predicates, we may still want to ask what it is in the natural facts that makes it intelligible that we should have this concept, and to ask this in the hope of a non-trivial answer.[4] I do not pretend to be able to satisfy this demand at all fully. But I may mention two very different things which might count as beginnings or fragments of an answer.

And, first, I think a beginning can be made by moving a certain class of P-predicates to a central position in the picture. They are predicates, roughly, which involve doing something, which clearly imply intention or a state of mind or at least consciousness in general, and which indicate a characteristic pattern, or range of patterns, of bodily movement, while not indicating at all precisely any very definite sensation or experience. I mean such things as "going for a walk," "furling a rope," "playing ball," "writing a letter." Such predicates have the interesting characteristic of many P-predicates that one does not, in general, ascribe them to oneself on the strength of observation, whereas one does ascribe them to others on the strength of observation. But, in the case of these predicates, one feels minimal reluctance to concede that what is ascribed in these two different ways is the same. And this is because of the marked dominance of a fairly definite pattern of bodily movement in what they ascribe, and the marked absence of any distinctive experience. They release us from the idea that the only things we can know about without observation, or inference, or both, are private experiences; we can know also, without telling by either of these means, about the present and future movements of a body. Yet bodily movements are certainly also things we can know about by observation and inference.

Among the things that we observe, as opposed to the things we know without observation, are the movements of bodies similar to that about which we have knowledge not based on observation. It is important that we understand such observed movements; they bear on and condition our own. And in fact we understand them, we interpret them, only by seeing them as elements in just such plans or schemes of action as those of which we know the present course and future development without observation of the relevant present movements. But this is to say that we see such movements (the observed movements of others) as *actions*, that we interpret them in terms of intention, that we see them as movements of individuals of a type to which also belongs that individual whose present and future movements we know about without observation; that we see others, as self-ascribers, not on the basis of observations, of what we ascribe to them on this basis.

Of course these remarks are not intended to suggest how the "problem of

---

[4] I mean, in the hope of an answer which does not *merely* say: Well, there are people in the world.

other minds" could be solved, or our beliefs about others given a general philosophical "justification." I have already argued that such a "solution" or "justification" is impossible, that the demand for it cannot be coherently stated. Nor are these remarks intended as a priori genetic psychology. They are simply intended to help to make it seem intelligible to us, at this stage in the history of the philosophy of this subject, that we have the conceptual scheme we have. What I am suggesting is that it is easier to understand how we can see each other (and ourselves) as persons, if we think first of the fact that we act, and act on each other, and act in accordance with a common human nature. "To see each other as persons" is a lot of things; but not a lot of separate and unconnected things. The class of P-predicates that I have moved into the center of the picture are not unconnectedly there, detached from others irrelevant to them. On the contrary, they are inextricably bound up with the others, interwoven with them. The topic of the mind does not divide into unconnected subjects.

I spoke just now of a common human nature. But there is also a sense in which a condition of the existence of the conceptual scheme we have is that human nature should not be common, should not be, that is, a community nature. Philosophers used to discuss the question of whether there was, or could be, such a thing as a "group mind." And for some the idea had a peculiar fascination, while to others it seemed utterly absurd and nonsensical and at the same time, curiously enough, pernicious. It is easy to see why these last found it pernicious: they found something horrible in the thought that people should cease to have toward individual persons the kind of attitudes that they did have, and instead have attitudes in some way analogous to those toward groups; and that they might cease to decide individual courses of action for themselves and instead merely participate in corporate activities. But their finding it pernicious showed that they understood the idea they claimed to be absurd only too well. The fact that we find it natural to individuate as persons the members of a certain class of what might also be individuated as organic bodies does not mean that such a conceptual scheme is inevitable for any class of beings not utterly unlike ourselves.

Might we not construct the idea of a special kind of social world in which the concept of an individual person has no employment, whereas an analogous concept for groups does have employment? Think, to begin with, of certain aspects of actual human existence. Think, for example, of two groups of human beings engaged in some competitive but corporate activity, such as battle, for which they have been exceedingly well trained. We may even suppose that orders are superfluous, though information is passed. It is easy to imagine that, while absorbed in such activity, the members of the groups make no references to individual persons at all, have no use for personal names or pronouns. They do, however, refer to the groups and apply to them predicates analogous to those predicates ascribing purposive activity which we normally apply to individual persons. They may, *in fact*, use in such circumstances the plural forms "we" and "they"; but these are not genuine plurals, they are plurals without a singular, such as we use in sentences like these: "We have taken the citadel," "We have lost the game." They may also refer to elements in the group, to members of the group, but exclusively in terms which get their sense from the parts played by these elements in the corporate activity. (Thus we sometimes refer to what are in fact persons as "stroke" or "tackle.")

When we think of such cases, we see that we ourselves, over a part of our social lives—not, I am thankful to say, a very large part—do operate conceptual schemes in which the idea of the individual person has no place, in which its place is taken, so to speak, by that of a group. But might we not think of communities or groups such that this part of the lives of their members was the dominant part—or was the whole? It sometimes happens, with groups of human beings, that, as we say, their members think, feel, and act "as one." The point I wish to make is that a condition for the existence, the use, of the concept of an individual person is that this should happen *only sometimes*.

It is absolutely useless to say, at this point: But all the same, even if this happened all the time, every member of the group would have an individual consciousness, would be an individual subject of experience. The point is, once more, that there is no sense in speaking of the individual consciousness just as such, of the individual subject of experience just as such: for there is no way of identifying such pure entities.[5] It is true, of course, that in suggesting this fantasy, I have taken our concept of an individual person as a starting point. It is this fact which makes the useless reaction a natural one. But suppose, instead, I had made the following suggestion: that each part of the human body, each organ and each member, had an individual consciousness, was a separate center of experiences. This, in the same way, but more obviously, would be a useless suggestion. Then imagine all the intermediate cases, for instance these. There is a class of moving natural objects, divided into groups, each group exhibiting the same characteristic pattern of activity. Within each group there are certain differentiations of appearance accompanying differentiations of function, and in particular there is one member of each group with a distinctive appearance. Cannot one imagine different sets of observations which might lead us, in the one case, to think of the particular member as the spokesman of the group, as its mouthpiece; and in the other case to think of him as its mouth, to think of the group as a single *scattered* body? The point is that as soon as we adopt the latter way of thinking then we want to drop the former; we are no longer influenced by the human analogy in its first form, but only in its second; and we no longer want to say: "Perhaps the members have consciousness." To understand the movement of our thought here, we need only remember the startling ambiguity of the phrase "a body and its members."

VI

I shall not pursue this attempt at explanation any further. What I have been mainly arguing for is that we should acknowledge the logical primitiveness of the concept of a person and, with this, the unique logical character of certain predi-

---

[5] More accurately: their identification is necessarily secondary to the identification of persons.

cates. Once this is acknowledged, certain traditional philosophical problems are seen not to be problems at all. In particular, the problem that seems to have perplexed Hume[6] does not exist—the problem of the principle of unity, of identity, of the particular consciousness, of the particular subject of "perceptions" (experiences) considered as a primary particular. There is no such problem and no such principle. If there were such a principle, then each of us would have to apply it in order to decide whether any contemporary experience of his was his or someone else's; and there is no sense in this suggestion. (This is not to deny, of course, that one *person* may be unsure of his own identity in some way, may be unsure, for example, whether some particular action, or series of actions, had been performed by him. Then he uses the same methods (the same in principle) to resolve the doubt about himself as anyone else uses to resolve the same doubt about him. And these methods simply involve the application of the ordinary criteria for *personal* identity. There remains the question of what exactly these criteria are, what their relative weights are, etc.; but, once disentangled from spurious questions, this is one of the easier problems in philosophy.)

Where Hume erred, or seems to have erred, both Kant and Wittgenstein had the better insight. Perhaps neither always expressed it in the happiest way. For Kant's doctrine that the "analytic unity of consciousness" neither requires nor entails any principle of unity is not as clear as one could wish. And Wittgenstein's remarks (at one time) to the effect that the data of consciousness are not owned, that "I" as used by Jones, in speaking of his own feelings, etc., does not refer to what "Jones" as used by another refers to, seem needlessly to flout the conceptual scheme we actually employ. It is needlessly paradoxical to deny, or seem to deny, that when Smith says "Jones has a pain" and Jones says "I have a pain," they are talking about the same entity and saying the same thing about it, needlessly paradoxical to deny that Jones can *confirm* that he has a pain. Instead of denying that self-ascribed states of consciousness are really ascribed at all, it is more in harmony with our actual ways of talking to say: For each user of the language, there is just one person in ascribing to whom states of consciousness he does not need to use the criteria of the observed behavior of that person (though he does not necessarily not do so); and that person is himself. This remark at least respects the structure of the conceptual scheme we employ, without precluding further examination of it.

---

[6] Cf. the Appendix to the *Treatise of Human Nature*.

8

Anthony Quinton
The Soul

Anthony Quinton, University Lecturer in Philosophy at New College, Oxford, is currently Professor of Philosophy at the New School for Social Research in New York City. He is the author of numerous articles, among the best-known of which are "The Soul" (1962) and "The Problem of Perception" (1955). He is also the editor of Political Philosophy (1972) *and the author of* On the Nature of Things (1973), *which propounds an essentially materialist theory of substance. He holds that material bodies are the fundamental constituents of the world; that the theoretical entities of science are material bodies or constructions out of them; that experiences are brain states; and that values are defined in terms of the responses of sensitive organisms.*

1. The Soul and Spiritual Substance

Philosophers in recent times have had very little to say about the soul. The word, perhaps, has uncomfortably ecclesiastical associations, and the idea seems to be bound up with a number of discredited or at any rate generally disregarded theories. In the history of philosophy the soul has been used for two distinct purposes: first, as an explanation of the vitality that distinguishes human beings, and also animals and plants, from the broad mass of material objects, and, secondly, as the seat of consciousness. The first of these, which sees the soul as an ethereal but nonetheless physical entity, a volatile collection of fire-atoms or a stream of animal spirits, on some views dissipated with the dissolution of the body, on others absorbed at death into the cosmic soul, and on others again as capable of independent existence, need not detain us. The second, however, the soul of Plato and Descartes, deserves a closer examination than it now usually receives. For it tends to be identified with the view that in each person there is to be found a spiritual substance which is the subject of his mental states and the bearer of his personal identity. But on its widest interpretation, as the nonphysical aspect of a person, its acceptance need not involve either the existence of a spiritual substance over and above the mental states that make up a person's inner, conscious life or the proposition that this spiritual substance is what ultimately determines a person's identity through time. When philosophers dismiss the soul it is usually because they reject one or both of these supposed consequences of belief in it.

It is worth insisting, furthermore, that the existence of a spiritual substance

Anthony Quinton, "The Soul," *The Journal of Philosophy*, LIX, 15 (July 19, 1962), 393–409. Reprinted by permission of the publisher and the author.

is logically distinct from its being the criterion of personal identity. So the strong, and indeed fatal, arguments against the substance theory of personal identity do not at the same time refute the proposition, self-evident to Berkeley and many others, that there can be no conscious state that is not the state of some subject.

As a criterion of identity spiritual substance has three main weaknesses. First, it is regressive in just the same way as is an account of the identity of a material object through time in terms of its physical components. No general account of the identity of a kind of individual thing can be given which finds that identity in the presence of another individual thing within it. For the question immediately arises, how is the identity through time of the supposed identifier to be established? It, like the thing it is supposed to identify, can present itself at any one time only as it is at that time. However alike its temporally separate phases may be, they still require to be identified as parts of the same, continuing thing. In practice we do identify some wholes through their parts, normally where the parts are more stable and persistent unities than the wholes they compose and where, in consequence, the parts are more readily identifiable, as, for example, when we pick out one person's bundle of laundry from the bundles of others after the labels have been lost. But this can be only a practical expedient, not a theoretical solution.

A second difficulty is to find any observable mental entity that can effectively serve as a criterion in this case. The only plausible candidate is that dim, inchoate background, largely composed of organic sensations, which envelops the mental states occupying the focus of attention. This organic background is a relatively unchanging environment for the more dramatic episodes of conscious life to stand out against. But both the fixity and the peripheral status of this background are only relative. It does change, and it, or its parts, can come or be brought into the focus of attention. Even if its comparatively undisturbed persistence of character suggests it as a criterion, its vagueness makes it even less accessible to public application than the general run of mental criteria and leaves it with little power to distinguish between one person and another. The organic background is, of course, as regressive a criterion as any other part of a person's mental life. Its only virtues are that it is observable and that it does seem to be a universal constituent of the momentary cross sections of a person's experience. In this last respect it is preferable to most distinguishable features of a person's mental life. For, generally speaking, the parts of a complex and enduring thing are not necessary to the identity of that thing. Just as a cathedral is still the same cathedral if a piece has been knocked off it, whatever the piece may be, so a person is the same person if he ceases to have a particular belief or emotion, whatever that belief or emotion may be.

Finally, if it is held that the spiritual substance is nevertheless a permanent and unaltering constituent of a person's conscious life, it follows that it must be unobservable and so useless for purposes of identification. Suppose that from its very first stirrings my consciousness has contained a continuous whistling sound of wholly unvarying character. I should clearly never notice it, for I can only notice what varies independently of my consciousness—the whistles that start and stop at times other than those at which I wake up and fall asleep. It is this fact that ensured from the outset that Hume's search for a self over and above his particular perceptions was bound to fail. The unobservability of spiritual substance, and its consequent inapplicability as a criterion, can also be held to follow directly from taking its status as substance seriously, as an uncharacterized substratum for qualities and relations to inhere in with no recognizable features of its own.

But to admit that spiritual substance cannot possibly be the criterion of a person's identity and that it cannot be identified with any straightforwardly observable part of a person's mental life does not mean that it does not exist. It has seemed self-evident to many philosophers that every mental state must have an owner. To believe this is not to commit onself to the existence of something utterly unobservable. If it is true, although both subjects and mental states are unobservable in isolation, each can be observed in conjunction with the other. There is a comparison here with the relations and observability of the positions and qualities of material things. One cannot be aware of a color except as present at some place and at some time or of a position except as the place and time where some discernible characteristics are manifested. So it might be argued that one can be aware of a conscious subject only as in some mental state or other and of a mental state only as belonging to some subject or other. Critics of the Berkeleyan principle sometimes suggest that it is no more than a faulty inference from the subject-object structure of the sentences in which mental facts are reported. It would certainly be a mistake to infer that a conscious subject is something entirely distinct from all its states from the linguistic fact that we commonly assign mental states to owners. We say of a chair that it has a back, a seat, arms, and legs, but this should not and does not lead us to conclude that the chair is something over and above the parts that it has, appropriately arranged. A more usual argument for the principle starts from the premise that mental states are acts that cannot be conceived without an agent in the same way as there cannot be a blow without a striker or a journey without a traveler. The premise of this argument has been much criticized by recent philosophers. A feeling of depression or a belief in the trustworthiness of a friend is not a precisely datable occurrence but a more or less persisting dispositional state. Nor is it an instance of agency in the sense of being the intentional execution of a decision. But these mistaken implications do not affect the validity of the argument under consideration. A disposition requires a possessor as much as an act requires an agent, and the blow I get from a swinging door still presupposes the existence of the door even though it did not mean to hit me.

The strength of the argument lies in the fact that we can assert the existence of some mental state, a feeling of anger let us say, only when we are in a position to assert either that we ourselves are angry or that somebody else is. We have given no sense to the words "discovering the existence of a mental state that is not my own or anyone else's." The nearest we come to speaking in this way is when we say, for example, "there is a sadness about the place," when walking about some ruins in a contemplative frame of mind. What we mean in this case is that the place inclines us to feel sad and might well give rise to the same inclination in others. And this capacity for producing sad feelings in myself and others, as a disposition, has its own substance, so to speak: the broken columns and collapsed walls with which it is bound up.

The subject in this rather thin and formal sense is not borne down in the ruin of that concept of spiritual substance in which it is proposed as the determinant of personal identity. It could be argued that it is a loose way of referring to the related series of other mental states or to the body or both with which any given mental state is universally associated by our manner of reporting such states. If it is something distinct from both of these, as it has traditionally been believed to be, it is not properly to be called the soul. It could not exist without any states at all, and even if it could it would be an emotionally useless form of survival of bodily death. Its existence, in fact, is irrelevant to the problem of the soul, which is that of whether a person is essentially mental in character and so distinct from his body, a connected sequence of mental states and not a physical object. It is irrelevant whether the sequence of mental states composing a person on this theory presupposes a distinguishable subject or not.

Spiritual substance cannot be the criterion of personal identity, and it may or may not be presupposed by the existence of conscious mental states. Whether as part or presupposition of our mental life, it should not be identified with the soul when this is conceived as the nonbodily aspect of a person. The well-founded conviction that there is no spiritual substance in the first sense and widespread doubts as to its existence in the second should not be allowed to obscure the issue of whether there is a unitary nonbodily aspect to a person and, if there is, whether it is the fundamental and more important aspect. Locke saw that spiritual substance could not account for personal identity and, although he believed in its existence, speculated whether it might not have been possible for God to endow a material substance with the power of thinking. Yet he clearly believed in the soul as the connected sequence of a person's conscious states, regarded this sequence as what a person essentially was, and held it to be capable of existing independently of the body. I want to consider whether an empirical concept of the soul, which, like Locke's, interprets it as a sequence of mental states logically distinct from the body and is neutral with regard to the problem of the subject, can be constructed.

2. The Empirical Concept of the Soul

It will be admitted that among all the facts that involve a person there is a class that can be described as mental in some sense or other. Is it enough to define the soul as the temporally extended totality of mental states and events that belong to a person? It will not be enough to provide a concept of the soul as something logically distinct from the body if the idea of the series of a person's mental states involves some reference to the particular human body that he possesses. In the first place, therefore, a nonbodily criterion of personal identity must be produced. For if the soul were the series of mental states associated with a given body, in the sense of being publicly reported by it and being manifested by its behavior, two temporally separate mental states could belong to the history of the same soul only if they were in fact associated with one and the same human body. This notion of the soul could have no application to mental states that were not associated with bodies. The soul must, then, be a series of mental states that is identified through time in virtue of the properties and relations of these mental states themselves. Both the elements of the complex and the relations that make an identifiable persisting thing out of them must be mental. To establish the possibility of such a mental criterion of identity will be the hardest part of the undertaking.

Locke's criterion of memory has been much criticized, and it is certainly untenable in some of the interpretations it has been given. It will not do to say that two mental states belong to the same soul if and only if whoever has the later one can recollect the earlier one if the possibility of recollection involved is factual and not formal. For people forget things, and the paradox of the gallant officer is generated in which he is revealed as identical with both his childish and his senile selves while these are not identical with each other. However, a more plausible criterion can be offered in terms of continuity of character and memory. Two soul-phases belong to the same soul, on this view, if they are connected by a continuous character and memory path. A soul-phase is a set of contemporaneous mental states belonging to the same momentary consciousness. Two soul-phases are directly continuous if they are temporally juxtaposed, if the character revealed by the constituents of each is closely similar, and if the later contains recollections of some elements of the earlier. Two soul-phases are indirectly continuous and connected by a continuous character and memory path if there is a series of soul-phases all of whose members are directly continuous with their immediate predecessors and successors in the series and if the original soul-phases are the two end points of the series. There is a clear analogy between this criterion and the one by means of which material objects, including human bodies, are identified. Two object-phases belong to the same object if they are connected by a continuous quality and position path. Direct continuity in this case obtains between two temporally juxtaposed object-phases which are closely similar in qualities and are in the same position or in closely neighboring positions. Indirect continuity is once again the ancestral of direct continuity. There is no limit to the amount of difference in position allowed by the criterion to two indirectly continuous object-phases, but in normal discourse a limit is set to the amount of qualitative difference allowed by the requirement that the two phases be of objects of the same kind. Character in the mental case corresponds to quality in the physical and memory to spatial position. The soul, then, can be defined empirically as a series of mental states connected by continuity of character and memory.

Now there is an objection to the idea that memory can be any sort of fundamental criterion of identity which rests on the view that a memory criterion presupposes a bodily criterion. I shall defer the consideration of this issue, however, until two less serious difficulties have been met. These are that the construction suggested requires an exploded Cartesian dualism about the nature of mental states and, arising out of this, that a person's character is not clearly distinguishable from his body. The former, Rylean, objection can be met without difficulty. Even if the most extreme and reductive version of logical behaviorism were correct, even if a person's mental states were simply and solely behavioral dispositions, actual or potential, his character a complex property of these dispositions, and his memory a particular disposition to make first-person statements in the past tense without inference or reliance on testimony, the empirical concept of the soul would still apply to something distinct from any particular human body, though some body or other, not necessarily human perhaps, would be required to manifest the appropriate dispositions in its behavior and speech. In other words, an extreme, reductive, logical behaviorism is perfectly compatible with reincarnation, with the manifestation by one body of the character and memories that were previously manifested by another body that no longer exists. The second objection is that the soul as here defined and the body cannot be clearly distinguished, since the possession of some sorts of character trait requires the possession of an appropriate sort of body. I do not see that there is much empirical foundation for this to start with. It would be odd for a six-year-old girl to display the character of Winston Churchill, odd indeed to the point of outrageousness, but it is not utterly inconceivable. At first, no doubt, the girl's display of dogged endurance, a world-historical comprehensiveness of outlook, and so forth, would strike one as distasteful and pretentious in so young a child. But if she kept it up the impression would wear off. We do not, after all, find the story of Christ disputing with the doctors in the temple literally unintelligible. And a very large number of character traits seem to presume nothing about the age, sex, build, and general physical condition of their host. However, even if this were an empirically well-founded point, it would not be a relevant one. It would merely show that the possession of a given trait of character required the possession of an appropriate *kind* of body, a large one or a male one or an old one, and not the possession of a *particular* body. As things are, characters can survive large and even emotionally disastrous alterations to the physical type of a person's body, and these changes may have the effect of making it hard to others to recognize the continuity of character that there is. But courage, for example, can perfectly well persist even though the bodily conditions for its more obvious manifestations do not.

3. Mental and Bodily Criteria of Identity

In recent philosophy there have been two apparently independent aspects to the view that the mind is logically dependent on the body. On the one hand, there are the doctrines that hold mental states either to be or necessarily to involve bodily states, whether bodily movement and dispositions thereto or neural events and configurations. With these doctrines, I have argued, the empirical concept of the soul can be reconciled. On the other hand, many philosophers have insisted that the basic and indispensable criterion of personal identity is bodily. Even mind-body dualists like [A. J.—Ed.] Ayer, who have accepted the existence of a categorically clear-cut class of mental events, have sometimes taken this position. In his first treatment of the problem he appears at first to give a mental account of the concept of a person as being a series of experiences. But the relation that connects them in his theory involves an indispensable reference to a particular persisting human body. A person is made up of those total mental states which contain organic sensations belonging to one particular human body, presumably to be identified itself in terms of continuity of qualities and spatial position. Ayer draws the conclusion that properly follows from this and from any other account of personal identity that involves reference to a particular human body, namely that the notion of a person's disembodied existence is a self-contradictory one and, further, that even the association of a personality with different bodies at different times is inconceivable. These conclusions may well seem to constitute a reductio ad absurdum of the bodily criterion of personal identity rather than a disproof of the possibility of a person's survival of death. To explore them a little further will help to present the claims of mental as against bodily criteria in a clearer light.

At the outset it must be admitted that the theory of a bodily criterion has a number of virtues. It has, first, the theoretical attraction of simplicity, in that it requires only one mode of treatment for the identification through time of all enduring things, treating human beings as just one variety of concrete objects. Second, it has a practical appeal, in that its application yields uncontentiously correct answers in the very great majority of the actual cases of personal identification with which we are called upon to deal. Finally, it has the merit of realism, for it is, in fact, the procedure of identification that we do most commonly apply. Even where, for lack of relevant evidence, it is inapplicable, as in the case of the Tichborne claimant, it would not be supposed that the result of applying other criteria such as memory would conflict with what the bodily evidence would have shown if it had been forthcoming. Is there anything better to set against these powerful recommendations in favor of a bodily criterion than that it entails that things many people have wanted very deeply to say about the survival of death are inconsistent? A supporter of the bodily criterion might argue that it was so much the worse for them, that their inconsistent assertions arose from attempting to assert and deny at the same time that a person no longer existed.

It does seem strange, all the same, to say that all statements about disembodied or reincarnated persons are self-contradictory. Is it really at all plausible to say this about such familiar things as the simpler type of classical ghost story? It may be argued that there are plenty of stories which are really self-contradictory and yet which can be, in a way, understood and enjoyed, stories about time machines, for example. To try to settle the case we had better consider some concrete instances. Suppose I am walking on the beach with my friend A. He walks off a fair distance, treads on a large mine that someone has forgotten to remove, and is physically demolished in front of my eyes. Others, attracted by the noise, draw near and help to collect the scattered remains of A for burial. That night, alone in my room, I hear A's voice and see a luminous but intangible object, of very much the shape and size of A, standing in the corner. The remarks that come from it are in A's characteristic style and refer to matters that only A could have known about. Suspecting a hallucination, I photograph it and call in witnesses who hear and see what I do. The apparition returns afterwards and tells of where it has been and what it has seen. It would be very peculiar to insist, in these circumstances, that A no longer existed, even though his body no longer exists except as stains on the rocks and in a small box in the mortuary. It is not essential for the argument that the luminous object look like A or that it speak in A's voice. If it were a featureless cylinder and spoke like a talking weighing machine we should simply take longer becoming convinced that it really was A. But if continuity of character and memory were manifested with normal amplitude, we surely should be convinced.

Consider a slightly different case. I know two men B and C. B is a dark, tall, thin, puritanical Scotsman of sardonic temperament with whom I have gone on bird-watching expeditions. C is a fair, short, plump, apolaustic Pole of indestructible enterprise and optimism with whom I have made a number of more urban outings. One day I come into a room where both appear to be, and the dark, tall, thin man suggests that he and I pursue tonight some acquaintances I made with C, though he says it was with him, a couple of nights ago. The short, fair, plump, cheerful-looking man reminds me in a strong Polish accent of a promise I had made to B, though he says it was to him, and which I had forgotten about, to go in search of owls on this very night. At first I suspect a conspiracy, but the thing continues far beyond any sort of joke, for good perhaps, and is accompanied by suitable amazement on their part at each other's appearance, their own reflections in the mirror, and so forth.

Now what would it be reasonable to say in these circumstances: that B and C have changed bodies (the consequence of a mental criterion), that they have switched character and memories (the consequence of a bodily criterion), or neither? It seems to me quite clear that we should not say that B and C had switched characters and memories. And if this is correct, it follows that bodily identity is not a logically complete criterion of personal identity; at best it could be a necessary condition of personal identity. Of the other alternatives, that of refusing to identify either of the psychophysical hybrids before us with B or C may seem the most scrupulous and proper. But the refusal might take a number of different forms. It might be a categorical denial that either of the hybrids is B or C. It might, more sophisticatedly, be an assertion that the concept of personal identity had broken down and that there was no correct answer, affirmative or negative, to the question: which of these two is B and which C? It might, uninterestingly, be a state of amazed and inarticulate confusion.

What support is there for the conclusion required by the empirical concept of the soul, that B and C have substituted bodies? First of all, the rather weak evidence of imaginative literature. In F. Anstey's story *Vice Versa* the corpulent and repressive Mr. Bultitude and his athletic and impulsive schoolboy son are the victims of a similar rearrangement. The author shows not the smallest trace of hesitation in calling the thing with the father's character and memories the father and the thing with the father's body the son. (Cf. also Conan Doyle's *Keinplatz Experiment.*) A solider support is to be found by reflecting on the probable attitude after the switch of those who are most concerned with our original pair, B and C, as persons, those who have the greatest interest in answering the question of their personal identity: their parents, their wives, their children, their closest friends. Would they say that B and C had ceased to exist, that they had exchanged characters and memories or that they had exchanged bodies? It is surely plain that if the character and memories of B and C really survived intact in their new bodily surroundings those closely concerned with them would say that the two had exchanged bodies, that the original persons were where the characters and memories were. For why, after all, do we bother to identify people so carefully? What is unique about individual people that is important enough for us to call them by individual proper names? In our general relations with other human beings their bodies are for the most part intrinsically unimportant. We use them as convenient recognition devices enabling us to locate without difficulty the persisting character and memory complexes in which we are interested, which we love or like. It would be upsetting if a complex with which we were emotionally involved came to have a monstrous or repulsive physical appearance, it would be socially embarrassing if it kept shifting from body to body while most such complexes stayed put, and it would be confusing and tiresome if such shifting around were generally widespread, for it would be a laborious business finding out where one's friends and family were. But that our concern and affection would follow the character and memory complex and not its original bodily associate is surely clear. In the case of general shifting about we should be in the position of people trying to find their intimates in the dark. If the shifts were both frequent and spatially radical we should no doubt give up the attempt to identify individual people, the whole character of relations between people would change, and human life would be like an unending sequence of shortish ocean trips. But, as long as the transfers did not involve large movements in space, the character and memory complexes we are concerned with could be kept track of through their audible identification of themselves. And there is no reason to doubt that the victim of such a bodily transfer would regard himself as the person whom he seems to remember himself as being. I conclude, then, that although, as things stand, our concept of a person is not called upon to withstand these strains and, therefore, that in the face of a psychophysical transfer we might at first not know what to say, we should not identify the people in question as those who now have the bodies they used to have and that it would be the natural thing to extend our concept of a person, given the purposes for which it has been constructed, so as to identify anyone present to us now with whoever it was who used to have the same character and memories as he has. In other words the soul, defined as a series of mental states connected by continuity of character and memory, is the essential constituent of personality. The soul, therefore, is not only logically distinct from any particular human body with which it is associated; it is also what a person fundamentally is.

It may be objected to the extension of the concept of personal identity that I have argued for that it rests on an incorrect and even sentimental view of the nature of personal relations. There are, it may be said, personal relationships which are of an exclusively bodily character and which would not survive a change of body but which would perfectly well survive a change of soul. Relations of a rather unmitigatedly sexual type might be instanced and also those where the first party to the relationship has violent racial feelings. It can easily be shown that these objections are without substance. In the first place, even the most tired of entrepreneurs is going to take some note of the character and memories of the companion of his later nights at work. He will want her to be docile and quiet, perhaps, and to remember that he takes two parts of water to one of scotch, and no ice. If she ceases to be plump and red-headed and vigorous he may lose interest in and abandon her, but he would have done so anyway in response to the analogous effects of the aging process. If he has any idea of her as a person at all, it will be as a unique cluster of character traits and recollections. As a body, she is simply an instrument of a particular type, no more and no less interesting to him than a physically identical twin. In the case of a purely sexual relationship no particular human body is required, only one of a more or less precisely demarcated kind. Where concern with the soul is wholly absent there is no interest in individual identity at all, only in identity of type. It may be said that this argument cuts both ways: that parents and children are concerned only that they should have round them children and parents with the same sort of character and memories as the children and parents they were with yesterday. But this is doubly incorrect. First, the memories of individual persons cannot be exactly similar, since even the closest of identical twins must see things from slightly different angles; they cannot be in the same place at the same time. More seriously, if more contingently, individual memories, even of identical twins, are seldom, if ever, closely similar. To put the point crudely, the people I want to be with are the people who remember me and the experiences we have shared, not those who remember someone more or less like me with whom they have shared more or less similar experiences. The relevant complexity of the memories of an individual person is of an altogether different order of magnitude from that of the bodily properties of an entrepreneur's lady friend. The lady friend's bodily type is simply enough defined for it to have a large number of instances. It is barely conceivable that two individual memories should be similar enough to be emotionally adequate substitutes for each other. There is the case of the absolutely identical twins who go everywhere together, side by side, and always have done so. Our tendency here would be to treat the pair as a physically dual single person. There would be no point in distinguishing one from the other. As soon as their ways parted sufficiently for the question of which was which to arise, the condition of different memories required for individuation would be satisfied.

It may be felt that the absolutely identical twins present a certain difficulty for the empirical concept of the soul. For suppose their characters and memories to be totally indistinguishable and their thoughts and feelings to have been precisely the same since the first dawning of consciousness in them. Won't the later phases of one of the twins be as continuous in respect of character and memory with the earlier phases of the other as they are with his own earlier phases? Should we even say that there are two persons there at all? The positional difference of the two bodies provides an answer to the second question. Although they are always excited and gloomy together, the thrills and pangs are manifested in distinct bodies and are conceivable as existing separately. We might ignore the duality of their mental states, but we should be able in principle to assert it. As to the matter of continuity, the environment of the two will be inevitably asymmetrical, each will at various times be nearer something than the other, each will block some things from the other's field of vision or touch; so there will always be some, perhaps trivial, difference in the memories of the two. But even if trivial, the difference will be enough to allow the application in this special case of a criterion that normally relies on radical and serious differences. However alike the character and memories of twin no. 1 on Tuesday and twin no. 2 on Wednesday, they will inevitably be less continuous than those of twin no. 2 on the two days.

4. Memory and Bodily Identity

I must now return to the serious objection to the use of memory as a criterion of personal identity whose consideration was postponed earlier. This has been advanced in an original and interesting article on personal identity recently published by Sydney S. Shoemaker in this *Journal*.[1] He argues that memory could not be the sole or fundamental criterion for the identity of other people, because in order to establish what the memories of other people are I have to be able to identify them in a bodily way. I cannot accept sentences offered by other people beginning with the words "I remember" quite uncritically. I must be assured, first, that these utterances really are memory claims, that the speaker understands the meaning of the sentences he is using, and, secondly, that his memory claims are reliable. Mr. Shoemaker contends that it is essential, if either of these requirements is to be satisfied, for me to be able to identify the maker of the apparent memory claims in an independent, bodily way. In order to be sure that his remarks really are intended as memory claims, I have to see that he generally uses the form of words in question in connection with antecedent states of affairs of which he has been a witness. And to do this I must be assured that he is at one time uttering a memory sentence and at another, earlier, time is a witness of the event he purports to describe; in other words I must be able to identify him at different times without taking his apparent memories into account. The point is enforced by the second requirement about the conditions under which I can take his memory claims as trustworthy. To do this I must be able to establish at least that he was physically present at and, thus, in a position to observe the state of affairs he now claims to recollect.

There is a good deal of force in these arguments, but I do not think they are sufficient to prove that the soul is not logically distinct from the particular body with which it happens to be associated at any given time. In the first place, the doubt about the significance of someone's current memory claims is not one that I must positively have laid to rest before taking these claims as evidence of his identity. The doubt could seriously arise only in very special and singular circumstances. If someone now says to me, "I remember the battle of Hastings," I will presume him to be slightly misusing the words, since I have good reasons for thinking that no one now alive was present at that remote event. I shall probably take him to be saying that he remembers that there was such a thing as the battle of Hastings, having learnt of it at school, or that it took place in 1066, that Harold was killed at it, that it was the crucial military

[1] "Personal Identity and Memory." *The Journal of Philosophy*, 56, 22 (Oct. 22, 1959): 868.

factor in the Norman conquest, and so forth. But if, on being questioned, he says that these reinterpretations distort the meaning he intended, that he remembers the battle of Hastings in the same way as he remembers having breakfast this morning, if perhaps a little more dimly, then I cannot reasonably suppose that he doesn't understand the meaning of his remark though I may well think that it is false, whether deliberately or not. Mr. Shoemaker admits that in a case of apparent bodily transfer the significance of a person's memory claims could be established by considering the way in which he used memory sentences after the transfer had taken place. So at best this part of his argument could prove that in order to identify people we need to be able to make at least local applications of the criterion of bodily identity. They must be continuous in a bodily way for a period of time sufficient to enable us to establish that they are using memory sentences correctly. But in view of the somewhat strained and artificial character of the doubt in question, I am inclined to reject even this modest conclusion. At best it is a practical requirement: people must be sufficiently stable in a bodily way for me to be able to accumulate a large enough mass of apparent memory claims that are prima facie there to infer from the coherence of these apparent claims that they really are memory claims and not senseless noises.

The reliability of the memory claims of others is a more substantial issue. For, unlike significance, it is a feature of apparent memory claims that we commonly do have serious reason to doubt. It must be admitted, further, that if I have independent reasons for believing that Jones's body was physically present at an event that Jones now claims to remember, I have a piece of strong evidence in support of the correctness of his claim. It is not, of course, conclusive. Even if he were looking in the direction at the time, he might have been in a condition of day-dreaming inattentiveness. The question is, however: is it in any sense a necessary condition for the correctness of my acceptance of a man's present memory claim that I should be able, in principle, to discover that the very same body from which the claim under examination now emerges was actually present at the event now purportedly remembered? I cannot see that it is. To revert to the example of a radical psychophysical exchange between B and C. Suppose that from B's body memory claims emerge about a lot of what I have hitherto confidently taken to be C's experiences. I may have good reason to believe that C's body was present at the events apparently recalled. If the claims are very numerous and detailed, if they involve the recollection of things I didn't know B had seen although I can now establish that they were really present for C to observe, and if the emission of apparent C memories from B's body and vice versa keeps up for a fair period, it would be unreasonable not to conclude that the memory claims emerging from B's body were in fact correct, that they were the memory claims of C not of B, and that therefore the person with B's body was in fact not now B but C. Here again a measure of local bodily continuity seems required. I shall not say that C inhabits B's body at all unless he seems to do so in a fairly substantial way and over a fair period of time. But as long as the possibility of psychophysical exchange is established by some salient cases in which the requirement of local bodily continuity is satisfied I can reasonably conjecture that such exchange has taken place in other cases where the translocation of memory claims is pretty short-lived. At any rate it is only the necessity of local bodily continuity that is established, not the necessary association of a person with one particular body for the whole duration of either. Bodily continuity with a witness is a test of the reliability of someone's memory claims, and it is an important one, but it is not a logically indispensable one.

5. *The Problem of Disembodiment*

Nothing that I have said so far has any direct bearing on the question whether the soul can exist in an entirely disembodied state. All I have tried to show is that there is no necessary connection between the soul as a series of mental states linked by character and memory and any particular continuing human body. The question now arises: must the soul be associated with some human body? The apparent intelligibility of my crude ghost story might seem to suggest that not even a body is required, let alone a human one. And the same point appears to be made by the intelligibility of stories in which trees, toadstools, pieces of furniture, and so on are endowed with personal characteristics. But a good deal of caution is needed here. In the first place, even where these personal characteristics are not associated with any sort of body in the physiological sense, they are associated with a body in the epistemological sense; in other words, it is an essential part of the story that the soul in question have physical manifestations. Only in our own case does it seem that strictly disembodied existence is conceivable, in the sense that we can conceive circumstances in which there would be some good reason to claim that a soul existed in a disembodied state. Now how tenuous and nonhuman could these physical manifestations be? To take a fairly mild example, discussed by Professor [Norman—Ed.] Malcolm, could we regard a tree as another person? He maintains with great firmness that we could not, on the rather flimsy ground that trees haven't got mouths and, therefore, could not be said to speak or communicate with us or make memory claims. But if a knothole in a tree trunk physically emitted sounds in the form of speech, why should we not call it a mouth? We may presume that ventriloquism, hidden record-players and microphones, dwarfs concealed in the foliage, and so forth have all been ruled out. If the remarks of the tree were coherent and appropriate to its situation and exhibited the type of continuity that the remarks of persons normally do exhibit, why shouldn't we regard the tree as a person? The point is that we might, by a serious conceptual effort, allow this in the case of one tree or even several trees or even a great many nonhuman physical things. But the sense of our attribution of personality to them would be logically parasitic on our attributions of personality to ordinary human bodies. It is from their utterances and behavior that we derive our concept of personality, and this concept would be applicable to nonhuman things only by more or less far-fetched analogy. That trees should be personal presupposes, then, the personality of human beings. The same considerations hold in the extreme case of absolutely minimal embodiment, as when a recurrent and localized voice of a recognizable tone is heard to make publicly audible remarks. The voice might give evidence of qualitative and positional continuity sufficient to treat it as an identifiable body, even if of an excessively diaphanous kind. The possibility of this procedure, however, is contingent on there being persons in the standard, humanly embodied sense to provide a clear basis for the acquisition of the concept that is being more or less speculatively applied to the voice.

Whatever the logic of the matter, it might be argued, the causal facts of the situation make the whole inquiry into the possibility of a soul's humanly or totally disembodied existence an entirely fantastic one. That people have the memories and characters that they do, that they have memories and characters at all, has as its causally necessary condition the relatively undisturbed persistence of a particular bit of physiological apparatus. One can admit this without concluding that the inquiry is altogether without practical point. For the bit of physiological apparatus in question is not the human body as a whole, but the brain. Certainly lavish changes in the noncerebral parts of the human body often affect the character and perhaps even to some extent the memories of the person whose body it is. But there is no strict relationship here. Now it is sometimes said that the last bit of the body to wear out is the brain, that the brain takes the first and lion's share of the body's nourishment, and that the brains of people who have starved to death are often found in perfectly good structural order. It is already possible to graft bits of one human body on to another, corneas, fingers, and, even, I believe, legs. Might it not be possible to remove the brain from an otherwise worn-out human body and replace it either in a manufactured human body or in a cerebrally untenanted one? In this case we should have a causally conceivable analogue of reincarnation. If this were to become possible and if the resultant creatures appeared in a coherent way to exhibit the character and memories previously associated with the brain that had been fitted into them, we could say that the original person was still in existence even though only a relatively minute part of its original mass and volume was present in the new physical whole. Yet if strict bodily identity is a necessary condition of personal identity, such a description of the outcome would be ruled out as self-contradictory. I conclude, therefore, not only that a logically adequate concept of the soul is constructible but that the construction has some possible utility even in the light of our knowledge of the causal conditions of human life.

The Mind and Knowledge
of Other Minds

9

Bertrand Russell
The Argument from Analogy

Bertrand Russell (1872–1970) was one of the most prolific as well as one of the greatest philosophers of the twentieth century. His reputation rests on a variety of accomplishments, not the least of them political and educational, on which he wrote as extensively as on philosophy. Because of his pacifist activity in Britain during World War I, he was jailed and dismissed from his post at Trinity College. In fact, he was dismissed from a number of posts and was not allowed to take up a promised post at City College in New York because of charges against his character. He stood unsuccessfully for Parliament; founded an experimental school; was jailed a second time in 1961, when he actively supported nuclear disarmament. He became Earl Russell in 1931 and received the Nobel Prize for Literature in 1950.

Working with Alfred North Whitehead, Russell produced Principia Mathematica *(3 vols., 1910–1913), in which arithmetic is subsumed within logic. He is distinguished in this regard by his discovery of a paradox of classes (sets), though his own conception of classes was itself the subject of considerable dispute. He maintained a lively exchange with G. E. Moore and befriended Ludwig Wittgenstein, for whose* Tractatus Logico-philosophicus *(1921, 1922) he wrote an introduction.*

Russell's influence has been extraordinary, all the more so given that he recast his views innumerable times, was not satisfied with the results, and has not attracted sustained adherents to his final philosophy. His early philosophical motivation seems to have been directed against Hegelianism, particularly against the British Hegelian F. H. Bradley. In fact, his opposition to the doctrine of internal relations and his advocacy of a doctrine of external relations led directly to his atomism. Relations, he held, could not be reduced to things identified only as related

From Bertrand Russell, *Human Knowledge: Its Scope and Limits* (London and New York: 1948), Part VI, Chap. VIII, pp. 482–486. Copyright 1948 by Bertrand Russell renewed © 1975, by the Estate of Bertrand Russell. Reprinted by permission of Simon & Schuster, Inc. and George Allen & Unwin Ltd.

to something else. *Bradley had held that a thing's apparently distinct attributes are what they are in virtue of a certain relation holding between them. But that relation must hold in virtue of a further relation, and so on. Russell held that attributes could be ascribed to things without entailing such relations. Furthermore, knowledge may be characterized, he maintained, in terms of our acquaintance with the separate items of sense experience and in terms of logical connections among the sentences affirming such acquaintance (logical atomism). Hence his theory of external relations and his atomism are closely connected.*

But emphasis on atomic facts (the independent facts regarding direct acquaintance with sense experience) and on the independent reality of what there is led to difficulties. Russell himself was aware of the limitations of atomism. Thus he rejected the view that generalizations (for instance, "All lemons are yellow") could be reduced to logical combinations of atomic sentences, though this appeared to be required by his own theory.

One of his early papers, "On Denoting" (1905) (see IV:8), may well be the most celebrated essay in twentieth-century Anglo-American philosophy. It is often cited as a specimen of the possibility of genuine philosophical progress, though it has actually spawned a substantial and controversial literature on the central problem of reference. Here, Russell uses the then relatively novel devices of quantification ("all" and "some") to eliminate definite descriptions and hence to suggest an economical way of reducing our commitments to what we take to be real. (The issue is taken up in Part IV.) This theme is one of the main strands of contemporary philosophical motivation.

In one of his best-known papers, "Knowledge by Acquaintance and Knowledge by Description" (1910–1911), Russell emphasized that knowledge rests on our direct acquaintance with whatever is given to immediate experience. Consistent with this, he maintained that our knowledge that other persons are in a particular mental state is based on an argument from analogy with our own case. As we see that our own pains and the like are correlated with distinct forms of behavior and physical conditions, he said, we infer that others must have similar mental states when they behave similarly or are in similar physical conditions. In Russell's view, first we are familiar with our own mental states and then we are obliged to bridge the gap between our own states and those we suppose to obtain in others, by means of a form of argument whose adequacy has come to be seriously challenged.

Among the more salient of Russell's publications are The Principles of Mathematics *(1903),* The Problems of Philosophy *(1912),* Our Knowledge of the External World *(1914),* Mysticism and Logic *(1918),* The Analysis of Mind *(1921),* An Inquiry into Meaning and Truth *(1940), and* Logic and Knowledge *(1956).*

The postulates hitherto considered have been such as are required for knowledge of the physical world. Broadly speaking, they have led us to admit a certain degree of knowledge as to the space-time structure of the physical world, while leaving us completely agnostic as regards its qualitative character. But where other human beings are concerned, we feel that we know more than this; we are convinced that other people have thoughts and feelings that are qualitatively fairly similar to our own. We are not content to think that we know only the space-time structure of our friends' minds, or their capacity for initiating causal chains that end in sensations of our own. A philosopher might pretend to think that he knew only this, but let him get cross with his wife and you will see that he does not regard her as a mere spatio-temporal edifice of which he knows the logical properties but not a glimmer of the intrinsic character. We are therefore justified in inferring that his skepticism is professional rather than sincere.

The problem with which we are concerned is the following. We observe in ourselves such occurrences as remembering, reasoning, feeling pleasure, and feeling pain. We think that sticks and stones do not have these experiences, but that other people do. Most of us have no doubt that the higher animals feel pleasure and pain, though I was once assured by a fisherman that "Fish have no sense nor feeling." I failed to find out how he had acquired this knowledge. Most people would disagree with him, but would be doubtful about oysters and starfish. However this may be, common sense admits an increasing doubt-fulness as we descend in the animal kingdom, but as regards human beings it admits no doubt.

It is clear that belief in the minds of others requires some postulate that is not required in physics, since physics can be content with a knowledge of struc-ture. My present purpose is to suggest what this further postulate may be.

It is clear that we must appeal to something that may be vaguely called "analogy." The behavior of other people is in many ways analogous to our own, and we suppose that it must have analogous causes. What people say is what we should say if we had certain thoughts, and so we infer that they probably have these thoughts. They give us information which we can sometimes sub-sequently verify. They behave in ways in which we behave when we are pleased (or displeased) in circumstances in which we should be pleased (or displeased). We may talk over with a friend some incident which we have both experienced, and find that his reminiscences dovetail with our own; this is particularly con-vincing when he remembers something that we have forgotten but that he recalls to our thoughts. Or again: you set your boy a problem in arithmetic, and with luck he gets the right answer; this persuades you that he is capable of arithmetical reasoning. There are, in short, very many ways in which my responses to stimuli differ from those of "dead" matter, and in all these ways other people resemble me. As it is clear to me that the causal laws governing my behavior have to do with "thoughts," it is natural to infer that the same is true of the analogous behavior of my friends.

The inference with which we are at present concerned is not merely that which takes us beyond solipsism, by maintaining that sensations have causes about which *something* can be known. This kind of inference, which suffices for physics, has already been considered. We are concerned now with a much more specific kind of inference, the kind that is involved in our knowledge of the thoughts and feelings of others—assuming that we have such knowledge. It is of course obvious that such knowledge is more or less doubtful. There is not only the general argument that we may be dreaming; there is also the possibility of ingenious automata. There are calculating machines that do sums much better than our schoolboy sons; there are gramophone records that remember impeccably what So-and-so said on such-and-such an occasion; there are people in the cinema who, though copies of real people, are not themselves alive. There is no theoretical limit to what ingenuity could achieve in the way of producing the illusion of life where in fact life is absent.

But, you will say, in all such cases it was the thoughts of human beings that produced the ingenious mechanism. Yes, but how do you know this? And how do you know that the gramophone does *not* "think"?

There is, in the first place, a difference in the causal laws of observable behavior. If I say to a student, "Write me a paper on Descartes' reasons for believing in the existence of matter," I shall, if he is industrious, cause a certain response. A gramophone record might be so constructed as to respond to this stimulus, perhaps better than the student, but if so it would be incapable of telling me anything about any other philosopher, even if I threatened to refuse to give it a degree. One of the most notable peculiarities of human behavior is change of response to a given stimulus. An ingenious person could construct an automaton which would always laugh at his jokes, however often it heard them; but a human being, after laughing a few times, will yawn, and end by saying, "How I laughed the first time I heard that joke."

But the differences in observable behavior between living and dead matter do not suffice to prove that there are "thoughts" connected with living bodies other than my own. It is probably possible theoretically to account for the behavior of living bodies by purely physical causal laws, and it is probably impossible to refute materialism by external observation alone. If we are to believe that there are thoughts and feelings other than our own, that must be in virtue of some inference in which our own thoughts and feelings are relevant, and such an inference must go beyond what is needed in physics.

I am, of course, not discussing the history of how we come to believe in other minds. We find ourselves believing in them when we first begin to reflect; the thought that Mother may be angry or pleased is one which arises in early infancy. What I am discussing is the possibility of a postulate which shall establish a rational connection between this belief and data, e.g., between the belief "Mother is angry" and the hearing of a loud voice.

The abstract schema seems to be as follows. We know, from observation of ourselves, a causal law of the form "A causes B," where A is a "thought" and B a physical occurrence. We sometimes observe a B when we cannot observe any A; we then infer an unobserved A. For example: I know that when I say, "I'm thirsty," I say so, usually, because I am thirsty, and therefore, when I hear the sentence "I'm thirsty" at a time when I am not thirsty, I assume that someone else is thirsty. I assume this the more readily if I see before me a hot, drooping body which goes on to say, "I have walked twenty desert miles in this heat with never a drop to drink." It is evident that my confidence in the "inference" is increased by increased complexity in the datum and also by increased certainty of the causal law derived from subjective observation, provided the causal law is such as to account for the complexities of the datum.

It is clear that in so far as plurality of causes is to be suspected, the kind of inference we have been considering is not valid. We are supposed to know "A causes B," and also to know that B has occurred; if this is to justify us in inferring A, we must know that *only* A causes B. Or, if we are content to infer that A is probable, it will suffice if we can know that in most cases it is A that causes B. If you hear thunder without having seen lightning, you confidently infer that there was lightning, because you are convinced that the sort of noise you heard is seldom caused by anything except lightning. As this example shows, our principle is not only employed to establish the existence of other minds but is habitually assumed, though in a less concrete form, in physics. I say "a less concrete form" because unseen lightning is only abstractly similar to seen lightning, whereas we suppose the similarity of other minds to our own to be by no means purely abstract.

Complexity in the observed behavior of another person, when this can all be accounted for by a simple cause such as thirst, increases the probability of the inference by diminishing the probability of some other cause. I think that in ideally favorable circumstances the argument would be formally as follows:

From subjective observation I know that A, which is a thought or feeling, causes B, which is a bodily act, e.g., a statement. I know also that, whenever B is an act of my own body, A is its cause. I now observe an act of the kind B in a body not my own, and I am having no thought or feeling of the kind A. But I still believe, on the basis of self-observation, that only A can cause B; I therefore infer that there was an A which caused B, though it was not an A that I could observe. On this ground I infer that other people's bodies are associated with minds, which resemble mine in proportion as their bodily behavior resembles my own.

In practice, the exactness and certainty of the above statement must be softened. We cannot be sure that, in our subjective experience, A is the only cause of B. And even if A is the only cause of B in our experience, how can we know that this holds outside our experience? It is not necessary that we should know this with any certainty; it is enough if it is highly probable. It is the assumption of probability in such cases that is our postulate. The postulate may therefore be stated as follows:

If, whenever we can observe whether A and B are present or absent, we find that every case of B has an A as a causal antecedent, then it is probable that most B's have A's as causal antecedents, even in cases where observation does not enable us to know whether A is present or not.

This postulate, if accepted, justifies the inference to other minds, as well as many other inferences that are made unreflectingly by common sense.

10

Franz Brentano

The Distinction Between Mental and Physical Phenomena

Franz Brentano (1838–1917) was one of the most original philosophers of nineteenth-century Germany. He taught at the University of Vienna and influenced Alexius Meinong and Edmund Husserl, who were his students. In fact, Brentano has long been thought of primarily as the teacher of Husserl. But his importance in his own right is becoming clear, and a good many of his works are now available in English translation. He became a Roman Catholic priest but left the church within ten years; and he went blind toward the end of his life.

His most influential book is Psychology from an Empirical Standpoint *(1874; posth. enl. ed., 1925), which provides his central conception of intentionality and the distinction between mental and physical phenomena. What was common to all forms of mental phenomena and absent in physical phenomena, he said, was "directedness upon an object" or "intentional inexistence." He maintained that mental relations were not relations in the strict sense, since one could think about something even if it did not exist.*

Brentano's important The True and the Evident *(posth. 1930) presents his distinctive theory of knowledge, whose central emphasis is that the evident precludes error and doubt. The most important contemporary descendant of Brentano's theory of knowledge may well be that of Chisholm.*

IV

The attempt has been made to give a perfectly unified definition which distinguishes all of the mental phenomena, as contrasted with the physical, by means of negation. All physical phenomena, it is said, manifest extension and definite spatial location, whether they are appearances to sight or another sense, or products of the imagination, which presents similar objects to us. The opposite, however, is true of mental phenomena; thinking, willing, and so on appear as unextended and without a situation in space.

According to this view, we would be in a position to characterize the physical phenomena easily and rigorously in contrast to the mental, if we were to say that they are those which appear extended and spatial. And, with the same exactitude, the mental phenomena would then be definable, as contrasted with

Franz Brentano, "The Distinction Between Mental and Physical Phenomena" (originally included in Brentano's *Psychologie vom empirischen Standpunkt*, Vol. I, Bk. II, Ch. i [1874]), translated by D. B. Terrell. Permission to reprint has been granted by D. B. Terrell and Roderick M. Chisholm, who edited *Realism and the Background of Phenomenology* (Glencoe, Ill.: Free Press, 1960), in which the translation first appeared.

the physical, as those which exhibit no extension or definite spatial location. One could call on Descartes and Spinoza in support of such a differentiation, but particularly on Kant, who declares space to be the form of intuition of outer sensation.

A. Bain has recently given the same definition: "The department of the Object, or Object-World," he says, "is exactly circumscribed by one property, Extension. The world of Subject-experience is devoid of this property.

"A tree or a river is said to possess extended magnitude. A pleasure has no length, breadth, or thickness; it is in no respect an extended thing. A thought or idea may refer to extended magnitudes, but it cannot be said to have extension in itself. Neither can we say that an act of the will, a desire, a belief, occupy dimensions in space. Hence all that comes within the sphere of the Subject is spoken of as the Unextended.

"Thus, if Mind, as commonly happens, is put for the sum total of Subject-experiences, we may define it negatively by a single fact—the absence of Extension."[9]

So it appears that we have found, negatively at least, a unified definition for the sum-total of mental phenomena.

But here, too, unanimity does not prevail among the psychologists, and for diverse reasons we often hear it denied that extension and the absence of extension are differentiating characteristics distinguishing physical and mental phenomena.

Many believe that the definition is false because not only mental, but also many physical phenomena, appear without extension. Thus, a large number of not unimportant psychologists teach that the phenomena of certain senses, or even of the senses in general, originally manifest themselves free of all extension and definite spatial character. This is very generally believed [to be true] of sounds and of the phenomena of smell. According to [George—Ed.] Berkeley, the same holds true of colors, and according to Platner, of the phenomena of the sense of touch. According to Herbart and [H.—Ed.] Lotze, as well as [D.—Ed.] Hartley, Brown, the two Mills, H. Spencer, and others, [it is true] of the phenomena of all the external senses. To be sure, it appears to us as if the phenomena which the external senses, particularly vision and the sense of touch, manifest to us were all spatially extended. But the reason for this, it is said, is the fact that on the basis of prior experience we connect with them our gradually developed presentation of *space*; originally without definite spatial location, they are later localized by us. If this should really be the only way in which physical phenomena attain definite spatial location, then we could plainly no longer distinguish the two realms by reference to this property. [The possibility of such a distinction] is decreased still more by the fact that mental phenomena are also localized by us in such a way, as, for example, when we mistakenly place a phenomenon of anger in the irritable lion, and our own thoughts in the space that is filled by us.

So that would be one way, from the point of view of a large number of

---

[9] *Mental Science*, Intro., chap. i.

important psychologists, in which the stated definition must be contested. When all is said, even Bain, who seems to advance it, is to be counted among these thinkers; for he follows Hartley's line of thought completely. He is able to speak as he has spoken only because (even though without complete consistency) he has not included the phenomena of the external senses, in and for themselves, among the physical phenomena.[10]

Others, as I have said, will reject the definition for contrary reasons. It is not so much the claim that all physical phenomena appear extended that arouses their opposition. It is the claim, rather, that all mental phenomena lack extension; according to them, certain mental phenomena also manifest themselves as extended. Aristotle appears to have been of this opinion when, in the first chapter of his treatise on sensation and the object of sense, he regards it as evident, immediately and without previous proof, that sense perception is the act of a physical organ.[11] Modern psychologists and physiologists express themselves similarly at times in connection with certain affects. They speak of feelings of pleasure and pain which appear in the external organs, sometimes, indeed, even after the amputation of the member; and surely, feeling, like perception, is a mental phenomenon. Many also say of sensual desires that they appear localized; and the fact that poets speak, perhaps not of thought, but of bliss and yearning which suffuse the heart and all the parts of the body, is in accord with that view.

So we see that the stated distinction is assailed with regard to both physical and mental phenomena. Perhaps both points raised against it are equally unfounded.[12] Nevertheless, a further definition common to mental phenomena is still desirable in any case. For conflict over the question whether certain mental and physical phenomena appear extended or not shows at once that the alleged attribute does not suffice for a distinct differentiation; furthermore, for the mental phenomena it is negative only.

V

What positive attribute will we now be able to advance? Or is there, perhaps, no positive definition at all which holds true of all mental phenomena generally?

A. Bain says that in fact there is none.[13] Nonetheless, psychologists of an earlier period have already directed attention to a particular affinity and analogy which exists among all mental phenomena, while the physical do not share in it. Every mental phenomenon is characterized by what the scholastics of the

---

[10] See note 1.

[11] *De sens, et sens* 1, p. 436, b, 7. See also what he says in *De anim.* I. 1. p. 403, a, 16 about the affects, especially those of fear.

[12] The claim that even mental phenomena appear extended rests plainly on a confusion between physical and mental phenomena similar to the one we became convinced of above, when we established that even sensory feelings are necessarily based on a presentation.

[13] *The Senses and the Intellect*, Intro.

Middle Ages called the intentional (and also mental)[14] inexistence (*Inexistenz*) of an object (*Gegenstand*), and what we could call, although in not entirely unambiguous terms, the reference to a content, a direction upon an object (by which we are not to understand a reality in this case), or an immanent objectivity. Each one includes something as object within itself, although not always in the same way. In presentation something is presented, in judgment something is affirmed or denied, in love [something is] loved, in hate [something] hated, in desire [something] desired, etc.[15]

This intentional inexistence is exclusively characteristic of mental phenomena. No physical phenomenon manifests anything similar. Consequently, we can define mental phenomena by saying that they are such phenomena as include an object intentionally within themselves.

But here, too, we come up against conflict and contradiction. And it is [Sir William—Ed.] Hamilton in particular who denies the alleged property of a whole broad class of mental phenomena, namely, of all those which he designates as feelings, of pleasure and pain in their most diverse shades and varieties. He is in agreement with us concerning the phenomena of thinking and desire. Obviously, there would be no thinking without an object which is thought, no desire without an object which is desired. "In the phenomena of Feeling—the phenomena of Pleasure and Pain—on the contrary, consciousness does not place the mental modification or state before itself; it does not contemplate it apart— as separate from itself—but is, as it were, fused into one. The peculiarity of Feeling, therefore, is that there is nothing but what is subjectively subjective; there is no object different from self—no objectification of any mode of self."[16] In the first case, there would be something there which, according to Hamilton's way of expression, is "objective"; in the second, something which is "objectively subjective," as in self-knowledge, whose object Hamilton therefore calls subject-

---

[14] They also use the expression "to be in something objectively," which, if we should wish to make use of it now, could possibly be taken in just the opposite sense, as the designation of a real existence outside of the mind. Nevertheless, it reminds one of the expression "to be immanently objective," which we sometimes use in a similar sense, and in which the "immanently" is intended to exclude the misunderstanding that was to be feared.

[15] Aristotle has already spoken of this mental inherence. In his books on the soul, he says that what is experienced, insofar as it is experienced, is in the one experiencing it, that sense contains what is experienced without its matter, that what is thought is in the thinking intellect. In Philo we likewise find the doctrine of mental existence and inexistence. In confusing this, however, with existence in the strict sense, he arrives at his doctrine of the Logos and Ideas, with its wealth of contradictions. The like holds true of the Neo-Platonists. Augustine touches on the same fact in his theory of the *Verbum mentis* and its internal origin. Anselm does so in his well-known ontological argument: and many have alleged the basis of his fallacy to be the fact that he regarded mental existence as if it were actual existence (see Ueberweg, *History of Philosophy*, Vol. II). Thomas Aquinas teaches that what is thought is intentionally in the one thinking, the object of love in the person loving, what is desired in the person desiring, and uses this for theological purposes. When the scripture speaks of an indwelling of the Holy Ghost, he explains this as an intentional indwelling by way of love. And he also seeks to find in intentional inexistence, in the cases of thinking and loving, a certain analogy for the mystery of the Trinity and the procession of the Word and Spirit.

[16] *Lect. on Metaph.*, I, 432.

object; Hamilton, in denying both with regard to feeling, most definitely denies any intentional inexistence to it.

However, what Hamilton says is surely not entirely correct. Certain feelings are unmistakably referred to objects, and language itself indicates these through the expressions it uses. We say that a person rejoices in or about something, that a person sorrows or grieves about something. And once again: that delights me, that pains me, that hurts me, and so on. Joy and sorrow, like affirmation and denial, love and hate, desire and aversion, distinctly ensue upon a presentation and are referred to what is presented in it.

At the utmost, one could be inclined to agree with Hamilton in *those* cases in which one succumbs most easily, as we saw before, to the illusion that feeling is not based on any presentation: the case of the pain which is aroused by a cut or burn, for example. But its basis is none other than the very temptation toward this hypothesis, which, as we saw, is erroneous. Moreover, even Hamilton recognizes with us the fact that, without exception, presentations form the basis of feelings, and consequently [do so] in these cases as well. Therefore, his denial that feelings have an object seems so much the more striking.

To be sure, one thing is to be granted. The object to which a feeling refers is not always an external object. Even when I hear a harmonious chord, the pleasure which I feel is not really a pleasure in the sound, but a pleasure in the hearing [of it]. Indeed, one might not be mistaken in saying that it even refers to itself in a certain way and, therefore, that what Hamilton asserts, namely, that the feeling is "fused into one" with its object, *does* occur more or less. But this is nothing which does not likewise hold true of many phenomena of presentation and knowledge, as we shall see in our study of inner consciousness. Nevertheless, in them there is still a mental inexistence, a subject-object, to speak Hamilton's language; and the same will therefore hold true of these feelings as well. Hamilton is mistaken when he says that, in them, everything is "subjectively subjective," an expression which is indeed really self-contradictory; for where we can no longer speak of an object, we can no longer speak of a subject either. Even when Hamilton spoke of a fusion-into-one of the feeling with the mental modification, he gave witness against himself if we consider the matter exactly. Every fusion is a unification of several things; and consequently the pictorial expression, which is intended to make us concretely aware of the distinctive character of feeling, still indicates a certain duality in the unity.

We may thus take it to be valid that the intentional inexistence of an object is a general distinguishing characteristic of mental phenomena, which differentiates this class of phenomena from the class of physical phenomena.

VI

It is a further general characteristic of all mental phenomena that they are perceived only in inner consciousness, while only outer perception is possible for the physical. Hamilton advances this distinguishing attribute.[17]

---

[17] *Ibid.*

One could believe that such a definition says little, since it would seem more natural to take the opposite course, defining the act by reference to its object, and so defining inner perception, in contrast to all others as perception of mental phenomena. But inner perception has still another characteristic, apart from the special nature of its object, which distinguishes it: namely, that immediate, infallible self-evidence, which pertains to it alone among all the cases in which we know objects of experience. Thus, if we say that mental phenomena are those which are grasped by means of inner perception, we have accordingly said that their perception is immediately evident.

Still more! Inner perception is not merely unique as immediately evident perception; it is really unique as perception (*Wahrnehmung*) in the strict sense of the word. We have seen that the phenomena of so-called outer perception can in no way be demonstrated to be true and real, even by means of indirect reasoning. Indeed, we have seen that anyone who placed confidence in them and took them to be what they presented themselves as being is misled by the way the phenomena hang together. Strictly speaking, so-called outer perception is thus not perception; and mental phenomena can accordingly be designated as the only ones of which perception in the strict sense of the word is possible.

Mental phenomena are also adequately characterized by means of this definition. It is not as if all mental phenomena are introspectively perceivable for everyone, and therefore that everything which a person cannot perceive he is to count among the physical phenomena. On the contrary, it is obvious, and was already expressly remarked by us earlier, that no mental phenomenon is perceived by more than a single individual: but on that occasion we also saw that every type of mental phenomenon is represented in the psychical life of every fully developed human being. For this reason, reference to the phenomena which constitute the realm of inner perception serves our purpose satisfactorily.

VII

We said that mental phenomena are the only ones of which a perception in the strict sense is possible. We could just as well say that they are the only phenomena to which actual, as well as intentional, existence pertains. Knowledge, joy, desire, exist actually; color, sound, heat, only phenomenally and intentionally.

There are philosophers who go so far as to say that it is self-evident that no actuality *could* correspond to a phenomenon such as we call a physical one. They maintain that anyone who assumes this and ascribes to physical phenomena any existence other than mental holds a view which is self-contradictory in itself. Bain, for example, says that some people have attempted to explain the phenomena of outer perception by the hypothesis of a material world, "in the first instance, detached from perception, and, afterwards, coming into perception, by operating upon the mind." "This view," he says, "involves a contradiction. The prevailing doctrine is that a tree is something in itself apart from all perception; that, by its luminous emanations, it impresses our mind and is then perceived; the perception being an effect, and the unperceived tree [i.e. the one which exists outside of perception] the cause. But the tree is known only through perception; what it may be anterior to, or independent of, perception, we cannot tell; we can think of it as perceived but not as unperceived. There is a manifest contradiction in the supposition; we are required at the same moment to perceive the thing and not to perceive it. We know the touch of iron, but we cannot know the touch apart from the touch."[18]

I must confess that I am not in a position to be convinced of the correctness of this argument. As certain as it is that a color only appears to us when it is an object of our presentation [*wenn wir sie vorstellen*], it is nevertheless not to be inferred from this that a color could not exist without being presented. Only if being presented were included as one factor in the color, just as a certain quality and intensity is included in it, would a color which is not presented signify a contradiction, since a whole without one of its parts is truly a contradiction. This, however, is obviously not the case. Otherwise it would be strictly inconceivable how the belief in the actual existence of the physical phenomenon outside of our presentation of it could have, not to say originated, but achieved the most general dissemination, been maintained with the utmost tenacity, and, indeed, even long been shared by thinkers of the first rank. If what Bain says were correct: "We can think of [a tree] as perceived, but not as unperceived. There is manifest contradiction in the supposition," then his further conclusion would surely no longer be subject to objection. But it is precisely this which is not to be granted. Bain explains his dictum by saying: "We are required at the same moment to perceive the thing and not to perceive it." But it is not true that this is required: For, in the first place, not every case of thinking is a perception; and further, even if this were the case, it would only follow that a person could only think of trees perceived by him, but not that he could only think of trees *as perceived by him*. To taste a white piece of sugar does not mean to taste a piece of sugar as *white*. The fallacy reveals itself quite distinctly when it is applied to mental phenomena. If one should say: "I cannot think of a mental phenomenon without thinking of it; and so I can only think of mental phenomena as thought by me; hence no mental phenomena exist outside of my thinking," this mode of inference would be exactly like the one Bain uses. Nonetheless, Bain himself will not deny that his individual mental life is not the only thing to which actual existence belongs. When Bain adds, "We know the touch of iron, but it is not possible that we should know the touch apart from the touch," he uses the word "touch," in the first place, obviously, in the sense of what is felt, and then in the sense of the feeling of it. These are different concepts even if they have the same name. Accordingly, only someone who permits himself to be deceived by the equivocation could make the concession of immediate evidence required by Bain.

It is not true, then, that the hypothesis that a physical phenomenon like those which exist intentionally in us exists outside of the mind in actuality includes a contradiction. It is only that, when we compare one with the other, conflicts are revealed, which show clearly that there is no actual existence cor-

---

[18] *Mental Science*, 3d ed., p. 198.

responding to the intentional existence in this case. And even though this holds true in the first instance only as far as our experience extends, we will, nevertheless, make no mistake if we quite generally deny to physical phenomena any existence other than intentional existence.

VIII

Still another circumstance has been taken as a distinguishing characteristic for physical and mental phenomena. It has been said that mental phenomena occur only one after the other, while many physical phenomena, on the other hand, occur at the same time. This has not always been asserted in one and the same sense; and not every sense which has been attached to the contention appears to be in accord with the truth.

H. Spencer expressed his opinion on this subject recently: "The two great classes of vital actions called Physiology and Psychology are broadly distinguished in this, that while the one includes both simultaneous and successive changes the other includes successive changes only. The phenomena forming the subject-matter of Physiology present themselves as an immense number of different series bound up together. Those forming the subject-matter of Psychology present themselves as but a single series. A glance at the many continuous actions constituting the life of the body at large, shows that they are synchronous—that digestion, circulation, respiration, excretion, secretion, etc., in all their many sub-divisions, are going on at one time in mutual dependence. And the briefest introspection makes it clear that the actions constituting thought occur, not together, but one after another."[19] Thus, in making his comparison, Spencer has particularly in view the physiological and physical phenomena within one and the same organism to which a consciousness is attached. If he had not done this, he would have had to grant that several series of mental phenomena can also run concurrently, since there is, surely, more than one living thing in the world endowed with consciousness. But even within the limits he gives, the contention he advances is still not entirely true. And Spencer himself is so far from failing to recognize this fact that he immediately calls attention to those kinds of lower animals, e.g., the *Radiata,* in which a manifold psychological life spins itself out within *one* body. Here, he says—something which others, however, will not readily admit—that there is little difference between mental and physical existence. And he makes still further concessions, according to which the alleged difference between physiological and mental phenomena is weakened to a matter of a mere more or less. Still more! If we ask ourselves what Spencer understands by physiological phenomena, alterations in which are supposed to occur simultaneously, in contrast to mental phenomena, it appears that he does not really mean physical phenomena by this term, but their causes, which are in themselves unknown; for with respect to the physical phenomena which present themselves in sensation,

---

[19] *Principles of Psychol.,* 2d ed., Vol. I, § 177, p. 395.

it may be undeniable that they could not vary simultaneously unless the sensations also admitted of simultaneous variations. Hence we could not arrive at a distinguishing characteristic for the two classes in this way.

Others have chosen to see a peculiarity of mental life in the fact that only *one* object can ever be grasped in consciousness, and never several at the same time. They point to the noteworthy case of error in time-determination which regularly occurs in astronomical observations, in that the simultaneous swing of the pendulum does not enter into consciousness simultaneously with, but earlier or later than, the moment when the observed star touches the hairline in the telescope.[20] Thus, mental phenomena always merely follow one another in a simple series. But certainly a person would be mistaken to generalize on the basis of what such a case (involving the utmost concentration of attention) shows, without any further evidence. Spencer, at least, says: "I find that there may sometimes be detected as many as five simultaneous series of nervous changes, which in various degrees rise into consciousness so far that we cannot call any of them absolutely unconscious. When walking, there is the locomotive series; there may be, under certain circumstances, a tactual series; there is very often (in myself at least) an auditory series, constituting some melody or fragment of a melody which haunts me; and there is the visual series: all of which, subordinate to the dominant consciousness formed by some train of reflection, are continually crossing it and weaving themselves into it."[21] Hamilton, [J. J.—Ed.] Cardaillac, and other psychologists make similar reports on the basis of their experiences. But if it were assumed to be correct that all cases of perception are like the astronomer's, would we not always have to grant at least that we often have a presentation of something and simultaneously make a judgment about it or desire it? So there would still be several simultaneous mental phenomena. Indeed, one could more correctly advance the opposite contention, that, often enough, several mental phenomena are present but never more than one physical phenomenon.

What is the only sense, then, in which we might say that invariably only one mental phenomenon is apparent but, on the other hand, that many physical phenomena appear simultaneously? We can say this insofar as the entire multiplicity of mental phenomena which appear to someone in inner perception always manifests itself to him as a unity, while this does not hold true of the physical phenomena which he simultaneously grasps by means of so-called outer perception. As is commonly the case elsewhere, many persons have confused unity with simplicity here and therefore maintain that they perceive themselves in inner consciousness as something simple. Others, in contradicting the simplicity of the phenomenon, at the same time denied its unity. But just as the former group could not maintain a consistent position, since, as soon as they described what was within them, a great number of different factors came

---

[20] Cf. [F. F. W.—Ed.] Bessel, *Astron. Beobachtungen* (Konigsberg, 1823). Intro., Part VIII; Struve, [W.—Ed.] *Expédition Chronometrique*, etc. (Petersburg, 1844), p. 29.

[21] *Ibid.*, p. 398. Likewise, Drobisch says, it is "a fact, that several series of presentations can go through the mind simultaneously, but at different levels, as it were" (*Empir. Psych.*, p. 140).

to be mentioned, so the latter could also not prevent themselves from testifying involuntarily to the unity of the mental phenomenon. They speak, as do others, of an "I" and not a "we," and sometimes call this entity a "bundle" of perceptions, sometimes by other names which describe a state of hanging-together in an internal unity. When we perceive simultaneously color, sound, heat, smell, nothing hinders us from ascribing each to a particular thing. On the other hand, we are obliged to take the diverse set of corresponding acts of sensation, seeing, hearing, sensing heat, and smelling, and with them the willing and feeling and considering going on at the same time, and the inner perception by which we are aware of all of them as well, to be partial phenomena of a unified phenomenon which includes them, and to take them to be a single, unified thing. We shall thoroughly discuss the reason we are obliged to do so somewhat later and shall present in greater detail and more fully at that time more that is pertinent to the question. For what we touched on here is nothing other than the so-called unity of consciousness, a fact of psychology which is one of the richest in its consequences and which is, nevertheless, still disputed.

IX

In conclusion, let us summarize the results of our comments on the distinction between physical and mental phenomena. First of all, we made ourselves concretely aware of the distinctive nature of the two classes by means of *examples*. We then defined mental phenomena as *presentations* and such phenomena which are *based upon presentations;* all the rest belong to the physical. We next spoke of the attribute of *extension*, which was taken by psychologists to be a distinctive characteristic of all physical phenomena; all mental phenomena were supposed to lack it. The contention had not remained uncontested, however, and only later investigations could decide the issue; that in fact mental phenomena do invariably appear unextended was all that could be confirmed now. We next found *intentional inexistence*, the reference to something as an object, to be a distinguishing feature of all mental phenomena; no physical phenomenon manifests anything similar. We further defined mental phenomena as the exclusive *object of inner perception;* they alone are therefore perceived with immediate evidence; indeed, they alone are perceived in the strict sense of the word. And with this there was bound up the further definition, that they alone are phenomena which possess *actual* existence besides their intentional existence. Finally, we advanced it as a distinguishing [feature] that the mental phenomena which someone perceives *always* appear *as a unity* despite their variety, while the physical phenomena which he may perceive simultaneously are not all presented in the same way as partial phenomena within a single phenomenon.

There can be no doubt but that the characteristic which is more distinctive of mental phenomena than any of the others is intentional inexistence. We may now regard them as distinctly defined, over against the physical phenomena, by this, as well as by the other properties which were introduced.

The definitions of mental and physical phenomena which have been given cannot fail to throw a brighter light on our earlier definitions of mental science and physical science (*psychischer und Naturwissenschaft*): indeed, we said of the latter that it is the science of physical phenomena and of the former that it is the science of mental phenomena. It is now easy to see that both definitions implicitly include certain limitations.

This holds true principally of the definition of physical science. For it is not concerned with all physical phenomena; not with those of imagination, but only with those which appear in sensation. And it determines laws for these only insofar as they depend upon physical stimulation of the sense organs. We could express the scientific task of physical science precisely by saying that physical science is the science which attempts to explain the succession of physical phenomena which are normal and pure (not influenced by any particular psychological states and events) on the basis of the hypothesis [that they are the effect] of the stimulation of our sense organs by a world which is quasi-spatially (*raumähnlich*) extended in three dimensions and which proceeds quasi-temporally (*zeitähnlich*) in *one* direction.[22] Without giving any particulars concerning the absolute nature of this world, [physical science] is satisfied to ascribe to it powers which evoke the sensations and mutually influence each other in their working, and to determine the laws of coexistence and succession for these powers. In those laws, it then indirectly gives the laws governing the succession of the physical phenomena of sensation when, by means of scientific abstraction from concomitant psychological conditions, these are regarded as pure and as occurring in relation to a constant sensory capacity. Hence, "science of physical phenomena" must be interpreted in this somewhat complicated way, if it is made synonymous with physical science.[23]

We have seen, along the way, how the expression "physical phenomenon" is sometimes misused by being applied to the above-mentioned powers themselves. And, since the object of a science is naturally designated as the one for which it determines laws directly and explicitly, I believe I make no mistake in also assuming with respect to the definition of physical science as the science of physical phenomena that there is ordinarily bound up with this term the concept of powers belonging to a world which is quasi-spatially extended and which proceeds quasi-temporally, powers which evoke sensations by their effect on the sense organs and which reciprocally influence one another, and for which physical science investigates the laws of coexistence and succession. If one regards these powers as the object [of physical science], this also has the convenient feature that something which truly and actually exists appears as object

---

[22] On this point see Ueberweg (*System der Logik*), in whose analysis, to be sure, not everything is deserving of approval. He is mistaken particularly when he considers the external causes to be spatial instead of quasi-spatial, temporal instead of quasi-temporal.

[23] The interpretation would not be quite as Kant would have it: nevertheless, it approximates his interpretations as far as is feasible. In a certain sense, it comes closer to the viewpoint of Mill in his book against Hamilton (chap. xi), but still without agreeing with him in all the essential respects. What Mill calls permanent possibilities of sensations has a close relationship with what we call powers. The relationhip to, as well as the most important departure from, Ueberweg's view was already touched upon in the preceding note.

of the science. This last would be just as attainable if we defined physical science as the science of sensations, implicitly adding the same limitation of which we just spoke. What made the expression "physical phenomenon" seem preferable was, probably, primarily the fact that the external causes of sensation were thought of as corresponding to the physical phenomena appearing in it, (whether this be in every respect, as was originally the case, or whether it be, as now, in respect at least to extension in three dimensions). From this, there also arose the otherwise inappropriate term, "outer perception." It is pertinent, however, that the act of sensation manifests, along with the intentional in-existence of the physical phenomenon, still other properties with which the physical scientist (*Naturforscher*) is not at all concerned, since sensation does not give through them similar information about the distinctive relationships of the external world.

With respect to the definition of psychology, it may be apparent in the first place that the concept of mental phenomena is to be broadened rather than narrowed. For the physical phenomena of imagination, at least, fall completely within its scope just as much as do mental phenomena, in the sense defined earlier; and those which appear in sensation can also not remain unconsidered in the theory of sensation. But it is obvious that they come into consideration only as the content of mental phenomena, when the characteristics of those phenomena are being described. And the same holds true of all mental phenomena which possess exclusively phenomenal existence. It is only mental phenomena in the sense of actual states which we shall have to regard as the true object of psychology. And it is exclusively with reference to them that we say psychology is the science of mental phenomena.

11

Norman Malcolm
Knowledge of Other Minds

*Norman Malcolm is Susan Linn Sage Professor of Philosophy at Cornell University.
He is the author of a number of books, including* Ludwig Wittgenstein: A Memoir
(1958), Knowledge and Certainty *(1963), and* Dreaming *(1959). But he is best
known as an interpreter of Wittgenstein's philosophy, particularly of that period
represented by Wittgenstein's* Philosophical Investigations. *A number of
Malcolm's papers—on certainty, on the interpretation of first-person reports of
pain and the like, on dreaming, on memory, on Anselm's ontological argument—
have provoked a great deal of interest and controversy. His work exhibits the
influence of the Wittgenstein of the* Investigations *along with G. E. Moore's
emphasis on commonsense certainty. In this regard, Malcolm seems to have had in
mind Wittgenstein's notion of a "form of life" in which certain truths could not
be doubted without calling into question the entire human mode of existing.
His interpretation of Wittgenstein has been controversial, but relatively authoritative.
In fact, many who have addressed themselves to such Wittgensteinian issues as
criteria and private languages have preferred Malcolm's lucid version. Recently,
Malcolm published several new collections of his papers.*

I

I believe that the argument from analogy for the existence of other minds still
enjoys more credit than it deserves, and my first aim will be to show that it leads
nowhere. J. S. Mill is one of many who have accepted the argument and I take
his statement of it as representative. He puts to himself the question, "By what
evidence do I know, or by what considerations am I led to believe, that there
exist other sentient creatures; that the walking and speaking figures which I see
and hear, have sensations and thoughts, or in other words, possess Minds?" His
answer is the following:

> I conclude that other human beings have feelings like me, because, first, they
> have bodies like me, which I know, in my own case, to be the antecedent con-
> dition of feelings; and because, secondly, they exhibit the acts, and other out-
> ward signs, which in my own case I know by experience to be caused by feelings.
> I am conscious in myself of a series of facts connected by an uniform sequence,
> of which the beginning is modifications of my body, the middle is feelings, the
> end is outward demeanor. In the case of other human beings I have the evidence
> of my senses for the first and last links of the series, but not for the intermediate
> link. I find, however, that the sequence between the first and last is as regular and

Norman Malcolm, "Knowledge of Other Minds," *Journal of Philosophy,* LV, 23 (Nov. 6,
1958), 969–978. Reprinted by permission of the publisher and the author.

constant in those other cases as it is in mine. In my own case I know that the first link produces the last through the intermediate link, and could not produce it without. Experience, therefore, obliges me to conclude that there must be an intermediate link; which must either be the same in others as in myself, or a different one: I must either believe them to be alive, or to be automatons: and by believing them to be alive, that is, by supposing the link to be of the same nature as in the case of which I have experience, and which is in all other respects similar, I bring other human beings, as phenomena, under the same generalizations which I know by experience to be the true theory of my own existence.[1]

I shall pass by the possible objection that this would be very *weak* inductive reasoning, based as it is on the observation of a single instance. More interesting is the following point: Suppose this reasoning could yield a conclusion of the sort "It is probable that that human figure" (pointing at some person other than oneself) "has thoughts and feelings." Then there is a question as to whether this conclusion can *mean* anything to the philosopher who draws it, because there is a question as to whether the sentence "That human figure has thoughts and feelings" can mean anything to him. Why should this be a question? Because the assumption from which Mill starts is that he has *no criterion* for determining whether another "walking and speaking figure" does or does not have thoughts and feelings. If he had a criterion he could apply it, establishing with certainty that this or that human figure does or does not have feelings (for the only plausible criterion would lie in behavior and circumstances that are open to view), and there would be no call to resort to tenuous analogical reasoning that yields at best a probability. If Mill has no criterion for the existence of feelings other than his own then in that sense he does not understand the sentence "That human figure has feelings" and therefore does not understand the sentence "It is *probable* that that human figure has feelings."

There is a familar inclination to make the following reply: "Although I have no criterion of verification still I *understand*, for example, the sentence 'He has a pain.' For I understand the meaning of 'I have a pain,' and 'He has a pain' means that he has the *same* thing I have when I have a pain." But this is a fruitless maneuver. If I do not know how to establish that someone has a pain then I do not know how to establish that he has the *same* as I have when I have a pain.[2] You cannot improve my understanding of "He has a pain" by this recourse to the notion of "the same," unless you give me a criterion for saying that someone *has* the same as I have. If you can do this you will have no use for the argument from analogy: and if you cannot then you do not understand the supposed conclusion of that argument. A philosopher who purports to rely on the analogical argument cannot, I think, escape this dilemma.

There have been various attempts to repair the argument from analogy.

---

[1] J. S. Mill, *An Examination of Sir William Hamilton's Philosophy*, 6th ed. (New York: Longmans, Green & Co., Inc., 1889), pp. 243–244.

[2] "It is no explanation to say: the supposition that he has a pain is simply the supposition that he has the same as I. For *that* part of the grammar is quite clear to me: that is, that one will say that the stove has the same experience as I, *if* one says: it is in pain and I am in pain" (Ludwig Wittgenstein, *Philosophical Investigations* [New York: The Macmillan Company, 1953], sec. 350).

Mr. Stuart Hampshire has argued[3] that its validity as a method of inference can be established in the following way: Others sometimes infer that I am feeling giddy from my behavior. Now I have direct, non-inferential knowledge, says Hampshire, of my own feelings. So I can check inferences made about me against the facts, checking thereby the accuracy of the "methods" of inference.

> All that is required for testing the validity of any method of factual inference is that each one of us should sometimes be in a position to confront the conclusions of the doubtful method of inference with what is known by him to be true independently of the method of inference in question. Each one of us is certainly in this position in respect of our common methods of inference about the feelings of persons other than ourselves, in virtue of the fact that each one of us is constantly able to compare the results of this type of inference with what he knows to be true directly and non-inferentially; each one of us is in the position to make this testing comparison, whenever he is the designated subject of a statement about feelings and sensations. I, Hampshire, know by what sort of signs I may be misled in inferring Jones's and Smith's feelings, because I have implicitly noticed (though probably not formulated) where Jones, Smith and others generally go wrong in inferring my feelings (op. cit., pp. 4–5).

Presumably I can also note when the inferences of others about my feelings do not go wrong. Having ascertained the reliability of some inference-procedures I can use them myself, in a guarded way, to draw conclusions about the feelings of others, with a modest but justified confidence in the truth of those conclusions.

My first comment is that Hampshire has apparently forgotten the purpose of the argument from analogy, which is to provide some probability that "the walking and speaking figures which I see and hear, have sensations and thoughts" (Mill). For the reasoning that he describes involves the assumption that other human figures *do* have thoughts and sensations: for they are assumed to *make inferences* about me from *observations* of my behavior. But the philosophical problem of the existence of other minds *is* the problem of whether human figures other than oneself do, among other things, make observations, inferences, and assertions. Hampshire's supposed defense of the argument from analogy is an *ignoratio elenchi* [failure to appreciate what needs to be proved—Ed.].

If we struck from the reasoning described by Hampshire all assumption of thoughts and sensations in others we should be left with something roughly like this: "When my behavior is such and such there come from nearby human figures the sounds 'He feels giddy.' And generally I do feel giddy at the time. Therefore when another human figure exhibits the same behavior and I say 'He feels giddy,' it is probable that he does feel giddy." But the reference here to the sentence-like sounds coming from other human bodies is irrelevant, since I must not assume that those sounds express inferences. Thus the reasoning becomes simply the classical argument from analogy: "When my behavior is such and such I feel giddy; so probably when another human figure behaves the same way he feels the same way." This argument, again, is caught in the dilemma about the criterion of the *same*.

---

[3] "The Analogy of Feeling," *Mind*, January 1952, pp. 1–12.

The version of analogical reasoning offered by Profesor H. H. Price[4] is more interesting. He suggests that "one's evidence for the existence of other minds is derived primarily from the understanding of language" (p. 429). His idea is that if another body gives forth noises one understands, like "There's the bus," and if these noises give one new information, this "provides some evidence that the foreign body which uttered the noises is animated by a mind like one's own. . . . Suppose I am often in its neighborhood, and it repeatedly produces utterances which I can understand, and which I then proceed to verify for myself. And suppose that this happens in many different kinds of situations. I think that my evidence for believing that this body is animated by a mind like my own would then become very strong" (p. 430). The body from which these informative sounds proceed need not be a human body. "If the rustling of the leaves of an oak formed intelligible words conveying new information to me, and if gorse-bushes made intelligible gestures, I should have evidence that the oak or the gorse-bush was animated by an intelligence like my own" (p. 436). Even if the intelligible and informative sounds did not proceed from a body they would provide evidence for the existence of a (disembodied) mind (p. 435).

Although differing sharply from the classical analogical argument, the reasoning presented by Price is still analogical in form: I know by introspection that when certain combinations of sounds come from me they are "symbols in acts of spontaneous thinking"; therefore similar combinations of sounds, not produced by me, "probably function as instruments to an act of spontaneous thinking, which in this case is not my own" (p. 446). Price says that the reasoning also provides an *explanation* of the otherwise mysterious occurrence of sounds which I understand but did not produce. He anticipates the objection that the hypothesis is nonsensical because unverifiable. "The hypothesis is a perfectly conceivable one," he says, "in the sense that I know very well what the world would have to be like if the hypothesis were true—what sorts of entities there must be in it, and what sorts of events must occur in them. I know from introspection what acts of thinking and perceiving are, and I know what it is for such acts to be combined into the unity of a single mind . . ." (pp. 446–447).

I wish to argue against Price that no amount of intelligible sounds coming from an oak tree or a kitchen table could create any probability that it has sensations and thoughts. The question to be asked is: What would show that a tree or table *understands* the sounds that come from it? We can imagine that useful warnings, true descriptions and predictions, even "replies" to questions, should emanate from a tree, so that it came to be of enormous value to its owner. How should we establish that it understood those sentences? Should we "question" it? Suppose that the tree "said" that there was a vixen in the neighborhood, and we "asked" it "What is a vixen?," and it "replied," "A vixen is a female fox." It might go on to do as well for "female" and "fox." This performance might incline us to say that the tree understood the words, in contrast to the possible case in which it answered "I don't know" or did not

---

[4] "Our Evidence for the Existence of Other Minds," *Philosophy*, XIII (1938), 425–456.

answer at all. But would it show that the tree understood the words in the same sense that a person could understand them? With a person such a performance would create a presumption that he could make correct *applications* of the word in question; but not so with a tree. To see this point think of the normal teaching of words (e.g., "spoon," "dog," "red") to a child and how one decides whether he understands them. At a primitive stage of teaching one does not require or expect definitions, but rather that the child should *pick out* reds from blues, dogs from cats, spoons from forks. This involves his looking, pointing, reaching for and going to the right things and not the wrong ones. That a child says "red" when a red thing and "blue" when a blue thing is put before him is indicative of a mastery of those words *only* in conjunction with the other activities of looking, pointing, trying to get, fetching, and carrying. Try to suppose that he says the right words but looks at and reaches for the wrong things. Should we be tempted to say that he has mastered the use of those words? No, indeed. The disparity between words and behavior would make us say that he does not understand the words. In the case of a tree there could be no disparity between its words and its "behavior" because it is logically incapable of behavior of the relevant kind.

Since it has nothing like the human face and body it makes no sense to say of a tree, or an electronic computer, that it is looking or pointing at or fetching something. (Of course one can always *invent* a sense for these expressions.) Therefore it would make no sense to say that it did or did not understand the above words. Trees and computers cannot either pass or fail the tests that a child is put through. They cannot take them. That an object was a source of intelligible sounds or other signs (no matter how sequential) would not be enough by itself to establish that it had thoughts or sensations. How informative sentences and valuable predictions could emanate from a gorse-bush might be a grave scientific problem, but the explanation could never be that the gorse-bush has a mind. Better no explanation than nonsense!

It might be thought that the above difficulty holds only for words whose meaning has a "perceptual content" and that if we imagined, for example, that our gorse-bush produced nothing but pure mathematical propositions we should be justified in attributing thought to it, although not sensation. But suppose there was a remarkable "calculating boy" who could give right answers to arithmetical problems but could not apply numerals to reality in empirical propositions, e.g., he could not *count* any objects. I believe that everyone would be reluctant to say that he *understood* the mathematical signs and truths that he produced. If he could count in the normal way there would not be this reluctance. And "counting in the normal way" involves looking, pointing, reaching, fetching, and so on. That is, it requires the human face and body, and human behavior—or something similar. Things which do not have the human form, or anything like it, not merely do not but *cannot* satisfy the criteria for thinking. I am trying to bring out part of what Wittgenstein meant when he said, "We only say of a human being and what is like one that it thinks" (*Investigations*, sec. 360), and "The human body is the best picture of the human soul" (*ibid.*, p. 178).

I have not yet gone into the most fundamental error of the argument from analogy. It is present whether the argument is the classical one (the analogy between my body and other bodies) or Price's version (the analogy between my language and the noises and signs produced by other things). It is the mistaken assumption that *one learns from one's own case* what thinking, feeling, sensation are. Price gives expression to this assumption when he says: "I know from introspection what acts of thinking and perceiving are . . ." (*op. cit.*, p. 447). It is the most natural assumption for a philosopher to make and indeed seems at first to be the only possibility. Yet Wittgenstein has made us see that it leads first to solipsism and then to nonsense. I shall try to state as briefly as possible how it produces those results.

A philosopher who believes that one must learn what thinking, fear, or pain is "from one's own case," does not believe that the thing to be observed is one's behavior, but rather something "inward." He considers behavior to be related to the inward states and occurrences merely as an accompaniment or possibly an effect. He cannot regard behavior as a *criterion* of psychological phenomena: for if he did he would have no use for the analogical argument (as was said before) and also the priority given to "one's own case" would be pointless. He believes that he notes something in himself that he calls "thinking" or "fear" or "pain," and then he tries to infer the presence of the *same* in others. He should then deal with the question of what his criterion of the *same* in others is. This he cannot do because it is of the essence of his viewpoint to reject circumstances and behavior as a criterion of mental phenomena in others. And what else could serve as a criterion? He ought, therefore, to draw the conclusion that the notion of thinking, fear, or pain in others is in an important sense meaningless. He has no idea of what would count for or against it.[5] "That there should be thinking or pain other than my own is unintelligible," he ought to hold. This would be a rigorous solipsism, and a correct outcome of the assumption that one can know only from one's own case what the mental phenomena are. An equivalent way of putting it would be: "When I say 'I am in pain,' by 'pain' I mean a certain inward state. When I say '*He* is in pain,' by 'pain' I mean *behavior*. I cannot attribute pain to others *in the same sense* that I attribute it to myself."

Some philosophers before Wittgenstein may have seen the solipsistic result of starting from "one's own case." But I believe he is the first to have shown how that starting point destroys itself. This may be presented as follows: One supposes that one inwardly picks out something as thinking or pain and thereafter identifies it whenever it presents itself in the soul. But the question to be pressed is, Does one make *correct* identifications? The proponent of these "private" identifications has nothing to say here. He feels sure that he identifies correctly the occurrences in his soul; but feeling sure is no guarantee of being right. Indeed he has no idea of what being *right* could mean. He does not know how to distinguish between actually making correct identifications and being under the impression that he does. (See *Investigations*, secs. 258–9.) Suppose

---

[5] One reason why philosophers have not commonly drawn this conclusion may be, as Wittgenstein acutely suggests, that they assume that they have "an infallible paradigm of identity in the identity of a thing with itself" (*Investigations*, sec. 215).

that he identified the emotion of anxiety as the sensation of pain? Neither he nor anyone else could know about this "mistake." Perhaps he makes a mistake *every* time! Perhaps all of us do! We ought to see now that we are talking nonsense. We do not know what a *mistake* would be. We have no standard, no examples, no customary practice, with which to compare our inner recognitions. The inward identification cannot hit the bull's-eye, or miss it either, because there is no bull's-eye. When we see that the ideas of correct and incorrect have no application to the supposed inner identification, the latter notion loses its appearance of sense. Its collapse brings down both solipsism and the argument from analogy.

II

The destruction of the argument from analogy also destroys the *problem* for which it was supposed to provide a solution. A philosopher feels himself in a difficulty about other minds because he assumes that first of all he is acquainted with mental phenomena "from his own case." What troubles him is how to make the transition from his own case to the case of others. When his thinking is freed of the illusion of the priority of his own case, then he is able to look at the familiar facts and to acknowledge that the circumstances, behavior, and utterances of others actually are his *criteria* (not merely his evidence) for the existence of their mental states. Previously this had seemed impossible.

But now he is in danger of flying to the opposite extreme of behaviorism, which errs by believing that through observation of one's own circumstances, behavior, and utterances one can find out that one is thinking or angry. The philosophy of "from one's own case" and behaviorism, though in a sense opposites, make the common assumption that the first-person, present-tense psychological statements are verified by self-observation. According to the "one's own case" philosophy the self-observation cannot be checked by others; according to behaviorism the self-observation would be by means of outward criteria that are available to all. The first position becomes unintelligible; the second is false for at least many kinds of psychological statements. We are forced to conclude that the first-person psychological statements are not (or hardly ever) verified by self-observation. It follows that they have no verification at all; for if they had a verification it would have to be by self-observation.

But if sentences like "My head aches" or "I wonder where she is" do not express observations then what do they do? What is the relation between my declaration that my head aches and the fact that my head aches, if the former is not the report of an observation? The perplexity about the existence of *other* minds has, as the result of criticism, turned into perplexity about the meaning of one's own psychological sentences about oneself. At our starting point it was the sentence "*His* head aches" that posed a problem; but now it is the sentence "*My* head aches" that puzzles us.

One way in which this problem can be put is by the question, "How does *one know when to say* the words 'My head aches'?" The inclination to ask this question can be made acute by imagining a fantastic but not impossible case of a person who has survived to adult years without ever experiencing pain. He is given various sorts of injections to correct this condition, and on receiving one of these one day, he jumps and exclaims, "Now I feel pain!" One wants to ask, "How did he *recognize* the new sensation as a *pain?*"

Let us note that if the man gives an answer (e.g., "I knew it must be pain because of the way I jumped") then he proves by that very fact that he has not mastered the correct use of the words "I feel pain." They cannot be used to state a *conclusion*. In telling us *how* he did it he will convict himself of a misuse. Therefore the question "How did he recognize his sensation?" requests the impossible. The inclination to ask it is evidence of our inability to grasp the fact that the use of this psychological sentence has nothing to do with recognizing or identifying or observing a state of oneself.

The fact that this imagined case produces an especially strong temptation to ask the "How?" question shows that we have the idea that it must be more difficult to give the right name of one's sensation *the first time*. The implication would be that it is not so difficult *after* the first time. Why should this be? Are we thinking that then the man would have a paradigm of pain with which he could compare his sensations and so be in a position to know right off whether a certain sensation was or was not a pain? But the paradigm would be either something "outer" (behavior) or something "inner" (perhaps a memory impression of the sensation). If the former then he is misusing the first-person sentence. If the latter then the question of whether he compared *correctly* the present sensation with the inner paradigm of pain would be without sense. Thus the idea that the use of the first-person sentences can be governed by paradigms must be abandoned. It is another form of our insistent misconception of the first-person sentence as resting somehow on the identification of a psychological state.

These absurdities prove that we must conceive of the first-person psychological sentences in some entirely different light. Wittgenstein presents us with the suggestion that the first-person sentences are to be thought of as similar to the natural nonverbal, behavioral expressions of psychological states. "My leg hurts," for example, is to be assimilated to crying, limping, holding one's leg. This is a bewildering comparison and one's first thought is that two sorts of things could not be more unlike. By saying the sentence one can make a *statement*; it has a *contradictory*; it is *true* or *false*; in saying it one *lies* or *tells the truth*; and so on. None of these things, exactly, can be said of crying, limping, holding one's leg. So how can there be any resemblance? But Wittgenstein knew this when he deliberately likened such a sentence to "the primitive, the natural, expressions" of pain, and said that it is "new pain-behavior" (*ibid.*, sec. 244). This analogy has at least two important merits: first, it breaks the hold on us of the question "How does one *know when to say* 'My leg hurts'?", for in the light of the analogy this will be as nonsensical as the question "How does one know when to cry, limp, or hold one's leg?"; second, it explains how the utterance of a first-person psychological sentence by another person can have *importance* for us, although not as an identification—for in the light of the analogy it will have the same importance as the natural behavior which serves as our pre-verbal criterion of the psychological states of others.

12

James Cornman

Intentionality and Intensionality

*James Cornman, Professor of Philosophy at the University of Pennsylvania, is a
frequent contributor to a wide variety of contemporary discussions chiefly
centered on metaphysics but with substantial links to the philosophy of science, the
mind–body problem, intentionality, and the analysis of sensation and perception.
He has published three volumes* (Metaphysics, Reference, and Language, *1966;*
Materialism and Sensations, *1971; and* Perception, Common Sense and Science,
1975), which appear to constitute phases of a systematic inquiry.

    *Cornman's work is distinguished by extraordinary attention to detail in working
out alternative possibilities. In the first volume, he develops the thesis that
metaphysical problems—the mind–body problem is taken as a paradigm—are
"external to the linguistic frameworks of the terms used to formulate them, because
they concern the nature of what is referred to by some of these terms." In the
second volume, Cornman considers the mind–body problem more closely, particularly
the question of how materialism can accommodate sensations. In the final volume,
he turns to questions posed by competing theories of perception. His general
aim, involving a reconciliation of science and common sense, is influenced by the
work of Wilfrid Sellars.*

Certain philosophers have held the thesis of the unity of science.[1] As often
conceived, this thesis has two parts: the thesis of physicalism and the thesis of
extensionality. For each of these two parts there is an outstanding problem, i.e.
the problem of intentionality and the problem of intensionality respectively.
The purpose of this paper is twofold: first, to make explicit the nature of these
two problems, and second, to show to what extent they can be said to be the
same problem. Thus I am not at all interested here either to defend or attack
this thesis or either of its parts. I shall first define the two theses.

Physicalism and the Problem of Intentionality

The thesis of physicalism has had several formulations. I shall interpret physicalism to be the thesis that the language of physics is adequate for a complete

James Cornman, "Intentionality and Intensionality," *The Philosophical Quarterly*, XII
(1962), 44–52. Reprinted by permission of the publisher and the author.

---

[1] Such a view in various forms has been held by men such as Neurath, Carnap, Schlick,
and Hempel. For example, see R. Carnap, *The Unity of Science*, (London: K. Paul, Trench,
Trubner & Co., 1934). See also the articles by Schlick and Hempel in Section VI of
Readings in Philosophical Analysis, (New York: Appleton-Century-Crofts, Inc., 1949), H.
Feigl and W. Sellars, editors.

description of the world. This view, then, is that the language of physics can be made the universal language of science. An obvious problem for this view is that one sub-domain of science, psychology, seems to require terms such as 'believe', 'assume', 'desire', 'hope', 'think', and 'doubt' which are quite unnecessary for physics. The problem of intentionality is the problem of showing that we do not need such "intentional" terms in order fully to describe the world.

We can define the problem of intentionality more precisely by stating what I shall call the thesis of intentionality as it is presented by R. M. Chisholm.

> Let us say (1) that we do not need to use intentional language when we describe non-psychological, or "physical", phenomena; we can express all that we know, or believe, about such phenomena in language which is not intentional. And let us say (2) that, when we wish to describe certain psychological phenomena—in particular, when we wish to describe thinking, believing, perceiving, seeing, knowing, wanting, hoping and the like—either (*a*) we must use language which is intentional or (*b*) we must use a vocabulary which we do not need to use when we describe non-psychological or "physical" phenomena.[2]

If the view that Chisholm has expressed here is correct, then the thesis of physicalism is mistaken. The problem of showing that this view is wrong is the problem of intentionality.

We must now explain what is meant by intentional language. According to Chisholm there are three individually sufficient criteria of intentionality. I shall paraphrase them in order to use terminology more appropriate than Chisholm's for comparing intentionality and intensionality. The three criteria are as follows:

1. A simple declarative sentence is intentional if it uses a substantive expression (a name or description) as the direct object of an action verb and in such a way that neither the sentence nor its contradictory implies whether or not the expression has a non-null extension, i.e. whether or not the expression truly applies to anything.[3]
2. A complex declarative sentence (a sentence containing a subordinate clause or an equivalent phrase) is intentional if neither the sentence nor its contradictory implies anything about the truth-value of the subordinate clause.
3. A declarative sentence is intentional if it contains a substantive expression which is such that its replacement in the sentence by an expression with the same extension, i.e. by an extensionally equivalent expression, results in a sentence, the truth-value of which will under certain conditions differ from that of the original sentence.[4]

---

[2] R. M. Chisholm, "Sentences about Believing", *Proceedings of the Aristotelian Society,* 56 (1955–1956), p. 129. This is also discussed in Chisholm's book, *Perceiving,* (Ithaca: Cornell University Press, 1957), pp. 168–173.

[3] I have not only paraphrased this criterion but also added to it the phrase "as the direct object of an action verb" which makes explicit what seems to be the point of such criteria, that is, that these are criteria of intentional activity. Thus, we are interested only in verbs expressing this kind of activity, and consequently only in those substantive expressions which occur as direct (grammatical) objects of these "intentional" verbs.

[4] For the way Chisholm expresses these three criteria, see "Sentences about Believing", pp. 126–128.

Chisholm says two additional things. First, he says that a compound sentence is intentional "if and only if one or more of the component sentences of its indicative version is intentional".[5] Second, he suggests that by adopting [Gottlob—Ed.] Frege's terminology we can make the third criterion "do the work of the first two".[6] Since I have paraphrased Chisholm's criteria using a terminology similar to Frege's, this will enable us to examine Chisholm's suggestion during our discussion of the relationship between intentionality and intensionality.

At this point let me give three examples each of which proves to be intentional by at least one of the three criteria. First, the sentence "John is thinking of Pegasus" is intentional by the first criterion because neither the sentence nor its contradictory implies anything about the extension of the substantive expression 'Pegasus'. That is, neither the sentence nor its contradictory implies whether or not 'Pegasus' truly applies to anything. Second, the sentence "John believes that Pegasus once lived" is intentional by the second criterion because neither this complex sentence nor its contradictory implies anything about the truth-values of 'Pegasus once lived'. Third, the sentence "John knows that Pegasus is a fictitious creature" is intentional by the third criterion because if we replace the substantive expression 'Pegasus' by the extensionally equivalent expression 'the winged horse captured by Bellerophon', the truth-value of the resulting sentence would differ from the original if, for example, John knew that Pegasus is a creature from Greek mythology but had never heard of Bellerophon.

Extensionality and the Problem of Intensionality

Let us now turn to the thesis of extensionality. This thesis states that a universal language of science may be extensional, or, as [Rudolf—Ed.] Carnap says, "for every given [non-extensional] language S_1 an extensional language S_2 may be constructed such that S_1 may be translated into S_2".[7] By an extensional language I mean a language such that each of its sentences is extensional. And I understand an extensional sentence to be a sentence the extension of which is a function of the extensions of its designative components.[8] Let me amplify this. First, let us take as the extension of a declarative sentence its truth-value. Thus the truth-value of a sentence is a function of the extensions of its components. Second, because the truth-value of such a sentence is a function of only the

---

[5] *Ibid.*, p. 129.

[6] *Ibid.*, p. 128.

[7] R. Carnap, *The Logical Syntax of Language*, (New York: Harcourt, Brace, 1937), p. 320.

[8] By a designative component of a sentence I mean a component which has independent meaning at least to some degree. Such components are to be distinguished from syncategorematic components. (See R. Carnap, *Meaning and Necessity*, (Chicago: The Univ. of Chicago Press, 1958), pp. 6–7 for this distinction.) Consequently a designative component of a sentence has an extension which, however, may be null. Hereafter in this paper when I speak of components of sentences I shall be referring to designative components.

extensions of its components, then if a sentence is extensional, the replacement of one of those components by another expression with the same extension, i.e. by an extensionally equivalent expression, will not change the truth-value of the sentence. Third, if certain of the components are sentential elements, i.e. clauses, then the truth-value of the sentence is a function of the truth-values, i.e. extensions, of the simple sentential elements which are its components.

With this characterization of extensionality in mind, let me now state two jointly sufficient necessary conditions of the extensionality of a sentence. A sentence is extensional if and only if:

1. The truth-value of a sentence which results from the replacement of any expression contained in the original sentence by an extensionally equivalent expression will not differ from that of the original under any conditions.
2. The truth-value of the sentence, if it is compound or complex, i.e. if it contains co-ordinate main clauses or at least one subordinate clause, is a function of the truth-values of the simple sentential elements which make up the compound or complex sentence.

I shall say that any sentence which fails to meet at least one of these conditions is a non-extensional or an intensional sentence. The problem of intensionality, then, arises because contrary to the thesis of extensionality, it does not seem that all intensional sentences utilized by science can be translated into extensional sentences. As an example let us examine the sentence "John believes that all humans are mortal". This sentence is not extensional because it fails to meet the first condition of extensionality. Suppose that the sentence is true and that John has a false anthropomorphic view of God. If this belief-sentence were extensional, then by replacing 'humans' with the extensionally equivalent expression 'featherless bipeds' the truth-value would not change. But under the above stated conditions it would be changed because John believes that there is a featherless biped who is immortal, i.e. God. Thus the new sentence is false and the original sentence intensional.

Another kind of intensional sentence is the kind which fails to meet the second condition. Contrary-to-fact or subjunctive conditionals are an important part of this class of sentences because of their relationship to scientific laws. For example, the sentence "If Socrates had pleaded guilty, he would not have had to drink hemlock" is a contrary-to-fact conditional, because it implies that its antecedent clause taken as a declarative sentence is false. If this conditional were extensional, and thus truth-functional, its truth-value would be a function of the truth-values of its antecedent and its consequent clauses. Thus, knowing the truth-value of these two clauses when taken as declarative sentences would be sufficient for calculating the truth-value of the conditional. However, for contrary-to-fact conditionals this is not sufficient. The two clauses are both false and, it seems, the conditional is true. Thus if the truth-value of this kind of conditional is a function of the truth-value of its two clauses, then all such conditionals should be true. But this is not the case. For example, the false conditional, "If Socrates had pleaded guilty, he would have been crowned queen of Sparta" has both clauses false. Thus such sentences are not truth-functional. Their truth-value seems to depend not merely on the truth-value of their component clauses, but also upon the "connection" among the expressions in the clauses. Contrary-to-fact conditionals, then, fail to meet the second condition of extensionality. They are intensional sentences.

Intentionality and Intensionality

What we have done so far is to characterize the thesis of the unity of science as consisting of two sub-theses, the thesis of physicalism and the thesis of extensionality. That is, the thesis of the unity of science is the claim that all expressions utilized by science can be translated into the physical language which itself can be made extensional. We have also described the two general problems for such a thesis, the problem of intentionality and the problem of intensionality. Let us now see to what extent these two problems overlap. To do so, let us examine the relationship of the three independently sufficient conditions of intentionality to the two jointly sufficient necessary conditions of extensionality. I shall begin with the third criterion of intentionality because it is the condition which Chisholm suggests can be made not only sufficient but necessary.

The third criterion of intentionality states that a sufficient condition of a sentence being intentional is that the truth-value of the sentence will change under certain conditions, when an expression in the sentence is replaced by an extensionally equivalent expression. Let us compare this with the first necessary condition of extensionality. This condition is that the truth-value of an extensional sentence will not change under any conditions when an expression in the sentence is replaced by an extensionally equivalent expression. Since this is a necessary condition of extensionality, then its denial is a sufficient condition for non-extensionality or intensionality. But this denial is the third criterion of intentionality. Thus any sentence intentional by the third criterion is also intensional because it fails to meet the first necessary condition of extensionality and any sentence which fails to meet this condition of extensionality is intensional. One consequence of this is that given a solution to the problem of intensionality, the problem of intentionality for those sentences intentional on the basis of the third criterion alone is also solved.

Another consequence is that if Chisholm's suggestion that the third criterion of intentionality can "do the work of the first two" is correct, then given the problem of intensionality there is no additional problem of intentionality. Intentional sentences would be a subclass, whether a proper subclass or not we shall have to see, of intensional sentences. This consequence, then, gives us an additional reason to examine Chisholm's suggestion. However, first let us consider the second criterion of intentionality.

The second criterion of intentionality states that a sufficient condition of a sentence being intentional is that neither the sentence nor its contradictory implies anything about the truth-value of a subordinate clause which is a component of the sentence. In other words, a sufficient condition of intentionality is that the truth-value of the sentence is completely independent of the truth-value of any subordinate clause in the sentence. This amounts to saying that a sufficient condition of intentionality is that the truth-value of the sentence is not a function of the truth-value of any subordinate clause in the sentence. If we look at the second necessary condition of extensionality and confine our attention to complex sentences, we can see that a necessary condition for the extensionality of a complex sentence is that the truth-value of the complex sentence is a function of the truth-values of the simple sentential elements of which it is composed. Thus, because a subordinate clause is a sentential element (either compound, complex, or simple), then a necessary condition of the extensionality of a complex sentence is that the truth-value of the sentence is a function of the truth-values of the subordinate clauses in it, which, if they are not simple themselves, are truth-functional with regard to the simple clauses of which they are composed.

The denial of this necessary condition of extensionality is a sufficient condition of intensionality. But this denial is that the truth-value of a complex sentence is not a function of the truth-value of the subordinate clauses in the sentence, which is the second sufficient condition of intentionality. Thus, as with the third criterion, any sentence intentional by the second criterion is also intensional because it fails to meet the second necessary condition of extensionality. Furthermore, any complex sentence which fails to meet the second necessary condition of extensionality is intentional. A consequence of this is that given a solution to the problem of intensionality the problem of intentionality for those sentences intentional on the basis of the second criterion alone is also solved.

We have so far found out that two of the three criteria of intentionality are also criteria of intensionality. Thus all sentences intentional by either the second or third criterion are also intensional. There are two questions left. First, are all sentences intentional by the first criterion also intensional? If they are, then we can conclude that all intentional sentences are intensional, and then proceed to examine Chisholm's suggestion which amounts to saying that the reason they are all intensional is that they fail to meet the first necessary condition of extensionality. Second, are all intensional sentences intentional? We have found that all simple and complex intensional sentences are. This leaves only compound sentences to be examined.

One way to approach the first question is to find out whether any sentences intentional by the first criterion are extensional. Unlike the second and third criteria there seems to be no necessary condition of extensionality comparable to this criterion. The first criterion concerns a certain kind of simple sentence which is not explicitly covered by either necessary condition of extensionality. It seems, then, that there should be an extensional sentence which is intentional by the first criterion. This is indeed the case. One example is the sentence "John is thinking of Alaska". This sentence is intentional by the first criterion because neither the sentence nor its contradictory implies whether or not the substantive expression 'Alaska' applies to anything, i.e. whether or not 'Alaska' has an extension.

However, the sentence is extensional because it is a simple sentence in which an expression may be replaced by an extensionally equivalent one under any conditions without change of truth-value. The only expression in the sentence which might seem to violate this condition is 'Alaska'. But when we say that John is thinking of Alaska we are claiming that he is thinking of a particular place and what name or description we use to express this claim is limited only by the condition that it indeed apply to the place. This is true of all expressions extensionally equivalent to 'Alaska'. Thus the sentence "John is thinking of Alaska" is true given and only given those conditions under which "John is thinking of the largest state of the United States" is true. In other words, substituting 'the largest state of the United States' for its extensionally equivalent 'Alaska' will not change the truth-value of the sentence under any conditions. The sentence will have the same truth-value as the original, for example, no matter what John is thinking about Alaska or what he thinks that the largest state is.

We have, therefore, found an example of an intentional sentence which is extensional. The class of intentional sentences and the class of intensional sentences are not co-extensive. This shows, incidentally, that Chisholm's suggestion about the applicability of the third criterion of intentionality is mistaken. If it were correct, then, as we have shown, all intentional sentences would be intensional. But we have just found an intentional sentence which is not intensional. Thus at least the first criterion of intentionality is not replaceable by the third.

Not all intentional sentences are intensional. Are all intensional sentences intentional? We have found all simple and complex intensional sentences to be intentional. However, certain intensional compound sentences do not seem to be intentional. Certain contrary-to-fact conditionals such as the example used previously are, as we have shown, intensional, but they are not all intentional. Thus the sentence "If Socrates had pleaded guilty, he would not have had to drink hemlock" is intensional because it violates the second necessary condition of extensionality. However, it is not intentional because it meets none of the three criteria of intentionality. It does not meet the third criterion because the two substantive expressions in the sentence, 'Socrates' and 'hemlock', can be replaced by extensionally equivalent expressions without change of truth-value. The second criterion does not apply because the sentence is not complex. It also fails to meet the first criterion. The only substantive expression which is the direct object of an action verb is 'hemlock', Although this sentence does not imply whether or not 'hemlock' has a non-null extension, its contradictory, i.e. "He had to drink hemlock", implies that 'hemlock' does have an extension, i.e. does apply to something.

We could, however, make the sentence intentional by changing the second criterion of intentionality so that it applies not only to subordinate clauses and thus complex sentences, but also to co-ordinate clauses and thus compound sentences. By so doing the second and third criteria of intentionality would be the contradictories of the second and first necessary conditions of extensionality. Thus, all intensional sentences would be intentional. However, there is another way to interpret the relationship among the various criteria and conditions which seems more appropriate. Intentionality, as Chisholm points out, has to do with certain activities which can take as objects things which do not exist. Thus to say that someone is performing such an activity with regard to some object, e.g. thinking of it, dreaming of it, looking for it, or hoping for it, is to imply nothing about the existence or non-existence of the object and, therefore, to imply nothing about the extension of the name or description of the object. Thus a criterion of intentionality should be one by which we can distinguish intentional from non-intentional activities, or, if it is a criterion relevant to language as those of Chisholm are, one by which we can distinguish verbs which express intentional activities and those which do not. It would seem, furthermore, that it should be a criterion which in some way considers the fact that intentional activities can take as objects things which do not exist.

This suggests two reasons why we might more profitably construe the first of Chisholm's three criteria as the one criterion of intentionality, and the other two as merely the contradictories of the two necessary conditions of extensionality, i.e. as the two sufficient conditions of intensionality. First, only the first criterion is concerned with the extensions of substantive expressions which are the direct objects of verbs expressing activities. Thus only the first criterion is directly concerned with matters related to "intentional inexistence". Second, the action verbs which are found to be intentional by the other two criteria, are, I believe, with the exception of one class of verbs also found intentional by the first criterion. Thus although the first criterion may not be sufficient to distinguish all intentional sentences, it seems to be sufficient to distinguish all intentional verbs, with the one possible exception. We must consider this apparent exception now.

There is a class of sentences which Chisholm calls "cognitive sentences", i.e. sentences using verbs such as 'know', 'perceive', and 'remember'. If we use just the first criterion, or even the second, such sentences and thereby such verbs will be excluded from the class of intentional expressions because they are intentional by the third criterion only. Let us take 'know' as an example. A simple sentence using 'know', such as "John knows the governor of Alaska", is not intentional by the first criterion because the sentence implies that the substantive expression 'the governor of Alaska' has an extension. Similarly a complex sentence such as "John knows that Alaska is the largest state" is not intentional by the second criterion because the sentence implies that the declarative sentence "Alaska is the largest state" is true. Thus if we merely use the first, or the first and second criteria, the verb 'know' would not be intentional. However, by the third criterion the sentence "John knows that Alaska is the largest state" is intentional and thereby so is 'know'. If we replace the substantive expression 'the largest state' by an extensionally equivalent expression, e.g. 'the forty-ninth state', then if John believes that Alaska is the fiftieth state the resulting sentence would be false although the original might well be true.

I have suggested that the first of Chisholm's criteria seems to be the appropriate criterion of intentionality. But, as we have just seen, cognitive sentences are not intentional by the criterion. This leads to the question of whether we should consider them intentional. There is, I believe, only one argument which would give us reason to think that we should. It goes as follows. All psychological or mental activities have the characteristic of intentionality. Cognitive verbs such as 'know', 'perceive', and 'remember' express mental activities. Therefore, such verbs are intentional. This argument can be attacked via either premiss, depending upon the interpretation given to cognitive verbs. If we assume that such verbs express mental activities, then the first premiss, i.e. all mental activities are intentional, seems to be false by the following argument. Intentional activities are those which can take as objects things which may never exist. Knowing, perceiving and remembering take as objects things which must exist at least at some time or other. Therefore, knowing, perceiving and remembering, and thus 'know', 'perceive', and 'remember', are not intentional.

The above argument is directed against the first premiss only if cognitive verbs express mental activities, i.e. if the second premiss is true. However, as certain philosophers have pointed out, there is good reason to believe that no matter what the truth-value of the first premiss, the second premiss is false. Cognitive verbs are not verbs which designate certain mental activities. In other words, there is no activity corresponding to 'know', for example, in the way the activity of desiring corresponds to the verb 'desire'. There is no unique activity (e.g. some certain infallible mental act which we can perform), such that its occurrence guarantees that we know and do not merely believe something.[9] Cognitive verbs are more like what Gilbert Ryle has called "achievement verbs"[10] because they express not that some activity has taken place but that over and above the occurrence of any activity some task, i.e. the achievement of knowledge, has been successfully completed. To know, to perceive, or to remember something are, as Ryle points out, analogous to winning rather than running a race. Winning a race, although it implies an activity such as running, is not itself an activity. It is an achievement. Furthermore, just as there is an activity essential to winning, there may be one essential to knowing (certainly believing seems to be necessary). However, just as 'win' does not express running or any other activity, neither does 'know' express any activity essential to it (e.g. 'believe' rather than 'know' express believing). Thus although cognitive verbs may imply and thus refer to certain mental activities, they do not express mental or any other kind of activity. They express achievements and achievements are not activities. Thus the second premiss in the above argument is false.

In the preceding discussion I have tried to show why cognitive verbs do not seem to be intentional and thus why there is no need for the third of Chisholm's criteria. There is, however, a reason not only against the need of using this criterion, but against considering it at all related to intentionality. This reason is, incidentally, an additional reason against considering cognitive verbs intentional, because they are intentional only by the third criterion. If the third criterion is properly a criterion of sentences expressing intentional activity, whether that kind of activity be mental or not, then certain modal sentences such as "It is necessary that Alaska is Alaska", which do not seem to

---

[9] See J. L. Austin, "Other Minds". *Proceedings of the Aristotelian Society.* Supplementary Volume XX, (1946) for a discussion of this point.

[10] See G. Ryle, *The Concept of Mind*, (London: Hutchinson, 1949), pp. 149–153.

express any activity, either mental or otherwise, would be intentional and thus express intentional activity.[11] For this reason as well as those above, I believe that the third of Chisholm's criteria should be interpreted merely as a criterion of intensionality, as should the second. Thus only the first criterion would be the criterion of intentionality. This interpretation, while maintaining the two problems distinct, as we have seen they are, not only allows us to reduce the number of criteria we must work with, but also, as I hope to have shown, pinpoints which of the criteria are relevant to the problem of intensionality and which to the problem of intentionality.

---

[11] It might be suggested that this objection could be avoided by adding to the third criterion a clause similar to the phrase which I added to the first criterion, e.g. "which is the direct object of an action verb". This would eliminate modal sentences from the class of intentional sentences. It would also, however, if the previous objections are sound, eliminate cognitive sentences because they would not contain action verbs. In such a case, I believe, the third criterion would become unnecessary because it would apply only to those action verbs found intentional by the first criterion.

Bibliography

ANDERSON, ALAN ROSS (ed.). *Minds and Machines*. Englewood Cliffs, N.J.: Prentice-Hall, 1964.*

ANSCOMBE, G. E. M. *Intentions*. Oxford: Blackwell, 1957.*

ARMSTRONG, D. M. *A Materialist Theory of the Mind*. London: Routledge & Kegan Paul, 1968.

AYER, A. J. *The Concept of a Person*. London: Macmillan, 1963. Chaps. 3–4.

————. *Philosophical Essays*. London: Macmillan, 1954. Chap. 8.†

————. *The Problem of Knowledge*. Harmondsworth: Penguin Books, 1956. Chap. 5.*

BRENTANO, FRANZ. *Psychology from an Empirical Standpoint*, ed. Oskar Kraus; English Edition, ed. Linda L. McAlister. London: Routledge & Kegan Paul, 1973.

BROAD, C.D. *The Mind and Its Place in Nature*. London: Routledge & Kegan Paul, 1925.†

CASTANEDA, H.–N. (ed.). *Intentionality, Minds, and Perception*. Detroit: Wayne State University Press, 1967.*

CHAPPELL, V. C. (ed.). *The Philosophy of Mind*. Englewood Cliffs, N.J.: Prentice-Hall, 1962.*

CORNMAN, JAMES. *Metaphysics, Reference, and Language*. New Haven: Yale University Press, 1966.

DENNETT, DANIEL. *Content and Consciousness*. London: Routledge & Kegan Paul, 1969.

FEIGENBAUM, E., and J. FELDMAN (eds.). *Computers and Thought*. New York: McGraw-Hill, 1963.

FEIGL, HERBERT. *The "Mental" and the "Physical"; The Essay and a Postscript*. Minneapolis: University of Minnesota Press, 1958, 1967.†

FEYERABEND, P. K., and G. MAXWELL (eds.). *Mind, Matter, and Method*. Minneapolis: University of Minnesota Press, 1966.

FLEW, ANTONY (ed.). *Body, Mind, and Death*. New York: Macmillan, 1964.*

FODOR, JERRY A. *Psychological Explanation*. New York: Random House, 1968.*

GEACH, PETER. *Mental Acts*. London: Routledge & Kegan Paul, 1957.

GUNDERSON, KEITH. *Mentality and Machines*. Garden City, N.Y.: Anchor Books, 1971.*

GUSTAFSON, DONALD (ed.). *Essays in Philosophical Psychology*. New York: Doubleday, 1964.*

HAMPSHIRE, STUART (ed.). *Philosophy of Mind*. New York: Harper & Row, 1966.*

HENZE, DONALD E., and JOHN TURK SAUNDERS. *The Private Language Problem*. New York: Random House, 1967.*

HOOK, SIDNEY (ed.). *Dimensions of Mind*. New York: New York University Press, 1960.†

LASLETT, P. (ed.). *The Physical Basis of Mind*. Oxford: Blackwell, 1951.

MACKAY, DONALD M. *Information, Mechanism and Meaning*. Cambridge: MIT Press, 1969.†

MALCOLM, NORMAN. *Dreaming*. London: Routledge & Kegan Paul, 1962.†

MARGOLIS, JOSEPH. *Persons and Minds*. Dordrecht: D. Reidel, 1977.†

MINSKY, MARVIN (ed.). *Semantic Information Processing*. Cambridge: MIT Press, 1968.

MUNITZ, M. K. (ed.). *Identity and Individuation*. New York: New York University Press, 1971.

O'CONNOR, JOHN (ed.). *Modern Ma-*

---

* Paperback edition.   † Also available in paperback edition.

terialism: *Readings on Mind–Body Identity.* New York: Harcourt, Brace & World, 1969.*

PENELHUM, TERENCE. *Survival and Disembodied Existence.* London: Routledge & Kegan Paul, 1970.

PERRY, JOHN (ed.). *Personal Identity.* Berkeley: University of California Press, 1975.*

PITCHER, GEORGE (ed.). *Wittgenstein. The Philosophical Investigations.* New York: Doubleday, 1966.*

PRICE, H. H. "Our Evidence for the Existence of Other Minds." *Philosophy,* XIII (1938), 425–456.

RORTY, AMELIE OKSENBERG (ed.). *The Identities of Persons.* Berkeley: University of California Press, 1976.

RYLE, GILBERT. *The Concept of Mind.* London: Hutchinson, 1949.†

SAYRE, K. *Recognition: A Study in the Philosophy of Artificial Intelligence.* Notre Dame: Notre Dame University Press, 1965.†

SHAFFER, JEROME A. "Recent Work on the Mind–Body Problem." *American Philosophical Quarterly,* II (1965), 81–104.

SHOEMAKER, SYDNEY. *Self-Knowledge and Self-Identity.* Ithaca, N.Y.: Cornell University Press, 1963.

SMART, J. J. C. *Philosophy and Scientific Realism.* London: Routledge & Kegan Paul, 1963. Chaps. 5–6.

SMYTHIES, J. R. (ed.). *Brain and Mind. Modern Concepts of the Nature of Mind.* London: Routledge & Kegan Paul, 1965.

SPICKER, STUART (ed.). *The Philosophy of the Body.* Chicago: University of Chicago Press, 1970.*

STRAWSON, P. F. *Individuals.* London: Methuen, 1959.†

VAN PEURSEN, C. A. *Body, Soul, Spirit.* London: Oxford University Press, 1966.

VESEY, G. N. A. *The Embodied Mind.* London: Allen & Unwin, 1964.

—— (ed.). *Body and Mind.* London: Allen & Unwin, 1964.

WHITE, ALAN R. *The Philosophy of Mind.* New York: Random House, 1967.*

WILLIAMS, BERNARD. *Problems of the Self.* Cambridge: Cambridge University Press, 1973.†

WISDOM, JOHN. *Other Minds.* Oxford: Blackwell, 1952.

WITTGENSTEIN, LUDWIG. *Philosophical Investigations.* G. E. M. Anscombe (trans.). New York: Macmillan, 1953.

II

KNOWLEDGE
AND
CERTAINTY

What is the nature of knowledge? This is a strategic and difficult question. First of all, human cognition is and must for us be the paradigm of what it is to search for and to have knowledge. An account of knowledge so oriented is bound to consider the relevant states of mind of human agents and what they are disposed to assert or claim.

Hence the theory of knowledge is inseparable from assumptions about the nature of persons and their mental states and about the complexities of language, particularly vis-à-vis belief (see Part I). The resulting theory would require adjustment if knowledge were to be ascribed to languageless creatures. But apart from that, the most influential contemporary analyses of knowledge tend to be restricted to the relatively formal features of what it is to know.

In our own time, one of the most strenuous disputes has concerned a refined version of an issue that Plato first broached in the *Theaetetus* (see Part III): whether the necessary and sufficient conditions of knowledge can be formulated. There are many versions of the recovered problem. But the question comes to this: In addition to the truth of what is alleged to be known, and in addition to one's belief in the things that happen to be true, what serves as a necessary condition of knowledge enabling us to distinguish between accidentally true belief and genuine knowledge?

The issue was revived by Roderick Chisholm. No sooner did Chisholm propose a solution, however, then counterinstances of an unusually stubborn sort began to proliferate. The search for these and their elimination by improvements in Chisholm's original formula (II:6) were triggered by a short paper by Edmund Gettier (II:5). In effect Gettier showed what is now called the Gettier problem. It is that there is no straightforward way to characterize the required third condition—that the knowing subject be in a position to know or be justified in his belief or the like—which would preclude even the most obvious counterinstances. Chisholm has also tried to improve the formula and has sketched the details of appraising the justification of belief (II:6). These are not, however, designed to eliminate the Gettier problem.

The effort goes on, but increasingly we face two alternatives. The first alternative is that ascriptions of knowledge may be inherently informal because only the condition of truth is beyond dispute and no necessary and sufficient conditions can or need be provided. The second alternative is that the satisfactory analysis of knowledge cannot be merely formal in the sense given, because perhaps only by turning to the foundations of knowledge and the conditions of certainty can the conditions of knowledge themselves be specified.

The first alternative suggests the relatively peripheral importance of ascriptions of knowledge *beyond* those instances in which the truth of some proposition is established. The second suggests the deeper convergence between the theory of mind and the theory of knowledge. Reference to foundations and certainty draws us on to consider whatever distinctive cognitive privilege human beings possess with respect to the contents of their own minds. Chisholm's contribution hints at the connection, at the same time that it addresses itself to the improvement of the justified-true-belief analysis of knowledge.

Historically, this is the focus of Descartes's philosophical venture (II:1), which accounts for the close connection between his theory of knowledge and certainty and his theory of the nature of the human mind. It was in fact Descartes, responding to the discoveries of early Renaissance science, who analyzed the sources of certainty that are central to his philosophy and the philosophy of those who followed. It is therefore Descartes who imposed on the philosophical community the quest for cognitive foundations. But what is distinctly premodern in Descartes, what aligns him with Plato and against Immanuel Kant (II:8), is his underlying assumption that knowledge is all of a piece, that the conditions for certain knowledge in mathematics, in empirical science, in morality, in metaphysics are the same.

Before pursuing this development, we may catch up several other strands of the theory of knowledge. The achievement of science and the ordinary or commonsense knowledge of all of us invite the question of what we have when we have knowledge and how we come to have it. The further question lurks: whether we are deluded, whether knowledge or certainty of knowledge is possible at all, and, if it is, what actually insures it. Here again, Descartes's investigations dominate; and here again, considerations of certainty and of the foundations of human knowledge suggest themselves.

One of the great troubles with characterizing the theory of knowledge is that it does not lend itself to the special ministrations of any science. First, all sciences presumably aim at knowing the truth. Second, the threat of the insecurity or impossibility of knowledge appears, if relevant, to be relevant to every science. Third, because science seems to presuppose a prior grasp of the nature of knowledge, its particular findings are marked as true and therefore as instances of true knowledge. Finally, the most secure of the conditions of knowledge—truth—cannot be investigated in any of the ways in which the truths of the empirical or formal sciences are established.

We attempt to propose a theory of truth that fits the main body of the system of true propositions. Truth must be a relationship of some sort, between language and the world, or among affirmed or affirmable propositions, or inherent in certain such propositions. Admitting the condition of truth precludes the possibility of construing knowledge as a psychological state, since whatever truth is, it is not a psychological state or a psychological feature of any state of affairs. Hence, even if the quest for certainty and cognitive foundations turns to the privilege or privileged access one has to the contents of his own mind, knowledge itself could not be a state directly open to some form of introspection.

Of course, it need not be, on the theory of self-evident truths or self-intimating states. And this is precisely the attraction of the quest for certainty and the foundations of knowledge. But if the truth of a proposition is an essential element of the "state" of knowledge, knowledge itself cannot be a psychological state of any sort. This is also why the search for the adequate criteria of knowledge is so difficult, since truth is the only condition of knowledge that makes no reference to any state of any would-be cognitive agent and the only condition that is beyond dispute.

The theory of truth is a curious concern. A grasp of the nature of truth does not directly bear on the appraisal of the truth or falsity of any proposition. Here we must distinguish between analyzing the nature of truth and providing criteria of truth. A grasp of the criteria of truth is obviously essential to ascriptions of truth and hence to ascriptions of knowledge. But it is possible to theorize about the meaning of the concept without descending to those procedural considerations with which the truth of propositions may be confirmed or contested.

The classical theories of truth are not inclined to link the two issues too closely. They attempt to be precise about the nature of truth and to suggest how the specific inquiries of the empirical and formal sciences would conform to the accounts given. But the liberty that seems to be fair here is not available in the analysis of knowledge. It makes no sense to say that we know what knowledge is, if we do not know how to decide in particular instances whether knowledge obtains. To know what knowledge is is to know how to determine that knowledge obtains; and to know how to determine that knowledge obtains is to know what knowledge is.

But the analogue respecting truth does not hold.

According to the most common view, truth is a relationship between what is affirmed in language and what is the case in the world or what the facts about the world are. This view, called the correspondence theory of truth, has been most forcefully debated in our own time by J. L. Austin (II:14) and P. F. Strawson (II:15).

This is the difficulty: It is unsatisfactory to affirm that, in truth, what is said corresponds to states of affairs in the world or facts about the world (since these must be specified linguistically). But to deny it is equally unsatisfactory (since truth would seem then not to concern the world at all). Strawson's solution draws on an earlier thesis, which suggests that the problem of truth is not separable from the problem of the analysis of informative judgments themselves.

Another much-discussed theory had been advanced by the American pragmatists. In the form in which William James advanced it (II:12), in effect, confusing C. S. Peirce's pragmatic theory of meaning (see Part IV), truth is construed as a species of goodness with respect to belief. The doctrine is seen by Bertrand Russell (II:13) as leading to intolerable paradox.

To return to knowledge and certainty, if Descartes represents the first stage in the development of modern theories of knowledge, Immanuel Kant (I:8) surely represents the second. It was Kant who broke the spell of the unity of knowledge, or the unity of the conditions on which knowledge depends. After Kant it is, for example, merely a refinement of the critical enterprise to explore the epistemic oddities of one's knowledge of one's own immediate experience (A. J. Ayer [II:3]).

Kant was prepared to admit a variety of propositions, each with its own conditions of truth. Part of the complexity of his account depends on combining the *a priori/a posteriori* distinction and the *analytic/synthetic* distinction. The first concerns different sources of knowledge, whether what is known derives from the exercise of reason without depending on sensory experience (the *a priori*) or whether it depends on sensory experience (the *a posteriori*). The second distinction concerns whether, given the meanings of the words and sentences conveying what is known, what is known is necessarily true or cannot but be true (the analytic) or whether it may be either true or false at least as far as the meanings of terms are concerned (the synthetic).

These considerations lead Kant to certain curious conclusions. First, mathematical judgments are thought to be synthetic even though they are not given *a posteriori*, and they are necessarily true even though they are not analytic. But empirical judgments, Kant holds, are all synthetic and *a posteriori* (both contingent judgments and judgments known only through sensory experience). Second, analytic judgments are all *a priori* and merely explain some identity relation involving the subject and the predicate, though not all such sentences actually appear to involve identity.

John Stuart Mill (II:9) reverses Kant's distinction, in a sense. As an empiricist he theorizes that so-called mathematical and empirical judgments rest on precisely the same conditions—for which reason even mathematical propositions are only contingently true (see also Part V). W. V. Quine (II:10) represents a newer and greater complication in a similar direction. In his view, even the demarcation between analytic and synthetic truths cannot be sharply established.

Saul Kripke (II:11) distinguishes between "a prioricity" and necessity, as between epistemological and metaphysical concepts. By this, he means to sort out a number of issues that have, through the tradition since Kant, been regularly interwoven. Kripke denies that if a proposition can be known *a priori*, it cannot be known *a posteriori*. He also denies that whatever is *a priori* is necessary and that whatever is necessary is *a priori*. Here, he goes directly contrary to Kant. Both claims depend on distinguishing what has to do with the source of our knowledge (epistemological issues) and what has to do with the nature of the real world (metaphysical issues).

In so arguing, Kripke reinstates the difference intended by the so-called analytic/synthetic distinction. As a matter of fact, he is even hospitable to the prospect of necessary *a posteriori* truths and of contingent *a priori* truths. The distinction is pursued in a fresh way to illuminate the intriguing problem of essentialism (which also bears on the analytic/synthetic distinction): whether particular things have certain properties necessarily or only contingently. It is here that Kripke's position collides with that of Quine, for Quine resists essentialism in holding that whether a property is or is not essential to a thing depends on how it is described.

Kripke's essentialism also bears directly on his theory of naming and of names as "rigid designators"; for the question arises whether for any property taken to be essential to it, a thing can or cannot be imagined to be one and the same without that property. The analytic/synthetic distinction, essentialism, and the theory of how particular things are effectively sorted and identified may therefore be seen to be systematically linked (see Part IV).

Behind these relatively formal considerations, which have more to do with the theory of truth and the analysis of propositions than with knowledge as such, there lurks the threat of skepticism. In Descartes's view, the possibility of error entails the impossibility of certain knowledge and hence the impossibility of knowledge itself.

In our own century G. E. Moore—and those, like Norman Malcolm (II:4), who combines Moore's view with Wittgenstein's—thought to combat the threat of skepticism by providing a great number of commonsense truths that Moore believed he knew with complete certainty. Moore stressed that it is not doubt (a psychological state) but doubtfulness that is essential to skepticism. But he never explained what he meant by complete certainty or even doubtfulness, and he never established that what he said we all know with certainty we actually do know thus.

The serious weakness of Moore's account, which reappears in Malcolm's, lies in the fact that he never linked his favored truths with anything that might count as the foundations of knowledge. Hence he never attempted to provide an account of a reasoned system of knowledge. The novelty and puzzle of Malcolm's view lies in this: His specimens of certain knowledge cross the division between mathematical and empirical truths and seemingly involve two distinct kinds of knowledge. Yet they fail to distinguish between the grounds of knowledge and biographical quirks (in particular, that one may refuse to identify anything as counterevidence under certain circumstances).

The commonsense tradition is forceful in the sense that to see what could be doubtful about certain propositions is difficult; but it fails to provide a reasoned basis for the certainty of any particular proposition. The main philosophical effort to establish certainty has always moved, rather, in the direction of foundationalism, the theory that knowledge is two-tiered and includes a range of truths, known in some privileged and reliable way, on which other sorts of knowledge depend.

The plausibility of Malcolm's account lies in its emphasis (drawn to some extent from Wittgenstein's views) on the impossibility of there being *any* system of knowledge or societal life in which *every* proposition is open to doubt. The thesis that the uncertainty of any particular proposition presupposes many propositions known with certainty is compatible with the thesis that particular propositions are actually open to doubt. The first thesis is the cornerstone of all so-called commonsense philosophies; the second is the thesis that foundationalism must oppose. But commonsense theories appear dubious whenever they posit specimen propositions as unquestionable, for, in ignoring foundationalist considerations, they ignore the necessary grounds for such claims.

Foundationalism need not be restricted to empirical knowledge. In fact, Quine's rejection of a demarcation between analytic and synthetic truths raises doubts about the viability of a foundationalist account, whether the foundations are taken to be empirical or analytic and self-evident. Still, the principal varieties of foundationalism have been concerned with the sources of empirical knowledge on which the great body of science depends. Predominantly, down to our own day, foundational propositions have been taken to be propositions about one's own experiences, thought to be self-justified, stronger in certainty than any other propositions, possibly even indubitable.

Sense-data theories (see Part III) represent a particularly persistent tradition of this sort, though they are opposed to commonsense philosophies. To repeat, by foundationalism one means in fact (Keither Lehrer [II:7]) that knowledge is two-tiered, that the basic foundation statements are either self-justifying or justified on the strength of other basic beliefs, that all other beliefs are justified or refuted by reference to basic beliefs. Hence, foundationalism searches for a range of experiences that may be regarded as self-intimating, as disclosing themselves in such a way that the truth about them is grasped at once when undergoing the relevant experience.

The tension between the quest for such certainty and the seeming impossibility of holding that any statements about material objects could be certain in that way is illustrated in the pragmatist account offered by C. I. Lewis (II:2). But the telltale feature of Lewis's account, which recalls the strategic importance of Ayer's distinction, is the ease with which Lewis oscillates between the *experiences* that are taken to be given and the *propositions* about such experience that are taken to insure certitude.

Against Lewis (and Moore), Lehrer eschews foundationalism altogether, admitting the inherent possibility of error in all forms of knowledge. To that extent, Lehrer credits the skeptic. Unlike Moore, however, he maintains that the skeptical position cannot be sustained unless it can be shown that if there is a chance of error in one's belief, one does not then have knowledge. But the logical possibility and even the empirical likelihood of error do not themselves entail these conclusions. In short, Lehrer embraces knowledge without certainty. Thus we are provided with a view diametrically opposed to Descartes's, which in effect generated the inquiry in the first place.

Knowledge, Certainty, and the Foundations of Knowledge

————◆————

1

René Descartes

The Sphere of the Doubtful

It is now some years since I detected how many were the false beliefs that I had from my earliest youth admitted as true, and how doubtful was everything I had since constructed on this basis; and from that time I was convinced that I must once for all seriously undertake to rid myself of all the opinions which I had formerly accepted, and commence to build anew from the foundation, if I wanted to establish any firm and permanent structure in the sciences. But as this enterprise appeared to be a very great one, I waited until I had attained an age so mature that I could not hope that at any later date I should be better fitted to execute my design. This reason caused me to delay so long that I should feel that I was doing wrong were I to occupy in deliberation the time that yet remains to me for action. To-day, then, since very opportunely for the plan I have in view I have delivered my mind from every care [and am happily agitated by no passions] and since I have procured for myself an assured leisure in a peaceable retirement, I shall at last seriously and freely address myself to the general upheaval of all my former opinions.

Now for this object it is not necessary that I should show that all of these are false—I shall perhaps never arrive at this end. But inasmuch as reason already persuades me that I ought no less carefully to withhold my assent from matters which are not entirely certain and indubitable than from those which appear to me manifestly to be false, if I am able to find in each one some reason to doubt, this will suffice to justify my rejecting the whole. And for that end it will not be requisite that I should examine each in particular, which would be an endless undertaking; for owing to the fact that the destruction of the foundations of necessity brings with it the downfall of the rest of the edifice, I shall

From "Meditations on First Philosophy," in *The Philosophical Works of Descartes*, E. S. Haldane and G. R. T. Ross, trans. (Cambridge: Cambridge University Press, 1931), Meditation I, pp. 144–149. Reprinted by permission of the publisher.

only in the first place attack those principles upon which all my former opinions rested.

All that up to the present time I have accepted as most true and certain I have learned either from the senses or through the senses; but it is sometimes proved to me that these senses are deceptive, and it is wiser not to trust entirely to anything by which we have once been deceived.

But it may be that although the senses sometimes deceive us concerning things which are hardly perceptible, or very far away, there are yet many others to be met with as to which we cannot reasonably have any doubt, although we recognise them by their means. For example, there is the fact that I am here, seated by the fire, attired in a dressing gown, having this paper in my hands and other similar matters. And how could I deny that these hands and this body are mine, were it not perhaps that I compare myself to certain persons, devoid of sense, whose cerebella are so troubled and clouded by the violent vapours of black bile, that they constantly assure us that they think they are kings when they are really quite poor, or that they are clothed in purple when they are really without covering, or who imagine that they have an earthenware head or are nothing but pumpkins or are made of glass. But they are mad, and I should not be any the less insane were I to follow examples so extravagant.

At the same time I must remember that I am a man, and that consequently I am in the habit of sleeping, and in my dreams representing to myself the same things or sometimes even less probable things, than do those who are insane in their waking moments. How often has it happened to me that in the night I dreamt that I found myself in this particular place, that I was dressed and seated near the fire, whilst in reality I was lying undressed in bed! At this moment it does indeed seem to me that it is with eyes awake that I am looking at this paper; that this head which I move is not asleep, that it is deliberately and of set purpose that I extend my hand and perceive it; what happens in sleep does not appear so clear nor so distinct as does all this. But in thinking over this I remind myself that on many occasions I have in sleep been deceived by similar illusions, and in dwelling carefully on this reflection I see so manifestly that there are no certain indications by which we may clearly distinguish wakefulness from sleep that I am lost in astonishment. And my astonishment is such that it is almost capable of persuading me that I now dream.

Now let us assume that we are asleep and that all these particulars, e.g. that we open our eyes, shake our head, extend our hands, and so on, are but false delusions; and let us reflect that possibly neither our hands nor our whole body are such as they appear to us to be. At the same time we must at least confess that the things which are represented to us in sleep are like painted representations which can only have been formed as the counterparts of something real and true, and that in this way those general things at least, i.e. eyes, a head, hands, and a whole body, are not imaginary things, but things really existent. For, as a matter of fact, painters, even when they study with the greatest skill to represent sirens and satyrs by forms the most strange and extraordinary, cannot give them natures which are entirely new, but merely make a certain medley of the members of different animals; or if their imagination is extravagant enough to invent something so novel that nothing similar has ever before been seen, and that then their work represents a thing purely fictitious and absolutely false, it is certain all the same that the colours of which this is composed are necessarily real. And for the same reason, although these general things, to wit, [a body], eyes, a head, hands, and such like, may be imaginary, we are bound at the same time to confess that there are at least some other objects yet more simple and more universal, which are real and true; and of these just in the same way as with certain real colours, all these images of things which dwell in our thoughts, whether true and real or false and fantastic, are formed.

To such a class of things pertains corporeal nature in general, and its extension, the figure of extended things, their quantity or magnitude and number, as also the place in which they are, the time which measures their duration, and so on.

That is possibly why our reasoning is not unjust when we conclude from this that Physics, Astronomy, Medicine and all other sciences which have as their end the consideration of composite things, are very dubious and uncertain; but that Arithmetic, Geometry and other sciences of that kind which only treat of things that are very simple and very general, without taking great trouble to ascertain whether they are actually existent or not, contain some measure of certainty and an element of the indubitable. For whether I am awake or asleep, two and three together always form five, and the square can never have more than four sides, and it does not seem possible that truths so clear and apparent can be suspected of any falsity [or uncertainty].

Nevertheless I have long had fixed in my mind the belief that an all-powerful God existed by whom I have been created such as I am. But how do I know that He has not brought it to pass that there is no earth, no heaven, no extended body, no magnitude, no place, and that nevertheless [I possess the perceptions of all these things and that] they seem to me to exist just exactly as I now see them? And, besides, as I sometimes imagine that others deceive themselves in the things which they think they know best, how do I know that I am not deceived every time that I add two and three, or count the sides of a square, or judge of things yet simpler, if anything simpler can be imagined? But possibly God has not desired that I should be thus deceived, for He is said to be supremely good. If, however, it is contrary to His goodness to have made me such that I constantly deceive myself, it would also appear to be contrary to His goodness to permit me to be sometimes deceived, and nevertheless I cannot doubt that He does permit this.

There may indeed be those who would prefer to deny the existence of a God so powerful, rather than believe that all other things are uncertain. But let us not oppose them for the present, and grant that all that is here said of a God is a fable; nevertheless in whatever way they suppose that I have arrived at the state of being that I have reached—whether they attribute it to fate or to accident, or make out that it is by a continual succession of antecedents, or by some other method—since to err and deceive oneself is a defect, it is clear that the greater will be the probability of my being so imperfect as to deceive myself ever, as is the Author to whom they assign my origin the less powerful. To these reasons I have certainly nothing to reply, but at the end I feel constrained to confess that there is nothing in all that I formerly believed to be true, of which I cannot in some measure doubt, and that not merely through want of thought or through levity, but for reasons which are very powerful and maturely considered; so that henceforth I ought not the less carefully to refrain from giving credence to these opinions than to that which is manifestly false, if I desire to arrive at any certainty [in the sciences].

But it is not sufficient to have made these remarks, we must also be careful to keep them in mind. For these ancient and commonly held opinions still revert frequently to my mind, long and familiar custom having given them the right to occupy my mind against my inclination and rendered them almost masters of my belief; nor will I ever lose the habit of deferring to them or of placing my confidence in them, so long as I consider them as they really are, i.e. opinions in some measure doubtful, as I have just shown, and at the same time highly probable, so that there is much more reason to believe in than to deny them. That is why I consider that I shall not be acting amiss, if, taking of set purpose a contrary belief, I allow myself to be deceived, and for a certain time pretend that all these opinions are entirely false and imaginary, until at last, having thus balanced my former prejudices with my latter [so that they cannot divert my opinions more to one side than to the other], my judgment will no longer be dominated by bad usage or turned away from the right knowledge of the truth. For I am assured that there can be neither peril nor error in this course, and that I cannot at present yield too much to distrust, since I am not considering the question of action, but only of knowledge.

I shall then suppose, not that God who is supremely good and the fountain of truth, but some evil genius not less powerful than deceitful, has employed his whole energies in deceiving me; I shall consider that the heavens, the earth, colours, figures, sound, and all other external things are nought but the illusions and dreams of which this genius has availed himself in order to lay traps for my credulity; I shall consider myself as having no hands, no eyes, no flesh, no blood, nor any senses, yet falsely believing myself to possess all these things; I shall remain obstinately attached to this idea, and if by this means it is not in my power to arrive at the knowledge of any truth, I may at least do what is in my power [i.e. suspend my judgment], and with firm purpose avoid giving credence to any false thing, or being imposed upon by this arch deceiver, however powerful and deceptive he may be. But this task is a laborious one, and insensibly a certain lassitude leads me into the course of my ordinary life. And just as a captive who in sleep enjoys an imaginary liberty, when he begins to suspect that his liberty is but a dream, fears to awaken, and conspires with these agreeable illusions that the deception may be prolonged, so insensibly of my own accord I fall back into my former opinions, and I dread awakening from this slumber, lest the laborious wakefulness which would follow the tranquillity of this repose should have to be spent not in daylight, but in the excessive darkness of the difficulties which have just been discussed.

2

C. I. Lewis

The Bases of Empirical Knowledge

C. I. Lewis was, until his retirement in 1953, Edgar Pierce Professor of Philosophy at Harvard University. He is particularly well known for his original work in the development of modal logic—the logic of possibility, necessity, and related modal notions. In epistemology he provides, in An Analysis of Knowledge and Valuation *(1946), a combination of foundationalist and pragmatic elements— elements that are naturally antithetical—since pragmatism emphasizes the continuity of cognitive and precognitive interaction of organism and environment, hence a resistence to foundationalism. Knowledge, for the pragmatist, is characterized in terms of the biological conditions for confidence in and reliance upon how the world appears to humans rather than in terms of some source of certainty identified without regard to the conditions of life.*

Lewis's pragmatic strain tends to emphasize the nonterminating nature of confirmation (precluding absolute certainty), and his foundationalist strain tends to favor the possibility of certainty and the absence of error at some point in the system of knowledge. But, rather puzzlingly, he also associates the impossibility of error with the absence of (the possibility of) knowledge; and he admits so-called terminating judgments that can be conclusively verified. He favors a distinctly pragmatist view of the testing of our conceptual schemes as well as of the validity of our value judgments.

1. If the conclusions of the preceding discussion are to be accepted, then all knowledge has an eventual empirical significance in that all which is knowable or even significantly thinkable must have reference to meanings which are sense-representable. But this conception that even what is analytically true and knowable *a priori* is to be assured by reference to sense meanings, does not, of course, abrogate the distinction between what may be known independently of given data of sense and that which cannot be so known. Analytic statements assert some relation of meanings amongst themselves: nonanalytic statements require relation of a meaning to what is found on particular occasions of experience. It is the latter class alone which may express empirical knowledge. They coincide with those the falsity of which is antecedently thinkable.

Empirical truth cannot be known except, finally, through presentations of sense. Most affirmations of empirical knowledge are to be justified, proximately, by others already accepted or believed: such justification involves a step or steps depending on logical truth. The classification as empirical will still be correct, however, if amongst such statements required to support the one in question, either deductively or inductively, there are some which cannot be assured by

From C. I. Lewis, An Analysis of Knowledge and Valuation (La Salle, Illinois: Open Court Publishing Company, 1946), Ch. 7, pp. 171–197. Reprinted by permission of the publisher.

logic or analysis of meaning but only by reference to the content of a given experience. Our empirical knowledge rises as a structure of enormous complexity, most parts of which are stabilized in measure by their mutual support, but all of which rest, at bottom, on direct findings of sense. Unless there should be some statements, or rather something apprehensible and statable, whose truth is determined by given experience and is not determinable in any other way, there would be no non-analytic affirmation whose truth could be determined at all, and no such thing as empirical knowledge. But also there could be no empirical knowledge if there were not meanings capable of being entertained without dependence on particular occasions. No experience or set of experiences will determine truth of a statement or a belief unless, prior to such experience, we know what we mean; know what experiences will corroborate our affirmation or supposition and what experiences will discredit it. Apprehension of the criteria by which what we intend may be recognized, must be antecedent to any verification or disproof.

We shall find, however, that most empirical statements—all those ordinarily made, in fact—are such that no single experience could decisively prove them true; and it can be doubted that any experience would conclusively prove them false. We *do* entertain assertable meanings of a sort which *can* be decisively determined to hold or not to hold; but statements having that kind of significance are not usually expressed, both because there is seldom occasion to express them and because there is no language in which they can be easily expressed without ambiguity. It is items which belong somewhere in the upper stories of our structure of empirical beliefs which can be clearly put: it is those which are at or near the bottom, required to support the whole edifice, which there is difficulty to state without implying what does not genuinely belong to the import of them. Thus the analysis of an ordinary empirical judgment such as might indicate the foundations of it in given experience, encounters a difficulty which is primarily one of formulation. The reason for this is something which must be understood and appreciated at the start, if we are not to fall into some kind of misconception which would be fatal for the understanding of empirical knowledge in general.

2. Let us turn to the simplest kind of empirical cognition; knowledge by direct perception. And let us take two examples.

I am descending the steps of Emerson Hall, and using my eyes to guide my feet. This is a habitual and ordinarily automatic action. But for this occasion, and in order that it may clearly constitute an instance of perceptual cognition instead of unconsidered behavior, I put enough attention on the process to bring the major features of it to clear consciousness. There is a certain visual pattern presented to me, a feeling of pressure on the soles of my feet, and certain muscle-sensations and feelings of balance and motion. And these items mentioned are fused together with others in one moving whole of presentation, within which they can be genuinely elicited but in which they do not exist as separate. Much of this presented content, I should find it difficult to put in words. I should find it difficult because, for one reason, if I tried to express it precisely in objectively intelligible fashion, I should have to specify such items as particular muscles which are involved and the behavior of them, and other things of this kind; and I do not in fact know which muscles I am using and just how. But one does not have to study physiology in order to walk down stairs. I know by my feelings when I am walking erect—or I think I do. And you, by putting yourself in my place, know how I feel—or think you do. That is all that is necessary, because we are here speaking of direct experience. You will follow me through the example by using your imagination, and understand what I mean—or what *you* would mean by the same language—in terms of your own experience.

The experience I have as I approach the steps and look down is familiar: it is qualitatively specific, and undoubtedly supplies the clues on which I act. For example, if I had approached the steps with eyes shut, I should have been obliged to behave quite differently in order to avoid falling. Let us single out the visual part of the presentation for particular consideration. Ordinarily I have no occasion to express empirical content of this sort: it performs its office of guiding my behavior and thereupon lapses from consciousness. But if I attempt to express it, I might say: "I see what looks like a flight of granite steps, fifteen inches wide and seven inches deep, in front of me." The locution 'looks like' represents my attempt to signalize the fact that I do not mean to assert that the steps *are* granite, or have the dimensions mentioned, or even that in point of absolutely certain fact there are any steps at all. Language is largely pre-empted to the assertion of objective realities and events. If I wish, as I now do, to confine it to expression of a presented content, my best recourse is, very likely, to express what I take to be the objective facts this presentation signalizes and use locutions such as 'looks like', 'tastes like', 'feels like', or some other contextual cue, to mark the intention on this occasion to restrict what I say to the fact of presentation itself as contrasted with the objective state of affairs more usually signified by the rest of my statement.

This given presentation—what looks like a flight of granite steps before me—leads to a prediction: "If I step forward and down, I shall come safely to rest on the step below." Ordinarily this prediction is unexpressed and would not even be explicitly thought. When so formulated, it is altogether too pedantic and portentous to fit the simple forward-looking quality of my conscious attitude. But unless I were prepared to assent to it, in case my attention were drawn to the matter, I should not now proceed as I do. Here again, the language I use would ordinarily be meant to express an objective process involving my body and a physical environment. But for the present occasion, I am trying to express the direct and indubitable content of my experience only, and, particularly, to elicit exemplary items which mark this conscious procedure as cognitive. As I stand momentarily poised and looking before me, the presented visual pattern leads me to predict that acting in a certain manner—stepping forward and down—will be followed by a further empirical content, equally specific and recognizable but equally difficult to express without suggesting more than I now mean—the felt experience of coming to balance on the step below.

I adopt the mode of action envisaged; and the expected empirical sequent actually follows. My prediction is verified. The cognitive significance of the visual presentation which operated as cue, is found valid. This functioning of it was a genuine case of perceptual knowledge.

Let us take another and different example; different not in any important character of the situation involved, but different in the manner in which we shall consider it.

I believe there is a piece of white paper now before me. The reason that I believe this is that I see it: a certain visual presentation is given. But my belief includes the expectation that so long as I continue to look in the same direction, this presentation, with its qualitative character essentially unchanged, will persist; that if I move my eyes right, it will be displaced to the left in the visual field; that if I close them, it will disappear; and so on. If any of these predictions should, upon trial, be disproved, I should abandon my present belief in a real piece of paper before me, in favor of belief in some extraordinary after-image or some puzzling reflection or some disconcerting hallucination.

I do look in the same direction for a time; then turn my eyes; and after that try closing them: all with the expected results. My belief is so far corroborated. And these corroborations give me even greater assurance in any further predictions based upon it. But theoretically and ideally it is not completely verified, because the belief in a real piece of white paper now before me has further implications not yet tested: that what I see could be folded without cracking, as a piece of celluloid could not; that it would tear easily, as architect's drawing-cloth would not; that this experience will not be followed by waking in quite different surroundings; and others too numerous to mention. If it is a real piece of paper before me now, then I shall expect to find it here tomorrow with the number I just put on the corner: its reality and the real character I attribute in my belief imply innumerable possible verifications, or partial verifications, tomorrow and later on.

But looking back over what I have just written, I observe that I have succumbed to precisely those difficulties of formulation which have been mentioned. I have here spoken of predictable results of further tests I am not now making; of folding the paper and trying to tear it, and so on. Finding these predictions borne out would, in each case, be only a partial test, theoretically, of my belief in a real piece of paper. But it was my intention to mention predictions which, though only partial verification of the objective fact I believe in, could themselves be decisively tested. And there I have failed. That the paper, upon trial, would really be torn, will no more be evidenced with perfect certainty than is the presence of real paper before me now. It—provided it take place—will be a real objective event about which, theoretically, my momentary experience could deceive me. What I meant to speak of was certain expected experiences—of the *appearance and feeling* of paper being folded; of its *seeming* to be torn. These predictions of *experience*, would be decisively and indubitably borne out or disproved if I make trial of them. But on this point, the reader will most likely have caught my intent and improved upon my statement as made.

· · ·

4. Let us now give attention to our two examples, and especially to the different manner in which the two have been considered. Both represent cases of knowledge by perception. And in both, while the sensory cues to this knowledge are provided by the given presentation, the cognitive significance is seen to

lie not in the mere givenness of these sensory cues but in prediction based upon them. In both cases, it is such prediction the verification of which would mark the judgment made as true or as false.

In the first case, of using my eyes to guide me down the steps, the prediction made was a single one. Or if more than one was made, the others would presumably be like the one considered and this was taken as exemplary. This judgment is of the form, "If I act in manner A, the empirical eventuation will include E." We found difficulty in expressing, in language which would not say more than was intended, the content of the presentation which functioned as sensory cue. We encountered the same difficulty in expressing the mode of action, A, as we envisaged it in terms of our own felt experience and as we should recognize it, when performed, as the act we intended. And again this difficulty attended our attempt to express that expected presentational eventuality, E, the accrual of which was anticipated in our prediction.

As we considered this first example, the attempt was to portray it as a case in which a directly apprehensible presentation of a recognizable sort functioned as cue to a single prediction; the prediction that a certain directly recognizable act would lead to a particular and directly recognizable result. If we are to describe this cognitive situation truly, all three of these elements—the presentation, the envisaged action, and the expected consequence—must be described in language which will denote immediately presented or directly presentable contents of experience. We attempted to make clear this intent of the language used by locutions such as 'looks like', 'feels like'; thus restricting it to what would fall completely within the passage of experience in question and what this passage of experience could completely and directly determine as true. For example, if I should say, "There is a flight of granite steps before me," I should not merely report my experience but assert what it would require a great deal of further experience to corroborate fully. Indeed, it is questionable whether any amount of further experience could put this assertion theoretically beyond all possibility of a rational doubt. But when I say, "I see what *looks like* granite steps before me," I restrict myself to what is given; and what I intend by this language is something of which I can have no possible doubt. And the only possible doubt *you* could have of it—since it concerns a present experience of mine—is a doubt whether you grasp correctly what I intend to report, or a doubt whether I am telling the truth or a lie.

This use of language to formulate a directly presented or presentable content of experience, may be called its *expressive* use. This is in contrast to that more common intent of language, exemplified by, "I see (what in fact *is*) a flight of granite steps before me," which may be called its *objective* use. The distinctive character of expressive language, or the expressive use of language, is that such language signifies *appearances*. And in thus referring to appearances, or affirming what appears, such expressive language *neither asserts any objective reality of what appears nor denies any.* It is confined to description of the content of presentation itself.

In such expressive language, the cognitive judgment, "If I act in manner A, the empirical eventuality will include E," is one which can be verified by putting it to the test—supposing I can in fact put it to the test; can act in manner A.

When the hypothesis of this hypothetical judgment is made true by my volition, the consequent is found true or found false by what follows; and this verification is decisive and complete, because nothing beyond the content of this passage of experience was implied in the judgment.

In the second example, as we considered it, what was judged was an *objective fact*: "A piece of white paper is now before me." This judgment will be false if the presentation is illusory; it will be false if what I see is not really paper; false if it is not really white but only looks white. This objective judgment also is one capable of corroboration. As in the other example, so here too, any test of the judgment would pretty surely involve some way of acting— *making* the test, as by continuing to look, or turning my eyes, or grasping to tear, etc.—and would be determined by finding or failing to find some expected result in experience. But in this example, if the result of any single test is as expected, it constitutes a partial verification of the judgment only; never one which is absolutely decisive and theoretically complete. This is so because, while the judgment, so far as it is significant, contains nothing which could not be tested, still it has a significance which outruns what any single test, or any limited set of tests, could exhaust. No matter how fully I may have investigated this objective fact, there will remain some theoretical possibility of mistake; there will be further consequences which must be thus and so if the judgment is true, and not all of these will have been determined. The possibility that such further tests, if made, might have a negative result, cannot be altogether precluded; and this possibility marks the judgment as, at the time in question, not fully verified and less than absolutely certain. To quibble about such possible doubts will not, in most cases, be common sense. But we are not trying to weigh the degree of theoretical dubiety which common-sense practicality should take account of, but to arrive at an accurate analysis of knowledge. This character of being further testable and less than theoretically certain characterizes every judgment of objective fact at all times; every judgment that such and such a real thing exists or has a certain objectively factual property, or that a certain objective event actually occurs, or that any objective state of affairs actually is the case.

A judgment of the type of the first example—prediction of a particular passage of experience, describable in expressive language—may be called *terminating*. It admits of decisive and complete verification or falsification. One of the type of the second example—judgment of objective fact which is always further verifiable and never completely verified—may be called *non-terminating*.

However, if the suggested account should be correct, then the judgment of objective fact implies nothing which is not theoretically verifiable. And since any, even partial, verification could be made only by something disclosed in *some* passage of experience, such an objective and non-terminating judgment must be translatable into judgments of the terminating kind. Only so could confirmation of it in experience come about. If particular experiences should not serve as its corroborations, then it cannot be confirmed at all; experience in general would be irrelevant to its truth or falsity; and it must be either analytic or meaningless. Its non-terminating character reflects the fact, not that the statement implies anything which is not expressible in some terminating judgment or other, but that no limited set of such terminating judgments could be sufficient to exhaust its empirical significance.

To be sure, the sense of 'verifiable' which is appropriate to the principle that a statement of supposed objective fact which should not be verifiable would be meaningless, is one which will call for further consideration. 'Verifiable', like most 'able' words, is a highly ambiguous term, connoting conditions which are implied but unexpressed. For example, the sense in which it is verifiable that there are lines on the other side of this paper, is somewhat different from the sense in which it is verifiable that there are mountains on the other side of the moon. But such various senses in which 'verifiable' may be taken, concern the sense in which the verifying experience is 'possible'; not the character of the experience which would constitute verification. And in general we may safely say that for *any* sense in which statement of objective fact is 'meaningful', there is a coordinate and indicated sense in which it is 'verifiable'.

It may also be the case that, for some judgments at least—those called 'practically certain'—a degree of verification may be attained such that no later confirmation can render what is presently judged more certain than it is at the moment. That turns on considerations which we are not yet ready to examine. But as will appear, these postponed considerations further corroborate, instead of casting doubt upon, the conclusion that no objective statement is theoretically and completely certain. For that conclusion—which is the present point—the grounds mentioned would seem to be sufficient.

5. The conception is, thus, that there are three classes of empirical statements. First, there are formulations of what is presently given in experience. Only infrequently are such statements of the given actually made: there is seldom need to formulate what is directly and indubitably presented. They are also difficult or—it might plausibly be said—impossible to state in ordinary language, which, as usually understood, carries implications of something more and further verifiable which *ipso facto* is not given. But this difficulty of formulating precisely and only a given content of experience, is a relatively inessential consideration for the analysis of knowledge. That which we should thus attempt to formulate plays the same role whether it is expressed, or could be precisely expressed, or not. Without such apprehensions of direct and indubitable content of experience, there could be no basis for any empirical judgment, and no verification of one.

To this there is no alternative. Even if one should wish to suppose that *all* empirical statements are affected by uncertainty; one could not—short of an absurd kind of skepticism—suppose them all to be doubtful in the same degree that they would be if there were no experience. And if there are some empirical statements not thus utterly doubtful, then there must be something which imparts to them this status of better-than-utterly-doubtful. And that something must be an apprehended fact, or facts, of experience. If facts of this order should not be clearly expressible in language, they would still be the absolutely essential bases of all empirical knowledge.

Those thinkers who approach all problems of analysis from the point of view of language, have raised numerous difficulties over this conception of the empirically given. We shall not pause to clear away all the irrelevant issues with which the point has thus been surrounded. That point is simply that there is such a thing as experience, the content of which we do not invent and cannot have as we will but merely find. And that this given is an element in perception but not the whole of perceptual cognition. Subtract, in what we say that we see, or hear, or otherwise learn from direct experience, *all that conceivably could be mistaken*; the remainder is the given content of the experience inducing this belief. If there were no such hard kernel in experience—e.g., what we *see* when we think we see a deer but there is no deer—then the word 'experience' would have nothing to refer to.

It is essential to remember that in the statement or formulation of what is given (if such formulation be attempted), one uses language to *convey* this content, but what is *asserted* is what the language is intended to convey, not the correctness of the language used. If, for example, one say, "I see a red round something," one assumes but does *not* assert, "The words 'red' and 'round' correctly apply to something now given." This last is not a given fact of present experience but a generalization from past experience indicating the customary use of English words. But one does not have to know English in order to see red; and that the word 'red' applies to this presently given appearance, is not a fact given in that experience.

Knowledge itself might well get on without the formulation of the immediately given: what is thus directly presented does not require verbalization. But the *discussion* of knowledge hardly can, since it must be able somehow to refer to such basic factualities of experience. If there should be no understood linguistic mode of telling what is given, the analysis of knowledge would have to invent one, if only by arbitrary figure of speech. But our situation is hardly so bad as that: such formulations can be made, in a manner the intent of which, at least, is recognizable by what we have called the expressive use of language, in which its reference is restricted to appearances—to what is given, as such.

Apprehensions of the given which such expressive statements formulate, are not judgments; and they are not here classed as knowledge, because they are not subject to any possible error. Statement of such apprehension is, however, true or false: there could be no doubt about the presented content of experience as such at the time when it is given, but it would be possible to tell lies about it.[1]

Second, there are terminating judgments, and statements of them. These

---

[1] It would be possible to take statements of the given as involving judgment of correspondence between the character of the given itself and a fixed (expressive) meaning of words. But a judgment, "What is given is what '———' expresses" is not expression of the given but of a relation between it and a certain form of words. There is such a 'judgment of formulation' in the case of *any* statable fact. Let 'P' be an empirical statement which says nothing about language. "This fact is correctly stated by 'P'" is then a different statement, stating a relation between the fact which 'P' asserts and the verbal formulation 'P'. Correlatively, it is always possible to make a mistake of formulation, even where there could be no possible error concerning what is formulated. (In Book I, where we were frequently concerned with matters of logic, we used small letters, p, q, etc., to represent statements, following the current logical usage. But from this point on, it will make for easier reading if we represent statements by capital letters, P, Q, etc.)

represent some prediction of further possible experience. They find their cue in what is given: but what they state is something taken to be verifiable by some test which involves a way of acting. Thus terminating judgments are, in general, of the form, "If A then E," or "S being given, if A then E," where 'A' represents some mode of action taken to be possible, 'E' some expected consequent in experience, and 'S' the sensory cue. The hypothesis 'A' must here express something which, if made true by adopted action, will be *indubitably* true, and not, like a condition of my musculature in relation to the environment, an objective state of affairs only partially verified and not completely certain at the time. And the consequent 'E' represents an eventuality of *experience*, directly and certainly recognizable in case it accrues; not a resultant objective event, whose factuality could have, and would call for, further verification. Thus both antecedent and consequent of this judgment, "If A then E," require to be formulated in expressive language; though we shall not call it an expressive statement, reserving that phrase for formulations of the given. Also, unlike statements of the given, what such terminating judgments express is to be classed as knowledge: the prediction in question calls for verification, and is subject to possible error.

Third, there are non-terminating judgments which assert objective reality; some state of affairs as actual. These are so named because, while there is nothing in the import of such objective statements which is intrinsically unverifiable, and hence nothing included in them which is not expressible by some terminating judgment, nevertheless no limited set of particular predictions of empirical eventualities can completely exhaust the significance of such an objective statement. This is true of the simplest and most trivial, as much as of the most important. The statement that something is blue, for example, or is square—as contrasted with merely looking blue or appearing to be square—has, always, implications of further possible experience, beyond what should, at any particular time, have been found true. Theoretically complete and absolute verification of any objective judgment would be a never-ending task: any actual verification of them is no more than partial; and our assurance of them is always, theoretically, less than certain.

Non-terminating judgments represent an enormous class; they include, in fact, pretty much all the empirical statements we habitually make. They range in type from the simplest assertion of perceived fact—"There is a piece of white paper now before me"—to the most impressive of scientific generalizations—"The universe is expanding." In general, the more important an assertion of empirical objective fact, the more remote it is from its eventual grounds. The laws of science, for example, are arrived at by induction from inductions from inductions - - -. But objective judgments are all alike in being non-terminating, and in having no other eventual foundation than data of given experience.

6. The point of distinguishing expressive statements of given data of experience from predictive and verifiable statements of terminating judgments, and both of them from statements of objective fact, representing non-terminating judgments, is that without such distinctions it is almost impossible so to analyze empirical knowledge as to discover the grounds of it in experience, and the manner of its derivation from such grounds.

All empirical knowledge rests ultimately upon this kind of evidence and calls for the corroboration constituted by the facts of presentation. The cue to any statement of perceived actuality is in such presentation; and if there is to be any further confirmation of such statement, that can come about only through some further presentation. But unless the fact of presentation itself be distinguished from the objective fact it is cue to or corroborates, we shall never be able to understand or formulate the manner in which objective belief receives its warrant, or to explain how a belief which has some justification may nevertheless prove later to have been mistaken.

One says, for example, "I see a sheet of white paper," "I hear a bell," "I smell honeysuckle." Some datum of sense gives rise to the belief expressed. But what is believed does not coincide with the fact of sense: the belief expressed may be mistaken and the experience, as we say, 'illusory'; whereas the actual character of the given datum as such, is indubitable. If the belief expressed is corroborated by further investigation, there will be, again, data of sense. But these additional and corroborating data will not be the totality of the objective fact believed in and corroborated; and expression of the verifying event of experience will not coincide with expression of this objective fact.

Again; if the statement of objective fact, in whatever degree it may have become already assured, is further significant—if it implies what could be further and empirically determined but is not strictly deducible from past and present findings—then always it signifies something verifiable but as yet unverified, and is, in corresponding measure, itself subject to some theoretical uncertainty. We have concluded that all statements of objective fact do have this character. That conclusion being premised, it becomes essential to distinguish statements of the given and presently certain, as well as statements of terminating judgments which later experience may render certain, from such statements of objective fact. Otherwise it becomes impossible to assure objective truth as even probable. If what is to confirm the objective belief and thus show it probable, were itself an objective belief and hence no more than probable, then the objective belief to be confirmed would only probably be rendered probable. Thus unless we distinguish the objective truths belief in which experience may render probable, from those presentations and passages of experience which provide this warrant, any citation of evidence for a statement about objective reality, and any mentionable corroboration of it, will become involved in an indefinite regress of the merely probable—or else it will go around in a circle—and the probability will fail to be genuine. If anything is to be probable, then something must be certain. The data which eventually support a genuine probability, must themselves be certainties. We do have such absolute certainties, in the sense data initiating belief and in those passages of experience which later may confirm it. But neither such initial data nor such later verifying passages of experience can be phrased in the language of objective statement—because what can be so phrased is never more than probable. Our sense certainties can only be formulated by the expressive use of language, in which what is signified is a content of experience and what is asserted is the givenness of this content.

·   ·   ·

3

A. J. Ayer

Are Mistakes About One's Own Immediate Experience Only Verbal?

A. J. Ayer has been Wykeham Professor of Logic at Oxford since 1959. He is best know as l'enfant terrible of English positivism. In 1936 he published his justly famous Language, Truth and Logic. *The work of the Vienna Circle, the original group committed to positivism, had developed autonomously over years. Yet in England and America particularly, where positivism was little known, Ayer's work was rapidly accepted as the most succinct and authoritative statement of the new radical philosophical movement.*

He has been extremely productive, and his books are marked by an unusual gracefulness of style without loss of precision. His effort to save the central doctrine of meaningfulness, on which the positivist program rests, gradually proved impossible. He himself was engaged in exploring some of the efforts to recast the doctrine in a viable form, but the failure of the enterprise rests on considerations that undercut all such endeavors.

Apart from his notable aptness in discussing a wide variety of issues in the context of the most current and best-informed accounts, Ayer is probably identified chiefly with his own effort to clarify the conditions under which sense-data theories are tenable and adequate to the purpose of rendering perceptual judgments in their most lucid form. His books include The Foundations of Empirical Knowledge *(1940),* Philosophical Essays *(1954),* The Problem of Knowledge *(1956), and* The Concept of a Person *(1963).*

For those who have the use of language, there is an intimate connection be-tween identifying an object and knowing what to call it. Indeed on many occa-sions one's recognizing whatever it may be is simply a matter of one's coming out with the appropriate word. Of course the word must be meant to designate the object in question, but there are not, or need not be, two separate processes, one of fixing the object and the other of labelling it. The intention is normally to be found in the way in which the label is put on. There is, however, a sense in which one can recognize an object without knowing how to describe it. One may be able to place the object as being of the same sort as such and such another, or as having appeared before on such and such occasions, although one forgets what it is called or even thinks that it is called something which it is not. To a certain extent this placing of the object is already a fashion of describing it: we are not now concerned with the cases where recognition, con-ceived in terms of adaptive behaviour, is independent of the use of any symbols at all: but our finding a description of this sort is consistent with our ignoring or infringing some relevant linguistic rule. And this can happen also when the rule is of one's own making, or at least constituted by one's own practice. When the usage which they infringe is private, such lapses can only be exceptional; for unless one's practice were generally consistent, there would be no rule to break: but it is to be envisaged that they should now and then occur.

If this is so, one can be mistaken, after all, in the characterization of one's present experience. One can at least misdescribe it in the sense that one applies the wrong word to it; wrong because it is not the word which by the rules of one's language is correlated with an 'object' of the sort in question. But the reply to this may be that one would then be making only a verbal mistake. One would be misusing words, but not falling into any error of fact. Those who maintain that statements which describe some feature of one's present experience are incorrigible need not deny that the sentences which express them may be incorrectly formulated. What they are trying to exclude is the possibility of one's being factually mistaken.

But what is supposed to be the difference in this context between a verbal and a factual mistake? The first thing to remark is that we are dealing with words which, though general in their application, are also ostensive: that is, they are meant to stand for features of what is directly given in experience. And with respect to words of this kind, it is plausible to argue that knowing what they mean is simply a matter of being disposed to use them on the right occasions, when these are presented. It then appears to follow that to be in doubt as to the nature of something which is given, to wonder, for example, what colour this looks to me to be, is to be in doubt about the meaning of a word. And, correspondingly, to misdescribe what is given is to misuse a word. If I am not sure whether this looks crimson, what I am doubting is whether 'crimson' is the right word to describe this colour: if I resolve this doubt wrongly I have used the word 'crimson' when I should not or failed to use it when I should. This example is made easier to accept because the word 'crimson' has a conventional use. It is harder to see how I can use a word improperly when it is I alone who set the standard of propriety: my mistake would then have to consist in the fact that I had made an involuntary departure from some consistent practice which I had previously followed. In any event, it is argued, my mistake is not factual. If I were to predict that something, not yet presented to me, was going to look crimson, I might very well be making a factual mistake. My use of the word 'crimson' may be quite correct. It properly expresses my expectation: only the expectation is not in fact fulfilled. But in such a case I venture beyond the description of my present experience: I issue a draft upon the facts which they may refuse to honour. But for them to frustrate me I must put myself in their power. And this it is alleged to fail to do when I am merely recording what is directly given to me. My mistakes then can only be verbal. Thus we see that the reason why it is held to be impossible to make a factual error in describing a feature of one's present experience is that there is nothing in these circumstances which is allowed to count as one's being factually mistaken.

Against this, some philosophers would argue that it is impossible to describe anything, even a momentary private experience, without venturing beyond it. If I say that what I seem to see is crimson, I am saying that it bears the appropriate resemblance in colour to certain other objects. If it does not so resemble them I have classified it wrongly, and in doing so I have made a factual mistake. But the answer to this is that merely from the statement that a given thing looks crimson, it cannot be deduced that anything else is coloured or even that anything else exists. The fact, if it be a fact, that the colour of the thing in question does not resemble that of other things which are properly described as crimson does indeed prove that in calling it crimson I am making a mistake; I am breaking a rule which would not exist unless there were, or at any rate could be, other things to which the word applied. But in saying that this is crimson, I am not explicitly referring to these other things. In using a word according to a rule, whether rightly or wrongly, I am not talking about the rule. I operate it but I do not say how it operates. From the fact that I have to refer to other things in order to show that my description of something is correct, it does not follow that my description itself refers to them. We may admit that to describe is to classify; but this does not entail that in describing something one is bound to go beyond it, in the sense that one actually asserts that it is related to something else.

Let us allow, then, that there can be statements which refer only to the contents of one's present experiences. Then, if it is made a necessary condition for being factually mistaken that one should make some claim upon the facts which goes beyond the content of one's present experience, it will follow that even when these statements misdescribe what they refer to the error is not factual: and then there appears no choice but to say that it is verbal. The question is whether this ruling is to be accepted.

The assumption which lies behind it is that to understand the meaning of an ostensive word one must be able to pick out the instances to which it applies. If I pick out the wrong instances, or fail to pick out the right ones, I show that I have not learned how to use the word. If I hesitate whether to apply it to a given case, I show that I am so far uncertain of its meaning. Now there is clearly some truth in this assumption. We should certainly not say that someone knew the meaning of an ostensive word if he had no idea how to apply it; more than that, we require that his use of it should, in general, be both confident and right. But this is not to say that in every single case in which he hesitates over the application of the word, he must be in doubt about its meaning. Let us consider an example. Suppose that two lines of approximately the same length are drawn so that they both come within my field of vision and I am then asked to say whether either of them looks to me to be the longer, and if so which. I think I might very well be uncertain how to answer. But it seems very strange to say that what, in such a case, I should be uncertain about would be the meaning of the English expression 'looks longer than'. It is not at all like the case where I know which looks to me the longer, but having to reply in French, and speaking French badly, I hesitate whether to say 'plus longue' or 'plus large'. In this case I am uncertain only about the proper use of words, but in the other surely I am not. I know quite well how the words 'looks longer than' are used in English. It is just that in the present instance I am not sure whether, as a matter of fact, either of the lines does look to me to be longer than the other.

But if I can be in doubt about this matter of fact, I can presumably also come to the wrong decision. I can judge that this line looks to me to be longer than the one when in fact it does not. This would indeed be a curious position to be in. Many would say that it was an impossible position, on the ground that there is no way of distinguishing between the way things look to someone and the way he judges that they look. After all he is the final authority on the way things look to him, and what criterion is there for deciding how things look to him except the way that he assesses them? But in allowing that he may be uncertain how a thing looks to him, we have already admitted this distinction. We have drawn a line between the facts and his assessment, or description, of them.[1] Even so, it may be objected, there is no sense in talking of there being a mistake unless it is at least possible that the mistake should be discovered. And how could it ever be discovered that one had made a mistake in one's account of some momentary, private experience? Clearly no direct test is possible. The experience is past: it cannot be produced for reinspection. But there may still be indirect evidence which would carry weight. To return to our example, if I look at the lines again, it may seem quite clear to me that A looks longer than B, whereas I had previously been inclined to think that B looked longer than A, or that they looked the same length. This does not prove that I was wrong before: it may be that they look to me differently now from the way they did then. But I might have indirect, say physiological, evidence that their appearance, that is the appearance that they offer to me, has not changed. Or I may have reason to believe that in the relevant conditions things look the same to certain other people as they do to me: and then the fact that the report given by these other people disagrees with mine may have some tendency to show that I am making a mistake. In any event it is common ground that one can misdescribe one's experience. The question is only whether such misdescription is always to be taken as an instance of a verbal mistake. My contention is that there are cases in which it is more plausible to say that the mistake is factual.

If I am right, there is then no class of descriptive statements which are incorrigible. However strong the experiential basis on which a descriptive statement is put forward, the possibility of its falsehood is not excluded. Statements which do no more than describe the content of a momentary, private experience achieve the greatest security because they run the smallest risk. But they do run some risk, however small, and because of this they too can come to grief. Complete security is attained only by statements like 'I exist' which function as gesticulations. But the price which they pay for it is the sacrifice of descriptive content.

We are left still with the argument that some statements must be incor-

---

[1] Yes, but it may still be argued that his assessment, when he reaches it, *settles* the question. The point is whether a meaning can be given to saying that he decides wrongly. I suggest that it can.

rigible, if any are ever to be verified. If the statements which have been taken as basic are fallible like all the rest, where does the process of verification terminate? The answer is that it terminates in someone's having some experience, and in his accepting the truth of some statement which describes it, or more commonly, the truth of some more far-reaching statement which the occurrence of the experience supports. There is nothing fallible about the experience itself. What may be wrong is only one's identification of it. If an experience has been misidentified, one will be misled into thinking that some statement has been verified when it has not. But this does not mean that we never verify anything. There is no reason to doubt that the vast majority of our experiences are taken by us to be what they are; in which case they do verify the statements which are construed as describing them. What we do not, and can not, have is a logical guarantee that our acceptance of a statement is not mistaken. It is chiefly the belief that we need such a guarantee that has led philosophers to hold that some at least of the statements which refer to what is immediately given to us in experience must be incorrigible. But, as I have already remarked, even if there could be such incorrigible statements, the guarantee which they provided would not be worth very much. In any given case it would operate only for a single person and only for the fleeting moment at which he was having the experience in question. It would not, therefore, be of any help to us in making lasting additions to our stock of knowledge.

In allowing that the descriptions which people give of their experiences may be factually mistaken, we are dissociating having an experience from knowing that one has it. To know that one is having whatever experience it may be, one must not only have it but also be able to identify it correctly, and there is no necessary transition from one to the other; not to speak of the cases when we do not identify our experiences at all, we may identify them wrongly. Once again, this does not mean that we never know, or never really know, what experiences we are having. On the contrary it is exceptional for us not to know. All that is required is that we should be able to give an account of our experiences which is both confident and correct; and these conditions are very frequently fulfilled. It is no rebuttal of our claim to knowledge that, in this as in other domains, it may sometimes happen that we think we know when we do not.

The upshot of our argument is that the philosopher's ideal of certainty has no application. Except in the cases where the truth of a statement is a condition of its being made, it can never in any circumstances be logically impossible that one should take a statement to be true when it is false; and this holds good whatever the statement may be, whether, for example, it is itself necessary or contingent. It would, however, be a mistake to express this conclusion by saying, lugubriously or in triumph, that nothing is really certain. There are a great many statements the truth of which we rightly do not doubt; and it is perfectly correct to say that they are certain. We should not be bullied by the sceptic into renouncing an expression for which we have a legitimate use. Not that the sceptic's argument is fallacious; as usual his logic is impeccable. But his victory is empty. He robs us of certainty only by so defining it as to make it certain that it cannot be obtained.

4

Norman Malcolm
Knowledge and Belief

"We must recognize that when we know something we either do, or by reflecting, can know that our condition is one of knowing that thing, while when we believe something, we either do or can know that our condition is one of believing and not of knowing: so that we cannot mistake belief for knowledge or vice versa."[1]

This remark is worthy of investigation. Can I discover *in myself* whether I know something or merely believe it?

Let us begin by studying the ordinary usage of "know" and "believe." Suppose, for example, that several of us intend to go for a walk and that you propose that we walk in Cascadilla Gorge. I protest that I should like to walk beside a flowing stream and that at this season the gorge is probably dry. Consider the following cases:

(1) You say "I believe that it won't be dry although I have no particular reason for thinking so." If we went to the gorge and found a flowing stream we should not say that you *knew* that there would be water but that you thought so and were right.

(2) You say "I believe that it won't be dry because it rained only three days ago and usually water flows in the gorge for at least that long after a rain." If we found water we should be inclined to say that you knew that there would be water. It would be quite natural for you to say "I knew that it wouldn't be dry"; and we should tolerate your remark. This case differs from the previous one in that here you had a *reason*.

(3) You say "I know that it won't be dry" and give the same reason as in (2). If we found water we should have very little hesitation in saying that you knew. Not only had you a reason, but you *said* "I know" instead of "I believe." It may seem to us that the latter should not make a difference—but it does.

(4) You say "I know that it won't be dry" and give a stronger reason, e.g., "I saw a lot of water flowing in the gorge when I passed it this morning." If we went and found water, there would be no hesitation at all in saying that you knew. If, for example, we later met someone who said "Weren't you surprised to see water in the gorge this afternoon?" you would reply "No, I *knew* that there would be water; I had been there earlier in the day." We should have no objection to this statement.

Norman Malcolm, "Knowledge and Belief," *Mind*, LXI, 242 (April 1952). Reprinted by permission of the publisher and the author.

[1] H. A. Prichard, *Knowledge and Perception* (Oxford: The Clarendon Press, 1950), p. 88.

(5) Everything happens as in (4), except that upon going to the gorge we find it to be dry. We should not say that you knew, but that you *believed* that there would be water. And this is true even though you declared that you knew, and even though your evidence was the same as it was in case (4) in which you did know.

I wish to make some comments on the usage of "know," "knew," "believe," and "believed," as illustrated in the preceding cases:

(a) Whether we should say that you knew, depends in part on whether you had grounds for your assertion and on the strength of those grounds. There would certainly be less hesitation to say that you knew in case (4) than in case (3), and this can be due only to the difference in the strength of the grounds.

(b) Whether we should say that you knew, depends in part on how *confident* you were. In case (2), if you had said "It rained only three days ago and usually water flows in the gorge for at least that long after a rain; but, of course, I don't feel absolutely sure that there will be water," then we should *not* have said that you knew that there would be water. If you lack confidence that p is true then others do not say that you know that p is true, even though *they* know that p is true. Being confident is a necessary condition for knowing.

(c) [H. A.—Ed.] Prichard says that if we reflect we cannot mistake belief for knowledge. In case (4) you knew that there would be water, and in case (5) you merely believed it. Was there any way that you could have discovered by reflection, in case (5), that you did not know? It would have been useless to have reconsidered your grounds for saying that there would be water, because in case (4), where you *did* know, your grounds were identical. They could be at fault in (5) only if they were at fault in (4), and they were not at fault in (4). Cases (4) and (5) differ in only one respect—namely, that in one case you did subsequently find water and in the other you did not. Prichard says that we can determine by reflection whether we know something or merely believe it. But where, in these cases, is the material that reflection would strike upon? There is none.

There is only one way that Prichard could defend his position. He would have to say that in case (4) you did *not* know that there would be water. And it is obvious that he would have said this. But this is false. It is an enormously common usage of language to say, in commenting upon just such an incident as (4), "He knew that the gorge would be dry because he had seen water flowing there that morning." It is a usage that all of us are familiar with. We so employ "know" and "knew" every day of our lives. We do not think of our usage as being loose or incorrect—and it is not. As philosophers we may be surprised to observe that it *can* be that the knowledge that p is true should differ from the belief that p is true *only* in the respect that in one case p is true and in the other false. But that is the fact.

There is an argument that one is inclined to use as a proof that you did not know that there would be water. The argument is the following: It could have turned out that you found no water; if it had so turned out you would have been mistaken in saying that you would find water; therefore you could have been mistaken; but if you could have been mistaken then you did not know.

Now it certainly *could* have turned out that the gorge was quite dry when you went there, even though you saw lots of water flowing through it only a few hours before. This does not show, however, that you did not know that there would be water. What it shows is that *although you knew you could have been mistaken.*[2] This would seem to be a contradictory result; but it is not. It seems so because our minds are fixed upon another usage of "know" and "knew"; one in which "It would have turned out that I was mistaken," implies "I did not know."

When is "know" used in this sense? I believe that Prichard uses it in this sense when he says that when we go through the proof of the proposition that the angles of a triangle are equal to two right angles we *know* that the proposition is true (p. 89). He says that if we put to ourselves the question: Is our condition one of knowing this, or is it only one of being convinced of it? then "We can only answer 'Whatever may be our state on other occasions, here we are knowing this.' And this statement is an expression of our *knowing* that we are knowing; for we do not *believe* that we are knowing this, we know that we are" (p. 89). He goes on to say that if someone were to object that we might be making a mistake "because for all we know we can later on discover some fact which is incompatible with a triangle's having angles that are equal to two right angles, we can answer that we *know* that there can be no such fact, for in knowing that a triangle must have such angles we also know that nothing can exist which is incompatible with this fact" (p. 90).

It is easy to imagine a non-philosophical context in which it would have been natural for Prichard to have said "I know that the angles of a triangle are equal to two right angles." Suppose that a young man just beginning the study of geometry was in doubt as to whether that proposition is true, and had even constructed an ingenious argument that appeared to prove it false. Suppose that Prichard was unable to find any error in the argument. He might have said to the young man: "There must be an error in it. I know that the angles of a triangle are equal to two right angles."

When Prichard says that "nothing can exist which is incompatible with" the truth of that proposition, is he prophesying that no one will ever have the ingenuity to construct a flawless-looking argument against it? I believe not. When Prichard says that "we" *know* (and implies that *he* knows) that the proposition is true and *know* that nothing can exist that is incompatible with its being true, he is not making any *prediction* as to what the future will bring in the way of arguments or measurements. On the contrary, he is asserting that *nothing* that the future might bring could ever count as evidence against the proposition. He is implying that he would not *call* anything "evidence" against

---

[2] [Some readers seem to have thought that I was denying here that "I knew that *p*" entails "that *p*." That was not my intention, and my words do not have that implication. If I had said "*Although you knew you were mistaken,*" I should have denied the above entailment and, also, I should have misused "knew." The difference between the strong and weak senses of "know" (and "knew") is not that this entailment holds for the strong but not for the weak sense. It holds for both. If it is false that *p*, then one does not (and did not) know that *p*.]

it. He is using "know" in what I shall call its "strong" sense. "Know" is used in this sense when a person's statement "I know that p is true" implies that the person who makes the statement would look upon nothing whatever as evidence that p is false.

It must not be assumed that whenever "know" is used in connection with mathematical propositions it is used in the strong sense. A great many people have *heard* of various theorems of geometry, e.g., the Pythagorean. These theorems are a part of "common knowledge." If a schoolboy doing his geometry assignment felt a doubt about the Pythagorean theorem, and said to an adult "Are you *sure* that it is true?" the latter might reply "Yes, I know that it is." He might make this reply even though he could not give proof of it and even though he had never gone through a proof of it. If subsequently he was presented with a "demonstration" that the theorem is false, or if various persons reputed to have a knowledge of geometry soberly assured him that it is false, he might be filled with doubt or even be convinced that he was mistaken. When he said "Yes, I know that it is true," he did not pledge himself to hold to the theorem through thick and thin. He did not absolutely exclude the possibility that something could prove it to be false. I shall say that he used "know" in the "weak" sense.

Consider another example from mathematics of the difference between the strong and weak senses of "know." I have just now rapidly calculated that 92 times 16 is 1472. If I had done this in the commerce of daily life where a practical problem was at stake, and if someone had asked "Are you sure that $92 \times 16 = 1472$?" I might have answered "I *know* that it is; I have just now calculated it." But also I might have answered "I know that it is; but I will calculate it again to *make sure*." And here my language points to a distinction. I say that I *know* that $92 \times 16 = 1472$. Yet I am willing to *confirm* it—that is, there is something that I should *call* "making sure"; and, likewise, there is something that I should *call* "finding out that it is false." If I were to do this calculation again and obtain the result that $92 \times 16 = 1372$, and if I were to carefully check this latter calculation without finding any error, I should be disposed to say that I was previously mistaken when I declared that $92 \times 16 = 1472$. Thus when I say that I know that $92 \times 16 = 1472$, I allow for the possibility of a *refutation*; and so I am using "know" in its weak sense.

Now consider propositions like $2 + 2 = 4$ and $7 + 5 = 12$. It is hard to think of circumstances in which it would be natural for me to say that I know that $2 + 2 = 4$, because no one ever questions it. Let us try to suppose, however, that someone whose intelligence I respect argues that certain developments in arithmetic have shown that $2 + 2$ does not equal 4. He writes out a proof of this in which I can find no flaw. Suppose that his demeanor showed me that he was in earnest. Suppose that several persons of normal intelligence became persuaded that his proof was correct and that $2 + 2$ does not equal 4. What would be my reaction? I should say "I can't see what is wrong with your proof; but it *is* wrong, because I *know* that $2 + 2 = 4$." Here I should be using "know" in its strong sense. I should not admit that any argument or any future development in mathematics could show that it is false that $2 + 2 = 4$.

The propositions $2 + 2 = 4$ and $92 \times 16 = 1472$ do not have the same status. There *can* be a demonstration that $2 + 2 = 4$. But a demonstration would be for me (and for any average person) only a curious exercise, a sort of *game*. We have no serious interest in proving that proposition.[3] It does not *need* a proof. It stands without one, and would not fall if a proof went against it. The case is different with the proposition that $92 \times 16 = 1472$. We take an interest in the demonstration (calculation) because that proposition *depends* upon its demonstration. A calculation may lead me to reject it as false. But $2 + 2 = 4$ does *not* depend on its demonstration. It does not depend on anything! And in the calculation that proves that $92 \times 16 = 1472$, there are steps that do not depend on any calculation (e.g., $2 \times 6 = 12$; $5 + 2 = 7$; $5 + 9 = 14$).

There is a correspondence between this dualism in the logical status of mathematical propositions and the two senses of "know." When I use "know" in the weak sense I am prepared to let an investigation (demonstration, calculation) determine whether the something that I claim to know is true or false. When I use "know" in the strong sense I am not prepared to look upon anything as an *investigation*; I do not concede that anything whatsoever could prove me mistaken; I do not regard the matter as open to any *question*; I do not admit that my proposition could turn out to be false, that any future investigation *could* refute it or cast doubt on it.[4]

We have been considering the strong sense of "know" in its application to mathematical propositions. Does it have application anywhere in the realm of *empirical* propositions—for example, to propositions that assert or imply that certain physical things exist? Descartes said that we have a "moral assurance" of the truth of some of the latter propositions but that we lack a "metaphysical certainty."[5] Locke said that the perception of the existence of physical things is not "so certain as our intuitive knowledge, or the deductions of our reason" although "it is an assurance that deserves the name of knowledge."[6] Some philosophers have held that when we make judgments of perception such as that there are peonies in the garden, cows in the field, or dishes in the cupboard, we are "taking for granted" that the peonies, cows, and dishes exist, but not knowing it in the "strict" sense. Others have held that all empirical proposi-

---

[3] Some logicians and philosophers have taken an interest in proving that $2 + 2 = 4$ (e.g., [Gottfried Wilhelm—Ed.] Leibniz, *New Essays on the Understanding*, Bk. IV, ch. 7, sec. 10; [Gottlob—Ed.] Frege, *The Foundations of Arithmetic*, sec. 6). They have wished to show that it can be deduced from certain premises, and to determine what premises and rules of inference are required in the deduction. Their interest has not been in the *outcome* of the deduction.

[4] Compare these remarks about the strong sense of "know" with some of Locke's statements about "intuitive knowledge": ". . . in this the mind is at no pains of proving or examining. . . ." "This part of knowledge . . . leaves no room for hesitation, doubt, or examination. . . ."

"It is on this intuition that depends all the certainty and evidence of all our knowledge; which certainty every one finds to be so great, that he cannot imagine, and therefore not require a greater. . . ." Locke, *Essay*, Bk. IV, ch. 2, sec. 1.

[5] Descartes, *Discourse on the Method*, Part IV.

[6] Locke, *Essay*, Book IV, ch. 11, sec. 3.

tions, including judgments of perception, are merely hypotheses.[7] The thought behind this exaggerated mode of expression is that any empirical proposition whatever *could* be refuted by future experience—that is, it *could* turn out to be false. Are these philosophers right?

Consider the following propositions:

(i) The sun is about ninety million miles from the earth.
(ii) There is a heart in my body.
(iii) Here is an ink-bottle.

In various circumstances I should be willing to assert of each of these propositions that I know it to be true. Yet they differ strikingly. This I see when, with each, I try to imagine the possibility that it is false.

(i) If in ordinary conversation someone said to me "The sun is about twenty million miles from the earth, isn't it?" I should reply "No, it is about ninety million miles from us." If he said "I think that you are confusing the sun with Polaris," I should reply, "I *know* that ninety million miles is roughly the sun's distance from the earth." I might invite him to verify the figure in an encyclopedia. A third person who overheard our conversation could quite correctly report that I knew the distance to the sun, whereas the other man did not. But this knowledge of mine is little better than hearsay. I have seen that figure mentioned in a few books. I know nothing about the observations and calculations that led astronomers to accept it. If tomorrow a group of eminent astronomers announced that a great error had been made and that the correct figure is twenty million miles, I should not insist that they were wrong. It would surprise me that such an enormous mistake could have been made. But I should no longer be willing to say that I *know* that ninety million is the correct figure. Although I should *now* claim that I know the distance to be about ninety million miles, it is easy for me to envisage the possibility that some future investigation will prove this to be false.

(ii) Suppose that after a routine medical examination the excited doctor reports to me that the X-ray photographs show that I have no heart. I should tell him to get a new machine. I should be inclined to say that the fact that I have a heart is one of the few things that I can count on as absolutely certain. I can feel it beat. I know it's there. Furthermore, how could my blood circulate if I didn't have one? Suppose that later on I suffer a chest injury and undergo a surgical operation. Afterwards the astonished surgeons solemnly declare that they searched my chest cavity and found no heart, and that they made incisions and looked about in other likely places but found it not. They are convinced that I am without a heart. They are unable to understand how circulation can occur or what accounts for the thumping in my chest. But they are in agreement and obviously sincere, and they have clear photographs of my interior spaces. What would be my attitude? Would it be to insist that they were all mistaken?

---

[7] E.g., ". . . no proposition, other than a tautology, can possibly be anything more than a probable hypothesis." A. J. Ayer, *Language, Truth and Logic*, second ed. (New York: Dover Publications, Inc., 1951), p. 38.

I think not. I believe that I should eventually accept their testimony and the evidence of the photographs. I should consider to be false what I now regard as an absolute certainty.

(iii) Suppose that as I write this paper someone in the next room were to call out to me "I can't find an ink-bottle; is there one in the house?" I should reply "Here is an ink-bottle." If he said in a doubtful tone "Are you sure? I looked there before," I should reply "Yes, I know there is; come and get it."

Now could it turn out to be false that there is an ink-bottle directly in front of me on this desk? Many philosophers have thought so. They would say that many things could happen of such a nature that if they did happen it would be proved that I am deceived. I agree that many extraordinary things could happen, in the sense that there is no logical absurdity in the supposition. It could happen that when I next reach for this ink-bottle my hand should seem to pass *through* it and I should not feel the contact of any object. It could happen that in the next moment the ink-bottle will suddenly vanish from sight; or that I should find myself under a tree in the garden with no ink-bottle about; or that one or more persons should enter this room and declare with apparent sincerity that they see no ink-bottle on this desk; or that a photograph taken now of the top of the desk should clearly show all of the objects on it except the ink-bottle. Having admitted that these things *could happen*,[8] am I compelled to admit that if they did happen then it would be proved that there is no ink-bottle here *now*? Not at all! I could say that when my hand seemed to pass through the ink-bottle I should *then* be suffering from hallucination; that if the ink-bottle suddenly vanished it would have miraculously ceased to exist; that the other persons were conspiring to drive me mad, or were themselves victims of remarkable concurrent hallucinations; that the camera possessed some strange flaw or that there was trickery in developing the negative. I admit that in the next moment I could find myself under a tree or in the bathtub. But this is not to admit that it could be revealed in the next moment that I am now dreaming. For what I admit is that I might be instantaneously transported to the garden, but not that in the next moment I might *wake up* in the garden. There is nothing that could happen to me in the next moment that I should call "waking up"; and therefore nothing that could happen to me in the next moment would be accepted by me now as proof that I now dream.

Not only do I not *have* to admit that those extraordinary occurrences would be evidence that there is no ink-bottle here; the fact is that I *do not* admit it. There is nothing whatever that could happen in the next moment or the next year that would by me be called *evidence* that there is not an ink-

---

[8] [My viewpoint is somewhat different here from what it is in "The Verification Argument." There I am concerned with bringing out the different ways in which such a remark as "these things *could* happen" can be taken. I wish to show, furthermore, that from none of the senses in which the remark is *true* does it follow that it is *not certain* that the things in question will *not happen*. Finally, I hold there, that it is perfectly certain that they will not happen. Here, I am not disagreeing with any of those points, but I am adding the further point that my admission that, in some sense, the things *could happen*, does not require me to admit that *if* they were to happen, that would be evidence that there is no ink-bottle here now.]

bottle here now. No future experience or investigation could prove to me that I am mistaken. Therefore, if I were to say "I know that there is an ink-bottle here," I should be using "know" in the strong sense.

It will appear to some that I have adopted an *unreasonable* attitude toward that statement. There is, however, nothing unreasonable about it. It seems so because one thinks that the statement that here is an ink-bottle *must* have the same status as the statements that the sun is ninety million miles away and that I have a heart and that there will be water in the gorge this afternoon. But this is a *prejudice*.

In saying that I should regard nothing as evidence that there is no ink-bottle here now, I am not *predicting* what I should do if various astonishing things happened. If other members of my family entered this room and, while looking at the top of this desk, declared with apparent sincerity that they see no ink-bottle, I might fall into a swoon or become mad. I *might* even come to believe that there is not and has not been an ink-bottle here. I cannot foretell with certainty how I should react. But if it is *not* a prediction, what is the meaning of my assertion that I should regard nothing as evidence that there is no ink-bottle here?

That assertion describes my *present* attitude towards the statement that here is an ink-bottle. It does not prophesy what my attitude *would* be if various things happened. My present attitude toward that statement is radically different from my present attitude toward those other statements (e.g., that I have a heart).[9] I do *now* admit that certain future occurrences would disprove the latter. Whereas no imaginable future occurrence would be considered by me *now* as proving that there is not an ink-bottle here.

These remarks are not meant to be autobiographical. They are meant to throw light on the common concepts of evidence, proof, and disproof. Every one of us upon innumerable occasions of daily life takes this same attitude towards various statements about physical things, e.g., that here is a torn page, that this dish is broken, that the thermometer reads 70, that no rug is on the floor. Furthermore, the concepts of proof, disproof, doubt, and conjecture *require* us to take this attitude. In order for it to be possible that any statements about physical things should *turn out to be false* it is necessary that some statements about physical things *cannot* turn out to be false.

This will be made clear if we ask ourselves the question, When do we *say* that something turned out to be false? When do we use those words? Someone asks you for a dollar. You say "There is one in this drawer." You open the drawer and look, but it is perfectly empty. Your statement turned out to be false. This can be said because you *discovered* an empty drawer. It could not

---

[9] [The word "attitude" is not very satisfactory, but I cannot think of another noun that would do the trick. By "my attitude" I mean, here, *what I should say and think* if various things were to happen. By "my *present* attitude" I mean what I should say and think now, when I imagine those things as happening, in contrast with what I should say and think at some future time if those things actually did happen at that time. It is this distinction that shows that my description of "my present attitude" is not a *prophecy*.]

be said if it were only probable that the drawer is empty or were still open to question. Would it make sense to say "I had better make sure that it is empty; perhaps there is a dollar in it after all?" Sometimes; but not always. Not if the drawer lies open before your eyes. That remark is the prelude to a search. What search can there be when the emptiness of the drawer confronts you? In certain circumstances there is nothing that you would call "making sure" that the drawer is empty; and likewise nothing that you would call "its turning out to be false" that the drawer is empty. You *made* sure that the drawer is empty. One statement about physical things *turned out to be false* only because you *made sure* of another statement about physical things. The two concepts cannot exist apart. Therefore it is impossible that *every* statement about physical things *could* turn out to be false.

In a certain important respect some a priori statements and some empirical statements possess the same logical character. The statements that $5 \times 5 = 25$ and that here is an ink-bottle, both lie beyond the reach of doubt. On both, my judgment and reasoning *rests*. If you could somehow undermine my confidence in either, you would not teach me *caution*. You would fill my mind with chaos! I could not even make *conjectures* if you took away those fixed points of certainty; just as a man cannot *try* to climb whose body has no support. A conjecture implies an understanding of what certainty would be. If it is not a certainty that $5 \times 5 = 25$ and that here is an ink-bottle, then I do not understand what it is. You cannot make me doubt either of these statements or treat them as hypotheses. You cannot persuade me that future experience could refute them. With both of them it is perfectly unintelligible to me to speak of a "possibility" that they are false. This is to say that I know both of them to be true, in the strong sense of "know." And I am inclined to think that the strong sense of "know" is what various philosophers have had in mind when they have spoken of "perfect," "metaphysical," or "strict certainty."[10]

It will be thought that I have confused a statement about my "sensations," or my "sense-data," or about the way something *looks* or *appears* to me, with a statement about physical things. It will be thought that the things that I have said about the statement "Here is an ink-bottle" could be true only if that statement is interpreted to mean something like "There appears to me to be an ink-bottle here," i.e., interpreted so as not to assert or imply that any physical thing exists. I wish to make it clear that my statement "Here is an ink-bottle" is *not* to be interpreted in that way. It would be utterly fantastic for me in my present circumstances to say "There appears to me to be an ink-bottle here."

If someone were to call me on the telephone and say that he urgently

---

[10] Descartes, for example, apparently took as his criterion for something's being "entirely certain" that he could not *imagine* in it the least ground of doubt: ". . . je pensai qu'il fallait . . . que je retasse comme absolument faux tout ce en quoi je pourrais imaginer le moindre doute, afin de voir s'il ne me resterait point après cela quelque chose en ma creánce qui fut entièrement indubitable" (*Discourse*, Part IV). And Locke (as previously noted) said of "intuitive knowledge" that one *cannot imagine* a greater certainty, and that it "leaves no room for hesitation, doubt, or examination." *Essay*, Bk. IV, ch. 2, sec. 1.

needed an ink-bottle I should invite him to come here and get this one. If he said that it was extremely urgent that he should obtain one immediately and that he could not afford to waste time going to a place where there might not be one, I should tell him that it is an absolute certainty that there is one here, that nothing could be more certain, that it is something I absolutely guarantee. But if my statement "There is an ink-bottle here" were a statement about my "sensations" or "sense-data," or if it meant that there *appears* to me to be an ink-bottle here or that something here *looks* to me like an ink-bottle, and if that is all that I meant by it—then I should react quite differently to his urgent request. I should say that there is probably an ink-bottle here but that I could not *guarantee* it, and that if he needs one very desperately and at once then he had better look elsewhere. In short, I wish to make it clear that my statement "Here is an ink-bottle" is strictly about physical things and not about "sensations," "sense-data," or "appearances."[11]

Let us go back to Prichard's remark that we can determine by reflection whether we know something or merely believe it. Prichard would think that "knowledge in the weak sense" is mere belief and not knowledge. This is wrong. But if we let ourselves speak this way, we can then see some justification for Prichard's remark. For then he would be asserting, among other things, that we can determine by reflection whether we know something in the strong sense or in the weak sense. This is not literally true; however, there is this truth in it—that reflection can make us realize that we are *using* "I know it" in the strong (or weak) sense in a particular case. Prichard says that reflection can show us that "our condition is one of knowing" a certain thing, or instead that "our condition is one of believing and not of knowing" that thing. I do not understand what could be meant here by "our condition." The way I should put it is that reflection on *what we should think* if certain things were to happen may make us realize that we should (or should not) call those things "proof" or "evidence" that what we claim to know is not so. I have tried to show that the distinction between strong and weak knowledge does not run parallel to the distinction between a priori and empirical knowledge but cuts across it, i.e., these two kinds of knowledge may be distinguished *within* a priori knowledge and *within* empirical knowledge.

Reflection can make me realize that I am using "know" in the strong sense; but can reflection show me that I *know* something in the strong sense (or in the weak)? It is not easy to state the logical facts here. On the one hand, if I make an assertion of the form "I know that *p*" it does not follow that *p*, whether or not I am using "know" in the strong sense. If I have said to someone outside my room "Of course, I know that Freddie is in here," and I am speaking in the strong sense, it does not *follow* that Freddie is where I claim

---

[11] [The remainder of the essay is newly written. The original conclusion was wrongly stated. The reader is referred to the following exchange between Richard Taylor and myself, in respect to the original paper: Taylor, "A Note on Knowledge and Belief," *Analysis*, XIII, June 1953; Malcolm, "On Knowledge and Belief," *Analysis*, XIV, March 1954; Taylor, "Rejoinder to Mr. Malcolm," *ibid.*]

he is. This logical fact would not be altered even if I *realized* that I was using "know" in the strong sense. My reflection on what I should say if . . . , cannot show me that I *know* something. From the fact that I should not call anything "evidence" that Freddie is not here, it does not follow that he *is* here; therefore, it does not follow that I *know* he is here.

On the other hand, in an actual case of my using "know" in the strong sense, I cannot envisage a possibility that what I say to be true should turn out to be not true. If I were speaking of *another person's* assertion about something, I *could* think both that he is using "know" in the strong sense and that nonetheless what he claims he knows to be so might turn out to be not so. But *in my own case* I cannot have this conjunction of thoughts, and this is a logical and not a psychological fact. When *I* say that I know something to be so, using "know" in the strong sense, it is unintelligible *to me* (although perhaps not to others) to suppose that anything could prove that it is not so and, therefore, that I do not know it.[12]

5

Edmund L. Gettier
Is Justified True Belief Knowledge?

Edmund Gettier is Professor of Philosophy at the University of Massachusetts. His paper, "Is Justified True Belief Knowledge?" (1963), has set off an entire industry devoted to improving the formal analysis of knowledge. Using several specimen cases, Gettier managed to show that the classical justified-true-belief conception of knowledge was incapable of excluding accidentally true and justified beliefs that

Edmund L. Gettier, "Is Justified True Belief Knowledge?," *Analysis*, 23 (1963), 121–123. Reprinted by permission of Basil Blackwell, Publisher.

---

[12] This is the best summary I can give of what is wrong and right in Prichard's claim that one can determine by reflection whether one knows something or merely believes it. A good part of the ideas in this essay were provoked by conversations with Wittgenstein. A brief and rough account of those talks is to be found in my *Ludwig Wittgenstein: A Memoir* (New York: Oxford University Press, 1958), pp. 87–92. Jaakko Hintikka provides an acute treatment of the topic of "knowing that one knows," with special reference to Prichard's claim. See his *Knowledge and Belief* (Ithaca: Cornell University Press, 1962), ch. 5.

depend on false beliefs; and that the correction of the definition was not simple or obvious. He has since attacked related difficulties in the analysis of knowledge.

Various attempts have been made in recent years to state necessary and sufficient conditions for someone's knowing a given proposition. The attempts have often been such that they can be stated in a form similar to the following:[1]

(a) S knows that P   IFF   (i) P is true,
                                             (ii) S believes that P, and
                                             (iii) S is justified in believing that P.

For example, [Roderick—Ed.] Chisholm has held that the following gives the necessary and sufficient conditions for knowledge:[2]

(b) S knows that P   IFF   (i) S accepts P,
                                             (ii) S has adequate evidence for P, and
                                             (iii) P is true.

[A. J.—Ed.] Ayer has stated the necessary and sufficient conditions for knowledge as follows:[3]

(c) S knows that P   IFF   (i) P is true,
                                             (ii) S is sure that P is true, and
                                             (iii) S has the right to be sure that P is true.

I shall argue that (a) is false in that the conditions stated therein do not constitute a *sufficient* condition for the truth of the proposition that S knows that P. The same argument will show that (b) and (c) fail if 'has adequate evidence for' or 'has the right to be sure that' is substituted for 'is justified in believing that' throughout.

I shall begin by noting two points. First, in that sense of 'justified' in which S's being justified in believing P is a necessary condition of S's knowing that P, it is possible for a person to be justified in believing a proposition that is in fact false. Secondly, for any proposition P, if S is justified in believing P, and P entails Q, and S deduces Q from P and accepts Q as a result of this deduction, then S is justified in believing Q. Keeping these two points in mind, I shall now present two cases in which the conditions stated in (a) are true for some proposition, though it is at the same time false that the person in question knows that proposition.

---

[1] Plato seems to be considering some such definition at *Theaetetus* 201, and perhaps accepting one at *Meno* 98.

[2] Roderick M. Chisholm, *Perceiving: a Philosophical Study*, Cornell University Press (Ithaca, New York, 1957), p. 16.

[3] A. J. Ayer, *The Problem of Knowledge*, Macmillan (London, 1956), p. 34.

Case I

Suppose that Smith and Jones have applied for a certain job. And suppose that Smith has strong evidence for the following conjunctive proposition:

(d) Jones is the man who will get the job, and Jones has ten coins in his pocket.

Smith's evidence for (d) might be that the president of the company assured him that Jones would in the end be selected, and that he, Smith, had counted the coins in Jones's pocket ten minutes ago. Proposition (d) entails:

(e) The man who will get the job has ten coins in his pocket.

Let us suppose that Smith sees the entailment from (d) to (e), and accepts (e) on the grounds of (d), for which he has strong evidence. In this case, Smith is clearly justified in believing that (e) is true.

But imagine, further, that unknown to Smith, he himself, not Jones, will get the job. And, also, unknown to Smith, he himself has ten coins in his pocket. Proposition (e) is then true, though proposition (d), from which Smith inferred (e), is false. In our example, then, all of the following are true: (*i*) (e) is true, (*ii*) Smith believes that (e) is true, and (*iii*) Smith is justified in believing that (e) is true. But it is equally clear that Smith does not *know* that (e) is true; for (e) is true in virtue of the number of coins in Smith's pocket, while Smith does not know how many coins are in Smith's pocket, and bases his belief in (e) on a count of the coins in Jones's pocket, whom he falsely believes to be the man who will get the job.

Case II

Let us suppose that Smith has strong evidence for the following proposition:

(f) Jones owns a Ford.

Smith's evidence might be that Jones has at all times in the past within Smith's memory owned a car, and always a Ford, and that Jones has just offered Smith a ride while driving a Ford. Let us imagine, now, that Smith has another friend, Brown, of whose whereabouts he is totally ignorant. Smith selects three place names quite at random and constructs the following three propositions:

(g) Either Jones owns a Ford, or Brown is in Boston.
(h) Either Jones owns a Ford, or Brown is in Barcelona.
(i) Either Jones owns a Ford, or Brown is in Brest-Litovsk.

Each of these propositions is entailed by (f). Imagine that Smith realizes the entailment of each of these propositions he has constructed by (f), and proceeds to accept (g), (h), and (i) on the basis of (f). Smith has correctly inferred (g), (h), and (i) from a proposition for which he has strong evidence. Smith is therefore completely justified in believing each of these three propositions. Smith, of course, has no idea where Brown is.

But imagine now that two further conditions hold. First, Jones does *not* own a Ford, but is at present driving a ʳented car. And secondly, by the sheerest coincidence, and entirely unknown to Smith, the place mentioned in proposition (h) happens really to be the place where Brown is. If these two conditions hold, then Smith does *not* know that (h) is true, even though (*i*) (h) *is* true, (*ii*) Smith does believe that (h) is true, and (*iii*) Smith is justified in believing that (h) is true.

These two examples show that definition (a) does not state a *sufficient* condition for someone's knowing a given proposition. The same cases, with appropriate changes, will suffice to show that neither definition (b) nor definition (c) do so either.

6

Roderick M. Chisholm
The Terms of Epistemic Appraisal

Roderick M. Chisholm, Romeo Elton Professor of Natural Theology and Professor of Philosophy at Brown University, is one of the most influential philosophers in the United States today. He is the author of a number of influential books, particularly bearing on the analysis and defense of the justified-true-belief account of knowledge, foundationalism, the theory of perception, and the analysis of intentionality and of intentional contexts. He is the author of Perceiving *(1957) and of* Theory of Knowledge *(1966), which has just appeared in revised form. And he is the editor of* Realism and the Background of Phenomenology *(1960) and of Brentano's* The True and the Evident *(1966). He is in fact largely responsible for awakening the interest of American philosophers in Brentano's distinctive views—notably concerning intentionality.*

Chisholm has been productive in a variety of fields and combines in an original way not only his familiarity with classical philosophy but also his interests in both Anglo-American and Continental philosophy. His discussions of the definition of knowledge and of the conditions of intentionality have set puzzles that are among the most discussed in the contemporary literature. He is certainly the best-known defender of a subtle version of foundationalism.

Chisholm brings to much-discussed issues an interpretation, always well worked out but subject to continuing and sustained revision, that is rarely supported by fashionable currents but that is nonetheless extremely difficult to defeat. This is

Roderick M. Chisholm, *Theory of Knowledge*, 2nd edition, © 1977, pp. 5–15. Reprinted by permission of Prentice-Hall, Inc., Englewood Cliffs, New Jersey.

*because he revises and tightens his formulations in the light of effective
counterinstances posed for earlier versions of his views. His production gives the
impression of leading vigorously to an as yet unformulated synthesis. But his
interests are so diverse that the form of the accumulating synthesis is not easily
anticipated.*

1. *Epistemic Appraisal*

The theory of knowledge could be said to have as its subject matter the *justification of belief*, or, more exactly, the justification of *believing*.

The sense of "believe" that is here intended may be illustrated by contrasting a theist, an atheist, and an agnostic. The theist believes that there is a God; the atheist believes that there is no God; and the agnostic doesn't believe either of these things. We may say that what it is that the theist believes contradicts what it is that the atheist believes. And so we may also say that there is something that the theist believes and there is another thing that the atheist believes; these two things contradict each other and the agnostic doesn't believe either one of them. Using a traditional terminology, we may say that the things in question are *propositions,* one of them being the proposition that there is a God and the other being the proposition that there is no God.[1]

What one believes, then, is always a proposition. Hence we might characterize propositions by saying that they are the sorts of things that can be believed. They are things that *could* be objects of belief.

In what follows, it will sometimes be convenient to replace the word "believe" by the word "accept" and then to speak of the propositions that a person *accepts.* It will also be convenient to introduce the word "withhold" and say that a person *withholds* a certain proposition provided he does not accept the proposition and also does not accept the negation or contradictory of the proposition. We could then say that the agnostic withholds the proposition that there is a God, for he does not believe that there is a God and he does not believe that there is no God. And since he thus withholds the proposition that there is a God, then, *ipso facto,* he withholds the proposition that there is no God.

So far as belief is concerned, then, there are three attitudes that one may take toward a given proposition at any particular time: (1) one may believe (or accept) the proposition; (2) one may disbelieve the proposition, and this is the same thing as accepting its negation; or (3) one may withhold or suspend belief—that is to say, one may refrain from believing and from disbelieving the proposition.

Philosophical language, as well as ordinary language, frequently obscures the distinction between disbelieving and withholding. If a philosopher tells us that we should "reject" a certain proposition, he may mean that we should disbelieve it, i.e., that we should believe its negation. Or he may mean that we

---

[1] Occasionally we will use the expression "state of affairs" in place of "proposition."

should withhold the proposition. And if the man in the street tells us that he "does not believe" a given proposition, he is likely to mean that he believes its negation, but he *may* mean instead that he is withholding the proposition.

What now of justification?

The term "justify," in its application to a belief, is used as a term of epistemic appraisal—a term that is used to say something about the reasonableness of belief. The term "reasonable" itself, therefore, may also be used as a term of epistemic appraisal. The same is so for such terms as "evident," "probable," "gratuitous," "certain," "unacceptable," and "indifferent." Let us begin by considering some of these terms and noting how they are related to each other.

Since they are terms of appraisal, we may best see their interrelations by introducing a comparative term—an expression that may be used to compare different beliefs with respect to reasonableness. Thus we may say that one belief is *more reasonable than* another, or, more exactly, that one belief is more reasonable for a given person at a given time than is another belief. As alternatives to "more reasonable than," we might also use "epistemically better than" or "epistemically preferable to."

Let us consider two rather clear-cut uses of "more reasonable than." The first expresses a suggestion made by St. Augustine: even though there might be ground to question the reliability of the senses, it is *more reasonable* for most of us most of the time to believe that we can safely rely upon them than to believe that we cannot.[2] The second is somewhat different: even if there is in fact life upon Venus, nevertheless, for most of us at the present time, it is more reasonable to withhold the proposition that there is life upon Venus than it is to accept it.

We may ask, then, with respect to any given proposition and any given subject at any given time, which is the most reasonable course: believing the proposition, disbelieving the proposition, or withholding the proposition? In considering such a question, we may refer to the following possibilities among others: (1) believing the proposition is more reasonable than withholding it; (2) believing it is more reasonable than disbelieving it; and (3) withholding it is more reasonable than believing it.

2. Some Basic Epistemic Concepts

Let us now consider what is suggested by these possibilities.

1. A proposition falling within the first category is one such that (for a given subject at a given time) believing it is more reasonable than withholding it. Any such proposition could be said to be one that is beyond reasonable

---

[2] This thesis is suggested by St. Augustine in his polemics against the skeptics. See his *Against the Academicians* (Milwaukee: Marquette Univerity Press, 1942). The thesis is explicitly formulated by Bertrand Russell in *An Inquiry into Meaning and Truth* (New York: W. W. Norton & Company, Inc., 1940), p. 166: ". . . . beliefs caused by perception are to be accepted unless there are positive grounds for rejecting them."

doubt (for that subject at that time). Since the concept of thus being beyond reasonable doubt is one we will often use in this book, we will put our definition of it somewhat more formally as follows:

D1.1   *h* is *beyond reasonable doubt* for *S* =Df Accepting *h* is more reasonable for *S* than is withholding *h*.[3]

In this definition and others like it that will follow, we will assume that there is also a reference to some specific time. What is beyond reasonable doubt for a given person at one time need not be beyond reasonable doubt for that person at other times.

"Beyond reasonable doubt," in the sense just defined, may be said to be a term of high epistemic praise. Of the three possibilities we have noted, this one puts the proposition in the best possible light.

The propositions that satisfy the negation of this first category—those propositions which are such that it is *not* more reasonable to believe them than it is to withhold them—may be said to be epistemically *gratuitous*. They are gratuitous for there is no need, epistemically, to accept them.

2. The second category comprises those propositions which are such that believing them is more reasonable than disbelieving them. If we say of a proposition that it falls within this category, we are expressing only faint epistemic praise. For in saying that believing is more reasonable than disbelieving we may be saying only that the former is the lesser evil, epistemically. Consider, for example, the proposition that the Pope will be in Rome on the third Tuesday in October five years from now. Believing it, given the information we now have, is more reasonable than *disbelieving* it, i.e., it is more reasonable to believe that the Pope will be in Rome at that time than it is to believe that he will *not* be there. But withholding the proposition, surely, is more reasonable still.

Let us say of any proposition thus falling within our second category that it is one having some *presumption in its favor*. Let us add this second definition:

D1.2   *h* has *some presumption in its favor* for *S* =Df Accepting *h* is more reasonable for *S* than accepting not-*h*.

The concepts defined in our first two definitions are such that the first implies the second, but not conversely. That is to say, whatever is beyond reasonable doubt is also such that it has some presumption in its favor, but some propositions having some presumption in their favor are not such that they are beyond reasonable doubt.

The negation of this second category yields a class of propositions having somewhat questionable epistemic status. The propositions belonging to this class are those which are such that believing them is *not* more reasonable than disbelieving them. These propositions, then, will be such that there is *no* presumption in their favor.

3. If we say of a proposition that it falls within our third category, we are expressing epistemic dispraise or condemnation, for we are saying of it that

---

[3] [Note omitted—Ed.]

withholding is more reasonable than believing. We are saying "Nay"—but in the sense of "Do not believe" and not in the sense of "Believe that not." Let us say that any proposition falling within this category is epistemically *unacceptable*.

Among the propositions that are thus unacceptable are, of course, those which are such that their negations are reasonable, in the sense of our first definition above. But the class of unacceptable propositions would seem to be considerably wider than the class of propositions that have reasonable negations. Sextus Empiricus tells us that, according to the skeptic Agrippa, "it is necessary to suspend judgment altogether with regard to *everything* that is brought before us."[4] Other, more moderate skeptics would have us suspend judgment with respect merely to those propositions that refer "beyond the appearances." But according to both types of skeptic, there are unacceptable propositions that have unacceptable negations; for example, the proposition that there are many things "beyond the appearances" is unacceptable and so is its negation. The older positivistic philosophers of the nineteenth century said of metaphysical propositions that both they and their negations are unacceptable.[5] And if what we shall say below is correct, there are still other unacceptable propositions that have unacceptable negations. Hence, although we can say that all reasonable propositions have unacceptable negations, we cannot say that all unacceptable propositions have reasonable negations.

If a proposition falls under the negation of this third category, it will be one such that withholding it is not more reasonable than believing it; hence, we may say of it that it is acceptable. We add, then, this definition:

D1.3   *h* is *acceptable* for *S* =Df Withholding *h* is not more reasonable for *S* than accepting *h*.

All propositions that are beyond reasonable doubt will, of course, be acceptable, but there are many acceptable propositions that are not beyond reasonable doubt. An adequate theory of perception, for example, might require us to say this: if I have that experience which might naturally be expressed by saying that I "seem to see" a certain state of affairs (e.g., "I seem to see a man standing there"), then the state of affairs that I thus seem to perceive (the proposition that a man is standing there) is one that is, for me, *ipso facto*, acceptable. It

---

[4] Sextus Empiricus, *Outlines of Pyrrhonism*, Book I, Chapter 15, p. 177. Epictetus, however, reminds us that believing is often more reasonable than withholding and says this of the person who accepts the skepticism of Agrippa: "He has sensation and pretends that he has not; he is worse than dead. One man does not see the battle; he is ill off. The other sees it but stirs not, nor advances; his state is still more wretched. His sense of shame and self-respect is cut out of him, and his reasoning faculty, though not cut away, is brutalized. Am I to call this 'strength'? Heaven forbid, unless I call it 'strength' in those who sin against nature, that makes them do and say in public whatever occurs to their fancy." *Discourses*, Book I, Chapter 6 ("August Followers of the Academy"); quoted from *The Stoic and Epicurean Philosophers*, ed. Whitney J. Oates (New York: Random House, 1940), p. 233.

[5] But the positivistic philosophers of the twentieth century have held that there *are* no metaphysical propositions and hence that sentences that purport to express them have no sense.

may be, however, that although the proposition is thus acceptable, it is not beyond reasonable doubt; i.e., although withholding it is not more reasonable than believing it, believing it cannot be said to be more reasonable than withholding it. "Acceptable," then, expresses less praise than does "reasonable." But it expresses more praise than does the doubtful compliment, "Believing is more reasonable than disbelieving," which tells us merely that the proposition has *some* presumption in its favor.[6]

3. Certainty

There is epistemic praise that is even higher than "beyond reasonable doubt." For example, we may say of a proposition not only that it is beyond reasonable doubt for a man at a certain time, but also that it is *certain*, or *absolutely certain*, for that man at that time. We could say that a proposition is certain if it is beyond reasonable doubt and if it is at least as reasonable as any other proposition. Our definition, then, is this:

> D1.4   *h* is *certain* for S =Df *h* is beyond reasonable doubt for S, and there is no *i* such that accepting *i* is more reasonable for S than accepting *h*.

The epistemic concept here defined should be distinguished from the psychological concept which might be expressed by saying, "S feels certain that *h* is true." The two concepts are logically independent of each other. To distinguish our epistemic sense of "certain" from the psychological concept expressed by "feels certain," we will sometimes use the expression "absolutely certain."

We have suggested that if I seem to see a man standing before me, then the proposition that there is a man standing before me is one that is for me, at that time, acceptable. But what of the proposition expressed by the words, "I *seem* to see a man standing before me"? As we shall see, such propositions as this, along with some of the propositions of logic and mathematics, are propositions which, at times, can be said to be absolutely certain.

4. The Evident

What now is the epistemic status of the ordinary things we know—the proposition, say, that the sun is now shining, or that it was shining yesterday, or that

---

[6] Another important epistemic concept is that of a proposition being *counterbalanced*. A proposition is counterbalanced if there is as much, or as little, to be said in favor of accepting it as there is to be said in favor of accepting its negation. We may say of any such proposition that there is no presumption in its favor and also no presumption in favor of its negation. Thus we could define "*h* is counterbalanced for S" by saying: "Accepting *h* is not more reasonable for S than accepting not-*h*, and accepting *not-h* is not more reasonable for S than accepting *h*." The followers of Pyrrho held that, if a proposition is counterbalanced, then it ought to be withheld. And they tried to show, as far as possible, that every proposition is counterbalanced. Compare Sextus Empiricus, *Outlines of Pyrrhonism*, Book I, Chapters 4, 6, 22, and 24.

we are now in a room with other people? If we look just to the epistemic concepts that have been singled out so far, we must choose between saying either that these propositions are absolutely certain or else that they are not certain but are beyond reasonable doubt. To say that they are absolutely certain, however, would seem to be saying too much. And to say only that they are beyond reasonable doubt would seem to be saying not quite enough.

If we say that these propositions are *certain*, then we must say that no other propositions are *more* respectable epistemically than they are. For if a proposition h is absolutely certain for a man at a given time, then there is no proposition i which is such that it is more reasonable for him to believe i at that time than it is for him to believe h. But even though we *know* that the sun is now shining, that it was shining yesterday, and that we are now in a room with other people, there are propositions which are even *more* reasonable for us to believe than they are. Among these would be the elementary truths of arithmetic, or the propositions that each of us could express in English by "I exist," or indeed that it *seems* to be the case that the sun is now shining or that it shone yesterday or that there are many people in the room.

To say, then, of these ordinary things we know, that we are absolutely certain of them would seem to be saying too much. And yet it is not enough to say that these things have the status merely of being beyond reasonable doubt, i.e., of being such that it is more reasonable for us to believe them than to withhold them. There is more to be said for them than this.

Consider the building next door which is usually occupied. For most of us, the proposition that *someone or other* is now in that building is beyond reasonable doubt. But even though that proposition is now beyond reasonable doubt and even if, moreover, it is true, we don't *know* that it is true. But we *do* now know that there is someone in *this* building.

Consider another sort of example. We do now know that the man who was President of France last year was in Paris more often than not last year. And I think we can say that, for most of us, it is beyond reasonable doubt that the man who will be President of France next year will be in Paris more often than not next year. But this latter is not a proposition that any of us now knows to be true.

When we say of a proposition that it is known to be true, then we are saying somewhat more than that it is true and beyond reasonable doubt, and we are saying somewhat less than that it is true and absolutely certain. What, then, is the epistemic status of the ordinary things we know?

One traditional term for this status is "evident," and let us use it in this connection. We will say, of the ordinary things we know, that these things are *evident*. The epistemic status of being evident is more impressive, epistemically, than that of being merely beyond reasonable doubt, and it is less impressive, epistemically, than that of being absolutely certain. What, then, do we mean by the expression "h is evident for S," and how are we to relate this concept to our other epistemic concepts?

Let us say that an evident proposition is a proposition which is beyond reasonable doubt and which is such that any proposition that is more reasonable than it is one that is certain. In other words:

D1.5 *h* is evident for *S* =Df (i) *h* is beyond reasonable doubt for *S* and (ii) for every *i*, if accepting *i* is more reasonable for *S* than accepting *h*, then *i* is certain for *S*.

This definition presupposes that being evident, like being certain, is not capable of degrees.

Although, as we have said, a proposition may be evident and yet not absolutely certain, we may assume that every proposition that is absolutely certain is also one that is evident.

5. On Epistemic Referability

We have been trying to explicate some of the basic concepts of the theory of knowledge. It is obvious that, if we are able to explicate any given concept, we can do so only by making use of certain other concepts. Or, to put the matter in a somewhat different way, if we are able to define any given expression, we can do so only by making use of other expressions that we do not define. We have been using the undefined technical expression, "*p* is more reasonable than *q* for *S* at *t*" (or, alternatively put, "*p* is epistemically preferable to *q* for *S* at *t*"). Can we throw any light upon this undefined expression?

There are two ways of throwing light upon what is intended by an undefined expression. One is to make explicit the basic principles it is used to formulate. The other is to try to paraphrase the undefined expression into a different terminology. Let us consider each of these two procedures.

What basic principles may be formulated as axioms of the concept expressed by "more reasonable than"? Another way of putting the question is to ask: What are the basic principles of epistemic logic, or the logic of epistemic appraisal? Among these principles, I suggest, are the following four:

1. *More reasonable than* is an intentional concept: If believing one proposition is more reasonable than believing another for any given subject *S*, then *S* is at least able to *understand* or *grasp* the first proposition. It follows from this that only rational beings—things that are capable of understanding—are such that, for them, some propositions are more reasonable than others. It also follows that, if a proposition has positive epistemic status for a given subject *S*, that is to say, if it is such that for *S* it has some presumption in its favor, or is acceptable, or is beyond reasonable doubt, or is evident, or is certain, then it is a proposition that *S* understands.

2. *More reasonable than* is a transitive relation: If one thing is more reasonable than another and the other more reasonable than a third, then the first thing is more reasonable than the third. Thus if for a given subject believing a certain proposition *h* is more reasonable than disbelieving a certain other proposition *i*, and if disbelieving *i* is more reasonable than withholding still another proposition *j*, than believing *h* is more reasonable than withholding *j*.

3. *More reasonable than* is also asymmetrical: If one thing is more reasonable for one subject than another, then the other is not more reasonable for him than the one. Thus if withholding a proposition is more reasonable than believing it, then believing it is not more reasonable than withholding it.

4. And, finally, if withholding is not more reasonable than believing, then believing is more reasonable than disbelieving. Or, more exactly, for any proposition *h* and any subject *S*, if it is not more reasonable for *S* to withhold *h* than it is for him to believe *h*, then it is more reasonable for *S* to believe *h* than it is for him to disbelieve *h*. An instance of this principle would be: if agnosticism is not more reasonable than theism, then theism is more reasonable than atheism.[7]

We have said that there is a second way of making clear what is intended by an undefined expression. This way is to try to paraphrase that expression into a different terminology.

Let us consider the concept of what might be called an "intellectual requirement." We may assume that every person is subject to a purely intellectual requirement—that of trying his best to bring it about that, for every proposition *h* that he considers, he accepts *h* if and only if *h* is true.[8] One might say that this is the person's responsibility or duty *qua* intellectual being. (But as a requirement it is only a *prima facie* duty; it may be, and usually is, overridden by others, nonintellectual requirements, and it may be fulfilled more or less adequately.[9]) One way, then, of re-expressing the locution "*p* is more reasonable than *q* for *S* at *t*" is to say this: "*S* is so situated at *t* that his intellectual requirement, his responsibility as an intellectual being, is better fulfilled by *p* than by *q*."

One might ask: "So far as our purely intellectual requirements are concerned, isn't the proper thing always to play it safe and restrict our beliefs to those propositions that are absolutely certain?" The following observation by William James reminds us that, even if one is subject only to purely intellectual requirements, one should not be motivated *merely* by the desire to play it safe: "There are two ways of looking at our duty in the matter of opinion—ways en-

---

[7] For a formal epistemic system in which the last three of these principles appear, see Roderick M. Chisholm and Robert Keim, "A System of Epistemic Logic," *Ratio*, XV (1973), 99–115. The third and fourth principles above are there taken as axioms; the second is replaced by the stronger principle according to which the relation expressed by "not epistemically preferable" (or "not more reasonable than") is transitive. There are four other axioms in that system which may be suggested by the following informal statements: "Believing *h* is preferable to believing *i*, if and only if, believing not-*i* is preferable to believing not-*h*"; "Withholding *h* is the same in epistemic value as withholding *i*, if and only if, either believing *h* is the same in epistemic value as believing *i* or believing not-*h* is the same in epistemic value as believing *i*" (two propositions are the same in epistemic value if neither one is epistemically preferable to the other); "If believing *i* is preferable to believing *h* and also preferable to believing not-*h*, then withholding *h* is preferable to withholding *i*"; and "Withholding *h* is the same as withholding not-*h*." Compare also Philip L. Quinn, "Some Epistemic Implications of 'Crucial Experiments,'" *Studies in the History and Philosophy of Science*, V (1975), 59–72; and Robert Keim, "Epistemic Values and Epistemic Viewpoints," in *Analysis and Metaphysics*, ed., Keith Lehrer (Dordrecht: D. Reidel, 1975), pp. 75–92.

[8] See J. T. Stevenson, "On Doxastic Responsibility," in *Analysis and Metaphysics*, ed. Lehrer, pp. 229–253.

[9] I have discussed the concept of requirement in detail in "Practical Reason and the Logic of Requirement," in *Practical Reason*, ed. Stephen Körner (Oxford: Basil Blackwell, 1974), pp. 40–53. The concepts of *overriding*, of *prima facie duty*, and of *absolute duty* are there defined in terms of requirement.

tirely different, and yet ways about whose difference the theory of knowledge seems hitherto to have shown very little concern. We *must know the truth*: and we *must avoid error*—these are our first and great commandments as would-be knowers; but they are not two ways of stating an identical commandment, they are two separable laws."[10]

Each person, then, is subject to two quite different requirements in connection with any proposition he considers: (1) he should try his best to bring it about that if that proposition is true then he believe it; and (2) he should try his best to bring it about that if that proposition is false then he not believe it. Each requirement by itself would be quite simple: to fulfill the first, our purely intellectual being could simply believe *every* proposition that comes along; to fulfill the second, he could *refrain* from believing *any* proposition that comes along. To fulfill both is more difficult. If he had only the second requirement—that of trying his best to bring it about that if a proposition is false then he not believe that proposition—then he could always play it safe and never act at all, doxastically. But sometimes more than just playing it safe is necessary if he is also to fulfill the first requirement: that of trying his best, with respect to the propositions he considers, to believe the ones that are true.

Obviously there are some *true* propositions which are such that it is more reasonable, for us now, to withhold those propositions than it is for us to believe them.

And are there some *false* propositions which are such that it is more reasonable, for us now, to believe those propositions than it is for us to withhold them? We will find that this may well be true. Or, more exactly, we will find that, if the skeptics are mistaken and if, as a matter of fact, we know pretty much the things about the world that we now think we know, then it is quite possible that some false propositions are such that it is more reasonable for us to believe those propositions than it is for us to withhold them.

Indeed, we will find this: it is possible that there are some propositions which are both *evident* and false.[11] This fact makes the theory of knowledge more difficult than it otherwise would be and it has led some philosophers to wonder whether, after all, the things we know might not be restricted to those things that are absolutely certain. (For we will not find it possible that what is absolutely certain might be false.) But if we do in fact know most of those ordinary things that we think we know (that there are such and such pieces of furniture in the room, that the sun was shining yesterday, that the earth, as G. E. Moore put it, has existed for many years past), then we must reconcile ourselves to the possibility that on occasion some of those things that are evident to us are also false.

This possibility will be clear when we consider the indirectly evident. But first we will consider the directly evident.

---

[10] William James, *The Will to Believe and Other Essays in Popular Philosophy* (New York: David McKay Co., Inc., 1911), p. 17.

[11] It may be that Pierre Bayle was the first to call attention to this fact. See his *Historical and Critical Dictionary: Selections*, ed. Richard H. Popkin (Indianapolis: Bobbs-Merrill Company, Inc., 1965), pp. 199–201.

7

Keith Lehrer
Skepticism and Conceptual Change

Keith Lehrer, Professor of Philosophy at the University of Arizona, is particularly well known for his close analysis of the literature regarding the justified-true-belief conception of knowledge and related issues—including the Gettier problem, foundationalism, and skepticism. His most systematic effort to date appears in Knowledge (1974), *in which he argues that justification of ascriptions of knowledge does not depend on foundationalism but on the coherence of the subjective beliefs of an agent, freed from error.* He is the editor of Philosophical Studies; *has edited a number of anthologies dealing with determinism, meaning, and philosophical analysis; and is the co-author (with James Cornman) of an introductory philosophy text,* Philosophical Problems and Arguments (1968).

People say they know. Almost no one doubts that he and others know for certain that at least some contingent statements are true. But I doubt it. Not only do I doubt that anyone knows for certain that any such statement is true, I also doubt that the lack of such knowledge is a serious epistemic loss. On the contrary, I believe that reasonable belief and action, reasonable theory and practice, do not depend on our knowing for certain that any contingent statement is true. I shall undertake to defend my skepticism and to explain why such knowledge is otiose. By so doing, I shall construct what James Ferrier called, an agnoiology, a theory of ignorance.[1]

I

There are immediate problems facing any would be skeptic. Language and the conventions of language are fraught with dangers. When a man asserts anything or argues for anything, it is natural to take him to be claiming to know. Skeptical speech must be understood differently. When I write something and argue, you must not take me as claiming to know anything but only as telling you what I believe with the hope that you will too. Even when I say that premisses logically imply a conclusion, you must not take me to be claiming to

Keith Lehrer, "Skepticism and Conceptual Change," in Roderick M. Chisholm and Robert J. Swartz (eds.), *Empirical Knowledge: Readings from Contemporary Sources* (Englewood Cliffs, New Jersey: Prentice-Hall, 1973), pp. 47–58. Reprinted by permission of the author.

---

[1] James F. Ferrier, *Institutes of Metaphysics* (Edinburgh and London: William Blackwood & Sons, 1854).

know. It is only a statement of what I believe. Of course, I have my reasons for believing what I do; you shall soon be told what they are.

Most of my argument for skepticism must be counterargument. The principal theses I shall advance have been advanced before and have been rejected as fallacious, unintelligible, inconsistent, and just plain false. Let me, therefore, lay down my premisses without comment and then turn to their defense. There are only two. First, if a man knows for certain that p is true, then there is no chance that he is wrong in thinking p to be true. Second, if a statement is contingent, then there is always some chance that one is wrong in thinking it to be true. Therefore, no one ever knows for certain that any contingent statement is true. If both premisses are conceded the conclusion is ineluctable. I now turn to a defense of the premisses.

The second premiss must be given some interpretation which makes the first premiss plausible. If by saying that there is some chance that a man was wrong in thinking something to be true, I meant no more than that it was logically possible that he was wrong; then, though the second premiss might be readily accepted, the first would become dubious. For it is doubtful that it need be logically impossible for a man to be wrong before he can know for certain that he is correct. Thus, we must find some stronger interpretation of the second premiss in order to sustain the first.

What, then, do I mean by saying that there is some chance that a man is wrong in thinking something to be true? Most simply put, I mean that there is some *probability* that he is wrong. Of course, introducing the notion of probability at this point is entirely unilluminating without some explanation of what is implied by that notion. What kind of probability is involved? Rather than giving a formal explication of the concept, I shall appeal to an intuitive conception of *objective* probability. Consider an ordinary penny and the statement that the probability is ½ that a fair toss of the coin will turn up heads. There are a number of possible interpretations of this statement. According to the subjective interpretation, it means the betting odds the agent would accept are one to one, according to the logical interpretation, it means one to one is a fair betting quotient, according to the frequency interpretation, it means that in an infinite sequence of tosses the limit of the relative frequency of heads in tosses would approach ½ as a limit. But all of these interpretations suggest a more fundamental idea, to wit, that the coin has a certain physical property which explains why we expect the relative frequency to approach ½, why we think ½ is a fair betting quotient, and why we would accept such odds. This physical property is dispositional, like the property of being magnetized. It is manifested in the relative frequency with which the coin turns up heads when tossed, just as the magnetism of a nail is manifested in the movement of iron toward it.[2] This propensity has an explanation in the structure of the coin just as the magnetism has an explanation in the structure of the nail.

---

[2] The propensity interpretation is advocated by Karl R. Popper in "The Propensity Interpretation of Probability," *British Journal for the Philosophy of Science*, Vol. 10, 1959–1960, pp. 25–42.

When I say that there is some chance that one is wrong, I mean that there is some probability that one is wrong in this last sense. The probability of being wrong is a property of the world which is manifested in cases of error concerning the truth value of contingent statements. It is this propensity to err that would lead me to reject any measure of probability as a fair betting quotient which assigned a probability of one or zero to any contingent statement. For I expect the relative frequency of error to be greater than zero no matter what kind of contingent statements one considered. However, it is no defense to argue that it is always logically possible that one is wrong. The logical possibility of error does not sustain the empirical claim that the world contains such a propensity.

I shall defend my claim with premises concerning human conception. By considering the role of concepts in thought, we shall find reason to think that the world contains the kind of propensity in question, and, at the same time, explain that propensity. Kant is famous for his remark that intuitions without concepts are blind.[3] The idea is that experience by itself tells us nothing. The application of concepts to experience is required for any belief or knowledge about the world. Without concepts, cognition is impossible. To think that something is true, is to think that some concept applies. Hence, to think that any contingent statement is true, is to think that some concept applies. If all this seems obvious and commonplace, so much the better for my argument.

Some philosophers have argued that the application of a concept entails the logical possibility of misapplication. I believe this to be true, but it will not suffice. For, once again, I am arguing that there is a genuine propensity of the world manifested in our errors, and I cannot conclude that I am right by appeal to the logical possibility of error. The stronger conclusion may be obtained by consideration of the implications of conceptual change. No matter how well entrenched a concept may be in our beliefs about the world, it remains always and constantly subject to total rejection. To obtain our objectives, scientific or other, we may discard a concept as lacking a denotation. Any concept may be thrown onto the junkheap of discarded concepts along with demons, entelechies, and the like. Indeed, some philosophers have even suggested that mental concepts may one day meet that fate. It is difficult to understand how to describe such a situation without incoherence. For example, it will not do to say that we mistakenly *believe* mental concepts to apply. However, some alternative way may be found to say what it seems incoherent for us to say the way we now conceive of ourselves. Any concept, even mental ones, or the concept of existence, may be retired from conceptual service and be replaced by other concepts better suited to the job.

A few qualifications are important. First, any discarded concept can be refurbished. From one's own place in the history of thought, one thinks of progress as linear. This is natural, but sometimes mistaken. The concepts we reject may be better than the ones that supplant them. We may have to recycle what we have discarded. Second, the goals and objectives of empirical

---

[3] Immanuel Kant, *Critique of Pure Reason*, A 51 = B 75.

science, explanation and prediction most notably, are the ones that guide conceptual shifts today. This has not always been so, and there is no guarantee it will be so in the future. Today we think of conceptual change as being instigated by scientific revolutions, tomorrow some other kind of revolution may be the source of new conceptions.

Now we may draw our conclusions. The chance that we are wrong about the truth value of any contingent statement is the probability that we are wrong. The probability that we are wrong is a property, or feature, or propensity of the world that manifests itself in error. This propensity is explained in terms of human conception which continually shifts as a result of our attempt to apply concepts in order to facilitate our goals and objectives. Concepts are discarded to satisfy the goals of the day, and, as the day changes, so do our objectives. The continual flux in our acceptance and rejection of concepts explains why there is some chance that any concept does not apply to what we think it does. No concept is immune from the ravishment of conceptual change leaving it without any application whatever. Whatever contingent statement you think is true, there is some chance, some probability, that a concept applied in the statement lacks application. Hence, there is some chance you are wrong. However slender and not worth worrying about the chance or error may be, it is real. The reality of that change is an objective feature of the world.

The foregoing is my argument in defense of the second premise, that, for any contingent statement, there is always some chance that one is wrong in thinking it to be true. This premise describes a dispositional property of the world rather than a mere logical possibility. It says that, whatever contingent statement one thinks is true, the probability that one is wrong is greater than zero.

This probability interpretation of the chance of being wrong makes it difficult to extend the skeptical argument beyond contingency, because the usual calculus of probability contains an axiom affirming that all logical truths have a probability of one, and, even without this axiom, it may be demonstrated that some statements have a probability of one. Thus, one cannot argue that there is always some probability that one is wrong no matter what sort of statement one thinks is true without abandoning standard conceptions of probability. Whether some nonstandard conception of probability can be developed to give expression to the chance that we are wrong no matter what we think is a matter of speculation. Hence, I restrict my skepticism to contingent statements and standard conceptions of probability.

II

Having clarified the meaning of our second premise, let us return to the first. If a man knows for certain that something is true, then there is no chance that he is wrong in thinking it to be true. It is difficult to muster direct support for this premise. Many philosophers have said things that support it. Malcolm has contended that if a man knows for certain that something is true, then there is nothing he would count as evidence proving him to be incorrect.[4] Hintikka has concurred.[5] Locke held a similar opinion.[6] Other than appealing to the opinions of other philosophers, I can only appeal to you directly. Imagine that we agree that a man thinks some statement is true but also agree that there is some chance that he is wrong. Would it be correct for us to describe the man as knowing for certain that the statement is true? Consider one's own case. If you admit that there is some chance that a statement is false, it would be incorrect for you to describe yourself as knowing for certain that the statement is true. If you ask me whether I know for certain that Oswald shot Kennedy, I would concede that there is *some* chance that Oswald did not shoot Kennedy, and hence, that I do not know for certain that he did. And you, I believe, would describe me in the same way for the same reason. It would be incorrect for you to describe me as knowing for certain that Oswald shot Kennedy, simply because there is some chance that I am wrong in thinking that he did.

The most important defense of the premise in question is a proper understanding of it. When I say that if a man knows something for certain, then there is no chance that he is wrong, what I have said may remind one of a simple fallacy. The plausibility of the premise depends on separating it from fallacious lines of thought. It follows from the statement that a man knows for certain that a statement is true, that the statement in question is true. Hence, it is logically impossible that a man should know for certain that something is true and be wrong, because his knowing for certain entails that he is right. It would be fallacious to argue from the logical impossibility of both knowing for certain and being wrong to the conclusion that if a man knows for certain, then there is no chance that he is wrong. I am not arguing in that way.

A second fallacious argument would be one based on conditional probability. When I have spoken of the probability of being wrong, I was speaking of the unconditional or antecedent probability, not conditional probability. Of course, a contingent statement may have a probability of one conditionally on the basis of some statement, for example, every contingent statement has a conditional probability of one on the basis of itself. When we speak of the probability or chance of being wrong, we may be speaking of the conditional probability of being wrong on the basis of what we know. If a man knows for certain that a statement is true, then the conditional probability of his being wrong on the basis of what he knows is zero, because the statement in question is included in what he knows. However, it is again fallacious to argue from this to the conclusion that if a man knows for certain, then there is no chance that he is wrong, where the chance of being wrong is an unconditional probability. I am not arguing in this way either.

It should now be somewhat clearer what I mean by the first premise of my original argument. I mean that if a man knows for certain that a statement is

---

[4] Norman Malcolm, "Knowledge and Belief," *Mind*, N. S., Vol. LXI, 1952, pp. 178–189, esp. pp. 179–180.

[5] Jaakko Hintikka, *Knowledge and Belief* (Ithaca: Cornell University Press, 1962), p. 20.

[6] John Locke, *An Essay Concerning Human Understanding*, A. S. Pringle-Pattison ed. (London: Oxford University Press, 1924), p. 261.

true, then there is no chance that he is wrong in the sense that the objective unconditional probability of his being wrong is greater than zero. The objective unconditional probability is the dispositional property of the world that is explained, at least in part, by the nature of human conception. Moreover, it should also be clear why it is that ordinary men commonly, though incorrectly, believe that they know for certain that some contingent statements are true. They believe that there is no chance whatever that they are wrong in thinking some contingent statements are true and thus feel sure they know for certain that those statements are true. One reason they feel sure is that they have not reflected upon the ubiquity of conceptual application and conceptual change in all human thought. Once these matters are brought into focus, we may reasonably conclude that no man knows for certain that any contingent statement is true.

III

Having laid down my premisses and drawn my conclusions, I shall now consider what I consider to be the strongest counterarguments.

The first objection to my skeptical argument is a semantic one. It might be argued that there is an oddity in the speech of a man who denies that he knows for certain that he exists, that he has a hand on the end of his arm, and so forth. And this oddity may be taken as indicating that a skeptic such as myself either speaks without meaning or else must mean something different by the words he utters than is customary. But this conclusion is ill drawn. Anyone who denies what most men assert speaks oddly. There is more than one way to explain the systematic oddity of a man's speech. One way is to suppose that the man does not use certain words to mean what is ordinarily meant, that he means something different than what we ordinarily mean by some of his words. The other way is to suppose that such a person means what we ordinarily mean but has beliefs that are systematically different from the beliefs of other men. In my case, the simplest and correct explanation of why I say I do not know for certain when most men say they do, is that I have different beliefs concerning what people know than most men do. Most men believe that people know for certain that a variety of contingent statements are true. I do not believe that anyone ever knows for certain that such statements are true. That is why I say, oddly enough, that no one knows for certain that he exists or has a hand at the end of his arm. There is no simpler explanation for my speech, and therefore, the conclusion that I mean something out of the ordinary by the locution 'know for certain' is unnecessary and unreasonable.

A more serious objection is based on the assumption that there are contingent statements a man may incorrigibly believe to be true. This assumption has been disputed, and the concept of incorrigibility requires some explication. However, there is one familiar conception of incorrigibility that supports the assumption. Suppose that by saying a belief is incorrigible we mean that it is logically impossible that a man should believe such a statement to be true and yet be mistaken. It surely is very rare for a belief that a contingent statement is true to be incorrigible in this sense. Indeed, even beliefs about one's own immediate present experiences are not, for the most part, incorrigible. The reason is that one may believe something about what one is presently experiencing on the basis of inference, for example, from a premise one accepts on medical authority affirming that whenever one is experiencing E, an itch say, one is also experiencing E*, a pain say. Consequently one may believe one is experiencing E* and be mistaken because a premise of the inference leading to the belief is false. However, if I believe that I believe something, then I am believing a contingent statement, to wit, the statement that I believe something, and it is logically impossible that I should believe that statement and yet be mistaken. If I believe that statement, then it logically follows I believe something, which is the statement believed. So, I concede that there are at least some contingent statements a man may incorrigibly believe to be true.

However, if a man incorrigibly believes contingent statements to be true, it does not follow either that he knows for certain that the statement is true or that there is no chance that he is wrong in what he believes. A belief that a contingent statement S is true is incorrigible if and only if the conclusion that S is true follows logically from the premise that S is believed to be true. However, the logical truth that a conclusion follows from a premise does not imply that the conclusion is known for certain or that there is no chance that the conclusion is false. First, it would need to be known for certain that the original conclusion did follow from the premise, and, second, it would have to be known for certain that the premise is true. Only then could the truth that the conclusion followed logically from the premise imply that the conclusion was known for certain. The incorrigibility of a belief can only yield the conclusion that the statement believed is known for certain *if* it is known for certain that the statement is believed. Put in the first person, the incorrigibility of my belief that S is true can yield the conclusion that I know for certain that S is true only if I know for certain that I believe S to be true. Thus, the incorrigibility of my belief that I believe something only warrants the conclusion that I know for certain that I believe something if we add the premise that I know for certain that I believe that I believe something. This cannot be established by appeal to the incorrigibility of the belief without arguing in a circle. Hence, the appeal to the incorrigibility of beliefs fails to show that we know anything for certain. All it shows is that if we know for certain that we believe certain things, then there is something we know for certain. I concede that much because the concession is entirely harmless. For, as I suggested above, there is some chance, one that philosophers have worried about, that no one believes anything.

The third objection comes from philosophers of common sense who claim that we are warranted in saying that we know for certain that various statements expressing common sense beliefs are true.[7] The basic assumption is that at least some common sense beliefs are to be considered innocent until proven guilty.

---

[7] Cf. Thomas Reid, *The Works of Thomas Reid*, D.D. William Hamilton ed. (Edinburgh: Maclaugh and Steward, 1863), p. 234.

We may then argue that we know for certain that such beliefs are true until some proof to the contrary is presented on the other side.

The reply to this counterargument is that I have offered an argument on the other side, and the burden of proof now rests with my opponents. I agree that many of the beliefs of common sense are reasonable, though I do not think they are reasonable because they are beliefs of common sense. There is nothing sacrosanct about common sense. All that can be said for the beliefs of common sense is that they are what is believed, but the principle that whatever is, is reasonable, is no better principle of epistemology than of politics. Moreover, even if the beliefs of common sense are all reasonable, it hardly follows that there is no chance that they are wrong. So long as the belief of common sense is formulated in a contingent statement, there is some chance that the belief is wrong, and consequently, no one knows for certain that it is true.

The fourth objection is derived from those philosophers who argue that a statement is known to be true because of its explanatory virtues. Such a philosopher might argue that we know for certain that some contingent statement is true because it provides the best explanation of what we seek to explain or fits best into our total explanatory account.[8] My reply to this objection is based on the distinction between a correct and an incorrect explanation. An explanation, even the best explanation we have, may be incorrect because the explanatory statement is false. If the best explanation is incorrect for this reason, then we do not know for certain that the statement supplying the explanation is true. Thus, the argument proceeding from the premiss that a statement provides the best explanation to the conclusion that we know for certain that the statement is true is invalid. Moreover, even if the statement supplying the best explanation is true, it still does not follow that we know for certain that it is true. There is always some chance that even the best explanation is incorrect, whether or not it in fact happens to be so, and consequently, for all we know, even the best explanation is incorrect. Therefore, we do not know for certain that a statement supplying the best explanation is true.

The fifth and last objection is closely related to the two preceding ones. Some philosophers have argued that if it is not only reasonable to believe something but also as reasonable to believe that statement as any other; then, if the statement is true, it is one we know for certain.[9] It might be added that there are some contingent statements that it is as reasonable to believe as any other. Thus, assuming some contingent statements of the kind in question are true, we know for certain they are true.

This objection is the most difficult to deal with in a satisfactory manner. The most tempting reply is that, no matter what statement one considers, we do not know for certain that it is true because there is some chance that we are wrong in thinking it to be true. However, this reply is not genuinely available

---

[8] Cf. Gilbert Harman, "Knowledge, Inference, and Explanation," *American Philosophical Quarterly*, Vol. 5, 1968, pp. 164–173.

[9] Cf. R. M. Chisholm, *Perceiving* (Ithaca: Cornell University Press, 1957), p. 19.

because, as I conceded earlier, I cannot offer any satisfactory probabilistic explication of the sense in which there is a chance of being wrong in thinking a statement is true which is a logical theorem. Nevertheless, from the premiss that a contingent statement is true and as reasonable for me to believe as any other statement, it does not follow that I know for certain that the statement is true. First, if, as I believe, there is no statement that we know for certain, then even those true statements that are as reasonable for us to believe as any other are not statements we know for certain to be true. Second, if even there are some noncontingent statements that we know for certain to be true, it does not follow that we know for certain each true contingent statement that it is as reasonable for us to believe as those noncontingent statements we know for certain. There is some chance that we are wrong in thinking any contingent statement to be true. Even if the contingent statement is one that is as reasonable for me to believe as any other statement, the chance that I am wrong about it precludes my knowing for certain that it is true.

Having defended my skepticism against the most plausible objections, I should note that my principle thesis applies to itself. I have argued that there is always some chance that we are wrong no matter what contingent statement we think is true. As I interpret this statement, it tells us something about an objective property of the world. It is therefore a contingent statement. I concede, therefore, that there is some chance that I am wrong in saying that it is true. If I am right, nobody knows for certain that any contingent statement is true. I do not believe that anyone knows for certain that I am wrong.

IV

The conclusions reached so far are negative, or largely so. It is now time to consider the positive program that motivates what has gone before, and to explain why we need not mourn the passing of certainty as a great loss. Rational belief and rational action have been thought to depend upon a foundation of certain knowledge and to be impossible in the absence of such a foundation. But this is a mistake. We can offer a theory of reasonable belief and action that does not presuppose that we know for certain that any contingent statement is true. The broad outlines of such a theory may be sketched in a few words. Whether a belief or action is reasonable depends on two factors. One factor is what one values. The other factor is the probability of obtaining what one values. Once both values and probabilities are assigned, the reasonable belief or reasonable action may be calculated. The reasonable belief or action is the one that gives you a maximum of expected values. By construing rational belief and action in this way we can safely abandon the quest for certainty without giving up our claims to rationality.

First let us consider the matter of probability. It may seem that to assign probability we need to know for certain that some contingent statements are true. But this is incorrect. We may interpret probability in this context as subjective probabilities, as degrees of belief conforming to the calculus of probability, and as constituting our estimate of the objective probabilities discussed earlier. If you agree that there is always some chance of being wrong about any contingent statement, then you will not estimate the probability of any such statement as being equal to one. So your subjective probability for any contingent statement will be less than one but greater than zero.[10] Such probabilities enable us to give an account of rationality without certainty.

A problem remains. It will often seem appropriate to consider the conditional probability of some outcome of belief or action relative to our evidence, and such evidence looks as though it must be both contingent and also be known for certain. The solution to this problem is to repudiate the idea that acceptance of statements as evidence means knowing them for certain or even assigning them a probability of one. On the contrary, a statement is accepted as evidence because it competes favorably, that is, has a higher subjective probability, than other statements with which it competes for the status of evidence. I have argued that a statement may be regarded as competing for that status with any statement with which it could conceivably conflict, and therefore, with any statement except its logical consequences. What is accepted as evidence may change the subjective probabilities, but accepting a statement as evidence need not change the subjective probability of the statement at all. Hence, we need not assign evidence statements a probability of one, nor need we know for certain that such statements are true.[11]

With these considerations before us, the consequences of our theory may be drawn. Thomas Reid once suggested that a true skeptic would require the constant attention of his friends to keep him from stepping into dog kennels and walking in front of carriages. But the sort of skeptic we have been considering needs no such attention. Given the value he attaches to being unsoiled and uninjured and the high subjective probability he attaches to the statement that he will be soiled or injured if he steps in dog kennels or walks in front of carriages, it is only reasonable for him to avoid such actions. If he is reasonable in his actions, he need not suffer any indignity or harm not suffered by less skeptical companions.

Similar remarks apply concerning what one believes. Being a skeptic, I may for the most part believe what others do, excluding, of course, the belief of others that they know for certain that contingent statements are true. It may be reasonable for me to believe some contingent statement, not because I am willing to act as though the statement is true or know for certain that it is true, but because of what I value epistemically. Epistemic values differ from practical ones. For example, I may attach great epistemic value to believing those statements that explain what I seek to explain, though I attach no practical importance to explanation. If I value the understanding obtained from explanations, then it may be reasonable for me to believe contingent statements because

---

[10] For such an account of subjective probability, see *The Logic of Decision* (New York: McGraw Hill, 1965).

[11] I elaborate such a theory of evidence in "Induction and Conceptual Change," forthcoming in *Synthese*.

of their explanatory utility. And, so, being a skeptic, it may be reasonable for me to believe what best explains what I find puzzling, though I do not assign a probability of one to what I believe or assume that I know for certain that it is true. In a skeptical world, rational belief and action are shaped against a panorama of shifting probabilities without need of a permanent foundation of certain knowledge.

Analytic and Synthetic Truths

8

Immanuel Kant

Analytic and Synthetic Judgments

Immanuel Kant (1724–1804) is thought by many to be the greatest philosopher of all time. He was apparently the first major philosopher to pursue an almost exclusively academic career, teaching at the University at Königsberg, where he eventually obtained a professorship. He never married and was decidedly poor through half his life. Though a man of wit and wide interests—he was particularly interested in the French Revolution—Kant was reputed to be pedantic and so regular in his habits that the inhabitants of Königsberg set their clocks by his walks.

In his principal writings (the three great critiques: Critique of Pure Reason, Critique of Practical Reason, Critique of Judgment) *he adopted the rather stifling academic fashion of the day, which required a certain schematism in the presentation of material. The puzzled reception of the first* Critique *led him to attempt a simplification (*Prolegomena to Any Future Metaphysics) *and a revision of portions of his argument. Nevertheless, his genius initiated the genuinely modern phase of philosophical development. He appears when Newtonian physics was triumphant and when the extreme alternatives of the rationalist and empiricist positions (See Part III) seemed clearly inadequate.*

The central concern of the first Critique *is to determine the limits of our cognitive sources, particularly of reason alone (the rationalist emphasis) and of reason joined to sensory experience (Kant's original blending of rationalist and empiricist themes). The modernity of his orientation is in large part due to his realization that different propositions or judgments, resting as they do on different cognitive sources, cannot have the same epistemic standing. He distinguishes between* a priori *and* a posteriori *sources of knowledge (that is, between a reliance on reason alone and a reliance on sensory experience). He also distinguishes between analytic judgments (judgments in which what is conceived by the use of the predicate is already*

From *Immanuel Kant's Critique of Pure Reason*, Norman Kemp Smith, trans. (London: 1933), the Introduction, pp. 41–55. Reprinted by permission of St. Martin's Press, Inc., and Macmillan London and Basingstoke.

*contained in what is conceived by the use of the subject term) and synthetic
judgments (judgments in which this relationship does not hold).*

*He introduces, here, the distinct category of synthetic a priori judgments.
Though both necessary and universal, these do not depend simply on the
analytic relation between the terms employed. The peculiarity of the synthetic a
priori is that its necessity is ascribed on the condition that we have the knowledge that
we have. There is therefore some additional strain in Kant's insistence that these
judgments are a priori in the same sense in which analytic judgments are said to be
a priori.*

*The upshot of Kant's examination of this central notion is to preclude
knowledge of metaphysics; that is, in his view, to hold that it is impossible to have
knowledge of "things-in-themselves," things apart from their appearances as given in
sensory experience, and that human understanding is restricted to knowing a priori
only certain conceptual conditions under which any sensory experience will be
possible at all. Nevertheless, Kant's larger purpose in writing the first Critique
was to preserve, against the threat of Newtonian physics, the domain of human
freedom and morality.*

*Here, the internal tensions of Kant's large system become most
apparent. The distinction between the appearances of things (of which we can have
knowledge) and things-in-themselves (of which we cannot) is invoked so that,
in the moral domain, we can think of ourselves as free of the deterministic order of
nature. The implausibility of the thesis of one and the same agent viewing himself
both as subject to the condition of things perceived by the senses and as a
thing-in-itself, which is not subject to those conditions, Kant never seems to have
satisfactorily resolved. His distinctive moral theory is elaborated in the*
Foundations of the Metaphysics of Morals.

The Distinction Between Pure and Empirical Knowledge

There can be no doubt that all our knowledge begins with experience. For how
should our faculty of knowledge be awakened into action did not objects affecting our senses partly of themselves produce representations, partly arouse the
activity of our understanding to compare these representations, and, by combining or separating them, work up the raw material of the sensible impressions
into that knowledge of objects which is entitled experience? In the order of
time, therefore, we have no knowledge antecedent to experience, and with
experience all our knowledge begins.

But though all our knowledge begins with experience, it does not follow
that it all arises out of experience. For it may well be that even our empirical
knowledge is made up of what we receive through impressions and of what
our own faculty of knowledge (sensible impressions serving merely as the
occasion) supplies from itself. If our faculty of knowledge makes any such
addition, it may be that we are not in a position to distinguish it from the raw
material, until with long practice of attention we have become skilled in
separating it.

This, then, is a question which at least calls for closer examination, and
does not allow of any off-hand answer:—whether there is any knowledge that is
thus independent of experience and even of all impressions of the senses. Such

knowledge is entitled *a priori*, and distinguished from the *empirical*, which has its sources *a posteriori*, that is, in experience.

The expression '*a priori*' does not, however, indicate with sufficient precision the full meaning of our question. For it has been customary to say, even of much knowledge that is derived from empirical sources, that we have it or are capable of having it *a priori*, meaning thereby that we do not derive it immediately from experience, but from a universal rule—a rule which is itself, however, borrowed by us from experience. Thus we would say of a man who undermined the foundations of his house, that he might have known *a priori* that it would fall, that is, that he need not have waited for the experience of its actual falling. But still he could not know this completely *a priori*. For he had first to learn through experience that bodies are heavy, and therefore fall when their supports are withdrawn.

In what follows, therefore, we shall understand by *a priori* knowledge, not knowledge independent of this or that experience, but knowledge absolutely independent of all experience. Opposed to it is empirical knowledge, which is knowledge possible only *a posteriori*, that is, through experience. A *priori* modes of knowledge are entitled pure when there is no admixture of anything empirical. Thus, for instance, the proposition, 'every alteration has its cause', while an *a priori* proposition, is not a pure proposition, because alteration is a concept which can be derived only from experience.

We Are in Possession of Certain Modes of A Priori Knowledge, and Even the Common Understanding Is Never Without Them

What we here require is a criterion [*Merkmal*] by which to distinguish with certainty between pure and empirical knowledge. Experience teaches us that a thing is so and so, but not that it cannot be otherwise. First, then, if we have a proposition which in being thought is thought as *necessary*, it is an *a priori* judgment; and if, besides, it is not derived from any proposition except one which also has the validity of a necessary judgment, it is an absolutely *a priori* judgment. Secondly, experience never confers on its judgments true or strict, but only assumed and comparative *universality*, through induction. We can properly only say, therefore, that, so far as we have hitherto observed, there is no exception to this or that rule. If, then, a judgment is thought with strict universality, that is, in such manner that no exception is allowed as possible, it is not derived from experience, but is valid absolutely *a priori*. Empirical universality is only an arbitrary extension of a validity holding in most cases to one which holds in all, for instance, in the proposition, 'all bodies are heavy'. When, on the other hand, strict universality is essential to a judgment, this indicates a special source of knowledge, namely, a faculty of *a priori* knowledge. Necessity and strict universality are thus sure criteria of *a priori* knowledge, and are inseparable from one another. But since in the employment of these criteria the contingency of judgments is sometimes more easily shown than their empirical limitation, or, as sometimes also happens, their unlimited universality can be more convincingly proved than their necessity, it is advisable to use the two criteria separately, each by itself being infallible.

Now it is easy to show that there actually are in human knowledge judgments which are necessary and in the strictest sense universal, and which are therefore pure *a priori* judgments. If an example from the sciences be desired, we have only to look to any of the propositions of mathematics; if we seek an example from the understanding in its quite ordinary employment, the proposition, 'every alteration must have a cause', will serve our purpose. In the latter case, indeed, the very concept of a cause so manifestly contains the concept of a necessity of connection with an effect and of the strict universality of the rule, that the concept would be altogether lost if we attempted to derive it, as Hume has done, from a repeated association of that which happens with that which precedes, and from a custom of connecting representations, a custom originating in this repeated association, and constituting therefore a merely subjective necessity. Even without appealing to such examples, it is possible to show that pure *a priori* principles are indispensable for the possibility of experience, and so to prove their existence *a priori*. For whence could experience derive its certainty, if all the rules, according to which it proceeds, were always themselves empirical, and therefore contingent? Such rules could hardly be regarded as first principles. At present, however, we may be content to have established the fact that our faculty of knowledge does have a pure employment, and to have shown what are the criteria of such an employment.

Such *a priori* origin is manifest in certain concepts, no less than in judgments. If we remove from our empirical concept of a body, one by one, every feature in it which is [merely] empirical, the colour, the hardness or softness, the weight, even the impenetrability, there still remains the space which the body (now entirely vanished) occupied, and this cannot be removed. Again, if we remove from our empirical concept of any object, corporeal or incorporeal, all properties which experience has taught us, we yet cannot take away that property through which the object is thought as substance or as inhering in a substance (although this concept of substance is more determinate than that of an object in general). Owing, therefore, to the necessity with which this concept of substance forces itself upon us, we have no option save to admit that it has its seat in our faculty of *a priori* knowledge.

Philosophy Stands in Need of a Science
Which Shall Determine the Possibility, the Principles,
and the Extent of All A Priori Knowledge

But what is still more extraordinary than all the preceding is this, that certain modes of knowledge leave the field of all possible experiences and have the appearance of extending the scope of our judgments beyond all limits of experience, and this by means of concepts to which no corresponding object can ever be given in experience.

It is precisely by means of the latter modes of knowledge, in a realm beyond the world of the senses, where experience can yield neither guidance nor correction, that our reason carries on those enquiries which owing to their importance we consider to be far more excellent, and in their purpose far more lofty, than all that the understanding can learn in the field of appearances. Indeed we prefer to run every risk of error rather than desist from such urgent enquiries, on the ground of their dubious character, or from disdain and indifference. These unavoidable problems set by pure reason itself are *God, freedom,* and *immortality*. The science which, with all its preparations, is in its final intention directed solely to their solution is metaphysics; and its procedure is at first dogmatic, that is, it confidently sets itself to this task without any previous examination of the capacity or incapacity of reason for so great an undertaking.

Now it does indeed seem natural that, as soon as we have left the ground of experience, we should, through careful enquiries, assure ourselves as to the foundations of any building that we propose to erect, not making use of any knowledge that we possess without first determining whence it has come, and not trusting to principles without knowing their origin. It is natural, that is to say, that the question should first be considered, how the understanding can arrive at all this knowledge *a priori*, and what extent, validity, and worth it may have. Nothing, indeed, could be more natural, if by the term 'natural' we signify what fittingly and reasonably ought to happen. But if we mean by 'natural' what ordinarily happens, then on the contrary nothing is more natural and more intelligible than the fact that this enquiry has been so long neglected. For one part of this knowledge, the mathematical, has long been of established reliability, and so gives rise to a favourable presumption as regards the other part, which may yet be of quite different nature. Besides, once we are outside the circle of experience, we can be sure of not being *contradicted* by experience. The charm of extending our knowledge is so great that nothing short of encountering a direct contradiction can suffice to arrest us in our course; and this can be avoided, if we are careful in our fabrications—which none the less will still remain fabrications. Mathematics gives us a shining example of how far, independently of experience, we can progress in *a priori* knowledge. It does, indeed, occupy itself with objects and with knowledge solely in so far as they allow of being exhibited in intuition. But this circumstance is easily overlooked, since this intuition can itself be given *a priori*, and is therefore hardly to be distinguished from a bare and pure concept. Misled by such a proof of the power of reason, the demand for the extension of knowledge recognises no limits. The light dove, cleaving the air in her free flight, and feeling its resistance, might imagine that its flight would be still easier in empty space. It was thus that Plato left the world of the senses, as setting too narrow limits to the understanding, and ventured out beyond it on the wings of the ideas, in the empty space of the pure understanding. He did not observe that with all his efforts he made no advance—meeting no resistance that might, as it were, serve as a support upon which he could take a stand, to which he could apply his powers, and so set his understanding in motion. It is, indeed, the common fate of human reason to complete its speculative structures as speedily as may be, and only afterwards to enquire whether the foundations are reliable. All sorts of excuses will then be appealed to, in order to reassure us of their solidity, or rather indeed to enable us to dispense altogether with so late and so dangerous an enquiry. But what keeps us, during the actual building, free from all apprehension and suspicion, and flatters us with a seeming thoroughness, in this other circumstance, namely, that a great, perhaps the greatest, part of the business of our reason consists in analysis of the concepts which we already have of objects. This analysis supplies us with a considerable body of knowledge, which, while nothing but explanation or elucidation of what has already been thought in our concepts, though in a confused manner, is yet prized as being, at least as regards its form, new insight. But so far as the matter or content is concerned, there has been no extension of our previously possessed concepts, but only an analysis of them. Since this procedure yields real knowledge *a priori*, which progresses in an assured and useful fashion, reason is so far misled as surreptitiously to introduce, without itself being aware of so doing, assertions of an entirely different order, in which it attaches to given concepts others completely foreign to them, and moreover attaches them *a priori*. And yet it is not known how reason can be in position to do this. Such a question is never so much as thought of. I shall therefore at once proceed to deal with the difference between these two kinds of knowledge.

The Distinction Between Analytic and Synthetic Judgments

In all judgments in which the relation of a subject to the predicate is thought (I take into consideration affirmative judgments only, the subsequent application to negative judgments being easily made), this relation is possible in two different ways. Either the predicate B belongs to the subject A, as something which is (covertly) contained in this concept A; or B lies outside the concept A, although it does indeed stand in connection with it. In the one case I entitle the judgment analytic, in the other synthetic. Analytic judgments (affirmative) are therefore those in which the connection of the predicate with the subject is thought through identity; those in which this connection is thought without identity should be entitled synthetic. The former, as adding nothing through the predicate to the concept of the subject, but merely breaking it up into those constituent concepts that have all along been thought in it, although confusedly, can also be entitled explicative. The latter, on the other hand, add to the concept of the subject a predicate which has not been in any wise thought in it, and which no analysis could possibly extract from it; and they may therefore be entitled ampliative. If I say, for instance, 'All bodies are extended', this is an analytic judgment. For I do not require to go beyond the concept which I connect with 'body' in order to find extension as bound up with it. To meet with this predicate, I have merely to analyse the concept, that is, to become conscious to myself of the manifold which I always think in that concept. The judgment is therefore analytic. But when I say, 'All bodies are heavy', the predicate is something quite different from anything that I think in the mere concept of body in general; and the addition of such a predicate therefore yields a synthetic judgment.

Judgments of experience, as such, are one and all synthetic. For it would be absurd to found an analytic judgment on experience. Since, in framing the judgment, I must not go outside my concept, there is no need to appeal to the testimony of experience in its support. That a body is extended is a proposition that holds *a priori* and is not empirical. For, before appealing to experience, I have already in the concept of body all the conditions required for my judgment. I have only to extract from it, in accordance with the principle of contradiction, the required predicate, and in so doing can at the same time become conscious of the necessity of the judgment—and that is what experience could never have taught me. On the other hand, though I do not include in the concept of a body in general the predicate 'weight', none the less this concept indicates an object of experience through one of its parts, and I can add to that part other parts of this same experience, as in this way belonging together with the concept. From the start I can apprehend the concept of body analytically through the characters of extension, impenetrability, figure, etc., all of which are thought in the concept. Now, however, looking back on the experience from which I have derived this concept of body, and finding weight to be invariably connected with the above characters, I attach it as a predicate to the concept; and in doing so I attach it synthetically, and am therefore extending my knowledge. The possibility of the synthesis of the predicate 'weight' with the concept of 'body' thus rests upon experience. While the one concept is not contained in the other, they yet belong to one another, though only contingently, as parts of a whole, namely, of an experience which is itself a synthetic combination of intuitions.

But in *a priori* synthetic judgments this help is entirely lacking. [I do not here have the advantage of looking around in the field of experience.] Upon what, then, am I to rely, when I seek to go beyond the concept A, and to know that another concept B is connected with it? Through what is the synthesis made possible? Let us take the proposition, 'Everything which happens has its cause'. In the concept of 'something which happens', I do indeed think an existence which is preceded by a time, etc., and from this concept analytic judgments may be obtained. But the concept of a 'cause' lies entirely outside the other concept, and signifies something different from 'that which happens', and is not therefore in any way contained in this latter representation. How come I then to predicate of that which happens something quite different, and to apprehend that the concept of cause, though not contained in it, yet belongs, and indeed necessarily belongs, to it? What is here the unknown = X which gives support to the understanding when it believes that it can discover outside the concept A a predicate B foreign to this concept, which it yet at the same time considers to be connected with it? It cannot be experience, because the suggested principle has connected the second representation with the first, not only with greater universality, but also with the character of necessity, and therefore completely *a priori* and on the basis of mere concepts. Upon such synthetic, that is, ampliative principles, all our *a priori* speculative knowledge must ultimately rest; analytic judgments are very important, and indeed necessary, but only for obtaining that clearness in the concepts which is requisite for such a sure and wide synthesis as will lead to a genuinely new addition to all previous knowledge.

In All Theoretical Sciences of Reason Synthetic
A Priori Judgments Are Contained as Principles

1. *All mathematical judgments, without exception, are synthetic.* This fact, though incontestably certain and in its consequences very important, has hitherto escaped the notice of those who are engaged in the analysis of human reason, and is, indeed, directly opposed to all their conjectures. For as it was found that all mathematical inferences proceed in accordance with the principle of contradiction (which the nature of all apodeictic certainty requires), it was supposed that the fundamental propositions of the science can themselves be known to be true through that principle. This is an erroneous view. For though a synthetic proposition can indeed be discerned in accordance with the principle of contradiction, this can only be if another synthetic proposition is presupposed, and if it can then be apprehended as following from this other proposition; it can never be so discerned in and by itself.

First of all, it has to be noted that mathematical propositions, strictly so called, are always judgments *a priori*, not empirical; because they carry with them necessity, which cannot be derived from experience. If this be demurred to, I am willing to limit my statement to *pure* mathematics, the very concept of which implies that it does not contain empirical, but only pure *a priori* knowledge.

We might, indeed, at first suppose that the proposition $7 + 5 = 12$ is a merely analytic proposition, and follows by the principle of contradiction from the concept of a sum of 7 and 5. But if we look more closely we find that the concept of the sum of 7 and 5 contains nothing save the union of the two numbers into one, and in this no thought is being taken as to what that single number may be which combines both. The concept of 12 is by no means already thought in merely thinking this union of 7 and 5; and I may analyse my concept of such a possible sum as long as I please, still I shall never find the 12 in it. We have to go outside these concepts, and call in the aid of the intuition which corresponds to one of them, our five fingers, for instance, or, as Segner does in his *Arithmetic*, five points, adding to the concept of 7, unit by unit, the five given in intuition. For starting with the number 7, and for the concept of 5 calling in the aid of the fingers of my hand as intuition, I now add one by one to the number 7 the units which I previously took together to form the number 5, and with the aid of that figure [the hand] see the number 12 come into being. That 5 should be added to 7, I have indeed already thought in the concept of a sum $= 7 + 5$, but not that this sum is equivalent to the number 12. Arithmetical propositions are therefore always synthetic. This is still more evident if we take larger numbers. For it is then obvious that, however we might turn and twist our concepts, we could never, by the mere analysis of them, and without the aid of intuition, discover what [the number is that] is the sum.

Just as little is any fundamental proposition of pure geometry analytic. That the straight line between two points is the shortest, is a synthetic proposition. For my concept of *straight* contains nothing of quantity, but only of quality. The concept of the shortest is wholly an addition, and cannot be derived, through any process of analysis, from the concept of the straight line. Intuition, therefore, must here be called in; only by its aid is the synthesis possible. What here causes us commonly to believe that the predicate of such apodeictic judgments is already contained in our concept, and that the judgment is therefore analytic, is merely the ambiguous character of the terms used. We are required to join in thought a certain predicate to a given concept, and this necessity is inherent in the concepts themselves. But the question is not what we *ought* to join in thought to the given concept, but what we *actually* think in it, even if only obscurely; and it is then manifest that, while the predicate is indeed attached necessarily to the concept, it is so in virtue of an intuition which must be added to the concept, not as thought in the concept itself.

Some few fundamental propositions, presupposed by the geometrician, are, indeed, really analytic, and rest on the principle of contradiction. But, as identical propositions, they serve only as links in the chain of method and not as principles; for instance, $a = a$; the whole is equal to itself; or $(a + b) > a$, that is, the whole is greater than its part. And even these propositions, though they are valid according to pure concepts, are only admitted in mathematics because they can be exhibited in intuition.

2. *Natural science (physics) contains* a priori *synthetic judgments as principles.* I need cite only two such judgments: that in all changes of the material world the quantity of matter remains unchanged; and that in all communication of motion, action and reaction must always be equal. Both propositions, it is evident, are not only necessary, and therefore in their origin *a priori*, but also synthetic. For in the concept of matter I do not think its permanence, but only its presence in the space which it occupies. I go outside and beyond the concept of matter, joining to it *a priori* in thought something which I have not thought *in* it. The proposition is not, therefore, analytic, but synthetic, and yet is thought *a priori*; and so likewise are the other propositions of the pure part of natural science.

3. *Metaphysics*, even if we look upon it as having hitherto failed in all its endeavours, is yet, owing to the nature of human reason, a quite indispensable science, and *ought to contain* a priori *synthetic knowledge*. For its business is not merely to analyse concepts which we make for ourselves *a priori* of things, and thereby to clarify them analytically, but to extend our *a priori* knowledge. And for this purpose we must employ principles which add to the given concept something that was not contained in it, and through *a priori* synthetic judgments venture out so far that experience is quite unable to follow us, as, for instance, in the proposition, that the world must have a first beginning, and such like. Thus metaphysics consists, at least *in intention*, entirely of *a priori* synthetic propositions.

9

John Stuart Mill

Of Demonstration and Necessary Truths

John Stuart Mill (1806–1873), possibly the most influential philosopher of the English-speaking world in the nineteenth century, was something of an infant prodigy. He was subjected to an unusually intensive intellectual training by his father, James Mill, who was in effect Jeremy Bentham's lieutenant in the organization of the radical movement associated with utilitarianism, the general theory that the greatest good is the good of the greatest number of persons.

The younger Mill was converted at fifteen to Bentham's persuasion; but at the age of twenty, a breakdown led him to explore other spiritual sources for emotional stability and social reform, which led him to develop his own distinctive version of utilitarianism. He was particularly attracted to the theories of Saint-Simon and Auguste Comte. He published extensively in philosophy and political economy and is best known for his System of Logic *(1843; eighth edition, 1872),* Utilitarianism *(1861), and* On Liberty *(1859).*

The System *was a great success and was used as a text at both Oxford and Cambridge. The most famous part of the* System *concerns Mill's methods of induction, the canons or procedures by which the data of particular experiences are thought to yield defensible generalizations regarding causal laws. These have formed a part of the standard training in induction since their appearance.*

Though Mill himself was disinclined to characterize his position as empiricist, his account shows the characteristic strength and weakness of empiricism. He holds that no knowledge is possible beyond experience. Within the empiricist framework he tries to avoid the regress of inferential knowledge; and, in a famous account, he denies public objects in terms of "possible sensations."

The radical nature of Mill's account of inference, deductive as well as inductive, is captured by his claim that all inference ultimately rests on our inference "from particulars to particulars." Deductive logic and mathematics are therefore not merely verbal but depend on inductive inferences that are not confined to what has been granted or observed. The theme finds its most prominent contemporary champion in W. V. Quine. *Mill also holds, however, that the principle of induction, the principle of the uniformity of nature, is similarly a particularly comprehensive empirical generalization.*

. . . If the foundation of all sciences, even deductive or demonstrative sciences, is Induction; if every step in the ratiocinations even of geometry is an act of induction; and if a train of reasoning is but bringing many inductions to bear upon the same subject of inquiry, and drawing a case within one induction by means of another; wherein lies the peculiar certainty always ascribed to the sciences which are entirely, or almost entirely, deductive? Why are they called

From John Stuart Mill, *A System of Logic*, 8th ed. (New York: Harper & Bros., 1874), Book II, Chaps. V–VI, pp. 168–170, 172–174, 187–191.

the Exact Sciences? Why are mathematical certainty, and the evidence of demonstration, common phrases to express the very highest degree of assurance attainable by reason? Why are mathematics by almost all philosophers, and (by some) even those branches of natural philosophy which, through the medium of mathematics, have been converted into deductive sciences, considered to be independent of the evidence of experience and observation, and characterized as systems of Necessary Truth?

The answer I conceive to be, that this character of necessity, ascribed to the truths of mathematics, and (even with some reservations to be hereafter made) the peculiar certainty attributed to them, is an illusion; in order to sustain which, it is necessary to suppose that those truths relate to, and express the properties of, purely imaginary objects. It is acknowledged that the conclusions of geometry are deduced, partly at least, from the so-called Definitions, and that those definitions are assumed to be correct representations, as far as they go, of the objects with which geometry is conversant. Now we have pointed out that, from a definition as such, no proposition, unless it be one concerning the meaning of a word, can ever follow; and that what apparently follows from a definition, follows in reality from an implied assumption that there exists a real thing conformable thereto. This assumption, in the case of the definitions of geometry, is not strictly true: there exist no real things exactly conformable to the definitions. There exist no points without magnitude; no lines without breadth, nor perfectly straight; no circles with all their radii exactly equal, nor squares with all their angles perfectly right. It will perhaps be said that the assumption does not extend to the actual, but only to the possible, existence of such things. I answer that, according to any test we have of possibility, they are not even possible. Their existence, so far as we can form any judgment, would seem to be inconsistent with the physical constitution of our planet at least, if not of the universe. To get rid of this difficulty, and at the same time to save the credit of the supposed system of necessary truth, it is customary to say that the points, lines, circles, and squares which are the subject of geometry, exist in our conceptions merely, and are part of our minds; which minds, by working on their own materials, construct an *a priori* science, the evidence of which is purely mental, and has nothing whatever to do with outward experience. By howsoever high authorities this doctrine may have been sanctioned, it appears to me psychologically incorrect. The points, lines, circles, and squares which any one has in his mind, are (I apprehend) simply copies of the points, lines, circles, and squares which he has known in his experience. Our idea of a point, I apprehend to be simply our idea of the *minimum visibile*, the smallest portion of surface which we can see. A line, as defined by geometers, is wholly inconceivable. We can reason about a line as if it had no breadth; because we have a power, which is the foundation of all the control we can exercise over the operations of our minds; the power, when a perception is present to our senses, or a conception to our intellects, of *attending* to a part only of that perception or conception, instead of the whole. But we can not *conceive* a line without breadth; we can form no mental picture of such a line: all the lines which we have in our minds are lines possessing breadth. If any one doubts this, we may refer him to his own experience. I much question if any one who fancies that he can conceive what is called a mathematical line, thinks so from the evidence of his consciousness: I suspect it is rather because he supposes that unless such a conception were possible, mathematics could not exist as a science: a supposition which there will be no difficulty in showing to be entirely groundless.

Since, then, neither in nature, nor in the human mind, do there exist any objects exactly corresponding to the definitions of geometry, while yet that science can not be supposed to be conversant about nonentities; nothing remains but to consider geometry as conversant with such lines, angles, and figures, as really exist; and the definitions, as they are called, must be regarded as some of our first and most obvious generalizations concerning those natural objects. The correctness of those generalizations, *as* generalizations, is without a flaw: the equality of all the radii of a circle is true of all circles, so far as it is true of any one: but it is not exactly true of any circle; it is only nearly true; so nearly that no error of any importance in practice will be incurred by feigning it to be exactly true. When we have occasion to extend these inductions, or their consequences, to cases in which the error would be appreciable—to lines of perceptible breadth or thickness, parallels which deviate sensibly from equidistance, and the like—we correct our conclusions, by combining with them a fresh set of propositions relating to the aberration; just as we also take in propositions relating to the physical or chemical properties of the material, if those properties happen to introduce any modification into the result; which they easily may, even with respect to figure and magnitude, as in the case, for instance, of expansion by heat. So long, however, as there exists no practical necessity for attending to any of the properties of the object except its geometrical properties, or to any of the natural irregularities in those, it is convenient to neglect the consideration of the other properties and of the irrregularities, and to reason as if these did not exist: accordingly, we formally announce in the definitions, that we intend to proceed on this plan. But it is an error to suppose, because we resolve to confine our attention to a certain number of the properties of an object, that we therefore conceive, or have an idea of, the object, denuded of its other properties. We are thinking, all the time, of precisely such objects as we have seen and touched, and with all the properties which naturally belong to them; but, for scientific convenience, we feign them to be divested of all properties, except those which are material to our purpose, and in regard to which we design to consider them.

The peculiar accuracy, supposed to be characteristic of the first principles of geometry, thus appears to be fictitious. The assertions on which the reasonings of the science are founded, do not, any more than in other sciences, exactly correspond with the fact; but we suppose that they do so, for the sake of tracing the consequences which follow from the supposition. The opinion of Dugald Stewart respecting the foundations of geometry, is, I conceive, substantially correct; that it is built on hypotheses; that it owes to this alone the peculiar certainty supposed to distinguish it; and that in any science whatever, by reasoning from a set of hypotheses, we may obtain a body of conclusions as certain as those of geometry, that is, as strictly in accordance with the hypotheses, and as irresistibly compelling assent, *on condition* that those hypotheses are true.[1]

When, therefore, it is affirmed that the conclusions of geometry are necessary truths, the necessity consists in reality only in this, that they correctly follow from the suppositions from which they are deduced. Those suppositions are so far from being necessary, that they are not even true; they purposely depart, more or less widely, from the truth. The only sense in which necessity can be ascribed to the conclusions of any scientific investigation, is that of legitimately following from some assumption, which, by the conditions of the inquiry, is not to be questioned. In this relation, of course, the derivative truths of every deductive science must stand to the inductions, or assumptions, on which the science is founded, and which, whether true or untrue, certain or doubtful in themselves, are always supposed certain for the purposes of the particular science. . . .

It remains to inquire, what is the ground of our belief in axioms—what is the evidence on which they rest? I answer, they are experimental truths; generalizations from observation. The proposition, Two straight lines can not inclose a space—or, in other words, Two straight lines which have once met, do not meet again, but continue to diverge—is an induction from the evidence of our senses.

.   .   .

It is not necessary to show that the truths which we call axioms are originally *suggested* by observation, and that we should never have known that two straight lines can not inclose a space if we had never seen a straight line: thus much being admitted by Dr. [William—Ed.] Whewell, and by all, in recent times, who have taken his view of the subject. But they contend, that it is not experience which *proves* the axiom; but that its truth is perceived *a priori*, by the constitution of the mind itself, from the first moment when the meaning of the proposition is apprehended; and without any necessity for verifying it by repeated trials, as is requisite in the case of truths really ascertained by observation.

---

[1] It is justly remarked by Professor Bain (*Logic*, ii., 134) that the word Hypothesis is here used in a somewhat peculiar sense. An hypothesis, in science, usually means a supposition not proved to be true, but surmised to be so, because if true it would account for certain known facts; and the final result of the speculation may be to prove its truth. The hypotheses spoken of in the text are of a different character; they are known not to be literally true, while as much of them as is true is not hypothetical, but certain. The two cases, however, resemble in the circumstance that in both we reason, not from a truth, but from an assumption, and the truth therefore of the conclusions is conditional, not categorical. This suffices to justify, in point of logical propriety, Stewart's use of the term. It is of course needful to bear in mind that the hypothetical element in the definitions of geometry is the assumption that what is very nearly true is exactly so. This unreal exactitude might be called a fiction, as properly as an hypothesis; but that appellation, still more than the other, would fail to point out the close relation which exists between the fictitious point or line and the points and lines of which we have experience.

They can not, however, but allow that the truth of the axiom, Two straight lines can not inclose a space, even if evident independently of experience, is also evident from experience. Whether the axiom needs confirmation or not, it receives confirmation in almost every instant of our lives; since we can not look at any two straight lines which intersect one another, without seeing that from that point they continue to diverge more and more. Experimental proof crowds in upon us in such endless profusion, and without one instance in which there can be even a suspicion of an exception to the rule, that we should soon have stronger ground for believing the axiom, even as an experimental truth, than we have for almost any of the general truths which we confessedly learn from the evidence of our senses. Independently of *a priori* evidence, we should certainly believe it with an intensity of conviction far greater than we accord to any ordinary physical truth: and this too at a time of life much earlier than that from which we date almost any part of our acquired knowledge, and much too early to admit of our retaining any recollection of the history of our intellectual operations at that period. Where then is the necessity for assuming that our recognition of these truths has a different origin from the rest of our knowledge, when its existence is perfectly accounted for by supposing its origin to be the same? when the causes which produce belief in all other instances, exist in this instance, and in a degree of strength as much superior to what exists in other cases, as the intensity of the belief itself is superior? The burden of proof lies on the advocates of the contrary opinion: it is for them to point out some fact, inconsistent with the supposition that this part of our knowledge of nature is derived from the same sources as every other part.[2]

This, for instance, they would be able to do, if they could prove chronologically that we had the conviction (at least practically) so early in infancy as to be anterior to those impressions on the senses, upon which, on the other

---

[2] Some persons find themselves prevented from believing that the axiom, Two straight lines can not inclose a space, could ever become known to us through experience, by a difficulty which may be stated as follows: If the straight lines spoken of are those contemplated in the definition—lines absolutely without breadth and absolutely straight—that such are incapable of inclosing a space is not proved by experience, for lines such as these do not present themselves in our experience. If, on the other hand, the lines meant are such straight lines as we do meet with in experience, lines straight enough for practical purposes, but in reality slightly zigzag, and with some, however trifling, breadth; as applied to these lines the axiom is not true: for two of them may, and sometimes do, inclose a small portion of space. In neither case, therefore, does experience prove the axiom.

Those who employ this argument to show that geometrical axioms can not be proved by induction, show themselves unfamiliar with a common and perfectly valid mode of inductive proof; proof by approximation. Though experience furnishes us with no lines so unimpeachably straight that two of them are incapable of inclosing the smallest space, it presents us with gradations of lines possessing less and less either of breadth or of flexure, of which series the straight line of the definition is the ideal limit. And observation shows that just as much, and as nearly, as the straight lines of experience approximate to having no breadth or flexure, so much and so nearly does the space-inclosing power of any two of them approach to zero. The inference that if they had no breadth or flexure at all, they would inclose no space at all, is a correct inductive inference from these facts, conformable to one of the four Inductive Methods hereinafter characterized, the Method of Concomitant Variations; of which the mathematical Doctrine of Limits presents the extreme case.

theory, the conviction is founded. This, however, can not be proved: the point being too far back to be within the reach of memory, and too obscure for external observation. The advocates of the *a priori* theory are obliged to have recourse to other arguments.

. . .

In [our] examination . . . into the nature of the evidence of those deductive sciences which are commonly represented to be systems of necessary truth, we have been led to the following conclusions. The results of those sciences are indeed necessary, in the sense of necessarily following from certain first principles, commonly called axioms and definitions; that is, of being certainly true if those axioms and definitions are so; for the word necessity, even in this acceptation of it, means no more than certainty. But their claim to the character of necessity in any sense beyond this, as implying an evidence independent of and superior to observation and experience, must depend on the previous establishment of such a claim in favor of the definitions and axioms themselves. With regard to axioms, we found that, considered as experimental truths, they rest on superabundant and obvious evidence. We inquired, whether, since this is the case, it be imperative to suppose any other evidence of those truths than experimental evidence, any other origin for our belief of them than an experimental origin. We decided, that the burden of proof lies with those who maintain the affirmative, and we examined, at considerable length, such arguments as they have produced. The examination having led to the rejection of those arguments, we have thought ourselves warranted in concluding that axioms are but a class, the most universal class, of inductions from experience; the simplest and easiest cases of generalization from the facts furnished to us by our senses or by our internal consciousness.

While the axioms of demonstrative sciences thus appeared to be experimental truths, the definitions, as they are incorrectly called, in those sciences, were found by us to be generalizations from experience which are not even, accurately speaking, truths; being propositions in which, while we assert of some kind of object, some property or properties which observation shows to belong to it, we at the same time deny that it possesses any other properties, though in truth other properties do in every individual instance accompany, and in almost all instances modify, the property thus exclusively predicated. The denial, therefore, is a mere fiction, or supposition, made for the purpose of excluding the consideration of those modifying circumstances, when their influence is of too trifling amount to be worth considering, or adjourning it, when important to a more convenient moment.

From these considerations it would appear that Deductive or Demonstrative Sciences are all, without exception, Inductive Sciences; that their evidence is that of experience; but that they are also, in virtue of the peculiar character of one indispensable portion of the general formulæ according to which their inductions are made, Hypothetical Sciences. Their conclusions are only true on certain suppositions, which are, or ought to be, approximations to the truth, but are seldom, if ever, exactly true; and to this hypothetical character is to be ascribed the peculiar certainty, which is supposed to be inherent in demonstration.

What we have now asserted, however, can not be received as universally true of Deductive or Demonstrative Sciences, until verified by being applied to the most remarkable of all those sciences, that of Numbers; the theory of the Calculus; Arithmetic and Algebra. It is harder to believe of the doctrines of this science than of any other, either that they are not truths a priori, but experimental truths, or that their peculiar certainty is owing to their being not absolute but only conditional truths. This, therefore, is a case which merits examination apart; and the more so, because on this subject we have a double set of doctrines to contend with; that of the a priori philosophers on one side; and on the other, a theory the most opposite to theirs, which was at one time very generally received, and is still far from being altogether exploded, among metaphysicians.

This theory attempts to solve the difficulty apparently inherent in the case, by representing the propositions of the science of numbers as merely verbal, and its processes as simple transformations of language, substitutions of one expression for another. The proposition, Two and one is equal to three, according to these writers, is not a truth, is not the assertion of a really existing fact, but a definition of the word three; a statement that mankind have agreed to use the name three as a sign exactly equivalent to two and one; to call by the former name whatever is called by the other more clumsy phrase. According to this doctrine, the longest process in algebra is but a succession of changes in terminology, by which equivalent expressions are substituted one for another; a series of translations of the same fact, from one into another language; though how, after such a series of translations, the fact itself comes out changed (as when we demonstrate a new geometrical theorem by algebra), they have not explained; and it is a difficulty which is fatal to their theory.

It must be acknowledged that there are peculiarities in the processes of arithmetic and algebra which render the theory in question very plausible, and have not unnaturally made those sciences the stronghold of Nominalism. The doctrine that we can discover facts, detect the hidden processes of nature, by an artful manipulation of language, is so contrary to common sense, that a person must have made some advances in philosophy to believe it: men fly to so paradoxical a belief to avoid, as they think, some even greater difficulty, which the vulgar do not see. What has led many to believe that reasoning is a mere verbal process, is, that no other theory seemed reconcilable with the nature of the Science of Numbers. For we do not carry any ideas along with us when we use the symbols of arithmetic or of algebra. In a geometrical demonstration we have a mental diagram, if not one on paper; AB, AC, are present to our imagination as lines, intersecting other lines, forming an angle with one another, and the like; but not so a and b. These may represent lines or any other magnitudes, but those magnitudes are never thought of; nothing is realized in our imagination but a and b. The ideas which, on the particular occasion, they happen to represent, are banished from the mind during every intermediate part of the process, between the beginning, when the premises are translated from things into signs, and the end, when the conclusion is translated back from signs into things. Nothing, then, being in the reasoner's mind but the symbols, what can seem more inadmissible than to contend that the reasoning process has to do with any thing more? We seem to have come to one of Bacon's Prerogative Instances; an *experimentum crucis* [crucial experiment—Ed.] on the nature of reasoning itself.

Nevertheless, it will appear on consideration, that this apparently so decisive instance is no instance at all; that there is in every step of an arithmetical or algebraical calculation a real induction, a real inference of facts from facts; and that what disguises the induction is simply its comprehensive nature, and the consequent extreme generality of the language. All numbers must be numbers of something; there are no such things as numbers in the abstract. *Ten* must mean ten bodies, or ten sounds, or ten beatings of the pulse. But though numbers must be numbers of something, they may be numbers of any thing. Propositions, therefore, concerning numbers, have the remarkable peculiarity that they are propositions concerning all things whatever; all objects, all existences of every kind, known to our experience. All things possess quantity; consist of parts which can be numbered; and in that character possess all the properties which are called properties of numbers. That half of four is two, must be true whatever the word four represents, whether four hours, four miles, or four pounds weight. We need only conceive a thing divided into four equal parts (and all things may be conceived as so divided), to be able to predicate of it every property of the number four, that is, every arithmetical proposition in which the number four stands on one side of the equation. Algebra extends the generalization still farther: every number represents that particular number of all things without distinction, but every algebraical symbol does more, it represents all numbers without distinction. As soon as we conceive a thing divided into equal parts, without knowing into what number of parts, we may call it *a* or *x*, and apply to it, without danger of error, every algebraical formula in the books. The proposition, $2(a + b) = 2a + 2b$, is a truth co-extensive with all nature. Since then algebraical truths are true of all things whatever, and not, like those of geometry, true of lines only or of angles only, it is no wonder that the symbols should not excite in our minds ideas of any things in particular. When we demonstrate the forty-seventh proposition of Euclid, it is not necessary that the words should raise in us an image of all right-angled triangles, but only of some one right-angled triangle: so in algebra we need not, under the symbol *a*, picture to ourselves all things whatever, but only some one thing; why not, then, the letter itself? The mere written characters, *a, b, x, y, z*, serve as well for representatives of Things in general, as any more complex and apparently more concrete conception. That we are conscious of them, however, in their character of things, and not of mere signs, is evident from the fact that our whole process of reasoning is carried on by predicating of them the properties of things. In resolving an algebraic equation, by what rules do we proceed? By applying at each step to *a, b*, and *x*, the proposition that equals added to equals make equals; that equals taken from equals leave equals; and other propositions founded on these two. These are not properties of language, or of signs as such, but of magnitudes, which is as much as to say, of all things. The inferences, therefore, which are successively drawn, are inferences concerning things, not symbols; though as any Things whatever will serve the turn, there is no necessity for keeping the idea of the Thing at all distinct, and consequently the process of thought may, in this case, be allowed without danger to do what all processes of thought, when they have been performed often, will do if permitted, namely, to become entirely mechanical. Hence the general language of algebra comes to be used familiarly without exciting ideas, as all other general language is prone to do from mere habit, though in no other case than this can it be done with complete safety. But when we look back to see from whence the probative force of the process is derived, we find that at every single step, unless we suppose ourselves to be thinking and talking of the things, and not the mere symbols, the evidence fails.

There is another circumstance, which, still more than that which we have now mentioned, gives plausibility to the notion that the propositions of arithmetic and algebra are merely verbal. That is, that when considered as propositions respecting Things, they all have the appearance of being identical propositions. The assertion, Two and one is equal to three, considered as an assertion respecting objects, as for instance, "Two pebbles and one pebble are equal to three pebbles," does not affirm equality between two collections of pebbles, but absolute identity. It affirms that if we put one pebble to two pebbles, those very pebbles are three. The objects, therefore, being the very same, and the mere assertion that "objects are themselves" being insignificant, it seems but natural to consider the proposition, Two and one is equal to three, as asserting mere identity of signification between the two names.

This, however, though it looks so plausible, will not bear examination. The expression "two pebbles and one pebble," and the expression "three pebbles," stand indeed for the same aggregation of objects, but they by no means stand for the same physical fact. They are names of the same objects, but of those objects in two different states: though they *de*note the same things, their *con*notation is different. Three pebbles in two separate parcels, and three pebbles in one parcel, do not make the same impression on our senses; and the assertion that the very same pebbles may by an alteration of place and arrangement be made to produce either the one set of sensations or the other, though a very familiar proposition, is not an identical one. It is a truth known to us by early and constant experience: an inductive truth; and such truths are the foundation of the science of Number. The fundamental truths of that science all rest on the evidence of sense; they are proved by showing to our eyes and our fingers that any given number of objects—ten balls, for example—may by separation and re-arrangement exhibit to our senses all the different sets of numbers the sums of which is equal to ten. All the improved methods of teaching arithmetic to children proceed on a knowledge of this fact. All who wish to carry the child's *mind* along with them in learning arithmetic; all who wish to teach numbers, and not mere ciphers—now teach it through the evidence of the senses, in the manner we have described.

We may, if we please, call the proposition, "Three is two and one," a definition of the number three, and assert that arithmetic, as it has been asserted that geometry, is a science founded on definitions. But they are definitions in the geometrical sense, not the logical; asserting not the meaning of a term only, but along with it an observed matter of fact. The proposition, "A circle is a figure bounded by a line which has all its points equally distant from a point within it," is called the definition of a circle; but the proposition from which so many consequences follow, and which is really a first principle in geometry, is, that figures answering to this description exist. And thus we may call "three is two and one" a definition of three; but the calculations which depend on that proposition do not follow from the definition itself, but from an arithmetical theorem presupposed in it, namely, that collections of objects exist, which while they impress the senses thus, $^\circ{}_\circ{}^\circ$, may be separated into two parts, thus, o o o. This proposition being granted, we term all such parcels Threes, after which the enunciation of the above-mentioned physical fact will serve also for a definition of the word Three.

The Science of Number is thus no exception to the conclusion we previously arrived at, that the processes even of deductive sciences are altogether inductive, and that their first principles are generalizations from experience. It remains to be examined whether this science resembles geometry in the further circumstance, that some of its inductions are not exactly true; and that the peculiar certainty ascribed to it, on account of which its propositions are called Necessary Truths, is fictitious and hypothetical, being true in no other sense than that those propositions legitimately follow from the hypothesis of the truth of premises which are avowedly mere approximations to truth.

. . .

10

W. V. Quine

A Dogma of Empiricism

W. V. *Quine, Edgar Pierce Professor of Philosophy at Harvard University, is the most influential philosopher in the United States today. He has contributed substantially to the development of set theory (Set Theory and Its Logic, 1963). But he is perhaps best known in philosophical circles for his systematic analysis of the sentences of ordinary language in such a way as to eliminate or at least neutralize intensional contexts (see the introduction to Part I). Based on the extensional features of the notation of symbolic logic, Quine has sketched a series of maneuvers to eliminate the constraints of natural languages on an improved canon that is designed to capture what is "important" in ordinary expression.*

His two principal publications in this respect are From a Logical Point of View

(1953) and Word and Object *(1960). The first of these contains the influential papers, "Two Dogmas of Empiricism" and "On What There Is." The second of these is among the most discussed books of the contemporary literature. But he has also filled out his account, more recently, with the Paul Carus Lectures* (The Roots of Reference, 1974), Ontological Relativity and Other Essays (1969), Philosophy of Logic (1970), *and* Web of Belief *(with J. S. Ullian, 1970).*

Quine's literary style has always been markedly graceful—all the more intriguing considering the difficulty of the puzzles he has addressed himself to. He is particularly known for his thesis that the analytic/synthetic distinction cannot be satisfactorily drawn. He shows that analyticity cannot be explained independently of synonymy, and that synonymy cannot be analyzed independently of analyticity or some equivalent concept. He has also argued that there is a certain "radical indeterminacy of translation" affecting communication within as well as between languages. In Quine's view, if the meaning of what is said is construed in terms of a speaker's behavioral response to a certain stimulus, alternative and incompatible interpretations of given linguistic utterances can be constructed that are compatible with such behavior. This indeterminacy is also linked to a more formidable theory, said to be a form of conventionalism, to the effect that not individual statements but only systems of statements may conflict with experience. Hence, the truth of any statement can be preserved provided that suitable adjustments are made elsewhere in the system.

Modern empiricism has been conditioned in large part by two dogmas. One is a belief in some fundamental cleavage between truths which are *analytic,* or grounded in meanings independently of matters of fact, and truths which are *synthetic,* or grounded in fact. The other dogma is *reductionism:* the belief that each meaningful statement is equivalent to some logical construct upon terms which refer to immediate experience. Both dogmas, I shall argue, are ill-founded. One effect of abandoning them is, as we shall see, a blurring of the supposed boundary between speculative metaphysics and natural science. Another effect is a shift toward pragmatism.

1. Background for Analyticity

Kant's cleavage between analytic and synthetic truths was foreshadowed in Hume's distinction between relations of ideas and matters of fact, and in Leibniz's distinction between truths of reason and truths of fact. Leibniz spoke of the truths of reason as true in all possible worlds. Picturesqueness aside, this is to say that the truths of reason are those which could not possibly be false. In the same vein we hear analytic statements defined as statements whose denials are self-contradictory. But this definition has small explanatory value; for the notion of self-contradictoriness, in the quite broad sense needed for this definition of analyticity, stands in exactly the same need of clarification as does the notion of analyticity itself. The two notions are the two sides of a single dubious coin.

Kant conceived of an analytic statement as one that attributes to its subject no more than is already conceptually contained in the subject. This formulation has two shortcomings: it limits itself to statements of subject-predicate form, and it appeals to a notion of containment which is left at a metaphorical level. But Kant's intent, evident more from the use he makes of the notion of analyticity than from his definition of it, can be restated thus: a statement is analytic when it is true by virtue of meanings and independently of fact. Pursuing this line, let us examine the concept of *meaning* which is presupposed.

Meaning . . . is not to be identified with naming. [Gottlob—Ed.] Frege's example of 'Evening Star' and 'Morning Star', and Russell's of 'Scott' and 'the author of *Waverley*', illustrate that terms can name the same thing but differ in meaning. The distinction between meaning and naming is no less important at the level of abstract terms. The terms '9' and 'the number of the planets' name one and the same abstract entity but presumably must be regarded as unlike in meaning; for astronomical observation was needed, and not mere reflection on meanings, to determine the sameness of the entity in question.

The above examples consist of singular terms, concrete and abstract. With general terms, or predicates, the situation is somewhat different but parallel. Whereas a singular term purports to name an entity, abstract or concrete, a general term does not; but a general term is *true of* an entity, or of each of many, or of none. The class of all entities of which a general term is true is called the *extension* of the term. Now paralleling the contrast between the meaning of a singular term and the entity named, we must distinguish equally between the meaning of a general term and its extension. The general terms 'creature with a heart' and 'creature with kidneys', for example, are perhaps alike in extension but unlike in meaning.

Confusion of meaning with extension, in the case of general terms, is less common than confusion of meaning with naming in the case of singular terms. It is indeed a commonplace in philosophy to oppose intension (or meaning) to extension, or, in a variant vocabulary, connotation to denotation.

The Aristotelian notion of essence was the forerunner, no doubt, of the modern notion of intension or meaning. For Aristotle it was essential in men to be rational, accidental to be two-legged. But there is an important difference between this attitude and the doctrine of meaning. From the latter point of view it may indeed be conceded (if only for the sake of argument) that rationality is involved in the meaning of the word 'man' while two-leggedness is not; but two-leggedness may at the same time be viewed as involved in the meaning of 'biped' while rationality is not. Thus from the point of view of the doctrine of meaning it makes no sense to say of the actual individual, who is at once a man and a biped, that his rationality is essential and his two-leggedness accidental or vice versa. Things had essences, for Aristotle, but only linguistic forms have meanings. Meaning is what essence becomes when it is divorced from the object of reference and wedded to the word.

For the theory of meaning a conspicuous question is the nature of its objects: what sort of things are meanings? A felt need for meant entities may derive from an earlier failure to appreciate that meaning and reference are distinct. Once the theory of meaning is sharply separated from the theory of reference, it is a short step to recognizing as the primary business of the theory of meaning simply the synonymy of linguistic forms and the analyticity of statements; meanings themselves, as obscure intermediary entities, may well be abandoned.

The problem of analyticity then confronts us anew. Statements which are analytic by general philosophical acclaim are not, indeed, far to seek. They fall into two classes. Those of the first class, which may be called *logically true*, are typified by:

(1) No unmarried man is married.

The relevant feature of this example is that it not merely is true as it stands, but remains true under any and all reinterpretations of 'man' and 'married'. If we suppose a prior inventory of *logical* particles, comprising 'no', 'un-', 'not', 'if', 'then', 'and', etc., then in general a logical truth is a statement which is true and remains true under all reinterpretations of its components other than the logical particles.

But there is also a second class of analytic statements, typified by:

(2) No bachelor is married.

The characteristic of such a statement is that it can be turned into a logical truth by putting synonyms for synonyms; thus (2) can be turned into (1) by putting 'unmarried man' for its synonym 'bachelor'. We still lack a proper characterization of this second class of analytic statements, and therewith of analyticity generally, inasmuch as we have had in the above description to lean on a notion of "synonymy" which is no less in need of clarification than analyticity itself.

In recent years [Rudolf—Ed.] Carnap has tended to explain analyticity by appeal to what he calls state-descriptions. A state-description is any exhaustive assignment of truth values to the atomic, or noncompound, statements of the language. All other statements of the language are, Carnap assumes, built up of their component clauses by means of the familiar logical devices, in such a way that the truth value of any complex statement is fixed for each state-description by specifiable logical laws. A statement is then explained as analytic when it comes out true under every state-description. This account is an adaptation of Leibniz's "true in all possible worlds." But note that this version of analyticity serves its purpose only if the atomic statements of the language are, unlike 'John is a bachelor' and 'John is married', mutually independent. Otherwise there would be a state-description which assigned truth to 'John is a bachelor' and to 'John is married', and consequently 'No bachelors are married' would turn out synthetic rather than analytic under the proposed criterion. Thus the criterion of analyticity in terms of state-descriptions serves only for languages devoid of extra-logical synonym-pairs, such as 'bachelor' and 'unmarried man'—synonym-pairs of the type which give rise to the "second class" of analytic statements. The criterion in terms of state-descriptions is a reconstruction at best of logical truth, not of analyticity.

I do not mean to suggest that Carnap is under any illusions on this point. His simplified model language with its state-descriptions is aimed primarily not at the general problem of analyticity but at another purpose, the clarification of probability and induction. Our problem, however, is analyticity; and here the major difficulty lies not in the first class of analytic statements, the logical truths, but rather in the second class, which depends on the notion of synonymy.

2. *Definition*

There are those who find it soothing to say that the analytic statements of the second class reduce to those of the first class, the logical truths, by *definition*; 'bachelor', for example, is *defined* as 'unmarried man'. But how do we find that 'bachelor' is defined as 'unmarried man'? Who defined it thus, and when? Are we to appeal to the nearest dictionary, and accept the lexicographer's formulation as law? Clearly this would be to put the cart before the horse. The lexicographer is an empirical scientist, whose business is the recording of antecedent facts; and if he glosses 'bachelor' as 'unmarried man' it is because of his belief that there is a relation of synonymy between those forms, implicit in general or preferred usage prior to his own work. The notion of synonymy presupposed here has still to be clarified, presumably in terms relating to linguistic behavior. Certainly the "definition" which is the lexicographer's report of an observed synonymy cannot be taken as the ground of the synonymy.

Definition is not, indeed, an activity exclusively of philologists. Philosophers and scientists frequently have occasion to "define" a recondite term by paraphrasing it into terms of a more familiar vocabulary. But ordinarily such a definition, like the philologist's, is pure lexicography, affirming a relation of synonymy antecedent to the exposition in hand.

Just what it means to affirm synonymy, just what the interconnections may be which are necessary and sufficient in order that two linguistic forms be properly describable as synonymous, is far from clear; but, whatever these interconnections may be, ordinarily they are grounded in usage. Definitions reporting selected instances of synonymy come then as reports upon usage.

There is also, however, a variant type of definitional activity which does not limit itself to the reporting of preëxisting synonymies. I have in mind what Carnap calls *explication*—an activity to which philosophers are given, and scientists also in their more philosophical moments. In explication the purpose is not merely to paraphrase the definiendum into an outright synonym, but actually to improve upon the definiendum by refining or supplementing its meaning. But even explication, though not merely reporting a preëxisting synonymy between definiendum and definiens, does rest nevertheless on *other* preëxisting synonymies. The matter may be viewed as follows. Any word worth explicating has some contexts which, as wholes, are clear and precise enough to be useful; and the purpose of explication is to preserve the usage of these favored contexts while sharpening the usage of other contexts. In order that a given definition be suitable for purposes of explication, therefore, what is required is not that the definiendum in its antecedent usage be synonymous with the definiens, but just that each of these favored contexts of the definiendum, taken as a whole in its antecedent usage, be synonymous with the corresponding context of the definiens.

Two alternative definientia may be equally appropriate for the purposes of a given task of explication and yet not be synonymous with each other; for they may serve interchangeably within the favored contexts but diverge elsewhere. By cleaving to one of these definientia rather than the other, a definition of explicative kind generates, by fiat, a relation of synonymy between definiendum and definiens which did not hold before. But such a definition still owes its explicative function, as seen, to preëxisting synonymies.

There does, however, remain still an extreme sort of definition which does not hark back to prior synonymies at all: namely, the explicitly conventional introduction of novel notations for purposes of sheer abbreviation. Here the definiendum becomes synonymous with the definiens simply because it has been created expressly for the purpose of being synonymous with the definiens. Here we have a really transparent case of synonymy created by definition; would that all species of synonymy were as intelligible. For the rest, definition rests on synonymy rather than explaining it.

The word 'definition' has come to have a dangerously reassuring sound, owing no doubt to its frequent occurrence in logical and mathematical writings. We shall do well to digress now into a brief appraisal of the role of definition in formal work.

In logical and mathematical systems either of two mutually antagonistic types of economy may be striven for, and each has its peculiar practical utility. On the one hand we may seek economy of practical expression—ease and brevity in the statement of multifarious relations. This sort of economy calls usually for distinctive concise notations for a wealth of concepts. Second, however, and oppositely, we may seek economy in grammar and vocabulary; we may try to find a minimum of basic concepts such that, once a distinctive notation has been appropriated to each of them, it becomes possible to express any desired further concept by mere combination and iteration of our basic notations. This second sort of economy is impractical in one way, since a poverty in basic idioms tends to a necessary lengthening of discourse. But it is practical in another way: it greatly simplifies theoretical discourse *about* the language, through minimizing the terms and the forms of construction wherein the language consists.

Both sorts of economy, though prima facie incompatible, are valuable in their separate ways. The custom has consequently arisen of combining both sorts of economy by forging in effect two languages, the one a part of the other. The inclusive language, though redundant in grammar and vocabulary, is economical in message lengths, while the part, called primitive notation, is economical in grammar and vocabulary. Whole and part are correlated by rules of translation whereby each idiom not in primitive notation is equated to some complex built up of primitive notation. These rules of translation are the so-called *definitions* which appear in formalized systems. They are best viewed not as adjuncts to one language but as correlations between two languages, the one a part of the other.

But these correlations are not arbitrary. They are supposed to show how the primitive notations can accomplish all purposes, save brevity and convenience, of the redundant language. Hence the definiendum and its definiens may be expected, in each case, to be related in one or another of the three ways lately noted. The definiens may be a faithful paraphrase of the definiendum into the narrower notation, preserving a direct synonymy[1] as of antecedent usage; or the definiens may, in the spirit of explication, improve upon the antecedent usage of the definiendum; or finally, the definiendum may be a newly created notation, newly endowed with meaning here and now.

In formal and informal work alike, thus, we find that definition—except in the extreme case of the explicitly conventional introduction of new notations—hinges on prior relations of synonymy. Recognizing then that the notion of definition does not hold the key to synonymy and analyticity, let us look further into synonymy and say no more of definition.

3. Interchangeability

A natural suggestion, deserving close examination, is that the synonymy of two linguistic forms consists simply in their interchangeability in all contexts without change of truth value—interchangeability, in [G.W.—Ed.] Leibniz's phrase, *salva veritate*. Note that synonyms so conceived need not even be free from vagueness, as long as the vaguenesses match.

But it is not quite true that the synonyms 'bachelor' and 'unmarried man' are everywhere interchangeable *salva veritate*. Truths which become false under substitution of 'unmarried man' for 'bachelor' are easily constructed with the help of 'bachelor of arts' or 'bachelor's buttons'; also with the help of quotation, thus:

'Bachelor' has less than ten letters.

Such counterinstances can, however, perhaps be set aside by treating the phrases 'bachelor of arts' and 'bachelor's buttons' and the quotation 'bachelor' each as a single indivisible word and then stipulating that the interchangeability *salva veritate* which is to be the touchstone of synonymy is not supposed to apply to fragmentary occurrences inside of a word. This account of synonymy, supposing it acceptable on other counts, has indeed the drawback of appealing to a prior conception of "word" which can be counted on to present difficulties of formulation in its turn. Nevertheless some progress might be claimed in having reduced the problem of synonymy to a problem of wordhood. Let us pursue this line a bit, taking "word" for granted.

The question remains whether interchangeability *salva veritate* (apart from occurrences within words) is a strong enough condition for synonymy, or whether, on the contrary, some heteronymous expressions might be thus interchangeable. Now let us be clear that we are not concerned here with synonymy in the sense of complete identity in psychological associations or poetic quality; indeed no two expressions are synonymous in such a sense. We are concerned

---

[1] According to an important variant sense of 'definition', the relation preserved may be the weaker relation of mere agreement in reference. . . . But definition in this sense is better ignored in the present connection, being irrelevant to the question of synonymy.

only with what may be called *cognitive* synonymy. Just what this is cannot be said without successfully finishing the present study; but we know something about it from the need which arose for it in connection with analyticity in § 1. The sort of synonymy needed there was merely such that any analytic statement could be turned into a logical truth by putting synonyms for synonyms. Turning the tables and assuming analyticity, indeed, we could explain cognitive synonymy of terms as follows (keeping to the familiar example): to say that 'bachelor' and 'unmarried man' are cognitively synonymous is to say no more nor less than that the statement:

(3) All and only bachelors are unmarried men

is analytic.[2]

What we need is an account of cognitive synonymy not presupposing analyticity—if we are to explain analyticity conversely with help of cognitive synonymy as undertaken in § 1. And indeed such an independent account of cognitive synonymy is at present up for consideration, namely, interchangeability *salva veritate* everywhere except within words. The question before us, to resume the thread at last, is whether such interchangeability is a sufficient condition for cognitive synonymy. We can quickly assure ourselves that it is, by examples of the following sort. The statement:

(4) Necessarily all and only bachelors are bachelors

is evidently true, even supposing 'necessarily' so narrowly construed as to be truly applicable only to analytic statements. Then, if 'bachelor' and 'unmarried man' are interchangeable *salva veritate*, the result:

(5) Necessarily all and only bachelors are unmarried men

of putting 'unmarried man' for an occurrence of 'bachelor' in (4) must, like (4), be true. But to say that (5) is true is to say that (3) is analytic, and hence that 'bachelor' and 'unmarried man' are cognitively synonymous.

Let us see what there is about the above argument that gives it its air of hocus-pocus. The condition of interchangeability *salva veritate* varies in its force with variations in the richness of the language at hand: The above argument supposes we are working with a language rich enough to contain the adverb 'necessarily', this adverb being so construed as to yield truth when and only when applied to an analytic statement. But can we condone a language which contains such an adverb? Does the adverb really make sense? To suppose that it does is to suppose that we have already made satisfactory sense of 'analytic'. Then what are we so hard at work on right now?

Our argument is not flatly circular, but something like it. It has the form, figuratively speaking, of a closed curve in space.

---

[2] This is cognitive synonymy in a primary, broad sense. Carnap . . . and [C. I.—Ed.] Lewis . . . have suggested how, once this notion is at hand, a narrower sense of cognitive synonymy which is preferable for some purposes can in turn be derived. But this special ramification of concept-building lies aside from the present purposes and must not be confused with the broad sort of cognitive synonymy here concerned.

Interchangeability *salva veritate* is meaningless until relativized to a language whose extent is specified in relevant respects. Suppose now we consider a language containing just the following materials. There is an indefinitely large stock of one-place predicates (for example, 'F' where 'Fx' means that x is a man) and many-place predicates (for example, 'G' where 'Gxy' means that x loves y), mostly having to do with extralogical subject matter. The rest of the language is logical. The atomic sentences consist each of a predicate followed by one or more variables 'x', 'y', etc.; and the complex sentences are built up of the atomic ones by truth functions ('not', 'and', 'or', etc.) and quantification. In effect such a language enjoys the benefits also of descriptions and indeed singular terms generally, these being contextually definable in known ways. Even abstract singular terms naming classes, classes of classes, etc., are contextually definable in case the assumed stock of predicates includes the two-place predicates of class membership. Such a language can be adequate to classical mathematics and indeed to scientific discourse generally, except in so far as the latter involves debatable devices such as contrary-to-fact conditionals or modal adverbs like 'necessarily'. Now a language of this type is extensional, in this sense: any two predicates which agree extensionally (that is, are true of the same objects) are interchangeable *salva veritate*.

In an extensional language, therefore, interchangeability *salva veritate* is no assurance of cognitive synonymy of the desired type. That 'bachelor' and 'unmarried man' are interchangeable *salva veritate* in an extensional language assures us of no more than that (3) is true. There is no assurance here that the extensional agreement of 'bachelor' and 'unmarried man' rests on meaning rather than merely on accidental matters of fact, as does the extensional agreement of 'creature with a heart' and 'creature with kidneys'.

For most purposes extensional agreement is the nearest approximation to synonymy we need care about. But the fact remains that extensional agreement falls far short of cognitive synonymy of the type required for explaining analyticity in the manner of § 1. The type of cognitive synonymy required there is such as to equate the synonymy of 'bachelor' and 'unmarried man' with the analyticity of (3), not merely with the truth of (3).

So we must recognize that interchangeability *salva veritate*, if construed in relation to an extensional language, is not a sufficient condition of cognitive synonymy in the sense needed for deriving analyticity in the manner of § 1. If a language contains an intensional adverb 'necessarily' in the sense lately noted, or other particles to the same effect, then interchangeability *salva veritate* in such a language does afford a sufficient condition of cognitive synonymy; but such a language is intelligible only in so far as the notion of analyticity is already understood in advance.

The effort to explain cognitive synonymy first, for the sake of deriving analyticity from it afterward as in § 1, is perhaps the wrong approach. Instead we might try explaining analyticity somehow without appeal to cognitive synonymy. Afterward we could doubtless derive cognitive synonymy from analyticity satisfactorily enough if desired. We have seen that cognitive synonymy of 'bachelor' and 'unmarried man' can be explained as analyticity of (3). The same explanation works for any pair of one-place predicates, of course, and it can be extended in obvious fashion to many-place predicates. Other syntactical categories can also be accommodated in fairly parallel fashion. Singular terms may be said to be cognitively synonymous when the statement of identity formed by putting '=' between them is analytic. Statements may be said simply to be cognitively synonymous when their biconditional (the result of joining them by 'if and only if') is analytic.[3] If we care to lump all categories into a single formulation, at the expense of assuming again the notion of "word" which was appealed to early in this section, we can describe any two linguistic forms as cognitively synonymous when the two forms are interchangeable (apart from occurrences within "words") *salva* (no longer *veritate* but) *analyticitate* [preserving analyticity—Ed.]. Certain technical questions arise, indeed, over cases of ambiguity or homonymy; let us not pause for them, however, for we are already digressing. Let us rather turn our backs on the problem of synonymy and address ourselves anew to that of analyticity.

4. Semantical Rules

Analyticity at first seemed most naturally definable by appeal to a realm of meanings. On refinement, the appeal to meanings gave way to an appeal to synonymy or definition. But definition turned out to be a will-o'-the-wisp, and synonymy turned out to be best understood only by dint of a prior appeal to analyticity itself. So we are back at the problem of analyticity.

I do not know whether the statement 'Everything green is extended' is analytic. Now does my indecision over this example really betray an incomplete understanding, an incomplete grasp of the "meanings" of 'green' and 'extended'? I think not. The trouble is not with 'green' or 'extended', but with 'analytic'.

It is often hinted—that the difficulty in separating analytic statements from synthetic ones in ordinary language is due to the vagueness of ordinary language and that the distinction is clear when we have a precise artificial language with explicit "semantical rules." This, however, as I shall now attempt to show, is a confusion.

The notion of analyticity about which we are worrying is a purported relation between statements and languages: a statement S is said to be *analytic for* a language L, and the problem is to make sense of this relation generally, that is, for variable 'S' and 'L'. The gravity of this problem is not perceptibly less for artificial languages than for natural ones. The problem of making sense of the idiom 'S is analytic for L', with variable 'S' and 'L', retains its stubbornness even if we limit the range of the variable 'L' to artificial languages. Let me now try to make this point evident.

For artificial languages and semantical rules we look naturally to the writings of Carnap. His semantical rules take various forms, and to make my point I shall have to distinguish certain of the forms. Let us suppose, to begin with, an artificial language L_0 whose semantical rules have the form explicitly of a specification, by recursion or otherwise, of all the analytic statements of L_0.

---

[3] The 'if and only if' itself is intended in the truth functional sense.

The rules tell us that such and such statements, and only those, are the analytic statements of L_0. Now here the difficulty is simply that the rules contain the word 'analytic', which we do not understand! We understand what expressions the rules attribute analyticity to, but we do not understand what the rules attribute to those expressions. In short, before we can understand a rule which begins 'A statement S is analytic for language L_0 if and only if . . .', we must understand the general relative term 'analytic for'; we must under 'S is analytic for L' where 'S' and 'L' are variables.

Alternatively we may, indeed, view the so-called rule as a conventional definition of a new simple symbol 'analytic-for-L_0', which might better be written untendentiously as 'K' so as not to seem to throw light on the interesting word 'analytic'. Obviously any number of classes K, M, N, etc. of statements of L_0 can be specified for various purposes or for no purpose; what does it mean to say that K, as against M, N, etc., is the class of the "analytic" statements of L_0?

By saying what statements are analytic for L_0 we explain 'analytic-for-L_0' but not 'analytic', not 'analytic for'. We do not begin to explain the idiom 'S is analytic for L' with variable 'S and L', even if we are content to limit the range of 'L' to the realm of artificial languages.

Actually we do know enough about the intended significance of 'analytic' to know that analytic statements are supposed to be true. Let us then turn to a second form of semantical rule, which says not that such and such statements are analytic but simply that such and such statements are included among the truths. Such a rule is not subject to the criticism of containing the un-understood word 'analytic'; and we may grant for the sake of argument that there is no difficulty over the broader term 'true'. A semantical rule of this second type, a rule of truth, is not supposed to specify all the truths of the language; it merely stipulates, recursively or otherwise, a certain multitude of statements which, along with others unspecified, are to count as true. Such a rule may be conceded to be quite clear. Derivatively, afterward, analyticity can be demarcated thus: a statement is analytic if it is (not merely true but) true according to the semantical rule.

Still there is really no progress. Instead of appealing to an unexplained word 'analytic', we are now appealing to an unexplained phrase 'semantical rule'. Not every true statement which says that the statements of some class are true can count as a semantical rule—otherwise *all* truths would be "analytic" in the sense of being true according to semantical rules. Semantical rules are distinguishable, apparently, only by the fact of appearing on a page under the heading 'Semantical Rules'; and this heading is itself then meaningless.

We can say indeed that a statement is *analytic-for-L_0* if and only if it is true according to such and such specifically appended "semantical rules," but then we find ourselves back at essentially the same case which was originally discussed: 'S is analytic-for-L_0 if and only if. . . .' Once we seek to explain 'S is analytic-for-L' generally for variable 'L' (even allowing limitation of 'L' to artificial languages), the explanation 'true according to the semantical rules of L' is unavailing; for the relative term 'semantical rule of' is as much in need of clarification, at least, as 'analytic for'.

It may be instructive to compare the notion of semantical rule with that of postulate. Relative to a given set of postulates, it is easy to say what a postulate is: it is a member of the set. Relative to a given set of semantical rules, it is equally easy to say what a semantical rule is. But given simply a notation, mathematical or otherwise, and indeed as thoroughly understood a notation as you please in point of the translations or truth conditions of its statements, who can say which of its true statements rank as postulates? Obviously the question is meaningless—as meaningless as asking which points in Ohio are starting points. Any finite (or effectively specifiable infinite) selection of statements (preferably true ones, perhaps) is as much *a* set of postulates as any other. The word 'postulate' is significant only relative to an act of inquiry; we apply the word to a set of statements just in so far as we happen, for the year or the moment, to be thinking of those statements in relation to the statements which can be reached from them by some set of transformations to which we have seen fit to direct our attention. Now the notion of semantical rule is as sensible and meaningful as that of postulate, if conceived in a similarly relative spirit—relative, this time, to one or another particular enterprise of schooling unconversant persons in sufficient conditions for truth of statements of some natural or artificial language L. But from this point of view no one signalization of a subclass of the truths of L is intrinsically more a semantical rule than another; and, if 'analytic' means 'true by semantical rules', no one truth of L is analytic to the exclusion of another.

It might conceivably be protested that an artificial language L (unlike a natural one) is a language in the ordinary sense *plus* a set of explicit semantical rules—the whole constituting, let us say, an ordered pair; and that the semantical rules of L then are specifiable simply as the second component of the pair L. But, by the same token and more simply, we might construe an artificial language L outright as an ordered pair whose second component is the class of its analytic statements; and then the analytic statements of L become specifiable simply as the statements in the second component of L. Or better still, we might just stop tugging at our bootstraps altogether.

Not all the explanations of analyticity known to Carnap and his readers have been covered explicitly in the above considerations, but the extension to other forms is not hard to see. Just one additional factor should be mentioned which sometimes enters: sometimes the semantical rules are in effect rules of translation into ordinary language, in which case the analytic statements of the artificial language are in effect recognized as such from the analyticity of their specified translations in ordinary language. Here certainly there can be no thought of an illumination of the problem of analyticity from the side of the artificial language.

From the point of view of the problem of analyticity the notion of an artificial language with semantical rules is a *feu follet par excellence* [nothing but a will-o-the-wisp—Ed.]. Semantical rules determining the analytic statements of an artificial language are of interest only in so far as we already understand the notion of analyticity; they are of no help in gaining this understanding.

Appeal to hypothetical languages of an artificially simple kind could conceivably be useful in clarifying analyticity, if the mental or behavioral or cultural factors relevant to analyticity—whatever they may be—were somehow sketched into the simplified model. But a model which takes analyticity merely as an irreducible character is unlikely to throw light on the problem of explicating analyticity.

It is obvious that truth in general depends on both language and extralinguistic fact. The statement 'Brutus killed Caesar' would be false if the world had been different in certain ways, but it would also be false if the word 'killed' happened rather to have the sense of 'begat'. Thus one is tempted to suppose in general that the truth of a statement is somehow analyzable into a linguistic component and a factual component. Given this supposition, it next seems reasonable that in some statements the factual component should be null; and these are the analytic statements. But, for all its a priori reasonableness, a boundary between analytic and synthetic statements simply has not been drawn. That there is such a distinction to be drawn at all is an unempirical dogma of empiricists, a metaphysical article of faith.

11

Saul A. Kripke
Naming and Necessity

Saul A. Kripke, Professor of Philosophy at Princeton University, is one of the most original contributors to contemporary philosophy. Even his pioneer work in modal logic ("A Completeness Theorem in Modal Logic," 1959; "Semantical Analysis of Modal Logic," 1963, 1965) (see C. I. Lewis) was carried out with a view to certain critical issues in metaphysics and philosophical logic, chiefly concerned with essentialism and the a priori (see introduction to Part I). In developing a modal logic with quantifiers ("all" and "some"), Kripke was led to defend, against W. V. Quine's views, a form of essentialism to this effect: A particular object has properties (an "individual essence") so associated with it that nothing else could have just those properties without being that object.

In "Naming and Necessity" (1972), excerpted below, Kripke clarifies his account of essentialism and reference. Regarding reference, names ("Nixon," for instance) are to be construed as rigid designators, or devices intended to single out one

From Saul A. Kripke, *Naming and Necessity*, published by Basil Blackwell, Oxford, England. Reprinted by permission of the publisher and the author.

individual, whatever the descriptive conditions with which that individual may be associated. But, Kripke holds, nothing can be observed merely to be what the name names (nothing can be observed merely to be Nixon). Thus when we refer (to Nixon) we must be able to identify him under alternative possible circumstances ("what might have happened to him"); hence, essentialism (see the introduction to Part I). Kripke has more recently begun a series of investigations into the concept of truth.

.   .   .

Philosophers have talked (and, of course, there has been considerable controversy in recent years over the meaningfulness of these notions) [about] various categories of truth, which are called 'a priori', 'analytic', 'necessary',— and sometimes even 'certain' is thrown into this batch. The terms are often used as if *whether* there are things answering to these concepts is an interesting question, but we might as well regard them all as meaning the same thing. Now, everyone remembers Kant (a bit) as making a distinction between 'a priori' and 'analytic'. So maybe this distinction is still made. In contemporary discussion very few people, if any, distinguish between the concepts of statements being *a priori* and their being necessary. At any rate I shall *not* use the terms 'a priori' and 'necessary' interchangeably here.

Consider what the traditional characterizations of such terms as 'a priori' and 'necessary' are. First the notion of a prioricity is a concept of epistemology. I guess the traditional characterization from Kant goes something like: *a priori* truths are those which can be known independently of any experience. This introduces another problem before we get off the ground, because there's another modality in the characterization of 'a priori', namely, it is supposed to be something which *can* be known independently of any experience. That means that in some sense it's *possible* (whether we do or do not in fact know it independently of any experience) to know this independently of any experience. And possible for whom? For God? For the Martians? Or just for people with minds like ours? To make this all clear might [involve] a host of problems all of its own about what sort of possibility is in question here. It might be best therefore, instead of using the phrase 'a priori truth', to the extent that one uses it at all, to stick to the question of whether a particular person or knower knows something *a priori* or believes it true on the basis of *a priori* evidence.

I won't go further too much into the problems that might arise with the notion of a prioricity here. I will say that some philosophers somehow change the modality in this characterization from *can* to *must*. They think that if something belongs to the realm of *a priori* knowledge, it couldn't possibly be known empirically. This is just a mistake. Something may belong in the realm of such statements that can be known *a priori* but still may be known by particular people on the basis of experience. To give a really common sense example: anyone who has worked with a computing machine knows that the computing machine may give an answer to whether such and such a number is prime. No one has calculated or proved that the number is prime; but the machine has given the answer: this number is prime. We, then, if we believe that the number is prime, believe it on the basis of our knowledge of the laws of physics, the construction of the machine, and so on. We therefore do not believe this on the basis of purely *a priori* evidence. We believe it (if anything is *a posteriori* at all) on the basis of *a posteriori* evidence. Nevertheless, maybe this could be known *a priori* by someone who made the requisite calculations. So '*can* be known *a priori*' doesn't mean '*must* be known *a priori*'.

The second concept which is in question is that of necessity. Sometimes this is used in an epistemological way and might then just mean *a priori*. And of course, sometimes it is used in a physical way when people distinguish between physical and logical necessity. But what I am concerned with here is a notion which is not a notion of epistemology but of metaphysics, in some (I hope) nonpejorative sense. We ask whether something might have been true, or might have been false. Well, if something is false, it's obviously not necessarily true. If it is true, might it have been otherwise? Is it possible that, in this respect, the world should have been different from the way it is? If the answer is 'no', then this fact about the world is a necessary one. If the answer is 'yes', then this fact about the world is a contingent one. This in and of itself has nothing to do with anyone's knowledge of anything. It's certainly a philosophical thesis, and not a matter of obvious definitional equivalence, either that everything *a priori* is necessary or that everything necessary is *a priori*. Both concepts may be vague. That may be another problem. But at any rate they are dealing with two different domains, two different areas, the epistemological and the metaphysical. Consider, say, Fermat's last theorem—or the Goldbach conjecture. The Goldbach conjecture says that an even number greater than 2 must be the sum of two prime numbers. If this is true, it is presumably necessary, and, if it is false, presumably necessarily false. We are taking the classical view of mathematics here and assume that in mathematical reality it is either true or false.

If the Goldbach conjecture is false, then there is an even number, n, greater than 2, and for no primes p_1 and p_2, both $< n$, does $n = p_1 + p_2$. This fact about n, if true, is verifiable by direct computation, and thus is necessary if the results of arithmetical computations are necessary. On the other hand, if the conjecture is true, then every even number exceeding 2 is the sum of two primes. Could it then be the case that, although in fact every even number is the sum of two primes, there might have been an even number which was not the sum of two primes? What would that mean? Such a number would have to be one of 4, 6, 8, 10, . . . ; and, by hypothesis, since we are assuming Goldbach's conjecture to be true, each of these can be shown, by direct computation, to be the sum of two primes. Goldbach's conjecture, then, cannot be contingently true or false; whatever truth-value it has belongs to it by necessity.

But what we can say of course is that right now as far as we know, the question can come out either way. So, in the absence of a mathematical proof deciding this question, none of us has any *a priori* knowledge about this question in either direction. We don't know whether Goldbach's conjecture is true or false. So right now we certainly don't know anything *a priori* about it.

Perhaps it will be alleged that we *can* in principle know *a priori* whether it is true. Well, maybe we can. Of course an infinite mind which can search through all the numbers can or could. But I don't know whether a finite mind can or could. Maybe there just is no mathematical proof whatsoever which decides the conjecture. At any rate this might or might not be the case. Maybe there is a mathematical proof deciding this question; maybe every mathematical question is decidable by an intuitive proof or disproof. [David—Ed.] Hilbert thought so; others have thought not; still others have thought the question unintelligible unless the notion of intuitive proof is replaced by that of formal proof in a single system. Certainly no one formal system decides all mathematical questions, as we know from [Kurt—Ed.] Gödel. At any rate, and this is the important thing, the question is not trivial; even though someone said that it's necessary, if true at all, that every even number is the sum of two primes, it doesn't follow that anyone knows anything *a priori* about it. It doesn't even seem to me to follow without some further philosophical argument (it is an interesting philosophical question) that anyone *could* know anything *a priori* about it. The 'could', as I said, involves some other modality. We mean that even if no one, perhaps even in the future, knows or will know *a priori* whether Goldbach's conjecture is right, in principle there is a way, which *could* have been used, of answering the question *a priori*. This assertion is not trivial.

The terms 'necessary' and '*a priori*', then, as applied to statements are *not* obvious synonyms. There may be a philosophical argument connecting them, perhaps even identifying them; but an argument is required, not simply the observation that the two terms are clearly interchangeable. (I will argue below that in fact they are not even co-extensive—that necessary *a posteriori* truths, and probably contingent *a priori* truths, both exist.)

I think people have thought that these two things must mean the same for these reasons. First, if something not only happens to be true in the actual world but is also true in all possible worlds, then, of course, just by running through all the possible worlds in our heads, we ought to be able with enough effort to see, if a statement is necessary, that it is necessary, and thus know it *a priori*. But really this is not so obviously feasible at all.

Secondly, I guess it's thought that, conversely, if something is known *a priori* it must be necessary, because it was known without looking at the world. If it depended on some contingent feature of the actual world, how could you know it without looking? Maybe the actual world is one of the possible worlds in which it would have been false. This depends on the thesis that there can't be a way of knowing about the actual world without looking which wouldn't be a way of knowing the same thing about every possible world. This involves problems of epistemology and the nature of knowledge; and of course it is very vague as stated. But it is not really *trivial* either. More important than any particular example of something which is alleged to be necessary and not *a priori* or *a priori* and not necessary, is to see that the notions are different, that it's not trivial to argue on the basis of something's being something which maybe we can only know *a posteriori*, that it's not a necessary truth. It's not trivial just because something is known in some sense *a priori*, that what is known is a necessary truth.

Another term used in philosophy is 'analytic'. Here it won't be too important to get any clearer about this in this talk. The common examples of analytic statements, nowadays, are like 'bachelors are unmarried'. Kant (someone just pointed out to me) gives as an example 'gold is a yellow metal', which seems to me an extraordinary one, because it's something I think that can turn out to be false. At any rate, let's just make it a matter of stipulation that an analytic statement is in some sense true by virtue of its meaning and true in all possible worlds by virtue of its meaning. Then something which is analytically true will be both necessary and *a priori*. (That's sort of stipulative.)

Another category I mentioned was that of certainty. Whatever certainty is, it's clearly not obviously the case that everything which is necessary is certain. Certainty is another epistemological notion. Something can be known, or at least rationally believed, *a priori*, without being quite certain. You've read a proof in the math book; and, though you think it's correct, maybe you've made a mistake. You often do make mistakes of this kind. You've made a computation, perhaps with an error.

There is one more question I want to go into in a preliminary way. Some philosophers have distinguished between essentialism, the belief in modality *de re* [in the nature of things—Ed.], and a mere advocacy of necessity, the belief in modality *de dicto* [regarding sentences or what is said—Ed.]. Now, some people say: Let's give you the concept of necessity.[11] A much worse thing, something creating great additional problems, is whether we can say of any particular that it has necessary or contingent properties, even make the distinction between necessary and contingent properties. Look, it's only a *statement* or a *state of affairs* which can be either necessary or contingent. Whether a *particular* necessarily or contingently has a certain property depends on the way it's described. This is perhaps closely related to the view that the way we refer to particular things is by a description. What is Quine's famous example? If we consider the number 9, does it have the property of necessary oddness? Has that number got to be odd in all possible worlds? Certainly it's true in all possible worlds, let's say, it couldn't have been otherwise, that *nine* is odd. Of course, 9 could also be equally well picked out as *the number of planets*. It is not necessary, not true in all possible worlds, that the number of planets is odd. For example if there had been eight planets, the number of planets would not have been odd. And so it's thought: Was it necessary or contingent that Nixon won the election? (It might seem contingent, unless one has some view of some inexorable processes. . . .) But this is a contingent property of Nixon only relative to our referring to him as 'Nixon' (assuming 'Nixon' doesn't mean 'the man who won the election at such and such a time'). But if we designate Nixon as 'the man who won the election in 1968', then it will be a necessary truth, of

---

[11] By the way, it's a common attitude in philosophy to think that one shouldn't introduce a notion until it's been rigorously defined (according to some popular notion of rigor). Here I am just dealing with an intuitive notion and will keep on the level of an intuitive notion. That is, we think that some things, though they are in fact the case, might have been otherwise. I might not have given these lectures today. If that's right, then it is *possible* that I wouldn't have given these lectures today. Quite a different question is the epistemological question, how any particular person knows that I gave these lectures today. I suppose in that case he does know this is *a posteriori*. But, if someone were born with an innate belief that I was going to give these lectures today, who knows? Right now, anyway, let's suppose that people know this *a posteriori*. At any rate, the two questions being asked are different.

course, that the man who won the election in 1968, won the election in 1968. Similarly whether an object has the same property in all possible worlds depends not just on the object itself but on how it is described. So it's argued.

It is even suggested in the literature, that though a notion of necessity may have some sort of intuition behind it (we do think some things could have been otherwise; other things we don't think could have been otherwise), this notion [of a distinction between necessary and contingent properties] is just a doctrine made up by some bad philosopher, who (I guess) didn't realize that there are several ways of referring to the same thing. I don't know if some philosophers have not realized this; but at any rate it is very far from being true that this idea [that a property can be held to be essential or accidental to an object independently of its description] is a notion which has no intuitive content, which means nothing to the ordinary man. Suppose that someone said, pointing to Nixon, 'That's the guy who might have lost'. Someone else says 'Oh no, if you describe him as 'Nixon', then he might have lost; but, of course, describing him as the winner, then it is not true that he might have lost'. Now which one is being the philosopher, here, the unintuitive man? It seems to me obviously to be the second. The second man has a philosophical theory. The first man would say, and with great conviction, "Well, of course, the winner of the election *might have been someone else*. The actual winner, had the course of the campaign been different, might have been the loser, and someone else the winner; or there might have been no election at all. So, such terms as 'the winner' and 'the loser' don't designate the same objects in all possible worlds. On the other hand, the term 'Nixon' is just a *name of this man*". When you ask whether it is necessary or contingent that *Nixon* won the election, you are asking the intuitive question whether in some counterfactual situation, *this man* would in fact have lost the election. If someone thinks that the notion of a necessary property (forget whether there *are* any necessary properties [and consider] just the *meaningfulness* of the notion[12]) is a philosopher's notion with no intuitive content, he is wrong. Of course, some philosophers think that something's having intuitive content is very inconclusive evidence in favor of it. I think it is very heavy evidence in favor of anything, myself. I really don't know in a way what more conclusive evidence one can have about anything, ultimately speaking. But, in any event, people who think the notion of accidental property unintuitive have intuition reversed, I think.

Why have they thought this? While there are many motivations for people thinking this, one is this: The question of essential properties so-called is supposed to be equivalent (and it is equivalent) to the question of identity across possible worlds. Suppose we have someone, Nixon, and there's another

---

[12] The example I gave asserts a certain property—electoral victory—to be *accidental* to Nixon, independently of how he is described. Of course, if the notion of accidental property is meaningful, the notion of essential property must be meaningful also. This is not to say that there *are* any essential properties—though, in fact, I think there are. The usual argument questions the *meaningfulness* of essentialism, and says that whether a property is accidental or essential to an object depends on how it is described. It is thus *not* the view that all properties are accidental. Of course, it is also not the view, held by some idealists, that all properties are essential, all relations internal.

possible world where there is no one with all the properties Nixon has in the actual world. Which one of these other people, if any, is Nixon? Surely you must give some criterion of identity here. If you have a criterion of identity, then you just look in the other possible worlds at the man who is Nixon and the question whether in that other possible world Nixon has certain properties is well defined. It is also supposed to be well defined, in terms of such notions, whether it's true in all possible worlds, or there are some possible worlds in which Nixon didn't win the election. But, it's said, the problems of giving such criteria of identity are very difficult. Sometimes in the case of numbers it might seem easier (but even here it's argued that it's quite arbitrary). For example, one might say, and this is surely the truth, that if position in the series of numbers is what makes the number 9 what it is, then if (in another world) the number of planets had been 8, the number of planets would be a different number from the one it actually is. You wouldn't say that that number then is to be identified with our number 9 in this world. In the case of other types of objects, say people, material objects, things like that, has anyone given a set of necessary and sufficient conditions for identity across possible worlds?

Really, adequate necessary and sufficient conditions for identity which do not beg the question are very rare in any case. Mathematics is the only case I really know of where they are given even *within* a possible world, to tell the truth. I don't know of such conditions for identity of material objects over time, or for people. Everyone knows what a problem this is. But, let's forget about that. What seems to be more objectionable is that this depends on the wrong way of looking at what a possible world is. One thinks, in this picture, of a possible world as if it were like a foreign country. One looks upon it as an observer. Maybe Nixon has moved to the other country and maybe he hasn't, but one is given only qualities. One can observe all his qualities, but of course, one doesn't observe that someone is Nixon. One observes that something has red hair (or green or yellow) but not whether something is Nixon. So we had better have a way of telling in terms of properties when we run into the same thing again as we saw before; we had better have a way of telling, when we come across one of these other possible worlds, who was Nixon.

Some logicians in their formal treatment of modal logic may encourage this picture. A prominent example, perhaps, is myself. Nevertheless, intuitively speaking, it seems to me not to be the right way of thinking about the possible worlds. A possible world isn't a distant country that we are coming across, or viewing through a telescope. Generally speaking, another possible world is too far away. Even if we travel faster than light, we won't get to it. A possible world is *given by the descriptive conditions we associate with it.* What do we mean when we say 'In some other possible worlds I might not have given this lecture today'? We just imagine the situation where I didn't decide to give this lecture or decided to give it on some other day. Of course, we don't imagine everything that is true or false, but only those things relevant to my giving the lecture; but, in theory, everything needs to be decided to make a total description of the world. We can't really imagine that except in part; that, then, is a 'possible world'. Why can't it be part of the *description* of a possible world that it contains *Nixon* and that in that world *Nixon* didn't win the election? It might be a question, of course, whether such a world *is* possible. (Here it would seem, *prima facie*, to be clearly possible.) But, once we see that such a situation is possible, then we are given that the man who might have lost the election or did lose the election in this possible world is Nixon, because that's part of the description of the world. 'Possible worlds' are *stipulated*, not *discovered* by powerful telescopes. There is no reason why we cannot *stipulate* that, in talking about what would have happened to Nixon in a certain counterfactual situation, we are talking about what would have happened to *him*.

Of course, if someone makes the demand that every possible world has to be described in a purely qualitative way, we can't say, 'Suppose Nixon had lost the election', we could say instead 'suppose a man with a dog named Checkers, who looks like a certain David Fry impersonation, is in a certain possible world and loses the election', Well, does he resemble Nixon enough to be identified with Nixon? A very explicit and blatant example of this way of looking at things is David Lewis's counterpart theory,[13] but the literature on quantified modality is replete with it.[14] Why need we make this demand? That is not the way we ordinarily think of counterfactual situations. We just say 'suppose this man had lost'. It is *given* that the possible world contains *this man*, and that in that world, he had lost. There may be a problem about what intuitions about pos-

---

[13] David K. Lewis, 'Counterpart Theory and Quantified Modal Logic', *Journal of Philosophy* 65 (1968), 113–126. Lewis's elegant paper also suffers from a purely formal difficulty: on his interpretation of quantified modality, the familiar law $(y) ((x)A(x) \supset A(y))$ fails, if $A(x)$ is allowed to contain modal operators. (For example, $(\exists y) ((x) \Diamond (x \neq y))$ is satisfiable but $(\exists y) \Diamond (y \neq y)$ is not.) Since Lewis's formal model follows rather naturally from his philosophical views on counterparts, and since the failure of universal instantiation for modal properties is intuitively bizarre, it seems to me that this failure constitutes an additional argument against the plausibility of his philosophical views. There are other, lesser, formal difficulties as well. I cannot elaborate here.

Strictly speaking, Lewis's view is not a view of 'transworld identification'. Rather, he thinks that similarities across possible worlds determine a counterpart relation which need be neither symmetric nor transitive. The counterpart of something in another possible world is *never* identical with the thing itself. Thus if we say "Humphrey might have won the election (if only he had done such-and-such), we are not talking about something that might have happened to *Humphrey* but to someone else, a 'counterpart'." Probably, however, Humphrey could not care less whether someone *else*, no matter how much resembling him, would have been victorious in another possible world. Thus, Lewis's view seems to me even more bizarre than the usual notions of transworld identification that it replaces. The important issues, however, are common to the two views: the supposition that other possible worlds are like other dimensions of a more inclusive universe, that they can be given only by purely qualitative descriptions, and that therefore either the identity relation or the counterpart relation must be established in terms of qualitative resemblance.

Many have pointed out to me that the father of counterpart theory is probably Leibniz. I will not go into such a historical question here. It would also be interesting to compare Lewis's views with the Wheeler-Everett interpretation of quantum mechanics. I suspect that this view of physics may suffer from philosophical problems analogous to Lewis's counterpart theory; it is certainly very similar in spirit.

[14] Another *locus classicus* of the views I am criticizing, with more philosophical exposition than Lewis's paper, is a paper by David Kaplan on transworld identification. This paper has unfortunately never been published and no longer represents Kaplan's position.

sibility come to. But, if we have such an intuition about the possibility of *that* (*this man's* electoral loss), then it is about the possibility of *that*. It need not be identified with the possibility of a man looking like such and such, or holding such and such political views, or otherwise qualitatively described, having lost. We can point to the *man*, and ask what might have happened to *him*, had events been different.

It might be said 'Let's suppose that this is true. It comes down to the same thing, because whether Nixon could have had certain properties, different from the ones he actually has, is equivalent to the question of whether the criteria of identity across possible worlds include that Nixon does not have these properties'. But it doesn't really come to the same thing, because the usual notion of a criterion of transworld identity demands that we give purely qualitative necessary and sufficient conditions for someone being Nixon. If we can't imagine a possible world in which Nixon doesn't have a certain property, then it's a necessary condition of someone being Nixon. Or a necessary property of Nixon that he [has] that property. For example, supposing Nixon is in fact a human being, we might not imagine that there could have been a possible world in which he was, say, an inanimate object; perhaps it is not even possible for him not to have been a human being. Then it will be a necessary fact about Nixon that in all possible worlds where he exists at all, he is human or anyway he is not an inanimate object. This has nothing to do with any requirement that there be purely qualitative *sufficient* conditions for Nixonhood which we can spell out. And should there be? Maybe there is some argument that there should be, but we can consider these questions about *necessary* conditions without going into any question about *sufficient* conditions. Further, even if there were a purely qualitative set of necessary and sufficient conditions for being Nixon, the view I advocate would not demand that we find these conditions before we can ask whether Nixon might have won the election, nor does it demand that we restate the question in terms of such conditions. We can simply consider Nixon and ask what might have happened to him had various circumstances been different. So the two views, the two ways of looking at things, do seem to me to make a difference.

Notice this question, whether Nixon could not have been a human being, is a clear case where the question asked is not epistemological. Suppose Nixon actually turned out to be an automaton. That might happen. We might need evidence for whether Nixon is a human being or an automaton. But that is a question about our knowledge. The question of whether Nixon might have not been a human being, given that he is one, is not a question about knowledge, *a posteriori* or *a priori*. It's a question about, even though such and such things are the case, what might have been the case otherwise.

This table is composed of molecules. Might it not have been composed of molecules? Certainly it was a scientific discovery of great moment that it was composed of molecules (or atoms). But could anything be this very object and not be composed of molecules? Certainly there is some feeling that the answer to that must be 'no'. At any rate it's hard to imagine under what circumstances you would have this very object and find that it is not composed of molecules.

A quite different question is whether it is in fact composed of molecules in the actual world and how we know this. (I will go into more detail about these questions about essence later on.)

I wish at this point to introduce something which I need in the methodology of discussing the theory of names that I'm talking about. We need the notion of 'identity across possible worlds' as it's usually and, as I think, somewhat misleadingly called,[15] to explicate one distinction that I want to make now. What's the difference between asking whether it's necessary that 9 is greater than 7 or whether it's necessary that the number of planets be greater than 7? Why does one show anything more about essence than the other? The answer to this might be intuitively 'Well, look, the number of planets might have been different from what it in fact is. It doesn't make any sense, though, to say that nine might have been different from what it in fact is'. Let's use some terms quasi-technically. Let's call something a *rigid designator* if in any possible world it designates the same object, a *non rigid* or *accidental designator* if that is not the case. Of course we don't require that the objects exist in all possible worlds. Certainly Nixon might not have existed if his parents had not gotten married, in the normal course of things. When we think of a property as essential to an object we usually mean that it is true of that object in any case where it would have existed. A rigid designator of a necessary existent can be called *strongly rigid*.

One of the intuitive theses I will maintain in these talks is that *names* are rigid designators. Certainly they seem to satisfy the intuitive test mentioned above: although someone other than the U.S. President in 1970 might have been the U.S. President in 1970 (e.g., Humphrey might have), no one other than Nixon might have been Nixon. In the same way, a designator rigidly designates a certain object if it designates that object wherever the object exists; if, in addition, the object is a necessary existent, the designator can be called *strongly rigid*. For example, 'the President of the U.S. in 1970' designates a certain man, Nixon; but someone else (e.g., Humphrey) might have been the President in 1970, and Nixon might not have; so this designator is not rigid.

In these lectures, I will argue, intuitively, that proper names are rigid designators, for although the man (Nixon) might not have been the President, it is not the case that he might not have been Nixon (though he might not have been *called* 'Nixon'). Those who have argued that to make sense of the notion of rigid designator, we must antecedently make sense of 'criteria of transworld identity' have precisely reversed the cart and the horse; it is *because* we can refer

---

[15] Misleadingly, because the phrase suggests that there is a special problem of 'transworld identification', that we cannot trivially stipulate whom or what we are talking about when we imagine another possible world. The term 'possible world' may also mislead; perhaps it suggests the 'foreign country' picture. I have sometimes used 'counter-factual situation' in the text; Michael Slote has suggested that 'possible state of the world' might be less misleading than 'possible world'. It is better still, to avoid confusion, not to say, 'In some possible world, Humphrey would have won' but rather, simply, 'Humphrey might have won'. The apparatus of possible worlds has (I hope) been very useful as far as the set-theoretic model-theory of quantified modal logic is concerned, but has encouraged philosophical pseudo-problems and misleading pictures.

(rigidly) to Nixon, and stipulate that we are speaking of what might have happened to *him* (under certain circumstances), that 'transworld identifications' are unproblematic in such cases.[16]

The tendency to demand purely qualitative descriptions of counterfactual situations has many sources. One, perhaps, is the confusion of the epistemological and the metaphysical, between a prioricity and necessity. If someone identifies necessity with a prioricity, and thinks that objects are named by means of uniquely identifying properties, he may think that it is the properties used to identify the object which, being known about it *a priori*, must be used to identify it in all possible worlds, to find out which object is Nixon. As against this, I repeat: (1) Generally, things aren't 'found out' about a counterfactual situation, they are stipulated; (2) possible worlds need not be given purely qualitatively, as if we were looking at them through a telescope. And we will see shortly that the properties an object has in a counterfactual world have nothing to do with the properties used to identify it in the actual world.[17]

Does the 'problem' of 'transworld identification' make any sense? Is it *simply* a pseudo-problem? The following, it seems to me, can be said for it. Although the statement that England fought Germany in 1943 perhaps cannot be *reduced* to any statement about individuals, nevertheless in some sense it is not a fact 'over and above' the collection of all facts about persons, and their behavior over history. The sense in which facts about nations are not facts 'over and above' those about persons can be expressed in the observation that a description of the world mentioning all facts about persons but omitting those about nations can be a *complete* description of the world, from which the facts about nations follow. Similarly, perhaps, facts about material objects are not facts 'over and above' facts about their constituent molecules. We may then ask, given a description of a non-actualized possible situation in terms of people, whether England still exists in that situation, or whether a certain nation (described, say, as the one where Jones lives) which would exist in that situation, is England. Similarly, given certain counterfactual vicissitudes in the history of the molecules of a table, T, one may ask whether T would exist, in that situation, or whether a certain bunch of molecules, which in that situation would constitute a table, constitute the very same table T. In each case, we ask criteria of identity across possible worlds for certain particulars in terms of those for other, more 'basic', particulars. If statements about nations (or tribes) are not *reducible* to those about other more 'basic' constituents, if there is some 'open texture' in the relationship between them, we can hardly expect to give hard and fast identity criteria; nevertheless, in concrete cases we may be able to answer whether a certain bunch of molecules would still constitute T, though in some cases the answer may be indeterminate. I think similar remarks apply to the problem of identity over time; here too we are usually concerned with

---

[16] Of course I don't imply that language contains a name for every object. Demonstratives can be used as rigid designators, and free variables can be used as rigid designators of unspecified objects. Of course when we specify a counterfactual situation, we do not describe the whole possible world, but only the portion which interests us.

[17] See Lecture I, p. 273 (on Nixon), and Lecture II, pp. 287–289.

determinacy, the identity of a 'complex' particular in terms of more 'basic' ones. (For example, if various parts of a table are replaced, is it the same object?[18])

Such conception of 'transworld identification', however, differs considerably from the usual one. First, although we can try to describe the world in terms of molecules, there is no impropriety in describing it in terms of grosser entities: the statement that *this table* might have been placed in another room is perfectly proper, in and of itself. We *need* not use the description in terms of molecules, or even grosser parts of the table, though we *may*. Unless we assume that some particulars are 'ultimate', 'basic' particulars, no type of description need be regarded as privileged. We can ask whether *Nixon* might have lost the election without further subtlety, and usually no further subtlety is required. Second, it is not assumed that necessary and sufficient conditions for what kinds of collections of molecules make up this table are possible; this fact I just mentioned. Third, the attempted notion deals with criteria of identity of particulars in terms of other *particulars*, not qualities. I can refer to the table before me, and ask what might have happened to it under certain circumstances; I can also refer to its molecules. If, on the other hand, it is demanded that I describe each counterfactual situation purely qualitatively, then I can only ask whether *a table*, of such and such color, and so on, would have certain properties; whether the table in question would be *this table*, table *T*, is indeed moot, since all reference to objects, as opposed to qualities, has disappeared. It is often said that, if a counterfactual situation is described as one which would have happened to *Nixon*, and if it is not assumed that such a description is reducible to a purely qualitative one, then mysterious 'bare particulars' are assumed, propertyless substrata underlying the qualities. This is not so: I think that Nixon is a Republican, not merely that he lies in back of Republicanism, whatever that means; I also think he might have been a Democrat. The same holds for any other properties Nixon may possess, except that some of these properties may be essential. What I do deny is that a particular is nothing but a 'bundle of qualities', whatever that may mean. If a quality is an abstract object, a bundle of qualities is an object of an even higher degree of abstraction, not a particular. Philosophers have come to the opposite view through a false dilemma: they have asked, are these objects *behind* the bundle of qualities, or is the object

---

[18] There is some vagueness here. If a chip, or molecule, of a given table had been replaced by another one, we would be content to say that we have the same table. But if too many chips were different, we would seem to have a different one. The same problem can, of course, arise for identity over time.

Where the identity relation is vague, it may seem intransitive: a claim of apparent identity may yield an apparent non-identity. Some sort of 'counterpart' notion (though not with Lewis's philosophical underpinnings of resemblance, foreign country worlds, etc.), may have more utility here. One could say that strict identity applies only to the particulars (the molecules), and the counterpart relation to the particulars 'composed' of them, the tables. The counterpart relation can then be declared to be vague and intransitive. It seems, however, utopian to suppose that we will ever reach a level of ultimate, basic particulars for which identity relations are never vague and the danger of intransitivity is eliminated. The danger usually does not arise in practice, so we ordinarily can speak simply of identity without worry. Logicians have not developed a logic of vagueness.

nothing but the bundle? Neither is the case; this table is wooden, brown, in the room, etc. It has all these properties and is not a thing without properties, behind them; but it should not therefore be identified with the set, or 'bundle', of its properties, nor with the subset of its essential properties. Don't ask: how can I identify this table in another possible world, except by its properties? I have the table in my hands, I can point to it, and when I ask whether *it* might have been in another room, I am talking, by definition, about *it*. I don't have to identify it after seeing it through a telescope. If I am talking about it, I am talking about *it*, in the same way as when I say that our hands might have been painted green, I have stipulated that I am talking about greenness. Some properties of an object may be essential to it, in that it could not have failed to have them; but these properties are not used to identify the object in another possible world, for such an identification is not needed; nor need the essential properties of an object be the properties used to identify it in the actual world, if indeed it is identified in the actual world by means of properties (I have up to now left the question open).

So: the question of transworld identification makes *some* sense, in terms of asking about the identity of an object *via* questions about its component parts. But these parts are not qualities, and it is not an object resembling the given one which is in question. Theorists have often said that we identify objects across possible worlds as objects resembling the given one in the most important respects. On the contrary, Nixon, had he decided to act otherwise, might have avoided politics like the plague, through privately harboring radical opinions. Most important, even when we can replace questions about an object by questions about its parts, we need not do so. We can refer to the object and ask what might have happened to *it*. So, we do not begin with worlds (which are supposed somehow to be real, and whose qualities, but not whose objects, are perceptible to us), and then ask about criteria of transworld identification; on the contrary, we begin with the objects, which we *have*, and can identify, in the actual world. We can then ask whether certain things might have been true of the objects.

.   .   .

Truth

———◄◉►———

12

William James
Pragmatism's Conception of Truth

William James (1842–1910) was, in his day, internationally regarded as the most representative American philosopher. He was in fact a somewhat eclectic philosopher, most famous for his interpretation of pragmatism (Pragmatism, *1907;* The Meaning of Truth, *1909), and of an original turn of mind despite his dependence on the larger conceptions of other thinkers. Despite C. S. Peirce's earlier, germinal publications, James seems to have been responsible for launching pragmatism. By pragmatism is meant the denial of foundationalism (see the introduction to Part I), emphasis on the continuity of an organism's interaction with its environment leading to the discovery of truth, and the insistence on our being in touch with the real world through science and ordinary experience. Yet, as Peirce himself observed, James misunderstood him, construing pragmatism largely as a theory of truth rather than a theory of meaning.*

James's range of interests was strongly scientific. He obtained a medical degree and taught anatomy, physiology, psychology, and philosophy at Harvard. His Principles of Psychology *(1890) remains a classic of that early literature in which the philosophical aspects of psychology loom large. The* Principles *is prized also for its careful attention to the description of mental states and for James's signal effort to treat psychology as a science.*

He wrote widely, always with a strong conversational tone, and his books were immensely popular. Among his best-known titles must be included The Will to Believe *(1897),* The Varieties of Religious Experience *(1902),* A Pluralistic Universe *(1909), and* Essays in Radical Empiricism *(1912). The unity of his thought is clearly centered on his empiricism, which draws together the* Psychology *and* Pragmatism. *The distinction of his account lies largely with his effort to apply the categories of experience to the whole of reality. In fact, in the essays "Does Consciousness Exist?" included in* Radical Empiricism, *James postulates that "pure experience" is the "primal stuff" from which all the particular things of the world are composed. This orientation provides as well the leverage for his well-known attack on Hegel.*

From William James, *Pragmatism* (New York: Longmans, Green & Co. Limited, 1907), Lecture VI, pp. 197–227.

When [James—Ed.] Clerk-Maxwell was a child it is written that he had a mania for having everything explained to him, and that when people put him off with vague verbal accounts of any phenomenon he would interrupt them impatiently by saying, 'Yes; but I want you to tell me the *particular go* of it!' Had his question been about truth, only a pragmatist could have told him the particular go of it. I believe that our contemporary pragmatists, especially Messrs. [F. C. S.—Ed.] Schiller and [John—Ed.] Dewey, have given the only tenable account of this subject. It is a very ticklish subject, sending subtle rootlets into all kinds of crannies, and hard to treat in the sketchy way that alone befits a public lecture. But the Schiller-Dewey view of truth has been so ferociously attacked by rationalistic philosophers, and so abominably misunderstood, that here, if anywhere, is the point where a clear and simple statement should be made.

. . .

Truth, as any dictionary will tell you, is a property of certain of our ideas. It means their 'agreement,' as falsity means their disagreement, with 'reality.' Pragmatists and intellectualists both accept this definition as a matter of course. They begin to quarrel only after the question is raised as to what may precisely be meant by the term 'agreement,' and what by the term 'reality,' when reality is taken as something for our ideas to agree with.

In answering these questions the pragmatists are more analytic and painstaking, the intellectualists more offhand and irreflective. The popular notion is that a true idea must copy its reality. Like other popular views, this one follows the analogy of the most usual experience. Our true ideas of sensible things do indeed copy them. Shut your eyes and think of yonder clock on the wall, and you get just such a true picture or copy of its dial. But your idea of its 'works' (unless you are a clock-maker) is much less of a copy, yet it passes muster, for it in no way clashes with the reality. Even though it should shrink to the mere word 'works,' that word still serves you truly; and when you speak of the 'timekeeping function' of the clock, or of its spring's 'elasticity,' it is hard to see exactly what your ideas can copy.

You perceive that there is a problem here. Where our ideas cannot copy definitely their object, what does agreement with that object mean? Some idealists seem to say that they are true whenever they are what God means that we ought to think about that object. Others hold the copy-view all through, and speak as if our ideas possessed truth just in proportion as they approach to being copies of the Absolute's eternal way of thinking.

These views, you see, invite pragmatistic discussion. But the great assumption of the intellectualists is that truth means essentially an inert static relation. When you've got your true idea of anything, there's an end of the matter. You're in possession; you *know*; you have fulfilled your thinking destiny. You are where you ought to be mentally; you have obeyed your categorical imperative; and nothing more need follow on that climax of your rational destiny. Epistemologically you are in stable equilibrium.

Pragmatism, on the other hand, asks its usual question. "Grant an idea or belief to be true," it says, "what concrete difference will its being true make in any one's actual life? How will the truth be realized? What experiences will be different from those which would obtain if the belief were false? What, in short, is the truth's cash-value in experiential terms?"

The moment pragmatism asks this question, it sees the answer: *True ideas are those that we can assimilate, validate, corroborate and verify. False ideas are those that we can not.* That is the practical difference it makes to us to have true ideas; that, therefore, is the meaning of truth, for it is all that truth is known-as.

This thesis is what I have to defend. The truth of an idea is not a stagnant property inherent in it. Truth *happens* to an idea. It *becomes* true, is *made* true by events. Its verity *is* in fact an event, a process: the process namely of its verifying itself, its veri-*fication*. Its validity is the process of its valid-*ation*.

But what do the words verification and validation themselves pragmatically mean? They again signify certain practical consequences of the verified and validated idea. It is hard to find any one phrase that characterizes these consequences better than the ordinary agreement-formula—just such consequences being what we have in mind whenever we say that our ideas 'agree' with reality. They lead us, namely, through the acts and other ideas which they instigate, into or up to, or towards, other parts of experience with which we feel all the while—such feeling being among our potentialities—that the original ideas remain in agreement. The connexions and transitions come to us from point to point as being progressive, harmonious, satisfactory. This function of agreeable leading is what we mean by an idea's verification. Such an account is vague and it sounds at first quite trivial, but it has results which it will take the rest of my [lecture] to explain.

Let me begin by reminding you of the fact that the possession of true thoughts means everywhere the possession of invaluable instruments of action; and that our duty to gain truth, so far from being a blank command from out of the blue, or a 'stunt' self-imposed by our intellect, can account for itself by excellent practical reasons.

The importance to human life of having true beliefs about matters of fact is a thing too notorious. We live in a world of realities that can be infinitely useful or infinitely harmful. Ideas that tell us which of them to expect count as the true ideas in all this primary sphere of verification, and the pursuit of such ideas is a primary human duty. The possession of truth, so far from being here an end in itself, is only a preliminary means towards other vital satisfactions. If I am lost in the woods and starved, and find what looks like a cowpath, it is of the utmost importance that I should think of a human habitation at the end of it, for if I do so and follow it, I save myself. The true thought is useful here because the house which is its object is useful. The practical value of true ideas is thus primarily derived from the practical importance of their objects to us. Their objects are, indeed, not important at all times. I may on another occasion have no use for the house; and then my idea of it, however verifiable, will be practically irrelevant, and had better remain latent. Yet since almost any object may some day become temporarily important, the advantage of having a general stock of *extra* truths, of ideas that shall be true of merely possible situations, is obvious. We store such extra truths away in our memories, and with the overflow we fill our books of reference. Whenever such an extra truth becomes practically relevant to one of our emergencies, it passes from cold-storage to do work in the world and our belief in it grows active. You can say of it then either that 'it is useful because it is true' or that 'it is true because it is useful.' Both these phrases mean exactly the same thing, namely that here is an idea that gets fulfilled and can be verified. True is the name for whatever idea starts the verification-process, useful is the name for its completed function in experience. True ideas would never have been singled out as such, would never have acquired a class-name, least of all a name suggesting value, unless they had been useful from the outset in this way.

From this simple cue pragmatism gets her general notion of truth as something essentially bound up with the way in which one moment in our experience may lead us towards other moments which it will be worth while to have been led to. Primarily, and on the common-sense level, the truth of a state of mind means this function of *a leading that is worth while*. When a moment in our experience, of any kind whatever, inspires us with a thought that is true, that means that sooner or later we dip by that thought's guidance into the particulars of experience again and make advantageous connexion with them. This is a vague enough statement, but I beg you to retain it, for it is essential.

Our experience meanwhile is all shot through with regularities. One bit of it can warn us to get ready for another bit, can 'intend' or be 'significant of' that remoter object. The object's advent is the significance's verification. Truth, in these cases, meaning nothing but eventual verification, is manifestly incompatible with waywardness on our part. Woe to him whose beliefs play fast and loose with the order which realities follow in his experience; they will lead him nowhere or else make false connexions.

By 'realities' or 'objects' here, we mean either things of common sense, sensibly present, or else common-sense relations, such as dates, places, distances, kinds, activities. Following our mental image of a house along the cow-path, we actually come to see the house; we get the image's full verification. *Such simply and fully verified leadings are certainly the originals and prototypes of the truth-process.* Experience offers indeed other forms of truth-process, but they are all conceivable as being primary verifications arrested, multiplied or substituted one for another.

Take, for instance, yonder object on the wall. You and I consider it to be a 'clock,' altho no one of us has seen the hidden works that make it one. We let our notion pass for true without attempting to verify. If truths mean verification-process essentially, ought we then to call such unverified truths as this abortive? No, for they form the overwhelmingly large number of the truths we live by. Indirect as well as direct verifications pass muster. Where circumstantial evidence is sufficient, we can go without eye-witnessing. Just as we here assume Japan to exist without ever having been there, because it *works* to do so, everything we know conspiring with the belief, and nothing interfering, so we assume that thing to be a clock. We *use* it as a clock, regulating the length of our lecture by it. The verification of the assumption here means its leading to no frustration or contradiction. Verif*ability* of wheels and weights and pendulum is as good as verification. For one truth-process completed there are a million in our lives that function in this state of nascency. They turn us *towards* direct verification; lead us into the *surroundings* of the objects they envisage; and then, if everything runs on harmoniously, we are so sure that verification is possible that we omit it, and are usually justified by all that happens.

Truth lives, in fact, for the most part on a credit system. Our thoughts and beliefs 'pass,' so long as nothing challenges them, just as bank-notes pass so long as nobody refuses them. But this all points to direct face-to-face verifications somewhere, without which the fabric of truth collapses like a financial system with no cash-basis whatever. You accept my verification of one thing, I yours of another. We trade on each other's truth. But beliefs verified concretely by *somebody* are the posts of the whole superstructure.

Another great reason—beside economy of time—for waiving complete verification in the usual business of life is that all things exist in kinds and not singly. Our world is found once for all to have that peculiarity. So that when we have once directly verified our ideas about one specimen of a kind, we consider ourselves free to apply them to other specimens without verification. A mind that habitually discerns the kind of thing before it, and acts by the law of the kind immediately, without pausing to verify, will be a 'true' mind in ninety-nine out of a hundred emergencies, proved so by its conduct fitting everything it meets, and getting no refutation.

Indirectly or only potentially verifying processes may thus be true as well as full verification-processes. They work as true processes would work, give us the same advantages, and claim our recognition for the same reasons. All this on the common-sense level of matters of fact, which we are alone considering.

But matters of fact are not our only stock in trade. *Relations among purely mental ideas* form another sphere where true and false beliefs obtain, and here the beliefs are absolute, or unconditional. When they are true they bear the name either of definitions or of principles. It is either a principle or a definition that 1 and 1 make 2, that 2 and 1 make 3, and so on; that white differs less from gray than it does from black; that when the cause begins to act the effect also commences. Such propositions hold of all possible 'ones,' of all conceivable 'whites' and 'grays' and 'causes.' The objects here are mental objects. Their relations are perceptually obvious at a glance, and no sense-verification is necessary. Moreover, once true, always true, of those same mental objects. Truth here has an 'eternal' character. If you can find a concrete thing anywhere that is 'one' or 'white' or 'gray' or 'effect,' then your principles will everlastingly apply to it. It is but a case of ascertaining the kind, and then applying the law of its kind to the particular object. You are sure to get truth if you can but name the kind rightly, for your mental relations hold good of everything of that kind without exception. If you then, nevertheless, failed to get truth concretely, you would say that you had classed your real objects wrongly.

In this realm of mental relations, truth again is an affair of leading. We relate one abstract idea with another, framing in the end great systems of logical and mathematical truth, under the respective terms of which the sensible facts of experience eventually arrange themselves, so that our eternal truths hold good of realities also. This marriage of fact and theory is endlessly fertile. What we say is here already true in advance of special verification, *if we have subsumed our objects rightly.* Our ready-made ideal framework for all sorts of possible objects follows from the very structure of our thinking. We can no more play fast and loose with these abstract relations than we can do so with our sense-experiences. They coerce us; we must treat them consistently, whether or not we like the results. The rules of addition apply to our debts as rigorously as to our assets. The hundredth decimal of π, the ratio of the circumference to its diameter, is predetermined ideally now, tho no one may have computed it. If we should ever need the figure in our dealings with an actual circle we should need to have it given rightly, calculated by the usual rules; for it is the same kind of truth that those rules elsewhere calculate.

Between the coercions of the sensible order and those of the ideal order, our mind is thus wedged tightly. Our ideas must agree with realities, be such realities concrete or abstract, be they facts or be they principles, under penalty of endless inconsistency and frustration.

So far, intellectualists can raise no protest. They can only say that we have barely touched the skin of the matter.

Realities mean, then, either concrete facts, or abstract kinds of thing and relations perceived intuitively between them. They furthermore and thirdly mean, as things that new ideas of ours must no less take account of, the whole body of other truths already in our possession. But what now does 'agreement' with such threefold realities mean?—to use again the definition that is current.

Here it is that pragmatism and intellectualism begin to part company. Primarily, no doubt, to agree means to copy, but we saw that the mere word 'clock' would do instead of a mental picture of its works, and that of many realities our ideas can only be symbols and not copies. 'Past time,' 'power,' 'spontaneity,'—how can our mind copy such realities?

To 'agree' in the widest sense with a reality *can only mean to be guided either straight up to it or into its surroundings, or to be put into such working touch with it as to handle either it or something connected with it better than if we disagreed.* Better either intellectually or practically! And often agreement will only mean the negative fact that nothing contradictory from the quarter of that reality comes to interfere with the way in which our ideas guide us elsewhere. To copy a reality is, indeed, one very important way of agreeing with it, but it is far from being essential. The essential thing is the process of being guided. Any idea that helps us to *deal*, whether practically or intellectually, with either the reality or its belongings, that doesn't entangle our progress in frustrations, that *fits*, in fact, and adapts our life to the reality's whole setting, will agree sufficiently to meet the requirement. It will hold true of that reality.

Thus, *names* are just as 'true' or 'false' as definite mental pictures are. They set up similar verification-processes, and lead to fully equivalent practical results.

All human thinking gets discursified; we exchange ideas; we lend and borrow verifications, get them from one another by means of social intercourse. All truth thus gets verbally built out, stored up, and made available for every one. Hence, we must *talk* consistently just as we must *think* consistently: for both in talk and thought we deal with kinds. Names are arbitrary, but once understood they must be kept to. We mustn't now call Abel 'Cain' or Cain 'Abel.' If we do, we ungear ourselves from the whole book of Genesis, and from all its connexions with the universe of speech and fact down to the present time. We throw ourselves out of whatever truth that entire system of speech and fact may embody.

The overwhelming majority of our true ideas admit of no direct or face-to-face verification—those of past history, for example, as of Cain and Abel. The stream of time can be remounted only verbally, or verified indirectly by the present prolongations or effects of what the past harbored. Yet if they agree with these verbalities and effects, we can know that our ideas of the past are true. *As true as past time itself was,* so true was Julius Cæsar, so true were antediluvian monsters, all in their proper dates and settings. That past time itself was, is guaranteed by its coherence with everything that's present. True as the present *is,* the past *was* also.

Agreement thus turns out to be essentially an affair of leading—leading that is useful because it is into quarters that contain objects that are important. True ideas lead us into useful verbal and conceptual quarters as well as directly up to useful sensible termini. They lead to consistency, stability and flowing human intercourse. They lead away from eccentricity and isolation, from foiled and barren thinking. The untrammelled flowing of the leading-process, its general freedom from clash and contradiction, passes for its indirect verification; but all roads lead to Rome, and in the end and eventually, all true processes must lead to the face of directly verifying sensible experiences *somewhere,* which somebody's ideas have copied.

Such is the large loose way in which the pragmatist interprets the word agreement. He treats it altogether practically. He lets it cover any process of conduction from a present idea to a future terminus, provided only it run prosperously. It is only thus that 'scientific' ideas, flying as they do beyond common sense, can be said to agree with their realities. It is, as I have already said, *as if* reality were made of ether, atoms or electrons, but we mustn't think so literally. The term 'energy' doesn't even pretend to stand for anything 'objective.' It is only a way of measuring the surface of phenomena so as to string their changes on a simple formula.

Yet in the choice of these man-made formulas we can not be capricious with impunity any more than we can be capricious on the common-sense practical level. We must find a theory that will *work;* and that means something extremely difficult; for our theory must mediate between all previous truths and certain new experiences. It must derange common sense and previous belief as little as possible, and it must lead to some sensible terminus or other that can be verified exactly. To 'work' means both these things; and the squeeze is so tight that there is little loose play for any hypothesis. Our theories are wedged and controlled as nothing else is. Yet sometimes alternative theoretic formulas are equally compatible with all the truths we know, and then we choose between them for subjective reasons. We choose the kind of theory to which we are already partial; we follow 'elegance' or 'economy.' Clerk-Maxwell somewhere says it would be 'poor scientific taste' to choose the more complicated of two equally well-evidenced conceptions; and you will all agree with him. Truth in science is what gives us the maximum possible sum of satisfactions, taste included, but consistency both with previous truth and with novel fact is always the most imperious claimant.

I have led you through a very sandy desert. But now, if I may be allowed so vulgar an expression, we begin to taste the milk in the coconut. Our rationalist critics here discharge their batteries upon us, and to reply to them will take us out from all this dryness into full sight of a momentous philosophical alternative.

Our account of truth is an account of truths in the plural, of processes of leading, realized *in rebus* [in things themselves—Ed.], and having only this quality in common, that they *pay*. They pay by guiding us into or towards some part of a system that dips at numerous points into sense-percepts, which we may copy mentally or not, but with which at any rate we are now in the kind of commerce vaguely designated as verification. Truth for us is simply a collective name for verification-processes, just as health, wealth, strength, etc., are names for other processes connected with life, and also pursued because it pays to pursue them. Truth is *made*, just as health, wealth and strength are made, in the course of experience.

Here rationalism is instantaneously up in arms against us. I can imagine a rationalist to talk as follows:

"Truth is not made," he will say; "it absolutely obtains, being a unique relation that does not wait upon any process, but shoots straight over the head of experience, and hits its reality every time. Our belief that yon thing on the wall is a clock is true already, altho no one in the whole history of the world should verify it. The bare quality of standing in that transcendent relation is what makes any thought true that possesses it, whether or not there be verification. You pragmatists put the cart before the horse in making truth's being reside in verification-processes. These are merely signs of its being, merely our lame ways of ascertaining after the fact, which of our ideas already has possessed the wondrous quality. The quality itself is timeless, like all essences and natures. Thoughts partake of it directly, as they partake of falsity or of irrelevancy. It can't be analyzed away into pragmatic consequences."

The whole plausibility of this rationalist tirade is due to the fact to which we have already paid so much attention. In our world, namely, abounding as it does in things of similar kinds and similarly associated, one verification serves for others of its kind, and one great use of knowing things is to be led not so much to them as to their associates, especially to human talk about them. The quality of truth, obtaining *ante rem* [prior to an examination of particular things in the world—Ed.], pragmatically means, then, the fact that in such a world innumerable ideas work better by their indirect or possible than by their direct and actual verification. Truth *ante rem* means only verifiability, then; or else it is a case of the stock rationalist trick of treating the *name* of a concrete phenomenal reality as an independent prior entity, and placing it behind the reality as its explanation.

.   .   .

In the case of 'wealth' we all see the fallacy. We know that wealth is but a name for concrete processes that certain men's lives play a part in, and not a natural excellence found in Messrs. Rockefeller and Carnegie, but not in the rest of us.

Like wealth, health also lives *in rebus.* It is a name for processes, as digestion, circulation, sleep, etc., that go on happily, tho in this instance we are more inclined to think of it as a principle and to say the man digests and sleeps so well *because* he is so healthy.

With 'strength' we are, I think, more rationalistic still, and decidedly inclined to treat it as an excellence pre-existing in the man and explanatory of the herculean performances of his muscles.

With 'truth' most people go over the border entirely, and treat the rationalistic account as self-evident. But really all these words in *th* are exactly similar. Truth exists *ante rem* just as much and as little as the other things do.

The scholastics, following Aristotle, made much of the distinction between habit and act. Health *in actu* [fully realized and actual—Ed.] means, among other things, good sleeping and digesting. But a healthy man need not always be sleeping, or always digesting, any more than a wealthy man need be always handling money, or a strong man always lifting weights. All such qualities sink to the status of 'habits' between their times of exercise; and similarly truth becomes a habit of certain of our ideas and beliefs in their intervals of rest from their verifying activities. But those activities are the root of the whole matter, and the condition of there being any habit to exist in the intervals.

'The true,' to put it very briefly, is only the expedient in the way of our thinking, just as 'the right' is only the expedient in the way of our behaving. Expedient in almost any fashion; and expedient in the long run and on the whole of course; for what meets expediently all the experience in sight won't necessarily meet all farther experiences equally satisfactorily. Experience, as we know, has ways of *boiling over*, and making us correct our present formulas.

The 'absolutely' true, meaning what no farther experience will ever alter, is that ideal vanishing-point towards which we imagine that all our temporary truths will some day converge. It runs on all fours with the perfectly wise man, and with the absolutely complete experience; and, if these ideals are ever realized, they will all be realized together. Meanwhile we have to live to-day by what truth we can get to-day, and be ready to-morrow to call it falsehood. Ptolemaic astronomy, euclidean space, aristotelian logic, scholastic metaphysics, were expedient for centuries, but human experience has boiled over those limits, and we now call these things only relatively true, or true within those borders of experience. 'Absolutely' they are false; for we know that those limits were casual, and might have been transcended by past theorists just as they are by present thinkers.

When new experiences lead to retrospective judgments, using the past tense, what these judgments utter *was* true, even tho no past thinker had been led there. We live forwards, a Danish thinker has said, but we understand backwards. The present sheds a backward light on the world's previous processes. They may have been truth-processes for the actors in them. They are not so for one who knows the later revelations of the story.

This regulative notion of a potential better truth to be established later, possibly to be established some day absolutely, and having powers of retroactive legislation, turns its face, like all pragmatist notions, towards concreteness of fact, and towards the future. Like the half-truths, the absolute truth will have to be *made*, made as a relation incidental to the growth of a mass of verification-experience, to which the half-true ideas are all along contributing their quota.

I have already insisted on the fact that truth is made largely out of previous truths. Men's beliefs at any time are so much experience *funded*. But the beliefs are themselves parts of the sum total of the world's experience, and become matter, therefore, for the next day's funding operations. So far as reality means experienceable reality, both it and the truths men gain about it are everlastingly in process of mutation—mutation towards a definite goal, it may be— but still mutation.

Mathematicians can solve problems with two variables. On the Newtonian theory, for instance, acceleration varies with distance, but distance also varies with acceleration. In the realm of truth-processes facts come independently and determine our beliefs provisionally. But these beliefs make us act, and as fast as they do so, they bring into sight or into existence new facts which re-determine the beliefs accordingly. So the whole coil and ball of truth, as it rolls up, is the product of a double influence. Truths emerge from facts; but they dip forward into facts again and add to them; which facts again create or reveal new truth (the word is indifferent) and so on indefinitely. The 'facts' themselves meanwhile are not *true*. They simply *are*. Truth is the function of the beliefs that start and terminate among them.

·　　·　　·

The most fateful point of difference between being a rationalist and being a pragmatist is now fully in sight. Experience is in mutation, and our psychological ascertainments of truth are in mutation—so much rationalism will allow; but never that either reality itself or truth itself is mutable. Reality stands complete and ready-made from all eternity, rationalism insists, and the agreement of our ideas with it is that unique unanalyzable virtue in them of which she has already told us. As that intrinsic excellence, their truth has nothing to do with our experiences. It adds nothing to the content of experience. It makes no difference to reality itself; it is supervenient, inert, static, a reflexion merely. It doesn't *exist*, it *holds* or *obtains*, it belongs to another dimension from that of either facts or fact-relations, belongs, in short, to the epistemological dimension—and with that big word rationalism closes the discussion.

Thus, just as pragmatism faces forward to the future, so does rationalism here again face backward to a past eternity. True to her inveterate habit, rationalism reverts to 'principles,' and thinks that when an abstraction once is named, we own an oracular solution.

·　　·　　·

13

Bertrand Russell
William James's Conception of Truth

.   .   .

[William—Ed.] James, like most philosophers, represents his views as mediating between two opposing schools. He begins by distinguishing two philosophic types called respectively the "tender-minded" and the "tough-minded." The "tender-minded" are "rationalistic, intellectualistic, idealistic, optimistic, religious, free-willist, monistic, dogmatical." The "tough-minded" are "empiricist, sensationalistic, materialistic, pessimistic, irreligious, fatalistic, pluralistic, sceptical." Traditionally, German philosophy was on the whole "tender-minded," British philosophy was on the whole "tough-minded." It will clear the ground for me to confess at once that I belong, with some reserves, to the "tough-minded" type. Pragmatism, William James avers, "can satisfy both kinds of demand. It can remain religious like the rationalisms, but at the same time, like the empiricisms, it can preserve the richest intimacy with facts." This reconciliation, to my mind, is illusory; I find myself agreeing with the "tough-minded" half of pragmatism and totally disagreeing with the "tender-minded" half. But the disentangling of the two halves must be postponed till we have seen how the reconciliation professes to be effected. Pragmatism represents, on the one hand, a method and habit of mind, on the other, a certain theory as to what constitutes truth. The latter is more nearly what Dr. [F. C. S.—Ed.] Schiller calls humanism; but this name is not adopted by James. We must, therefore, distinguish the pragmatic *method* and the pragmatic *theory of truth*. The former, up to a point, is involved in all induction, and is certainly largely commendable. The latter is the essential novelty and the point of real importance. But let us first consider the pragmatic method.

"Pragmatism," says James, "represents a perfectly familiar attitude in philosophy, the empiricist attitude, but it represents it, as it seems to me, both in a more radical and in a less objectionable form than it has ever yet assumed. A pragmatist turns his back resolutely and once for all upon a lot of inveterate habits dear to professional philosophers. He turns away from abstraction and insufficiency, from verbal solutions, from bad *a priori* reasons, from fixed principles, closed systems, and pretended absolutes and origins. He turns towards concreteness and adequacy, towards facts, towards action and towards power. That means the empiricist temper regnant and the rationalist temper sincerely given up. It means the open air and possibilities of nature, as against dogma, artificiality, and the pretence of finality in truth."

From Bertrand Russell, *Philosophical Essays* (London: Longmans, Green, and Co., 1910), pp. 128–144. Copyright 1966 by George Allen & Unwin, Ltd. Reprinted by permission of George Allen & Unwin, Ltd., and Simon & Schuster, Inc.

The temper of mind here described is one with which I, for my part, in the main cordially sympathise. But I think there is an impression in the mind of William James, as of some other pragmatists, that pragmatism involves a more open mind than its opposite. As regards scientific questions, or even the less important questions of philosophy, this is no doubt more or less the case. But as regards the fundamental questions of philosophy—especially as regards what I consider *the* fundamental question, namely, the nature of truth— pragmatism is absolutely dogmatic. The hypothesis that pragmatism is erroneous is not allowed to enter for the pragmatic competition; however well it may work, it is not to be entertained. To "turn your back resolutely and once for all" upon the philosophy of others may be heroic or praiseworthy, but it is not undogmatic or open-minded. A modest shrinking from self-assertion, a sense that all our theories are provisional, a constant realisation that after all the hypothesis of our opponents may be the right one—these characterise the truly empirical temper, but I do not observe that they invariably characterise the writings of pragmatists. Dogmatism in fundamentals is more or less unavoidable in philosophy, and I do not blame pragmatists for what could not be other- wise; but I demur to their claim to a greater open-mindedness than is or may be possessed by their critics.

William James, however, it must be admitted, is about as little pontifical as a philosopher well can be. And his complete absence of unction is most re- freshing. "In this real world of sweat and dirt," he says, "it seems to me that when a view of things is 'noble,' that ought to count as a presumption against its truth and as a philosophic disqualification." Accordingly his contentions are never supported by "fine writing"; he brings them into the market-place, and is not afraid to be homely, untechnical, and slangy. All this makes his books refreshing to read, and shows that they contain what he really lives by, not merely what he holds in his professional capacity.

But it is time to return to the pragmatic method.

"The pragmatic method," we are told, "is primarily a method of settling metaphysical disputes that otherwise might be interminable. Is the world one or many?—fated or free?—material or spiritual?—here are notions either of which may or may not hold good of the world; and disputes over such notions are unending. The pragmatic method in such cases is to try to interpret each notion by tracing its respective practical consequences. What difference would it practically make to any one if this notion rather than that notion were true? If no practical difference whatever can be traced, then the alternatives mean practically the same thing, and all dispute is idle. Whenever a dispute is serious, we ought to be able to show some practical difference that must follow from one side or the other's being right." And again: "To attain perfect clear- ness in our thoughts of an object, then, we need only consider what conceivable effects of a practical kind the object may involve—what sensations we are to expect from it, and what reactions we must prepare. Our conception of these effects, whether immediate or remote, is then for us the whole of our concep- tion of the object, so far as that conception has positive significance at all."

To this method, applied within limits and to suitable topics, there is no ground for objecting. On the contrary, it is wholesome to keep in touch with concrete facts, as far as possible, by remembering to bring our theories constantly into connection with them. The method, however, involves more than is stated in the extract which I quoted just now. It involves also the suggestion of the pragmatic criterion of truth: a belief is to be judged true in so far as the practical consequences of its adoption are good. Some pragmatists, for example, [Edouard—Ed.] Le Roy (who has lately suffered Papal condemnation), regard the pragmatic test as giving *only* a criterion;[1] others, notably Dr. Schiller, regard it as giving the actual *meaning* of truth. William James agrees on this point with Dr. Schiller, though, like him, he does not enter into the question of criterion *versus* meaning.

The pragmatic theory of truth is the central doctrine of pragmatism, and we must consider it at some length. William James states it in various ways, some of which I shall now quote. He says: "Ideas (which themselves are but parts of our experience) become true just in so far as they help us to get into satisfactory relation with other parts of our experience." Again: "Truth is *one species of good*, and not, as is usually supposed, a category distinct from good, and co-ordinate with it. *The true is the name of whatever proves itself to be good in any way of belief, and good, too, for definite, assignable reasons.*" That truth means "agreement with reality" may be said by a pragmatist as well as by any one else, but the pragmatist differs from others as to what is meant by *agreement*, and also (it would seem) as to what is meant by *reality*. William James gives the following definition of agreement: "To 'agree' in the widest sense with a reality *can only mean to be guided either straight up to it or into its surroundings, or to be put into such working touch with it as to handle either it or something connected with it better than if we disagreed.*" This language is rather metaphorical, and a little puzzling; it is plain, however, that "agreement" is regarded as practical, not as merely intellectual. This emphasis on practice is, of course, one of the leading features of pragmatism.

In order to understand the pragmatic notion of truth, we have to be clear as to the basis of *fact* upon which truths are supposed to rest. Immediate sensible experience, for example, does not come under the alternative of *true* and *false*. "Day follows day," says James, "and its contents are simply added. The new contents themselves are not true, they simply *come* and *are*. Truth is *what we say about* them." Thus when we are merely aware of sensible objects, we are not to be regarded as knowing any truth, although we have a certain kind of contact with reality. It is important to realise that the *facts* which thus lie outside the scope of truth and falsehood supply the material which is presupposed by the pragmatic theory. Our beliefs have to agree with matters of fact: it is an essential part of their "satisfactoriness" that they should do so. James also mentions what he calls "relations among purely mental ideas" as part of our stock-in-trade with which pragmatism starts. He mentions as instances "1 and 1 make 2," "white differs less from grey than it does from black," and so on. All such propositions as these, then, we are supposed to know

---

[1] Cf., e.g., Le Roy, "Comment se pose le problème de Dieu," *Revue de Métaphysique et de Morale*, xv. 4 (July, 1907), pp. 506, 507 *n*.

for certain before we can get under way. As James puts it: "Between the coercions of the sensible order and those of the ideal order, our mind is thus wedged tightly. Our ideas must agree with realities, be such realities concrete or abstract, be they facts or be they principles, under penalty of endless inconsistency and frustration." Thus it is only when we pass beyond plain matters of fact and *a priori* truisms that the pragmatic notion of truth comes in. It is, in short, the notion to be applied to doubtful cases, but it is not the notion to be applied to cases about which there can be no doubt. And that there are cases about which there can be no doubt is presupposed in the very statement of the pragmatist position. "Our account of truth," James tells us, "is an account . . . of processes of leading, realised *in rebus* [among actual things—Ed.], and having only this quality in common, that they *pay*." We may thus sum up the philosophy in the following definition: "A truth is anything which it pays to believe." Now, if this definition is to be useful, as pragmatism intends it to be, it must be possible to know that it pays to believe something without knowing anything that pragmatism would call a truth. Hence the knowledge that a certain belief pays must be classed as knowledge of a sensible fact or of a "relation among purely mental ideas," or as some compound of the two, and must be so easy to discover as not to be worthy of having the pragmatic test applied to it. There is, however, some difficulty in this view. Let us consider for a moment what it means to say that a belief "pays." We must suppose that this means that the consequences of entertaining the belief are better than those of rejecting it. In order to know this, we must know what are the consequences of entertaining it, and what are the consequences of rejecting it; we must know also what consequences are good, what bad, what consequences are better, and what worse. Take, say, belief in the Roman Catholic Faith. This, we may agree, causes a certain amount of happiness at the expense of a certain amount of stupidity and priestly domination. Such a view is disputable and disputed, but we will let that pass. But then comes the question whether, admitting the effects to be such, they are to be classed as on the whole good or on the whole bad; and this question is one which is so difficult that our test of truth becomes practically useless. It is far easier, it seems to me, to settle the plain question of fact: "Have Popes been always infallible?" than to settle the question whether the effects of thinking them infallible are on the whole good. Yet this question, of the truth of Roman Catholicism, is just the sort of question that pragmatists consider specially suitable to their method.

The notion that it is quite easy to know when the consequences of a belief are good, so easy, in fact, that a theory of knowledge need take no account of anything so simple—this notion, I must say, seems to be one of the strangest assumptions for a theory of knowledge to make. Let us take another illustration. Many of the men of the French Revolution were disciples of Rousseau, and their belief in his doctrines had far-reaching effects, which make Europe at this day a different place from what it would have been without that belief. If, on the whole, the effects of their belief have been good, we shall have to say that their belief was true; if bad, that it was false. But how are we to strike the balance? It is almost impossible to disentangle what the effects have been; and even if we could ascertain them, our judgment as to whether they have been good or bad would depend upon our political opinions. It is surely far easier to discover by direct investigation that the *Contrat Social* is a myth than to decide whether belief in it has done harm or good on the whole.

Another difficulty which I feel in regard to the pragmatic meaning of "truth" may be stated as follows: Suppose I accept the pragmatic criterion, and suppose you persuade me that a certain belief is useful. Suppose I thereupon conclude that the belief is true. Is it not obvious that there is a transition in my mind from seeing that the belief is useful to actually holding that the belief is true? Yet this could not be so if the pragmatic account of truth were valid. Take, say, the belief that other people exist. According to the pragmatists, to say "it is true that other people exist" *means* "it is useful to believe that other people exist." But if so, then these two phrases are merely different words for the same proposition; therefore when I believe the one I believe the other. If this were so, there could be no transition from the one to the other, as plainly there is. This shows that the word "true" represents for us a different idea from that represented by the phrase "useful to believe," and that, therefore, the pragmatic definition of truth ignores, without destroying, the meaning commonly given to the word "true," which meaning, in my opinion, is of fundamental importance, and can only be ignored at the cost of hopeless inadequacy.

This brings me to the difference between *criterion* and *meaning*—a point on which neither James nor Dr. Schiller is very clear. I may best explain the difference, to begin with, by an instance. If you wish to know whether a certain book is in a library, you consult the catalogue: books mentioned in the catalogue are presumably in the library, books not mentioned in it are presumably not in the library. Thus the catalogue affords a *criterion* of whether a book is in the library or not. But even supposing the catalogue perfect, it is obvious that when you say the book is in the library you do not *mean* that it is mentioned in the catalogue. You mean that the actual book is to be found somewhere in the shelves. It therefore remains an intelligible hypothesis that there are books in the library which are not yet catalogued, or that there are books catalogued which have been lost and are no longer in the library. And it remains an inference from the discovery that a book is mentioned in the catalogue to the conclusion that the book is in the library. Speaking abstractly, we may say that a property A is a *criterion* of a property B when the same objects possess both; and A is a *useful* criterion of B if it is easier to discover whether an object possesses the property A than whether it possesses the property B. Thus being mentioned in the catalogue is a *useful* criterion of being in the library, because it is easier to consult the catalogue than to hunt through the shelves.

Now if pragmatists only affirmed that utility is a *criterion* of truth, there would be much less to be said against their view. For there certainly seem to be few cases, if any, in which it is clearly useful to believe what is false. The chief criticism one would then have to make on pragmatism would be to deny that utility is a *useful* criterion, because it is so often harder to determine whether a belief is useful than whether it is true. The arguments of pragmatists are almost wholly directed to proving that utility is a *criterion*; that utility is the *meaning* of truth is then supposed to follow. But, to return to our illustration of the library, suppose we had conceded that there are no mistakes in the British Museum catalogue: would it follow that the catalogue would do without the books? We can imagine some person long engaged in a comparative study of libraries, and having, in the process, naturally lost all taste for reading, declaring that the catalogue is the only important thing—as for the books, they are useless lumber; no one ever wants them, and the principle of economy should lead us to be content with the catalogue. Indeed, if you consider the matter with an open mind, you will see that the catalogue *is* the library, for it tells you everything you can possibly wish to know about the library. Let us, then, save the taxpayers' money by destroying the books: allow free access to the catalogue, but condemn the desire to read as involving an exploded dogmatic realism.

This analogy of the library is not, to my mind, fantastic or unjust, but as close and exact an analogy as I have been able to think of. The point I am trying to make clear is concealed from pragmatists, I think, by the fact that their theories start very often from such things as the general hypotheses of science—ether, atoms, and the like. In such cases, we take little interest in the hypotheses themselves, which, as we well know, are liable to rapid change. What we care about are the inferences as to sensible phenomena which the hypotheses enable us to make. All we ask of the hypotheses is that they should "work"— though it should be observed that what constitutes "working" is not the general agreeableness of their results, but the conformity of these results with observed phenomena. But in the case of these general scientific hypotheses, no sensible man believes that they are true as they stand. They are believed to be true in part, and to work because of the part that is true; but it is expected that in time some element of falsehood will be discovered, and some truer theory will be substituted. Thus pragmatism would seem to derive its notion of what constitutes belief from cases in which, properly speaking, belief is absent, and in which—what is pragmatically important—there is but a slender interest in truth or falsehood as compared to the interest in what "works."

But when this method is extended to cases in which the proposition in question has an emotional interest on its own account, apart from its working, the pragmatic account becomes less satisfactory. This point has been well brought out by Prof. [G. F.—Ed.] Stout in *Mind*,[2] and what I have to say is mostly contained in his remarks. Take the question whether other people exist. It seems perfectly possible to suppose that the hypothesis that they exist will always work, even if they do not in fact exist. It is plain, also, that it makes for happiness to believe that they exist—for even the greatest misanthropist would not wish to be deprived of the objects of his hate. Hence the belief that other people exist is, pragmatically, a true belief. But if I am troubled by solipsism, the discovery that a belief in the existence of others is "true" in the pragmatist's sense is not enough to allay my sense of loneliness: the

---

[2] October, 1907, pp. 586–8. This criticism occurs in the course of a very sympathetic review of Dr. Schiller's *Studies in Humanism*.

perception that I should profit by rejecting solipsism is not alone sufficient to make me reject it. For what I desire is not that the belief in solipsism should be false in the pragmatic sense, but that other people should in fact exist. And with the pragmatist's meaning of truth, these two do not necessarily go together. The belief in solipsism might be false even if I were the only person or thing in the universe.

This paradoxical consequence would, I presume, not be admitted by pragmatists. Yet it is an inevitable outcome of the divorce which they make between *fact* and *truth*. Returning to our illustration, we may say that "facts" are represented by the books, and "truths" by the entries in the catalogue. So long as you do not wish to read the books, the "truths" will do in place of the "facts," and the imperfections of your library can be remedied by simply making new entries in the catalogue. But as soon as you actually wish to read a book, the "truths" become inadequate, and the "facts" become all-important. The pragmatic account of truth assumes, so it seems to me, that no one takes any interest in facts, and that the truth of the proposition that your friend exists is an adequate substitute for the fact of his existence. "Facts," they tell us, are neither true nor false, therefore truth cannot be concerned with them. But the truth "A exists," if it is a truth, is concerned with A, who in that case is a fact; and to say that "A exists" may be true even if A does not exist is to give a meaning to "truth" which robs it of all interest. Dr. Schiller is fond of attacking the view that truth must correspond with reality; we may conciliate him by agreeing that *his* truth, at any rate, need not correspond with reality. But we shall have to add that reality is to us more interesting than such truth.

I am, of course, aware that pragmatists minimise the basis of "fact," and speak of the "making of reality" as proceeding *pari passu* with the "making of truth." It is easy to criticise the claim to "make reality" except within obvious limits. But when such criticisms are met by pointing to the pragmatist's admission that, after all, there must be a basis of "fact" for our creative activity to work upon, then the opposite line of criticism comes into play. Dr. Schiller, in his essay on "the making of reality," minimises the importance of the basis of "fact," on the ground (it would seem) that "facts" will not submit to pragmatic treatment, and that, if pragmatism is true, they are unknowable.[3] Hence, on pragmatistic principles, it is useless to think about facts. We therefore return to fictions with a sigh of relief, and soothe our scruples by calling them "realities." But it seems something of a *petitio principii* [begging of the question—Ed.] to condemn "facts" because pragmatism, though it finds them necessary, is unable to deal with them. And William James, it should be said, makes less attempt than Dr. Schiller does to minimise facts. In this essay, therefore, I have considered the difficulties which pragmatism has to face if it admits "facts" rather than those (no less serious) which it has to face if it denies them.

It is chiefly in regard to religion that the pragmatist use of "truth" seems to me misleading. Pragmatists boast much of their ability to reconcile religion and science, and William James, as we saw, professes to have discovered a

---

[3] Cf. *Studies in Humanism*, pp. 434–6.

position combining the merits of tender-mindedness and tough-mindedness. The combination is really effected, if I am not mistaken, in a way of which pragmatists are not themselves thoroughly aware. For their position, if they fully realised it, would, I think, be this: "We cannot know whether, in fact, there is a God or a future life, but we can know that the belief in God and a future life is true." This position, it is to be feared, would not afford much comfort to the religious if it were understood, and I cannot but feel some sympathy with the Pope in his condemnation of it.

"On pragmatic principles," James says, "we cannot reject any hypothesis if consequences useful to life flow from it." He proceeds to point out that consequences useful to life flow from the hypothesis of the Absolute, which is therefore so far a true hypothesis. But it should be observed that these useful consequences flow from the hypothesis that the Absolute is a fact, not from the hypothesis that useful consequences flow from belief in the Absolute. But we cannot believe the hypothesis that the Absolute is a fact merely because we perceive that useful consequences flow from this hypothesis. What we can believe on such grounds is that this hypothesis is what pragmatists call "true," i.e. that it is useful; but it is not from this belief that the useful consequences flow, and the grounds alleged do not make us believe that the Absolute is a fact, which is the useful belief. In other words, the useful belief is that the Absolute is a fact, and pragmatism shows that this belief is what it calls "true." Thus pragmatism persuades us that belief in the Absolute is "true," but does not persuade us that the Absolute is a fact. The belief which it persuades us to adopt is therefore not the one which is useful. In ordinary logic, if the belief in the Absolute is true, it follows that the Absolute is a fact. But with the pragmatist's meaning of "true" this does not follow; hence the proposition which he proves is not, as he thinks, the one from which comforting consequences flow.

In another place James says: "On pragmatistic principles, if the hypothesis of God works satisfactorily in the widest sense of the word, it is true." This proposition is, in reality, a mere tautology. For we have laid down the definition: "The word 'true' means 'working satisfactorily in the widest sense of the word.'" Hence the proposition stated by James is merely a verbal variant on the following: "On pragmatistic principles, if the hypothesis of God works satisfactorily in the widest sense of the word, then it works satisfactorily in the widest sense of the word." This would hold even on other than pragmatistic principles; presumably what is peculiar to pragmatism is the belief that this is an important contribution to the philosophy of religion. The advantage of the pragmatic method is that it decides the question of the truth of the existence of God by purely mundane arguments, namely, by the effects of belief in His existence upon our life in this world. But unfortunately this gives a merely mundane conclusion, namely, that belief in God is true, i.e. useful, whereas what religion desires is the conclusion that God exists, which pragmatism never even approaches. I infer, therefore, that the pragmatic philosophy of religion, like most philosophies whose conclusions are interesting, turns on an unconscious play upon words. A common word—in this case, the word "true"—is taken at the outset in an uncommon sense, but as the argument proceeds the usual sense of the word gradually slips back, and the conclusions arrived at seem, therefore, quite different from what they would be seen to be if the initial definition had been remembered.

The point is, of course, that, so soon as it is admitted that there are things that exist, it is impossible to avoid recognising a distinction, to which we may give what name we please, between believing in the existence of something that exists and believing in the existence of something that does not exist. It is common to call the one belief true, the other false. But if, with the pragmatists, we prefer to give a different meaning to the words "true" and "false," that does not prevent the distinction commonly called the distinction of "true" and "false" from persisting. The pragmatist attempt to ignore this distinction fails, as it seems to me, because a basis of fact cannot be avoided by pragmatism, and this basis of fact demands the *usual* antithesis of "true" and "false." It is hardly to be supposed that pragmatists will admit this conclusion. But it may be hoped that they will tell us in more detail how they propose to avoid it.

.   .   .

14

J. L. Austin

Truth

J. L. Austin was White's Professor of Moral Philosophy at Oxford until his death in 1960. Apart from his influential philosophical papers, a fair portion of which were published posthumously, Austin had distinguished himself as a British intelligence officer during World War II and as a specialist in Greek philosophy, Leibniz, and Frege. He was greatly admired and feared as an extraordinarily incisive critic in personal exchange. The informal once-a-week meetings he initiated at Oxford and continued in America in the last year of his life (when he was Visiting Professor at the University of California, Berkeley) became an important part of the oral tradition of Anglo-American philosophy.

Since his production is somewhat small, his influence must be credited to the brilliance and originality of his style. It has been said that Austin had the most acute ear for the nuances of English, and indeed his method of analysis rested on a respect for the conceptual distinctions that could be marked by a collection of relevant specimens of the language. In the lecture room, for instance, Austin tested "what we would say" in an immense number of subtly varying situations.

J. L. Austin, "Truth," *Proceedings of the Aristotelian Society*, Supplementary Vol. **XXIV** (1950), 111–128. Reprinted by courtesy of the Editor of The Aristotelian Society. © 1950, The Aristotelian Society.

He seems to have had a kind of evolutionary theory regarding the changes in
ordinary language. Though he expressly denied that philosophy is nothing but the
analysis of the conceptual functions of expressions in ordinary language, he
was equally insistent that such analysis was at least the "begin-all" of philosophy.
In "A Plea for Excuses" he confirms the remarkable force of suitably arraying
linguistic distinctions collected in the literature of the law.

Austin's two principal volumes were Sense and Sensibilia *(1962) and* How to
Do Things with Words *(the William James lectures at Harvard, 1955, published*
1962). Both exhibit his own brand of ordinary-language analysis—notably
independent of Wittgenstein's style and method of proceeding, which had become
so influential in England when Austin lectured—and introduce his most
penetrating discoveries. In the first, for instance, Austin demonstrated the variety
of ways in which the epithet "real" is employed, the dialectic nature of contrasting
how things seem *and how they* are, *and the special status of illusions. The second*
book is almost single-handedly responsible for the great vogue, now pursued in
ways rather different from Austin's, of analyzing language in the context of speech.
Austin is clearly responsible for the terminological distinctions that have facilitated
that development.

1. 'What is truth?' said jesting Pilate, and would not stay for an answer. Pilate
was in advance of his time. For 'truth' itself is an abstract noun, a camel, that
is, of a logical construction, which cannot get past the eye even of a grammarian.
We approach it cap and categories in hand: we ask ourselves whether Truth
is a substance (the Truth, the Body of Knowledge), or a quality (something
like the colour red, inhering in truths), or a relation ('correspondence').[1] But
philosophers should take something more nearly their own size to strain at.
What needs discussing rather is the use, or certain uses, of the word 'true'. *In
vino*, possibly, *'veritas'* ['truth'—Ed.], but in a sober symposium *'verum'* ['true'
—Ed.].

2. What is it that we say is true or is false? Or, how does the phrase 'is
true' occur in English sentences? The answers appear at first multifarious. We
say (or are said to say) that beliefs are true, that descriptions or accounts are
true, that propositions or assertions or statements are true, and that words or
sentences are true: and this is to mention only a selection of the more obvious
candidates. Again, we say (or are said to say) 'It is true that the cat is on the
mat', or 'It is true to say that the cat is on the mat', or ' "The cat is on the mat"
is true'. We also remark on occasion, when someone else has said something,
'Very true' or 'That's true' or 'True enough'.

Most (though not all) of these expressions, and others besides, certainly
do occur naturally enough. But it seems reasonable to ask whether there is
not some use of 'is true' that is primary, or some generic name for that which
at bottom we are always saying 'is true'. Which, if any, of these expressions is
to be taken *au pied de la lettre* [quite literally—Ed.]? To answer this will not
take us long, nor, perhaps, far: but in philosophy the foot of the letter is the
foot of the ladder.

---

[1] It is sufficiently obvious that 'truth' is a substantive, 'true' an adjective and 'of' in
'true of' a preposition.

I suggest that the following are the primary forms of expression:

It is true (to say) that the cat is on the mat.
That statement (of his, &c.) is true.
The statement that the cat is on the mat is true.

But first for the rival candidates.

(*a*) Some say that 'truth is primarily a property of beliefs'. But it may be doubted whether the expression 'a true belief' is at all common outside philosophy and theology: and it seems clear that a man is said to hold a true belief when and in the sense that he believes (in) *something which* is true, or believes that *something which* is true is true. Moreover if, as some also say, a belief is 'of the nature of a picture', then it is of the nature of what cannot be true, though it may be, for example, faithful.[2]

(*b*) True descriptions and true accounts are simply varieties of true statements or of collections of true statements, as are true answers and the like. The same applies to propositions too, in so far as they are genuinely said to be true (and not, as more commonly, sound, tenable and so on).[3] A proposition in law or in geometry is something portentous, usually a generalization, that we are invited to accept and that has to be recommended by argument: it cannot be a direct report on current observation—if you look and inform me that the cat is on the mat, that is not a proposition though it is a statement. In philosophy, indeed, "proposition' is sometimes used in a special way for 'the meaning or sense of a sentence or family of sentences': but whether we think a lot or little of this usage, a proposition in this sense cannot, at any rate, be what we say is true or false. For we never say 'The meaning (or sense) of this sentence (or of these words) is true': what we do say is what the judge or jury says, namely that 'The words taken in this sense, or if we assign to them such and such a meaning, or so interpreted or understood, *are true'*.

(*c*) Words and sentences are indeed said to be true, the former often, the latter rarely. But only in certain senses. Words as discussed by philologists, or by lexicographers, grammarians, linguists, phoneticians, printers, critics (stylistic or textual) and so on, are not true or false: they are wrongly formed, or ambiguous or defective or untranslatable or unpronounceable or mis-spelled or archaistic or corrupt or what not.[4] Sentences in similar contexts are elliptic or involved or alliterative or ungrammatical. We may, however, genuinely say 'His closing words were very true' or 'The third sentence on page 5 of his speech is quite

---

[2] A likeness is true *to* life, but not true *of* it. A *word* picture can be true, just because it is *not* a picture.

[3] Predicates applicable also to 'arguments', which we likewise do not say are true, but, for example, valid.

[4] [C. S.—Ed.] Peirce made a beginning by pointing out that there are two (or three) different senses of the word 'word', and adumbrated a technique ('counting' words) for deciding what is a 'different sense'. But his two senses are not well defined, and there are many more—the 'vocable' sense, the philologist's sense in which 'grammar' is the same word as 'glamour', the textual critic's sense in which the 'the' in 1. 254 has been written twice, and so on. With all his 66 divisions of signs, Peirce does not, I believe, distinguish between a sentence and a statement.

false': but here 'words' and 'sentence' refer, as is shown by the demonstratives (possessive pronouns, temporal verbs, definite descriptions, &c.), which in this usage consistently accompany them, to the words or sentence *as used by a certain person on a certain occasion*. That is, they refer (as does 'Many a true word spoken in jest') to *statements*.

A statement is made and its making is an historic event, the utterance by a certain speaker or writer of certain words (a sentence) to an audience with reference to an historic situation, event or what not.[5]

A sentence is made *up of* words, a statement is made *in* words. A sentence is not English or not good English, a statement is not in English or not in good English. Statements are made, words or sentences are used. We talk of *my* statement, but of *the English* sentence (if a sentence is mine, I coined it, but I do not coin statements). The *same* sentence is used in making *different* statements (I say 'It is mine', you say 'It is mine'): it may also be used on two occasions or by two persons in making the *same* statement, but for this the utterance must be made with reference to the same situation or event.[6] We speak of 'the statement that S,' but of 'the sentence "S" ', not of 'the sentence that S'.[7]

When I say that a statement is true, I have no wish to become wedded to one word. 'Assertion', for example, will in most contexts do just as well, though perhaps it is slightly wider. Both words share the weakness of being rather solemn (much more so than the more general 'what you said' or 'your words')— though perhaps we are generally being a little solemn when we discuss the truth of anything. Both have the merit of clearly referring to the historic use of a sentence by an utterer, and of being therefore precisely not equivalent to 'sentence'. For it is a fashionable mistake to take as primary '(The sentence) "S" is true (in the English language)'. Here the addition of the words 'in the English language' serves to emphasize that 'sentence' is not being used as equivalent to 'statement', so that it precisely is not what can be true or false (and moreover, 'true in the English language' is a solecism, mismodelled presumably, and with deplorable effect, on expressions like 'true in geometry').

3. When is a statement true? The temptation is to answer (at least if we

---

[5] 'Historic' does not, of course, mean that we cannot speak of future or possible statements. A 'certain' speaker need not be any definite speaker. 'Utterance' need not be public utterance—the audience may be the speaker himself.

[6] 'The same' does not always mean the same. In fact it has no meaning in the way that an 'ordinary' world like 'red' or 'horse' has a meaning: it is a (the typical) device for establishing and distinguishing the meanings of ordinary words. Like 'real', it is part of our apparatus *in* words for fixing and adjusting the semantics *of* words.

[7] Inverted commas show that the words, though uttered (in writing), are not to be taken as a statement by the utterer. This covers two possible cases, (i) where what is to be discussed is the sentence, (ii) where what is to be discussed is a statement made elsewhere in the words 'quoted'. Only in case (i) is it correct to say simply that the token is doing duty for the type (and even here it is quite incorrect to say that 'The cat is on the mat' is the *name* of an English sentence—though possibly *The Cat is on the Mat* might be the title of a novel, or a bull might be known as *Catta est in matta*). Only in case (ii) is there something true or false, *viz.* (not the quotation but) the statement made in the words quoted.

confine ourselves to 'straightforward' statements): 'When it corresponds to the facts'. And as a piece of standard English this can hardly be wrong. Indeed, I must confess I do not really think it is wrong at all: the theory of truth is a series of truisms. Still, it can at least be misleading.

If there is to be communication of the sort that we achieve by language at all, there must be a stock of symbols of some kind which a communicator ('the speaker') can produce 'at will' and which a communicatee ('the audience') can observe: these may be called the 'words', though, of course, they need not be anything very like what we should normally call words—they might be signal flags, &c. There must also be something other than the words, which the words are to be used to communicate about: this may be called the 'world'. There is no reason why the world should not include the words, in every sense except the sense of the actual statement itself which on any particular occasion is being made about the world. Further, the world must exhibit (we must observe) similarities and dissimilarities (there could not be the one without the other): if everything were either absolutely indistinguishable from anything else or completely unlike anything else, there would be nothing to say. And finally (for present purposes—of course there are other conditions to be satisfied too) there must be two sets of conventions:

> *Descriptive* conventions correlating the words (= sentences) with the *types* of situation, thing, event, &c., to be found in the world.
> *Demonstrative* conventions correlating the words (= statements) with the *historic* situations, &c., to be found in the world.[8]

A statement is said to be true when the historic state of affairs to which it is correlated by the demonstrative conventions (the one to which it 'refers') is of a type[9] with which the sentence used in making it is correlated by the descriptive conventions.[10]

---

[8] Both sets of conventions may be included together under 'semantics'. But they differ greatly.

[9] 'Is of a type with which' means 'is sufficiently like those standard states of affairs with which'. Thus, for a statement to be true one state of affairs must be *like* certain others, which is a natural relation, but also *sufficiently* like to merit the same 'description', which is no longer a purely natural relation. To say 'This is red' is not the same as to say 'This is like those', nor even as to say 'This is like those which were called red'. That things are *similar*, or even 'exactly' similar, I may literally see, but that they are the *same* I cannot literally see—in calling them the same colour a convention is involved additional to the conventional choice of the name to be given to the colour which they are said to be.

[10] The trouble is that sentences contain words or verbal devices to serve both descriptive and demonstrative purposes (not to mention other purposes), often both at once. In philosophy we mistake the descriptive for the demonstrative (theory of universals) or the demonstrative for the descriptive (theory of monads). A sentence as normally distinguished from a mere word or phrase is characterized by its containing a minimum of verbal demonstrative devices (Aristotle's 'reference to time'); but many demonstrative conventions are non-verbal (pointing, &c.), and using these we can make a statement in a single word which is not a 'sentence'. Thus, 'languages' like that of (traffic, &c.) *signs* use quite distinct media for their descriptive and demonstrative elements (the sign on the post, the site of the post). And however many verbal demonstrative devices we use as auxiliaries, there must *always* be a non-verbal *origin* for these co-ordinates, which is the point of utterance of the statement.

3*a*. Troubles arise from the use of the word 'facts' for the historic situations, events, &c., and in general, for the world. For 'fact' is regularly used in conjunction with 'that' in the sentences 'The fact is that S' or 'It is a fact that S' and in the expression 'the fact that S', all of which imply that it would be true to say that S.[11]

This may lead us to suppose that

(i) 'fact' is only an alternative expression for 'true statement'. We note that when a detective says 'Lets look at the facts' he does not crawl round the carpet, but proceeds to utter a string of statements: we even talk of 'stating the facts';

(ii) for every true statement there exists 'one' and its own precisely corresponding fact—for every cap the head it fits.

It is (i) which leads to some of the mistakes in 'coherence' or formalist theories; (ii) to some of those in 'correspondence' theories. Either we suppose that there is nothing there but the true statement itself, nothing to which it corresponds, or else we populate the world with linguistic *Doppelgänger* [doubles —Ed.] (and grossly overpopulate it—every nugget of 'positive' fact overlaid by a massive concentration of 'negative' facts, every tiny detailed fact larded with generous general facts, and so on).

When a statement is true, there is, *of course*, a state of affairs which makes it true and which is *toto mundo* [entirely—Ed.] distinct from the true statement about it: but equally of course, we can only *describe* that state of affairs *in words* (either same or, with luck, others). I can only describe the situation in which it is true to say that I am feeling sick by saying that it is one in which I am feeling sick (or experiencing sensations of nausea):[12] yet between stating, however truly, that I am feeling sick and feeling sick there is a great gulf fixed.[13]

'Fact that' is a phrase designed for use in situations where the distinction between a true statement and the state of affairs about which it is a truth is neglected; as it often is with advantage in ordinary life, though seldom in philosophy—above all in discussing truth, where it is precisely our business to

---

[11] I use the following *abbreviations*:
S for the cat is on the mat.
ST for it is true that the cat is on the mat.
tst for the statement that.

I take tstS as my example throughout and not, say, tst Julius Caesar was bald or tst all mules are sterile, because these latter are apt in their different ways to make us overlook the distinction between sentence and statement: we have, apparently, in the one case a sentence capable of being used to refer to only one historic situation, in the other a statement without reference to at least (or to any particular) one.

If space permitted other types of statement (existential, general, hypothetical, &c.) should be dealt with: these raise problems rather of meaning than of truth, though I feel uneasiness about hypotheticals.

[12] If this is what was meant by ' "It is raining" is true if and only if it is raining', so far so good.

[13] It takes two to make a truth. Hence (obviously) there can be no criterion of truth in the sense of some feature detectable in the statement itself which will reveal whether it is true or false. Hence, too, a statement cannot without absurdity refer to itself.

prise the words off the world and keep them off it. To ask 'Is the fact that S the true statement that S or that which it is true of?' may beget absurd answers. To take an analogy: although we may sensibly ask 'Do we *ride* the word "elephant" or the animal?' and equally sensibly 'Do we *write* the word or the animal?' it is nonsense to ask 'Do we *define* the word or the animal?' For defining an elephant (supposing we ever do this) is a compendious description of an operation involving both word and animal (do we focus the image or the battleship?); and so speaking about 'the fact that' is a compendious way of speaking about a situation involving both words and world.[14]

3*b*. 'Corresponds' also gives trouble, because it is commonly given too restricted or too colourful a meaning, or one which in this context it cannot bear. The only essential point is this: that the correlation between the words (= sentences) and the type of situation, event, &c. which is to be such that when a statement in those words is made with reference to an historic situation of that type the statement is then true, is *absolutely and purely* conventional. We are absolutely free to appoint *any* symbol to describe *any* type of situation, so far as merely being true goes. In a small one-spade language tst nuts might be true in exactly the same circumstances as the statement in English that the National Liberals are the people's choice.[15] There is no need whatsoever for the words used in making a true statement to 'mirror' in any way, however indirect, any feature whatsoever of the situation or event; a statement no more needs, in order to be true, to reproduce the 'multiplicity,' say, or the 'structure' or 'form' of the reality, than a word needs to be echoic or writing pictographic. To suppose that it does, is to fall once again into the error of reading back into the world the features of language.

The more rudimentary a language, the more, very often, it will tend to have a 'single' word for a highly 'complex' type of situation: this has such disadvantages as that the language becomes elaborate to learn and is incapable of dealing with situations which are non-standard, unforeseen, for which there may just be no word. When we go abroad equipped only with a phrase-book, we may spend long hours learning by heart—

A'-moest-fa'nd-ᵉtschâʳwoumᵉn,
Ma'hwîl-iz-wauʳpt (bènt),

and so on and so on, yet faced with the situation where we have the pen of our aunt, find ourselves quite unable to say so. The characteristics of a more developed language (articulation, morphology, syntax, abstractions, &c.), do not make statements in it any more capable of being true or capable of being any more true, they make it more adaptable, more learnable, more comprehensive, more precise, and so on; and *these* aims may no doubt be furthered by

---

[14] 'It is true that S' and 'It is a fact that S' are applicable in the same circumstances; the cap fits when there is a head it fits. Other words can fill the same role as 'fact': we say, e.g. 'The situation is that S'.

[15] We could use 'nuts' even now as a code-word: but a code, as transformation of a language, is distinguished from a language, and a code-word dispatched is not (called) 'true'.

making the language (allowance made for the nature of the medium) 'mirror' in conventional ways features descried in the world.

Yet even when a language does 'mirror' such features very closely (and does it ever?) the truth of statements remains still a matter, as it was with the most rudimentary languages, of the words used being the ones *conventionally appointed* for situations of the type to which that referred to belongs. A picture, a copy, a replica, a photograph—these are *never* true in so far as they are reproductions, produced by natural or mechanical means: a reproduction can be accurate or lifelike (true *to* the original), as a gramophone recording or a transcription may be, but not true (*of*) as a record of proceedings can be. In the same way a (natural) sign *of* something can be infallible or unreliable but only an (artificial) sign *for* something can be right or wrong.[16]

There are many intermediate cases between a true account and a faithful picture, as here somewhat forcibly contrasted, and it is from the study of these (a lengthy matter) that we can get the clearest insight into the contrast. For example, maps: these may be called pictures, yet they are highly conventionalized pictures. If a map can be clear or accurate or misleading, like a statement, why can it not be true or exaggerated? How do the 'symbols' used in map-making differ from those used in statement-making? On the other hand, if an air-mosaic is not a map, why is it not? And when does a map become a diagram? These are the really illuminating questions.

4. Some have said that—

To say that an assertion is true is not to make any further assertion at all.
In all sentences of the form '*p* is true' the phrase 'is true' is logically superfluous. To say that a proposition is true is just to assert it, and to say that it is false is just to assert its contradictory.

But wrongly. TstS (except in paradoxical cases of forced and dubious manufacture) refers to the world or any part of it exclusive of tstS, i.e. of itself.[17] TstST refers to the world or any part of it *inclusive* of tstS, though once again exclusive of itself, i.e. of tstST. That is, tstST refers to something to which tstS cannot refer. TstST does not, certainly, include any statement referring to the world exclusive of tstS which is not included already in tstS— more, it seems doubtful whether it does include that statement about the world exclusive of tstS which is made when we state that S. (If I state that tstS is true, should we really agree that I have stated that S? Only 'by implication'.)[18] But all this does not go any way to show that tstST is not a statement different

---

[16] [George—Ed.] Berkeley confuses these two. There will not be books in the running brooks until the dawn of hydro-semantics.

[17] A statement may refer to 'itself' in the sense, for example, of the sentence used or the utterance uttered in making it ('statement' is not exempt from all ambiguity). But paradox does result if a statement purports to refer to itself in a more full-blooded sense, purports, that is, to state that it itself is true, or to state what it itself refers to ('This statement is about Cato').

[18] And 'by implication' tstST asserts something about the making of a statement which tstS certainly does not assert.

from tstS. If Mr. Q writes on a notice-board 'Mr. W is a burglar', then a trial is held to decide whether Mr. Q's published statement that Mr. W is a burglar is a libel: finding 'Mr. Q's statement was true (in substance and in fact)'. Thereupon a second trial is held, to decide whether Mr. W. is a burglar, in which Mr. Q's statement is no longer under consideration: verdict 'Mr. W is a burglar'. It is an arduous business to hold a second trial: why is it done if the verdict is the same as the previous finding?[19]

What is felt is that the evidence considered in arriving at the one verdict is the same as that considered in arriving at the other. This is not strictly correct. It is more nearly correct that whenever tstS is true then tstST is also true and conversely, and that whenever tstS is false tstST is also false and conversely.[20] And it is argued that the words 'is true' are logically superfluous because it is believed that generally if any two statements are always true together and always false together then they must mean the same. Now whether this is in general a sound view may be doubted: but even if it is, why should it not break down in the case of so obviously 'peculiar' a phrase as 'is true'? Mistakes in philosophy notoriously arise through thinking that what holds of 'ordinary' words like 'red' or 'growls' must also hold of extraordinary words like 'real' or 'exists'. But that 'true' is just such another extraordinary word is obvious.[21]

There is something peculiar about the 'fact' which is described by tstST, something which may make us hesitate to call it a 'fact' at all; namely, that the relation between tstS and the world which tstST asserts to obtain is a *purely conventional* relation (one which 'thinking makes so'). For we are aware that this relation is one which we could alter at will, whereas we like to restrict the word 'fact' to *hard* facts, facts which are natural and unalterable, or anyhow not alterable at will. Thus, to take an analogous case, we may not like calling it a fact that the word elephant means what it does, though we can be induced to call it a (soft) fact—and though, of course, we have no hesitation in calling it a fact that contemporary English speakers use the word as they do.

An important point about this view is that it confuses falsity with negation: for according to it, it is the same thing to say 'He is not at home' as to say 'It is false that he is at home'. (But what if no one has said that he *is* at home? What if he is lying upstairs dead?) Too many philosophers maintain, when anxious to explain away negation, that a negation is just a second order affirmation (to the effect that a certain first order affirmation is false), yet, when anxious to explain away falsity, maintain that to assert that a statement is

---

[19] This is not quite fair: there are many legal and personal reasons for holding two trials—which, however, do not affect the point that the issue being tried is not the same.

[20] Not *quite* correct, because tstST is only in place at all when tstS is envisaged as made and has been verified.

[21] *Unum, verum, bonum* [one, true, good—Ed.]—the old favourites deserve their celebrity. There is something odd about each of them. Theoretical theology is a form of onomatolatry.

false is just to assert its negation (contradictory). It is impossible to deal with so fundamental a matter here.[22] Let me assert the following merely. Affirmation and negation are exactly on a level, in this sense, that no language can exist which does not contain conventions for both and that both refer to the world equally directly, not to statements about the world: whereas a language can quite well exist without any device to do the work of 'true' and 'false'. Any satisfactory theory of truth must be able to cope equally with falsity:[23] but 'is false' can only be maintained to be logically superfluous by making this fundamental confusion.

5. There is another way of coming to see that the phrase 'is true' is not logically superfluous, and to appreciate what sort of a statement it is to say that a certain statement is true. There are numerous other adjectives which are in the same class as 'true' and 'false', which are concerned, that is, with the relations between the words (as uttered with reference to an historic situation) and the world, and which nevertheless no one would dismiss as logically superfluous. We say, for example, that a certain statement is exaggerated or vague or bald, a description somewhat rough or misleading or not very good, an account rather general or too concise. In cases like these it is pointless to insist on deciding in simple terms whether the statement is 'true or false'. Is it true or false that Belfast is north of London? That the galaxy is the shape of a fried egg? That Beethoven was a drunkard? That Wellington won the battle of Waterloo? There are various *degrees and dimensions* of success in making statements: the

---

[22] The following two sets of logical axioms are, as Aristotle (though not his successors) makes them, quite distinct:
   (*a*) No statement can be both true and false.
        No statement can be neither true nor false.
   (*b*) Of two contradictory statements—
        Both cannot be true.
        Both cannot be false.
The second set demands a definition of contradictories, and is usually joined with an unconscious postulate that for every statement there is one and only one other statement such that the pair are contradictories. It is doubtful how far any language does or must contain contradictories, however defined, such as to satisfy both this postulate and the set of axioms (*b*).

Those of the so-called 'logical paradoxes' (hardly a genuine class) which concern 'true' and 'false' are *not* to be reduced to cases of self-contradiction, any more than 'S but I do not believe it' is. A statement to the effect that it is itself true is every bit as absurd as one to the effect that it is itself false. There are *other* types of sentence which offend against the fundamental conditions of all communication in ways *distinct* from the way in which 'This is red and is not red' offends—e.g. 'This does (I do) not exist', or equally absurd 'This exists (I exist)'. There are more deadly sins than one; nor does the way to salvation lie through any hierarchy.

[23] To be false is (not, of course, to correspond to a non-fact, but) to mis-correspond with a fact. Some have not seen how, then, since the statement which is false does not describe the fact with which it mis-corresponds (but mis-describes it), we know which fact to compare it with: this was because they thought of all linguistic conventions as descriptive— but it is the demonstrative conventions which fix which situation it is to which the statement refers. No statement can state what it itself refers to.

statements fit the facts always more or less loosely, in different ways on different occasions for different intents and purposes. What may score full marks in a general knowledge test may in other circumstances get a gamma. And even the most adroit of languages may fail to 'work' in an abnormal situation or to cope, or cope reasonably simply, with novel discoveries: is it true or false that the dog goes round the cow?[24] What, moreover, of the large class of cases where a statement is not so much false (or true) as out of place, inept ('All the signs of bread' said when the bread is before us)?

We become obsessed with 'truth', when discussing statements, just as we become obsessed with 'freedom' when discussing conduct. So long as we think that what has always and alone to be decided is whether a certain action was done freely or was not, we get nowhere: but so soon as we turn instead to the numerous other adverbs used in the same connexion ('accidentally', 'unwillingly', 'inadvertently', &c.), things become easier, and we come to see that no concluding inference of the form 'Ergo, it was done freely (or not freely)' is required. Like freedom, truth is a bare minimum or an illusory ideal (the truth, the whole truth and nothing but the truth about, say, the battle of Waterloo or the *Primavera*).

6. Not merely is it jejune to suppose that all a statement aims to be is 'true', but it may further be questioned whether every 'statement' does aim to be true at all. The principle of Logic, that 'Every proposition must be true or false', has too long operated as the simplest, most persuasive and most pervasive form of the descriptive fallacy. Philosophers under its influence have forcibly interpreted all 'propositions' on the model of the statement that a certain thing is red, as made when the thing concerned is currently under observation.

Recently, it has come to be realized that many utterances which have been taken to be statements (merely because they are not, on grounds of grammatical form, to be classed as commands, questions, &c.) are not in fact descriptive, nor susceptible of being true or false. When is a statement not a statement? When it is a formula in a calculus: when it is a performatory utterance: when it is a value-judgment: when it is a definition: when it is part of a work of fiction—there are many such suggested answers. It is simply not the business of such utterances to 'correspond to the facts' (and even genuine statements have other businesses besides that of so corresponding).

It is a matter for decision how far we should continue to call such masquerades 'statements' at all, and how widely we should be prepared to extend the uses of 'true' and 'false' in 'different senses'. My own feeling is that it is better, when once a masquerader has been unmasked, *not* to call it a statement

---

[24] Here there is much sense in 'coherence' (and pragmatist) theories of truth, despite their failure to appreciate the trite but central point that truth is a matter of the relation between words and world, and despite their wrong-headed *Gleichschaltung* [assimilation—Ed.] of all varieties of statemental failure under the lone head of 'partly true' (thereafter wrongly equated with 'part of the truth'). 'Correspondence' theorists too often talk as one would who held that every map is either accurate or inaccurate; that accuracy is a single and the sole virtue of a map; that every country can have but one accurate map; that a map on a larger scale or showing different features must be a map of a different country; and so on.

and *not* to say it is true or false. In ordinary life we should not call most of them statements at all, though philosophers and grammarians may have come to do so (or rather, have lumped them all together under the term of art 'proposition'). We make a difference between 'You said you promised' and 'You stated that you promised': the former can mean that you said 'I promise', whereas the latter must mean that you said 'I promised': the latter, which we say you 'stated', is something which is true or false, whereas for the former, which is not true or false, we use the wider verb to 'say'. Similarly, there is a difference between 'You say this is (call this) a good picture' and 'You state that this is a good picture'. Moreover, it was only so long as the real nature of arithmetical formulae, say, or of geometrical axioms remained unrecognized, and they were thought to record information about the world, that it was reasonable to call them 'true' (and perhaps even 'statements'—though were they ever so called?): but, once their nature has been recognized, we no longer feel tempted to call them 'true' or to dispute about their truth or falsity.

In the cases so far considered the model 'This is red' breaks down because the 'statements' assimilated to it are not of a nature to correspond to facts at all—the words are not descriptive words, and so on. But there is also another type of case where the words *are* descriptive words and the 'proposition' does in a way have to correspond to facts, but precisely not in the way that 'This is red' and similar statements setting up to be true have to do.

In the human predicament, for use in which our language is designed, we may wish to speak about states of affairs which have not been observed or are not currently under observation (the future, for example). And although we *can* state anything 'as a fact' (which statement will then be true or false[25]) we need not do so: we need only say 'The cat *may be* on the mat'. This utterance is quite different from tstS—it is not a statement at all (it is not true or false; it is compatible with 'The cat may *not* be on the mat'). In the same way, the situation in which we discuss whether and state that tstS is *true* is different from the situation in which we discuss whether it is *probable* that S. Tst it is probable that S is out of place, inept, in the situation where we can make tstST, and, I think, conversely. It is not our business here to discuss probability: but is worth observing that the phrases 'It is true that' and 'It is probable that' are in the same line of business,[26] and in so far incompatibles.

7. In a recent article in *Analysis* Mr. [P. F.—Ed.] Strawson has propounded a view of truth which it will be clear I do not accept. He rejects the 'semantic' account of truth on the perfectly correct ground that the phrase 'is true' is not used in talking about *sentences*, supporting this with an ingenious hypothesis as to how meaning may have come to be confused with truth: but this will not suffice to show what he wants—that 'is true' is not used in talking about (or that 'truth is not a property of') *anything*. For it *is* used in talking about *statements* (which in his article he does not distinguish clearly from sentences).

---

[25] Though it is not yet in place to call it either. For the same reason, one cannot lie or tell the truth about the future.

[26] Compare the odd behaviours of 'was' and 'will be' when attached to 'true' and to 'probable'.

Further, he supports the 'logical superfluity' view to this extent, that he agrees that to say that ST is not to make any further assertion at all, beyond the assertion that S: but he disagrees with it in so far as he thinks that to say that ST *is* to *do* something more than just to assert that S—it is namely to *confirm* or to *grant* (or something of that kind) the assertion, made or taken as made already, that S. It will be clear that and why I do not accept the first part of this: but what of the second part? I agree that to say that ST 'is' very often, and according to the all-important linguistic occasion, to confirm tstS or to grant it or what not; but this cannot show that to say that ST is not also and at the same time to make an assertion about tstS. To say that I believe you 'is' on occasion to accept your statement; but it is also to make an assertion, which is not made by the strictly performatory utterance 'I accept your statement'. It is common for quite ordinary statements to have a performatory 'aspect': to say that you are a cuckold may be to insult you, but it is also and at the same time to make a statement which is true or false. Mr. Strawson, moreover, seems to confine himself to the case where I *say* 'Your statement is true' or something similar—but what of the case where you state that S and I *say* nothing but '*look and see*' that your statement is true? I do not see how this critical case, to which nothing analogous occurs with strictly performatory utterances, could be made to respond to Mr. Strawson's treatment.

One final point: if it is admitted (*if*) that the rather boring yet satisfactory relation between words and world which has here been discussed does genuinely occur, why should the phrase 'is true' not be our way of describing it? And if it is not, what else is?

15

P. F. Strawson

Truth

Mr. [J. L.—Ed.] Austin offers us a purified version of the correspondence theory of truth. On the one hand he disclaims the semanticists' error of supposing that "true" is a predicate of sentences; on the other, the error of supposing that the relation of correspondence is other than purely conventional, the error which models the word on the world or the world on the word. His own theory is, roughly, that to say that a statement is true is to say that a certain speech-episode is related in a certain conventional way to something in the world exclusive of itself. But neither Mr. Austin's account of the two terms of the truth-conferring relation, nor his account of the relation itself, seems to me satisfactory. The correspondence theory requires, not purification, but elimination.

1. *Statements*

It is, of course, indisputable that we use various substantival expressions as grammatical subjects of "true." These are, commonly, noun-phrases like "What he said" or "His statement"; or pronouns or noun-phrases, with a "that"-clause in apposition, *e.g.*, "It . . . that *p*" and "The statement that *p*." Austin proposes that we should use "statement" to do general duty for such expressions as these. I have no objection. This will enable us to say, in a philosophically non-committal way, that, in using "true," we are talking about statements. By "saying this in a non-committal way," I mean saying it in a way which does not commit us to any view about the nature of statements so talked about; which does not commit us, for example, to the view that statements so talked about are historic events.

The words "assertion" and "statement" have a parallel and convenient duplicity of sense. "My statement" may be either what I say or my saying it. My saying something is certainly an episode. What I say is not. It is the latter, not the former, we declare to be true. (Speaking the truth is not a manner of speaking: it is saying something true.) When we say "His statement was received with thunderous applause" or "His vehement assertion was followed by a startled silence," we are certainly referring to, characterising, a historic event, and placing it in the context of others. If I say that the same statement

P. F. Strawson, "Truth," *Proceedings of the Aristotelian Society*, Supplementary Vol. XXIV (1950), 129–156. Reprinted by courtesy of the Editor of The Aristotelian Society.

was first whispered by John and then bellowed by Peter, uttered first in French and repeated in English, I am plainly still making historical remarks about utterance-occasions; but the word "statement" has detached itself from reference to any particular speech-episode. The episodes I am talking about are the whisperings, bellowings, utterings and repetitions. The statement is not something that figures in all these episodes. Nor, when I say that the statement is true, as opposed to saying that it was, in these various ways, made, am I talking indirectly about these episodes or any episodes at all. (Saying of a statement that it is true is not related to saying of a speech-episode that it was true as saying of a statement that it was whispered is related to saying of a speech-episode that it was a whisper.) It is futile to ask what thing or event I *am* talking about (over and above the subject-matter of the statement) in declaring a statement to be true; for there is no such thing or event. The word "statement" and the phrase "What he said," like the conjunction "that" followed by a noun clause, are convenient, grammatically substantival, devices, which we employ, on certain occasions, for certain purposes, notably (but not only) the occasions on which we use the word "true." What these occasions are I shall try later to elucidate. To suppose that, whenever we use a singular substantive, we are, or ought to be, using it to refer to something, is an ancient, but no longer a respectable, error.

More plausible than the thesis that in declaring a statement to be true I am talking about a speech-episode is the thesis that in order for me to declare a statement true, there must have occurred, within my knowledge, at least one episode which was a making of that statement. This is largely, but (as Austin sees) not entirely, correct. The occasion of my declaring a statement to be true may be not that someone has made the statement, but that I am envisaging the possibility of someone's making it. For instance, in discussing the merits of the Welfare State, I might say: "It is true that the general health of the community has improved (that p), but this is due only to the advance in medical science." It is not necessary that anyone should have said that p, in order for this to be a perfectly proper observation. In making it, I am not talking *about* an actual or possible speech-episode. I am myself asserting that p, in a certain way, with a certain purpose. I am anticipatorily conceding, in order to neutralize, a possible objection. I forestall someone's making the statement that p by making it myself, with additions. It is of prime importance to distinguish the fact that the use of "true" always glances backwards or forwards to the actual or envisaged making of a statement by someone, from the theory that it is used to characterise such (actual or possible) episodes.

It is not easy to explain the non-episodic and non-committal sense of "statement" in which "statement" = "what is said to be true or false." But, at the risk of being tedious, I shall pursue the subject. For if Austin is right in the suggestion that it is basically of speech-episodes that we predicate "true," it should be possible to "reduce" assertions in which we say of a statement in the non-episodic sense that it is true to assertions in which we are predicating truth of episodes. Austin points out that the same sentence may be used to make different statements. He would no doubt agree that different sentences may be used to make the same statement. I am not thinking only of different languages or synonymous expressions in the same language; but also of such occasions as that on which you say of Jones "He is ill," I say *to* Jones "You are ill" and Jones says "I am ill." Using, not only different sentences, but sentences with different meanings, we all make "the same statement"; and this is the sense of "statement" we need to discuss, since it is, *prima facie,* of statements in this sense that we say that they are true or false (*e.g.,* "What they all said, namely, that Jones was ill, was quite true."). We could say: people make the same statement when the words they use in the situations in which they use them are such that they must (logically) either all be making a true statement or all be making a false statement. But this is to use "true" in the elucidation of "same statement." Or we could say, of the present case: Jones, you and I all make the same statement because, using the words we used in the situation in which we used them, we were all applying the same description to the same person at a certain moment in his history; anyone applying that description to that person (etc.), would be making that statement. Mr. Austin might then wish to analyse (A) "The statement that Jones was ill is true" in some such way as the following: "If anyone has uttered, or were to utter, words such that in the situation in which they are uttered, he is applying to a person the same description as I apply to that person when I now utter the words 'Jones was ill,' then the resulting speech-episode was, or would be, true." It seems plain, however, that nothing but the desire to find a metaphysically irreproachable first term for the correspondence relation could induce anyone to accept this analysis of (A) as an elaborate general hypothetical. It would be a plausible suggestion only if the grammatical subjects of "true" were *commonly* expressions referring to particular, uniquely dateable, speech-episodes. But the simple and obvious fact is that the expressions occurring as such grammatical subjects ("What they said," "It . . . that *p*" and so on) never do, in these contexts, stand for such episodes.[1] *What they said* has no date, though their several sayings of it are dateable. *The statement that p* is not an event, though it had to be made for the first time and made within my knowledge if I am to talk of its truth or falsity. If I endorse Plato's view, wrongly attributing it to Lord [Bertrand—Ed.] Russell ("Russell's view that *p* is quite true"), and am corrected, I have not discovered that I was talking of an event separated by centuries from the one I imagined I was talking of. (Corrected, I may say: "Well it's true, whoever said it.") My *implied* historical judgment is false; that is all.

2. Facts

What of the second term of the correspondence relation? For this Mr. Austin uses the following words or phrases: "thing," "event," "situation," "state of affairs," "feature" and "fact." All these are words which should be handled

---

[1] And the cases where such phrases might most plausibly be exhibited as having an episode-referring rôle are precisely those which yield most readily to another treatment; *viz.,* those in which one speaker corroborates, confirms or grants what another has just said (*see* Section 4 below).

with care. I think that through failing to discriminate sufficiently between them, Mr. Austin (1) encourages the assimilation of facts to things, or (what is approximately the same thing) of stating to referring; (2) misrepresents the use of "true"; and (3) obscures another and more fundamental problem.

In section 3 of his paper, Mr. Austin says, or suggests, that all stating involves both referring ("demonstration") and characterizing ("description"). It is questionable whether all statements do involve both,[2] though it is certain that some do. The following sentences, for example, could all be used to make such statements; *i.e.*, statements in the making of which both the referring and describing functions are performed, the performance of the two functions being approximately (though not exclusively) assignable to different parts of the sentences as uttered:—

> The cat has the mange.
> That parrot talks a lot.
> Her escort was a man of medium build, clean-shaven, well-dressed and with a North Country accent.

In using such sentences to make statements, we refer to a thing or person (object) in order to go on to characterize it: (we demonstrate in order to describe). A *reference* can be correct or incorrect. A *description* can fit, or fail to fit, the thing or person to which it is applied.[3] When we refer correctly, there certainly is a conventionally established relation between the words, so used, and the thing to which we refer. When we describe correctly, there certainly is a conventionally established relation between the words we use in describing and the type of thing or person we describe. These relations, as Mr. Austin emphasizes, are different. An expression used referringly has a different logical rôle from an expression used describingly. They are differently related to the object. And *stating* is different from referring, and different from describing; for it is (in such cases) both these at once. Statement (*some* statement) is reference-cum-description. To avoid cumbersome phrasing, I shall speak henceforward of *parts* of statements (the referring part and the describing part); though parts of statements are no more to be equated with parts of sentences (or parts of speech-episodes) than statements are to be equated with sentences (or speech-episodes).

That (person, thing, etc.) to which the referring part of the statement refers, and which the describing part of the statement fits or fails to fit, is that which the statement is *about*. It is evident that there is nothing else in the world for the statement itself to be related to either in some further way of its own or in either of the different ways in which these different parts of the statement are related to what the statement is about. And it is evident that

---

[2] *See* Section 5 below. The thesis that all statements involve both demonstration and description is, roughly, the thesis that all statements are, or involve, subject-predicate statements (not excluding relational statements).

[3] *Cf.* the phrase "He is described as . . ." What fills the gap is not a sentence (expression which could normally be used to make a statement), but a phrase which could occur as a part of an expression so used.

the demand that there should be such a relatum is logically absurd: a logically fundamental type-mistake. But the demand for something in the world *which makes the statement true* (Mr. Austin's phrase), or *to which the statement corresponds when it is true*, is just this demand. And the answering theory that to say that a statement is true is to say that a speech-episode is conventionally related in a certain way to such a relatum reproduces the type-error embodied in this demand. For while we certainly say that a statement corresponds to (fits, is borne out by, agrees with) the facts, as a variant on saying that it is true, we *never* say that a statement corresponds to the thing, person, etc., it is about. What "makes the statement" that the cat has mange "true," is not the cat, but the *condition* of the cat, *i.e.*, the fact that the cat has mange. The only plausible candidate for the position of what (in the world) makes the statement true is the fact it states; but the fact it states is not something in the world.[4] It is not an object; not even (as some have supposed) a complex object consisting of one or more particular elements (constituents, parts) and a universal element (constituent, part). I can (perhaps) hand you, or draw a circle round, or time with a stop-watch the things or incidents that are referred to when a statement is made. Statements are about such objects; but they state facts. Mr. Austin seems to ignore the complete difference of type between, *e.g.*, "fact" and "thing"; to talk as if "fact" were just a very general word (with, unfortunately, some misleading features) for "event," "thing," etc., instead of being (as it is) both wholly different from these, and yet the only possible candidate for the desired non-linguistic correlate of "statement." Roughly: the thing, person, etc., referred to is the material correlate of the referring part of the statement; the quality or property the referent is said to "possess" is the *pseudo*-material correlate of its describing part; and the fact to which the statement "corresponds" is the *pseudo*-material correlate of the statement as a whole.

These points are, of course, reflected in the behaviour of the word "fact" in ordinary language; behaviour which Mr. Austin notes, but by which he is insufficiently warned. "Fact," like "true," "states" and "statement" is wedded to "that"-clauses; and there is nothing unholy about this union. Facts are known, stated, learnt, forgotten, overlooked, commented on, communicated or noticed. (Each of these verbs may be followed by a "that"-clause or a "the fact that"-clause.) Facts are what statements (when true) state; they are not what statements are about. They are not, like things or happenings on the face of the globe, witnessed or heard or seen, broken or overturned, interrupted or prolonged, kicked, destroyed, mended or noisy. Mr. Austin notes the expression "fact that," warns us that it may tempt us to identify facts with true statements and explains its existence by saying that for certain purposes in ordinary life

---

[4] This is not, of course, to deny that there is that in the world which a statement of this kind is about (true or false *of*), which is *referred to* and *described* and which the description fits (if the statement is true) or fails to fit (if it is false). This truism is an inadequate introduction to the task of elucidating, not our use of "true," but a certain general way of using language, a certain type of discourse, *viz.*, the fact-stating type of discourse. What confuses the issue about the use of the word "true" is precisely its entanglement with this much more fundamental and difficult problem. (*See* (ii) of this section.)

we neglect, or take as irrelevant, the distinction between saying something true and the thing or episode of which we are talking. It would indeed be wrong— but not for Mr. Austin's reasons—to identify "fact" and "true statement"; for these expressions have different rôles in our language, as can be seen by the experiment of trying to interchange them in context. Nevertheless their rôles— or those of related expressions—overlap. There is no nuance, except of style, between "That's true" and "That's a fact"; nor between "Is it true that . . . ?" and "Is it a fact that . . . ?"[5] But Mr. Austin's reasons for objecting to the identification seem mistaken, as does his explanation of the usage which (he says) tempts us to make it. Because he thinks of a statement as something in the world (a speech-episode) and a fact as something else in the world (what the statement either "corresponds to" or "is about"), he conceives the distinction as of overriding importance in philosophy, though (surprisingly) sometimes negligible for ordinary purposes. But I can conceive of no occasion on which I could possibly be held to be "neglecting or taking as irrelevant" the distinction between, say, my wife's bearing me twins (at midnight) and my saying (ten minutes later) that my wife had borne me twins. On Mr. Austin's thesis, however, my announcing "The fact is that my wife has borne me twins" would be just such an occasion.

Elsewhere in his paper, Mr. Austin expresses the fact that there is no theoretical limit to what could truly be said about things in the world, while there are very definite practical limits to what human beings actually can and do say about them, by the remark that statements "always fit the facts more or less loosely, in different ways for different purposes." But what could fit more perfectly the fact that it is raining than the statement that it is raining? Of course, statements and facts fit. They were made for each other. If you prise the statements off the world you prise the facts off it too; but the world would be none the poorer. (You don't also prise off the world what the statements are about—for this you would need a different kind of lever.)

A symptom of Mr. Austin's uneasiness about facts is his preference for the expressions "situation" and "state of affairs"; expressions of which the character and function are a little less transparent than those of "fact." They are more plausible candidates for inclusion in the world. For while it is true that situations and states of affairs are not seen or heard (any more than facts are), but are rather *summed up* or *taken in at a glance* (phrases which stress the connection with statement and "that"-clause respectively), it is also true that there is a sense of "about' in which we do talk about, do describe, situations and states of affairs. We say, for example, "The international situation is serious" or "This state of affairs lasted from the death of the King till the dissolution of Parliament." In the same sense of "about," we talk about facts; as when we say "I am alarmed by the fact that kitchen expenditure has risen by 50 per cent

---

[5] I think in general the difference between them is that while the use of "true," as already acknowledged, glances backwards or forwards at an actual or envisaged making of a statement, the use of "fact" does not generally do this though it may do it sometimes. It certainly does not do it in, *e.g.*, the phrase "The fact is that . . ." which serves rather to prepare us for the unexpected and unwelcome.

in the last year." But whereas "fact" in such usages is linked with a "that-clause (or connected no less obviously with "statement," as when we "take down the facts" or hand someone the facts on a sheet of paper), "situation" and "state of affairs" stand by themselves, states of affairs are said to have a beginning and an end, and so on. Nevertheless, situations and states of affairs so talked of are (like facts so talked of), abstractions that a logician, if not a grammarian, should be able to see through. Being alarmed by a fact is not like being frightened by a shadow. It is being alarmed because. . . . One of the most economical and pervasive devices of language is the use of substantival expressions to abbreviate, summarize and connect. Having made a series of descriptive statements, I can comprehensively connect with these the remainder of my discourse by the use of such expressions as "this situation" or "this state of affairs"; just as, having produced what I regard as a set of reasons for a certain conclusion I allow myself to draw breath by saying "Since *these things* are so, then . . . ," instead of prefacing the entire story by the conjunction. A situation or state of affairs is, roughly, a set of facts not a set of things.

A point which it is important to notice in view of Mr. Austin's use of these expressions (in sections 3a and 3b of his paper) is that when we *do* "talk about" situations (as opposed to things and persons) the situation we talk about is not, as he seems to think it is, correctly identified with the fact we state (with "what makes the statement true"). If a situation is the "subject" of our statement, then what "makes the statement true" is not the situation, but the fact that the situation has the character it is asserted to have. I think much of the persuasivness of the phrase "talking about situations" derives from that use of the word on which I have just commented. But if a situation is treated as the "subject" of a statement, then it will not serve as the non-linguistic term, for which Mr. Austin is seeking, of the "relation of correspondence"; and if it is treated as the non-linguistic term of this relation, it will not serve as the subject of the statement.

Someone might now say: "No doubt 'situation,' 'state of affairs,' 'facts' are related in this way to 'that'-clauses and assertive sentences; can serve, in certain ways and for certain purposes, as indefinite stand-ins for specific expressions of these various types. So also is 'thing' related to some nouns; 'event' to some verbs, nouns and sentences; 'quality' to some adjectives; 'relation' to some nouns, verbs and adjectives. Why manifest this prejudice in favour of things and events as alone being parts of the world or its history? Why not situations and facts as well?" The answer to this (implicit in what has gone before) is twofold.

(i) The first part of the answer[6] is that the whole charm of talking of situations, states of affairs or facts as included in, or parts of, the world, consists in thinking of them as things, and groups of things; that the temptation to talk of situations, etc., in the idiom appropriate to talking of things and events is,

---

[6] Which could be more shortly expressed by saying that if we read "world" (a sadly corrupted word) as "heavens and earth," talk of facts, situations and states of affairs, as "included in" or "parts of" the world is, obviously, metaphorical. The world is the totality of things, not of facts.

once this first step is taken, overwhelming. Mr. Austin does not withstand it. He significantly slips in the word "feature" (noses and hills are *features*, of faces and landscapes) as a substitute for "facts." He says that the reason why photographs and maps are not "true" in the way that statements are true is that the relation of a map or a photograph to what it is a map or a photograph of is not wholly (in the first case) and not all (in the second) a conventional relation. But this is not the only, or the fundamental, reason. (The relation between the Prime Minister of England and the phrase "the Prime Minister of England" *is* conventional; but it doesn't make sense to say that someone uttering the phrase out of context is saying something true or false.) The (for present purposes) fundamental reason is that "being a map of" or "being a photograph of" *are* relations, of which the non-photographic, non-cartographical, relata are, say, personal or geographical *entities*. The trouble with correspondence theories of truth is not primarily the tendency to substitute non-conventional relations for what is really a wholly conventional relation. It is the misrepresentation of "correspondence between statement and fact" *as a relation, of any kind, between events or things or groups of things* that is the trouble. Correspondence theorists think of a statement as "describing that which makes it true" (fact, situation, state of affairs) in the way a descriptive predicate may be used to describe, or a referring expression to refer to, a thing.[7]

(ii) The second objection to Mr. Austin's treatment of facts, situations, states of affairs as "parts of the world" which we declare to stand in a certain relation to a statement when we declare that statement true, goes deeper than the preceding one but is, in a sense, its point. Mr. Austin rightly says or implies (section 3) that for some of the purposes for which we use language, there must be conventions correlating the words of our language with what is to be found in the world. Not all the linguistic purposes for which this necessity holds, however, are identical. Orders, as well as information, are conventionally communicated. Suppose "orange" always meant what we mean by "Bring me an orange" and "that orange" always meant what we mean by "Bring me that orange," and, in general, our language contained only sentences in some such

---

[7] Suppose the pieces set on a chessboard, a game in progress. And suppose someone gives, in words, an exhaustive statement of the position of the pieces. Mr. Austin's objection (or one of his objections) to earlier correspondence theories is that they would represent the relation between the description and the board with the pieces on it as like, say, the relation between a newspaper diagram of a chess-problem and a board with the pieces correspondingly arranged. He says, rather, that the relation is a purely conventional one. My objection goes farther. It is that there is no thing or event called "a statement" (though there is the making of the statement) and there is no thing or event called "a fact" or "situation" (though there is the chessboard with the pieces on it) which stand to one another in any, even a purely conventional, relation as the newspaper diagram stands to the board-and-pieces. The facts (situation, state of affairs) cannot, like the chessboard-and-pieces, have coffee spilt on them or be upset by a careless hand. It is because Mr. Austin needs such events and things for his theory that he takes the making of the statement as the statement, and that which the statement is about as the fact which it states.

Events can be dated and things can be located. But the facts which statements (when true) state can be neither dated or located. (Nor can the statements, though the making of them can be.) Are they included in the world?

way imperative. There would be no less need for a conventional correlation between the word and the world. Nor would there be any less to be found in the world. But those pseudo-entities which *make statements true* would not figure among the non-linguistic correlates. They would no more be found; (they never were found, and never did figure among the non-linguistic correlates). The point is that the word "fact" (and the "set-of-facts" words like "situation," "state of affairs") have, like the words "statement" and "true" themselves, a certain type of word-world-relating discourse (the informative) *built in* to them. The occurrence in ordinary discourse of the words "fact," "state-ment," "true" signalizes the occurrence of this type of discourse; just as the occurrence of the words "order," "obeyed" signalizes the occurrence of another kind of conventional communication (the imperative). If our task were to elucidate the nature of the first type of discourse, it would be futile to attempt to do it in terms of the words "fact," "statement," "true," for these words contain the problem, not its solution. It would, for the same reason, be equally futile to attempt to elucidate any one of these words (in so far as the elucidation of *that* word would be the elucidation of *this* problem) in terms of the others. And it is, indeed, very strange that people have so often proceeded by saying "Well, we're pretty clear what a statement is, aren't we? Now let us settle *the further question, viz.,* what it is for a statement to be true." This is like "Well, we're clear about what a command is: now what is it for a command to be obeyed?" As if one could divorce statements and commands from the point of making or giving them!

Suppose we had in our language the word "execution" meaning "action which is the carrying out of a command." And suppose someone asked the philosophical question: What is *obedience?* What is it for a command to be *obeyed?* A philosopher might produce the answer: "Obedience is a conventional relation between a command and an execution. A command is obeyed when it corresponds to an execution."

This is the Correspondence Theory of Obedience. It has, perhaps, a little less value as an attempt to elucidate the nature of one type of communication than the Correspondence Theory of Truth has as an attempt to elucidate that of another. In both cases, the words occurring in the solution incorporate the problem. And, of course, this intimate relation between "statement" and "fact" (which is understood when it is seen that they both incorporate this problem) explains why it is that when we seek to explain *truth* on the model of naming or classifying or any other kind of conventional or non-conventional relation between one thing and another, we always find ourselves landed with "fact," "situation," "state of affairs" as the non-linguistic terms of the relation.

But why should the problem of Truth (the problem about our use of "true") be seen as this problem of elucidating the fact-stating type of discourse? The answer is that it shouldn't be; but that the Correspondence Theory can only be fully seen through when it is seen as a barren attempt on this second prob-lem. Of course, a philosopher concerned with the second problem, concerned to elucidate a certain general type of discourse, must stand back from language and talk about the different ways in which utterances are related to the world (though he must get beyond "correspondence of statement and fact" if his talk is to be fruitful). But—to recur to something I said earlier—the occurrence *in ordinary discourse* of the words "true," "fact," etc., signalizes, without commenting on, the occurrence of a certain way of using language. When we use these words in ordinary life, we are talking within, and not about, a certain frame of discourse; we are precisely not talking about the way in which utterances are, or may be, conventionally related to the world. We are talking about persons and things, but in a way in which we could not talk about them if conditions of certain kinds were not fulfilled. The problem about the use of "true" is to see how this word fits into that frame of discourse. The surest route to the wrong answer is to confuse this problem with the question: What type of discourse is this?[8]

3. Conventional Correspondence

It will be clear from the previous paragraph what I think wrong with Mr. Austin's account of the relation itself, as opposed to its terms. In section 4 of his paper he says that, when we declare a statement to be true, the relation between the statement and the world which our declaration "asserts to obtain" is "a purely conventional relation" and "one which we could alter at will." This remark reveals the fundamental confusion of which Mr. Austin is guilty between:—

(*a*) the semantic conditions which must be satisfied for the statement that a certain statement is true to be itself true; and
(*b*) what is asserted when a certain statement is stated to be true.

Suppose A makes a statement, and B declares A's statement to be true. Then for B's statement to be true, it is, *of course*, necessary that the words used by A in making the statement should stand in a certain conventional (semantical) relationship with the world; and that the "linguistic rules" underlying this relationship should be rules "observed" by both A and B. It should be remarked that these conditions (with the exception of the condition about B's observance of linguistic rules) are equally necessary conditions of A's having made a true statement in using the words he used. *It is no more and no less absurd to suggest that B, in making his statement, asserts that these semantic conditions are fulfilled than it is to suggest that A, in making his statement, asserts that these semantic conditions are fulfilled* (i.e., that we can never use words without mentioning them). *If Mr. Austin is right in suggesting that to say that a statement is true is to say that "the historic state of affairs to which it [i.e., for Mr. Austin, the episode of making it] is correlated by the demonstrative conventions (the one it 'refers to') is of a type with which the sentence used in making the statement is correlated by the descriptive conventions," then* (and this is shown quite clearly by his saying that the relation we assert to obtain is a "purely

---

[8] A parallel mistake would be to think that in our ordinary use (as opposed to a philosopher's use) of the word "quality," we were talking about people's uses of words; on the ground (correct in itself) that this word would have no use but for the occurrence of a certain general way of using words.

conventional one" which "could be altered at will") in declaring a statement to be true, we are either:—

(*a*) talking about the meanings of the words used by the speaker whose making of the statement is the occasion for our use of "true" (*i.e.*, profiting by the occasion to give semantic rules); or

(*b*) saying that the speaker has used correctly the words he did use.

It is *patently* false that we are doing either of these things. Certainly, we use the word "true" when the semantic conditions described by Austin[9] are fulfilled; but we do not, in using the word, *state* that they are fulfilled. (And this, incidentally, is the answer to the question with which Mr. Austin concludes his paper.) The damage is done (the two problems distinguished at the end of the previous section confused) by asking the question: *When* do we use the word "true"? instead of the question: *How* do we use the word "true"?

Someone says: "It's true that French Governments rarely last more than a few months, but the electoral system is responsible for that." Is the fact he states in the first part of his sentence alterable by changing the conventions of language? It is not.

4. Uses of "That" Clauses; and of "Statement," "True," "Fact," "Exaggerated," etc.

(*a*) There are many ways of making an assertion about a thing, X, besides the bare use of the sentence-pattern "X is Y." Many of these involve the use of "that"-clauses. For example:—

How often shall I have to tell you
Today I learnt
It is surprising
The fact is
I have just been reminded of the fact
It is indisputable
It is true
It is established beyond question

---

[9] In what, owing to his use of the words "statement," "fact," "situation," etc., is a misleading form. The quoted account of the conditions of truthful statement is more nearly appropriate as an account of the conditions of correct descriptive reference. Suppose, in a room with a bird cage, I say "That parrot is very talkative." Then my use of the referring expression ("That parrot") with which my sentence begins is correct when the token-object (bird) with which my token-expression (event) is correlated by the conventions of demonstration is of a kind with which the type-expression is correlated by the conventions of description. Here we do have an event and a thing and a (type-mediated) conventional relation between them. If someone corrects me, saying "That's not a parrot; it's a cockatoo," he may be correcting either a linguistic or a factual error on my part. (The question of which he is doing is the question of whether I would have stuck to my story on a closer examination of the bird.) Only in the former case is he declaring a certain semantic condition to be unfulfilled. In the latter case, he is talking about the bird. He asserts that it is a cockatoo and not a parrot. This he could have done whether I had spoken or not. He also *corrects* me, which he could not have done if I had not spoken.

These are all ways of asserting, in very different context and circumstances, that X is Y.[10] Some of them involve autobiographical assertions as well; others do not. In the grammatical sense already conceded, all of them are "about" facts or statements. In no other sense is any of them about either, though some of them carry *implications* about the *making* of statements.

(*b*) There are many different circumstances in which the simple sentence-pattern "X is Y" may be used to do things which are not merely stating (though they all involve stating) that X is Y. In uttering words of this simple pattern we may be encouraging, reproving or warning someone; reminding someone; answering, or replying to, someone; denying what someone has said; confirming, granting, corroborating, agreeing with, admitting what someone has said. Which of these, if any, we are doing depends on the circumstances in which, using this simple sentence-pattern, we assert that X is Y.

(*c*) In many of the cases in which we are doing something besides merely stating that X is Y, we have available, for use in suitable contexts, certain abbreviatory devices which enable us to state that X is Y (to make our denial, answer, admission or whatnot) *without* using the sentence-pattern "X is Y." Thus, if someone asks us "Is X Y?", we may state (in the way of reply) that X is Y by saying "Yes." If someone says "X is Y," we may state (in the way of denial) that X is not Y, by saying "It is not" or by saying "That's not true"; or we may state (in the way of corroboration, agreement, granting, etc.) that X is Y by saying "It is indeed" or "That is true." In all these cases (of reply, denial and agreement) the context of our utterance, as well as the words we use, must be taken into account if it is to be clear what we are asserting, *viz.*, that X is (or is not) Y. It seems to me plain that in these cases "true" and "not true" (we rarely use "false") are functioning as abbreviatory statement-devices of the same general kind as the others quoted. And it seems also plain that the *only* difference between these devices which might tempt us, while saying of some ("Yes," "It is indeed," "It is not") that, in using them, we were talking about X, to say of others ("That's true," "That's not true") that, in using them, we were talking about something quite different, *viz.*, the utterance which was the occasion for our use of these devices, is their difference in grammatical structure, *i.e.*, the fact that 'true" occurs as a grammatical predicate.[11] (It is obviously not a predicate of X.) If Mr. Austin's thesis, that in using the word "true" we make an assertion about a statement, were no more than the thesis that the word "true" occurs as a grammatical predicate, with, as gram-

---

[10] One might prefer to say that in some of these cases one was asserting only *by implication* that X is Y; though it seems to me more probable that in all these cases we should say, of the speaker, not "What he said implied that X is Y," but "He *said* that X was Y."

[11] Compare also the English habit of making a statement followed by an interrogative appeal for agreement in such forms as "isn't it?", "doesn't he?" etc., with the corresponding German and Italian idioms, "Nicht wahr?", "non è vero?' There is surely no significant difference between the phrases which do not employ the word for "true" and those which do: they all appeal for agreement in the same way.

matical subjects, such words and phrases as "That," "What he said," "His state-ment," etc., then, of course, it would be indisputable. It is plain, however, that he means more than this, and I have already produced my objections to the more that he means.

(*d*) It will be clear that, in common with Mr. Austin, I reject the thesis that the phrase "is true" is logically superfluous, together with the thesis that to say that a proposition is true is *just* to assert it and to say that it is false is *just* to assert its contradictory. "True" and "not true" have jobs of their own to do, *some*, but by no means all, of which I have characterized above. In using them, we are not *just* asserting that X is Y or that X is not Y. We are asserting this in a way in which we could not assert it unless certain conditions were fulfilled; we may also be granting, denying, confirming, etc. It will be clear also that the rejection of these two theses does not entail acceptance of Mr. Austin's thesis that in using "true" we are making an assertion about a statement. Nor does it entail the rejection of the thesis which Mr. Austin (in Section 4 of his paper) couples with these two, *viz.*, the thesis that to say that an assertion is true is not to make any further *assertion* at all. This thesis holds for many uses, but requires modification for others.

(*e*) The occasions for using "true" mentioned so far in this section are evidently not the only occasions of its use. There is, for example, the generally concessive employment of "It is true that *p* . . .", which it is difficult to see how Mr. Austin could accommodate. All these occasions have, however, a certain contextual immediacy which is obviously absent when we utter such sentences as "What John said yesterday is quite true" and "What La Rochefoucauld said about friendship is true." Here the context of our utterance does not identify for us the statement we are talking about (in the philosophically non-committal sense in which we *are* "talking about statements" when we use the word "true"), and so we use a descriptive phrase to do the job. But the descriptive phrase does not identify an event; though the statement we make carries the implication (in some sense of "implication") that there occurred an event which was John's making yesterday (or Rochefoucauld's making sometime) the statement that *p* (*i.e.*, the statement we declare to be true). We are certainly not telling our audience that the event occurred, *e.g.*, that John made the statement that *p*, for (i) we do not state, either by way of quotation or otherwise, what it was that John said yesterday, and (ii) our utterance achieves its main purpose (that of making, by way of confirmation or endorsement, the statement that *p*) only if our audience already knows that John yesterday made the statement that *p*. The abbreviatory function of "true" in cases such as these becomes clearer if we compare them with what we say in the case where (i) we want to assert that *p*; (ii) we want to indicate (or display our knowledge that) an event occurred which was John's making yesterday the statement that *p*; (iii) we believe our audience ignorant or forgetful of the fact that John said yesterday that *p*. We then use the formula "As John said yesterday, *p*" or "It is true, as John said yesterday, that *p*," or "What John said yesterday, namely that *p*, is true." (Of course the words represented by the letter *p*, which we use, may be—sometimes, if we are to make the same statement, must be—different from the words which John used.) Sometimes, to embarrass, or test, our audience, we use, in cases where the third of these conditions is fulfilled, the formula appropriate to its non-fulfillment, *viz.*, "What John said yesterday is true."

(*f*) In criticism of my view of truth put forward in *Analysis*,[12] and presumably in support of his own thesis that "true" is used to assert that a certain relation obtains between a speech-episode and something in the world exclusive of that episode, Mr. Austin makes, in Section 7 of his paper, the following point. He says: "Mr. Strawson seems to confine himself to the case when I say "Your statement is true" or something similar—but what of the case when you state that S and I say nothing, but *look and see* that your statement is true?" The point of the objection is, I suppose, that since I *say* nothing, I cannot be making any performatory use of "true"; yet I can see *that* your statement is true. The example, however, seems to have a force precisely contrary to what Mr. Austin intended. Of course, "true" has a different rôle in "X sees that Y's statement is true" from its rôle in "Y's statement is true." What is this rôle? Austin says in my hearing "There is a cat on the mat" and I look and see a cat on the mat. Someone (Z) reports: "Strawson saw that Austin's statement was true." What is he reporting? He is reporting that I have seen a cat on the mat; but he is reporting this in a way in which he could not report it except in certain circumstances, *viz.*, in the circumstances of Austin's having said in my hearing that there was a cat on the mat. Z's remark also carries the implication that Austin made a statement, but cannot be regarded as *reporting* this by implication since it fulfills its main purpose only if the audience already knows that Austin made a statement and what statement he made; and the implication (which *can* be regarded as an implied report) that I heard and understood what Austin said.[13] The man who looks and sees that the statement that there is a cat on the mat is true, sees no more and no less than the man who looks and sees that there is a cat on the mat, or the man who looks and sees that there is *indeed* a cat on the mat. But the *settings* of the first and third cases may be different from that of the second.

This example has value, however. It emphasizes the importance of the concept of the "occasion" on which we may make use of the assertive device which is the subject of this symposium (the word "true"); and minimizes (what I was inclined to over-emphasize) the performatory character of our uses of it.

(*g*) Mr. Austin stresses the differences between negation and falsity; rightly, in so far as to do so is to stress the difference (of occasion and context) between asserting that X is not Y and denying the assertion that X is Y. He also exaggerates the difference; for, if I have taken the point of his example, he suggests that there are cases in which "X is not Y" is inappropriate to a situation in which, if anyone stated that X was Y, it would be correct to say that the statement that X was Y was false. These are cases where the question of whether X is or is not Y does not arise (where the conditions of its arising are

---

[12] Vol. 9, No. 6, June, 1949.

[13] If *I* report: "I see that Austin's statement is true," this is simply a first-hand corroborative report that there is a cat on the mat, made in a way in which it could not be made except in these circumstances.

not fulfilled). They are equally, it seems to me, cases when the question of the truth or falsity of the statement that X is Y does not arise.

(*h*) A qualification of my general thesis, that in using "true" and "untrue" we are not talking about a speech-episode, is required to allow for those cases where our interest is not primarily in what the speaker asserts, but in the speaker's asserting it, in, say, the fact of his having *told the truth* rather than in the fact which he reported in doing so. (We may, of course, be interested in both; or our interest in a man's evident truthfulness on one occasion may be due to our concern with the degree of his reliability on others.)

But this case calls for no special analysis and presents no handle to any theorist of truth; for to use "true" in this way is simply to characterize a certain *event* as *the making*, by someone, of a true statement. The problem of analysis remains.

(*i*) Mr. Austin says that we shall find it easier to be clear about "true" if we consider other adjectives "in the same class," such as "exaggerated," "vague," "rough," "misleading," "general," "too concise." I do not think these words *are* in quite the same class as "true" and "false." In any language in which statements can be made at all, it must be possible to make true and false statements. But statements can suffer from the further defects Mr. Austin mentions only when language has attained a certain richness. Imagine one of Mr. Austin's rudimentary languages with "single words" for "complex situations" of totally different kinds. One could make true or false statements; but not statements which were exaggerated, over-concise, too general or rather rough. And even given a language as rich as you please, whereas all statements made in it could be true or false, not all statements could be exaggerated. When can we say that the statement that *p* is exaggerated? *One* of the conditions is this: that, if the sentence S_1 is used to make the statement that *p*, there should be some sentence S_2 (which could be used to make the statement that *q*) such that S_1 and S_2 are related somewhat as "There were 200 people there" is related to "There were 100 people there." (To the remark "We got married yesterday," you cannot, except as a joke, reply: "You're exaggerating.")

Mr. Austin's belief, then, that the word "exaggerated" stands for a relation between a statement and something in the world exclusive of the statement, would at least be an over-simplification, even if it were not objectionable in other ways. But it is objectionable in other ways. The difficulties about statement and fact recur; and the difficulties about the relation. Mr. Austin would not want to say that the relation between an exaggerated statement and the world was like that between a globe and a hand too small for it. He would say that the relation was a conventional one. But the fact that the statement that *p* is exaggerated is not in any sense a conventional fact. (It is, perhaps, the fact that there were 1,200 people there and not 2,000.) If a man says: "There were at least 2,000 people there," you may reply (A) "No, there were not so many (far more)," or you may reply (B) "That's an exaggeration (understatement)." (A) and (B) say the same thing. Look at the situation more closely. In saying (A), you are not merely asserting that there were fewer than 2,000 people there: you are also correcting the first speaker, and correcting him in a certain general way, which you could not have done if he had not spoken as he did, though you could merely have asserted that there were fewer than 2,000 there without his having spoken. Notice also that what is being asserted by the use of (A)—that there were fewer than 2,000 there—cannot be understood without taking into account the original remark which was the occasion for (A). (A) has both contextually-assertive and performatory features. (B) has the same features, and does the same job as (A), but more concisely and with greater contextual reliance.

· Not all the words taken by Austin as likely to help us to be clear about "true" are in the same class as one another. "Exaggerated" is, of those he mentions, the one most relevant to his thesis; but has been seen to yield to my treatment. Being "over-concise" and "too general" are not ways of being "not quite true." These obviously relate to the specific purposes of specific makings of statements; to the unsatisfied wishes of specific audiences. No alteration in things in the world, nor any magical replaying of the course of events, could bring statements so condemned into line, in the way that an "exaggerated assessment" of the height of a building could be brought into line by inorganic growth. Whether the statement (that p) is true or false is a matter of the way things are (of whether p); whether a statement is exaggerated (if the question arises—which depends on the type of statement and the possibilities of the language) is a matter of the way things are (e.g., of whether or not there were fewer than 2,000 there). But whether a statement is over-concise[14] or too general depends on what the hearer wants to know. The world does not demand to be described with one degree of detail rather than another.

5. The Scope of "Statement," "True," "False" and "Fact"

Commands and questions, obviously, do not claim to be statements of fact: they are not true or false. In Section 6 of his paper, Mr. Austin reminds us that there are many expressions neither interrogative nor imperative in form which we use for other purposes than that of reportage or forecast. From our employment of these expressions he recommends that we withhold (suspects that we do, in practice, largely withhold) the appellation "stating facts," the words "true" and "false." Philosophers, even in the sphere of language, are not legislators; but I have no wish to challenge the restriction, in some philosophical contexts, of the words "statement," "true," "false," to what I have myself earlier called the "fact-stating" type of discourse.

What troubles me more is Mr. Austin's own incipient analysis of this type of discourse. It seems to me such as to force him to carry the restriction further than he wishes or intends. And here there are two points which, though connected, need to be distinguished. First, there are difficulties besetting the relational theory of truth as such; second, there is the persistence of these difficulties

---

[14] "Concise" is perhaps less often used of what a man says than of the way he says it (e.g., "concisely put," "concisely expressed," "a concise formulation"). A may take 500 words to say what B says in 200. Then I shall say that B's formulation was more concise than A's, meaning simply that he used fewer words.

in a different form when this "theory of truth" is revealed as, rather, an incipient analysis of the statement-making use of language.

First then, facts of the cat-on-the-mat-type are the favoured species for adherents of Mr. Austin's type of view. For here we have one thing (one chunk of reality) sitting on another: we can (if we are prepared to commit the errors commented on in Section (2) above) regard the two together as forming a single chunk, if we like, and call it a fact or state of affairs. The view may then seem relatively plausible that to say that the statement (made by me to you) that the cat is on the mat is true is to say that the three-dimensional state of affairs with which the episode of my making the statement is correlated by the demonstrative conventions is of a type with which the sentence I use is correlated by the descriptive conventions. Other species of fact, however, have long been known to present more difficulty: the fact that the cat is not on the mat, for example, or the fact that there are white cats, or that cats persecute mice, or that if you give my cat an egg, it will smash it and eat the contents. Consider the simplest of these cases, that involving negation. With what type of state-of-affairs (chunk of reality) is the sentence "The cat is not on the mat" correlated by conventions of description? With a mat *simpliciter* [merely—Ed.]? With a dog on a mat? With a cat up a tree? The amendment of Mr. Austin's view to which one might be tempted for negative statements (*i.e.,* "S is true" = "The state of affairs to which S is correlated by the demonstrative conventions is *not* of a type with which *the affirmative form of* S is correlated by the descriptive conventions") destroys the simplicity of the story by creating the need for a different sense of "true" when we discuss negative statements. And worse is to follow. Not all statements employ conventions of demonstration. Existential statements don't, nor do statements of (even relatively) unrestricted generality. Are we to deny that these are statements, or create a further sense of "true"? And what has become of the non-linguistic correlate, the chunk of reality? Is this, in the case of existential or general statements, the entire world? Or, in the case of negatively existential statements, an ubiquitous non-presence?

As objections to a correspondence theory of truth, these are familiar points; though to advance them as such is to concede too much to the theory. What makes them of interest is their power to reveal how such a theory, in addition to its intrinsic defects, embodies too narrow a conception of the fact-stating use of language. Mr. Austin's description of the conditions under which a statement is true, regarded as an analysis of the fact-stating use, applies only to affirmative subject-predicate statements, *i.e.,* to statements in making which we refer to some one or more localized thing or group of things, event or set of events, and characterize it or them in some positive way (identify the object or objects and affix the label). It does not apply to negative, general and existential statements nor, straight-forwardly, to hypothetical and disjunctive statements. I agree that any language capable of the fact-stating use must have some devices for performing the function to which Mr. Austin exclusively directs his attention, and that other types of statements of fact can be understood only in relation to this type. But the other types *are* other types. For example, the word "not" can usefully be regarded as a kind of crystallizing-out of something *implicit* in all use of descriptive language (since no predicate would have any descriptive force if it were compatible with everything). But from this it does not follow that negation (*i.e.*, the *explicit* exclusion of some characteristic) is a kind of affirmation, that negative statements are properly discussed in the language appropriate to affirmative statements. Or take the case of existential statements. Here one needs to distinguish two kinds of demonstration or reference. There is, first, the kind whereby we enable our hearer to identify the thing or person or event or set of these which we then go on to characterize in some way. There is, second, the kind by which we simply indicate a locality. The first (*"Tabby* has the mange") answers the question "Who (which one, what) are you talking about?" The second (*"There's* a cat") the question "Where?" It is plain that no part of an existential statement performs the first function; though Austin's account of reference-cum-description is appropriate to reference of this kind rather than to that of the other. It is clear also that a good many existential statements do not answer the question "Where?" though they may license the enquiry. The difference between various types of statement, and their mutual relations, is a matter for careful description. Nothing is gained by lumping them all together under a description appropriate only to one, even though it be the basic, type.

6. Conclusion

My central objection to Mr. Austin's thesis is this. He describes the conditions which must obtain if we are correctly to declare a statement true. His detailed description of these conditions is, with reservations, correct as far as it goes, though in several respects too narrow. The central mistake is to suppose that in using the word "true" we are asserting such conditions to obtain. That this is a mistake is shown by the detailed examination of the behaviour of such words as "statement," "fact," etc., and of "true" itself, and by the examination of various different types of statement. This also reveals some of the ways in which "true" actually functions as an assertive device. What supremely confuses the issue is the failure to distinguish between the task of elucidating the nature of a certain type of communication (the empirically informative) from the problem of the actual functioning of the word "true" within the framework of that type of communication.

Bibliography

ARMSTRONG, D. M. *Knowledge, Belief, and Thought*. Cambridge: Cambridge University press, 1973.*

AYER, A. J. *Lauguage, Truth and Logic* (2nd ed., rev.). London: Gollancz, 1946.†

——. *The Problem of Knowledge*. Harmondsworth: Penguin, 1956.*

——. (ed.) *Logical Positivism*. New York: Free Press, 1959.†

BENACERRAF, P., and H. PUTNAM (eds.). *Philosophy of Mathematics*. Englewood Cliffs, N.J.: Prentice-Hall, 1964.

BOUWSMA, O. K. "Descartes' Skepticism of the Senses," *Mind*, LIV (1945), 313–322.

CANFIELD, J. V., and F. H. DONNELL (eds.). *Readings in the Theory of Knowledge*. New York: Appleton-Century-Crofts, 1964.

CHISHOLM, R. M. "Theory of Knowledge." In R. M. CHISHOLM et al. *Philosophy*. Englewood Cliffs, N.J.: Prentice-Hall, 1964.

——. *Theory of Knowledge*. Englewood Cliffs, N.J.: Prentice-Hall, 1966.*

—— and ROBERT J. SWARTZ (eds.) *Empirical Knowledge. Readings from Contemporary Sources*. Englewood Cliffs, N.J.: Prentice-Hall, 1973.

COPI, IRVING M., and JAMES A. GOULD (eds.). *Readings in Logic*. New York: Macmillan, 1964.*

DRETSKE, FRED I. *Seeing and Knowing*. Chicago: University of Chicago Press, 1969.

GRIFFITHS, A. PHILLIPS. *Knowledge and Belief*. London: Oxford University Press, 1967.*

HARMAN, GILBERT. *Thought*. Princeton: Princeton University Press, 1973.

HILL, T. E. *Contemporary Theories of Knowledge*. New York: Macmillan, 1959.

HINTIKKA, JAAKKO. *Knowledge and Belief*. Ithaca, N.Y.: Cornell University Press, 1962.

HINTIKKA, JAAKKO (ed.). *The Philosophy of Mathematics*. London: Oxford University Press, 1969.*

KÖRNER, S. *The Philosophy of Mathematics*. New York: Harper & Row, 1960.*

KUHN, THOMAS S. *The Structure of Scientific Revolutions* (2nd ed., enl.). Chicago: University of Chicago Press, 1962, 1970.*

LEHRER, KEITH. *Knowledge*. Oxford: Clarendon Press, 1974.

LEWIS, C. I. *An Analysis of Knowledge and Valuation*. LaSalle, Ill.: Open Court, 1946.

MALCOLM, NORMAN. *Knowledge and Certainty*. Englewood Cliffs, N.J.: Prentice-Hall, 1963.

MARGOLIS, JOSEPH. *Knowledge and Existence*. New York: Oxford University Press, 1973.

MORICK, HAROLD (ed.). *Challenges to Empiricism*. Belmont, Calif.: Wadsworth, 1972.*

PAP, ARTHUR. *Semantics and Necessary Truth*. New Haven: Yale University Press, 1958.†

PEARS, DAVID. *What Is Knowledge?* New York: Harper Torchbooks, 1971.*

PITCHER, GEORGE (ed.). *Truth*. Englewood Cliffs, N.J.: Prentice-Hall, 1964.*

POLLOCK, JOHN L. *Knowledge and Justification*. Princeton: Princeton University Press, 1974.

RESCHER, NICHOLAS. *The Coherence Theory of Truth*. Oxford: Clarendon Press, 1973.

---

* Paperback edition.   † Also available in paperback edition.

ROLLINS, C. D. (ed.). *Knowledge and Experience*. Pittsburgh: University of Pittsburgh Press, 1963.

ROTH, MICHAEL D., and LEON GALIS (eds.). *Knowing. Essays in the Analysis of Knowledge*. New York: Random House, 1970.*

STROLL, AVRUM (ed.). *Epistemology*. New York: Harper & Row, 1967.*

SUMNER, L. W., and JOHN WOODS (eds.). *Necessary Truth: A Book of Readings*. New York: Random House, 1969.*

SWARTZ, R. J. (ed.). *Perceiving, Sensing, and Knowing*. New York: Doubleday, 1965.*

TARSKI, ALFRED. "The Semantic Conception of Truth," *Philosophy and Phenomenological Research*, IV (1944), 341–375.

UNGER, PETER. *Ignorance*. Oxford: Clarendon Press, 1975.

WITTGENSTEIN, LUDWIG. *Remarks on the Foundations of Mathematics*. Oxford: Blackwell, 1956.

———. *Tractatus Logico-philosophicus*. London: Routledge & Kegan Paul, 1962.

WOOZLEY, A. D. *Theory of Knowledge*. London: Hutchinson, 1949.

III

PERCEPTION
AND THOUGHT

If we think of the human being as having mastered an enormous collection of truths about the real world, we are bound to ask for the sources of such information. Historically, the relevant philosophical developments from the sixteenth to the eighteenth centuries leading to the Kantian synthesis lie with the traditions known in Europe as rationalism and in Britain as empiricism (see Part II). The emphasis of that period tended to link the origin of the propositions we believe with the validity of those beliefs. Both traditions tended to risk not being able to account for our knowledge of the external world adequately by beginning with the putatively immediate data of our minds. An assured connection with the external world is traded for a measure of certainty.

To some extent, the relevant faculties of the mind remain a pertinent question to this day; though the cognitive status of perception and thought is characteristically appraised independently of genetic criteria, except where some form of foundationalism (see Part II) is posited. The master theme here is the dependence of our knowledge of the external world on sensory perception.

Plato's *Theaetetus* (III:1) is the first great classical investigation of the distinction between knowledge and right opinion or true belief (see Part II), with special attention to the sense in which perception may or may not be counted as knowledge. We are accustomed to speak of perceptual knowledge, because we suppose a real world exists that is somehow accessible to the senses. We also suppose that in exercising our senses effectively we come to know at least some properties of the things of the world. Further, we suppose that other of their properties (for example, those captured by so-called laws of nature) depend upon our first having discerned the former.

But Plato questions whether perception and knowledge *can* be the same. He himself inclines toward a negative conclusion, because perception seems an inferior faculty that cannot be directed to reality or being—or even similarity and difference. Plato links the phenomena of perceptual illusion and the variability of perceptual reports. What this shows is that a theory of perception is at least a partial commitment to a theory of the nature of the real world. At the present time, it is more usual to construe veridical perception— that is, perception yielding true beliefs—as having existential import. In effect, a perceptual statement's being true entails that what is perceived exists. But this shows only that different ontologies, different theories of the nature of the real world, may be fitted to perceptual phenomena.

The modern discussion of sensory perception achieves its first flowering in the British empiricist tradition. There, beginning with the pioneer work of John Locke (III:2), the extraordinary attempt is made to account for all the knowledge and concepts of the mind solely in terms of the initial data of "sensation or perception" and in terms of how the mind was activated to work upon these initial data (empiricism). The issue of empiricism was at once seen to be controversial by a rationalist contemporary of Locke's, Gottfried Leibniz (III:8). For Leibniz, the mind had concepts that could not be generated solely from sensory experience; it must be endowed with innate capacities for ordering and discriminating the data of the senses and even for arriving at certain necessary truths on its own power. Concepts like that of God, Leibniz thought, could not but be innate; and general truths could not be accounted for in terms of the passivity of the mind (Locke's thesis).

So the classical quarrel between rationalists and empiricists centered on the activity or passivity of the human mind, on the tenability of the doctrine of innate ideas. Locke's rejection of the thesis is obscured both by the uncertainty regarding the target of his attack and by the certainty that his own thesis was not adequately defended against a similar charge. But the contrast between rationalists and empiricists is also obscured in the next phase of the empiricist tradition, for George Berkeley (III:3) insisted on the inherent activity of the mind.

Berkeley was not an empiricist in Locke's sense, since he construed the reality of the world as consisting of ideas in the mind of God (a dependency that could not be established in sensory terms itself). What Berkeley attempted to do was to construct a more consistent but limited empiricism than Locke's, in terms of such central problems as the idea of material substance, the distinction between primary and secondary qualities, the nature of universal terms, and the meaning of immediate perception—problems which Berkeley found somewhat muddled in Locke.

In a sense, Locke's achievement lay in having formulated a first pass at an empiricist resolution of the problem of knowledge relative to the new experimental science of Isaac Newton. Ultimately, Locke's theory foreshadowed a causal theory of perceptual knowledge, which was to be refined in our own day. Berkeley was really more concerned with eliminating what he regarded as skepticism connected with the empiricist program (generated by the materialist concerns of Locke) than with perfecting a Lockean sort of empiricism itself. So there is an implicit sense of the limitation of empiricism in Berkeley's work as well as an interest in the extent to which Locke's account could be amended. Despite Berkeley's clever solution, there is as much difficulty in choosing his form of idealism as in choosing Locke's reliance on the causal efficacy of physical bodies external to the mind.

The emphasis on the immediate data of sensory experience persisted through much of the nineteenth and twentieth centuries. The reason is undoubtedly connected with the formulation of what were thought to be the cognitive foundations of scientific knowledge itself (see Part II). In the first half of the twentieth century, empiricist foundationalism was well entrenched. The essential question, it was thought, was to render a correct account of the immediate given of sensory experience, sense data. The problem became one of explaining the relationship between sense data and material objects.

G. E. Moore's account (III:4) is one of the classic early attempts to specify the relationship. But there are uncertainties that Moore acknowledges in his candid way—about whether, say, the sense datum of the edge of an object can be regarded as *part* of that object. This is entirely due to Moore's bifocal commitment to a commonsense philosophy and to empiricism. Thus Moore generated a whole series of puzzles concerned with the differences between the sense data I perceive and those that you perceive, as well as with the relationship between sense data and material objects. The issue is obviously inherited from the British empiricists. In fact, in the form in which early empiricism was finally presented by David Hume, it was opposed by an almost forgotten (and only now recovered) Scottish philosopher, Thomas Reid, who prefigured Moore as well as Malcolm in championing the commonsense opposition to empiricist "ideas."

A. J. Ayer's numerous and changing accounts of the analysis of sense-datum language make it difficult to assign him one simple thesis. In our selection (III:5) he sketches the lines of a so-called phenomenalist position. In it a sense-datum language is taken to be basic to perceptual knowledge, and physical objects are construed as theoretical entities posited relative to information derived from directly perceived sense data. Most philosophers have seriously doubted that the phenomenalist program is logically possible. Many even supposed the program's impossibility has been demonstrated, inasmuch as a sense-datum language can be shown to depend on a physical-object language, even though the latter is supposed to depend on the former.

The demonstration of this relationship is part of Wilfrid Sellars' endeavor (III:6), which also includes refuting the thesis that anything is initially *given* in a cognitively pertinent sense. Sellars' account is one of the most persistent examinations of the central puzzles posed by sense data; it trades on the confusion as to whether it is *facts* or *particulars* that are said to be sensed (see Part II).

A somewhat different attack on Ayer's sense-datum position is mounted by J. L. Austin (I:7), in a celebrated discussion within the confines of an "ordinary-language" approach and with particular attention to the use of such expressions as "looks," "appears," and "really." What Austin demonstrates is the inherently realistic cast of our perceptual discourse. The various ways in which we hedge our perceptual reports show not a retreat to a more fundamental level of "direct" perception (sense data) but alternative, efficient adjustments in what we wish to claim about the macroscopically perceivable world. Closely reviewed, what Austin demonstrates is not the indefensibility of sense-datum theories but the inadequacy of Ayer's line of argument.

The rationalist thesis has been vigorously revived in our own day by Noam Chomsky (III:9), particularly with regard to the acquisition of a natural language. There are questions as to whether Chomsky's concept is a version of the seventeenth-century notion of innate ideas. Chomsky himself has been increasingly careful to emphasize resemblances, where actual revival has been contested.

Chomsky's thesis is arresting in its own right. The acquisition of natural language is too efficient, he contends, too rapidly developed from incomplete samples, too clearly not dependent on any standard form of learning, too much convergent across the range of experience of speakers of every natural language to be accounted for in empiricist terms. In order to learn the variable details of some particular language, the mind must already be provided with the linguistic regularities basic to every natural language—the so-called linguistic universals. In this sense, the mind is primed by experience; its native linguistic competence comes to be exhibited in actual performance, under the pressures of social existence. Here, "competence" signifies the innate capacity to acquire any natural language; and "performance" signifies the ability to speak such a language under the conditions of social experience and the absence of physical handicap.

Human beings are said innately to *know* the deep rules common to every natural language. Although even a competent speaker normally cannot formulate such rules on demand, empirical research would show that our ability to speak creatively—to produce sentences that we have never heard before—argues our reliance on a command of these underlying rules. The empirical evidence itself is incomplete since no rules of language are demonstrably universal for all known languages.

But the ultimate question concerns what linguistic regularities would signify, whether the kind of competence Chomsky considers can be a form of knowledge, or whether the accomplishment is itself an artifact of his theory. These are issues of the sort that Hilary Putnam (III:10) presses against Chomsky, representing the empiricist objection. The puzzling feature of Chomsky's thesis depends in large measure on what sense can be made of innate rulelike regularities as opposed to lawlike regularities. And this may itself be taken to provide the contemporary distinction between rationalism and empiricism.

It is but a step from Chomsky's thesis to argue that thought itself must have a comparable underlying and innate structure. Jerry Fodor (III:11), who has been sympathetically associated with Chomsky's work, attempts to provide a positive demonstration. The argument is not that only creatures capable of explicit speech or of an explicit use of language are capable of thought and perception. It is rather that cognition in general must be inherently computational. If cognition *is* computational (as in making inferences from given data), it must depend on some internal representational system. But if cognition is itself a representational system, there must be an internal language with which the representations may be made. Hence, in Fodor's view, thought and perception are inherently linguistic, even where the agent is unaware of the rules by which its computations must be regulated.

Neither Chomsky nor Fodor adequately reckons with the possibility that both in the acquisition of speech and in the exercise of thought and perception our performance may be functionally equivalent to what they postulate in terms of some innate and determinate system of representation, without such a system's actually obtaining. Joseph Margolis (III:12) pursues this in terms of first-language acquisition. The ascription of propositional content to thought and perception, modeled on linguistic reports, need only be heuristically indebted to that model in order to preserve the functional import of particular episodes. That a bird sees that there is a worm on the ground may be inferred from the bird's behavior, assuming its needs and related mental states. It need never be the case that the bird computes, in any cognitively or linguistically relevant sense, that there is a worm on the ground.

In this respect at least empiricism gains another inning. The heuristic element concerns the representation of a nonlinguistic creature's thought and perception, not the fictional provision of such thought and perception. In other words, though languageless animals think and perceive, we are obliged to construe the content of their thought on the model of our own language (the heuristic element). There is no empiricist alternative, but even that is enough to avoid a rationalist account in the manner of Chomsky and Fodor.

Perception

1

Plato

Knowledge and Perception

Plato (b. 5th century B.C.), the author of the famous Dialogues, *is unknown to us in a personal sense. There is extraordinarily little reference to him or his life and circumstances in the statements of his contemporaries, including those of Aristotle, who was at the Academy during Plato's later life. For the most part the* Dialogues *feature Socrates, who is also difficult to identify in the sense of sorting out the historical figure from the voice of Plato's discourses. Still, Plato is not just the great precursor of Aristotle but one of the greatest philosophers of all time. We do have some information about him from the gossip Diogenes Laertius, and there remain some letters, many thought to be forgeries, that show Plato to have been occupied in a practical way with political life in Sicily.*

The distinctive method used particularly in the early dialogues involves a debating technique associated with the traveling sophists, perhaps an innovation of Protagoras himself. This technique restricts exchange so that yes and no serve as the only satisfactory answers. It also hints at, without approaching, Aristotle's syllogistic model. The most famous of the dialogues is surely the Republic, *which integrates all of Plato's interests.*

Plato's most characteristic doctrine, the theory of Forms, is nowhere more clearly articulated than in Phaedo *and* Symposium *or more tellingly queried than in* Parmenides *and* Sophist. *The Forms seem to be required to ensure both what is real among particular things and what can be known of them. Their distinction lies in their independent reality, their immutability, and their capacity to be "participated in" timelessly by endless things of the same kind. They are emphatically not concepts, since concepts are mental. They may perhaps be characterized as that to which concepts conform, and grasping them renders knowledge possible.*

It was the independent existence of the Forms that Aristotle attacked and Plato himself came to question. In the Meno, *the doctrine of recollection suggests (in today's terms) a recognition of innate ideas respecting knowledge. In* Phaedo, *the doctrine is linked to the theory of Forms.*

The problem of knowledge, in particular the contrast between knowledge and opinion or belief, is pursued in Theaetetus, *with the insistence that knowledge and opinion are not addressed to the same objects. The Forms seem, once again, to give point to the thesis. The issue is of some importance, given the intended recovery of Plato's so-called justified-true-belief interpretation of knowledge in recent American philosophy (see Part II). The* Theaetetus *is also prized for its exploration of a great many of the standard puzzles of perception. Plato argues there that knowledge is not sense perception. He seems to have in mind particularly that knowledge requires thought—in other words, that to know something is to know* that *something is the case. But that is just the feature that makes the definition of knowledge so difficult.*

.   .   .

SOCRATES   ... Theaetetus, ... you [said—Ed.] that knowledge is perception?

THEAETETUS.   I did.

SOC.   And if any one were to ask you: With what does a man see black and white colours? and with what does he hear high and low sounds?—you would say, if I am not mistaken, 'With the eyes and with the ears.'

THEAET.   I should.

SOC.   The free use of words and phrases, rather than minute precision, is generally characteristic of a liberal education, and the opposite is pedantic; but sometimes precision is necessary, and I believe that the answer which you have just given is open to the charge of incorrectness; for which is more correct, to say that we see or hear with the eyes and with the ears, or through the eyes and through the ears.

THEAET.   I should say 'through', Socrates, rather than 'with'.

SOC.   Yes, my boy, for no one can suppose that in each of us, as in a sort of Trojan horse, there are perched a number of unconnected senses, which do not all meet in some one nature, the soul or whatever we please to call it, of which they are the instruments, and with which through them we perceive objects of sense.

THEAET.   I agree with you in that opinion.

SOC.   The reason why I am thus precise is, because I want to know whether, when we perceive black and white through the eyes, and again, other qualities through other organs, we do not perceive them with one and the same part of ourselves; and whether, if you were asked, you could refer all such perceptions to the body. Perhaps, however, I had better allow you to answer for yourself and not interfere. Tell me, then, are not the organs through which you perceive warm and hard and light and sweet, organs of the body?

THEAET.   Of the body, certainly.

SOC.   And you would admit that what you perceive through one faculty you cannot perceive through another; the objects of hearing, for example, cannot be perceived through sight, or the objects of sight through hearing?

THEAET.   Of course not.

SOC.   If you have any thought about both of them, this common perception cannot come to you, either through the one or the other organ?

THEAET.   It cannot.

soc. How about sounds and colours: in the first place you may reflect that they both *exist?*

THEAET. Yes.

soc. And that either of them is different from the other, and the same with itself?

THEAET. Certainly.

soc. And that both are two and each of them one?

THEAET. Yes.

soc. You can further observe whether they are like or unlike one another?

THEAET. I dare say.

soc. But through what do you perceive all this about them? for neither through hearing nor yet through seeing can you apprehend that which they have in common. Let me give you an illustration of the point at issue:—If there were any meaning in asking whether sounds and colours are saline or not, you would be able to tell me what faculty would consider the question. It would not be sight or hearing, but some other.

THEAET. Certainly; the faculty of taste.

soc. Very good; and now tell me what is the power which discerns, not only in sensible objects, but in all things, universal properties, such as those which are called being and not-being, and those others about which we were just asking—what organs will you assign for the perception of these by the appropriate power in us?

THEAET. You are thinking of being and not-being, likeness and unlikeness, sameness and difference, and also of unity and any other number which occurs in our judgement of objects. And evidently your question applies to odd and even numbers and other arithmetical conceptions—through what bodily organ the soul perceives them.

soc. You follow me excellently, Theaetetus; that is precisely what I am asking.

THEAET. Indeed, Socrates, I cannot answer; my only notion is, that these, unlike objects of sense, have no separate organ, but that the mind, by a power of her own, contemplates such common properties in all things.

soc. You are a beauty, Theaetetus, and not ugly, as Theodorus was saying; for he who utters the beautiful is himself beautiful and good. And besides being beautiful, you have done me a kindness in releasing me from a very long discussion, if you believe that the soul views some things by herself and others through the bodily organs. For that was my own opinion, and I wanted you to agree with me.

THEAET. Indeed, I do believe it.

soc. And to which class would you refer being or essence; for this, of all our notions, is the most universal?

THEAET. I should say, to that class which the soul aspires to know of herself.

soc. And would you say this also of like and unlike, same and other?

THEAET. Yes.

soc. And would you say the same of the noble and base, and of good and evil?

THEAET. These also I conceive to be among the chief instances of those relative terms whose nature the soul perceives by comparing in herself things past and present with the future.

SOC. Hold! does she not perceive the hardness of that which is hard by the touch, and the softness of that which is soft equally by the touch?

THEAET. Yes.

SOC. But their *being*, I mean the fact that they are, and their opposition to one another, and the being (to repeat that term) of this opposition, the soul herself endeavours to decide for us by the review and comparison of them?

THEAET. Certainly.

SOC. The simple sensations which reach the soul through the body are given at birth to men and animals by nature, but their reflections on the being and use of them are slowly and hardly gained, if they are ever gained, by education and long experience.

THEAET. Assuredly.

SOC. And can a man attain truth who fails of attaining being?

THEAET. Impossible.

SOC. And can he who misses the truth of anything, have a knowledge of that thing?

THEAET. He cannot.

SOC. Then knowledge does not consist in impressions of sense, but in reasoning about them; in that only, and not in the mere impression, truth and being can be attained?

THEAET. Apparently.

SOC. And would you call the two processes by the same name, when there is so great a difference between them?

THEAET. That would certainly not be right.

SOC. And what name would you give to seeing, hearing, smelling, being cold and being hot?

THEAET. I should call all of them perceiving—what other name could be given to them?

SOC. Perception would be the collective name of them?

THEAET. Certainly.

SOC. Which, as we say, has no part in the attainment of truth, since it does not attain to being?

THEAET. Certainly not.

SOC. And therefore not in knowledge?

THEAET. No.

SOC. Then perception, Theaetetus, can never be the same as knowledge?

THEAET. Apparently not, Socrates; and knowledge has now been most distinctly proved to be different from perception.

.   .   .

2

John Locke
Knowledge and Perception

John Locke (1632–1704) is the first of the great early British empiricists. His
The Essay Concerning Human Understanding, *first published in 1690 though it*
had been drafted at least three times in the twenty years before its appearance,
is the wellspring of empiricism. It is a prolix and even inconsistent book, and it was
the butt of skillful critics, notably Leibniz and Berkeley.

Locke was a man of many talents. He served as personal physician to the
Earl of Shaftesbury, collaborated with the physician Thomas Sydenham, framed
(for Shaftesbury) a constitution for the colony of Carolina, served in a number of
politically sensitive ways including adviser to William of Orange before his ascent to
the throne and became a fellow of the Royal Society. His A Letter Concerning
Toleration *and* Two Treatises of Government *were published anonymously.*

Locke seems to have been particularly fearful of his political fortunes, being
associated with Shaftesbury. He fled England when Shaftesbury's fortunes became
uncertain; and he returned, from Holland, accompanying the Princess of Orange.
His own statement of the purpose of the Essay *is instructive: "to inquire into*
the original, certainty, and extent of human knowledge, together with the grounds
and degrees of belief, opinion, and assent."

The main thrust of his effort was to determine what ensured knowledge of
"ideas," sufficient for the normal affairs of men but at a distance from the real
world that produced them in us. For Locke, ideas are objects of awareness. The result
is that he inclined toward a skepticism about the nature of things (which Berkeley
stressed) and tended to confuse what the mind is aware of and how the mind
operates with what it is aware of (which Leibniz stressed).

Locke assumes the existence of an external world that produces sensations in
us. He insists that we have no innate ideas, that all our ideas come from original
experience. But if the mind is distinguished solely by its capacity to receive
impressions, then Locke has no account of the characteristic activity of the mind
working with such materials. Locke also introduced the distinction between primary
and secondary qualities—that is, the "inseparable" properties of physical bodies
and the powers of those properties to produce ideas in us (as of color and sound)
that do not resemble the qualities of external bodies. Locke's Newtonian bias
resisted the idea of theoretical hypotheses. Yet his insistence on the existence of the
theoretical entities of the new physics has attracted contemporary philosophers
speculating about the nature of what is perceived from the vantage of recent science.

From John Locke, *An Essay Concerning Human Understanding*, A. C. Fraser, ed. (Oxford: The Clarendon Press, 1894), Book II, Chap. VIII, Secs. 7–26, Vol. I, pp. 168–182; Book IV, Chap. XI, Secs. 1–10, Vol. II, pp. 325–336.

Chapter VIII. Simple Ideas of Sensation

.   .   .

To discover the nature of our *ideas* the better, and to discourse of them intelligibly, it will be convenient to distinguish them *as they are ideas or perceptions in our minds*; and *as they are modifications of matter in the bodies that cause such perceptions in us:* that so we may not think (as perhaps usually is done) that they are exactly the images and resemblances of something inherent in the subject; most of those of sensation being in the mind no more the likeness of something existing without us, than the names that stand for them are the likeness of our ideas, which yet upon hearing they are apt to excite in us.

Whatsoever the mind perceives *in itself*, or is the immediate object of perception, thought, or understanding, that I call *idea*; and the power to produce any idea in our mind, I call *quality* of the subject wherein that power is. Thus a snowball having the power to produce in us the ideas of white, cold, and round,—the power to produce those ideas in us, as they are in the snowball, I call qualities; and as they are sensations or perceptions in our understandings, I call them ideas; which *ideas*, if I speak of sometimes as in the things themselves, I would be understood to mean those qualities in the objects which produce them in us.

[Qualities thus considered in bodies are, *First*, such as are utterly inseparable from the body, in what state soever it be;] and such as in all the alterations and changes it suffers, all the force can be used upon it, it constantly keeps; and such as sense constantly finds in every particle of matter which has bulk enough to be perceived; and the mind finds inseparable from every particle of matter, though less than to make itself singly be perceived by our senses:, v.g. Take a grain of wheat, divide it into two parts; each part has still solidity, extension, figure, and mobility: divide it again, and it retains still the same qualities; and so divide it on, till the parts become insensible; they must retain still each of them all those qualities. For division (which is all that a mill, or pestle, or any other body, does upon another, in reducing it to insensible parts) can never take away either solidity, extension, figure, or mobility from any body, but only makes two or more distinct separate masses of matter, of that which was but one before; all which distinct masses, reckoned as so many distinct bodies, after division, make a certain number. [These I call *original* or *primary qualities* of body, which I think we may observe to produce simple ideas in us, viz. solidity, extension, figure, motion or rest, and number.

Secondly, such qualities which in truth are nothing in the objects themselves but powers to produce various sensations in us by their primary qualities, i.e. by the bulk, figure, texture, and motion of their insensible parts, as colours, sounds, tastes, &c. These I call *secondary qualities*. To these might be added a *third* sort, which are allowed to be barely powers; though they are as much real qualities in the subject as those which I, to comply with the common way of speaking, call qualities, but for distinction, secondary qualities. For the power in fire to produce a new colour, or consistency, in *wax* or *clay*,—by its primary qualities, is as much a quality in fire, as the power it has to produce in *me* a new idea or sensation of warmth or burning, which I felt not before,—by the same primary qualities, viz. the bulk, texture, and motion of its insensible parts.]

[The next thing to be considered is, how bodies produce ideas in us; and that is manifestly by impulse, the only way which we can conceive bodies to operate in.]

If then external objects be not united to our minds when they produce ideas therein; and yet we perceive these *original* qualities in such of them as singly fall under our senses, it is evident that some motion must be thence continued by our nerves, or animal spirits, by some parts of our bodies, to the brain or the seat of sensation, there to produce in our minds the particular ideas we have of them. And since the extension, figure, number, and motion of bodies of an observable bigness, may be perceived at a distance by the sight, it is evident some singly imperceptible bodies must come from them to the eyes, and thereby convey to the brain some motion; which produces these ideas which we have of them in us.

After the same manner that the ideas of these original qualities are produced in us, we may conceive that the ideas of *secondary* qualities are also produced, viz. by the operation of insensible particles on our senses. For, it being manifest that there are bodies and good store of bodies, each whereof are so small, that we cannot by any of our senses discover either their bulk, figure, or motion,—as is evident in the particles of the air and water, and others extremely smaller than those; perhaps as much smaller than the particles of air and water, as the particles of air and water are smaller than peas or hail-stones; —let us suppose at present that the different motions and figures, bulk and number, of such particles, affecting the several organs of our senses, produce in us those different sensations which we have from the colours and smells of bodies; v.g. that a violet, by the impulse of such insensible particles of matter, of peculiar figures and bulks, and in different degrees and modifications of their motions, causes the ideas of the blue colour, and sweet scent of that flower to be produced in our minds. It being no more impossible to conceive that God should annex such ideas to such motions, with which they have no similitude, than that he should annex the idea of pain to the motion of a piece of steel dividing our flesh, with which that idea hath no resemblance.

What I have said concerning colours and smells may be understood also of tastes and sounds, and other the like sensible qualities; which, whatever reality we by mistake attribute to them, are in truth nothing in the objects themselves, but powers to produce various sensations in us; and depend on those primary qualities, viz. bulk, figure, texture, and motion of parts [as I have said].

From whence I think it easy to draw this observation,—that the ideas of primary qualities of bodies are resemblances of them, and their patterns do really exist in the bodies themselves, but the ideas produced in us by these secondary qualities have no resemblance of them at all. There is nothing like our ideas, existing in the bodies themselves. They are, in the bodies we denominate from them, only a power to produce those sensations in us: and what is sweet, blue, or warm in idea, is but the certain bulk, figure, and motion of the insensible parts, in the bodies themselves, which we call so.

Flame is denominated hot and light; snow, white and cold; and manna, white and sweet, from the ideas they produce in us. Which qualities are commonly thought to be the same in those bodies that those ideas are in us, the one the perfect resemblance of the other, as they are in a mirror, and it would by most men be judged very extravagant if one should say otherwise. And yet he that will consider that the same fire that, at one distance produces in us the sensation of warmth, does, at a nearer approach, produce in us the far different sensation of pain, ought to bethink himself what reason he has to say—that this idea of warmth, which was produced in him by the fire, is *actually in the fire*; and his idea of pain, which the same fire produced in him the same way, is *not* in the fire. Why are whiteness and coldness in snow, and pain not, when it produces the one and the other idea in us; and can do neither, but by the bulk, figure, number, and motion of its solid parts?

The particular bulk, number, figure, and motion of the parts of fire or snow are really in them,—whether any one's senses perceive them or no: and therefore they may be called *real* qualities, because they really exist in those bodies. But light, heat, whiteness, or coldness, are no more really in them than sickness or pain is in manna. Take away the sensation of them; let not the eyes see light or colours, nor the ears hear sounds; let the palate not taste, nor the nose smell, and all colours, tastes, odours, and sounds, *as they are such particular ideas*, vanish and cease, and are reduced to their causes, i.e. bulk, figure, and motion of parts.

A piece of manna of a sensible bulk is able to produce in us the idea of a round or square figure; and by being removed from one place to another, the idea of motion. This idea of motion represents it as it really is in manna moving: a circle or square are the same, whether in idea or existence, in the mind or in the manna. And this, both motion and figure, are really in the manna, whether we take notice of them or no: this everybody is ready to agree to. Besides, manna, by the bulk, figure, texture, and motion of its parts, has a power to produce the sensations of sickness, and sometimes of acute pains or gripings in us. That these ideas of sickness and pain are *not* in the manna, but effects of its operations on us, and are nowhere when we feel them not; this also every one readily agrees to. And yet men are hardly to be brought to think that sweetness and whiteness are not really in manna; which are but the effects of the operations of manna, by the motion, size, and figure of its particles, on the eyes and palate: as the pain and sickness caused by manna are confessedly nothing but the effects of its operations on the stomach and guts, by the size, motion, and figure of its insensible parts, (for by nothing else can a body operate, as has been proved): as if it could not operate on the eyes and palate, and thereby produce in the mind particular distinct ideas, which in itself it has not, as well as we allow it can operate on the guts and stomach, and thereby produce distinct ideas, which in itself it has not. These ideas, being all effects of the operations of manna on several parts of our bodies, by the size, figure, number, and motion of its parts;—why those produced by the eyes and palate should rather be thought to be really in the manna, than those produced by the stomach and guts; or why the pain and sickness, ideas that are the effect of manna, should be thought to be nowhere when they are not felt; and yet the sweetness and whiteness, effects of the same manna on other parts of the body, by ways equally as unknown, should be thought to exist in the manna, when they are not seen or tasted, would need some reason to explain.

Let us consider the red and white colours in porphyry. Hinder light from striking on it, and its colours vanish; it no longer produces any such ideas in us: upon the return of light it produces these appearances on us again. Can any one think any real alterations are made in the porphyry by the presence or absence of light; and that those ideas of whiteness and redness are really in porphyry in the light, when it is plain *it has no colour in the dark?* It has, indeed, such a configuration of particles, both night and day, as are apt, by the rays of light rebounding from some parts of that hard stone, to produce in us the idea of redness; and from others the idea of whiteness; but whiteness or redness are not in it at any time, but such a texture that hath the power to produce such a sensation in us.

Pound an almond, and the clear white colour will be altered into a dirty one, and the sweet taste into an oily one. What real alteration can the beating of the pestle make in any body, but an alteration of the texture of it?

Ideas being thus distinguished and understood, we may be able to give an account how the same water, at the same time, may produce the idea of cold by one hand and of heat by the other: whereas it is impossible that the same water, if those ideas were really in it, should at the same time be both hot and cold. For, if we imagine *warmth*, as it is in our hands, to be nothing but a certain sort and degree of motion in the minute particles of our nerves or animal spirits, we may understand how it is possible that the same water may, at the same time, produce the sensations of heat in one hand and cold in the other; which yet *figure* never does, that never producing the idea of a square by one hand which has produced the idea of a globe by another. But if the sensation of heat and cold be nothing but the increase or diminution of the motion of the minute parts of our bodies, caused by the corpuscles of any other body, it is easy to be understood, that if that motion be greater in one hand than in the other; if a body be applied to the two hands, which has in its minute particles a greater motion than in those of one of the hands, and a less than in those of the other, it will increase the motion of the one hand and lessen it in the other; and so cause the different sensations of heat and cold that depend thereon.

I have in what just goes before been engaged in physical inquiries a little further than perhaps I intended. But, it being necessary to make the nature of sensation a little understood; and to make the difference between the *qualities* in bodies, and the *ideas* produced by them in the mind, to be distinctly conceived, without which it were impossible to discourse intelligibly of them;— I hope I shall be pardoned this little excursion into natural philosophy; it being necessary in our present inquiry to distinguish the *primary* and *real* qualities of bodies, which are always in them (viz. solidity, extension, figure, number, and motion, or rest, and are sometimes perceived by us, viz. when the bodies they are in are big enough singly to be discerned), from those *secondary* and *imputed* qualities, which are but the powers of several combinations of those primary ones, when they operate without being distinctly discerned,—whereby we may also come to know what ideas are, and what are not, resemblances of something really existing in the bodies we denominate from them.

The qualities, then, that are in bodies, rightly considered, are of three sorts:—

First, The bulk, figure, number, situation, and motion or rest of their solid parts. Those are in them, whether we perceive them or not; and when they are of that size that we can discover them, we have by these an idea of the thing as it is in itself; as is plain in artificial things. These I call *primary qualities.*

Secondly, The power that is in any body, by reason of its insensible primary qualities, to operate after a peculiar manner on any of our senses, and thereby produce in *us* the different ideas of several colours, sounds, smells, tastes, &c. These are usually called *sensible qualities.*

Thirdly, The power that is in any body, by reason of the particular constitution of its primary qualities, to make such a change in the bulk, figure, texture, and motion of *another body,* as to make it operate on our senses differently from what it did before. Thus the sun has a power to make wax white, and fire to make lead fluid. [These are usually called *powers.*]

The first of these, as has been said, I think may be properly called real, original, or primary qualities; because they are in the things themselves, whether they are perceived or not: and upon their different modifications it is that the secondary qualities depend.

The other two are only powers to act differently upon other things: which powers result from the different modifications of those primary qualities.

But, though the two latter sorts of qualities are powers barely, and nothing but powers, relating to several other bodies, and resulting from the different modifications of the original qualities, yet they are generally otherwise thought of. For the *second* sort, viz. the powers to produce several ideas in us, by our senses, are looked upon as real qualities in the things thus affecting us: but the *third* sort are called and esteemed barely powers. v.g. The idea of heat or light, which we receive by our eyes, or touch, from the sun, are commonly thought real qualities existing in the sun, and something more than mere powers in it. But when we consider the sun in reference to wax, which it melts or blanches, we look on the whiteness and softness produced in the wax, not as qualities in the sun, but effects produced by powers in it. Whereas, if rightly considered, these qualities of light and warmth, which are perceptions in me when I am warmed or enlightened by the sun, are no otherwise in the sun, than the changes made in the wax, when it is blanched or melted, are in the sun. They are all of them equally *powers in the sun, depending on its primary qualities*; whereby it is able, in the one case, so to alter the bulk, figure, texture, or motion of some of the insensible parts of my eyes or hands, as thereby to produce in me the idea of light or heat; and in the other, it is able so to alter the bulk, figure, texture, or motion of the insensible parts of the wax, as to make them fit to produce in me the distinct ideas of white and fluid.

The reason why the one are ordinarily taken for real qualities, and the other only for bare powers, seems to be, because the ideas we have of distinct colours, sounds, &c., containing nothing at all in them of bulk, figure, or motion, we are not apt to think them the effects of these primary qualities; which appear not, to our senses, to operate in their production, and with which they have not any apparent congruity or conceivable connexion. Hence it is that we are so forward to imagine, that those ideas are the resemblances of something really existing in the objects themselves: since sensation discovers nothing of bulk, figure, or motion of parts in their production; nor can reason show how bodies, *by their bulk, figure, and motion,* should produce in the mind the ideas of blue or yellow, &c. But, in the other case, in the operations of bodies changing the qualities one of another, we plainly discover that the quality produced hath commonly no resemblance with anything in the thing producing it; wherefore we look on it as a bare effect of power. For, through receiving the idea of heat or light from the sun, we are apt to think *it* is a perception and resemblance of such a quality in the sun; yet when we see wax, or a fair face, receive change of colour from the sun, we cannot imagine that to be the reception or resemblance of anything in the sun, because we find not those different colours in the sun itself. For, our senses being able to observe a likeness or unlikeness of sensible qualities in two different external objects, we forwardly enough conclude the production of any sensible quality in any subject to be an effect of bare power, and not the communication of any quality which was really in the efficient, when we find no such sensible quality in the thing that produced it. But our senses, not being able to discover any unlikeness between the idea produced in us, and the quality of the object producing it, we are apt to imagine that our ideas are resemblances of something in the objects, and not the effects of certain powers placed in the modification of their primary qualities, with which primary qualities the ideas produced in us have no resemblance.

To conclude. Beside those before-mentioned primary qualities in bodies, viz. bulk, figure, extension, number, and motion of their solid parts; all the rest, whereby we take notice of bodies, and distinguish them one from another, are nothing else but several powers in them, depending on those primary qualities; whereby they are fitted, either by immediately operating on our bodies to produce several different ideas in us; or else, by operating on other bodies, so to change their primary qualities as to render them capable of producing ideas in us different from what before they did. The former of these, I think, may be called secondary qualities *immediately perceivable*: the latter, secondary qualities, *mediately perceivable*.

Chapter XI. Of Our Knowledge of the Existence of Other Things

The knowledge of our own being we have by intuition. The existence of a God, reason clearly makes known to us . . .

The knowledge of the existence of *any other thing* we can have only by *sensation*: for there being no necessary connexion of real existence with any *idea* a man hath in his memory; nor of any other existence but that of God with the existence of any particular man: no particular man can know the existence of any other being, but only when, by actual operating upon him, it makes itself perceived by him. For, the having the idea of anything in our mind, no more proves the existence of that thing, than the picture of a man evidences his being in the world, or the visions of a dream make thereby a true history.

It is therefore the *actual receiving* of ideas from without that gives us notice of the existence of other things, and makes us know, that something doth exist at that time without us, which causes that idea in us; though perhaps we neither know nor consider how it does it. For it takes not from the certainty of our senses, and the ideas we receive by them, that we know not the manner wherein they are produced: v.g. whilst I write this, I have, by the paper affecting my eyes, that idea produced in my mind, which, whatever object causes, I call *white*; by which I know that that quality or accident (i.e. whose appearance before my eyes always causes that idea) doth really exist, and hath a being without me. And of this, the greatest assurance I can possibly have, and to which my faculties can attain, is the testimony of my eyes, which are the proper and sole judges of this thing; whose testimony I have reason to rely on as so certain, that I can no more doubt, whilst I write this, that I see white and black, and that something really exists that causes that sensation in me, than that I write or move my hand; which is a certainty as great as human nature is capable of, concerning the existence of anything, but a man's self alone, and of God.

The notice we have by our senses of the existing of things without us, though it be not altogether so certain as our intuitive knowledge, or the deductions of our reason employed about the clear abstract ideas of our own minds; yet it is an assurance that deserves the name of *knowledge*. If we persuade ourselves that our faculties act and inform us right concerning the existence of those objects that affect them, it cannot pass for an ill-grounded confidence: for I think nobody can, in earnest, be so sceptical as to be uncertain of the existence of those things which he sees and feels. At least, he that can doubt so far, (whatever he may have with his own thoughts,) will never have any controversy with me; since he can never be sure I say anything contrary to his own opinion. As to myself, I think God has given me assurance enough of the existence of things without me: since, by their different application, I can produce in myself both pleasure and pain, which is one great concernment of my present state. This is certain: the confidence that our faculties do not herein deceive us, is the greatest assurance we are capable of concerning the existence of material beings. For we cannot act anything but by our faculties; nor talk of knowledge itself, but by the help of those faculties which are fitted to apprehend even what knowledge is.

But besides the assurance we have from our senses themselves, that they do not err in the information they give us of the existence of things without us, when they are affected by them, we are further confirmed in this assurance by other concurrent reasons:—

I. It is plain those perceptions are produced in us by exterior causes affecting our senses: because those that want the *organs* of any sense, never can have the ideas belonging to that sense produced in their minds. This is too evident to be doubted: and therefore we cannot but be assured that they come in by the organs of that sense, and no other way. The organs themselves, it is plain, do not produce them: for then the eyes of a man in the dark would produce colours, and his nose smell roses in the winter: but we see nobody gets the relish of a pineapple, till he goes to the Indies, where it is, and tastes it.

II. Because sometimes I find that *I cannot avoid the having those ideas produced in my mind.* For though, when my eyes are shut, or windows fast, I can at pleasure recall to my mind the ideas of light, or the sun, which former sensations had lodged in my memory; so I can at pleasure lay by *that* idea, and take into my view that of the smell of a rose, or taste of sugar. But, if I turn my eyes at noon towards the sun, I cannot avoid the ideas which the light or sun then produces in me. So that there is a manifest difference between the ideas laid up in my memory, (over which, if they were there only, I should have constantly the same power to dispose of them, and lay them by at pleasure,) and those which force themselves upon me, and I cannot avoid having. And therefore it must needs be some exterior cause, and the brisk acting of some objects without me, whose efficacy I cannot resist, that produces those ideas in my mind, whether I will or no. Besides, there is nobody who doth not perceive the difference in himself between contemplating the sun, as he hath the idea of it in his memory, and actually looking upon it: of which two, his perception is so distinct, that few of his ideas are more distinguishable one from another. And therefore he hath certain knowledge that they are not *both* memory, or the actions of his mind, and fancies only within him; but that actual seeing hath a cause without.

III. Add to this, that many of those ideas are *produced in us with pain,* which afterwards we remember without the least offence. Thus, the pain of heat or cold, when the idea of it is revived in our minds, gives us no disturbance; which, when felt, was very troublesome; and is again, when actually repeated: which is occasioned by the disorder the external object causes in our bodies when applied to them: and we remember the pains of hunger, thirst, or the headache, without any pain at all; which would either never disturb us, or else constantly do it, as often as we thought of it, were there nothing more but ideas floating in our minds, and appearances entertaining our fancies, without the real existence of things affecting us from abroad. The same may be said of *pleasure,* accompanying several actual sensations. And though mathematical demonstration depends not upon sense, yet the examining them by diagrams gives great credit to the evidence of our sight, and seems to give it a certainty approaching to that of demonstration itself. For it would be very strange, that a man should allow it for an undeniable truth, that two angles of a figure, which he measures by lines and angles of a diagram, should be bigger one than the other, and yet doubt of the existence of those lines and angles, which by looking on he makes use of to measure that by.

IV. Our *senses* in many cases *bear witness to the truth of each other's report,* concerning the existence of sensible things without us. He that *sees* a fire, may, if he doubt whether it be anything more than a bare fancy, *feel* it too; and be convinced, by putting his hand in it. Which certainly could never be put into such exquisite pain by a bare idea or phantom, unless that the pain be a fancy too: which yet he cannot, when the burn is well, by raising the idea of it, bring upon himself again.

Thus I see, whilst I write this, I can change the appearance of the paper; and by designing the letters, tell *beforehand* what new idea it shall exhibit the very next moment, by barely drawing my pen over it: which will neither appear (let me fancy as much as I will) if my hands stand still; or though I move my pen, if my eyes be shut: nor, when those characters are once made on the paper, can I choose afterwards but see them as they are; that is, have the ideas of such letters as I have made. Whence it is manifest, that they are not barely the sport and play of my own imagination, when I find that the characters that were made at the pleasure of my own thoughts, do not obey them; nor yet cease to be, whenever I shall fancy it, but continue to affect my senses constantly and regularly, according to the figures I made them. To which if we will add, that the sight of those shall, from another man, draw such sounds as I beforehand design they shall stand for, there will be little reason left to doubt that those words I write do really exist without me, when they cause a long series of regular sounds to affect my ears, which could not be the effect of my imagination, nor could my memory retain them in that order.

But yet, if after all this any one will be so sceptical as to distrust his senses, and to affirm that all we see and hear, feel and taste, think and do, during our whole being, is but the series and deluding appearances of a long dream, whereof there is no reality; and therefore will question the existence of all things, or our knowledge of anything: I must desire him to consider, that, if all be a dream, then he doth but dream that he makes the question, and so it is not much matter that a waking man should answer him. But yet, if he pleases, he may dream that I make him this answer, That the certainty of things existing in *rerum natura* [in the nature of things—Ed.] when we have the testimony of our senses for it is not only as great as our frame can attain to, but as our condition needs. For, our faculties being suited not to the full extent of being, nor to a perfect, clear, comprehensive knowledge of things free from all doubt and scruple; but to the preservation of us, in whom they are; and accommodated to the use of life: they serve to our purpose well enough, if they will but give us certain notice of those things, which are convenient or inconvenient to us. For he that sees a candle burning, and hath experimented the force of its flame by putting his finger in it, will little doubt that this is something existing without him, which does him harm, and puts him to great pain: which is assurance enough, when no man requires greater certainty to govern his actions by than what is as certain as his actions themselves. And if our dreamer pleases to try whether the glowing heat of a glass furnace be barely a wandering imagination in a drowsy man's fancy, by putting his hand into it, he may perhaps be wakened into a certainty greater than he could wish, that it is something more than bare imagination. So that this evidence is as great as we can desire, being as certain to us as our pleasure or pain, i.e. happiness or misery; beyond which we have no concernment, either of knowing or being. Such an assurance of the existence of things without us is sufficient to direct us in the attaining the good and avoiding the evil which is caused by them, which is the important concernment we have of being made acquainted with them.

In fine, then, when our senses do actually convey into our understandings any idea, we cannot but be satisfied that there doth something *at that time* really exist without us, which doth affect our senses, and by them give notice of itself to our apprehensive faculties, and actually produce that idea which we then perceive: and we cannot so far distrust their testimony, as to doubt that such *collections* of simple ideas as we have observed by our senses to be united together, do really exist together. But this knowledge extends as far as the present testimony of our senses, employed about particular objects that do then affect them, and no further. For if I saw such a collection of simple ideas as is wont to be called *man*, existing together one minute since, and am now alone, I cannot be certain that the same man exists now, since there is no *necessary connexion* of his existence a minute since with his existence now: by a thousand ways he may cease to be, since I had the testimony of my senses for his existence. And if I cannot be certain that the man I saw last to-day is now in being, I can less be certain that he is so who hath been longer removed from my senses, and I have not seen since yesterday, or since the last year: and much less can I be certain of the existence of men that I never saw. And, therefore, though it be highly probable that millions of men do now exist, yet, whilst I am alone, writing this, I have not that certainty of it which we strictly call knowledge; though the great likelihood of it puts me past doubt, and it be reasonable for me to do several things upon the confidence that there are men (and men also of my acquaintance, with whom I have to do) now in the world: but this is but probability, not knowledge.

Whereby yet we may observe how foolish and vain a thing it is for a man of a narrow knowledge, who having reason given him to judge of the different evidence and probability of things, and to be swayed accordingly; how vain, I say, it is to expect demonstration and certainty in things not capable of it; and refuse assent to very rational propositions, and act contrary to very plain and clear truths, because they cannot be made out so evident, as to surmount every the least (I will not say reason, but) pretence of doubting. He that, in the ordinary affairs of life, would admit of nothing but direct plain demonstration, would be sure of nothing in this world, but of perishing quickly. The wholesomeness of his meat or drink would not give him reason to venture on it: and I would fain know what it is he could do upon such grounds as are capable of no doubt, no objection.

.   .   .

3

George Berkeley
The Reality of Sensible Things

*George Berkeley (1685–1753), eventually Bishop of Cloyne in Ireland, earlier the
promoter of an ill-fated project for a Christian college in Bermuda for Indians and
Negro as well as white settlers, was the most brilliant Anglo-Irish philosopher of
the Newtonian era. By the age of twenty-five he had already published* An Essay
Towards a New Theory of Vision *and the first part of* A Treatise Concerning the
Principles of Human Knowledge; *the second part seems to have been lost in
transit. The force of his novel doctrine, which he himself called immaterialism
but others usually termed idealism, was focused in* Three Dialogues Between Hylas
and Philonous. *He wrote extensively, but his later work does not seem to have
sustained the freshness and analytic power of his early production.*

*Berkeley's key thesis is that to exist is to be perceived or to perceive. But
since what we perceive, borrowing from Locke, are "ideas," or "sensible qualities,"
Berkeley was obliged to distinguish what was capable of perception by other terms
("spirits" of various sorts). Ideas cannot, he insisted, exist outside the mind. But
he did not give a satisfactory account of the independent existence of perceptible
objects, because he failed to account for the difference between the ideas in
God's mind (which insured the independence of the external world) and the
ideas in our own minds.*

*What we know we know by the senses; what God knows he knows otherwise.
Hence what we know directly (sensible ideas) cannot be the same as what God knows.
Since perception involves passivity, Berkeley thought, God does not know his
own ideas by perceptual means and they cannot as such be sensible ideas.
Correspondingly, we lack a full account from Berkeley about the difference between
sensible ideas and our notions (not able to be captured in the way ideas are) of
minds or spirits. Nevertheless, Berkeley brilliantly exposed the difficulty in Locke's
distinction between primary and secondary qualities, his treatment of universals, and
the lurking skepticism of the earlier empiricist formulations.*

.   .   .

PHILONOUS.   Shall we . . . examine which of us it is that denies the reality
of sensible things, or professes the greatest ignorance of them; since, if I take
you rightly, he is to be esteemed the greatest *sceptic?*

.   .   .

HYLAS.   That is what I desire.

PHILONOUS.   What mean you by sensible things?

From *Three Dialogues between Hylas and Philonous,* in *The Works of George Berkeley,
Bishop of Cloyne,* T. E. Jessop, ed. (London: Thomas Nelson & Sons Ltd., 1949), Vol. II,
First Dialogue, pp. 173–191, 193–195. Reprinted by permission of the publisher.

HYLAS. Those things which are perceived by the senses. Can you imagine that I mean any thing else?

PHILONOUS. Pardon me, Hylas, if I am desirous clearly to apprehend your notions, since this may much shorten our inquiry. Suffer me then to ask you this farther question. Are those things only perceived by the senses which are perceived immediately? Or may those things properly be said to be *sensible*, which are perceived mediately, or not without the intervention of others?

HYLAS. I do not sufficiently understand you.

PHILONOUS. In reading a book, what I immediately perceive are the letters, but mediately, or by means of these, are suggested to my mind the notions of God, virtue, truth, &c. Now, that the letters are truly sensible things, or perceived by sense, there is no doubt: but I would know whether you take the things suggested by them to be so too.

HYLAS. No certainly, it were absurd to think *God* or *Virtue* sensible things, though they may be signified and suggested to the mind by sensible marks, with which they have an arbitrary connexion.

PHILONOUS. It seems then, that by *sensible things* you mean those only which can be perceived immediately by sense.

HYLAS. Right.

PHILONOUS. Doth it not follow from this, that though I see one part of the sky red, and another blue, and that my reason doth thence evidently conclude there must be some cause of that diversity of colours, yet that cause cannot be said to be a sensible thing, or perceived by the sense of seeing?

HYLAS. It doth.

PHILONOUS. In like manner, though I hear variety of sounds, yet I cannot be said to hear the causes of those sounds.

HYLAS. You cannot.

PHILONOUS. And when by my touch I perceive a thing to be hot and heavy, I cannot say with any truth or propriety, that I feel the cause of its heat or weight.

HYLAS. To prevent any more questions of this kind, I tell you once for all, that by *sensible things* I mean those only which are perceived by sense, and that in truth the senses perceive nothing which they do not perceive immediately: for they make no inferences. The deducing therefore of causes or occasions from effects and appearances, which alone are perceived by sense, entirely relates to reason.

PHILONOUS. The point then is agreed between us, that *sensible things are those only which are immediately perceived by sense*. You will farther inform me, whether we immediately perceive by sight any thing beside light, and colours, and figures: or by hearing, any thing but sounds: by the palate, any thing beside tastes: by the smell, beside odours: or by the touch, more than tangible qualities.

HYLAS. We do not.

PHILONOUS. It seems therefore, that if you take away all sensible qualities, there remains nothing sensible.

HYLAS. I grant it.

PHILONOUS. Sensible things therefore are nothing else but so many sensible qualities, or combinations of sensible qualities.

HYLAS. Nothing else.

PHILONOUS. Heat then is a sensible thing.

HYLAS. Certainly.

PHILONOUS. Doth the reality of sensible things consist in being perceived? or, is it something distinct from their being perceived, and that bears no relation to the mind?

HYLAS. To *exist* is one thing, and to be *perceived* is another.

PHILONOUS. I speak with regard to sensible things only: and of these I ask, whether by their real existence you mean a subsistence exterior to the mind, and distinct from their being perceived?

HYLAS. I mean a real absolute being, distinct from, and without any relation to their being perceived.

PHILONOUS. Heat therefore, if it be allowed a real being, must exist without the mind.

HYLAS. It must.

PHILONOUS. Tell me, Hylas, is this real existence equally compatible to all degrees of heat, which we perceive: or is there any reason why we should attribute it to some, and deny it others? And if there be, pray let me know that reason.

HYLAS. Whatever degree of heat we perceive by sense, we may be sure the same exists in the object that occasions it.

PHILONOUS. What, the greatest as well as the least?

HYLAS. I tell you, the reason is plainly the same in respect of both: they are both perceived by sense; nay, the greater degree of heat is more sensibly perceived; and consequently, if there is any difference, we are more certain of its real existence than we can be of the reality of a lesser degree.

PHILONOUS. But is not the most vehement and intense degree of heat a very great pain?

HYLAS. No one can deny it.

PHILONOUS. And is any unperceiving thing capable of pain or pleasure?

HYLAS. No certainly.

PHILONOUS. Is your material substance a senseless being, or a being endowed with sense and perception?

HYLAS. It is senseless, without doubt.

PHILONOUS. It cannot therefore be the subject of pain.

HYLAS. By no means.

PHILONOUS. Nor consequently of the greatest heat perceived by sense, since you acknowledge this to be no small pain.

HYLAS. I grant it.

PHILONOUS. What shall we say then of your external object; is it a material substance, or no?

HYLAS. It is a material substance with the sensible qualities inhering in it.

PHILONOUS. How then can a great heat exist in it, since you own it cannot in a material substance? I desire you would clear this point.

HYLAS. Hold, Philonous, I fear I was out in yielding intense heat to be a pain. It should seem rather, that pain is something distinct from heat, and the consequence or effect of it.

PHILONOUS. Upon putting your hand near the fire, do you perceive one simple uniform sensation, or two distinct sensations?

HYLAS. But one simple sensation.

PHILONOUS. Is not the heat immediately perceived?

HYLAS. It is.

PHILONOUS. And the pain?

HYLAS. True.

PHILONOUS. Seeing therefore they are both immediately perceived at the same time, and the fire affects you only with one simple, or uncompounded idea, it`follows that this same simple idea is both the intense heat immediately perceived, and the pain; and consequently, that the intense heat immediately perceived, is nothing distinct from a particular sort of pain.

HYLAS. It seems so.

PHILONOUS. Again, try in your thoughts, Hylas, if you can conceive a vehement sensation to be without pain, or pleasure.

HYLAS. I cannot.

PHILONOUS. Or can you frame to yourself an idea of sensible pain or pleasure in general, abstracted from every particular idea of heat, cold, tastes, smells? &c.

HYLAS. I do not find that I can.

PHILONOUS. Doth it not therefore follow, that sensible pain is nothing distinct from those sensations or ideas, in an intense degree?

HYLAS. It is undeniable; and to speak the truth, I begin to suspect a very great heat cannot exist but in a mind perceiving it.

PHILONOUS. What! are you then in that *sceptical* state of suspense, between affirming and denying?

HYLAS. I think I may be positive in the point. A very violent and painful heat cannot exist without the mind.

PHILONOUS. It hath not therefore, according to you, any real being.

HYLAS. I own it.

PHILONOUS. Is it therefore certain, that there is no body in nature really hot?

HYLAS. I have not denied there is any real heat in bodies. I only say, there is no such thing as an intense real heat.

PHILONOUS. But did you not say before, that all degrees of heat were equally real: or if there was any difference, that the greater were more un-doubtedly real than the lesser?

HYLAS. True: but it was, because I did not then consider the ground there is for distinguishing between them, which I now plainly see. And it is this: because intense heat is nothing else but a particular kind of painful sensation; and pain cannot exist but in a perceiving being; it follows that no intense heat can really exist in an unperceiving corporeal substance. But this is no reason why we should deny heat in an inferior degree to exist in such a substance.

PHILONOUS. But how shall we be able to discern those degrees of heat which exist only in the mind, from those which exist without it?

HYLAS. That is no difficult matter. You know, the least pain cannot exist unperceived; whatever therefore degree of heat is a pain, exists only in the mind. But as for all other degrees of heat, nothing obliges us to think the same of them.

PHILONOUS. I think you granted before, that no unperceiving being was capable of pleasure, any more than of pain.

HYLAS. I did.

PHILONOUS. And is not warmth, or a more gentle degree of heat than what causes uneasiness, a pleasure?

HYLAS. What then?

PHILONOUS. Consequently it cannot exist without the mind in any unperceiving substance, or body.

HYLAS. So it seems.

PHILONOUS. Since therefore, as well those degrees of heat that are not painful, as those that are, can exist only in a thinking substance; may we not conclude that external bodies are absolutely incapable of any degree of heat whatsoever?

HYLAS. On second thoughts, I do not think it so evident that warmth is a pleasure, as that a great degree of heat is a pain.

PHILONOUS. I do not pretend that warmth is as great a pleasure as heat is a pain. But if you grant it to be even a small pleasure, it serves to make good my conclusion.

HYLAS. I could rather call it an *indolence*. It seems to be nothing more than a privation of both pain and pleasure. And that such a quality or state as this may agree to an unthinking substance, I hope you will not deny.

PHILONOUS. If you are resolved to maintain that warmth, or a gentle degree of heat, is no pleasure, I know not how to convince you otherwise, than by appealing to your own sense. But what think you of cold?

HYLAS. The same that I do of heat. An intense degree of cold is a pain; for to feel a very great cold, is to perceive a great uneasiness: it cannot therefore exist without the mind; but a lesser degree of cold may, as well as a lesser degree of heat.

PHILONOUS. Those bodies therefore, upon whose application to our own, we perceive a moderate degree of heat, must be concluded to have a moderate degree of heat or warmth in them: and those, upon whose application we feel a like degree of cold, must be thought to have cold in them.

HYLAS. They must.

PHILONOUS. Can any doctrine be true that necessarily leads a man into an absurdity?

HYLAS. Without doubt it cannot.

PHILONOUS. Is it not an absurdity to think that the same thing should be at the same time both cold and warm?

HYLAS. It is.

PHILONOUS. Suppose now one of your hands hot, and the other cold, and that they are both at once put into the same vessel of water, in an intermediate state; will not the water seem cold to one hand, and warm to the other?

HYLAS. It will.

PHILONOUS. Ought we not therefore by your principles to conclude, it is really both cold and warm at the same time, that is, according to your own concession, to believe an absurdity.

HYLAS. I confess it seems so.

PHILONOUS. Consequently, the principles themselves are false, since you have granted that no true principle leads to an absurdity.

HYLAS. But after all, can any thing be more absurd than to say, *there is no heat in the fire?*

PHILONOUS. To make the point still clearer; tell me, whether in two cases exactly alike, we ought not to make the same judgment?

HYLAS. We ought.

PHILONOUS. When a pin pricks your finger, doth it not rend and divide the fibres of your flesh?

HYLAS. It doth.

PHILONOUS. And when a coal burns your finger, doth it any more?

HYLAS. It doth not.

PHILONOUS. Since therefore you neither judge the sensation itself occasioned by the pin, nor any thing like it to be in the pin; you should not, conformably to what you have now granted, judge the sensation occasioned by the fire, or any thing like it, to be in the fire.

HYLAS. Well, since it must be so, I am content to yield this point, and acknowledge, that heat and cold are only sensations existing in our minds: but there still remain qualities enough to secure the reality of external things.

PHILONOUS. But what will you say, Hylas, if it shall appear that the case is the same with regard to all other sensible qualities, and that they can no more be supposed to exist without the mind, than heat and cold?

HYLAS. Then indeed you will have done something to the purpose; but that is what I despair of seeing proved.

PHILONOUS. Let us examine them in order. What think you of tastes, do they exist without the mind, or no?

HYLAS. Can any man in his senses doubt whether sugar is sweet, or wormwood bitter?

PHILONOUS. Inform me, Hylas. Is a sweet taste a particular kind of pleasure or pleasant sensation, or is it not?

HYLAS. It is.

PHILONOUS. And is not bitterness some kind of uneasiness or pain?

HYLAS. I grant it.

PHILONOUS. If therefore sugar and wormwood are unthinking corporeal substances existing without the mind, how can sweetness and bitterness, that is, pleasure and pain, agree to them?

HYLAS. Hold, Philonous, I now see what it was deluded me all this time. You asked whether heat and cold, sweetness and bitterness, were not particular sorts of pleasure and pain; to which I answered simply, that they were. Whereas I should have thus distinguished: those qualities, as perceived by us, are pleasures or pains, but not as existing in the external objects. We must not therefore conclude absolutely, that there is no heat in the fire, or sweetness in the sugar, but only that heat or sweetness, as perceived by us, are not in the fire or sugar. What say you to this?

PHILONOUS. I say it is nothing to the purpose. Our discourse proceeded altogether concerning sensible things, which you defined to be the things we *immediately perceived by our senses.* Whatever other qualities therefore you speak of, as distinct from these, I know nothing of them, neither do they at all belong to the point in dispute. You may indeed pretend to have discovered certain qualities which you do not perceive, and assert those insensible qualities exist in fire and sugar. But what use can be made of this to your present purpose, I am at a loss to conceive. Tell me then once more, do you acknowledge that heat and cold, sweetness and bitterness (meaning those qualities which are perceived by the senses) do not exist without the mind?

HYLAS. I see it is to no purpose to hold out, so I give up the cause as to those mentioned qualities. Though I profess it sounds oddly, to say that sugar is not sweet.

PHILONOUS. But for your farther satisfaction, take this along with you: that which at other times seems sweet, shall to a distempered palate appear bitter. And nothing can be plainer, than that divers persons perceive different tastes in the same food, since that which one man delights in, another abhors. And how could this be, if the taste was something really inherent in the food?

HYLAS. I acknowledge I know not how.

PHILONOUS. In the next place, odours are to be considered. And with regard to these, I would fain know, whether what hath been said of tastes doth not exactly agree to them? Are they not so many pleasing or displeasing sensations?

HYLAS. They are.

. . .

PHILONOUS. May we not therefore conclude of smells, as of the other forementioned qualities, that they cannot exist in any but a perceiving substance or mind?

HYLAS. I think so.

PHILONOUS. Then as to sounds, what must we think of them: are they accidents really inherent in external bodies, or not?

HYLAS. That they inhere not in the sonorous bodies, is plain from hence; because a bell struck in the exhausted receiver of an air-pump, sends forth no sound. The air therefore must be thought the subject of sound.

PHILONOUS. What reason is there for that, Hylas?

HYLAS. Because when any motion is raised in the air, we perceive a sound greater or lesser, in proportion to the air's motion; but without some motion in the air, we never hear any sound at all.

PHILONOUS. And granting that we never hear a sound but when some motion is produced in the air, yet I do not see how you can infer from thence, that the sound itself is in the air.

HYLAS. It is this very motion in the external air, that produces in the mind the sensation of *sound.* For, striking on the drum of the ear, it causeth a vibration, which by the auditory nerves being communicated to the brain, the soul is thereupon affected with the sensation called *sound.*

PHILONOUS. What! is sound then a sensation?

HYLAS. I tell you, as perceived by us, it is a particular sensation in the mind.

PHILONOUS. And can any sensation exist without the mind?

HYLAS. No certainly.

PHILONOUS. How then can sound, being a sensation exist in the air, if by the *air* you mean a senseless substance existing without the mind?

HYLAS. You must distinguish, Philonous, between sound as it is perceived by us, and as it is in itself; or (which is the same thing) between the sound we immediately perceive, and that which exists without us. The former indeed is a particular kind of sensation, but the latter is merely a vibrative or undulatory motion in the air.

PHILONOUS. I thought I had already obviated that distinction by the answer I gave when you were applying it in a like case before. But to say no more of that; are you sure then that sound is really nothing but motion?

HYLAS. I am.

PHILONOUS. Whatever therefore agrees to real sound, may with truth be attributed to motion.

HYLAS. It may.

PHILONOUS. It is then good sense to speak of *motion,* as of a thing that is *loud, sweet, acute,* or *grave.*

HYLAS. I see you are resolved not to understand me. Is it not evident, those accidents or modes belong only to sensible sound, or *sound* in the common acceptation of the word, but not to *sound* in the real and philosophic sense, which, as I just now told you, is nothing but a certain motion of the air?

PHILONOUS. It seems then there are two sorts of sound, the one vulgar, or that which is heard, the other philosophical and real.

HYLAS. Even so.

PHILONOUS. And the latter consists in motion.

HYLAS. I told you so before.

PHILONOUS. Tell me, Hylas, to which of the senses think you, the idea of motion belongs: to the hearing?

HYLAS. No certainly, but to the sight and touch.

PHILONOUS. It should follow then, that according to you, real sounds may possibly be *seen* or *felt,* but never *heard.*

HYLAS. Look you, Philonous, you may if you please make a jest of my opinion, but that will not alter the truth of things. I own indeed, the inferences you draw me into, sound something oddly; but common language, you know, is framed by, and for the use of the vulgar: we must not therefore wonder, if expressions adapted to exact philosophic notions, seem uncouth and out of the way.

PHILONOUS. Is it come to that? I assure you, I imagine myself to have gained no small point, since you make so light of departing from common phrases and opinions; it being a main part of our inquiry, to examine whose notions are widest of the common road, and most repugnant to the general sense of the world. But can you think it no more than a philosophical paradox, to say that *real sounds are never heard*, and that the idea of them is obtained by some other sense. And is there nothing in this contrary to nature and the truth of things?

HYLAS.   To deal ingenuously, I do not like it. And after the concessions already made, I had as well grant that sounds too have no real being without the mind.

PHILONOUS.   And I hope you will make no difficulty to acknowledge the same of colours.

HYLAS.   Pardon me: the case of colours is very different. Can any thing be plainer, than that we see them on the objects?

PHILONOUS.   The objects you speak of are, I suppose, corporeal substances existing without the mind.

HYLAS.   They are.

PHILONOUS.   And have true and real colours inhering in them?

HYLAS.   Each visible object hath that colour which we see in it.

PHILONOUS.   How! Is there any thing visible but what we perceive by sight?

HYLAS.   There is not.

PHILONOUS.   And do we perceive anything by sense, which we do not perceive immediately?

HYLAS.   How often must I be obliged to repeat the same thing? I tell you, we do not.

PHILONOUS.   Have patience, good Hylas; and tell me once more, whether there is any thing immediately perceived by the senses, except sensible qualities. I know you asserted there was not: but I would now be informed, whether you still persist in the same opinion.

HYLAS.   I do.

PHILONOUS.   Pray, is your corporeal substance either a sensible quality, or made up of sensible qualities?

HYLAS.   What a question that is! who ever thought it was?

PHILONOUS.   My reason for asking was, because in saying, *each visible object hath that colour which we see in it*, you make visible objects to be corporeal substances; which implies either that corporeal substances are sensible qualities, or else that there is something beside sensible qualities perceived by sight: but as this point was formerly agreed between us, and is still maintained by you, it is a clear consequence, that your corporeal substance is nothing distinct from sensible qualities.

HYLAS.   You may draw as many absurd consequences as you please, and endeavour to perplex the plainest things; but you shall never persuade me out of my senses. I clearly understand my own meaning.

PHILONOUS.   I wish you would make me understand it too. But since you are unwilling to have your notion of corporeal substance examined, I shall urge that point no farther. Only be pleased to let me know, whether the same colours which we see, exist in external bodies, or some other.

HYLAS. The very same.

PHILONOUS. What! are then the beautiful red and purple we see on yonder clouds, really in them? Or do you imagine they have in themselves any other form, than that of a dark mist or vapour?

HYLAS. I must own, Philonous, those colours are not really in the clouds as they seem to be at this distance. They are only apparent colours.

PHILONOUS. *Apparent* call you them? how shall we distinguish these apparent colours from real?

HYLAS. Very easily. Those are to be thought apparent, which appearing only at a distance, vanish upon a nearer approach.

PHILONOUS. And those I suppose are to be thought real, which are discovered by the most near and exact survey.

HYLAS. Right.

PHILONOUS. Is the nearest and exactest survey made by the help of a microscope, or by the naked eye?

HYLAS. By a microscope, doubtless.

PHILONOUS. But a microscope often discovers colours in an object different from those perceived by the unassisted sight. And in case we had microscopes magnifying to any assigned degree; it is certain, that no object whatsoever viewed through them, would appear in the same colour which it exhibits to the naked eye.

HYLAS. And what will you conclude from all this? You cannot argue that there are really and naturally no colours on objects: because by artificial managements they may be altered, or made to vanish.

PHILONOUS. I think it may evidently be concluded from your own concessions, that all the colours we see with our naked eyes, are only apparent as those on the clouds, since they vanish upon a more close and accurate inspection, which is afforded us by a microscope. Then as to what you say by way of prevention: I ask you, whether the real and natural state of an object is better discovered by a very sharp and piercing sight, or by one which is less sharp?

HYLAS. By the former without doubt.

PHILONOUS. Is it not plain from *dioptrics*, that microscopes make the sight more penetrating, and represent objects as they would appear to the eye, in case it were naturally endowed with a most exquisite sharpness?

HYLAS. It is.

PHILONOUS. Consequently the microscopical representation is to be thought that which best sets forth the real nature of the thing, or what it is in itself. The colours therefore by it perceived, are more genuine and real, than those perceived otherwise.

HYLAS. I confess there is something in what you say.

PHILONOUS. Besides, it is not only possible but manifest, that there actually are animals, whose eyes are by Nature framed to perceive those things, which by reason of their minuteness escape our sight. What think you of those inconceivably small animals perceived by glasses? Must we suppose they are all stark blind? Or, in case they see, can it be imagined their sight hath not the same use in preserving their bodies from injuries, which appears in that of all other animals? And if it hath, is it not evident, they must see particles less than their own bodies, which will present them with a far different view in each object, from that which strikes our senses? Even our own eyes do not always represent objects to us after the same manner. In the *jaundice,* every one knows that all things seem yellow. Is it not therefore highly probable, those animals in whose eyes we discern a very different texture from that of ours, and whose bodies abound with different humours, do not see the same colours in every object that we do? From all which, should it not seem to follow, that all colours are equally apparent, and that none of those which we perceive are really inherent in any outward object?

HYLAS.   It should.

PHILONOUS.   The point will be past all doubt, if you consider, that in case colours were real properties or affections inherent in external bodies, they could admit of no alteration, without some change wrought in the very bodies themselves: but is it not evident from what hath been said, that upon the use of microscopes, upon a change happening in the humours of the eye, or a variation of distance, without any manner of real alteration in the thing itself, the colours of any object are either changed, or totally disappear? Nay all other circumstances remaining the same, change but the situation of some objects, and they shall present different colours to the eye. The same thing happens upon viewing an object in various degrees of light. And what is more known, than that the same bodies appear differently coloured by candle-light, from what they do in the open day? Add to these the experiment of a prism, which separating the heterogeneous rays of light, alters the colour of any object; and will cause the whitest to appear of a deep blue or red to the naked eye. And now tell me, whether you are still of opinion, that every body hath its true real colour inhering in it; and if you think it hath, I would fain know farther from you, what certain distance and position of the object, what peculiar texture and formation of the eye, what degree or kind of light is necessary for ascertaining that true colour, and distinguishing it from apparent ones.

HYLAS.   I own myself entirely satisfied, that they are all equally apparent; and that there is no such thing as colour really inhering in external bodies, but that it is altogether in the light. And what confirms me in this opinion is, that in proportion to the light, colours are still more or less vivid; and if there be no light, then are there no colours perceived. Besides, allowing there are colours on external objects, yet how is it possible for us to perceive them? For no external body affects the mind, unless it act first on our organs of sense. But the only action of bodies is motion; and motion cannot be communicated otherwise than by impulse. A distant object therefore cannot act on the eye, nor consequently make itself or its properties perceivable to the soul. Whence it plainly follows, that it is immediately some contiguous substance, which operating on the eye occasions a perception of colours: and such is light.

PHILONOUS.   How! is light then a substance?

HYLAS.   I tell you, Philonous, external light is nothing but a thin fluid substance, whose minute particles being agitated with a brisk motion, and in various manners reflected from the different surfaces of outward objects to the eyes, communicate different motions to the optic nerves; which being propagated to the brain, cause therein various impressions: and these are attended with the sensations of red, blue, yellow, &c.

PHILONOUS. It seems then, the light doth no more than shake the optic nerves.

HYLAS. Nothing else.

PHILONOUS. And consequent to each particular motion of the nerves the mind is affected with a sensation, which is some particular colour.

HYLAS. Right.

PHILONOUS. And these sensations have no existence without the mind.

HYLAS. They have not.

PHILONOUS. How then do you affirm that colours are in the light, since by *light* you understand a corporeal substance external to the mind?

HYLAS. Light and colours, as immediately perceived by us, I grant cannot exist without the mind. But in themselves they are only the motions and configurations of certain insensible particles of matter.

PHILONOUS. Colours then in the vulgar sense, or taken for the immediate objects of sight, cannot agree to any but a perceiving substance.

HYLAS. That is what I say.

PHILONOUS. Well then, since you give up the point as to those sensible qualities, which are alone thought colours by all mankind beside, you may hold what you please with regard to those invisible ones of the philosophers. It is not my business to dispute about them; only I would advise you to bethink your self, whether considering the inquiry we are upon, it be prudent for you to affirm, *the red and blue which we see are not real colours, but certain unknown motions and figures which no man ever did or can see, are truly so.* Are not these shocking notions, and are not they subject to as many ridiculous inferences, as those you were obliged to renounce before in the case of sounds?

HYLAS. I frankly own, Philonous, that it is in vain to stand out any longer. Colours, sounds, tastes, in a word, all those termed *secondary qualities*, have certainly no existence without the mind. But by this acknowledgment I must not be supposed to derogate any thing from the reality of matter or external objects, seeing it is no more than several philosophers maintain, who nevertheless are the farthest imaginable from denying matter. For the clearer understanding of this, you must know sensible qualities are by philosophers divided into *primary* and *secondary*. The former are extension, figure, solidity, gravity, motion, and rest. And these they hold exist really in bodies. The latter are those above enumerated; or briefly, all sensible qualities beside the primary, which they assert are only so many sensations or ideas existing no where but in the mind. But all this, I doubt not, you are already apprised of. For my.part, I have been a long time sensible there was such an opinion current among philosophers, but was never thoroughly convinced of its truth till now.

PHILONOUS. You are still then of opinion, that extension and figures are inherent in external unthinking substances.

HYLAS. I am.

PHILONOUS. But what if the same arguments which are brought against secondary qualities, will hold good against these also?

HYLAS. Why then I shall be obliged to think, they too exist only in the mind.

PHILONOUS. Is it your opinion, the very figure and extension which you perceive by sense, exist in the outward object or material substance?

HYLAS. It is.

PHILONOUS. Have all other animals as good grounds to think the same of the figure and extension which they see and feel?

HYLAS. Without doubt, if they have any thought at all.

PHILONOUS. Answer me, Hylas. Think you the senses were bestowed upon all animals for their preservation and well-being in life? or were they given to men alone for this end?

HYLAS. I make no question but they have the same use in all other animals.

PHILONOUS. If so, is it not necessary they should be enabled by them to perceive their own limbs, and those bodies which are capable of harming them?

HYLAS. Certainly.

PHILONOUS. A mite therefore must be supposed to see his own foot, and things equal or even less than it, as bodies of some considerable dimension; though at the same time they appear to you scarce discernible, or at best as so many visible points.

HYLAS. I cannot deny it.

PHILONOUS. And to creatures less than the mite they will seem yet larger.

HYLAS. They will.

PHILONOUS. Insomuch that what you can hardly discern, will to another extremely minute animal appear as some huge mountain.

HYLAS. All this I grant.

PHILONOUS. Can one and the same thing be at the same time in itself of different dimensions?

HYLAS. That were absurd to imagine.

PHILONOUS. But from what you have laid down it follows, that both the extension by you perceived, and that perceived by the mite itself, as likewise all those perceived by lesser animals, are each of them the true extension of the mite's foot, that is to say, by your own principles you are led into an absurdity.

HYLAS. There seems to be some difficulty in the point.

PHILONOUS. Again, have you not acknowledged that no real inherent property of any object can be changed, without some change in the thing itself?

HYLAS. I have.

PHILONOUS. But as we approach to or recede from an object, the visible extension varies, being at one distance ten or an hundred times greater than at another. Doth it not therefore follow from hence likewise, that it is not really inherent in the object?

HYLAS. I own I am at a loss what to think.

PHILONOUS. Your judgment will soon be determined, if you will venture to think as freely concerning this quality, as you have done concerning the rest. Was it not admitted as a good argument, that neither heat nor cold was in the water, because it seemed warm to one hand, and cold to the other?

HYLAS. It was.

PHILONOUS. Is it not the very same reasoning to conclude, there is no extension or figure in an object, because to one eye it shall seem little, smooth, and round, when at the same time it appears to the other, great, uneven, and angular?

HYLAS.   The very same. But doth this latter fact ever happen?

PHILONOUS.   You may at any time make the experiment, by looking with one eye bare, and with the other through a microscope.

HYLAS.   I know not how to maintain it, and yet I am loth to give up *extension*, I see so many odd consequences following upon such a concession.

PHILONOUS.   Odd, say you? After the concessions already made, I hope you will stick at nothing for its oddness. But on the other hand should it not seem very odd, if the general reasoning which includes all other sensible qualities did not also include extension? If it be allowed that no idea nor any thing like an idea can exist in an unperceiving substance, then surely it follows, that no figure or mode of extension, which we can either perceive or imagine, or have any idea of, can be really inherent in matter; not to mention the peculiar difficulty there must be, in conceiving a material substance, prior to and distinct from extension, to be the *substratum* of extension. Be the sensible quality what it will, figure, or sound, or colour; it seems alike impossible it should subsist in that which doth not perceive it.

HYLAS.   I give up the point for the present, reserving still a right to retract my opinion, in case I shall hereafter discover any false step in my progress to it.

PHILONOUS.   That is a right you cannot be denied. Figures and extension being dispatched, we proceed next to *motion*. Can a real motion in any external body be at the same time both very swift and very slow?

HYLAS.   It cannot.

PHILONOUS.   Is not the motion of a body swift in a reciprocal proportion to the time it takes up in describing any given space? Thus a body that describes a mile in an hour, moves three times faster than it would in case it described only a mile in three hours.

HYLAS.   I agree with you.

PHILONOUS.   And is not time measured by the succession of ideas in our minds?

HYLAS.   It is.

PHILONOUS.   And is it not possible ideas should succeed one another twice as fast in your mind, as they do in mine, or in that of some spirit of another kind.

HYLAS.   I own it.

PHILONOUS.   Consequently the same body may to another seem to perform its motion over any space in half the time that it doth to you. And the same reasoning will hold as to any other proportion: that is to say, according to your principles (since the motions perceived are both really in the object) it is possible one and the same body shall be really moved the same way at once, both very swift and very slow. How is this consistent either with common sense, or with what you just now granted?

HYLAS.   I have nothing to say to it.

PHILONOUS.   Then as for *solidity*; either you do not mean any sensible quality by that word, and so it is beside our inquiry: or if you do, it must be either hardness or resistance. But both the one and the other are plainly relative to our senses: it being evident, that what seems hard to one animal, may appear soft to another, who hath greater force and firmness of limbs. Nor is it less plain, that the resistance I feel is not in the body.

. . .

HYLAS. I wonder, Philonous, if what you say be true, why those philosophers who deny the secondary qualities any real existence, should yet attribute it to the primary. If there is no difference between them, how can this be accounted for?

. . .

PHILONOUS. Can you even separate the ideas of extension and motion, from the ideas of all those qualities which they who make the distinction, term *secondary*.

. . .

. . . Since therefore it is impossible even for the mind to disunite the ideas of extension and motion from all other sensible qualities, doth it not follow, that where the one exist, there necessarily the other exist likewise?

HYLAS. It should seem so.

PHILONOUS. Consequently the very same arguments which you admitted, as conclusive against the secondary qualities, are without any farther application of force against the primary too. Besides, if you will trust your senses, is it not plain all sensible qualities coexist, or to them, appear as being in the same place? Do they ever represent a motion, or figure, as being divested of all other visible and tangible qualities?

HYLAS. You need say no more on this head. I am free to own, if there be no secret error or oversight in our proceedings hitherto, that all sensible qualities are alike to be denied existence without the mind. But my fear is, that I have been too liberal in my former concessions, or overlooked some fallacy or other. In short, I did not take time to think.

PHILONOUS. For that matter, Hylas, you may take what time you please in reviewing the progress of our inquiry. You are at liberty to recover any slips you might have made, or offer whatever you have omitted, which makes for your first opinion.

HYLAS. One great oversight I take to be this: that I did not sufficiently distinguish the *object* from the *sensation*. Now though this latter may not exist without the mind, yet it will not thence follow that the former cannot.

PHILONOUS. What object do you mean? the object of the senses?

HYLAS. The same.

PHILONOUS. It is then immediately perceived.

HYLAS. Right.

PHILONOUS. Make me to understand the difference between what is immediately perceived, and a sensation.

HYLAS. The sensation I take to be an act of the mind perceiving; beside which, there is something perceived; and this I call the *object*. For example, there is red and yellow on that tulip. But then the act of perceiving those colours is in me only, and not in the tulip.

PHILONOUS.   What tulip do you speak of? is it that which you see?

HYLAS.   The same.

PHILONOUS.   And what do you see beside colour, figure, and extension?

HYLAS.   Nothing.

PHILONOUS.   What you would say then is, that the red and yellow are coexistent with the extension; is it not?

HYLAS.   That is not all; I would say, they have a real existence without the mind, in some unthinking substance.

PHILONOUS.   That the colours are really in the tulip which I see, is manifest. Neither can it be denied, that this tulip may exist independent of your mind or mine; but that any immediate object of the senses, that is, any idea, or combination of ideas, should exist in an unthinking substance, or exterior to all minds, is in itself an evident contradiction. Nor can I imagine how this follows from what you said just now, to wit that the red and yellow were on the tulip *you saw*, since you do not pretend to *see* that unthinking substance.

.   .   .

4

G. E. Moore

Sense-Data

G. E. Moore, who died in 1958, was, with Bertrand Russell and Ludwig Wittgenstein, one of the three most important and most influential philosophers of the British world of the twentieth century. His career was almost uneventful in a public sense. From 1892, when he entered Trinity College, Cambridge, he remained almost entirely absorbed in his academic and professional activities. After having left Cambridge at the end of his fellowship in 1904 (though he lectured there in the interim), he returned to assume a professorship in 1925. His personal manner and lack of pretense earned for him a reputation as a philosopher's philosopher. Most of his work appeared in the form of separate essays collected in a series of volumes (Philosophical Studies, 1922; Some Main Problems of Philosophy, 1953; Philosophical Papers, 1959; The Common Place Books, 1919–1953, 1962).

From G. E. Moore, *Some Main Problems of Philosophy* (London: George Allen & Unwin Ltd., 1953), Chap. II, pp. 28–38, 40, 42–44. Reprinted by permission of the publisher.

Moore published two volumes in ethics. The first of these, Principia Ethica *(1903), had a vogue and influence unequaled by any other volume in the field in the twentieth century. His writing betrays extraordinary care in tracking down every conceivable lead in the development of a theme. He wrote on nearly every topic of central philosophical interest in his day with the exception of formal logic and the philosophy of science. The twin themes of his philosophical orientation, if any can be assigned with confidence, are a persistent realism—extended even to sense data, which occasioned many a puzzle for Moore—and an epistemology devoted to commonsense certainty ("The Refutation of Idealism," "The Status of Sense-data," "A Defense of Common Sense"). He also developed, at least implicitly, a conceptual analysis of a concept into its constituent parts. This appears most prominently in* Principia Ethica *and forms the basis of Moore's now famous (and notorious) thesis that "good" is a simple quality. Moore served as editor of* Mind *from 1921 to 1947.*

. . . I shall . . . begin discussing the various ways in which we know of the existence of material objects—*supposing* that we do know of their existence. I do not want to assume, to begin with, that we *certainly do* know that they exist. I only want to consider what sort of a thing our knowledge of them is, *supposing* that it is really knowledge. . . .

And I . . . should begin with the most primitive sort of way in which we commonly suppose that we have knowledge of them—namely, that kind of knowledge, which we should call knowledge *by means of the senses*—the knowledge which we have, for instance, by seeing and feeling, as when we feel an object over with our hands. This way of knowing material objects, by means of the senses, is, of course, by no means the only way in which we commonly suppose we know of their existence. For instance, each of us knows of the past existence of many material objects by means of memory; we remember the existence of objects which we are no longer perceiving by any of our senses. We know of others again, which we ourselves have never perceived by our senses and cannot therefore remember, by the testimony of other persons who *have* perceived them by their senses. And we know also, we suppose, by means of inference, of others which nobody has ever perceived by his senses: we know, for instance, in this way that there is another surface of the moon, different from that which is constantly turned to the earth. All these other ways of knowing material objects, I shall have presently to consider, and to contrast them with sense-perception. But all these other ways do seem, in a sense, to be *based* upon sense-perception, so that *it* is, in a sense, the most primitive way of knowing material objects: it seems, in fact, to be true, that if I had not known of *some* material objects by means of sense-perception, I could never possibly have known of any others in any of these other ways; and this seems to be true universally: no man could ever know of the existence of any material objects at all, unless he first knew of *some* by means of his senses. The evidence of the senses is, therefore, the evidence upon which all our other ways of knowing material objects seems to be based.

And what I want first to consider is what sort of a thing this evidence of the senses is; or in other words what it is that happens when (as we should say) we see, or feel, a material object, or perceive one by any other sense. And

I propose to take as an instance, for the sake of simplicity, a single sense *only*—namely, the sense of sight: I shall use what happens when we *see*, as an illustration of what happens in sense-perception generally. All the general principles which I point out with regard to the sense of seeing, will, I think, be easily transferable, *mutatis mutandis* [in comparable circumstances—Ed.], to all the other senses by which we can be said to perceive material objects.

My first question is, then: What exactly is it that happens, when (as we should say) we *see* a material object? And I should explain, perhaps, to avoid misunderstanding, that the occurrence which I mean here to analyse is merely the *mental* occurrence—the act of consciousness—which we call *seeing*. I do not mean to say anything at all about the bodily processes which occur in the eye and the optic nerves and the brain. I have no doubt, myself, that these bodily processes *do* occur, when we see; and that physiologists really do *know* a great deal about them. But all that I shall mean by '*seeing*', and all that I wish to talk about, is the mental occurrence—the act of consciousness—which occurs (as is supposed) as a consequence of or accompaniment of these bodily processes. This mental occurrence, which I call 'seeing', is known to us in a much more simple and direct way, than are the complicated physiological processes which go on in our eyes and nerves and brains. A man cannot directly observe the minute processes which go on in his own eyes and nerves and brain when he sees; but all of us who are not blind can directly observe this mental occurrence, which we mean by seeing. And it is solely with *seeing*, in this sense—seeing, as an act of consciousness which we can all of us directly observe as happening in our own minds—that I am now concerned.

And I wish to illustrate what I have to say about seeing by a direct practical example; because, though I dare say many of you are perfectly familiar with the sort of points I wish to raise, it is, I think, very important for every one, in these subjects, to consider carefully single concrete instances, so that there may be no mistake as to exactly what it is that is being talked about. Such mistakes are, I think, very apt to happen, if one talks merely in generalities; and moreover one is apt to overlook important points. I propose, therefore, to hold up an envelope in my hand, and to ask you all to look at it for a moment; and then to consider with me exactly what it is that happens, when you see it: *what* this occurrence, which we call the *seeing* of it, *is*.

I hold up this envelope, then: I look at it, and I hope you all will look at it. And now I put it down again. Now what has happened? We should certainly say (if you have looked at it) that we all *saw* that envelope, that we all saw *it*, *the same* envelope: I saw it, and you all saw it. We all saw *the same* object. And by the *it*, which we all saw, we mean an object, which, at any one of the moments when we were looking at it, occupied just *one* of the many places that constitute the whole of space. Even during the short time in which we were looking at it, it may have moved—occupied successively several different places; for the earth, we believe, is constantly going round on its axis, and carrying with it all the objects on its surface, so that, even while we looked at the envelope, it probably moved and changed its position in space, though we did not see it move. But at any *one* moment, we should say, this *it*, the envelope, which we say we all saw, was at some *one* definite place in space.

But now, what happened to each of us, when we saw that envelope? I will begin by describing *part* of what happened to me. I saw a patch[1] of a particular whitish colour, having a certain size, and a certain shape, a shape with rather sharp angles or corners and bounded by fairly straight lines. These things: this patch of a whitish color, and its size and shape I did actually see. And I propose to call these things, the colour and size and shape, *sense-data*,[2] things *given* or presented by the senses—given, in this case, by my sense of sight. Many philosophers have called these things which I call sense-data, *sensations*. They would say, for instance, that that particular patch of colour was a sensation. But it seems to me that this term 'sensation' is liable to be misleading. We should certainly say that I *had* a sensation, when I saw that colour. But when we say that I *had* a sensation, what we mean is, I think, that I had the experience which consisted in my *seeing* the colour. That is to say, what we mean by a 'sensation' in this phrase, is my *seeing* of the colour, not the colour which I saw: this colour does not seem to be what I mean to say that I *had*, when I say I *had* a sensation of colour. It is very unnatural to say that I *had* the colour, that I *had* that particular whitish grey or that I *had* the patch which was of that colour. What I certainly did *have* is the experience which consisted in my seeing the colour and the patch. And when, therefore, we talk of *having* sensations, I think what we mean by 'sensations' is the experiences which consist in apprehending certain sense-data, *not* these sense-data themselves. I think, then, that the term 'sensation' is liable to be misleading, because it may be used in two different senses, which it is very important to distinguish from one another. It may be used *either* for the colour which I saw or for the experience which consisted in my seeing it. And it is, I think very important, for several reasons, to distinguish these two things. I will mention only two of these reasons. In the first place, it is, I think, quite conceivable (I do not say it is actually true) but *conceivable* that the patch of colour which I saw may have continued to exist after I saw it: whereas, of course, when I ceased to see it, *my seeing* of it ceased to exist. I will illustrate what I mean, by holding up the envelope again, and looking at it. I look at it, and I again see a *sense-datum*, a patch of a whitish colour. But now I immediately turn away my eyes, and I no longer see that sense-datum: my seeing of it has ceased to exist. But I am by no means sure that the sense-datum—that very same patch of whitish colour which I saw—is not still *existing* and still there. I do not say, for certain, that it is: I think very likely it is not. But I have a strong inclination to believe that it is. And it seems to me at least *conceivable* that it should be still existing, whereas my *seeing* of it certainly has ceased to exist. This is one reason for distinguishing between the sense-data which I see, and my seeing of them. And

---

[1] I am so extending the use of the word 'patch' that, *e.g.*, the very small black dot which I directly apprehend when I see a full-stop, or the small black line which I directly apprehend when I see a hyphen, are, each of them, in the sense in which I am using the word, a 'patch of colour'. (1952).

[2] I should now make, and have for many years made, a sharp distinction between what I have called the 'patch', on the one hand, and the colour, size and shape, of which it is, on the other; and should call, and have called, *only* the patch, *not* its colour, size or shape, a 'sense-datum'. (1952).

here is another. It seems to me *conceivable*—here again I do not say it is true but *conceivable*—that some sense-data—this whitish colour for instance—are in the place in which the material object—the envelope, is. It seems to me *conceivable* that this whitish colour is really on the surface of the material envelope. Whereas it does not seem to me that my *seeing* of it is in that place. My seeing of it is in another place—somewhere within my body. Here, then, are two reasons for distinguishing between the *sense-data* which I see, and my *seeing* of them. And it seems to me that both of these two very different things are often meant when people talk about "sensations". In fact, when you are reading any philosopher who is talking about sensations (or about sense-*impressions* or *ideas* either), you need to look very carefully to see which of the two he is talking about in any particular passage—whether of the sense-data themselves or of our apprehension of them: you will, I think, almost invariably find that he is talking now of the one and now of the other, and very often that he is assuming that what is true of the one must also be true of the other—an assumption which does not seem to be at all justified. I think, therefore, that the term 'sensation' is liable to be very misleading. And I shall, therefore, never use it. I shall always talk of *sense-data*, when what I mean is such things as this colour and size and shape or the patch which is *of* this colour and size and shape, which I actually see. And when I want to talk of my seeing of them, I shall expressly call this the seeing of sense-data; or, if I want a term which will apply equally to all the senses, I shall speak of the *direct apprehension* of sense-data. Thus when I see this whitish colour, I am *directly apprehending* this whitish colour: my seeing of it, as a mental act, an act of consciousness, just consists in my direct apprehension of it;—so too when I hear a sound, I directly apprehend the sound; when I feel a toothache I directly apprehend the ache: and all these things—the whitish colour, the sound and the ache are *sense-data*.

To return, then, to what happened to us, when we all saw the same envelope. Part, at least, of what happened to me, I can now express by saying that I saw certain sense-data: I saw a whitish patch of colour, of a particular size and shape. And I have no doubt whatever that this is part, at least, of what happened to all of you. You also saw certain sense-data; and I expect also that the sense-data which you saw were more or less similar to those which I saw. You also saw a patch of colour which might be described as whitish, of a size not very different from the size of the patch which I saw, and of a shape similar at least in this that it had rather sharp corners and was bounded by fairly straight lines. But now, what I want to emphasize is this. Though we all did (as we should say) see *the same* envelope, no two of us, in all probability, saw exactly the *same sense-data*. Each of us, in all probability, saw, to begin with, a slightly different shade of colour. All these colours may have been whitish; but each was probably at least slightly different from all the rest, according to the way in which the light fell upon the paper, relatively to the different positions you are sitting in; and again according to differences in the strength of your eye-sight, or your distance from the paper. And so too, with regard to the size of the patch of colour which you saw: differences in the strength of your eyes and in your distance from the envelope probably made slight differences in the size of the patch of colour, which you saw. And so again with regard to the shape. Those of you on that side of the room will have seen a rhomboidal figure, while those in front of me will have seen a figure more nearly rectangular. Those on my left will have seen a figure more like this which you in front now see, and which you see is different from *this* which you then saw. And those in front of me will have seen a figure like that which you on the left now see, and which, you see, is different from *this*, which you saw before. Those directly in front of me, may, indeed, have all seen very nearly the same figure—perhaps, even, exactly the same. But we should not say we *knew* that any two did; whereas we should say we did *know* that we all saw the *same* envelope. That you did all see the same envelope, would, indeed, be accepted in ordinary life as a certainty of the strongest kind. Had you all seen me commit a murder, as clearly as you all saw this envelope, your evidence would be accepted by any jury as sufficient to hang me. Such evidence would be accepted in any court of law as quite conclusive; we should take such a responsibility as that of hanging a man, upon it. It would be accepted, that is, that you had all seen me, *the same man*, commit a murder; and not merely that you had all seen some man or other, possibly each of you a different man in each case, commit one. And yet, in this case, as in the case of the envelope, the sense-data which you had all seen, would have been different sense-data: you could not swear in a court of law that you had all seen exactly the *same sense-data*.

Now all this seems to me to shew very clearly, that, *if* we *did* all see the same envelope, the envelope which we saw was not *identical with* the sense-data which we saw: the envelope cannot be exactly the same thing as each of the sets of sense-data, which we each of us saw; for these were in all probability each of them slightly different from all the rest, and they cannot, therefore, *all* be exactly the same thing as the envelope.

But it might be said: Of course, when we say that we all saw the envelope, we do not mean that we all saw the *whole* of it. I, for instance, only saw *this* side of it, whereas all of you only saw *that* side. And generally, when we talk of seeing an object we only mean seeing some *part* of it. There is always more in any object which we see, than the *part* of it which we see.

And this, I think, is quite true. Whenever we talk roughly of seeing any object, it is true that, in another and stricter sense of the word *see*, we only see *a part of* it. And it might, therefore, be suggested that why we say we all saw this envelope, when we each, in fact, saw a different set of sense-data, is because each of these *sets of sense-data* is, in fact, a *part* of the envelope.

But it seems to me there is a great difficulty even in maintaining that the different sense-data we all saw are parts of the envelope. What do we mean by a *part* of a material object? We mean, I think, at least this. What we call a part of a material object must be something which occupies a part of the volume in space occupied by the whole object. For instance, this envelope occupies a certain volume in space: that is to say, it occupies a space which has breadth and thickness as well as length. And anything which is a *part* of the envelope at any moment, must be *in* some part of the volume of space occupied by the whole envelope at that moment: it must be somewhere within that volume, or at some point in the surfaces bounding that volume.

Are, then, any of the sense-data we saw *parts* of the envelope in this sense?

The sense-data I mentioned were these three—the colour—the whitish colour; the *size* of this colour; its *shape*.[3] And of these three it is only the colour, which could, in the sense defined, possibly be supposed to be a *part* of the envelope. The colour might be supposed to occupy a *part* of the volume occupied by the envelope—one of its bounding surfaces,[4] for instance. But the size and shape could hardly be said to *occupy* any part of this volume. What might be true of them is that the size I saw *is* the size of one surface of the envelope; and that the shape *is* the shape of this surface of the envelope. The side of the envelope which I say I saw certainly *has* some size and some shape; and the sense-data—the size and shape, which I saw as the size and shape of a patch of colour—might possibly *be* the size and shape of this side of the envelope.

Let us consider whether these things are so.

And, first, as to the colours. Can these possibly be parts of the envelope? What we supposed is that each of you probably saw a slightly different colour. And if we are to suppose that *all* those colours are parts of the envelope, then we must suppose that *all* of them are in the same place. We must suppose that ever so many different colours all of them occupy the same surface—this surface of the envelope which you now see. And I think it is certainly difficult to suppose this, though not absolutely impossible. It is not absolutely impossible, I think, that all the different colours which you see are really all of them in the same place. But I myself find it difficult to believe that this is so; and you can understand, I think, why most philosophers should have declared it to be impossible. They have declared, chiefly, I think, on grounds like this, that none of the colours which any of us ever see are ever parts of material objects: they have declared that none of them are ever in any part of the places where material objects (if there are any material objects) are. This conclusion does, indeed, go beyond what the premises justify, even if we accept the premiss that several different colours cannot all be in exactly the same place. For it remains possible that the colour, which some *one* of you sees, is really on the surface of the envelope; whereas the colours which all the rest of you see are *not* there. But if so, then we must say that though all of you are seeing the same side of the envelope, yet only one of you is seeing a sense-datum which is a part of that side: the sense-data seen by all the rest are *not* parts of the envelope. And this also, I think, is difficult to believe. It might be, indeed, that those of you who are seeing a colour, which is *not* a part of the envelope, might yet be seeing a size and a shape which really *is* the size and shape of one side of the envelope; and we will go on to consider whether *this* is so.

And, first, as to the size. I assumed that the sense-given sizes, which you see, are all of them probably slightly different from one another. And, if this be so, then certainly it seems to be absolutely impossible that they should *all*

---

[3] I had here forgotten that one of the sense-data mentioned was the *patch* which *has* that colour and shape and size—the *patch* which, I should now say, is the *only* 'sense-datum', having to do with the envelope, which I then saw. (1952).

[4] I should now say that any part of the *surface* of a volume is *not* a part of the volume, because it is not itself a volume. (1952).

of them be the size of this side of the envelope. This side of the envelope can only really have *one* size; it cannot have several different sizes. But it may not seem quite clear, that you all do see different sizes; the differences between the different distances at which you are from the envelope are not so great, but what the patches of colour you all see might be, at least, of *much the same* size. So I will give a hypothetical instance to make my point clearer. Suppose this room were so large that I could carry the envelope two or three hundred yards away from you. The sense-given size which you would then see, when I was three hundred yards off, would certainly be appreciably smaller than what you see now. And yet you would still be seeing this same envelope. It seems quite impossible that these two very different sizes should both of them be *the* size of the envelope. So that here the *only* possibility is that the size which you see at some *one* definite distance or set of distances, should be the envelope's real size, *if* you ever see its real size at all. This may be so: it may be that some one of the sense-given sizes which we see is the envelope's real size. But it seems also possible that none of them are; and in any case we all see the envelope, just the same, *whether* we see its real size or not.

And now for the shape. Here again it seems quite impossible that *all* the shapes we see can be the envelope's real shape. This side of the envelope can have but *one* shape: it cannot be both rhomboidal, as is the shape which you on the left see, and also rectangular, as is the shape seen by those in front; the angles at its corners cannot be both right angles and also very far from right angles. Certainly, therefore, the sense-given shape which some of you see is *not* the shape of this side of the envelope. But here it may be said, it is plain enough that one of the sense-given shapes seen *is* its real shape. You may say: The shape seen by those in front *is* its real shape; the envelope *is* rectangular. And I quite admit that this is so: I think we do know, in fact, that the envelope really is *roughly* rectangular. But here I want to introduce a distinction. There are two different senses in which we may talk of *the* shape of anything. A rectangle of the size of this envelope, and a rectangle of the size of this black-board, may both, in a sense, have exactly *the same* shape. They may have the same shape in the sense, that all the angles of both are right angles, and that the proportions between the sides of the one, and those between the sides of the other, are the same. They may, in fact, have the same shape, in the sense in which a big square always has the same shape as a small square, however big the one may be and however small the other. But there is another sense in which *the* shape of a big square is obviously not *the same* as that of a small square. We may mean by *the* shape of a big square the actual lines bounding it; and if we mean this, *the* shape of a big square cannot possibly be the *same* as *the* shape of a smaller one. The lines bounding the two cannot possibly be the *same* lines. And the same thing may be true, even when there is no difference in size between two shapes. Imagine *two* squares, of the same size, side by side. The lines bounding the one are *not* the same lines as those bounding the other: though each is both *of* the same shape and *of* the same size as the other. The difference between these two senses in which we may talk of *the* shape of anything, may be expressed by saying that the shape of the big square is the same *in quality*—qualitatively identical—with that of the small square, but is not *numerically* the same—not numerically identical: the shape of the big square is *numerically* different from that of the small, in the sense that they are *two* shapes, and not one only, of which we are talking, though both are the same in quality: both are *squares*, but the one is *one* square and the other is *another* square. There is, then, a difference between two different kinds of identity: qualitative identity and numerical identity; and we are all perfectly familiar with the difference between the two, though the names may sound strange. I shall in future use these names: qualitative identity and numerical identity. And now to return to the case of the envelope. Even supposing that the sense-given shape which you in front see is rectangular, and that the real shape of the envelope is also rectangular, and that both are rectangles of exactly the same shape; it still does not follow that the sense-given shape which you see is *the* shape of the envelope. The sense-given shape and the shape of the envelope, even if they are qualitatively the same, *must* still be *two* different shapes, *numerically* different, unless they are *of the same size*; just as *the* shape of a large square must be numerically different from *the* shape of a smaller one. And we saw before how difficult it was to be sure that any of the sizes which you saw were the *real* size of the envelope. And even if the sense-given size which some one of you sees *is* the real size of the envelope, it still does not follow that the sense-given *shape* which you see is numerically the same as the shape of the envelope. The two may be numerically different, just as in the case of two different squares, side by side, of the same shape and size, *the* shape of the one *is* not *the* shape of the other; they are two numerically different shapes. We may say, then, that if those of you who see rectangular shapes, do see rectangular shapes of different sizes, only one of these can possibly be *the* shape of the envelope: all the others may be *of* the same shape—the same in quality—but they cannot be *the* shape of the envelope. And even if some *one* of you does see a shape, which is of the same size as *the* shape of the envelope, as well as being of the same shape (and it is very doubtful whether any of you does) it would yet be by no means certain that this sense-given shape which you saw was *the* shape of the envelope. It might be a shape *numerically* different from *the* shape of the envelope, although exactly similar both in shape and size. And finally there is some reason to suppose that none of the sense-given shapes which any of you see are *exactly* the same, even in quality, as *the* shape of the envelope. The envelope itself probably has a more or less irregular edge; there are probably ups and downs in the line bounding its side, which you at that distance cannot see.

Of the three kinds of sense-data,[5] then, which you all of you saw, when I held up the envelope, namely, the whitish colour, its size, and its shape, the following things seem to be true. First, as regards the colour, no one of you can be sure that the exact colour which you saw was really a part of the envelope—was really in any part of the space, which the real envelope (if there was a real envelope) occupied. Then as regards the size, no one of you can be sure that the size which you saw was the real size of the envelope. And finally

---

[5] The *patch* itself, which *has* that colour and shape and size, again forgotten! (1952).

as regards the shape, no one of you can be sure that the shape which you saw was really of exactly the same shape as that of the envelope; still less can you be sure that it *was the* shape of the envelope, that the bounding lines which composed it were numerically the same bounding lines as those which enclosed the envelope. And not only can none of you be sure of these things. As regards the sizes and shapes which you saw, it seems quite certain that some of you saw sizes and shapes which were *not* the real size and shape of the envelope; because it seems quite certain that some of you saw sizes and shapes different from those seen by others, and that these different sizes and shapes cannot possibly *all* be *the* size and shape of the envelope. And as regards the colours it seems fairly certain, that the colours which you saw cannot all have been *in* the envelope; since it seems fairly certain that you all saw slightly different colours, and it is difficult to believe, though not absolutely impossible, that all these different colours were really in the same place at the same time.

This seems to be the state of things with regard to these sense-data—the colour, the size and the shape. They seem, in a sense, to have had very little to do with the real envelope, if there *was* a real envelope. It seems very probable that *none* of the colours seen was really a part of the envelope; and that *none* of the sizes and shapes seen were the size or the shape of the real envelope.

. . .

Well now: Chiefly, I think, for reasons of the sort which I have given you, an overwhelming majority of philosophers have adopted the following views.

. . .

. . . They have held, that is (1) that absolutely every sense-datum that any person ever directly apprehends exists only so long as he apprehends it, (2) that no sense-datum which any one person directly apprehends ever is directly apprehended by any other person, and (3) that no sense-datum that is directly apprehended by one person can be in *the same space with* any sense-datum apprehended by any other person—that no sense-datum that is seen or heard or felt by me can possibly be either in the same place with or at any distance from any that is seen or heard or felt by any one else. These three things are, I think, the chief things that are meant, when it is said that all sense-data exist only *in the mind of* the person who apprehends them; and it is certainly the common view in philosophy that all sense-data do only exist *in our minds.* I do not think myself that this is a good way of expressing what is meant. Even if all these three things are true of all the sense-data which I ever directly apprehend; it does not seem to me to follow that they exist only in my mind, or indeed are *in* my mind in any sense at all except that they are apprehended by me. They are, so far as I can see, not in my mind in the sense in which my apprehension of them is in my mind: for instance, this whitish colour, even if it does only exist while I see it, and cannot be seen by any one else, does not seem to me to be *in* my mind in the sense in which my seeing of it is *in my mind.* My seeing of it is, it seems to me, related to my mind in a way in which this which I see is not related to it: and I should prefer to confine the phrase 'in the mind' to those things which are related to my mind, in the way in which my seeing of this colour, and my other acts of consciousness are related to it. But whether they could be properly said to be in my mind or not, certainly all the sense-data, which I ever directly apprehend, are, if these three things are true of them, *dependent* upon my mind in a most intimate sense. If it is really true of all of them that they exist only while I am conscious of them, that nobody else ever is directly conscious of them, and that they are situated only in a private space of my own, which also exists only while I am conscious of it, and of which no one else is ever directly conscious—then certainly nothing could well be more thoroughly dependent on my mind than they are. Most philosophers have, I think, certainly held that all sense-data are dependent on our minds in this sense. This has been held both by philosophers who believe that there are material objects and that we know of their existence, and by those who believe that there are no such things as material objects, or, that, if there are, we do not know it. It has, in fact, an overwhelming weight of authority in its favour. And I am going to call it for the moment *the accepted view*.

And as regards the question whether this accepted view is true or not, I confess I cannot make up my mind. I think it may very likely be true. But I have never seen any arguments in its favour which seem to me to be absolutely conclusive. . . .

.　　.　　.

5

A. J. Ayer
Concerning Phenomenalism

The problem of specifying the relationship of material things to sense-data . . . is apt to be obscured by being represented as a problem about the interrelationship of two different classes of objects. There is, indeed, a sense in which it is correct to say that both sense-data and material things exist, inasmuch as sentences that are used to describe sense-data and sentences that are used to describe material things both very frequently express true propositions. But it would not be correct to infer from this that there really were both material things and sense-data, in the sense in which it can truly be said that there really are chairs as well as tables, or that there are tastes as well as sounds. For whereas, in these cases, the existential propositions refer to different empirical

From A. J. Ayer, *The Foundations of Empirical Knowledge* (London: 1940), Chap. V, Sec. 22, pp. 229–243. Reprinted by permission of St. Martin's Press Inc. and Macmillan London and Basingstoke.

"facts", this does not hold good in the case of sense-data and material things. All the same, the term "material thing" is not synonymous with any term or set of terms that stand for species of sense-data. It is indeed logically necessary that any situation that in any degree establishes the existence of a material thing should also establish the existence of a sense-datum; for we have constructed the sense-datum language in such a way that whenever it is true that a material thing is perceived, it must also be true that a sense-datum is sensed; and this applies also to the cases where the existence of the material thing is inferred from observations of its "physical effects". But it is not wholly a matter of convention that a situation which establishes the existence of a sense-datum should also be evidence in some degree for the existence of a material thing. For this depends . . . upon certain special features of our sensory experience, which it might conceivably not have possessed. Moreover, while a situation which directly establishes the existence of a sense-datum does so conclusively, no such situations can conclusively establish the existence of a material thing. The degree to which the existence of the material thing is established will depend upon the character of the sense-data in question, and especially upon the nature of the contexts in which they occur; but whatever the strength of this evidence may be, it will always be logically compatible with the hypothesis that this material thing is not in all respects what it appears to be, or even that it does not exist at all. Additional evidence may weaken this hypothesis to an extent that makes it very foolish still to entertain it; but it may also substantiate it, as the fact that there are illusions shows. At the same time, it is to be remarked that this additional evidence, whether favourable or not, will always consist in the occurrence of further sense-data. Indeed there is nothing else in which one can legitimately suppose it to consist, once one has accepted the rule that the word "sense-datum" is to be used to stand for whatever is, in fact, observed. And since it is impossible, by any valid process of inference, to make a transition from what is observed to anything that is conceived as being, in principle, unobservable, all that the evidence in question will be evidence for or against is the possible occurrence of further sense-data still. And from this it seems to follow that, even though the term "material thing" is not synonymous with any set of terms that stand for species of sense-data, any proposition that refers to a material thing must somehow be expressible in terms of sense-data, if it is to be empirically significant.

A common way of expressing this conclusion is to say that material things are nothing but collections of actual and possible sense-data. But this is a misleading formula and one that provokes objections which a more accurate way of speaking might avoid. Thus, it is sometimes argued, by those who reject this "phenomenalistic" analysis of the nature of material things, that to conceive of such things as houses or trees or stones as mere collections of actual and possible sense-data is to ignore their "unity" and "substantiality", and that, in any case, it is hard to see how anything can be composed of so shadowy a being as a possible sense-datum. But these objections are founded upon the mistaken assumption that a material thing is supposed to consist of sense-data, as a patchwork quilt consists of different coloured pieces of silk. To remove this misconception, it must be made clear that what the statement that material things consist of sense-data must be understood to designate is not a factual but a linguistic relationship. What is being claimed is simply that the propositions which are ordinarily expressed by sentences which refer to material things could also be expressed by sentences which referred exclusively to sense-data; and the inclusion of possible as well as actual sense-data among the elements of the material things must be taken only to imply a recognition that some of these statements about sense-data will have to be hypothetical. As for the belief in the "unity" and "substantiality" of material things, . . . it may be correctly represented as involving no more than the attribution to visual and actual sense-data of certain relations which do, in fact, obtain in our experience. And . . . it is only the contingent fact that there are these relations between sense-data that makes it profitable to describe the course of our experience in terms of the existence and behavior of material things.

It may seem that an attempt to carry out this plan of "reducing" material things to sense-data would be at variance with my previous attempt to draw a sharp distinction between them. But the purpose of making this distinction was simply to increase the utility and clarity of the sense-datum language by ensuring that its sentences should not be of the same logical form as those that refer to material things. And here it may be explained that two sentences may be said to have the same logical form if they can be correlated in such a way that to each expression that occurs in either one of them there corresponds in the other an expression of the same logical type; and that two expressions may be said to be of the same logical type if any sentence that significantly contains either one of them remains significant when the other is put in its place. It follows that if sentences referring to sense-data are of a different logical form from sentences referring to material things, it must not be assumed that precisely the same things can be said about them. To say, for example, that this was being written with a "pennish" group of sense-data, instead of saying that it was being written with a pen, would be neither true nor false but nonsensical. But this does not rule out the possibility that a proposition which is expressed by a sentence referring to a material thing can equally well be expressed by an entirely different set of sentences, which refer to sense-data; and this is what those who assert that material things are "logical constructions" out of sense-data must be understood to claim. Their view is sometimes put in the form of an assertion that "to say anything about a material thing is to say something, but not the same thing about classes of sense-data";[1] but if this is taken to imply that any significant statement about a material thing can actually be translated, without alteration of meaning, into a definite set of statements about sense data, it is not strictly accurate, for a reason I shall presently give.

An objection which is often brought against phenomenalists is that they begin with a false conception of the nature of "perceptual situations". Thus, it is held by some philosophers that what is directly observed is usually not a sense-datum at all, but a material thing; so that the view that material things

---

[1] *Vide* A. E. Duncan-Jones, "Does Philosophy Analyse Common Sense?" *Aristotelian Society Supplementary Proceedings*, 1937, pp. 140–41.

must be reducible to sense-data, on the ground that these alone are observable, is fundamentally erroneous. But this . . . is not the expression of a disagreement about any matter of fact, but only of a preference for a different form of language. It is indeed legitimate to use the phrase "direct observation" in such a way that things like houses and trees and stones can properly be said to be directly observable; and this usage can perfectly well be made to cover the case of delusive as well as veridical perceptions, provided that it is allowed that what is "directly observed" may not in fact exist, and that it may not really have the properties that it appears to have. But . . . it is also legitimate to use the phrase "direct observation" in such a way that it is only what is designated by the term "sense-datum", or some equivalent term, that can be said to be directly observable; and that it is this usage that, for my present purpose, is to be preferred. And one reason why it is to be preferred is to be found in the fact, which I have already mentioned, that whereas the proposition that a sense-datum is veridically sensed does not entail that any material thing is veridically perceived, the proposition that a material thing is veridically perceived can always be represented as entailing that some sense-datum or other is veridically sensed. Indeed, it is inconceivable that any sense-datum should not be sensed veridically, since it has been made self-contradictory to say of an experienced sense-datum that it does not exist or that it does not really have the properties that it appears to have. And because there is this logical relationship between "perceiving a material thing" and "sensing a sense-datum", it follows that, while a reference to a material thing will not elucidate the meaning of a sentence which is used to describe a sense-datum, except in so far as the poverty of our language may make it convenient to identify this sense-datum as one of a type that is ordinarily associated with a special sort of material thing, a reference to sense-data will provide a general elucidation of the meaning of statements about material things by showing what is the kind of evidence by which they may be verified. And this may be regarded as the purpose of the phenomenalist analysis.

Besides the philosophers who maintain that material things are themselves "directly observed", there are others who object to phenomenalism on the ground that even if the occurrence of illusions shows that what is directly observed is not a material thing, it is still not just a sense-datum. Thus Professor [G. F.—Ed.] Stout, for one, has argued that "the evidence of sense-perception flatly contradicts phenomenalism", on the ground that to regard what is immediately experienced as being just a sensible appearance is to ignore an essential factor which he calls "perceptual seeming".[2] According to him, it is because of "perceptual seeming" that one is able to "perceive one thing as behind another, although it is so hidden that there is no sensible appearance of it", or that one can "perceive things as having insides, when they are not transparent".[3] But while this line of argument may have some force against those who employ a physiological criterion for determining the character of

---

[2] "Phenomenalism", *Proceedings of the Aristotelian Society*, 1938–39, pp. 1–18.
[3] *Loc. cit.*, pp. 10–11.

sense-data, it does not affect us at all, inasmuch as our use of the word sense-datum is not bound up with any special empirical theory about the nature of what is given. If one accepts the view of certain psychologists that there are experiences that may properly be described as experiences of "seeing the inside of a solid object" or "seeing an object when it is screened by another," then the inference one must draw is not that what is observed on such occasions is "more than a mere sense-datum", but that the character of people's visual sense-fields is empirically different from what a misplaced attention to the laws of physiology might lead one to suppose. It is true that the terms in which the psychologists describe such experiences are not purely sensory; but the reason for this is that it is only by referring to material things that they can actually expect to make their meaning understood. We must not, therefore, be misled into supposing that what they are intending to describe is anything more than a sensory phenomenon. The statement that someone is having the experience of "seeing the inside of a solid object" must not, in this context, be taken to exclude the possibility that no such physical object is actually there.

It may, however, be admitted that not only in cases of this sort, but in the vast majority of cases in which one senses a visual or tactual sense-datum, one tends to take it for granted that there is a physical object "there"; and it may be that this is what Professor Stout is referring to when he talks of "perceptual seeming". But this is a fact that I do not think any phenomenalist would wish to deny. The view that material things are, in the sense I have just explained, logical constructions out of sense-data does not imply that "perceiving a material thing" need involve any conscious process of inference from the occurrence of one sense-datum to the possible occurrence of another. The phenomenalist is perfectly free to admit that the sensing of a visual or tactual sense-datum is, in most cases, accompanied by an unreflecting assumption of the existence of some material thing. But the question in which he is interested is, What exactly is it that is here unreflectingly assumed? And his answer, which certainly cannot be refuted by any such appeal to psychology as Professor Stout relies on, is that it is the possibility of obtaining further sense-data.

It would seem that the best way to justify the claim that "to say anything about a material thing is always to say something, though not the same thing, about certain sense-data", would be to provide a number of specimen translations. But this is what no one has ever yet been able to do. It may be suggested that the reason why it has never been done is that no one has yet devised a sufficiently elaborate vocabulary. With our current resources of language we are able to classify visual sense-data only in a very general way, tactual data even less specifically, and kinaesthetic data hardly at all: and the result is that when we wish to distinguish the sense-data that belong to one sort of material thing from those that belong to another we are unable to achieve it except by referring to the material things in question. But suppose that someone took the trouble to name all the different varieties of sensible characteristics with which he was acquainted. Even so, he would still not be able to translate any statement about a material thing into a finite set of statements about sense-data. It is not inconceivable that someone should construct and make use of such a sensory language, though in practice he would find it very difficult to make himself understood; but what he succeeded in expressing by these means would never be precisely equivalent even to the singular statement that we make about material things. For when statements are equivalent to one another, they can always be represented as standing in a relationship of mutual entailment. And, in the case I am now considering, this condition cannot be fulfilled.

I have indeed already admitted that no finite set of singular statements about sense-data can ever formally entail a statement about a material thing, inasmuch as I have recognized that statements about material things are not conclusively verifiable. For when we try to reproduce the content of a statement about a material thing by specifying the empirical situations that would furnish us with direct tests of its validity, we find that the number of these possible tests is infinite. Admittedly, when someone makes a statement of this kind he does not actually envisage an infinite series of possible verifications. He may very well be satisfied, in familiar circumstances, with the single sense-experience on which his statement is based; and if he does think it necessary to test it further, the subsequent occurrence, in the appropriate conditions, of only a limited number of "favourable" sense-data will be sufficient, in the absence of contrary evidence, to convince him that it is true. And this is an entirely reasonable procedure . . . But the fact remains that however many favourable tests he may make he can never reach a stage at which it ceases to be conceivable that further sense-experience will reverse the verdict of the previous evidence. He will never be in a position to demonstrate that he will not subsequently have experiences that will entitle him to conclude that his original statement was false after all. And this implies that the content of a statement about a material thing cannot be exhaustively specified by any finite number of references to sense-data. This difficulty could indeed be met by introducing into the sense-datum language a suitable set of expressions which would be understood to refer to infinite series of sense-data. But I am afraid that most philosophers would not admit that this gave them the sort of translation that they wanted. For all that would seem to be achieved by the introduction of these new expressions would be a mere renaming of material things.

But not only is the occurrence of any one particular, finite series of sense-data never formally sufficient to establish the truth of a statement about a material thing; it is never even necessary. There is, indeed, a sense in which it can be said that every statement about a material thing entails some set of statements or other about sense-data, inasmuch as it is only by the occurrence of some sense-datum that any statement about a material thing is ever in any degree verified. But there is no set of statements about the occurrence of particular sense-data of which it can truly be said that precisely this is entailed by a given statement about a material thing. And the reason for this is that what is required to verify a statement about a material thing is never just the occurrence of a sense-datum of an absolutely specific kind, but only the occurrence of one or another of the sense-data that fall within a fairly indefinite range. In other words, not only can we go on testing a statement about a material thing as long as we like without being able to arrive at a formal demonstration of its truth; but for any test that we actually do carry out there are always an indefinite number of other tests, differing to some extent either in respect of their conditions or their results, which would have done just as well. And this means that if we try to describe what at any given moment would afford us direct evidence for the truth of a statement about a material thing by putting forward a disjunction of statements about sense-data, we shall find once again that this disjunction will have to be infinite.[4]

But if one infers from this that sentences referring to material things cannot be translated, without alteration of meaning, into sentences referring to sense-data, one must not then conclude that to speak about a material thing is to speak about something altogether different from sense-data, or that it is to speak about sense-data but about something else besides. For that would be a mistake analogous to that of supposing that because sentences referring indefinitely to what is red cannot be translated into a finite number of sentences referring to particular red things, therefore "redness" is the name of an object with a distinct existence of its own, or that because sentences referring to "someone" cannot be translated into a finite disjunction of sentences referring to particular persons, therefore "someone" is the name of a peculiar being, a "subsistent entity" perhaps, who is distinct from any person that one can actually meet. If we cannot produce the required translations of sentences referring to material things into sentences referring to sense-data, the reason is not that it is untrue that "to say anything about a material thing is always to say something about sense-data", but only that one's references to material things are vague in their application to phenomena and that the series of sense-data that they may be understood to specify are composed of infinite sets of terms.

This does not mean, however, that nothing can be done in the way of "analysing material things in terms of sense-data". It would not, indeed, be profitable to seek in any such analysis a means of distinguishing one material thing from another. It is not by a verbal analysis in terms of sense-data that one can hope to make clear what is meant, for example, by "a pen" as opposed to "a pencil", or by "a steamship" as opposed to "a canoe". One can give a verbal, as well as an ostensive, indication of the meaning of such words; but it will not exclude the use of other expressions that belong to a physical rather than to a purely sensory terminology. At the same time, there are certain general features about the way in which any expression referring to a material thing applies to phenomena that one can profitably undertake to analyse. That is to say, one may be able to explain what are the relations between sense-data that make it possible for us successfully to employ the physical terminology that we do. If I may now use the metaphor of construction without being misunderstood, I can describe the task [in question] as that of showing what are the general principles on which, from our resources of sense-data, we "construct" the world of material things.

---

[4] Cf. John Wisdom, "Metaphysics and Verification", *Mind*, October 1938, pp. 478–81.

6

Wilfrid Sellars
Empiricism and the Philosophy of Mind

*Wilfrid Sellars is University Professor of Philosophy at the University of Pittsburgh.
With Herbert Feigl he founded the well-known journal* Philosophical Studies,
*which he edited for many years. He was John Locke Lecturer at Oxford 1965–
1966. A voluminous writer of somewhat difficult style, he also is reputed to be
an unusually gifted teacher. Sellars has contributed detailed papers on a remarkable
variety of issues, and he is one of the most important and influential philosophers
in the United States today. There is a strong dialectical character to his style of
argument. Though he appears committed to a form of reductive materialism
(see Part I), his program gives an impression of unusual amplitude.*

His first book, Science, Perception and Reality *(1963), is still perhaps his
best-known work, though he has published and lectured a great deal since its
appearance. Perhaps his most characteristic papers are "Philosophy and the Scientific
Image of Man" and "Empiricism and the Philosophy of Mind," both included in
his first volume. The first of these papers stresses the historical dimension of
philosophy and the way conceptual systems change in the face of experience. There,
Sellars draws attention to the central problem of his entire philosophical endeavor:
the reconciliation, under conditions of reasoned conceptual change, of our
commonsense categories and the categories of scientific explanation. The theme is
also central to his later publications and is characteristically viewed as Kantian
in spirit* (Science and Metaphysics, *1968).*

*The second paper, excerpted here, attacks versions of what he calls the
"Myth of the Given." Though largely concerned with a subtle inspection of the
sense-datum idiom, this attack fits neatly with his larger thesis regarding conceptual
change. There is a difficulty in his intended reconciliation, however, since the
"manifest image"—the ordinary conceptual scheme relatively uninformed by
advanced science—makes the concept of a person central to its explanatory
endeavors. Sellars is inclined to construe the psychological and linguistic capacities
of persons as adequately rendered in terms of the nature of language itself. He
believes he can reconcile the two "images" (the manifest and the scientific)
merely by assigning linguistic roles to physical bodies. His reason is that language
cannot be suitably reduced but need not be, since the admission of language does
not require ontological adjustment, only what might be called a forensic one.
But it is not clear that the analysis of language is equivalent to the analysis of
human linguistic abilities. In that respect, Sellars' entire endeavor focuses the
central difficulty of reductive materialism.*

Wilfred Sellars, "Empiricism and the Philosophy of Science," Volume 1, *Minnesota
Studies in the Philosophy of Science.* The University of Minnesota Press, Minneapolis. ©
Copyright 1956 by The University of Minnesota. Reprinted by permission of the publisher
and the author.

I. An Ambiguity in Sense-Datum Theories

I presume that no philosopher who has attacked the philosophical idea of givenness or, to use the Hegelian term, immediacy, has intended to deny that there is a difference between *inferring* that something is the case and, for example, *seeing* it to be the case. If the term "given" referred merely to what is observed as being observed, or, perhaps, to a proper subset of the things we are said to determine by observation, the existence of "data" would be as noncontroversial as the existence of philosophical perplexities. But, of course, this just isn't so. The phrase "the given" as a piece of professional—epistemological—shoptalk carries a substantial theoretical commitment, and one can deny that there are "data" or that anything is, in this sense, "given" without flying in the face of reason.

Many things have been said to be "given": sense contents, material objects, universals, propositions, real connections, first principles, even givenness itself. And there is, indeed, a certain way of construing the situations which philosophers analyze in these terms which can be said to be the framework of givenness. This framework has been a common feature of most of the major systems of philosophy, including, to use a Kantian turn of phrase, both "dogmatic rationalism" and "skeptical empiricism." It has, indeed, been so pervasive that few, if any, philosophers have been altogether free of it; certainly not Kant, and, I would argue, not even Hegel, that great foe of "immediacy." Often what is attacked under its name are only specific varieties of "given." Intuited first principles and synthetic necessary connections were the first to come under attack. And many who today attack "the whole idea of givenness"—and they are an increasing number—are really only attacking sense data. For they transfer to other items, say physical objects or relations of appearing, the characteristic features of the "given." If, however, I begin my argument with an attack on sense-datum theories, it is only as a first step in a general critique of the entire framework of givenness.

2. Sense-datum theories characteristically distinguish between an act of awareness and, for example, the color patch which is its *object*. The act is usually called *sensing*. Classical exponents of the theory have often characterized these acts as "phenomenologically simple" and "not further analyzable." But other sense-datum theorists—some of them with an equal claim to be considered "classical exponents"—have held that sensing is analyzable. And if some philosophers seem to have thought that if sensing is analyzable, then it can't be an *act*, this has by no means been the general opinion. There are, indeed, deeper roots for the doubt that sensing (if there is such a thing) is an act, roots which can be traced to one of two lines of thought tangled together in classical sense-datum theory. For the moment, however, I shall simply assume that however complex (or simple) the fact that x is sensed may be, it has the form, whatever exactly it may be, by virtue of which for x to be sensed is for it to be the object of an act.

Being a sense datum, or sensum, is a relational property of the item that is sensed. To refer to an item which is sensed in a way which does not entail that it *is* sensed, it is necessary to use some other locution. *Sensibile* [sensible item—Ed.] has the disadvantage that it implies that sensed items could exist without being sensed, and this is a matter of controversy among sense-datum theorists. *Sense content* is, perhaps, as neutral a term as any.

There appear to be varieties of sensing, referred to by some as *visual sensing, tactual sensing*, etc., and by others as *directly seeing, directly hearing*, etc. But it is not clear whether these are species of sensing in any full-blooded sense, or whether "x is visually sensed" amounts to no more than "x is a color patch which is sensed," "x is directly heard" than "x is a sound which is sensed" and so on. In the latter case, being a *visual sensing* or a *direct hearing* would be a relational property of an act of sensing, just as being a sense datum is a relational property of a sense content.

3. Now if we bear in mind that the point of the epistemological category of the given is, presumably, to explicate the idea that empirical knowledge rests on a 'foundation' of non-inferential knowledge of matter of fact, we may well experience a feeling of surprise on noting that according to sense-datum theorists, it is *particulars* that are sensed. For what is *known*, even in non-inferential knowledge, is *facts* rather than particulars, items of the form *something's being thus-and-so* or *something's standing in a certain relation to something else*. It would seem, then, that the sensing of sense contents *cannot* constitute knowledge, inferential *or* non-inferential; and if so, we may well ask, what light does the concept of a sense datum throw on the 'foundations of empirical knowledge?' The sense-datum theorist, it would seem, must choose between saying:

(a) It is *particulars* which are sensed. Sensing is not knowing. The existence of sense-data does not *logically* imply the existence of knowledge.

or

(b) Sensing *is* a form of knowing. It is *facts* rather than *particulars* which are sensed.

On alternative (a) the fact that a sense content was sensed would be a *non-epistemic* fact about the sense content. Yet it would be hasty to conclude that this alternative precludes *any* logical connection between the sensing of sense contents and the possession of non-inferential knowledge. For even if the sensing of sense contents did not logically imply the existence of non-inferential knowledge, the converse might well be true. Thus, the non-inferential knowledge of a particular matter of fact might logically imply the existence of sense data (for example, *seeing that a certain physical object is red* might logically imply *sensing a red sense content*) even though the sensing of a red sense content were not itself a cognitive fact and did not imply the possession of non-inferential knowledge.

On the second alternative, (b), the sensing of sense contents would logically imply the existence of non-inferential knowledge for the simple reason that it would *be* this knowledge. But, once again, it would be facts rather than particulars which are sensed.

4. Now it might seem that when confronted by this choice, the sense-datum theorist seeks to have his cake and eat it. For he characteristically insists *both*

that sensing is a knowing *and* that it is particulars which are sensed. Yet his position is by no means as hopeless as this formulation suggests. For the 'having' and the 'eating' *can* be combined without logical nonsense provided that he uses the word *know* and, correspondingly, the word *given* in two senses. He must say something like the following:

> The non-inferential knowing on which our world picture rests is the knowing that certain items, e.g. red sense contents, are of a certain character, e.g. red. When such a fact is non-inferentially known about a sense content, I will say that the sense content is sensed as *being*, e.g., *red*. I will then say that a sense content is *sensed* (full stop) if it is *sensed as being* of a certain character, e.g. red. Finally, I will say of a sense content that it is *known* if it is sensed (full stop), to emphasize that sensing is a *cognitive* or *epistemic* fact.

Notice that, given these stipulations, it is logically necessary that if a sense content be *sensed*, it be *sensed as being of a certain character*, and that if it be *sensed as being of a certain character*, the *fact that it is of this character* be *non-inferentially known*. Notice also that the being sensed of a sense content would be *knowledge* only in a stipulated sense of *know*. To say of a *sense content* —a color patch, for example—that it was 'known' would be to say that *some fact about it* was non-inferentially known, e.g. that it was red. This *stipulated* use of *know* would, however, receive aid and comfort from the fact that there is, in ordinary usage, a sense of *know* in which it is followed by a noun or descriptive phrase which refers to a particular, thus

Do you know John?
Do you know the President?

Because these questions are equivalent to "Are you acquainted with John?" and "Are you acquainted with the President?" the phrase "knowledge by acquaintance" recommends itself as a useful metaphor for this stipulated sense of *know* and, like other useful metaphors, has congealed into a technical term.

5. We have seen that the fact that a sense content is a *datum* (if, indeed, there are such facts) will logically imply that someone has non-inferential knowledge *only* if to say that a sense content is given is contextually defined in terms of non-inferential knowledge of a fact about this sense content. If this is not clearly realized or held in mind, sense-datum theorists may come to think of the givenness of sense contents as the *basic* or *primitive* concept of the sense-datum framework, and thus sever the logical connection between sense data and non-inferential knowledge to which the classical form of the theory is committed. This brings us face to face with the fact that in spite of the above considerations, many if not most sense-datum theorists *have* thought of the givenness of sense contents as the basic notion of the sense-datum framework. What, then, of the logical connection in the direction *sensing sense contents →* *having non-inferential knowledge?* Clearly it is severed by those who think of sensing as a unique and unanalyzable act. Those, on the other hand, who conceive of sensing as an *analyzable* fact, while they have prima facie severed this connection (by taking the sensing of sense contents to be the basic concept of the sense-datum framework) will nevertheless, in a sense, have maintained

it, if the result they get by analyzing *x is a red sense datum* turns out to be the same as the result they get when they analyze *x is non-inferentially known to be red*. The entailment which was thrown out the front door would have sneaked in by the back.

It is interesting to note, in this connection, that those who, in the classical period of sense-datum theories, say from [G. E.—Ed.] Moore's "Refutation of Idealism" until about 1938, analyzed or sketched an analysis of sensing, did so in *non-epistemic* terms. Typically it was held that for a sense content to be sensed is for it to be an element in a certain kind of relational array of sense contents, where the relations which constitute the array are such relations as spatiotemporal juxtaposition (or overlapping), constant conjunction, mnemic causation—even real connection and belonging to a self. There is, however, one class of terms which is conspicuous by its absence, namely *cognitive* terms. For these, like the 'sensing' which was under analysis, were taken to belong to a higher level of complexity.

Now the idea that epistemic facts can be analyzed without remainder—even "in principle"—into non-epistemic facts, whether phenomenal or behavioral, public or private, with no matter how lavish a sprinkling of subjunctives and hypotheticals is, I believe, a radical mistake—a mistake of a piece with the so-called "naturalistic fallacy" in ethics. I shall not, however, press this point for the moment, though it will be a central theme in a later stage of my argument. What I do want to stress is that whether classical sense-datum philosophers have conceived of the givenness of sense contents as analyzable in non-epistemic terms, or as constituted by acts which are somehow both irreducible *and* knowings, they have without exception taken them to be fundamental in another sense.

6. For they have taken givenness to be a fact which presupposes no learning, no forming of associations, no setting up of stimulus-response connections. In short, they have tended to equate *sensing sense contents* with *being conscious*, as a person who has been hit on the head is *not* conscious whereas a new-born babe, alive and kicking, *is* conscious. They would admit, of course, that the ability to know that a *person*, namely oneself, is *now*, at a certain time, feeling a pain, *is* acquired and does presuppose a (complicated) process of concept formation. But, they would insist, to suppose that the simple ability to *feel a pain* or *see a color*, in short, to sense sense contents, is *acquired* and involves a process of concept formation, would be very odd indeed.

But if a sense-datum philosopher takes the ability to sense sense contents to be unacquired, he is clearly precluded from offering an analysis of *x senses a sense content* which presupposes acquired abilities. It follows that he could analyze *x senses red sense content* s as *x non-inferentially knows that s is red* only if he is prepared to admit that the ability to have such non-inferential knowledge as that, for example, a red sense content is red, is itself unacquired. And this brings us face to face with the fact that most empirically minded philosophers are strongly inclined to think that all classificatory consciousness, all knowledge *that something is thus-and-so*, or, in logicians' jargon, all subsumption of particulars under universals, involves learning, concept formation, even the use of symbols. It is clear from the above analysis, therefore, that *classical* sense-datum theories—I emphasize the adjective, for there are other, 'heterodox,' sense-datum theories to be taken into account—are confronted by an inconsistent triad made up of the following three propositions:

A. *X senses red sense content s* entails *x non-inferentially knows that s is red.*
B. The ability to sense sense contents is unacquired.
C. The ability to know facts of the form *x is ϕ* is acquired.

A and B together entail not-C; B and C entail not-A; A and C entail not-B.

Once the classical sense-datum theorist faces up to the fact that A, B, and C do form an inconsistent triad, which of them will he choose to abandon?

1) He can abandon A, in which case the sensing of sense contents becomes a noncognitive fact—a noncognitive fact, to be sure which may be a necessary condition, even a *logically* necessary condition, of non-inferential knowledge, but a fact, nevertheless, which cannot *constitute* this knowledge.

2) He can abandon B, in which case he must pay the price of cutting off the concept of a sense datum from its connection with our ordinary talk about sensations, feelings, afterimages, tickles and itches, etc., which are usually thought by sense-datum theorists to be its common sense counterparts.

3) But to abandon C is to do violence to the predominantly nominalistic proclivities of the empiricist tradition.

7. It certainly begins to look as though the classical concept of a sense datum were a mongrel resulting from a crossbreeding of two ideas:

(1) The idea that there are certain inner episodes—e.g. sensations of red or of C♯ which can occur to human beings (and brutes) without any prior process of learning or concept formation; and without which it would *in some sense* be impossible to see, for example, that the facing surface of a physical object is red and triangular, or *hear* that a certain physical sound is C♯.

(2) The idea that there are certain inner episodes which are the non-inferential knowings that certain items are, for example, red or C♯ and that these episodes are the necessary conditions of empirical knowledge as providing the evidence for all other empirical propositions.

And I think that once we are on the lookout for them, it is quite easy to see how these two ideas came to be blended together in traditional epistemology. The *first* idea clearly arises in the attempt to explain the facts of sense perception in scientific style. How does it happen that people can have the experience which they describe by saying "It is as though I were seeing a red and triangular physical object" when either there is no physical object there at all, or, if there is, it is neither red nor triangular? The explanation, roughly, posits that in every case in which a person has an experience of this kind, whether veridical or not, he has what is called a 'sensation' or 'impression' 'of a red triangle.' The core idea is that the proximate cause of such a sensation is *only for the most part* brought about by the presence in the neighborhood of the perceiver of a red and triangular physical object; and that while a baby, say, can have the 'sensation of a red triangle' without either *seeing* or *seeming to see that the facing side of a physical object is red and triangular*, there usually *looks*, to adults, *to be* a physical object with a red and triangular facing surface, when they are caused to have a 'sensation of a red triangle'; while *without* such a sensation, no such experience can be had.

. . . What I want to emphasize for the moment . . . is that, as far as the above formulation goes, there is no reason to suppose that having the sensation of a red triangle is a *cognitive* or *epistemic* fact. There is, of course, a temptation to assimilate "having a sensation of a red triangle" to "thinking of a celestial city" and to attribute to the former the epistemic character, the 'intentionality' of the latter. But this temptation *could* be resisted, and it *could* be held that having a sensation of a red triangle is a fact *sui generis*, neither epistemic nor physical, having its own logical grammar. Unfortunately, the idea that there are such things as sensations of red triangles—in itself, as we shall see, quite legitimate, though not without its puzzles—seems to fit the requirements of another, and less fortunate, line of thought so well that it has almost invariably been distorted to give the latter a reinforcement without which it would long ago have collapsed. This unfortunate, but familiar, line of thought runs as follows:

> The seeing that the facing surface of a physical object is red and triangular is a *veridical* member of a class of experiences—let us call them 'ostensible seeings'—some of the members of which are non-veridical; and there is no inspectible hallmark which guarantees that *any* such experience is veridical. To suppose that the non-inferential knowledge on which our world picture rests consists of such ostensible seeings, hearings, etc., as *happen* to be veridical is to place empirical knowledge on too precarious a footing—indeed, to open the door to skepticism by making a mockery of the word *knowledge* in the phrase "empirical knowledge."
>
> Now it is, of course, possible to delimit subclasses of ostensible seeings, hearings, etc., which are progressively less precarious, i.e. more reliable, by specifying the circumstances in which they occur, and the vigilance of the perceiver. But the possibility that any given ostensible seeing, hearing, etc., is non-veridical can never be entirely eliminated. Therefore, given that the foundation of empirical *knowledge* cannot consist of the veridical members of a class not all the members of which are veridical, and from which the non-veridical members cannot be weeded out by 'inspection,' this foundation cannot consist of such items as *seeing that the facing surface of a physical object is red and triangular*.

Thus baldly put, scarcely anyone would accept this conclusion. Rather they would take the contrapositive of the argument, and reason that *since* the foundation of empirical knowledge *is* the non-inferential knowledge of such facts, it *does* consist of members of a class which contains non-veridical members. But before it is thus baldly put, it gets tangled up with the first line of thought. The idea springs to mind that *sensations of red triangles* have exactly the virtues which *ostensible seeings of red triangular physical surfaces* lack. To begin with, the grammatical similarity of 'sensation of a red triangle' to 'thought of a celestial city' is interpreted to mean, or, better, gives rise to the presupposition, that *sensations* belong in the same general pigeonhole as *thoughts*—in short, are cognitive facts. *Then*, it is noticed that sensations are *ex hypothesi* far more intimately related to mental processes than external physical objects. It would seem easier to "get at" a red triangle of which we are having a sensation, than to "get at" a red and triangular physical surface. But, above all, it is the fact that it *doesn't make sense* to speak of unveridical sensations which strikes these philosophers, though for it to strike them as it does, they must overlook the fact that if it makes sense to speak of an experience as *veridical* it must correspondingly make sense to speak of it as *unveridical*. Let me emphasize that not *all* sense-datum theorists—even of the classical type—have been guilty of *all* these confusions; nor are these *all* the confusions of which sense-datum theorists have been guilty. . . . But the confusions I have mentioned are central to the tradition, and will serve my present purpose. For the upshot of blending all these ingredients together is the idea that a sensation of a red triangle is the very paradigm of empirical knowledge. And I think that it can readily be seen that this idea leads straight to the orthodox type of sense-datum theory and accounts for the perplexities which arise when one tries to think it through.

. . .

III. The Logic of 'Looks'

10. . . . I . . . concluded that classical sense-datum theories, when pressed, reveal themselves to be the result of a mismating of two ideas: (1) The idea that there are certain "inner episodes," e.g. the sensation of a red triangle or of a C♯ sound, which occur to human beings and brutes without any prior process of learning or concept formation, and without which it would—in *some* sense—be impossible to *see*, for example, that the facing surface of a physical object is red and triangular, or *hear* that a certain physical sound is C♯; (2) The idea that there are certain "inner episodes" which are the non-inferential knowings that, for example, a certain item is red and triangular, or, in the case of sounds, C♯, which inner episodes are the necessary conditions of empirical knowledge as providing the evidence for all other empirical positions. If this diagnosis is correct, a reasonable next step would be to examine these two ideas and determine how that which survives criticism in each is properly to be combined with the other. Clearly we would have to come to grips with the idea of *inner episodes*, for this is common to both.

Many who attack the idea of the given seem to have thought that the central mistake embedded in this idea is exactly the idea that there are inner episodes, whether thoughts or so-called "immediate experiences," to which each of us has privileged access. I shall argue that this is just not so, and that the Myth of the Given can be dispelled without resorting to the crude verification-isms or operationalisms characteristic of the more dogmatic forms of recent empiricism. Then there are those who, while they do not reject the idea of inner episodes, find the Myth of the Given to consist in the idea that knowledge of these episodes furnishes *premises* on which empirical knowledge rests as on a foundation. But while this idea has, indeed, been the most widespread form of the Myth, it is far from constituting its essence. Everything hinges on *why* these philosophers reject it. If, for example, it is on the ground that the learning of a language is a *public* process which proceeds in a domain of *public* objects and is governed by *public* sanctions, so that *private* episodes—with the exception of a mysterious nod in their direction—must needs escape the net of rational discourse, then, while these philosophers are immune to the form of the myth which has flowered in sense-datum theories, they have no defense against the myth in the form of the givenness of such facts as that *physical object x looks red to person S at a time t*, or that *there looks to person S at a time to be a red physical object over there.* It will be useful to pursue the Myth in this direction for a while before more general issues are raised.

11. Philosophers have found it easy to suppose that such a sentence as "The tomato looks red to Jones" says that a certain triadic relation, *looking* or *appearing*, obtains among a physical object, a person, and a quality.* "A looks φ to S" is assimilated to "x gives y to z"—or, better, since giving is, strictly speaking, an action rather than a relation—to "x is between y and z," and taken to be a case of the general form "R(x,y,z)." Having supposed this, they turn without further ado to the question, "Is this relation analyzable?" Sense-datum theorists have, on the whole, answered "Yes," and claimed that facts of the form x looks red to X are to be analyzed in terms of sense data. Some of them, without necessarily rejecting this claim, have argued that facts of this kind are, at the very least, to be *explained* in terms of sense data. Thus, when [C. D.—Ed.] Broad (4) writes "If, in fact, nothing elliptical is before my mind, it is very hard to understand why the penny should seem *elliptical* rather than of any other shape (p. 240)," he is appealing to sense data as a means of *explaining* facts of this form. The difference, of course, is that whereas if *x looks φ to S* is correctly *analyzed* in terms of sense data, then no one could believe that x looks φ to S without believing that S has sense data, the same need not be true if *x looks φ to S* is explained in terms of sense data, for, in the case of some types of explanation, at least, one can believe a fact without believing its explanation.

On the other hand, those philosophers who reject sense-datum theories in favor of so-called theories of appearing have characteristically held that facts of the form *x looks φ to S* are ultimate and irreducible, and that sense data are needed neither for their analysis nor for their explanation. If asked, "Doesn't the statement 'x looks red to S' have as part of its meaning the idea that S stands in some relation to something that *is* red?" their answer is in the negative, and, I believe, rightly so.

12. I shall begin my examination of "X looks red to S at t" with the simple but fundamental point that the sense of "red" in which things *look* red is, on the face of it, the same as that in which things *are* red. When one glimpses an object and decides that it looks red (to *me, now,* from here) and wonders whether it really *is* red, one is surely wondering whether the color—red—which it looks to have is the one it really does have. This point can be obscured by

---

* A useful discussion of views of this type is to be found in (9) and (13).

such verbal manipulations as hyphenating the words "looks" and "red" and claiming that it is the insoluble unity "looks-red" and not just "looks" which is the relation. Insofar as this dodge is based on insight, it is insight into the fact that *looks* is not a relation between a person, a thing, and a quality. Unfortunately, as we shall see, the reason for this fact is one which gives no comfort at all to the idea that it is *looks-red* rather than *looks* which is the relation.

I have, in effect, been claiming that *being red* is logically prior, is a logically simpler notion, than *looking red*; the function "x is red" to "x looks red to y." In short, that it just won't do to say that x *is red* is analyzable in terms of x *looks red to y*. But what, then, are we to make of the necessary truth—and it is, of course, a necessary truth—that

x *is* red $\cdot \equiv \cdot$ x would *look* red to standard observers in standard conditions?

There is certainly some sense to the idea that this is at least the schema for a definition of *physical redness* in terms of *looking red*. One begins to see the plausibility of the gambit that *looking-red* is an insoluble unity, for the minute one gives "red" (on the right-hand side) an independent status, it becomes what it obviously is, namely "red" as a predicate of physical objects, and the supposed definition becomes an obvious circle.

13. The way out of this troubling situation has two parts. The *second* is to show how "x is red" can be necessarily equivalent to "x would *look* red to standard observers in standard situations" without this being a definition of "x is red" in terms of "x looks red." But the *first*, and logically prior, step is to show that "x looks red to S" does not assert either an unanalyzable triadic relation to obtain between x, red, and S, or an unanalyzable dyadic relation to obtain between x and S. Not, however, because it asserts an *analyzable* relation to obtain, but because *looks* is not a relation at all. Or, to put the matter in a familiar way, one can say that *looks* is a relation if he likes, for the sentences in which this word appears show some grammatical analogies to sentences built around words which we should not hesitate to classify as relation words; but once one has become aware of certain other features which make them very unlike ordinary relation sentences, he will be less inclined to view his task as that of *finding the answer* to the question "Is looks a relation?"

14. To bring out the essential features of the use of "looks," I shall engage in a little historical fiction. A young man, whom I shall call John, works in a necktie shop. He has learned the use of color words in the usual way, with this exception. I shall suppose that he has never looked at an object in other than standard conditions. As he examines his stock every evening before closing up shop, he says "This is red," "That is green," "This is purple," etc., and such of his linguistic peers as happen to be present nod their heads approvingly.

Let us suppose, now, that at this point in the story, electric lighting is invented. His friends and neighbors rapidly adopt this new means of illumination, and wrestle with the problems it presents. John, however, is the last to succumb. Just after it has been installed in his shop, one of his neighbors, Jim, comes in to buy a necktie.

"Here is a handsome green one," says John.

"But it *isn't* green," says Jim, and takes John outside.

"Well," says John, "it was green in there, but now it is blue."

"No," says Jim, "you know that neckties don't change their color merely as a result of being taken from place to place."

"But perhaps electricity changes their color and they change back again in daylight?"

"That would be a queer kind of change, wouldn't it?" says Jim.

"I suppose so," says bewildered John. "But we *saw* that it was green *in there*."

"No, we didn't see that it was green in there, because it wasn't green, and you can't see what isn't so!"

"Well, this is a pretty pickle," says John. *"I just don't know what to say."*

The next time John picks up this tie in his shop and someone asks what color it is, his first impulse is to say "It is green." He suppresses this impulse, and, remembering what happened before, comes out with "It is blue." He doesn't *see* that it is blue, nor would he say that he sees it to be blue. What does he see? Let us ask him.

"I don't know *what* to say. If I didn't know that the tie is blue—and the alternative to granting this is odd indeed—I would swear that I was seeing a green tie and seeing that it is green. It is *as though* I were seeing the necktie to be green."

If we bear in mind that such sentences as "This is green" have both a *fact-stating* and a *reporting* use, we can put the point I have just been making by saying that once John learns to stifle the *report* "This necktie is green" when looking at it in the shop, there is no other *report* about color and the necktie which he knows how to make. To be sure, he now says "This necktie is blue." But he is not making a *reporting* use of this sentence. He uses it as the conclusion of an inference.

15. We return to the shop after an interval, and we find that when John is asked "What is the color of this necktie?" he makes such statements as "It looks green, but take it outside and see." It occurs to us that perhaps in learning to say "This tie *looks* green" when in the shop, he has learned to make a new kind of report. Thus, it might seem as though his linguistic peers have helped him to notice a new kind of *objective* fact, one which, though a relational fact involving a perceiver, is as logically independent of the beliefs, the conceptual framework of the perceiver, as the fact that the necktie is blue; but a *minimal* fact, one which it is safer to report because one is less likely to be mistaken. Such a minimal fact would be the fact that the necktie looks green to John on a certain occasion, and it would be properly reported by using the sentence "This necktie *looks* green." It is this type of account, of course, which I have already rejected.

But what is the alternative? If, that is, we are not going to adopt the sense-datum analysis. Let me begin by noting that there certainly seems to be something to the idea that the sentence "This looks green to me now" has a reporting role. Indeed, it would seem to be essentially a report. But if so, *what* does it report, if not a minimal objective fact, and if what it reports is not to be analyzed in terms of sense data?

16. Let me next call attention to the fact that the experience of having something look green to one at a certain time is, insofar as it is an experience, obviously very much like that of seeing something to be green, insofar as the latter is an experience. But the latter, of course, is not *just* an experience. And this is the heart of the matter. For to say that a certain experience is a *seeing that* something is the case, is to do more than describe the experience. It is to characterize it as, so to speak, making an assertion or claim, and—which is the point I wish to stress—to *endorse* that claim. As a matter of fact, as we shall see, it is much more easy to see that the statement "Jones sees that the tree is green" ascribes a propositional claim to Jones' experience and endorses it, than to specify how the statement *describes* Jones' experience.

I realize that by speaking of experiences as containing propositional claims, I may seem to be knocking at closed doors. I ask the reader to bear with me, however, as the justification of this way of talking is one of my major aims. If I am permitted to issue this verbal currency now, I hope to put it on the gold standard before concluding the argument.

It is clear that the experience of seeing that something is green is not *merely* the occurrence of the propositional claim 'this is green'—not even if we add, as we must, that this claim is, so to speak, evoked or wrung from the perceiver by the object perceived. Here Nature—to turn Kant's simile (which he uses in another context) on its head—puts us to the question. The something more is clearly what philosophers have in mind when they speak of "visual impressions" or "immediate visual experiences." What exactly is the logical status of these "impressions" or "immediate experiences" is a problem which will be with us for the remainder of this argument. For the moment it is the propositional claim which concerns us.

I pointed out above that when we use the word "see" as in "S sees that the tree is green" we are not only ascribing a claim to the experience, but endorsing it. It is this endorsement which [Gilbert—Ed.] Ryle has in mind when he refers to *seeing that something is thus and so* as an *achievement*, and to "sees" as an *achievement word*. I prefer to call it a "so it is" or "just so" word, for the root idea is that of *truth*. To characterize S's experience as a *seeing* is, in a suitably broad sense—which I shall be concerned to explicate—to apply the semantical concept of truth to that experience.

Now the suggestion I wish to make is, in its simplest terms, that the statement "X looks green to Jones" differs from "Jones sees that x is green" in that whereas the latter both ascribes a propositional claim to Jones' experience *and endorses it*, the former ascribes the claim but does not endorse it. This is the essential difference between the two, for it is clear that two experiences may be identical *as experiences*, and yet one be properly referred to as a *seeing that* something is green, and the other *merely* as a case of something's *looking* green. Of course, if I say "X *merely looks* green to S" I am not only failing to endorse the claim, I am rejecting it.

Thus, when I say "X looks green to me now" I am *reporting* the fact that my experience is, so to speak, intrinsically, *as an experience*, indistinguishable from a veridical one of seeing that x is green. Involved in the report is the ascription to my experience of the claim 'x is green'; and the fact that I make this report rather than the simple report "X is green" indicates that certain considerations have operated to raise, so to speak in a higher court, the question 'to endorse or not to endorse.' I may have reason to think that x may not after all be green.

If I make at one time the report "X looks to be green"—which is not only a report, but the withholding of an endorsement—I may later, when the original reasons for withholding endorsement have been rebutted, endorse the original claim by saying "I saw that it was green though at the time I was only sure that it looked green." Notice that I will only say "I see that x is green" (as opposed to "X is green") when the question "to endorse or not to endorse" has come up. "I see that x is green" belongs, so to speak, on the same level as "X looks green" and "X merely *looks* green."

17. . . . Now one of the chief merits of this account is that it permits a parallel treatment of 'qualitative' and 'existential' seeming or looking. Thus, when I say "The tree looks bent" I am endorsing that part of the claim involved in my experience which concerns the existence of the tree, but withholding endorsement from the rest. On the other hand, when I say "There looks to be a bent tree over there" I am refusing to endorse any but the most general aspect of the claim, namely, that there is an 'over there' as opposed to a 'here.' Another merit of the account is that it explains how a necktie, for example, can look red to S at t, without looking scarlet or crimson or any other determinate shade of red. In short it explains how things can have a *merely generic* look, a fact which would be puzzling indeed if looking red were a *natural* as opposed to *epistemic* fact about objects. The core of the explanation, of course, is that the propositional claim involved in such an experience may be, for example, either the more determinable claim 'This is red' or the more determinate claim 'This is crimson.' The complete story is more complicated, and requires some account of the role in these experiences of the 'impressions' or 'immediate experiences' the logical status of which remains to be determined. But even in the absence of these additional details, we can note the resemblance between the fact that x can look red to S, without it being true of some specific shade of red that x looks to S to be of that shade, and the fact that S can believe that Cleopatra's Needle is tall, without its being true of some determinate number of feet that S believes it to be that number of feet tall.

18. The point I wish to stress at this time, however, is that the concept of *looking green*, the ability to recognize that something *looks green*, presupposes the concept of *being green*, and that the latter concept involves the ability to tell what colors objects have by looking at them—which, in turn, involves knowing in what circumstances to place an object if one wishes to ascertain its color by looking at it. Let me develop this latter point. As our friend John becomes more and more sophisticated about his own and other people's visual experiences, he learns under what conditions it is as though one were seeing a necktie to be of one color when in fact it is of another. Suppose someone asks him "Why does this tie look green to me?" John may very well reply "Because it is blue, and blue objects look green in this kind of light." And if someone asks this question when looking at the necktie in plain daylight, John may very

well reply "Because the tie *is* green"—to which he may add "We are in plain daylight, *and in daylight things look what they are.*" We thus see that

x is red · ≡ · x looks red to standard observers in standard conditions

is a necessary truth *not* because the right-hand side is the definition of "x is red," but because "standard conditions" means conditions in which things look what they are. And, of course, *which* conditions are standard for a given mode of perception is, at the common-sense level, specified by a list of conditions which exhibit the vagueness and open texture characteristic of ordinary discourse.

· · ·

References

4. Broad, C. D. *Scientific Thought*. London: Kegan Paul, 1923.
9. Chisholm, Roderick. "The Theory of Appearing," in Max Black (ed.), *Philosophical Analysis*, pp. 102–18. Ithaca: Cornell Univ. Pr., 1950.
13. Price, H. H. *Perception*. London: Methuen, 1932.

7

J. L. Austin
The Argument from Illusion

The primary purpose of the argument from illusion is to induce people to accept 'sense-data' as the proper and correct answer to the question what they perceive on certain *abnormal, exceptional* occasions; but in fact it is usually followed up with another bit of argument intended to establish that they *always* perceive sense-data. Well, what is the argument?

In [A. J.—Ed.] Ayer's statement[1] it runs as follows. It is 'based on the fact that material things may present different appearances to different observers, or to the same observer in different conditions, and that the character of these appearances is to some extent causally determined by the state of the conditions

From J. L. Austin, *Sense and Sensibilia* (Oxford: 1962), Chap. III, pp. 20–32. Reprinted by permission of The Oxford University Press.

---

[1] Ayer, *The Foundations of Empirical Knowledge*, pp. 3–5.

and the observer'. As illustrations of this alleged fact Ayer proceeds to cite perspective ('a coin which looks circular from one point of view may look elliptical
from another'); refraction ('a stick which normally appears straight looks bent
when it is seen in water'); changes in colour-vision produced by drugs ('such
as mescal'); mirror-images; double vision; hallucination; apparent variation in
tastes; variations in felt warmth ('according as the hand that is feeling it is
itself hot or cold'); variations in felt bulk ('a coin seems larger when it is
placed on the tongue than when it is held in the palm of the hand'); and the
oft-cited fact that 'people who have had limbs amputated may still continue to
feel pain in them'.

He then selects three of these instances for detailed treatment. First,
refraction—the stick which normally 'appears straight' but 'looks bent' when
seen in water. He makes the 'assumptions' (a) that the stick does not *really
change its shape* when it is placed in water, and (b) that it *cannot be* both
crooked and straight.[2] He then concludes ('it follows') that 'at least one of the
visual appearances of the stick is *delusive*'. Nevertheless, even when 'what we
see is not the *real quality* of a *material thing*, it is supposed that we are still
seeing something'—and this something is to be called a 'sense-datum'. A sense-
datum is to be 'the object of which we are *directly* aware, in perception, if it is
not *part* of any *material thing*'. (The italics are mine throughout this and the
next two paragraphs.)

Next, mirages. A man who sees a mirage, he says, is 'not perceiving any
material thing; for the oasis which he thinks he is perceiving *does not exist*'.
But 'his *experience* is not an experience of nothing'; thus 'it is said that he is
experiencing sense-data, which are similar in character to what he would be
experiencing if he were seeing a real oasis, but are delusive in the sense that
the material thing which they appear to present is not *really there*'.

Lastly, reflections. When I look at myself in a mirror 'my body *appears to
be* some distance behind the glass'; but it cannot actually be in two places at
once; thus, my perceptions in this case 'cannot all be *veridical*'. But I do see
something; and if 'there really is no such material thing as my body in the place
where it appears to be, what is it that I am seeing?' Answer—a sense-datum.
Ayer adds that 'the same conclusion may be reached by taking any other of
my examples'.

Now I want to call attention, first of all, to the name of this argument—
the 'argument from *illusion*', and to the fact that it is produced as establishing
the conclusion that some at least of our 'perceptions' are *delusive*. For in this
there are two clear implications—(a) that all the cases cited in the argument
are cases of *illusions*; and (b) that *illusion* and *delusion* are the same thing.
But both of these implications, of course, are quite wrong; and it is by no means
unimportant to point this out, for, as we shall see, the argument trades on
confusion at just this point.

---

[2] It is not only strange, but also important, that Ayer calls these 'assumptions'. Later on
he is going to take seriously the notion of denying at least one of them, which he could
hardly do if he had recognized them here as the plain and incontestable facts that they are.

What, then, would be some genuine examples of illusion? (The fact is that hardly any of the cases cited by Ayer is, at any rate without stretching things, a case of illusion at all.) Well, first, there are some quite clear cases of *optical* illusion—for instance the case we mentioned earlier in which, of two lines of equal length, one is made to look longer than the other. Then again there are illusions produced by professional 'illusionists', conjurors—for instance the Headless Woman on the stage, who is made to look headless, or the ventriloquist's dummy which is made to appear to be talking. Rather different—not (usually) produced on purpose—is the case where wheels rotating rapidly enough in one direction may look as if they were rotating quite slowly in the opposite direction. Delusions, on the other hand, are something altogether different from this. Typical cases would be delusions of persecution, delusions of grandeur. These are primarily a matter of grossly disordered beliefs (and so, probably, behaviour) and may well have nothing in particular to do with perception.[3] But I think we might also say that the patient who sees pink rats has (suffers from) delusions—particularly, no doubt, if, as would probably be the case, he is not clearly aware that his pink rats aren't real rats.[4]

The most important differences here are that the term 'an illusion' (in a perceptual context) does not suggest that something totally unreal is *conjured up*—on the contrary, there just is the arrangement of lines and arrows on the page, the woman on the stage with her head in a black bag, the rotating wheels; whereas the term 'delusion' *does* suggest something totally unreal, not really there at all. (The convictions of the man who has delusions of persecution can be *completely* without foundation.) For this reason delusions are a much more serious matter—something is really wrong, and what's more, wrong *with* the person who has them. But when I see an optical illusion, however well it comes off, there is nothing wrong with me personally, the illusion is not a little (or a large) peculiarity or idiosyncrasy of my own; it is quite public, anyone can see it, and in many cases standard procedures can be laid down for producing it. Furthermore, if we are not actually to be taken in, we need to be *on our guard*; but it is no use to tell the sufferer from delusions to be on his guard. He needs to be cured.

Why is it that we tend—if we do—to confuse illusions with delusions? Well, partly, no doubt the terms are often used loosely. But there is also the point that people may have, without making this explicit, different views or theories about the facts of some cases. Take the case of seeing a ghost, for example. It is not generally known, or agreed, what seeing ghosts *is*. Some people think of seeing ghosts as a case of something being conjured up, perhaps by the disordered nervous system of the victim; so in their view seeing ghosts is a case of delusion. But other people have the idea that what is called seeing ghosts is a case of being taken in by shadows, perhaps, or reflections, or a trick of the light—that is, they assimilate the case in their minds to illusion. In this way,

---

[3] The latter point holds, of course, for *some* uses of "illusion" too; there are the illusions which some people (are said to) lose as they grow older and wiser.

[4] Cp. the white rabbit in the play called *Harvey*.

seeing ghosts, for example, may come to be labelled sometimes as 'delusion', sometimes as 'illusion'; and it may not be noticed that it makes a difference which label we use. Rather, similarly, there seem to be different doctrines in the field as to what mirages are. Some seem to take a mirage to be a vision conjured up by the crazed brain of the thirsty and exhausted traveller (delusion), while in other accounts it is a case of atmospheric refraction, whereby something below the horizon is made to appear above it (illusion). (Ayer, you may remember, takes the delusion view, although he cites it along with the rest as a case of illusion. He says not that the oasis appears to be where it is not, but roundly that 'it does not exist'.)

The way in which the 'argument from illusion' positively trades on not distinguishing illusions from delusions is, I think, this. So long as it is being suggested that the cases paraded for our attention are cases of *illusion*, there is the implication (from the ordinary use of the word) that there really is something there that we perceive. But then, when these cases begin to be quietly called delusive, there comes in the very different suggestion of something being conjured up, something unreal or at any rate 'immaterial'. These two implications taken together may then subtly insinuate that in the cases cited there really is something that we are perceiving, but that this is an immaterial something; and this insinuation, even if not conclusive by itself, is certainly well calculated to edge us a little closer toward just the position where the sense-datum theorist wants to have us.

So much, then—though certainly there could be a good deal more—about the differences between illusions and delusions and the reasons for not obscuring them. Now let us look briefly at some of the other cases Ayer lists. Reflections, for instance. No doubt you *can* produce illusions with mirrors, suitably disposed. But is just *any* case of seeing something in a mirror an illusion, as he implies? Quite obviously not. For seeing things in mirrors is a perfectly *normal* occurrence, completely familiar, and there is usually no question of anyone being taken in. No doubt, if you're an infant or an aborigine and have never come across a mirror before, you may be pretty baffled, and even visibly perturbed, when you do. But is that a reason why the rest of us should speak of illusion here? And just the same goes for the phenomena of perspective—again, one *can* play tricks with perspective, but in the ordinary case there is no question of illusion. That a round coin should 'look elliptical' (in one sense) from some points of view is exactly what we expect and what we normally find; indeed, we should be badly put out if we ever found this not to be so. Refraction again—the stick that looks bent in water—is far too familiar a case to be properly called a case of illusion. We may perhaps be prepared to agree that the stick looks bent; but then we can see that it's partly submerged in water, so that is exactly how we should expect it to look.

It is important to realize here how familiarity, so to speak, takes the edge off illusion. Is the cinema a case of illusion? Well, just possibly the first man who ever saw moving pictures may have felt inclined to say that here was a case of illusion. But in fact it's pretty unlikely that even he, even momentarily, was actually taken in; and by now the whole thing is so ordinary a part of our lives that it never occurs to us even to raise the question. One might as well ask whether producing a photograph is producing an illusion—which would plainly be just silly.

Then we must not overlook, in all this talk about illusions and delusions, that there are plenty of more or less unusual cases, not yet mentioned, which certainly aren't either. Suppose that a proof-reader makes a mistake—he fails to notice that what ought to be 'causal' is printed as 'casual'; does he have a delusion? Or is there an illusion before him? Neither, of course; he simply *misreads*. Seeing after-images, too, though not a particularly frequent occurrence and not just an ordinary case of seeing, is neither seeing illusions nor having delusions. And what about dreams? Does the dreamer see illusions? Does he have delusions? Neither; dreams are *dreams*.

Let us turn for a moment to what [H. H.—Ed.] Price has to say about illusions. He produces,[5] by way of saying 'what the term "illusion" means', the following 'provisional definition': 'An illusory sense-datum of sight or touch is a sense-datum which is such that we tend to take it to be part of the surface of a material object, but if we take it so we are wrong.' It is by no means clear, of course, what this dictum itself means; but still, it seems fairly clear that the definition doesn't actually fit all the cases of illusion. Consider the two lines again. Is there anything here which we tend to take, wrongly, to be part of the surface of a material object? It doesn't seem so. We just see the two lines, we don't think or even tend to think that we see anything else, we aren't even raising the question whether anything is or isn't 'part of the surface' of—what, anyway? the lines? the page?—the trouble is just that one line looks longer than the other, though it isn't. Nor surely, in the case of the Headless Woman, is it a question whether anything is or isn't part of her surface; the trouble is just that she looks as if she had no head.

It is noteworthy, of course, that, before he even begins to consider the 'argument from illusion', Price has already incorporated in this 'definition' the idea that in such cases there is something to be seen *in addition to* the ordinary things—which is part of what the argument is commonly used, and not uncommonly taken, to *prove*. But this idea surely has no place in an attempt to say what 'illusion' *means*. It comes in again, improperly I think, in his account of perspective (which incidentally he also cites as a species of illusion)—'a distant hillside which is full of protuberances, and slopes upwards at quite a gentle angle, will appear flat and vertical. . . . This means that the sense-datum, the colour-expanse which we sense, actually *is* flat and vertical.' But why should we accept this account of the matter? Why should we say that there is *anything* we see which *is* flat and vertical, though not 'part of the surface' of any material object? To speak thus is to assimilate all such cases to cases of delusion, where there *is* something not 'part of any material thing'. But we have already discussed the undesirability of this assimilation.

Next, let us have a look at the account Ayer himself gives of some at least of the cases he cites. (In fairness we must remember here that Ayer has a number of quite substantial reservations of his own about the merits and efficacy of

---

[5] *Perception*, p. 27.

the argument from illusion, so that it is not easy to tell just how seriously he intends his exposition of it to be taken; but this is a point we shall come back to.)

First, then, the familiar case of the stick in water. Of this case Ayer says (a) that since the stick looks bent but is straight, 'at least one of the visual appearances of the stick is *delusive*'; and (b) that 'what we see [directly anyway] is not the real quality of [a few lines later, not part of] a material thing'. Well now: does the stick 'look bent' to begin with? I think we can agree that it does, we have no better way of describing it. But of course it does *not* look *exactly* like a bent stick, a bent stick out of water—at most, it may be said to look rather like a bent stick partly immersed *in* water. After all, we can't help seeing the water the stick is partly immersed in. So exactly what in this case is supposed to be *delusive?* What is wrong, what is even faintly surprising, in the idea of a stick's being straight but looking bent sometimes? Does anyone suppose that if something is straight, then it jolly well has to *look* straight at all times and in all circumstances? Obviously no one seriously supposes this. So what mess are we supposed to get into here, what is the difficulty? For of course it has to be suggested that there *is* a difficulty—a difficulty, furthermore, which calls for a pretty radical solution, the introduction of sense-data. But what is the problem we are invited to solve in this way?

Well, we are told, in this case you are seeing *something*; and what is this something 'if it is not part of any material thing'? But this question is, really, completely mad. The straight part of the stick, the bit not under water, is presumably part of a material thing; don't we see that? And what about the bit *under* water?—we can see that too. We can see, come to that, the water itself. In fact what we see is *a stick partly immersed in water*; and it is particularly extraordinary that this should appear to be called in question—that a question should be raised about *what* we are seeing—since this, after all, is simply the description of the situation with which we started. It was, that is to say, agreed at the start that we were looking at a stick, 'a material thing', part of which was under water. If, to take a rather different case, a church were cunningly camouflaged so that it looked like a barn, how could any serious question be raised about what we see when we look at it? We see, of course, *a church* that now *looks like a barn*. We do *not* see an immaterial barn, an immaterial church, or an immaterial anything else. And what in this case could seriously tempt us to say that we do?

Notice, incidentally, that in Ayer's description of the stick-in-water case, which is supposed to be prior to the drawing of any philosophical conclusions, there has already crept in the unheralded but important expression 'visual appearances'—it is, of course, ultimately to be suggested that all we *ever* get when we see is a visual appearance (whatever that may be).

Consider next the case of my reflection in a mirror. My body, Ayer says, 'appears to be some distance behind the glass'; but as it's in front, it can't really be behind the glass. So what am I seeing? A sense-datum. What about this? Well, once again, although there is no objection to saying that my body 'appears to be some distance behind the glass', in saying this we must remember what sort of situation we are dealing with. It does not 'appear to be' there in a way which might tempt me (though it might tempt a baby or a savage) to go round the back and look for it, and be astonished when this enterprise proved a failure. (To say that A is *in* B doesn't always mean that if you open B you will find A, just as to say that A is *on* B doesn't always mean that you could pick it off—consider 'I saw my face in the mirror', 'There's a pain in my toe', 'I heard him on the radio', 'I saw the image on the screen', &c. Seeing something in a mirror is not like seeing a bun in a shop-window.) But does it follow that, since my body is not actually located behind the mirror, I am not seeing a material thing? Plainly not. For one thing, I can see the mirror (nearly always anyway). I can see my own body 'indirectly', *sc.* in the mirror. I can also see the reflection of my own body or, as some would say, a mirror-image. And a mirror-image (if we choose this answer) is not a 'sense-datum'; it can be photographed, seen by any number of people, and so on. (Of course there is no question here of either illusion or delusion.) And if the question is pressed, what actually *is* some distance, five feet say, behind the mirror, the answer is, not a sense-datum, but some region of the adjoining room.

The mirage case—at least if we take the view, as Ayer does, that the oasis the traveller thinks he can see 'does not exist'—is significantly more amenable to the treatment it is given. For here we are supposing the man to be genuinely deluded, he is *not* 'seeing a material thing'.[6] We don't actually have to say, however, even here that he is 'experiencing sense-data'; for though, as Ayer says above, 'it is convenient to give a name' to what he is experiencing, the fact is that it already has a name—a *mirage*. Again, we should be wise not to accept too readily the statement that what he is experiencing is '*similar in character* to what he would be experiencing if he were seeing a real oasis'. For is it at all likely, really, to be very similar? And, looking ahead, if we were to concede this point we should find the concession being used against us at a later stage— namely, at the stage where we shall be invited to agree that we see sense-data always, in normal cases too.

---

[6] Not even 'indirectly', no such thing is 'presented'. Doesn't this seem to make the case, though more amenable, a good deal less useful to the philosopher? It's hard to see how normal cases could be said to be *very like* this.

Thought and Innate Ideas

8

Gottfried Wilhelm Leibniz
Leibniz's Critique of Locke

Gottfried Wilhelm Leibniz (1646–1716) was a man of unusually diverse skills. He formulated a version of the calculus independently of Newton, though in his later years he engaged in bitter quarrels about who discovered it first. He invented an advanced calculating machine. He performed diplomatic missions at various important courts. He wrote a history of the house of Brunswick, speculated about revisions in Roman law, and theorized about the nature of physical motion particularly in connection with the work of Huygens, whom he met in Paris. He attempted, hopelessly, to construct a universal language for the codification of all thought (his "alphabet of knowledge" is perhaps an ancestor of Russell's logical atomism), endorsed the conception of a universal encyclopedia of knowledge, promoted cooperation among the learned, and attempted to formulate a set of doctrines that Christians of all sects could adopt.

In 1700, on the institution of what was to become the Prussian Royal Academy, Leibniz became president for life. His thought underwent a series of transformations under the impact of the new science and his growing awareness of prevailing intellectual currents, particularly after his stay in Paris. The Theodicy (1710) was one of the few important philosophical works that he managed to publish in his lifetime. His New Essays *were published in 1765 and the* Discourse on Metaphysics, *in 1846.*

Leibniz developed an intriguing and altogether distinctive metaphysics, influenced as much by the currents of Newtonian science as by Cartesian philosophy. The theory is marked by his adherence to "the way of pre-established harmony," or the view that every substance acts in a spontaneous way independently of external influence, that everything that happens to it depends on its own nature, but that whatever happens to any substance happens in harmony with what happens to every other substance.

He is particularly known for his account of the "identity of indiscernibles," which applies, on his own view, to the monads, the individual distinctive substances of his pre-established harmony. He held (in Discourse on Metaphysics) *that two*

Reprinted from *New Essays Concerning Human Understanding*, Gottfried Leibniz, trans. Alfred Gideon Langley, by permission of Open Court Publishing Company, La Salle, Illinois.

*different substances cannot be alike in all respects. The issue is of importance in
contemporary discussions of identity. Leibniz's New Essays on Human Understanding
(1765), directed against Locke's Essay, have had a new vogue with the recent revival
of innatist conceptions of knowledge.*

. . . The question is to know whether the soul in itself is entirely empty as
the tablets upon which as yet nothing has been written (*tabula rasa*) according
to Aristotle, and [John Locke—Ed.] the author of the Essay, and whether all
that is traced thereon comes solely from the senses and from experience; or
whether the soul contains originally the principles of many ideas and doctrines
which external objects merely call up on occasion, as I believe with Plato,
and even with the schoolmen, and with all those who interpret in this way
the passage of St. Paul (Rom. 2: 15) where he states that the law of God is
written in the heart. The Stoics call these principles *prolepses, i.e.* fundamental assumptions, or what is taken for granted in advance. The Mathematicians call them *general notions.* . . . Modern philosophers give them other
beautiful names, and Julius Scaliger in particular named them *semina æternitatis,*
also *zopyra, i.e.* living fires, luminous flashes, concealed within us, but which
the encounter of the senses makes appear like the sparks which the blow makes
spring from the steel. And the belief is not without reason, that these glitterings
indicate something divine and eternal which appears especially in the necessary truths. Whence another question arises, whether all truths depend upon
experience, *i.e.* upon induction and examples, or whether there are some which
have still another foundation. For if some events can be foreseen prior to any
proof which may have been made of them, it is manifest that we ourselves contribute something thereto. The senses, although necessary for all our actual
knowledge, are not sufficient to give it all to us, since the senses never give us
anything but examples, *i.e.* particular or individual truths. Now all the examples
which confirm a general truth, whatever their number, do not suffice to establish the universal necessity of that same truth, for it does not follow that what
has happened will happen in the same way. For example, the Greeks and the
Romans, and all the other peoples of the earth known to the ancients, have
always observed that before the lapse of twenty-four hours day changes into
night, and night into day. But we would be deceived, if we believed that the
same law holds good everywhere else; for since then, the contrary has been
experienced in the region of Nova Zembla. And he would still be in error who
believed that, in our climates at least, this is a necessary and eternal truth,
which will always endure, since we must think that the earth, and the sun
even, do not necessarily exist, and that there will perhaps be a time when this
beautiful star, together with its whole system, will not longer exist, at least in
its present form. Whence it appears that necessary truths such as are found in
pure mathematics, and particularly in arithmetic and in geometry, must have
principles whose proof does not depend upon examples, nor consequently upon
the testimony of the senses, although without the senses it would never have
occurred to us to think of them. This distinction must be carefully made, and
was so well understood by Euclid, that he often proved by the reason, what

is sufficiently seen through experience and by sensible images. Logic also, together with metaphysics and ethics, one of which shapes theology and the other jurisprudence, both natural (sciences), are full of such truths, and consequently their proof can come only from internal principles which are called innate. It is true that we must not imagine that these eternal laws of the reason can be read in the soul as in an open book, as the prætor's edict is read upon his *album* without difficulty and research; but it is sufficient that they can be discovered in us by dint of attention, for which the senses furnish occasions, and successful experience serves to confirm reason, in much the same way as proofs in arithmetic serve for the better avoidance of error in calculating when the reasoning is long. Herein, also, human knowledge differs from that of the brutes: the brutes are purely empirics and only guide themselves by examples; for, so far as we can judge of them, they never attain to the formation of necessary propositions; while men are capable of demonstrative sciences. It is also for this reason that the faculty the brutes have for making *consecutions* is something inferior to the reason of man. The consecutions of the brutes are merely like those of simple empirics, who claim that what has sometimes happened will happen again in a case where something strikes them as similar, without being able to judge whether the same reasons hold good. This is why it is so easy for men to entrap the brutes, and so easy for simple empirics to make mistakes. This is why persons who have become skilful through age and experience are not exempt (from error) when they depend too much upon their past experience, as has happened to many in civil and military affairs; because they do not consider sufficiently that the world changes, and that men become more skilful by finding a thousand new dexterities, while the deer and hares of the present do not become more cunning than those of the past. The consecutions of the brutes are only a shadow of reasoning, *i.e.* are only connections of the imagination and passages from one image to another, because in a new juncture which appears similar to the preceding they expect anew that connection which they formerly met with, as if things were united in fact because their images are united in the memory. It is true that reason also counsels us to expect ordinarily to see that happen in the future which is conformed to a long past experience, but it is not on this account a necessary and infallible truth, and success may cease when least expected, when the reasons change which have sustained it. Therefore the wisest men do not so commit themselves to it as not to try to discover, if possible, something of the reason of this fact in order to judge when it is necessary to make exceptions. For reason is alone capable of establishing sure rules, and supplying what is wanting to those which were not such by inserting their exceptions; and of finding at length certain connections in the force of necessary consequences, which often furnish the means of foreseeing the result without the necessity of experiencing the sense-connections of images, to which the brutes are reduced, so that that which justifies the internal principles of necessary truths also distinguishes man from the brutes.

Perhaps our clever author will not wholly differ from my view. For after having employed the whole of his first book in rejecting innate intelligence, taken in a certain sense, he nevertheless, at the beginning of the second and in the sequel, admits that ideas, which do not originate in sensation, come from reflection. Now reflection is nothing else than attention to what is in us, and the senses do not give us what we already carry with us. That being so, can it be denied that there is much that is innate in our mind, since we are innate, so to speak, in ourselves? and that there is in us: being, unity, substance, duration, change, action, perception, pleasure, and a thousand other objects of our intellectual ideas? And these objects being immediate to our understanding and always present (although they cannot always be perceived by reason of our distractions and need), what wonder that we say that these ideas with all depending upon them are innate in us? I have made use also of the comparison of a block of marble which has veins, rather than of a block of marble wholly even, or of blank tablets, *i.e.* of what is called among philosophers a *tabula rasa*. For if the soul resembled these blank tablets, truths would be in us as the figure of Hercules is in the marble, when the marble is wholly indifferent to the reception of this figure or some other. But if there were veins in the block which should indicate the figure of Hercules rather than other figures, this block would be more determined thereto, and Hercules would be in it as in some sense innate, although it would be needful to labor to discover these veins, to clear them by polishing, and by cutting away what prevents them from appearing. Thus it is that ideas and truths are for us innate, as inclinations, dispositions, habits, or natural potentialities, and not as actions; although these potentialities are always accompanied by some actions, often insensible, which correspond to them.

It seems that our clever author claims that there is nothing *virtual* in us, and indeed nothing of which we are not always actually conscious; but he cannot take this rigorously, otherwise his opinion would be too paradoxical; since, moreover, acquired habits and the stores of our memory are not always perceived and do not even always come to our aid at need, although we often easily recall them to the mind upon some slight occasion which makes us remember them, just as we need only the beginning of a song to remember it. He limits his thesis also in other places, by saying that there is nothing in us of which we have not at least formerly been conscious. But besides the fact that no one can be assured by reason alone how far our past *apperceptions*, which we may have forgotten, may have gone, especially according to the Platonic doctrine of reminiscence which, wholly fabulous as it is, is in no respect incompatible at least in part with reason wholly pure; besides this, I say, why must we acquire all through the perception of external things, and nothing be unearthed in ourselves? Is our soul then by itself such a blank that besides the images borrowed from without, it is nothing? This is not an opinion (I am sure) that our judicious author could approve. And where do we find tablets that have no variety in themselves? For we never see a plane perfectly even and uniform. Why, then, could we not furnish also ourselves with something of thought from our own depths if we should dig therein? Thus I am led to believe that at bottom his opinion upon this point is not different from mine, or rather from the common view, inasmuch as he recognizes two sources of our knowledge, the Senses and Reflection.

I do not know whether it will be so easy to harmonize him with us and with the Cartesians, when he maintains that the mind does not always think, and particularly that it is without perception when we sleep without dreaming; and he objects that since bodies can exist without motion, souls can also exist without thought. But here I make a somewhat different reply than is customary, for I hold that naturally a substance cannot exist without action, and that there is indeed never a body without movement. Experience already favors me, and you have only to consult the book of the distinguished Mr. [Robert—Ed.] Boyle against absolute rest, to be convinced of it; but I believe reason favors it also, and this is one of the proofs I have for doing away with atoms.

Moreover, there are a thousand indications which make us think that there are at every moment an infinite number of *perceptions* in us, but without apperception and reflection, *i.e.* changes in the soul itself of which we are not conscious, because the impressions are either too slight and too great in number, or too even, so that they have nothing sufficiently distinguishing them from each other; but joined to others, they do not fail to produce their effect and to make themselves felt at least confusedly in the mass. Thus it is that habit makes us take no notice of the motion of a mill or a waterfall when we have lived quite near it for some time. It is not that the motion does not always strike our organs, and that something no longer enters into the soul corresponding thereto, in virtue of the harmony of the soul and the body, but these impressions which are in the soul and the body, being destitute of the attractions of novelty, are not strong enough to attract our attention and our memory, attached to objects more engrossing. For all attention requires memory, and often when we are not admonished, so to speak, and warned to take note of some of our own present perceptions, we allow them to pass without reflection, and even without being noticed; but if any one directs our attention to them immediately after, and makes us notice, for example, some noise which was just heard, we remember it, and are conscious of having had at the time some feeling of it. Thus there were perceptions of which we were not conscious at once, consciousness arising in this case only from the warning after some interval, however small it may be. And to judge still better of the minute perceptions which we cannot distinguish in the crowd, I am wont to make use of the example of the roar or noise of the sea which strikes one when on its shore. To understand this noise as it is made, it would be necessary to hear the parts which compose this whole, *i.e.* the noise of each wave, although each of these little noises makes itself known only in the confused collection of all the others, *i.e.* in the roar itself, and would not be noticed if the wave which makes it were alone. For it must be that we are affected a little by the motion of this wave, and that we have some perception of each one of these noises, small as they are; otherwise we would not have that of a hundred thousand waves, since a hundred thousand nothings cannot make something. One never sleeps so soundly as not to have some feeble and confused sensation, and one would never be awakened by the greatest noise in the world if he did not have some perception of its small beginning; just as one would never break a rope by the greatest effort in the world if it were not stretched and lengthened a little by smaller efforts, although the slight extension they produce is not apparent. . . .

9

Noam Chomsky

Recent Contributions
to the Theory of Innate Ideas

Summary of Oral Presentation

Noam Chomsky, who is Farrari P. Ward Professor of Linguistics at the Massachusetts Institute of Technology, is the most influential and controversial figure in contemporary linguistics. With the publication of Syntactic Structures (1957) *he launched a revolution in the study of language, which before the advent of his theories was viewed, perhaps not entirely accurately, as a classificatory discipline, rather like botany.*

Chomsky's work tends to combine two themes that need not be as closely linked as he himself is persuaded they are. For one thing, he has sought to formulate innate (so-called transformational) rules that particular sentences used in natural languages can be seen to depend upon. These internal rules are thought to be embedded in our minds in some sense, to be more deep-rooted than the surface grammar of our language, and to be normally not consciously recoverable by native speakers. Here, the effort strains toward the discovery of the "linguistic universals" of all natural languages.

Chomsky also construes his linguistic studies as the groundwork of a cognitive psychology, in the sense that the human mind is somehow programmed for language, that the linguistic universals of his theory (the rulelike regularities of all natural languages) are genetically transmitted from generation to generation. Here, he favors nativism or the doctrine of innate ideas (which, in Cartesian Linguistics, 1966, *he thought closely linked to seventeenth-century rationalism). In this connection, he has substantially criticized empiricist and behaviorist learning theories, notably B. F. Skinner's (in a famous article, "A Review of B. F. Skinner's* Verbal Behavior," 1959) *and, by implication, W. V. Quine's theory of language acquisition. His reasoning is that children learn languages too quickly and efficiently from fragmentary specimens, that speakers produce and understand sentences they have never heard or spoken before, and that all natural languages appear to converge in what Chomsky calls their "deep structure"; only the admission of innate linguistic universals, he believes, could account for these features.*

Chomsky was extraordinarily active in the anti-Vietnam War campaign, when he made himself something of an expert on American foreign policy commitments. He has written almost as extensively in this area as in linguistics (notably, in American Power and the New Mandarins, 1967, 1969). *His own summary of the thrust of his linguistic theories is best given in* Language and Mind (1968, 1972 enl.) *and* Reflections on Language (1975). *Particularly in the latter, he suggests the social and political analogue of his linguistic conception of innate ideas.*

From *Boston Studies in the Philosophy of Science*, vol. III, Robert S. Cohen and Marx W. Wartofsky (eds.) (The Humanities Press, 1968), pp. 81–90. Reprinted by permission of the author and D. Reidel Publishing Company.

I think that it will be useful to separate two issues in the discussion of our present topic—one is the issue of historical interpretation, namely, what in fact was the content of the classical doctrine of innate ideas, let us say, in Descartes and Leibniz; the second is the substantive issue, namely, in the light of the information presently available, what can we say about the prerequisites for the acquisition of knowledge—what can we postulate regarding the psychologically a priori principles that determine the character of learning and the nature of what is acquired.

These are independent issues; each is interesting in its own right, and I will have a few things to say about each. What I would like to suggest is that contemporary research supports a theory of psychological a priori principles that bears a striking resemblance to the classical doctrine of innate ideas. The separateness of these issues must, nevertheless, be kept clearly in mind.

The particular aspect of the substantive issue that I will be concerned with is the problem of acquisition of language. I think that a consideration of the nature of linguistic structure can shed some light on certain classical questions concerning the origin of ideas.

To provide a framework for the discussion, let us consider the problem of designing a model of language acquisition, an abstract 'language-acquisition device' that duplicates certain aspects of the achievement of the human who succeeds in acquiring linguistic competence. We can take this device to be an input-output system

$$\text{data} \rightarrow \boxed{\text{LA}} \rightarrow \text{knowledge}$$

To study the substantive issue, we first attempt to determine the nature of the output in many cases, and then to determine the character of the function relating input to output. Notice that this is an entirely empirical matter; there is no place for any dogmatic or arbitrary assumptions about the intrinsic, innate structure of the device LA. The problem is quite analogous to the problem of studying the innate principles that make it possible for a bird to acquire the knowledge that expresses itself in nest-building or in song-production. On a priori grounds, there is no way to determine the extent to which an instinctual component enters into these acts. To study this question, we would try to determine from the behavior of the mature animal just what is the nature of its competence, and we would then try to construct a second-order hypothesis as to the innate principles that provide this competence on the basis of presented data. We might deepen the investigation by manipulating input conditions, thus extending the information bearing on this input-output relation. Similarly, in the case of language-acquisition, we can carry out the analogous study of language-acquisition under a variety of different input conditions, for example, with data drawn from a variety of languages.

In either case, once we have developed some insight into the nature of the resulting competence, we can turn to the investigation of the innate mental functions that provide for the acquisition of this competence. Notice that the conditions of the problem provide an upper bound and a lower bound on the structure that we may suppose to be innate to the acquisition device. The upper bound is provided by the diversity of resulting competence—in our case, the diversity of languages. We cannot impose so much structure on the device that acquisition of some attested language is ruled out. Thus we cannot suppose that the specific rules of English are innate to the device and these alone, since this would be inconsistent with the observation that Chinese can be learned as readily as English. On the other hand, we must attribute to the device a sufficiently rich structure so that the output can be attained within the observed limits of time, data, and access.

To repeat, there is no reason for any dogmatic assumptions about the nature of LA. The only conditions we must meet in developing such a model of innate mental capacity are those provided by the diversity of language, and by the necessity to provide empirically attested competence within the observed empirical conditions.

When we face the problem of developing such a model in a serious way, it becomes immediately apparent that it is no easy matter to formulate a hypothesis about innate structure that is rich enough to meet the condition of empirical adequacy. The competence of an adult, or even a young child, is such that we must attribute to him a knowledge of language that extends far beyond anything that he has learned. Compared with the number of sentences that a child can produce or interpret with ease, the number of seconds in a lifetime is ridiculously small. Hence the data available as input is only a minute sample of the linguistic material that has been thoroughly mastered, as indicated by actual performance. Furthermore, great diversity of input conditions does not lead to a wide diversity in resulting competence, so far as we can detect. Furthermore, vast differences in intelligence have only a small effect on resulting competence. We observe further that the tremendous intellectual accomplishment of language acquisition is carried out at a period of life when the child is capable of little else, and that this task is entirely beyond the capacities of an otherwise intelligent ape. Such observations as these lead one to suspect, from the start, that we are dealing with a species-specific capacity with a largely innate component. It seems to me that this initial expectation is strongly supported by a deeper study of linguistic competence. There are several aspects of normal linguistic competence that are crucial to this discussion.

I. Creative Aspect of Language Use

By this phrase I refer to the ability to produce and interpret new sentences in independence from 'stimulus control'—i.e., external stimuli or independently identifiable internal states. The normal use of language is 'creative' in this sense, as was widely noted in traditional rationalist linguistic theory. The sentences used in everyday discourse are not 'familiar sentences' or 'generalizations of familiar sentences' in terms of any known process of generalization. In fact, even to speak of 'familiar sentences' is an absurdity. The idea that sentences or sentence-forms are learned by association or conditioning or 'training' as proposed in recent behaviorist speculations, is entirely at variance with obvious fact. More generally, it is important to realize that in no technical sense of these words can language use be regarded as a matter of 'habit' or can language be regarded as 'a complex of dispositions to respond'.

A person's competence can be represented by a *grammar*, which is a system of rules for pairing semantic and phonetic interpretations. Evidently, these rules operate over an infinite range. Once a person has mastered the rules (unconsciously, of course), he is capable, in principle, of using them to assign semantic interpretations to signals quite independently of whether he has been exposed to them or their parts, as long as they consist of elementary units that he knows and are composed by the rules he has internalized. The central problem in designing a language-acquisition device is to show how such a system of rules can emerge, given the data to which the child is exposed. In order to gain some insight into this question, one naturally turns to a deeper investigation of the nature of grammars. I think real progress has been made in recent years in our understanding of the nature of grammatical rules and the manner in which they function to assign semantic interpretations to phonetically represented signals, and that it is precisely in this area that one can find results that have some bearing on the nature of a language-acquisition device.

II. *Abstractness of Principles of Sentence Interpretation*

A grammar consists of syntactic rules that generate certain underlying abstract objects, and rules of semantic and phonological interpretation that assign an intrinsic meaning and an ideal phonetic representation to these abstract objects.

Concretely, consider the sentence 'The doctor examined John'. The phonetic form of this sentence depends on the intrinsic phonological character of its minimal items ('The', 'doctor', 'examine', 'past tense', 'John'), the bracketing of the sentence (that is, as [[[the] [doctor]] [[examined] [John]]]), and the categories to which the bracketed elements belong (that is, the categories 'Sentence', 'Noun-Phrase', 'Verb-Phrase', 'Verb', 'Noun', 'Determiner', in this case). We can define the 'surface structure' of an utterance as its labeled bracketing, where the brackets are assigned appropriate categorial labels from a fixed, universal set. It is transparent that grammatical relations (e.g., 'Subject-of', 'Object-of', etc.) can be defined in terms of such a labeled bracketing. With terms defined in this way, we can assert that there is very strong evidence that the phonetic form of a sentence is determined by its labeled bracketing by phonological rules that operate in accordance with certain very abstract but quite universal principles of ordering and organization.

The meaning of the sentence 'the doctor examined John' is, evidently, determined from the meanings of its minimal items by certain general rules that make use of the grammatical relations expressed by the labeled bracketing. Let us define the 'deep structure' of a sentence to be that labeled bracketing that determines its intrinsic meaning, by application of these rules of semantic interpretation. In the example just given, we would not be far wrong if we took the deep structure to be identical with the surface structure. But it is obvious that these cannot in general be identified. Thus consider the slightly more complex sentences: 'John was examined by the doctor'; 'someone persuaded the doctor to examine John'; 'the doctor was persuaded to examine John'; 'John was persuaded to be examined by the doctor'. Evidently, the grammatical relations among *doctor, examine,* and *John,* as expressed by the deep structure, must be the same in all of these examples as the relations in 'the doctor examined John'. But the surface structures will differ greatly.

Furthermore, consider the two sentences:

someone expected the doctor to examine John
someone persuaded the doctor to examine John.

It is clear, in this case, that the similarity of surface structure masks a significant difference in deep structure, as we can see, immediately, by replacing 'the doctor to examine John' by 'John to be examined by the doctor' in the two cases.

So far, I have only made a negative point, namely, that deep structure is distinct from surface structure. Much more important is the fact that there is very strong evidence for a particular solution to the problem of how deep and surface structures are related, and how deep and surface structures are formed by the syntactic component of the grammar. The details of this theory need not concern us for the present. A crucial feature of it, and one which seems inescapable, is that it involves formal manipulations of structures that are highly abstract, in the sense that their relation to signals is defined by a long sequence of formal rules, and that, consequently, they have nothing remotely like a point by point correspondence to signals. Thus sentences may have very similar underlying structures despite great diversity of physical form, and diverse underlying structures despite similarity of surface form. A theory of language acquisition must explain how this knowledge of abstract underlying forms and the principles that manipulate them comes to be acquired and freely used.

III. Universal Character of Linguistic Structure

So far as evidence is available, it seems that very heavy conditions on the form of grammar are universal. Deep structures seem to be very similar from language to language, and the rules that manipulate and interpret them also seem to be drawn from a very narrow class of conceivable formal operations. There is no a priori necessity for a language to be organized in this highly specific and most peculiar way. There is no sense of 'simplicity' in which this design for language can be intelligibly described as 'most simple'. Nor is there any content to the claim that this design is somehow 'logical'. Furthermore, it would be quite impossible to argue that this structure is simply an accidental consequence of 'common descent'. Quite apart from questions of historical accuracy, it is enough to point out that this structure must be rediscovered by each child who learns the language. The problem is, precisely, to determine how the child determines that the structure of his language has the specific characteristics that empirical investigation of language leads us to postulate, given the meagre evidence available to him. Notice, incidentally, that the evidence is not only meagre in scope, but very degenerate in quality. Thus the child learns the principles of sentence formation and sentence interpretation on the basis of a corpus of data that consists, in large measure, of sentences that deviate in form from the idealized structures defined by the grammar that he develops.

Let us now return to the problem of designing a language-acquisition device. The available evidence shows that the output of this device is a system of recursive rules that provide the basis for the creative aspect of language use and that manipulate highly abstract structures. Furthermore, the underlying abstract structures and the rules that apply to them have highly restricted properties that seem to be uniform over languages and over different individuals speaking the same language, and that seem to be largely invariant with respect to intelligence and specific experience. An engineer faced with the problem of designing a device meeting the given input-output conditions would naturally conclude that the basic properties of the output are a consequence of the design of the device. Nor is there any plausible alternative to this assumption, so far as I can see. More specifically, we are led by such evidence as I have mentioned to suppose that this device in some manner incorporates: a phonetic theory that defines the class of possible phonetic representations; a semantic theory that defines the class of possible semantic representations; a schema that defines the class of possible grammars; a general method for interpreting grammars that assigns a semantic and phonetic interpretation to each sentence, given a grammar; a method of evaluation that assigns some measure of 'complexity' to grammars.

Given such a specification, the device might proceed to acquire knowledge of a language in the following way: the given schema for grammar specifies the class of possible hypotheses; the method of interpretation permits each hypothesis to be tested against the input data; the evaluation measure selects the highest valued grammar compatible with the data. Once a hypothesis—a particular grammar—is selected, the learner knows the language defined by this grammar; in particular, he is capable of pairing semantic and phonetic interpretations over an indefinite range of sentences to which he has never been exposed. Thus his knowledge extends far beyond his experience and is not a 'generalization' from his experience in any significant sense of 'generalization' (except, trivially, the sense defined by the intrinsic structure of the language-acquisition device).

Proceeding in this way, one can seek a hypothesis concerning language acquisition that falls between the upper and lower bounds, discussed above, that are set by the nature of the problem. Evidently, for language learning to take place the class of possible hypotheses—the schema for grammar—must be heavily restricted.

This account is schematic and idealized. We can give it content by specifying the language-acquisition system along the lines just outlined. I think that very plausible and concrete specifications can be given, along these lines, but this is not the place to pursue this matter, which has been elaborately discussed in many publications on transformational generative grammar.

I have so far been discussing only the substantive issue of the prerequisites for acquisition of knowledge of language, the a priori principles that determine how and in what form such knowledge is acquired. Let me now try to place this discussion in its historical context.

First, I mentioned three crucial aspects of linguistic competence: (1) creative aspect of language use; (2) abstract nature of deep structure; (3) apparent universality of the extremely special system of mechanisms formalized now as transformational grammar. It is interesting to observe that these three aspects of language are discussed in the rationalist philosophy of the 17th century and its aftermath, and that the linguistic theories that were developed within the framework of this discussion are, in essence, theories of transformational grammar.

Consequently, it would be historically accurate to describe the views regarding language structure just outlined as a rationalist conception of the nature of language. Furthermore, I employed it, again, in the classical fashion, to support what might fairly be called a rationalist conception of acquisition of knowledge, if we take the essence of this view to be that the general character of knowledge, the categories in which it is expressed or internally represented, and the basic principles that underlie it, are determined by the nature of the mind. In our case, the schematism assigned as an innate property to the language-acquisition device determines the form of knowledge (in one of the many traditional senses of 'form'). The role of experience is only to cause the innate schematism to be activated, and then to be differentiated and specified in a particular manner.

In sharp contrast to the rationalist view, we have the classical empiricist assumption that what is innate is (1) certain elementary mechanisms of peripheral processing (a receptor system), and (2) certain analytical mechanisms or inductive principles or mechanisms of association. What is assumed is that a preliminary analysis of experience is provided by the peripheral processing mechanisms and that one's concepts and knowledge, beyond this, are acquired by application of the innate inductive principles to this initially analyzed experience. Thus only the procedures and mechanisms for acquisition of knowledge constitute an innate property. In the case of language acquisition, there has been much empiricist speculation about what these mechanisms may be, but the only relatively clear attempt to work out some specific account of them is in modern structural linguistics, which has attempted to elaborate a system of inductive analytic procedures of segmentation and classification that can be applied to data to determine a grammar. It is conceivable that these methods might be somehow refined to the point where they can provide the surface structures of many utterances. It is quite inconceivable that they can be developed to the point where they can provide deep structures or the abstract principles that generate deep structures and relate them to surface structures. This is not a matter of further refinement, but of an entirely different approach to the question. Similarly, it is difficult to imagine how the vague suggestions about conditioning and associative nets that one finds in philosophical and psychological speculations of an empiricist cast might be refined or elaborated so as to provide for attested competence. A system of rules for generating deep structures and relating them to surface structures, in the manner characteristic of natural language, simply does not have the properties of an associative net or a habit family; hence no elaboration of principles for developing such structures can be appropriate to the problem of designing a language-acquisition device.

I have said nothing explicit so far about the doctrine that there are innate ideas and innate principles of various kinds that determine the character of what can be known in what may be a rather restricted and highly organized way. In the traditional view a condition for these innate mechanisms to become activated is that appropriate stimulation must be presented. This stimulation provides the occasion for the mind to apply certain innate interpretive principles, certain concepts that proceed from 'the power of understanding' itself, from the faculty of thinking rather than from external objects. To take a typical example from Descartes (Reply to Objections, V): ". . . When first in infancy we see a triangular figure depicted on paper, this figure cannot show us how a real triangle ought to be conceived, in the way in which geometricians consider it, because the true triangle is contained in this figure, just as the statue of Mercury is contained in a rough block of wood. But because we already possess within us the idea of a true triangle, and it can be more easily conceived by our mind than the more complex figure of the triangle drawn on paper, we, therefore, when we see the composite figure, apprehend not it itself, but rather the authentic triangle" (Haldane and Ross, vol. II, p. 227). In this sense, the idea of triangle is innate. For Leibniz what is innate is certain principles (in general, unconscious), that "enter into our thoughts, of which they form the soul and the connection". "Ideas and truths are for us innate as inclinations, dispositions, habits, or natural potentialities." Experience serves to elicit, not to form, these innate structures. Similar views are elaborated at length in rationalist speculative psychology.

It seems to me that the conclusions regarding the nature of language acquisition, discussed above, are fully in accord with the doctrine of innate ideas, so understood, and can be regarded as providing a kind of substantiation and further development of this doctrine. Of course, such a proposal raises nontrivial questions of historical interpretation.

What does seem to me fairly clear is that the present situation with regard to the study of language learning, and other aspects of human intellectual achievement of comparable intricacy, is essentially this. We have a certain amount of evidence about the grammars that must be the output of an acquisition model. This evidence shows clearly that knowledge of language cannot arise by application of step-by-step inductive operations (segmentation, classification, substitution procedures, 'analogy', association, conditioning, and so on) of any sort that have been developed or discussed within linguistics, psychology, or philosophy. Further empiricist speculations contribute nothing that even faintly suggests a way of overcoming the intrinsic limitations of the methods that have so far been proposed and elaborated. Furthermore, there are no other grounds for pursuing these empiricist speculations, and avoiding what would be the normal assumption, unprejudiced by doctrine, that one would formulate if confronted with empirical evidence of the sort sketched above. There is, in particular, nothing known in psychology or physiology that suggests that the empiricist approach is well-motivated, or that gives any grounds for skepticism concerning the rationalist alternative sketched above.

10

Hilary Putnam

The 'Innateness Hypothesis' and Explanatory Models in Linguistics

I. The Innateness Hypothesis

The 'innateness hypothesis' (henceforth, the 'I.H.') is a daring—or apparently daring; it may be meaningless, in which case it is not daring—hypothesis proposed by Noam Chomsky. I owe a debt of gratitude to Chomsky for having repeatedly exposed me to the I.H.; I have relied heavily in what follows on oral communications from him; and I beg his pardon in advance if I misstate the I.H. in any detail, or misrepresent any of the arguments for it. In addition to relying upon oral communications from Chomsky, I have also relied upon Chomsky's paper 'Explanatory Models in Linguistics', in which the I.H. plays a considerable rôle.

To begin, then, the I.H. is the hypothesis that the human brain is 'programmed' at birth in some quite *specific* and *structured* aspects of human natural language. The details of this programming are spelled out in some detail in 'Explanatory Models in Linguistics'. We should assume that the speaker has 'built in'[1] a function which assigns weights to the grammars G_1, G_2, G_3, . . . in a certain class Σ of transformational grammars. Σ is not the class of all *possible* transformational grammars; rather all the members of Σ have some quite strong similarities. These similarities appear as 'linguistic universals' —i.e., as characteristics of *all* human natural languages. If intelligent non-terrestrial life—say, Martians—exists, and if the 'Martians' speak a language whose grammar does not belong to the subclass Σ of the class of all transformational grammars, then, I have heard Chomsky maintain, humans (except possibly for a few geniuses or linguistic experts) would be unable to learn

From *Boston Studies in the Philosophy of Science*, Vol. III, Robert S. Cohen and Marx W. Wartofsky (eds.) (The Humanities Press, 1968), pp. 91–101. Reprinted by permission of the author and D. Reidel Publishing Company.

---

[1] What 'built in' means is highly unclear in this context. The weighting function by itself determines only the relative ease with which various grammars can be learned by a human being. If a grammar G_1 can be learned more easily than a grammar G_2, then doubtless this is 'innate' in the sense of being a fact about human learning *potential*, as opposed to a fact about what has been learned. But this sort of fact is what learning theory tries to account for; *not* the explanation being sought. It should be noticed that Chomsky has never offered even a schematic account of the sort of device that is supposed to be present in the brain, and that is supposed to do the job of selecting the highest weighted grammar compatible with the data. But only a description, or at least a theory, of such a device could properly be called an innateness *hypothesis* at all.

Martian; a human child brought up by Martians would fail to acquire language; and Martians would, conversely, experience similar difficulties with human tongues. (Possible difficulties in *pronunciation* are not at issue here, and may be assumed *not* to exist for the purposes of this argument.) As examples of the similarities that all grammars of the subclass Σ are thought to possess (above the level of phonetics), we may mention the *active-passive* distinction, the existence of a *non-phrase-structure* portion of the grammar, the presence of such major categories as *concrete noun, verb taking an abstract subject*, etc. The project of delimiting the class Σ may also be described as the project of defining a *normal form for grammars*. Conversely, according to Chomsky, any non-trivial normal form for grammars, such that correct and perspicuous grammars of all human languages can and should be written in that normal form, "constitutes, in effect, a hypothesis concerning the innate intellectual equipment of the child".[2]

Given such a highly *restricted* class Σ of grammars (highly restricted in the sense that grammars not in the class are perfectly conceivable, not more 'complicated' in any absolute sense than grammars in the class, and may well be employed by non-human speakers, if such there be), the performance of the human child in learning his native language may be understood as follows, according to Chomsky. He may be thought of as operating on the following 'inputs'[3]: a list of utterances, containing both grammatical and ungrammatical sentences; a list of corrections, which enable him to classify the input utterances *as* grammatical or ungrammatical; and some information concerning which utterances count as *repetitions* of earlier utterances. Simplifying slightly, we may say that, on this model, the child is supplied with a list of grammatical sentence *types* and a list of ungrammatical sentence *types*. He then 'selects' the grammar in Σ compatible with this information to which his weighting function assigns the highest weight. On this scheme, the general *form* of grammar is not learned from experience, but is 'innate', and the 'plausibility ordering' of grammars compatible with given data of the kinds mentioned is likewise 'innate'.

So much for a statement of the I.H. If I have left the I.H. vague at many points, I believe that this is no accident—for the I.H. seems to me to be *essentially* and *irreparably* vague—but this much of a statement may serve to indicate *what* belief it is that I stigmatize as irreparably vague.

A couple of remarks may suffice to give some idea of the rôle that I.H. is supposed to play in linguistics. Linguistics relies heavily, according to Chomsky, upon 'intuitions' of grammaticality. But *what* is an intuition of 'grammaticality' an intuition *of*? According to Chomsky, the sort of theory-construction programmatically outlined above is what is needed to give this question the only answer it can have or deserves to have. Presumably, then, to 'intuit' (or assert, or conjecture, etc.) that a sentence is grammatical is to 'intuit' (or assert, or conjecture, etc.) that the sentence is generated by the highest-valued G_i in the class Σ which is such that it generates all the grammatical sentence types with

[2] E. M. in L., p. 550.
[3] E. M. in L., pp. 530–531.

which we have been supplied by the 'input' and none of the ungrammatical sentence types listed in the 'input'.[4]

Chomsky also says that the G_i which receives the highest value must do *more* than agree with 'intuitions' of grammaticality; it must account for certain ambiguities, for example.[5] At the same time, unfortunately, he lists no semantical information in the input, and he conjectures[6] that a child needs semantical information only to "provide motivation for language learning", and not to arrive at the *formal* grammar of its language. Apparently, then, the fact that a grammar which agrees with a sufficient amount of 'input' must be in the class Σ to be 'selected' by the child is what rules out grammars that generate all and only the grammatical sentences of a given natural language, but fail to correctly 'predict'[7] ambiguities (cf. E. M. in L., p. 533).

In addition to making clear what it *is* to be grammatical, Chomsky believes that the I.H. confronts the linguist with the following tasks: To *define* the normal form for grammars described above, and to *define* the weighting function. In *Syntactic Structures* Chomsky, indeed, gives this as an objective for linguistic theory: to give an *effective* procedure for choosing between rival grammars.

Lastly, the I.H. is supposed to justify the claim that what the linguist provides is "a hypothesis about the innate intellectual equipment that a child brings to bear in language learning".[8] Of course, even if language is *wholly* learned, it is still true that linguistics "characterizes the linguistic abilities of the mature speaker",[9] and that a grammar "could properly be called an explanatory model of the linguistic intuition of the native speaker".[10] However, one could with equal truth say that a driver's manual "characterizes the car-driving abilities of the mature driver" and that a calculus text provides "an explanatory model of the calculus-intuitions of the mathematician". Clearly, it is the idea that *these* abilities and *these* intuitions are close to the human *essence*, so to speak, that gives linguistics its 'sex appeal', for Chomsky at least.

II. *The Supposed Evidence for the I.H.*

A number of empirical facts and alleged empirical facts have been advanced to support the I.H. Since limitations of space make it impossible to describe all of them here, a few examples will have to suffice.

---

[4] I doubt that the child really is told which sentences it hears or utters are *ungrammatical*. At most it is told which are *deviant*—but it may not be told which are deviant for *syntactical* and which for *semantical* reasons.

[5] Many of these—e.g., the alleged 'ambiguity' in 'the shooting of the elephants was heard'—*require coaching to detect*. The claim that grammar "explains the ability to recognize ambiguities" thus lacks the impressiveness that Chomsky believes it to have. I am grateful to Paul Ziff and Stephen Leeds for calling this point to my attention.

[6] E. M. in L., p. 531, n. 5.

[7] A grammar 'predicts' an ambiguity, in Chomsky's formalism, whenever it assigns two or more structural descriptions to the same sentence.

[8] E. M. in L., p. 530.

[9] E. M. in L., p. 530.

[10] E. M. in L., p. 533.

(a) The *ease* of the child's original language learning "A young child is able to gain perfect mastery of a language with incomparably greater ease [*than an adult*—H.P.] and without any explicit instruction. Mere exposure to the language, and for a remarkably short period, seems to be all that the normal child requires to develop the competence of the native speaker".[11]

(b) The fact that reinforcement, "in any interesting sense", seems to be unnecessary for language learning. Some children have apparently even learned to speak without *talking*[12], and then displayed this ability at a relatively late age to startled adults who had given them up for mutes.

(c) The ability to "develop the competence of the native speaker" has been said not to depend on the intelligence level. Even quite low I.Q.'s 'internalize' the grammar of their native language.

(d) The 'linguistic universals' mentioned in the previous section are allegedly accounted for by the I.H.

(e) Lastly, of course, there is the 'argument' that runs "*what* else could account for language learning?" The task is so incredibly complex (analogous to learning, at least implicitly, a complicated physical theory, it is said), that it would be miraculous if even one tenth of the human race accomplished it without 'innate' assistance. (This is like Marx's 'proof' of the Labour Theory of Value in *Capital*, vol. III, which runs, in essence, "*What else* could account for the fact that commodities have different value *except* the fact that the labor-content is different?".)

III. *Criticism of the Alleged Evidence*

A. *The Irrelevance of Linguistic Universals*

1. NOT SURPRISING ON ANY THEORY. Let us consider just how surprising the 'linguistic universals' cited above really are. Let us assume for the purpose a community of Martians whose 'innate intellectual equipment' may be supposed to be as different from the human as is compatible with their being able to speak a language at all. What could we expect to find in their language?

If the Martians' brains are not vastly richer than ours in complexity, then they, like us, will find it possible to employ a practically infinite set of expressions only if those expressions possess a 'grammar'—i.e., if they are built up by recursive rules from a limited stock of basic forms. Those basic forms need not be built up out of a *short* list of phonemes—the Martians might have vastly greater memory capacity than we do—but if Martians, like humans, find rote learning difficult, it will not be surprising if they too have *short* lists of phonemes in their languages.

Are the foregoing reflections arguments *for* or *against* the I.H.? I find it difficult to tell. If belief in 'innate intellectual equipment' is *just* that, then

---

[11] E. M. in L., p. 529.

[12] Macaulay's *first* words, it is said, were: "Thank you, Madam, the agony has somewhat abated" (to a lady who had spilled hot tea on him).

how *could* the I.H. be false? How could something with *no* innate intellectual equipment *learn* anything? *To be sure,* human 'innate intellectual equipment' is relevant to language learning; if this means that such parameters as memory span and memory capacity play a crucial role. But what rank Behaviorist is supposed to have ever denied *this*? On the other hand, that a particular mighty arbitrary set Σ of grammars is 'built in' to the brain of *both* Martians and Humans is *not* a hypothesis we would have to invoke to account for *these* basic similarities.

But for what similarities above the level of phonetics, where constitutional factors play a large role for obvious reasons, *would* the I.H. have to be invoked *save* in the trivial sense that memory capacity, intelligence, needs, interests, etc., are all relevant to language learning, and all depend, in part, on the biological makeup of the organism? If Martians are such strange creatures that they have no interest in physical objects, for example, their language will contain no concrete nouns; but would not this be *more*, not *less* surprising, on any *reasonable* view, than their having an interest in physical objects? (Would it be surprising if Martian contained devices for forming truth-functions and for quantification?)

Two more detailed points are relevant here. Chomsky has pointed out that no natural language has a phrase structure grammar. But this too is not surprising. The sentence 'John and Jim came home quickly' is not generated by a phrase-structure rule, in Chomsky's formalization of English grammar. But the sentence 'John came home quickly and Jim came home quickly' *is* generated by a phrase-structure rule in the grammar of mathematical logic, and Chomsky's famous 'and-transformation' is just an abbreviation rule. Again, the sentence 'That was the lady I saw you with last night' is not generated by a phrase-structure rule in English, or at least not in Chomsky's description of English. But the sentence 'That is ix (x is a lady and I saw you with x last night)' is generated by a phrase-structure rule in the grammar of mathematical logic. And again the idiomatic English sentence *can* be obtained from its phrase-structure counterpart by a simple rule of abbreviation. Is it really surprising, does it really point to anything more interesting than *general intelligence*, that these operations which break the bounds of phrase-structure grammar appear in every natural language?[13]

Again, it may appear startling at first blush that such categories as noun, verb, adverb, etc. have 'universal' application. But, as Curry has pointed out, it is too easy to multiply 'facts' here. If a language contains nouns—that is,

---

[13] Another example of a transformation is the 'active-passive' transformation (cf. *Syntactic Structures*). But (a) the presence of this, if it *is* a part of the grammar, is not surprising—why should not there be a systematic way of expressing the *converse* of a relation?— and (b) the argument for the existence of such a 'transformation' at all is extremely slim. It is contended that a grammar which 'defines' active and passive forms separately (this can be done by even a phrase-structure grammar) fails to represent something that every speaker knows, *viz.* that active and passive forms are *related*. But why must every *relation* be mirrored by *syntax*? Every 'speaker' of the canonical languages of mathematical logic is aware that each sentence (x) $(Fx \supset Gx)$ is related to a sentence (x) $(\overline{G}x \supset Fx)$; yet the definition of 'well formed formula' fails to mirror 'what every speaker knows' in this respect, and is not inadequate on that account.

a phrase-structure category which contains the proper names—it contains noun phrases, that is, phrases which occupy the environments of nouns. If it contains noun phrases it contains verb phrases—phrases which when combined with a noun phrase by a suitable construction yield sentences. If it contains verb phrases, it contains adverb phrases—phrases which, when combined with a verb phrase yield a verb phrase. Similarly, adjective phrases, etc., can be defined in terms of the *two* basic categories 'noun' and 'sentence'. Thus the existence of nouns is all that has to be explained. And this reduces to explaining two facts: (1) The fact that all natural languages have a large phrase-structure portion in their grammar, in the sense just illustrated, in spite of the effect of what Chomsky calls 'transformations'. (2) The fact that all natural languages contain proper names. But (1) is not surprising in view of the fact that phrase-structure rules are extremely simple algorithms. Perhaps Chomsky would reply that 'simplicity' is subjective here, but this is just not so. The fact is that all the natural measures of complexity of an algorithm—size of the machine table, length of computations, time, and space required for the computation—lead to the same result here, quite independently of the detailed structure of the computing machine employed. Is it surprising that algorithms which are 'simplest' for virtually any computing system we can conceive of are also simplest for naturally evolved 'computing systems'? And (2)—the fact that all natural languages contain proper names—is not surprising in view of the utility of such names, and the difficulty of always finding a definite description which will suffice instead.

Once again, 'innate' factors are relevant *to be sure*—if choosing *simple* algorithms as the basis of the grammar is 'innate', and if the need for identifying persons rests on something innate—but what Behaviorist would or should be surprised? Human brains are computing systems and subject to some of the constraints that effect all computing systems; human beings have a natural interest in one another. If *that* is 'innateness', well and good!

2. LINGUISTIC UNIVERSALS COULD BE ACCOUNTED FOR, EVEN IF SURPRISING, WITHOUT INVOKING THE I.H.   Suppose that language-using human beings evolved *independently* in two or more places. Then, if Chomsky were *right*, there should be two or more *types* of human beings descended from the two or more original populations, and normal children of each type should fail to learn the languages spoken by the other types. Since we do not observe this, since there is only *one* class Σ built into *all* human brains, we have to conclude (if the I.H. is true) that language using is an evolutionary 'leap' that occurred only *once*. But in that case, it is overwhelmingly likely that all human languages are descended from a single original language, and that the existence today of what are called 'unrelated' languages is accounted for by the great lapse of time and by countless historical changes. This is, indeed, likely even if the I.H. is false, since the human race itself is now generally believed to have resulted from a single evolutionary 'leap', and since the human population was extremely small and concentrated for millennia, and only gradually spread from Asia to other continents. Thus, even if language using was learned or invented rather than 'built in', or even if only some general dispositions in the direction of language

using are 'built in',[14] it is likely that some one group of humans first developed language as we know it, and then spread this through conquest or imitation to the rest of the human population. Indeed, we do know that this is just how *alphabetic* writing spread. In any case, I repeat, this hypothesis—a single origin for human language—is certainly *required* by the I.H., but much weaker than the I.H.

But just this *consequence* of the I.H. is, in fact, enough to account for 'linguistic universals'! For, if all human languages are descended from a common parent, then just such highly useful features of the common parent as the presence of some kind of quantifiers, proper names, nouns, and verbs, etc., would be expected to survive. Random variation may, indeed, alter many things; but that it should fail to strip language of proper names, or common nouns, or quantifiers, is not *so* surprising as to require the I.H.

B. The 'Ease' of Language Learning Is Not Clear

Let us consider somewhat closely the 'ease' with which children do learn their native language. A typical 'mature' college student seriously studying a foreign language spends three hours a week in lectures. In fourteen weeks of term he is thus exposed to forty-two hours of the language. In four years he may pick up over 300 hours of language, very little of which is actual listening to native informants. By contrast, direct method teachers estimate that 300 hours of direct-method teaching will enable one to converse fluently in a foreign language. Certainly 600 hours—say, 300 hours of direct-method teaching and 300 hours of reading—will enable any adult to speak and read a foreign language with ease, and to use an incomparably larger vocabulary than a young child.

It will be objected that the adult does not acquire a perfect accent. So what? The adult has been speaking one way all of his life, and has a huge set of habits to unlearn. What can equally well be accounted for by learning theory should not be cited as evidence for the I.H.

Now the child by the time it is four or five years old has been exposed to *vastly* more than 600 hours of direct-method instruction. Moreover, even if 'reinforcement' is not necessary, most children are consciously and repeatedly reinforced by adults in a host of ways—e.g., the constant repetition of simple one-word sentences ('cup', 'doggie') in the presence of babies. Indeed, any foreign adult living with the child for those years would have an incomparably better grasp of the language than the child does. The child indeed has a better accent. Also, the child's grammatical mistakes, which are numerous, arise not from carrying over previous language habits, but from not having fully acquired the first set. But it seems to me that this 'evidence' for the I.H. stands the facts on their head.

---

[14] It is very difficult to account for such phenomena as the spontaneous babbling of infants without *this* much 'innateness'. But this is not to say that a class Σ and a function f are 'built in', as required by the I.H.

C. Reinforcement Another Issue

As Chomsky is aware, the evidence is today slim that *any* learning requires reinforcement "in any interesting sense". Capablanca, for example, learned to play chess by simply watching adults play. This is comparable to Macaulay's achievement in learning language without speaking. Nongeniuses normally do require practice both to speak correctly and to play chess. Yet probably anyone *could* learn to speak *or* to play chess without practice if muffled, in the first case, or not allowed to play, in the second case, with sufficiently prolonged observation.

D. Independence of Intelligence Level an Artifact

Every child learns to speak the native language. What does this mean? If it means that children do not make serious grammatical blunders, even by the standards of descriptive as opposed to prescriptive grammar, this is just not true for the young child. By nine or ten years of age this has ceased to happen, perhaps (I speak as a parent), but nine or ten years is enough time to become pretty darn good at *anything*. What is more serious is what 'grammar' *means* here. It does not include mastery of vocabulary, in which even many adults are deficient, nor ability to understand *complex* constructions, in which many adults are *also* deficient. It means purely and simply the ability to learn what every *normal* adult learns. Every normal adult learns what every normal adult learns. What this 'argument' reduces to is "Wow! How complicated a skill every normal adult learns. What else could it be but *innate*." Like the preceding argument, it reduces to the 'What Else' argument.

But what of the 'What Else?' argument? Just how impressed should we be by the failure of current learning theories to account for complex learning processes such as those involved in the learning of language? If Innateness were a *general* solution, perhaps we should be impressed. But the I.H. *cannot*, by its very nature, *be* generalized to handle all complex learning processes. Consider the following puzzle (called 'jump'):

```
            *   *   *
            *   *   *
    *   *   *   *   *   *   *
    *   *   *   ●   *   *   *
    *   *   *   *   *   *   *
            *   *   *
            *   *   *
```

To begin with, all the holes but the center one are filled. The object of the game is to remove all the pegs but one by 'jumping' (as in checkers) and to end with the one remaining peg in the center. A clever person can get the solution in perhaps eight or ten hours of experimentation. A not so clever person can get a 'near-solution'—two pegs left—in the same time. No program exists, to my knowledge, that would enable a computer to solve even the 'near solution' problem without running out of both time and space, even though the machine can spend the equivalent of many human lifetimes in experimentation. When we come to the discovery of even the simplest mathematical theorem the situation is even more striking. The theorems of mathematics, the solutions to puzzles, etc., cannot on *any* theory be *individually* 'innate'; what must be 'innate' are heuristics, i.e., learning strategies. In the absence of any knowledge of what *general multipurpose learning strategies* might even look like, the assertion that such strategies (which absolutely must exist and be employed by all humans) cannot account for this or that learning process, that the answer or an answer schema must be 'innate', is utterly unfounded.

I will be told, of course, that *everyone* learns his native language (as well as everyone does), and that not everyone solves puzzles or proves theorems. But everyone does learn pattern recognition, automobile driving, etc., and everyone in fact can solve many problems that no computer can solve. In conversation Chomsky has repeatedly used precisely such skills as these to support the idea that humans have an "innate conceptual space". Well and good, if true. *But that is no help. Let a complete 17th-century Oxford University education be innate if you like;* still the solution to 'jump' was not innate; the Prime Number Theorem was not innate; and so on. *Invoking 'Innateness' only postpones the problem of learning; it does not solve it.* Until we understand the strategies which make general learning possible—and vague talk of 'classes of hypotheses'— and 'weighting functions' is utterly useless here—no discussion of the *limits* of learning can even begin.

11

Jerry A. Fodor
Private Language, Public Languages

*Jerry A. Fodor is a member of the philosophy and psychology departments at MIT and of MIT's Research Laboratory of Electronics. He has been associated with the program of linguistic research initiated by Noam Chomsky and has collaborated with Jerrold Katz in the preparation of an important anthology (*The Structure of Language, 1964*). His first book,* Psychological Explanation *(1968), is addressed to the conceptual puzzles involved in explaining an organism's behavior by reference to its psychological states.*

In particular, Fodor introduces the concept of mentalism, defined as the denial of the central thesis of behaviorism. By behaviorism he means the thesis that it is a necessary truth that mental predicates that can enter into psychological explanation are logically connected with at least one description of behavior. He advocates mentalism, notes that it is compatible with both dualism and materialism, and ultimately opts for the alternative of materialism.

Fodor's most recent book, The Language of Thought *(1975), argues that plausible theories represent cognitive processes as computational and that computational processes require a medium of computation—that is, a representational system. Applied to organisms and in particular to human beings, Fodor presses the thesis that we are led to suppose that organisms have internal representational systems. In effect, this constitutes Fodor's extension of Chomskyan nativism to the processes of thought.*

The inner is not the outer.
    SØREN KIERKEGAARD

Why There Has To Be a Private Language

The discussion thus far might be summarized as follows: One of the essential variables in any theory of higher cognitive processes that we can now imagine is the character of the representation that the organism assigns to features of its environment and to its response options. This is, of course, a very traditional remark to make. Gestalt psychologists, for example, used to emphasize the salience of the *proximal* stimulus in the causation of behavior. Their point was that if you want to know how the organism will respond to an environmental

event, you must first find out what properties it takes the event to have.[1]
They might, with equal propriety, have emphasized the salience of the proximal
response; if you want to know why the organism behaved the way it did, you
must first find out what description it intended its behavior to satisfy; what it
took itself to be doing. [Earlier I—Ed.] sought to make explicit one of the
presuppositions of this line of argument: The 'proximal stimulus' is a proximal
representation of the *distal* stimulus, and the 'proximal response' *stands for*
an overt act. But representation presupposes a medium of representation, and
there is no symbolization without symbols. In particular, there is no internal
representation without an internal language.

I think, myself, that this conclusion is both true and extremely important.
There are, however, ways of construing it which would make it true but not
very important. For example, one might argue as follows:

> Of course there is a medium in which we think, and of course it is a language.
> In fact, it is a natural language: English for English speakers, French for French
> speakers, Hindi for Hindi speakers, and so on. The argument which seemed to
> lead to exciting and paradoxical conclusions thus leads only to one's own front
> door. Your 'traditional remarks' rest, in short, on a traditional confusion. You
> suppose that natural language is the medium in which we *express* our thoughts;
> in fact, it is the medium in which we *think* them.

This is a kind of view which has appealed to very many philosophers and
psychologists. Indeed, it *is* appealing, for it allows the theorist both to admit the
essential role of computation (and hence of representation) in the production
of behavior and to resist the more scarifying implications of the notion of a
language of thought. It is, for example, all right for hypothesis formation to
be essential to learning, and for hypotheses to presuppose a language to couch
them in, so long as the language presupposed is, e.g., English. For English is a
representational system to whose existence we are committed independent of our
views about cognitive psychology; ask any English speaker. We can in short
allow that cognitive processes are defined over linguistic objects and we can do
so without raising anybody's methodological hackles. All we need to do is
assume that the linguistic objects that cognitive processes are defined over are
drawn from one of the *public* languages.

The only thing that's wrong with this proposal is that it isn't possible to
take it seriously: So far as I can see, the radical consequences of the internal
language view will have to be lived with. The obvious (and, I should have
thought, sufficient) refutation of the claim that natural languages are the
medium of thought is that there are nonverbal organisms that think. I don't

---

[1] Not only because behavior is sometimes based on false beliefs (e.g., on misassignments
of properties to the stimulus) but also because the behaviorally salient properties of the
stimulus are a *selection* from the properties that belong to it: Of all the indefinitely many
properties the stimulus *does* have, only those can be behaviorally salient which the organism
represents the stimulus as having. That is why, in practice, it is usually only by attending to
the behavior of the organism that we can tell what the (proximal) stimulus is.

propose to quibble about what's to count as thinking, so I shall make the point in terms of the examples discussed [earlier—Ed.]. All three of the processes . . . examined . . .—considered action, concept learning, and perceptual integration— are familiar achievements of infrahuman organisms and preverbal children. The least that can be said, therefore, is what we have been saying all along: Computational models of such processes are the only ones we've got. Computational models presuppose representational systems. But the representational systems of preverbal and infrahuman organisms surely cannot be natural languages. So either we abandon such preverbal and infrahuman psychology as we have so far pieced together, or we admit that some thinking, at least, isn't done in English.

Notice that although computation presupposes a representational language, it does *not* presuppose that that language must be one of the ones which function as vehicles of communication between speakers and hearers: e.g., that it must be a natural language. So, on the one hand, there is no internal reason for supposing that our psychology applies only to organisms that talk, and if we do decide to so restrict its application we shall have no model at all for learning, choosing, and perceiving in populations other than fluent human beings. On the other hand, to extend our psychology to infrahuman species is thereby to commit ourselves to cognitive processes mediated by representational systems other than natural languages.

I think many philosophers are unimpressed by these sorts of considerations because they are convinced that it is not a question of fact but, as it were, of linguistic policy whether such psychological predicates as have their paradigmatic applications to fluent human beings ought to be 'extended' to the merely infraverbal. I was once told by a very young philosopher that it is a matter for *decision* whether animals can (can be said to) hear. 'After all,' he said, 'it's *our* word.'

But this sort of conventionalism won't do; the issue isn't whether we ought to be polite to animals. In particular, there are homogeneities between the mental capacities of infraverbal organisms and those of fluent human beings which, so far as anybody knows, are inexplicable except on the assumption that infraverbal psychology is relevantly homogeneous with our psychology.

To take just one example, . . . human subjects typically have more trouble mastering disjunctive concepts than they do with conjunctive or negative ones. But we remarked, too, that the notion of the form of a concept needs to be relativized to whatever system of representation the subject employs. For one thing, disjunction is interdefinable with conjunction and negation and, for another, which concepts are disjunctive depends upon which kind terms the vocabulary of the representational system acknowledges. *Color* isn't, I suppose, a disjunctive concept despite the fact that colors come in different colors. Whereas, 'red or blue' *is* a disjunctive concept; i.e., is disjunctively represented in English and, presumably, in whatever system of representation mediates the integration of our visual percepts.

The point is that these remarks apply wholesale to infraverbal concept learning. Animals, too, typically find (what *we* take to be) disjunctive concepts hard to master. We can account for this fact if we assume that the representational system that *they* employ is relevantly like the one that *we* employ (e.g., that an animal conditioned to respond positive to either-a-triangle-or-a-square represents the reinforcement contingencies disjunctively, just as the experimenter does).[2] Since no alternative account suggests itself (since, so far as I know, no alternative account has ever been suggested) it would seem to be the behavioral facts, and not our linguistic policies, which require us to hypothesize the relevant homogeneities between our representational system and the ones infraverbal organisms use.[3]

As one might expect, these sorts of issues become critical when we consider the preverbal child learning a first language. The first point to make is that we have no notion at all of how a first language might be learned that does not come down to some version of learning by hypothesis formation and confirmation. This is not surprising since, as we remarked [earlier—Ed.] barring the cases where what is learned is something explicitly taught, we have no notion of how *any* kind of concept is learned except by hypothesis formation and confirmation. And learning a language L must at least involve learning such concepts as 'sentence of L'.

If, for example, [Noam—Ed.] Chomsky is right (see Chomsky, [*Aspects of the Theory of Syntax*—Ed.] 1965; for detailed discussion of Chomsky's views of syntax acquisition, see Fodor et al., [*The Psychology of Language*—Ed.] 1974), then learning a first language involves constructing grammars consonant with some innately specified system of language universals and testing those grammars against a corpus of observed utterances in some order fixed by an innate simplicity metric. And, of course, there must be a language in which the universals, the candidate grammars, and the observed utterances are represented. And, of course, this language cannot be a natural language since, by hypothesis, it is his first language that the child is learning.[4]

---

[2] For an experimental demonstration that preverbal human infants have differential difficulties with disjunctive contingencies of reinforcement, see Fodor, Garrett and Brill, ["Pe, ka, pu: the perception of speech sounds in prelinguistic infants," *M.I.T. Quarterly Progress Report*, January—Ed.] 1975.

[3] It is worth emphasizing that this example is in no way special. The widespread homogeneity of human and infrahuman mental processes has been the main theme of psychological theorizing since Darwin. The interesting, exciting, and exceptional cases are, in fact, the ones where interspecific differences emerge. Thus, for example, there are situations in which infrahuman organisms treat as homogeneous stimuli which *we* take to be disjunctive. It is very difficult to train *octopus* to discriminate diagonal lines which differ (only) in left-right orientation. The natural assumption is that the representational system the animal employs does not distinguish between (i.e., assigns identical representations to) mirror images. For ingenious elaboration, see [N. S.—Ed.] Sutherland [Theories of Shape Discrimination in Octopus," *Nature*, 186—Ed.] (1960).

[4] Chomsky's argument infers the innateness of linguistic information (and hence of the representational system in which it is couched) from the universality of language structure across historically unrelated communities and from the complexity of the information the child must master if he is to become fluent. Versions of this argument can be found in [J. J.—Ed.] Katz [*The Philosophy of Language*—Ed.] (1966) and [Zeno—Ed.] Vendler [*Res Cogitans*—Ed.] (1972). I think it is a good argument, though it leaves a number of questions pending. Until we know *which* features of language are universal, it gives us no way of telling which aspects of the child's representation of his native language are innate.

In fact, however, for these purposes it doesn't matter whether Chomsky is right, since the same sort of point can be made on the basis of much more modest assumptions about what goes on in language acquisition. I want to discuss this claim in considerable detail.

To begin with, I am going to take three things for granted: (1) that learning a first language is a matter of hypothesis formation and confirmation . . . ; (2) that learning a first language involves at least learning the semantic properties of its predicates; (3) that S learns the semantic properties of P only if S learns some generalization which determines the extension of P (i.e., the set of things that P is true of).

These assumptions are unequally tendentious. Item 1 rests on . . . arguments reviewed [earlier.—Ed.]. I take it that item 2 will be granted by anyone who is willing to suppose that there is anything at all to the notion of semantic properties as psychologically real. Item 3, on the other hand, is serious; but I shan't argue for it, since, as will presently become apparent, it is assumed primarily for purposes of exposition. Suffice it to remark here that many philosophers have found it plausible that one understands a predicate only if one knows the conditions under which sentences that contain it would be true. But if this is so, and if, as we have supposed, language learning is a matter of testing and confirming hypotheses, then among the generalizations about a language that the learner must hypothesize and confirm are some which determine the extensions of the predicates of that language. A generalization that effects such a determination is, by stipulation, a *truth rule*. I shall henceforth abbreviate all this to "S learns P only if S learns a truth rule for P."[5]

Since I propose to work these assumptions very hard, I had better get my

---

And: *How* complex does learning have to be for the hypothesis of a task specific innate contribution to be plausible?

The considerations I shall be developing seek to delineate aspects of the child's innate contribution to language learning in ways that avoid these sorts of difficulties. But I shall be assuming what Chomsky et al. have always assumed and what Vendler has made explicit: There is an analogy between learning a second language on the basis of a first and learning a first language on the basis of an innate endowment. In either case, some previously available representational system must be exploited to formulate the generalizations that structure the system that is being learned. Out of nothing nothing comes.

---

[5] I shall, throughout, employ the following format for truth rules. Where P is a predicate in the language to be learned, T is a truth rule for P iff (a) it is of the same form as F, and (b) all of its *substitution instances are*

F: $\ulcorner P_y \urcorner$ is true (in L) iff x is G

true. The substitution instances of F are the formulae obtained by:

1. Replacing the angles by quotes. (In effect, variables in angles are taken to range over the expressions of the object language.)
2. Replacing 'P_y' by a sentence whose predicate is P and whose subject is a name or other referring expression.
3. Replacing 'x' by an expression which designates the individual referred to by the subject of the quoted sentence. (This condition yields a nonsyntactic notion of *substitution instance* since whether one formula bears that relation to another will depend, in part, on what their referring expressions refer to. This is, however, both convenient and harmless for our purposes.)

caveats in early. There are three. First, though it is, for my purposes, convenient to identify learning the semantic properties of P with learning a truth rule for P, nothing fundamental to the argument I want to give depends on doing so. Readers who object to the identification are free to substitute some other notion of semantic property or to take that notion as unanalyzed. Second, to say that someone has learned a truth rule for a predicate is not to say that he has learned a procedure for determining when the predicate applies, or even that there is such a procedure. Third, if there were anything to dispositional accounts of what is involved in understanding a predicate, we would have an alternative to the theory that learning a predicate involves learning a rule. So the whole discussion will proceed on the assumption that there is, in fact, nothing to be said for dispositional accounts of what is involved in understanding a predicate. I shall expand each of these points at some length before returning to the main argument.

1. Many philosophers think that truth conditions provide too weak a construal of what we learn when we learn a predicate; e.g., that what we learn must be what sentences containing the predicate entail and are entailed by, not what they materially imply and are materially implied by. I have, in fact, considerable sympathy with such views. But the point I want to stress is that the arguments that follow are entirely neutral so far as those views are concerned. That is, these arguments are neutral vis-à-vis the controversy between extensionalist and intensionalist semantics. If you are an extensionalist, then surely you believe that the semantic properties of a predicate determine its extension. If you are an intensionalist, then presumably you believe that the semantic properties of a predicate determine its *in*tension and that intensions determine extensions. Either way, then, you believe what I have wanted to assume.

Another way of putting it is this: Both intensionalists and extensionalists hold that semantic theories pair object language predicates with their metalinguistic counterparts. Extensionalists hold that the critical condition on the paired expressions is coextensivity. Intensionalists hold that the critical condition is logical equivalence or, perhaps, synonymy. But if either of these latter conditions is satisfied, then the former condition is satisfied too. So, once again, how the extensionalist/intentionalist question is resolved doesn't matter for the purposes I have in mind.

There are, however, philosophers who hold not only that the semantic

---

So, suppose that L is English and P is the predicate 'is a philosopher'. Then, a plausible truth rule for P is ⌜*y is a philosopher*⌝ *is true iff* x *is a philosopher*. Substitution instances of this truth rule would include '*Fred is a philosopher' is true iff Fred is a philosopher*; '*the man on the corner is a philosopher' is true iff the man on the corner is a philosopher*; and '*Fred is a philosopher' is true iff the man on the corner is a philosopher* (assuming Fred is the man on the corner) . . . etc.

Of course, nothing requires that the expression which forms the right-hand side of a truth rule (or its instances) should be drawn from the same language as the sentence quoted on the left. On the contrary, we shall see that that assumption is quite *im*plausible when *learning* truth rules is assumed to be involved in learning a language. (For a useful introduction to the general program of analyzing meaning in terms of truth, see [Donald—Ed.] Davidson, ["Truth and Meaning," *Synthese*, 17—Ed.] 1967).

properties of a predicate don't determine its *in*tension but that they don't determine its *ex*tension either. Such philosophers claim (very roughly) that what we know about the meanings of predicates determines at most their *putative* extensions, but that whether the putative extension of a predicate is in fact its *real* extension is, in the long run, at the mercy of empirical discoveries.

Thus, [Hilary—Ed.] Putnam (to be published) [*Mind, Language and Reality. Philosophical Papers, Vol. 2* (Cambridge: Cambridge University Press, 1975)—Ed.] argues that when we learn 'gold', 'cat', 'water', etc. we learn socially accepted stereotypes such that it is *reasonable to believe* of things that conform to the stereotypes that they satisfy the predicates. But what it is reasonable to believe need not prove, in the long run, to be true. Perhaps there was a time when only liquid water was known to *be* water. Perhaps it was then discovered that ice is water in a solid state. (Surely this is ontogenetically plausible even if it's a historical fairy tale.) To discover this would be to discover something about what the extension of 'water' *really* is (viz., that ice is in it). But if it *is* an empirical discovery that ice is water, then it is hard to see how the fact that 'water' applies to ice could have been determined, in any substantive sense, by what one learns when one learns what 'water' means. And if that is right, then it is hard to see how learning what 'water' means could involve learning something that determines the extension of 'water' in advance of such discoveries. In short, on this view, either the semantic properties of a word aren't what you learn when you learn the word, or the semantic properties of a word don't determine its extension.

I don't want to become involved in assessing these suggestions because, right or wrong, they are largely irrelevant to the main points that I shall make. I will argue, primarily, that you cannot learn a language whose terms express semantic properties not expressed by the terms of some language you are already able to use. In formulating this argument, it is convenient to assume that the semantic properties expressed by a predicate are those which determine its extension, since, whatever its faults may be, that assumption at least yields a sharp sense of identity of semantic properties (two predicates have the same semantic properties if they apply to the same set of things.) If, however, that assumption fails, then the same sort of argument can be constructed given any other notion of semantic property, so long as its semantic properties are what you learn when you learn a word. If, for example, what you learn when you learn P is (only) that it would be reasonable to believe that P applies iff S, then, according to my argument, in order to learn the language containing P you must already be able to use some (other) language which contains some (other) term such that it would be reasonable to believe that *it* applies iff it would be reasonable to believe that P applies. And so on, *mutatis mutandis*, for construals of *semantic property*.

I shall, then, continue to do what it is convenient to do: take the extension of a predicate to be what its semantic properties primarily determine. But only on the understanding that alternative readings of 'semantic property' may be substituted ad lib.

2. To endorse the view that learning a predicate involves learning a

generalization which determines its extension is not to subscribe to any species of verificationism, though the literature has exhibited an occasional tendency to confuse the two doctrines.

Consider the English predicate 'is a chair'. The present view is, roughly, that no one has mastered that predicate unless he has learned that it falls under some such generalization as ⌜*y is a chair*⌝ is true iff Gx. (For a discussion of the notation, see footnote 5 above.) But, of course, it does not follow that someone who knows what 'is a chair' means is therefore in command of a general procedure for sorting stimuli into chairs and non-chairs. That *would* follow only on the added assumption that he has a general procedure for sorting stimuli into those which do, and those which do not, satisfy G. But that assumption is no part of the view that learning a language involves learning truth rules for its predicates.

If, e.g., it is true that 'chair' means 'portable seat for one', then it is plausible that no one has mastered 'is a chair' unless he has learned that it falls under the truth rule "⌜*y is a chair*⌝ is true iff x is a portable seat for one.' But someone might well know this about 'is a chair' and still not be able to *tell* about some given object (or, for that matter, about any object) whether or not *it* is a chair. He would be in this situation if, e.g., his way of telling whether a thing is a chair is to find out whether it satisfies the right-hand side of the truth rule, and if he is unable to tell about *this* (or any) thing whether it is a portable seat for one.

I make these remarks in light of Wittgenstein's observation that many (perhaps all) ordinary language predicates are open-textured; e.g., that there are indefinitely many objects about which we cannot tell whether they are chairs; not just because the lighting is bad or some of the facts aren't in, but because 'is a chair' is, as it were, undefined for objects of those kinds, so that whether they are chairs isn't a question of fact at all (cf. the chair (sic) made of soap bubbles; the packing case that is used as a chair, etc.). This is all true and well taken, but the present point is that it doesn't prejudice the notion that learning truth rules is essential to language learning, or the point that truth rules are expressed by biconditional formulae. All it shows is that *if* the truth condition on 'is a chair' is expressed by 'is a portable seat for one', then 'portable seat for one' must be open-textured, undefined, etc., for just those cases where 'is a chair' is.

One can get into no end of trouble by confusing this point. For example, [H. L.—Ed.] Dreyfus [*What Computers Can't Do*—Ed.] (1972), if I understand him correctly, appears to endorse the following argument against the possibility of machine models of human linguistic capacities: (a) Machine models would presumably employ rules to express the extensions of the predicates they use. (b) Such rules would presumably be biconditionals (e.g., truth rules). But (c) Wittgenstein has shown that the extension of natural language predicates cannot be expressed by such rules because such predicates are inherently fuzzy-edged. So (d) people can't be modeled by machines and (e) a fortiori, people can't *be* machines.

But Wittgenstein showed no such thing. The most that can be inferred from the existence of open texture is that if a formula expresses the truth conditions on *P*, then its truth value must be indeterminate wherever the truth value of *P* is indeterminate. To put it slightly differently, if a machine simulates a speaker's use of a predicate, then (the machine ought to be unable to determine whether the predicate applies) iff (the speaker is unable to determine whether the predicates applies). But there is nothing at all in the notion of machines as rule-following devices that suggests that that condition cannot be met. Correspondingly, there is nothing in the notion that people's use of language is rule governed which suggests that every predicate in a language must have a determinate applicability to every object of predication.

3. I have assumed not only that learning a predicate involves learning something which determines its extension, but also that 'learning something which determines the extension of *P*' should be analyzed as learning that *P* falls under a certain rule (viz., a truth rule). Now, someone could accept the first assumption while rejecting the second: e.g., by postulating some sort of behavior analysis of '*S* knows the extension of *P*.' Equivalently for these purposes he could accept both assumptions and postulate a dispositional analysis of knowing a rule. Thus, if the truth rule for *P* is ''*Py*' is true iff *Gx*', then to know the truth rule might be equated with having a disposition to say *P* just in cases where *G* applies. Similarly, learning the truth conditions on *P* would be a matter (not of hypothesizing and confirming that the corresponding truth rule applies, but just) of having one's response dispositions appropriately shaped.

A number of philosophers who ought to know better do, apparently, accept such views. Nevertheless, I shall not bother running through the standard objections since it seems to be that if *anything* is clear it is that understanding a word (predicate, sentence, language) isn't a matter of how one behaves or how one is disposed to behave. Behavior, and behavioral disposition, are determined by the interactions of a variety of psychological variables (what one believes, what one wants, what one remembers, what one is attending to, etc.). Hence, in general, any behavior whatever is compatible with understanding, or failing to understand, any predicate whatever. Pay me enough and I will stand on my head iff you say 'chair'. But I know what 'is a chair' means all the same.

So much for caveats. Now I want to draw the moral. Learning a language (including, of course, a first language) involves learning what the predicates of the language mean. Learning what the predicates of a language mean involves learning a determination of the extension of these predicates. Learning a determination of the extension of the predicates involves learning that they fall under certain rules (i.e., truth rules). But one cannot learn that *P* falls under *R* unless one has a language in which *P* and *R* can be represented. So one cannot learn a language unless one has a language. In particular, one cannot learn a first language unless one already has a system capable of representing the predicates in that language *and their extensions*. And, on pain of circularity, that system cannot be the language that is being learned. But first languages *are* learned. Hence, at least some cognitive operations are carried out in languages other than natural languages.

[Ludwig—Ed.] Wittgenstein, commenting upon some views of Augustine's, says:

Augustine describes the learning of human languages as if the child came into a strange country and did not understand the language of the country;[6] that is, as if it already had a language, only not this one. Or again, as if the child could already *think*, only not yet speak. And 'think' would here mean something like 'talk to itself', ([*Philosophical Investigations*–Ed.] 1953, para. 32).

Wittgenstein apparently takes it that such a view is transparently absurd. But the argument that I just sketched suggests, on the contrary, that Augustine was precisely and demonstrably right and that seeing that he was is prerequisite to any serious attempts to understand how first languages are learned.

.   .   .

12

Joseph Margolis

First- and Second-Language Acquisition and the Theory of Thought and Perception

Joseph Margolis is Professor of Philosophy at Temple University and editor of Philosophical Monographs. *He has written extensively on the theory of knowledge and philosophy of mind. His early work was in aesthetics and value theory, which led to a distinctive form of nonreductive materialism (see Part I). In* Art and Philosophy (1978) *he introduced the concept of embodiment, a relation distinct from identity and composition, best illustrated by such phenomena as Michelangelo's* David's *being a culturally emergent entity (a sculpture) not identical with and not composed of the marble in which it is embodied.*

*In Margolis's view, the irreducibility of intentionality (see Part I) is already admitted by reductive materialists. He therefore sees a close analogy between the theory of art and the theory of persons, distinguished by their mastery of language. That is to say, embodiment is a relationship that obtains among all culturally emergent entities: works of art, persons, words and sentences, machines (*Persons and Minds, *1977). He has worked extensively in ethics, psychotherapy, medicine,*

From Joseph Margolis, "First- and Second-Language Acquisition and the Theory of Thought and Perception," to appear in slightly revised form in *Studies in Language*, I (1977). Printed with the permission of the editor.

6 For example, Augustine represents the child as trying to figure out what the adults are referring to when they use the referring expressions of their language. Wittgenstein's point is that this picture could make sense only on the assumption that the child has access to a linguistic system in which the 'figuring out' is carried on.

war, and related social issues (Psychotherapy and Morality, 1966; Values and Conduct, 1971; Negativities, 1975). *Here, he has pursued the thesis that only certain minima can be provided for the testing of normative commitments, that there is an ideological element that cannot be eliminated in all such commitments. Hence, he sees his theory of norms and values as convergent with the view that persons are culturally emergent entities who have no natural function.*

One of the most strategic questions about linguistic mastery asks whether acquiring a first or natural language is like acquiring a second. Since some of the salient features of acquiring a second language are reasonably clear, the move to construe acquiring a first in terms appropriate to acquiring a second suggests the resolution of a deep puzzle. The affirmative view need not be exclusively favored by so-called linguistic empiricists, who concede only innate lawlike dispositions of the mind—as opposed to linguistic rationalists, who concede also innate rulelike dispositions.[1]

Perhaps empiricists about language acquisition should forego that view and search for an alternative theory of language learning. And perhaps rationalists about language should construe a child's learning a first language as presupposing its grasp of certain antecedent essentials of language.

Colin Turbayne is strongly attracted to empiricism and opposed to linguistic rationalism of the sort associated with the work of Noam Chomsky.[2] Turbayne speaks quite straightforwardly of "the 'code' of visual language," which he admits is "chaotic." But, Turbayne thinks, one eventually "learns to 'read' this language [the 'code' of visual discrimination] like a native 'decoder,' and finally manages to fuse or complicate the items of two languages [the visual and haptic 'codes' —the haptic includes the sense of touch, pressure, kinaesthesia, and the like]." This yields a theory of vision rather like Berkeley's.[3]

Turbayne says that perceiving is "modelled on reading," by which he obviously does not mean that it may be *heuristically* useful to construe perceiving (cognitively) in propositional and therefore linguistic terms. Rather, he means that perceiving entails mastering a skill that is *essentially* one of reading a kind of visual code or language. Turbayne summarizes his view in the following way:

> According to the [traditional rationalist doctrine resurrected in recent years], the mind comes equipped with certain innate ideas or principles in the form of knowledge of language structure. This knowledge it applies to the mastery of its first language. It seems to me, however, that we are able to acquire this

---

[1] Cf. Joseph Margolis, "Mastering a Natural Language: Rationalists versus Empiricists," *Diogenes*, 84 (1973), 41–57.

[2] Noam Chomsky, *Language and Mind*, rev. ed. (New York: Harcourt Brace Jovanovich, 1972).

[3] Colin Murray Turbayne, "Metaphors for the Mind," in Richard Rudner and Israel Scheffler (eds.), *Language and Art. Essays in Honor of Nelson Goodman* (Indianapolis: Bobbs-Merrill, 1972), p. 75. Cf. also Turbayne, "Visual Language from the Verbal Model," *Journal of Typographic Research*, III (1969), 345–370. Turbayne there holds that "visual objects constitute *a written* language" (351)—following Plato's and Berkeley's view that "the visible world is a script, presented in alphabetical form, which we have to learn to read" (345). But he also says a "convention or mutual compact [is] necessary for language" (365), which undermines his thesis.

"first" language, not through knowledge of any innate ideas, but because all of us have been mastering code-breaking and encoding skills from earliest infancy. Some of us more readily broke the code of written English because we had already broken the simpler code of I.T.A. [Sir James Pitman's Initial Teaching Alphabet]. Most of us were helped to acquire our "first" language because we had already broken the code of visual language in the first months of life.[4]

Turbayne is particularly agile in sorting out the metaphoric ways in which the mind is described—which he strenuously resists. It is fair to say, therefore, that he intends his account quite literally. He draws attention as well to a similar view held by Nelson Goodman.

True, Goodman holds that "acquisition of an initial language is acquisition of a secondary symbolic system" and consequently is rather like the acquisition of a second language.[5] But Chomsky has strenuously opposed Goodman's position. Chomsky stresses Goodman's confidence that "once one language is available and can be used for giving explanation and instruction," the acquisition of a second language poses no difficulties and obviates the need for an appeal to innate ideas.

Chomsky holds that Goodman must be speaking metaphorically for two reasons. (1) There is no ground for supposing that "the specific properties of grammar—say the distinction of deep and surface structure, the specific properties of grammatical transformations and phonological rules, the principles of rule ordering, and so on—are present in these already acquired prelinguistic 'symbolic systems.'" (2) These putative systems "cannot 'be used for giving explanation and instruction' *in the way in which a first language can be used in second-language acquisition.*"[6]

Hence from the empiricist's vantage the problem of first-language acquisition remains unresolved—at least when it is based on construing first-language acquisition as a variety of second-language acquisition. In fact, Goodman holds elsewhere, languages are symbol systems "of a particular kind" that satisfy minimally the "syntactic requirements of disjointness and differentiation." Roughly, the first of these requirements is that replicas of given marks or inscription be syntactically equivalent to one another and that "no mark may belong to more than one character." The second of these requirements is that for any given mark or inscription that does not belong to two given characters, it may be determined that the mark does not belong to the one character or to the other.[7]

Apart from the strenuousness of applying these criteria to natural languages, it is difficult to see how Goodman could conclude, on his own grounds, that we possess initial "symbol systems" sufficiently like linguistic systems that we may

---

[4] Turbayne, "Metaphors for the Mind," p. 76.

[5] Nelson Goodman, "The Epistemological Argument," *Synthese*, XVII (1967), 23–28. The argument is presented in dialogue form.

[6] Noam Chomsky, "Linguistics and Philosophy," in *Language and Mind*, pp. 175–176; compare Goodman, "The Epistemological Argument," p. 25.

[7] Nelson Goodman, *Languages of Art* (Indianapolis: Bobbs-Merrill, 1968), pp. xii, 40n, 131–133, 135–136, 225f.

thereby undercut the plausibility of "the claim that there are rigid limitations upon initial-language acquisition."[8]

The rationalist tends to speak in much the same way, though for different reasons. David McNeill, for example, pursuing a position explicitly indebted to Chomsky's, begins his account of first-language acquisition by holding that "virtually everything that occurs in language acquisition depends on *prior* knowledge of the basic aspects of sentence structure. The concept of a sentence may be part of man's innate mental capacity."[9] McNeill says, "Children everywhere begin with exactly the same initial hypothesis; sentences consist of single words."[10] The upshot, he thinks, is "that children begin speaking underlying structure directly" because they do not initially grasp the idiosyncratic aspects of the different natural languages.[11]

This is tantalizingly close to providing a rationalist counterpart to Goodman's and Turbayne's empiricist accounts. Here, more compellingly than for the empiricist, explaining and instructing are no problem because what is essential in acquiring a second language *or* a first is already innate in the infant. In particular, this hypothesis takes care of Chomsky's objection to empiricism, since in instruction one no longer needs "enough explicit knowledge about [the universal deep] structure [of a first or second language]."[12] No one has that knowledge but no one needs it for the task at hand.

Arguing along somewhat different lines but as a rationalist, Zeno Vendler holds that all thought is propositional. Since he means this in the literal sense that, although we do not need to think in terms of some particular natural language, we do think in terms of the deep structure that underlies language, it follows that animals cannot think.

Vendler concludes from this that "a child must learn his native tongue in a way similar to the way one learns a second language," by means of something like Chomsky's deep structure.[13] What we see, then, is how the first- and second-language problem is strategically connected to the theory of thought and perception.

The trouble is not only that linguistic universals are difficult to specify *if*, as Chomsky apparently wishes,[14] they are to be made suitably explicit. McNeill's concept of a *sentence* is obviously inadequate and begs the question (particularly allegedly holophrastic—one word—sentences). Furthermore, what to make of the notion of *rulelike* dispositions in infants is problematic. Certainly, no straightforwardly materialistic account of genetics could countenance the inheritance of rulelike as opposed to lawlike regularities. And no remotely plausible conceptual model accounts for the transmission of such an organiza-

---

[8] Goodman, "The Epistemological Argument," p. 25.

[9] David McNeill, *The Acquisition of Language* (New York: Harper & Row, 1970), p. 2.

[10] *Ibid.*

[11] *Ibid.*, p. 72.

[12] Chomsky, "Linguistics and Philosophy," pp. 174–175.

[13] Zeno Vendler, *Res Cogitans* (Ithaca: Cornell University Press, 1972), pp. 140, 161, 165.

[14] Cf. Noam Chomsky and Morris Halle, *The Sound Pattern of English* (New York: Harper & Row, 1968).

tion.[15] But the rationalist and empiricist discussions of first- and second-language acquisition are so problematic as to suggest the need for more fundamental distinctions.

A promising beginning may be made by considering the relationship between speech and thought. Empiricists like Turbayne and Goodman evidently take for granted a strong structural similarity between cognitive perception and reading a language. But a rationalist like Zeno Vendler also holds that "you can say whatever you think, and you can think *almost* whatever you can say" (where the restriction is irrelevant to our concern). This is because, as Vendler argues, the structure of thought and speech is the same—literally, the same.[16] He means by this that speech and thought both rest on innate ideas, in Descartes's sense; though he seems also to hold that we think directly in terms of Chomskyan linguistic universals.[17]

Now, the trouble with all such views—whether empiricist or rationalist—is that, on the face of it, (1) animals may be said to perceive (cognitively), though there is no reason to suppose that in learning to discriminate perceptually they are learning to master some prelinguistic "symbolic system"; and (2) *if* animals are conceded to perceive in a cognitively pertinent sense, their ability to have beliefs and, in that sense, to think cannot be denied, despite their lack of language and of the capacity to master language.[18]

There is, furthermore, the intriguing recent evidence of the ability of chimpanzees to master a portion of natural language. Roger Brown cites the early views of Chomsky and Eric Lenneberg against animal language. "Acquisition of even [the] barest rudiments [of language] is quite beyond the capacities of an otherwise intelligent ape" (Chomsky). "There is no evidence that any nonhuman form has the capacity to acquire even the most primitive stages of language development" (Lenneberg).[19] Brown himself had held essentially the same view and has revised it cautiously in light of reports from the Gardners and Premack.[20]

---

[15] Cf. Margolis, "Mastering a Natural Language."

[16] Vendler, *Res Cogitans*, pp. 36, 166–182.

[17] This appears to have been his message in a lecture at Temple University (1973).

[18] Cf. the interesting reply to Vendler by Norman Malcolm, "Thoughtless Brutes," *Proceedings and Addresses of the American Philosophical Association*, XLVI (1972–1973), (Clinton, N.Y.: American Philosophical Association, 1973). I have explored some further aspects of this question in "Knowledge and Belief; Facts and Propositions," forthcoming in *Grazer Philosophische Studien*.

[19] Cited by Roger Brown, *A First Language* (Cambridge: Harvard University Press, 1973), pp. 32–33.

[20] Cf. Roger Brown, "The First Sentences of Child and Chimpanzee," in *Psycholinguistics: Selected Papers* (New York: Free Press, 1970). An anecdotal account of the early reception of the Gardners' work may be found in Eugene Linden, *Apes, Men, and Language* (New York: Saturday Review Press/Dutton, 1974), Chs. 3–4. Cf. also Beatrice T. Gardner and R. Allen Gardner, "Two-way Communication with an Infant Chimpanzee" and David Premack, "On the Assessment of Language Competence in the Chimpanzee," both in Allan M. Schreier and Fred Stolnitz (eds.), *Behavior of Nonhuman Primates. Modern Research Trends* (Vol. 4) (New York: Academic Press, 1971); and "An Unbuttoned Introduction," in *A First Language*.

In any case, professional doubts as to whether chimpanzees can learn to perform linguistically imply that the learning of a first language cannot be like the learning of a second. In particular, they imply that the perceptual competence of the chimpanzee cannot be construed as the mastery of a symbolic system sufficiently like a language to make the mastery of a first language likely. Alternatively, if it is held (against the evidence) that chimpanzees do not exhibit a minimal command of language, it could hardly be supposed that the prelinguistic perceptual abilities of the human infant render likely *its* eventual mastery of language.

There is, then, little reason to suppose either (1) that perceptual discrimination is or entails the mastery of a symbolic system or symbol system structurally similar to a language; or (2) that prelinguistic thinking or even nonverbal thinking on the part of linguistically qualified subjects exhibits the structure of speech.

Point 1 seems to be the thesis favored by empiricists in order to overtake the difficulty of first-language acquisition. Point 2 seems to be the thesis favored by rationalists in order to overtake that same difficulty. Furthermore, point 1 suggests a parallel between visual and haptic perception [the sense of touch, pressure, kinaesthesia, and the like] corresponding to that between spoken and written language, but it does not provide an analysis of perception as such. And point 2 suggests that speech and thought have the same structure because they rest on the innate conditions on which language acquisition itself depends, but it does not provide a way of determining independently what the structure of thinking is.

These omissions are so remarkably similar that, since we have no plausible account of the genetic conditions of innate ideas and we have no detailed linguistic model for the characterization of vision, it seems reasonable to turn to other alternatives. Here, the similarities between perceptual cognition and thought are instructive.

Even if we debate the nature of chimpanzee linguistic competence, we cannot doubt that these creatures are intelligent and capable of perceptual cognition. Even if we are not sure what to make of Washoe's protolinguistic responses to linguistic cues, we cannot deny that Washoe *sees what* the Gardners are doing on the occasion of her linguistic attempts. In other words, we cannot deny that Washoe sees *that* this or that occurs. Obviously, then, in ascribing perceptual cognition to Washoe, we are obliged to formulate her perceptual discriminations *propositionally*, whether or not we are prepared to ascribe linguistic abilities to her. A *fortiori*, we do the same for human infants and for adults who have mastered language, without supposing that when human beings perceive *that* such-and-such is the case, they must have formulated—or must have been capable of formulating linguistically—whatever propositional content is assigned to their perception.

Similarly, if Washoe may be said to *believe that* such-and-such is the case, for instance on the basis of perception, then since to believe that such-and-such is the case is to think or to be able to think or to have thoughts, Washoe's thoughts may be linguistically formulated whether or not we ascribe linguistic abilities to her. A *fortiori*, we do the same for human infants and for adults who have mastered language, without supposing that when human beings think *that* such-and-such is the case, they must have formulated—or must have been capable of formulating linguistically—whatever propositional content is assigned to their thought.

In a word, cognitive states cannot be ascribed to any subject without specifying the content of such states propositionally. And *propositions—on any theory* —cannot be specified independently of *sentences* by which they are conveyed. But, since we can ascribe cognitive states (perception and thought) not only to animals that lack language but also to human beings when they lack language or when they have not used their linguistic abilities, it is reasonable to suppose that linguistic formulations of the propositional content of their cognitive states, in the absence of explicit speech acts, must be construed *heuristically*.

Three things are meant by this. (1) No propositional structure can be independently discerned in perception or thought as such, and no independent access to such structures is needed.[21] (2) Perception and thought must be assigned propositional content.[22] (3) In using the sentences of some natural language in order to convey the propositional content of perception and thought, no assumptions need be made about the correspondences between the grammar of that language and the propositional structure of either perception or thought.

If this is so, then attempts by both rationalists and empiricists to link first- and second-language acquisition are not required in order to make sense out of perception and thought. Contrary to Turbayne and Goodman, language does not depend on a visual code; it is itself characterized in linguistic terms. And, contrary to Vendler and Geach, though thoughts may be linguistically expressed, the linguistic reporting of thought by means of *oratio obliqua* constructions (indirect speech) does not entail an independently accessible structure of thought that is the same as or analogous with the structure of language.

The thesis that the propositional content of cognitive perception and thought may be heuristically ascribed accommodates the relevant reporting, since our very theory of cognitive states justifies the ascription of propositional objects to perception and thought. In other words, our theory assigns objects of such a sort that only a model for reporting propositional objects will suffice, and our only model for formulating or fixing propositions expressed or conveyed requires sentences. (This does not mean that propositions can be conveyed or expressed only verbally.)

Should it turn out, on independent empirical investigation, that there is indeed a discernible propositional structure to perception and thought (the meaning of which possibility is by no means entirely clear), the heuristic thesis may be replaced by the literal one. What is here being argued is only that the heuristic thesis is both economical and reasonable and that there is no inde-

---

[21] Contrast P. T. Geach, *Mental Acts* (London: Routledge and Kegan Paul, 1956); and D. M. Armstrong, *Belief, Truth and Knowledge* (Cambridge: Cambridge University Press, 1973).

[22] Compare Roderick Chisholm, *Theory of Knowledge* (Englewood Cliffs: Prentice-Hall, 1966); and Vendler, *loc. cit.*

pendent evidence or evidence free of question-begging interpretations that points to grammatical structures somehow embedded in the processes of perception and thought.

Roger Brown, who has qualified resistance to chimpanzee language, draws three conclusions. (1) Chomsky's view of the "barest rudiments" of language is far too restrictive. (2) On that view even children are not producing language at the levels Brown distinguishes as Stages I–III. (3) In general, "what goes before 'language' in development is only linguistic by courtesy of its continuity with a system which in fully elaborated form is indeed a language."[23]

Washoe, it now turns out, compares rather favorably with so-called Stage I "linguistic" performance, because "appropriate word order is not strictly *necessary* for purposes of communication for either the Stage I child or the Stage I chimpanzee." The reason? "Because most of these sequences are produced concurrently with a referent situation which would ordinarily admit of only one sensible interpretation whether the order was right or wrong."[24]

Washoe's accomplishment seems to entail "enough of a linguistic capacity to have supported a considerable degree of cultural evolution," Brown concludes. "I would not rule out the possibility that chimpanzees in fact make more use of a linguistic capacity than has generally been supposed."[25] What does this really mean? Even in the context of language acquisition, a heuristic model of first-language learning is inescapable.

Brown himself draws attention to but does not elucidate the important fact that "first-language learning . . . is a process of cognitive socialization," by which he means "the taking on of culture."[26] Here, the difference between first-language and second-language learning is impossible to ignore.

Still, when he introduces what he calls "the Original Word Game," by which some tutor trains a player in at least a first language, Brown says, "the player forms hypotheses about the nonlinguistic categories eliciting particular utterances."[27] Clearly, to admit that the acquisition of a first language is part of the first "taking on of culture" entails a reliance on a heuristic model of propositional ascriptions.

Failure to recognize the adequacy of a heuristic model for assigning propositional content to the perception and belief of creatures that lack language is just what has obliged *both* rationalists and empiricists to construe the learning of a first language on the model of learning a second. How else, one can imagine them asking, can languageless creatures *understand* the nature of the first language they acquire? But how, we may ask in turn, are we to understand the notion of prelinguistic hypotheses?

---

[23] Brown, A *First Language*, p. 37.

[24] *Ibid.*, pp. 40–41.

[25] *Ibid.*, p. 43.

[26] Roger W. Brown, "Language and Categories," in Jerome S. Bruner, Jacqueline J. Goodnow, and George A. Austin, A *Study of Thinking* (New York: Wiley, 1956), Appendix, pp. 247–248.

[27] *Ibid.*, p. 284.

Essentially the same point is succinctly pressed against the theories of William Stern by the Russian theorist L. S. Vygotsky. Attacking Stern's intellectualistic conception of language learning, Vygotsky remarks:

> One might expect . . . that much light would be thrown on the relation between speech and thought when the meaningfulness of language is regarded as a result of an intellectual operation. Actually, such an approach, stipulating as it does an *already formed* intellect, blocks an investigation of the involved dialectical interactions of thought and speech.[28]

Clearly, both empiricists and rationalists here considered are struggling to preserve the futile intellectualism that Vygotsky has exposed.

The heuristic model itself generates a good many questions that deserve a separate airing. Two considerations may be mentioned that will at least suggest the resilience and power of the model. For one thing, heuristic ascriptions of propositional content to thought and perception entail a richer conception of the use of *oratio obliqua* constructions (indirect discourse) than is usually conceded. *Oratio obliqua* may be used to report the propositional content (1) of what someone *said* and (2) of what someone *perceived* or *thought*, even when the subject is incapable of speech or has not exercised or been disposed to exercise his linguistic ability. Vendler concedes as much, though for a different purpose, when he acknowledges that indirect discourse may be used "for the reproduction of someone else's, or my own, thought as well" as for reporting the message or propositional content of someone's speech-act.[29]

If thinking does not presuppose the capacity to speak, *oratio obliqua* must have this larger (and heuristic) function. Only a rationalist could avoid the conclusion. *Which* propositions to assign to a creature on the occasion of a particular ascription of perception or thinking will depend on our theory of the biologically developed capabilities of the creature in question. In fact, the very notion that a given creature is capable of cognitive perception and thought entails some constraint on the creature's conceptual capacities. Hence, in determining what range of perception and thought may be ascribed to a given creature, we determine as well the repertory of propositions that may be assigned as the pertinent content of particular perceptions and thoughts *and*, at the same time, the range of concepts that the creature is capable of using.[30] The elucidation of these issues is obviously strenuous. The point at stake here

---

[28] L. S. Vygotsky, *Thought and Language*, trans. Eugenia Hanfmann and Gertrude Vakar (Cambridge: MIT Press, 1962), p. 29. I had not considered Vygotsky's views when I drafted this account; I must thank the anonymous reader for *Foundations of Language* for suggesting the relevance of Vygotsky's work. But, as will be seen, I believe there is a crucial gap in Vygotsky's account. His contribution lies with (1) his grasping the close connection between thought and speech, which nevertheless have separate sources, and (2) his steadfast refusal to allow any line of argument that obscures the *gradual*, genetic, sociohistorical development of speech out of prelinguistic patterns of responsiveness and communication.

[29] *Res Cogitans*, pp. 55–57.

[30] This goes against the accounts of Geach, *Mental Acts*, and Armstrong, *Belief, Truth and Knowledge*.

is to sketch the orienting features of the theory within which heuristic ascriptions are actually made.

The second consideration concerns the intensionality of mental states like belief, thought, mood, and attitude as well as of cognition in general. Schematically, to believe *that a&b* does not entail and is not the same as believing *that b&a*. The puzzles of intensionality are regarded as particularly troublesome for a thoroughgoing materialistic interpretation of the mind.[31]

Be that as it may, the heuristic model obviates the paradoxes of intensionality. Mental states remain intentional, in the sense that they may be "about" or "directed to" propositions. But the ascription of propositional content need not generate any intensional puzzles.

The reason is elementary. Since the heuristic model does not presuppose a mastery of language or the use of any existing linguistic competence, no intensional consideration bearing on relations between sentences is the least bit relevant. Suppose, for a given creature, we wish to ascribe the belief that *a&b* and the belief that *b&a*. We cannot do so on the basis of what is entailed or logically equivalent among sets of sentences. We can do so only on the evidence —for instance, behavioral evidence relative to our theory of the interests, desires, skills, capacities, and the like of the creature in question—that (1) both may be independently confirmed; or that (2) the ascription is indifferent to either formulation.

In short, the heuristic model illuminates this important finding: The puzzles of intensionality arise not where ascriptions of mental states are involved but only where such ascriptions are made of creatures actively employing or disposed to employ speech in expressing or reporting their thoughts and perceptions.

Here again, enormous conceptual complications arise. Nevertheless, the considerations provided suggest that we may pursue these without danger of an immediate stalemate. And we may pursue them without resolving the rationalist/empiricist controversy and without confusing first- and second-language acquisition with the capacity for cognitive perception and thought. Still, the conditions for successful first-language acquisition remain a profound empirical mystery.

Vygotsky's views are instructive here. He says,

> If we compare the early development of speech and intellect—which, as we have seen, develop along separate lines both in animals and in very young children—with the development of inner speech and of verbal thought, we must conclude that the later stage is not a simple continuation of the earlier. *The nature of the development itself changes*, from biological to sociohistorical. Verbal thought is not an innate, natural form of behavior but is determined by a historical–cultural process and has specific properties and laws that cannot be found in the natural forms of thought and speech.[32]

---

[31] Cf. particularly Daniel Dennett, *Content and Consciousness* (London: Routledge and Kegan Paul, 1969); and Armstrong, *Belief, Truth and Knowledge.*

[32] Vygotsky, *Thought and Language*, p. 51.

In effect, these are Vygotsky's points. First, there can be no purely bio-logical accounting for the culturally distinctive, rulelike regularities of language. Second, ascriptions of prelinguistic communication by sound and gesture (what he calls animal language) and prelinguistic thought (which develops separately, as evidenced by the solution of problems and the expression of emotion by voice and gesture) provide the genetic basis for the *gradual* emergence of "verbal thought" and "intellectual speech."

Vygotsky means by verbal thought "inner, soundless speech"—*functionally* considered, the result of gradual "molecular" changes culminating in the "fusion" of the separate and linguistically altered processes of prelinguistic thought and prelinguistic "speech." By intellectual speech Vygotsky means "external speech" (the mastery of "the correct use of grammatical forms and structures," which may precede a grasp of "the logical operations for which they stand") *plus* the requisite grasp of their logical function.

One of Vygotsky's principal concerns is to demonstrate that the transi-tional phase in this development is precisely what Jean Piaget characterized as "the child's egocentric speech" (though reversing Piaget's own explanatory account).[33] Here, the emphasis is placed on the social character of learning even the forms and structures of a language, though the language learned is used in a way that is not socialized but "incommunicable," or egocentric.

What Vygotsky says is suggestive, leading on to an account of "inner speech" (verbally informed thought). But it too presupposes an essential feature of the learning of a first language that is not supplied. For one thing, what it is to say that a child comes to *grasp* the functional properties of language is never explained. Here, Vygotsky is in the same position as Stern, though he has cautioned us to attend to a gradual process. For another thing, Vygotsky has nothing to say about the inescapability of analyzing prelinguistic thought and perception in terms of a linguistic model. Hence he provides no ground on which to facilitate our understanding of the transition from the prelinguistic to the linguistic.

Even in his investigation of concept formation, Vygotsky confines himself to "the new significative use of the word, its use *as a means of concept forma-tion*." In opposition both to associative theorists and to those who favor tele-ological causation by way of cultural tasks, he says this use "is the immediate psychological cause of the radical change in the intellectual process that occurs on the threshold of adolescence."[34]

The point is that, along Vygotskyan lines precisely, the connection between a child's grasp of language and its use of prelinguistic thought and perception must lie with their functional convergence. An *awareness* of the propositional function of language and all it entails cannot pop up out of nothing. So the only reasonable assumption is that such an awareness results from a dawning and reflexive grasp of what is already functionally present in the prelinguistic material from which it emerges. Only a theory like the heuristic analysis of

---

[33] Cf. *ibid.*, Ch. 2.
[34] *Ibid.*, p. 59.

prelinguistic thought and perception could sustain an empirical account like Vygotsky's, which eschews the charge that learning a first language is like learning a second.

Here, then, Vygotsky fails to examine the implications of concept formation on the part of prelinguistic animals or human infants. He concerns himself only with the threshold phenomenon of learning to conceive by means of words.

Hence he specifies neither the nature of linguistic mastery nor the functional nature of prelinguistic conception on which verbal conception must depend. He is primarily concerned with the continuity between the two phases of development, but he has no way of specifying the functional resemblance among the developing stages.

The force of this conclusion may be appreciated by considering this. In "thinking in complexes," which Vygotsky calls "the second major phase on the way to concept formation," a child "unites" objects by way of "bonds actually existing between these objects" whenever the child notices that one object is similar to a nuclear or sample object—say, "in shape or in size, *or in any other attribute that happens to strike him.*"[35] But to say this is to fix the puzzle that needs to be explicated.

One may therefore agree, with Vygotsky, that "there is no rigid correspondence between the units of thought and speech."[36] But the question remains: What is the structure of thought? One may agree that "a word devoid of thought is a dead thing." But it is either false or trivially true to hold that "a thought unembodied in words remains a shadow."[37]

Vygotsky's own genetic method precludes the claim and calls for an explanation that he apparently fails to supply. The heuristic model accommodates the "different structures" of thought and speech. It obviates the need to reduce first-language learning to second-language learning. And it provides for the functional continuity of prelinguistic and linguistic competences.

---

[35] *Ibid.*, pp. 61–62. Italics added.
[36] *Ibid.*, p. 149.
[37] *Ibid.*, p. 153.

Bibliography

ARMSTRONG, D. M. *Perception and the Physical World*. London: Routledge & Kegan Paul, 1961.

AUSTIN, J. L. *Sense and Sensibilia*. G. J. Warnock (ed.). Oxford: Clarendon Press, 1962.†

AYER, A. J. *The Foundations of Empirical Knowledge*. London: Macmillan, 1940.*

———. *The Problem of Knowledge*. Harmondsworth: Penguin, 1956.*

CHISHOLM, RODERICK M. *Perceiving*. Ithaca, N.Y.: Cornell University Press, 1957.

———. *Theory of Knowledge*. Englewood Cliffs, N.J.: Prentice-Hall, 1966.*

CHOMSKY, NOAM. *Cartesian Linguistics*. New York: Harper & Row, 1966.†

DRETSKE, FRED I. *Seeing and Knowing*. Chicago: University of Chicago Press, 1969.

HAMLYN, D. W. *The Psychology of Perception*. London: Routledge & Kegan Paul, 1957.

———. *Sensation and Perception*. London: Routledge & Kegan Paul, 1961.

HILL, T. E. *Contemporary Theories of Knowledge*. New York: Ronald Press, 1961.

HIRST, R. J. *The Problems of Perception*. London: Allen & Unwin, 1959.

——— (ed.). *Perception and the External World*. New York: Macmillan, 1965.*

LOCKE, DON. *Perception and Our Knowledge of the External World*. London: Allen & Unwin, 1967.

MERLEAU-PONTY, M. *Phenomenology of Perception*, trans. Colin Smith. London: Routledge & Kegan Paul, 1962.

MOORE, G. E. *Some Main Problems of Philosophy*. London: Allen & Unwin, 1953.†

PITCHER, GEORGE. *The Causal Theory of Perception*. Princeton: Princeton University Press, 1969.

PRICE, H. H. *Perception* (2nd ed.). London: Methuen, 1950.

QUINTON, ANTHONY. "The Problem of Perception." *Mind*, LXIV (1955), 18–51.

ROLLINS, C. D. (ed.). *Knowledge and Experience*. Pittsburgh: University of Pittsburgh Press, 1963.

RYLE, GILBERT. *Dilemmas*. Cambridge: Cambridge University Press, 1954.†

SIBLEY, F. N. (ed.). *Perceiving. A Philosophical Symposium*. London: Methuen, 1971.

SMYTHIES, J. R. *Analysis of Perception*. London: Routledge & Kegan Paul, 1956.

SOLTIS, J. F. *Seeing, Knowing, and Believing*. London: Allen & Unwin, 1966.

STICH, STEPHEN P. (ed.). *Innate Ideas*. Berkeley: University of California Press, 1975.*

SWARTZ, R. J. (ed.). *Perceiving, Sensing, and Knowing*. New York: Doubleday, 1965.*

VESEY, GODFREY. *Perception*. Garden City, N.Y.: Anchor Books, 1971.*

WARNOCK, G. J. (ed.). *The Philosophy of Perception*. London: Oxford University Press, 1967.*

* Paperback edition.   † Also available in paperback edition.

IV

LANGUAGE
AND MEANING

Language is man's most distinctive accomplishment. There is evidence that chimpanzees can learn a portion of human language, but by and large language is uniquely human. It is *par excellence* the medium for representing the features of the external world as well as for representing the mental states of speakers. It is a shared medium.

With language a community of speakers can state, query, direct, and the like. With language what is represented is linked to characteristic human concerns—assignment of truth values, compliance with requests or orders, disclosure of feelings, ceremonial acknowledgment. In this respect, language is an admittedly specialized though varied form of human interaction and use and exploitation of a public world. So seen, it has an undoubted survival value. The characteristic purposes, interests, intentions of human existence must inform the special activity of speech.

The thesis that speech can be characterized only in terms of the activity of human societies may be taken to qualify all aspects of the theory of language. First of all is the question of precisely what kinds of acts can be performed using language. The issue must surely have concerned philosophers from ancient times. But only recently have the beginnings of a theory of speech acts, acts performed distinctively by using language, been formulated in a way that directly and profoundly affects other parts of the theory of language.

The pioneer effort, here, belongs to the late J. L. Austin (IV:8). He introduced the distinction between illocutionary acts performed merely *in* using language (stating or querying, for instance) and perlocutionary acts employing language *by* which an intended effect on others is produced (warning or threatening, for instance). The distinction is difficult to maintain. Even with illocutionary acts, some sort of successful "uptake" is required. Furthermore, a reasoned scheme for the classification of all speech acts is needed.

Austin's earliest schema (presented in our selection) contrasts the performative and the constative utterance (the first, an utterance by which to perform an action; the second, an utterance that can be true or false), but Austin's dissatisfaction is already explicit in that account. The performative utterance, Austin was persuaded, could not be adequately identified by any purely verbal means, though, as with promising, advising, and the like, he remained fascinated with the peculiar role of performative *verbs*, whereby in relevant utterances one performs a certain act in using the appropriate verb in the first person.

At the same time, Austin had to concede that constative utterances were a kind of performance or act, what in his more mature account he sorted out as illocutionary and perlocutionary acts. Utterances using performative verbs yield a subdivision of illocutionary acts (though they may also yield perlocutionary acts). One can advise another with or without using the locution "I advise," though the asymmetry of "I advise" and "He advises," with regard to acts performed, remains obvious.

Austin's developed account of the variety of speech acts was intuitive and not altogether systematic. The effort to formulate the necessary and sufficient conditions of (at least) a specimen speech act, in Austin's sense of a speech act, has been pursued by John Searle (IV:10). But Searle's effort shows the extraordinary difficulties plaguing the venture. For one thing, it requires attention to speakers' intentions. Another difficulty is that the analysis of promising (Searle's specimen speech act) requires attention to many other nonverbal aspects of the circumstances under which speakers perform the acts they do. The result is that we are obliged to note the impossibility of freeing the theory of language from larger considerations bearing on the theory of human action.

The limitation of the speech-act model, on the linguistic side, is best seen in pursuing two fundamental notions in the theory of language: meaning and reference. Notwithstanding the larger bearing of the puzzles of human action and cognition on the explanation of its functioning through changes over time, language may be dissected without the intrusion of the speaker's intention at every point of analysis.

The various theories of meaning and of reference formulated during the nineteenth and twentieth centuries tend to favor that approach. Their advocates are not satisfied that a speech-act model provides an adequate basis for the analysis of language. Among the more relevant recent accounts are Hilary Putnam's theory of the meaning of words (IV:4) and Saul Kripke's theory of reference (see Part II). In somewhat similar ways, both eschew the speech-act model in order to isolate a more fundamental sense in which particular words have assignable meanings (Putnam) or particular names and descriptions designate things or persons about which we may speak and hold beliefs (Kripke).

Putnam provides a strategy for distinguishing changes in meaning and changes in belief. He shows how the meaning of a "natural kind" term like "lemon" or "whale" may be fixed, atypical specimens may be admitted, and beliefs about the things denoted may change with time and new discovery. For example, Putnam wishes to regard the expression "one-legged man" as not self-contradictory even though men normally have two legs. Again, it may well be proved that lemons are yellow when mature only because of a prevalent disease.

Putnam shows that the meaning of a term need not determine its reference. On the other hand the analytic/synthetic distinction (the distinction between truths that depend on the meaning of a string of words and truths that depend on states of affairs) may be supported in a relativized form. The second issue is explored in greater detail in Part II—which also explains our attention here to Kripke's view.

Kripke's account shows in an equally inventive way why a proper name cannot be replaced by purely qualitative predicates, no matter how complex. Thus, insofar as "Nixon" designates the man Nixon, it cannot be supposed that "Nixon" means any of the things that befell Nixon. For instance, "Nixon was named 'Nixon,'" "Nixon was President of the United States," "Nixon married Pat" all affirm what might have been false of Nixon.

If any of these predicates were taken to give the meaning of "Nixon," the relevant sentences would become tautological—which would be anomalous. The only thing that could not befall Nixon is that Nixon might not have been Nixon. Here, Kripke does not wish to deny that Nixon might never have existed or that there might never have existed anyone having the characteristics of Nixon. He insists on only one point. Given that there is an actual individual, Nixon (not necessarily an individual named "Nixon"), that individual cannot fail to be the individual he is. A *fortiori*, he cannot fail to possess whatever properties are essential to his being that individual. This is the sense in which Kripke introduces what he himself terms essentialism (mentioned in Part II).

Descriptions, then, may be contingently or even necessarily true of what is named, but purely qualitative or descriptive predicates can neither give the meaning nor determine the referent of a name. Both explicitly and implicitly, Kripke's account is directed against the traditional views of Gottlob Frege (IV:5) and Bertrand Russell (IV:6) as well as the intended reform of P. F. Strawson's (IV:7) and the influential view offered by W. V. Quine (IV:9).

Frege's account is generally regarded as beginning the modern resolution of the problem of reference. His principal concern, in this respect, was to explain how sentences using codesignative terms (names or descriptions designating the same thing), as in "Aristotle is Aristotle" and "Aristotle was the Stagirite teacher of Alexander the Great," could yet differ in being or not being tautological.

Frege attempts to resolve the puzzle by distinguishing between the object a name designates and the characterization under which the object is so designated. His thesis is that two names or terms may designate one thing. But he also insists that two such distinct names or terms designate the same thing because different criteria are applied, thus making the names differ in their sense. "Aristotle is Aristotle" and "Aristotle is the Stagirite teacher of Alexander the Great" are thus both true because there was an actual man Aristotle, and he was born in Stagira. But although "Aristotle" and "the Stagirite teacher of Alexander the Great" designate Aristotle, they do so in different ways.

Still, Frege did not show how to fix the assignable sense of a given proper name, and he admits that people may disagree about the sense that a proper name expresses. He also holds that where a name has no bearer, where it designates nothing, the sentence in which it appears is neither true nor false. This introduces the vexing problem of so-called truth-value gaps.

In one of the most celebrated of modern philosophical papers, Bertrand Russell attempts to deal with Frege's problem by providing a scheme for paraphrasing "denoting phrases." Russell thinks this avoids the anomaly of appearing to refer to nonexistent entities ("the present King of France") and thereby clarifies the sense in which related statements are false ("The present King of France is bald").

The point is retrospectively important because Strawson, in criticizing Russell's account, introduces truth-value gaps for sentences like "The present King of France is bald" when the referring expression is purportedly *used to refer* to the present King of France. Since there is none, the speech act (in effect) is thwarted and what was said can be neither true nor false—hence, truth-value gaps. But this maneuver is extremely inconvenient if we maintain that it should be possible to assign truth-conditions to any sentence, even if we cannot determine its truth or falsity.

Strawson's approach further complicates the picture by distinguishing between referring and denoting as well as between expressions and their use. Russell, Strawson believes, wrongly blends these distinctions and in effect fails to take into account the speech-act features of the situation. Thus Russell is misled into thinking that the actual referring *use* of a proper name or definite description can be captured by a descriptive expression.

Quine's concern in the present essay, which predates Strawson's by several years, lies chiefly with replacing apparent names like "Pegasus" with frankly invented "unanalyzable irreducible attributes" like "being Pegasus" or "pegasizing." This device eliminates truth-value gaps and the inconvenience of "possible entities" or "unactualized possibles." But apart from whether one could refer to what is not yet actual ("the house that my contractor will build here"), Quine goes contrary to Strawson's and Kripke's views and treats proper names as if they could be replaced by purely qualitative predicates. Quine's solution may promise aid with respect to apparent reference to nonexistent entities. But the generalized practice he proposes either suggests essential properties (which Quine would wish to avoid) or produces tautologies where normally they would not be expected.

The problems of the theory of meaning and language pervade the history of philosophy, but they have been focused in a systematic way largely in our own century. The distinctive work of contemporary philosophy has centered on the nature of language and the relationship between language and the world. Charles Sanders Peirce (IV:1) is perhaps the first philosopher of importance to have made the analysis of meaning the pivotal question of his professional endeavor. His main philosophical contribution was pragmatism, which he believed his followers misread as a theory of truth rather than of meaning (see Part II). Interestingly, pragmatism anticipates versions of the verifiability theory of meaning advanced by the positivists or logical empiricists (see Moritz Schlick [IV:2]).

Peirce's account enables us to appreciate the strategy of testing proposed theories of meaning. Ironically, he had difficulty with the management of dispositional terms (for instance, the hardness of a diamond that is destroyed before it can be tested). And this difficulty points prophetically to the characteristic difficulties of the verifiability theory, as well as of Peirce's own concept of "the long run."

The appeal of Peirce's account lies with the broadly biological context of meaning that he provides more than with any of his criteria for determining the meaning of any notion. This is perhaps the most hospitable way in which to understand his pronouncement that the meaning of our concepts is completely given by a tally of the habits they produce.

The verifiability theory of meaning is the most sustained cooperative effort to puzzle out what we mean by the "meaning" of sentences. Actually, among the logical positivists and their close critics, two rather different questions have been regulary confused with one another. The first is the question of criteria of significance—that is, conditions for deciding that given sentences *are meaningful*. The second is the question of sense itself—that is, rules by which to specify *the meaning* of given sentences. Considerations of both sorts have led to doctrines of what we mean by the "meaning" of sentences. Yet to give the meaning of sentences is to presuppose that the sentences are meaningful, but to determine that they *are* meaningful is not to give their meaning.

Moritz Schlick was, with Rudolf Carnap, the most prominent among the logical positivists. In advancing his own version of the verifiability theory of meaning, Schlick appears to be providing a rule for specifying the meaning of sentences as well as a criterion for determining whether given sentences are meaningful. However, several irreversible entailments are evident in the theory of meaning. First of all, to verify that a given statement is true entails that the test be relevant to the meaning. Second, to determine the meaning of a statement entails that the statement have a meaning.

These considerations pose a difficulty for Schlick's thesis—and to all verificationist theories. Assigning a way to verify a given statement or proposition entails being able to determine that the verification mode is relevant to the statement. This suggests that a statement's meaning cannot be its mode of verification. Its being verifiable, in fact, seems to depend on its being meaningful.

It may be that any meaningful statement is verifiable, though this is debatable. For one thing, we might conceive of circumstances under which a given statement would be true yet not be able to formulate any way to verify the statement. We might, for instance, understand how the conjecture that every even number greater than two is the sum of two primes (Goldbach's conjecture) could be true but not have any idea how to verify it.

For another thing, the verifiability theory itself is presumably meaningful but unverifiable. Apart from such general objections, no advocate of the verifiability theory has formulated a version that does not exhibit serious flaws.

Schlick's approach fails to mark off nonsense sentences as a class. Also, it presupposes a class of basic sentences as paradigms of meaningfulness without accounting for their privileged status (see Part II).

Finally, sentences important for the systematization of science are especially difficult to reconcile with the verifiability thesis—in particular, so-called nomic universals (laws of nature), counterfactual statements (subjunctive conditionals), and negative existentials (for example, "There are no unicorns"). Carl Hempel (IV:3) comprehensively surveys the various transformations of the empiricist criterion of meaning that the positivists (and critics such as Karl Popper) adopted.

In effect, the verifiability theory survives only as a monument of an excessive requirement on meaningfulness. Yet it represents the most sustained philosophical effort to formulate the conditions of meaningfulness in the spirit of the empirical sciences and of logic and mathematics. In that regard, it represents the unavoidable attraction of linking the concepts of meaning and truth.

Meaning

1

C. S. Peirce
How to Make Our Ideas Clear

Charles Sanders Peirce (1839–1914) is generally regarded as the greatest native American philosopher. He had a decisive influence on William James, Josiah Royce, and John Dewey—all of whom acknowledged their debt explicitly—as well as on a host of others. He was an extraordinarily productive man of extraordinarily diverse abilities. He made original contributions to astronomy and physics and seems to have made discoveries regarding logical quantifiers independently of, but a few years later than, Frege.

His voluminous Collected Papers (1931–1935; 1958) cover nearly every topic in philosophy and reflect substantial periodic changes. He himself was an original who found it difficult to remain within the academic community, though he taught briefly at Johns Hopkins and though William James, who befriended him, tried to help him at Harvard.

Many doctrines are distinctively Peirce's, some more productive than others; it is not always easy to sort the eccentric from the genuinely inventive in his work. But among the inventive, one must include Peirce's original theory of signs. In it knowledge and meaning presuppose a triadic relationship involving what serves as a sign, what it signifies, and what (or whom) it serves. Signhood proves to be a particularly important instance of a pure triadic relation.

Peirce was occupied during much of his productive life with the categories he called Firstness, Secondness, and Thirdness, which were concerned with monadic ascriptions and dyadic and triadic relations. He was insistent on the irreducibility of triadic relations, but held that higher n–adic relations could be generated from the others. The material aspect of these categories Peirce associated respectively with quality or suchness, thisness, and a conceptual mediation of which signhood is a leading instance.

Peirce also subscribed to synechism, a doctrine that the world contained series that could not be restricted to discrete elements (although discrete elements might be generated from them). He subscribed as well to a doctrine he called tychism, that

Reprinted by permission of the publishers from Charles Hartshorne and Paul Weiss, editors, *The Collected Papers of Charles Sanders Peirce*, Vol. V (Cambridge, Mass.: The Belknap Press of Harvard University Press), Secs. 2–3, pp. 255–265, Copyright © 1934, 1962 by the President and Fellows of Harvard College.

there is absolute chance in the real universe. In view of his evolutionism, this led to the thesis that the world evolves from an original chaos, through developing "habits," so that the laws of nature are hardly fixed.

His most characteristic contribution, pragmatism (see Part II), was itself understood in terms of an evolutionary harmony of inquiry in accord with the evolution of the world. This gives Peirce's conception of "the long run" a distinctive import. Most of this superstructure of occasionally bizarre theory was ignored in the wider reception of pragmatism.

The most tantalizing of Peirce's conceptions involves the pragmatic anticipation of positivist and operationalist theories of meaning and the conception of abduction. In the first, Peirce links the meaning of a term or concept to test conditions under which its "practical effects" may be discerned. But he failed to solve the implicit problem of conditional statements (if . . . then . . .) in which the antecedent of a given statement is known to be contrary to fact and yet the entire statement need not be false or meaningless.

With the conception of abduction Peirce made a fresh start on the logical constraints of plausibility that bear on the selection of promising hypotheses from among an infinitude of possible hypotheses.

The Pragmatic Maxim

And what, then, is belief? It is the demi-cadence which closes a musical phrase in the symphony of our intellectual life. We have seen that it has just three properties: First, it is something that we are aware of; second, it appeases the irritation of doubt, which is the motive for thinking, thought relaxes, and comes to rest for a moment when belief is reached. But, since belief is a rule for action, the application of which involves further doubt and further thought, at the same time that it is a stopping-place, it is also a new starting-place for thought. That is why I have permitted myself to call it thought at rest, although thought is essentially an action. The *final* upshot of thinking is the exercise of volition, and of this thought no longer forms a part; but belief is only a stadium of mental action, an effect upon our nature due to thought, which will influence future thinking.

The essence of belief is the establishment of a habit; and different beliefs are distinguished by the different modes of action to which they give rise. If beliefs do not differ in this respect, if they appease the same doubt by producing the same rule of action, then no mere differences in the manner of consciousness of them can make them different beliefs, any more than playing a tune in different keys is playing different tunes. Imaginary distinctions are often drawn between beliefs which differ only in their mode of expression;—the wrangling which ensues is real enough, however. To believe that any objects are arranged among themselves as in Fig. 1, and to believe that they are arranged [as] in Fig. 2, are one and the same belief; yet it is conceivable that a man should assert one proposition and deny the other. Such false distinctions do as much harm as the confusion of beliefs really different, and are among the pitfalls of which we ought constantly to beware, especially when we are upon metaphysical ground. One singular deception of this sort, which often occurs, is

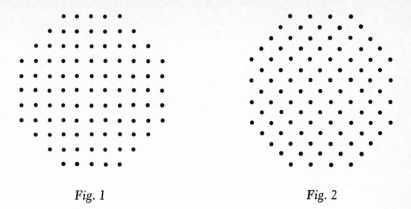

Fig. 1   Fig. 2

to mistake the sensation produced by our own unclearness of thought for a character of the object we are thinking. Instead of perceiving that the obscurity is purely subjective, we fancy that we contemplate a quality of the object which is essentially mysterious; and if our conception be afterward presented to us in a clear form we do not recognize it as the same, owing to the absence of the feeling of unintelligibility. So long as this deception lasts, it obviously puts an impassable barrier in the way of perspicuous thinking; so that it equally interests the opponents of rational thought to perpetuate it, and its adherents to guard against it.

Another such deception is to mistake a mere difference in the grammatical construction of two words for a distinction between the ideas they express. In this pedantic age, when the general mob of writers attend so much more to words than to things, this error is common enough. When I just said that thought is an *action,* and that it consists in a *relation,* although a person performs an action but not a relation, which can only be the result of an action, yet there was no inconsistency in what I said, but only a grammatical vagueness.

From all these sophisms we shall be perfectly safe so long as we reflect that the whole function of thought is to produce habits of action; and that whatever there is connected with a thought, but irrelevant to its purpose, is an accretion to it, but no part of it. If there be a unity among our sensations which has no reference to how we shall act on a given occasion, as when we listen to a piece of music, why we do not call that thinking. To develop its meaning, we have, therefore, simply to determine what habits it produces, for what a thing means is simply what habits it involves. Now, the identity of a habit depends on how it might lead us to act, not merely under such circumstances as are likely to arise, but under such as might possibly occur, no matter how improbable they may be. What the habit is depends on *when* and *how* it causes us to act. As for the *when,* every stimulus to action is derived from perception; as for the *how,* every purpose of action is to produce some sensible result. Thus, we come down to what is tangible and conceivably practical, as the root of every real distinction of thought, no matter how subtle it may be;

and there is no distinction of meaning so fine as to consist in anything but a possible difference of practice.

To see what this principle leads to, consider in the light of it such a doctrine as that of transubstantiation. The Protestant churches generally hold that the elements of the sacrament are flesh and blood only in a tropical sense; they nourish our souls as meat and the juice of it would our bodies. But the Catholics maintain that they are literally just meat and blood; although they possess all the sensible qualities of wafer-cakes and diluted wine. But we can have no conception of wine except what may enter into a belief, either—

1. That this, that, or the other, is wine; or,
2. That wine possesses certain properties.

Such beliefs are nothing but self-notifications that we should, upon occasion, act in regard to such things as we believe to be wine according to the qualities which we believe wine to possess. The occasion of such action would be some sensible perception, the motive of it to produce some sensible result. Thus our action has exclusive reference to what affects the senses, our habit has the same bearing as our action, our belief the same as our habit, our conception the same as our belief; and we can consequently mean nothing by wine but what has certain effects, direct or indirect, upon our senses; and to talk of something as having all the sensible characters of wine, yet being in reality blood, is senseless jargon. Now, it is not my object to pursue the theological question; and having used it as a logical example I drop it, without caring to anticipate the theologian's reply. I only desire to point out how impossible it is that we should have an idea in our minds which relates to anything but conceived sensible effects of things. Our idea of anything *is* our idea of its sensible effects; and if we fancy that we have any other we deceive ourselves, and mistake a mere sensation accompanying the thought for a part of the thought itself. It is absurd to say that thought has any meaning unrelated to its only function. It is foolish for Catholics and Protestants to fancy themselves in disagreement about the elements of the sacrament, if they agree in regard to all their sensible effects, here and hereafter.

It appears, then, that the rule for attaining . . . clearness of apprehension is as follows: Consider what effects, that might conceivably have practical bearings, we conceive the object of our conception to have. Then, our conception of these effects is the whole of our conception of the object.

Some Applications of the Pragmatic Maxim

Let us illustrate this rule by some examples; and, to begin with the simplest one possible, let us ask what we mean by calling a thing *hard*. Evidently that it will not be scratched by many other substances. The whole conception of this quality, as of every other, lies in its conceived effects. There is absolutely no difference between a hard thing and a soft thing so long as they are not brought to the test. Suppose, then, that a diamond could be crystallized in the midst of a cushion of soft cotton, and should remain there until it was finally burned up. Would it be false to say that that diamond was soft? This seems a foolish question, and would be so, in fact, except in the realm of logic. There such questions are often of the greatest utility as serving to bring logical principles into sharper relief than real discussions ever could. In studying logic we must not put them aside with hasty answers, but must consider them with attentive care, in order to make out the principles involved. We may, in the present case, modify our question, and ask what prevents us from saying that all hard bodies remain perfectly soft until they are touched, when their hardness increases with the pressure until they are scratched. Reflection will show that the reply is this: there would be no *falsity* in such modes of speech. They would involve a modification of our present usage of speech with regard to the words hard and soft, but not of their meanings. For they represent no fact to be different from what it is; only they involve arrangements of facts which would be exceedingly maladroit. This leads us to remark that the question of what would occur under circumstances which do not actually arise is not a question of fact, but only of the most perspicuous arrangement of them. For example, the question of free-will and fate in its simplest form, stripped of verbiage, is something like this: I have done something of which I am ashamed; could I, by an effort of the will, have resisted the temptation, and done otherwise? The philosophical reply is, that this is not a question of fact, but only of the arrangement of facts. Arranging them so as to exhibit what is particularly pertinent to my question—namely, that I ought to blame myself for having done wrong—it is perfectly true to say that, if I had willed to do otherwise than I did, I should have done otherwise. On the other hand, arranging the facts so as to exhibit another important consideration, it is equally true that, when a temptation has once been allowed to work, it will, if it has a certain force, produce its effect, let me struggle how I may. There is no objection to a contradiction in what would result from a false supposition. The *reductio ad absurdum* consists in showing that contradictory results would follow from a hypothesis which is consequently judged to be false. Many questions are involved in the free-will discussion, and I am far from desiring to say that both sides are equally right. On the contrary, I am of opinion that one side denies important facts, and that the other does not. But what I do say is, that the above single question was the origin of the whole doubt; that, had it not been for this question, the controversy would never have arisen; and that this question is perfectly solved in the manner which I have indicated.

Let us next seek a clear idea of Weight. This is another very easy case. To say that a body is heavy means simply that, in the absence of opposing force, it will fall. This (neglecting certain specifications of how it will fall, etc., which exist in the mind of the physicist who uses the word) is evidently the whole conception of weight. It is a fair question whether some particular facts may not *account* for gravity; but what we mean by the force itself is completely involved in its effects.

This leads us to undertake an account of the idea of Force in general. This is the great conception which, developed in the early part of the seventeenth century from the rude idea of a cause, and constantly improved upon since, has shown us how to explain all the changes of motion which bodies experience, and how to think about all physical phenomena; which has given birth to modern science, and changed the face of the globe; and which, aside from its more special uses, has played a principal part in directing the course of modern thought, and in furthering modern social development. It is, therefore, worth some pains to comprehend it. According to our rule, we must begin by asking what is the immediate use of thinking about force; and the answer is, that we thus account for changes of motion. If bodies were left to themselves, without the intervention of forces, every motion would continue unchanged both in velocity and in direction. Furthermore, change of motion never takes place abruptly; if its direction is changed, it is always through a curve without angles; if its velocity alters, it is by degrees. The gradual changes which are constantly taking place are conceived by geometers to be compounded together according to the rules of the parallelogram of forces. If the reader does not already know what this is, he will find it, I hope, to his advantage to endeavor to follow the following explanation; but if mathematics are insupportable to him, pray let him skip three paragraphs rather than we should part company here.

A *path* is a line whose beginning and end are distinguished. Two paths are considered to be equivalent, which, beginning at the same point, lead to the same point. Thus the two paths, A B C D E and A F G H E (Fig. 3), are equivalent. Paths which do *not* begin at the same point are considered to be equivalent, provided that, on moving either of them without turning it, but keeping it always parallel to its original position, when its beginning coincides with that of the other path, the ends also coincide. Paths are considered as geometrically added together, when one begins where the other ends; thus the path A E is conceived to be a sum of A B, B C, C D, and D E. In the parallelogram of Fig. 4 the diagonal A C is the sum of A B and B C; or, since A D is geometrically equivalent to B C, A C is the geometrical sum of A B and A D.

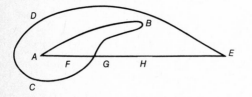

Fig. 3

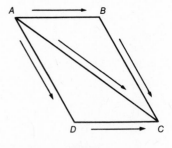

Fig. 4

All this is purely conventional. It simply amounts to this: that we choose to call paths having the relations I have described equal or added. But, though it is a convention, it is a convention with a good reason. The rule for geometrical addition may be applied not only to paths, but to any other things which can be represented by paths. Now, as a path is determined by the varying direction and distance of the point which moves over it from the starting-point, it follows that anything which from its beginning to its end is determined by a varying direction and a varying magnitude is capable of being represented by a line. Accordingly, *velocities* may be represented by lines, for they have only directions and rates. The same thing is true of *accelerations*, or changes of velocities. This is evident enough in the case of velocities; and it becomes evident for accelerations if we consider that precisely what velocities are to positions—namely, states of change of them—that accelerations are to velocities.

The so-called "parallelogram of forces" is simply a rule for compounding accelerations. The rule is, to represent the accelerations by paths, and then to geometrically add the paths. The geometers, however, not only use the "parallelogram of forces" to compound different accelerations, but also to resolve one acceleration into a sum of several. Let A B (Fig. 5) be the path which represents a certain acceleration—say, such a change in the motion of a body that at the end of one second the body will, under the influence of that change, be in a position different from what it would have had if its motion had continued unchanged such that a path equivalent to A B would lead from the latter position to the former. This acceleration may be considered as the sum of the accelerations represented by A C and C B. It may also be considered as the sum of the very different accelerations represented by A D and D B, where A D is almost the opposite of A C. And it is clear that there is an immense variety of ways in which A B might be resolved into the sum of two accelerations.

After this tedious explanation, which I hope, in view of the extraordinary interest of the conception of force, may not have exhausted the reader's patience, we are prepared at last to state the grand fact which this conception embodies. This fact is that if the actual changes of motion which the different particles of bodies experience are each resolved in its appropriate way, each component

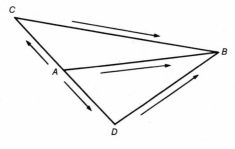

Fig. 5

acceleration is precisely such as is prescribed by a certain law of Nature, according to which bodies, in the relative positions which the bodies in question actually have at the moment,[1] always receive certain accelerations, which, being compounded by geometrical addition, give the acceleration which the body actually experiences.

This is the only fact which the idea of force represents, and whoever will take the trouble clearly to apprehend what this fact is, perfectly comprehends what force is. Whether we ought to say that a force *is* an acceleration, or that it *causes* an acceleration, is a mere question of propriety of language, which has no more to do with our real meaning than the difference between the French idiom "*Il fait froid*" and its English equivalent "*It is cold.*" Yet it is surprising to see how this simple affair has muddled men's minds. In how many profound treatises is not force spoken of as a "mysterious entity," which seems to be only a way of confessing that the author despairs of ever getting a clear notion of what the word means! In a recent admired work on *Analytic Mechanics* it is stated that we understand precisely the effect of force, but what force itself is we do not understand! This is simply a self-contradiction. The idea which the word force excites in our minds has no other function than to affect our actions, and these actions can have no reference to force otherwise than through its effects. Consequently, if we know what the effects of force are, we are acquainted with every fact which is implied in saying that a force exists, and there is nothing more to know. The truth is, there is some vague notion afloat that a question may mean something which the mind cannot conceive; and when some hair-splitting philosophers have been confronted with the absurdity of such a view, they have invented an empty distinction between positive and negative conceptions, in the attempt to give their non-idea a form not obviously nonsensical. The nullity of it is sufficiently plain from the considerations given a few pages back; and, apart from those considerations, the quibbling character of the distinction must have struck every mind accustomed to real thinking.

. . .

---

[1] Possibly the velocities also have to be taken into account.

2

Moritz Schlick
Meaning and Verification

Moritz Schlick (1882–1936) was Professor of Philosophy at the University of Vienna. He was shot to death by a deranged student, who apparently had once before attempted to take Schlick's life.

Schlick founded the famous Vienna Circle and arranged for Rudolf Carnap's lectureship at Vienna. The Circle was the center for the influential movement of the 1920s and 1930s known as logical positivism, which Schlick and Carnap led; it was dissolved with Schlick's tragic death. Schlick was motivated early to oppose the Kantian emphasis on the synthetic a priori (see Part II). He denied that there were such truths about the empirical world, though he seems to have hedged with respect to mathematics.

Schlick's extensive writings are gradually being translated. These include Space and Time in Contemporary Physics. An Introduction to the Theory of Relativity and Gravitation *(1917, 1919);* General Theory of Knowledge *(1918, 1925);* Vom Sinn des Lebens *(1927);* Problems of Ethics *(1930);* The Future of Philosophy *(1932);* Gesetz, Kausalität und Wahrscheinlichkeit *(1948); and* Philosophy of Nature *(1948). He is best known for his papers bearing on the verifiability theory of meaning (in particular, "Meaning and Verification," 1936, included here).*

Schlick stressed that verifiability means possibility of verification. But he failed to meet objections regarding the relevance of procedures for verifying a given proposition. He was drawn to but not satisfied with the thesis that natural laws are not verifiable propositions but directives of a sort. Generally, he sought to refine the sense in which analytic and empirical statements could be distinguished on the one hand, and metaphysics and the empirical sciences could be distinguished on the other. He seems to have favored a somewhat pragmatic solution, not actually satisfactory from the vantage point of his strenuous thesis.

I

Philosophical questions, as compared with ordinary scientific problems, are always strangely paradoxical. But it seems to be an especially strange paradox that the question concerning the meaning of a proposition should constitute a serious philosophical difficulty. For is it not the very nature and purpose of every proposition to express its own meaning? In fact, when we are confronted with a proposition (in a language familiar to us) we usually know its meaning immediately. If we do not, we can have it explained to us, but the explanation

From Moritz Schlick, "Meaning and Verification," *The Philosophical Review,* XLV (1936), 339–349, 352–353. Reprinted by permission of *The Philosophical Review.*

will consist of a new proposition; and if the new one is capable of expressing the meaning, why should not the original one be capable of it? So that a snippy person when asked what he meant by a certain statement might be perfectly justified in saying, 'I meant exactly what I said!'

It is logically legitimate and actually the normal way in ordinary life and even in science to answer a question concerning the meaning of a proposition by simply repeating it either more distinctly or in slightly different words. Under what circumstances, then, can there be any sense in asking for the meaning of a statement which is well before our eyes or ears?

Evidently the only possibility is that we have not *understood* it. And in this case what is actually before our eyes or ears is nothing but a series of words which we are unable to handle; we do not know how to use it, how to 'apply it to reality'. Such a series of words is for us simply a complex of signs 'without meaning', a mere sequel of sounds or a mere row of marks on paper, and we have no right to call it 'a proposition' at all; we may perhaps speak of it as 'a sentence'.

If we adopt this terminology we can now easily get rid of our paradox by saying that we cannot inquire after the meaning of a proposition, but can ask about the meaning of a sentence, and that this amounts to asking, 'What proposition does the sentence stand for?' And this question is answered either by a proposition in a language with which we are already perfectly familiar; or by indicating the logical rules which will makes a proposition out of the sentence, *i.e.*, will tell us exactly in what circumstances the sentence is to be *used*. These two methods do not actually differ in principle; both of them give meaning to the sentence (transform it into a proposition) by locating it, as it were, within the system of a definite language; the first method making use of a language which is already in our possession, the second one building it up for us. The first method represents the simplest kind of ordinary 'translation'; the second one affords a deeper insight into the nature of meaning, and will have to be used in order to overcome philosophical difficulties connected with the understanding of sentences.

The source of these difficulties is to be found in the fact that very often we do not know how to handle our own words; we speak or write without having first agreed upon a definite logical grammar which will constitute the signification of our terms. We commit the mistake of thinking that we know the meaning of a sentence (*i.e.*, understand it as a proposition) if we are familiar with all the words occurring in it. But this is not sufficient. It will not lead to confusion or error as long as we remain in the domain of everyday life by which our words have been formed and to which they are adapted, but it will become fatal the moment we try to think about abstract problems by means of the same terms without carefully fixing their signification for the new purpose. For every word has a definite signification only within a definite context into which it has been fitted; in any other context it will have no meaning unless we provide new rules for the use of the word in the new case, and this may be done, at least in principle, quite arbitrarily.

Let us consider an example. If a friend should say to me, 'Take me to a country where the sky is three times as blue as in England!' I should not know how to fulfill his wish; his phrase would appear nonsensical to me, because the word 'blue' is used in a way which is not provided for by the rules of our language. The combination of a numeral and the name of a color does not occur in it; therefore my friend's sentence has no meaning, although its exterior linguistic form is that of a command or a wish. But he can, of course, give it a meaning. If I ask him, 'What do you mean by "three times as blue"?', he can arbitrarily indicate certain definite physical circumstances concerning the serenity of the sky which he wants his phrase to be the description of. And then, perhaps, I shall be able to follow his directions, his wish will have become meaningful for me.

Thus, whenever we ask about a sentence, 'What does it mean?', what we expect is instruction as to the circumstances in which the sentence is to be used; we want a description of the conditions under which the sentence will form a *true* proposition, and of those which will make it *false*. The meaning of a word or a combination of words is, in this way, determined by a set of rules which regulate their use and which, following [Ludwig—Ed.] Wittgenstein, we may call the rules of their *grammar*, taking this word in its widest sense.

(If the preceding remarks about meaning are as correct as I am convinced they are, this will, to a large measure, be due to conversations with Wittgenstein which have greatly influenced my own views about these matters. I can hardly exaggerate my indebtedness to this philosopher. I do not wish to impute to him any responsibility for the contents of this article, but I have reason to hope that he will agree with the main substance of it.)

Stating the meaning of a sentence amounts to stating the rules according to which the sentence is to be used, and this is the same as stating the way in which it can be verified (or falsified). The meaning of a proposition is the method of its verification.

The 'grammatical' rules will partly consist of ordinary definitions, *i.e.*, explanations of words by means of other words, partly of what are called 'ostensive' definitions, *i.e.*, explanations by means of a procedure which puts the words to actual use. The simplest form of an ostensive definition is a pointing gesture combined with the pronouncing of the word, as when we teach a child the signification of the sound 'blue' by showing a blue object. But in most cases the ostensive definition is of more complicated form; we cannot point to an object corresponding to words like 'because', 'immediate', complex situations, and the meaning of the words is defined by the way we use them in these different situations.

It is clear that in order to understand a verbal definition we must know the signification of the explaining words beforehand, and that the only explanation which can work without any previous knowledge is the ostensive definition. We conclude that there is no way of understanding any meaning without ultimate reference to ostensive definitions, and this means, in an obvious sense, reference to 'experience' or 'possibility of verification'.

This is the situation, and nothing seems to me simpler or less questionable. It is this situation and nothing else that we describe when we affirm that the meaning of a proposition can be given only by giving the rules of its verification in experience. (The addition, 'in experience', is really superfluous, as no other kind of verification has been defined.)

This view has been called the "experimental theory of meaning"; but it certainly is no theory at all, for the term 'theory' is used for a set of hypotheses about a certain subject-matter, and there are no hypotheses involved in our view, which proposes to be nothing but a simple statement of the way in which meaning is *actually* assigned to propositions, both in everyday life and in science. There has never been any other way, and it would be a grave error to suppose that we believe we have discovered a new conception of meaning which is contrary to common opinion and which we want to introduce into philosophy. On the contrary, our conception is not only entirely in agreement with, but even derived from, common sense and scientific procedure. Although our criterion of meaning has always been employed in practice, it has very rarely been formulated in the past, and this is perhaps the only excuse for the attempts of so many philosophers to deny its feasibility.

The most famous case of an explicit formulation of our criterion is [Albert —Ed.] Einstein's answer to the question, What do we mean when we speak of two events at distant places happening simultaneously? This answer consisted in a description of an experimental method by which the simultaneity of such events was actually ascertained. Einstein's philosophical opponents maintained —and some of them still maintain—that they knew the meaning of the above question independently of any method of verification. All I am trying to do is to stick consistently to Einstein's position and to admit no exceptions from it. (Professor [P.—Ed.] Bridgman's book on *The Logic of Modern Physics* is an admirable attempt to carry out this program for all concepts of physics.) I am not writing for those who think that Einstein's philosophical opponents were right.

II

Professor C. I. Lewis, in a remarkable address on "Experience and Meaning" (published in . . . [*Philosophical*] *Review*, March 1934), has justly stated that the view developed above (he speaks of it as the "empirical-meaning requirement") forms the basis of the whole philosophy of what has been called the "logical positivism of the Viennese Circle". He criticizes this basis as inadequate chiefly on the ground that its acceptance would impose certain limitations upon "significant philosophic discussion" which, at some points, would make such discussion altogether impossible and, at other points, restrict it to an intolerable extent.

.   .   .

The mere statement that no sentence has meaning unless we are able to indicate a way of testing its truth or falsity is not very useful if we do not explain very carefully the signification of the phrases 'method of testing' and 'verifiability'.

.   .   .

How do we define verifiability?

In the first place I should like to point out that when we say that "a proposition has meaning only if it is verifiable" we are not saying ". . . if it is *verified*". This simple remark does away with one of the chief objections; the "here and now predicament", as Professor Lewis calls it, does not exist any more. We fall into the snares of this predicament only if we regard verification itself as the criterion of meaning, instead of 'possibility of verification' (= verifiability); this would indeed lead to a "reduction to absurdity of meaning". Obviously the predicament arises through some fallacy by which these two notions are confounded. I do not know if [Bertrand—Ed.] Russell's statement, "Empirical knowledge is confined to what we actually observe" (quoted by Professor Lewis), must be interpreted as containing this fallacy, but it would certainly be worth while to discover its genesis.

Let us consider the following argument which Professor Lewis discusses, but which he does not want to impute to anyone:

> Suppose it maintained that no issue is meaningful unless it can be put to the test of decisive verification. And no verification can take place except in the immediately present experience of the subject. Then nothing can be meant except what is actually present in the experience in which that meaning is entertained.

This argument has the form of a conclusion drawn from two premisses. Let us for the moment assume the second premiss to be meaningful and true. You will observe that even then the conclusion does *not* follow. For the first premiss assures us that the issue has meaning if it *can* be verified; the verification does not have to take place, and therefore it is quite irrelevant whether it can take place in the future or in the present only. Apart from this, the second premiss is, of course, nonsensical; for what fact could possibly be described by the sentence 'verification can take place only in present experience'? Is not verifying an act or process like hearing or feeling bored? Might we not just as well say that I can hear or feel bored only in the present moment? And what could I mean by this? The particular nonsense involved in such phrases will become clearer when we speak of the 'egocentric predicament' later on; at present we are content to know that our empirical-meaning postulate has nothing whatever to do with the now-predicament. 'Verifiable' does not even mean 'verifiable here now'; much less does it mean 'being verified now'.

Perhaps it will be thought that the only way of making sure of the verifiability of a proposition would consist in its actual verification. But we shall soon see that this is not the case.

There seems to be a great temptation to connect meaning and the 'immediately given' in the wrong way; and some of the Viennese positivists may have yielded to this temptation, thereby getting dangerously near to the fallacy we have just been describing. Parts of [Rudolph—Ed.] Carnap's *Logischer Aufbau der Welt* [*The Logical Structure of the World*], for instance, might be interpreted as implying that a proposition about future events did not really refer to the future at all but asserted only the present existence of certain expectations (and, similarly, speaking about the past would really mean speaking about present memories). But it is certain that the author of that book does not hold such a view now, and that it cannot be regarded as a teaching of the new positivism. On the contrary, we have pointed out from the beginning that our definition of meaning does not imply such absurd consequences, and when someone asked, "But how can you verify a proposition about a future event?", we replied, "Why, for instance, by waiting for it to happen! 'Waiting' is a perfectly legitimate method of verification".

.   .   .

III

Verifiability means possibility of verification. Professor Lewis justly remarks that to "omit all examination of the wide range of significance which could attach to 'possible verification', would be to leave the whole conception rather obscure". For our purpose it suffices to distinguish between two of the many ways in which the word 'possibility' is used. We shall call them 'empirical possibility' and 'logical possibility'. Professor Lewis describes two meanings of 'verifiability' which correspond exactly to this difference; he is fully aware of it, and there is hardly anything left for me to do but carefully to work out the distinction and show its bearing upon our issue.

I propose to call 'empirically possible' anything that does not contradict the laws of nature. This is, I think, the largest sense in which we may speak of empirical possibility; we do not restrict the term to happenings which are not only in accordance with the laws of nature but also with the actual state of the universe (where 'actual' might refer to the present moment of our own lives, or to the condition of human beings on this planet, and so forth). If we chose the latter definition (which seems to have been in Professor Lewis's mind when he spoke of "possible experience as conditioned by the actual") we should not get the sharp boundaries we need for our present purpose. So 'empirical possibility' is to mean 'compatibility with natural laws'.

Now, since we cannot boast of a complete and sure knowledge of nature's laws, it is evident that we can never assert with certainty the empirical possibility of any fact, and here we may be permitted to speak of *degrees* of possibility. Is it possible for me to lift this book? Surely!—This table? I think so!—This billiard table? I don't think so!—This automobile? Certainly not!—It is clear that in these cases the answer is given by *experience*, as the result of experiments performed in the past. Any judgment about empirical possibility is based on experience and will often be rather uncertain; there will be no sharp boundary between possibility and impossibility.

Is the possibility of verification which we insist upon of this empirical sort? In that case there would be different degrees of verifiability, the question of meaning would be a matter of more or less, not a matter of yes or no. In many disputes concerning our issue it is the empirical possibility of verification which is discussed; the various examples of verifiability given by Professor Lewis, *e.g.*, are instances of different empirical circumstances in which the verification is carried out or prevented from being carried out. Many of those who refuse to accept our criterion of meaning seem to imagine that the procedure of its application in a special case is somewhat like this: A proposition is presented to us ready made, and in order to discover its meaning we have to try various methods of verifying or falsifying it, and if one of these methods works we have found the meaning of the proposition; but if not, we say it has no meaning. If we really had to proceed in this way, it is clear that the determination of meaning would be entirely a matter of experience, and that in many cases no sharp and ultimate decision could be obtained. How could we ever know that we had tried long enough, if none of our methods were successful? Might not future efforts disclose a meaning which we were unable to find before?

This whole conception is, of course, entirely erroneous. It speaks of meaning as if it were a kind of entity inherent in a sentence and hidden in it like a nut in its shell, so that the philosopher would have to crack the shell or sentence in order to reveal the nut or meaning. We know from our considerations in section I that a proposition cannot be given 'ready made'; that meaning does not inhere in a sentence where it might be discovered, but that it must be bestowed upon it. And this is done by applying to the sentence the rules of the logical grammar of our language, as explained in section I. These rules are not facts of nature which could be 'discovered', but they are prescriptions stipulated by acts of definition. And these definitions have to be known to those who pronounce the sentence in question and to those who hear or read it. Otherwise they are not confronted with any proposition at all, and there is nothing they could try to verify, because you can't verify or falsify a mere row of words. You cannot even start verifying before you know the meaning, *i.e.*, before you have established the possibility of verification.

In other words, the possibility of verification which is relevant to meaning cannot be of the empirical sort; it cannot be established *post festum* [after the fact—Ed.]. You have to be sure of it before you can consider the empirical circumstances and investigate whether or no or under what conditions they will permit of verification. The empirical circumstances are all-important when you want to know if a proposition is *true* (which is the concern of the scientist), but they can have no influence on the *meaning* of the proposition (which is the concern of the philosopher). Professor Lewis has seen and expressed this very clearly, and our Vienna positivism, as far as I can answer for it, is in complete agreement with him on this point. It must be emphasized that when we speak of verifiability we mean *logical* possibility of verification, and nothing but this.

. . .

The dividing line between logical possibility and impossibility of verification is absolutely sharp and distinct; there is no gradual transition between meaning and nonsense. For either you have given the grammatical rules for verification, or you have not; *tertium non datur* [there is no third possibility—Ed.].

Empirical possibility is determined by the laws of nature, but meaning and verifiability are entirely independent of them. Everything that I can describe or define is logically possible—and definitions are in no way bound up with natural laws. The proposition 'Rivers flow uphill' is meaningful, but happens to be false because the fact it describes is *physically* impossible. It will not deprive a proposition of its meaning if the conditions which I stipulate for its verification are incompatible with the laws of nature; I may prescribe conditions, for instance, which could be fulfilled only if the velocity of light were greater than it actually is, or if the Law of Conservation of Energy did not hold, and so forth.

An opponent of our view might find a dangerous paradox or even a contradiction in the preceding explanations, because on the one hand we insisted so strongly on what has been called the *"empirical*-meaning requirement"*, and on the other hand we assert most emphatically that meaning and verifiability do not depend on any empirical conditions whatever, but are determined by purely logical possibilities. The opponent will object: if meaning is a matter of experience, how can it be a matter of definition and logic?

In reality there is no contradiction or difficulty. The word 'experience' is ambiguous. Firstly, it may be a name for any so-called 'immediate data'—which is a comparatively modern use of the word—and secondly we can use it in the sense in which we speak *e.g.*, of an 'experienced traveller', meaning a man who has not only seen a great deal but also knows how to profit from it for his actions. It is in this second sense (by the way, the sense the word has in Hume's and Kant's philosophy) that verifiability must be declared to be independent of experience. The possibility of verification does not rest on any 'experiential truth', on a law of nature or any other true general proposition, but is determined solely by our definitions, by the rules which have been fixed for our language, or which we can fix arbitrarily at any moment. All of these rules ultimately point to ostensive definitions, as we have explained, and through them verifiability is linked to *experience* in the *first* sense of the word. No rule of expression presupposes any law or regularity in the world (which is the condition of 'experience' as Hume and Kant use the word), but it does presuppose data and situations, to which names can be attached. The rules of language are rules of the application of language; so there must be something to which it can be applied. Expressibility and verifiability are one and the same thing. There is no antagonism between logic and experience. Not only can the logician be an empiricist at the same time; he *must* be one if he wants to understand what he himself is doing.

·　　·　　·

3

Carl G. Hempel

Empiricist Criteria of Cognitive Significance: Problems and Changes

Carl G. Hempel was originally a member of the so-called Berlin group, which was associated with the Vienna Circle in the 1930s. He has been Stuart Professor of Philosophy at Princeton University since 1955. He is particularly known for authoritatively examining the internal difficulties of the verifiability theory of meaning advanced by the positivists ("Problems and Changes in the Empiricist Criterion of Meaning," 1950) and for developing the so-called covering law model of scientific explanation ("Studies in the Logic of Explanation," 1948, in collaboration with P. Oppenheim). He extended the model later to accommodate , probabilistic laws and also attempted to apply his account to explanation in historical contexts. On the model, events are explained in that statements describing them are deduced from general laws and statements of antecedent conditions.

Hempel is also noted for his discovery of the so-called paradoxes of confirmation (also known as the raven paradoxes). These concern the fact that certain statements appear to be confirmatory of some hypothesis when equivalent statements are not. The seemingly anomalous results Hempel took to be illusory, but deeper questions remain as to whether what accords with a hypothesis actually confirms it.

Hempel explored the distinction between observational and theoretical terms, adopting a more flexible conception of meaningfulness than the positivists, by conceding the intelligibility of theories that yield a partial interpretation in observational terms. His most compendious effort appears in Aspects of Scientific Explanation (1965).

1. The General Empiricist Conception of Cognitive and Empirical Significance

It is a basic principle of contemporary empiricism that a sentence makes a cognitively significant assertion, and thus can be said to be either true or false, if and only if either (1) it is analytic or contradictory—in which case it is said to have purely logical meaning or significance—or else (2) it is capable, at least potentially, of test by experiential evidence—in which case it is said to have

From Carl G. Hempel, *Aspects of Scientific Explanation* (New York and London: 1965), Essay IV, pp. 101–119. This essay combines, with certain omissions and some other changes, the contents of two articles: "Problems and Changes in the Empiricist Criterion of Meaning," *Revue Internationale de Philosophie*, No. 11 (1950), 41–63; and "The Concept of Cognitive Significance: A Reconsideration," *Proceedings of the American Academy of Arts and Sciences*, 80 (1951), 61–77. Reprinted by permission of the Director of *Revue Internationale de Philosophie*; *Daedalus*, Journal of the American Academy of Arts and Sciences; and the author.

empirical meaning or significance. The basic tenet of this principle, and especially of its second part, the so-called testability criterion of empirical meaning (or better: meaningfulness), is not peculiar to empiricism alone: it is characteristic also of contemporary operationism, and in a sense of pragmatism as well; for the pragmatist maxim that a difference must make a difference to be a difference may well be construed as insisting that a verbal difference between two sentences must make a difference in experiential implications if it is to reflect a difference in meaning.

How this general conception of cognitively significant discourse led to the rejection, as devoid of logical and empirical meaning, of various formulations in speculative metaphysics, and even of certain hypotheses offered within empirical science, is too well known to require recounting. I think that the general intent of the empiricist criterion of meaning is basically sound, and that notwithstanding much oversimplification in its use, its critical application has been, on the whole, enlightening and salutary. I feel less confident, however, about the possibility of restating the general idea in the form of precise and general criteria which establish sharp dividing lines (a) between statements of purely logical and statements of empirical significance, and (b) between those sentences which do have cognitive significance and those which do not.

In the present paper, I propose to reconsider these distinctions as conceived in recent empiricism, and to point out some of the difficulties they present. The discussion will concern mainly the second of the two distinctions; in regard to the first, I shall limit myself to a few brief remarks.

2. The Earlier Testability Criteria of Meaning and Their Shortcomings

Let us note first that any general criterion of cognitive significance will have to meet certain requirements if it is to be at all acceptable. Of these, we note one, which we shall consider here as expressing a necessary, though by no means sufficient, *condition of adequacy* for criteria of cognitive significance.

(A) If under a given criterion of cognitive significance, a sentence N is nonsignificant, then so must be all truth-functional compound sentences in which N occurs nonvacuously as a component. For if N cannot be significantly assigned a truth value, then it is impossible to assign truth values to the compound sentences containing N; hence, they should be qualified as nonsignificant as well.

We note two corollaries of requirement (A):

(A1) If under a given criterion of cognitive significance, a sentence S is nonsignificant, then so must be its negation, $\sim S$.

(A2) If under a given criterion of cognitive significance, a sentence N is nonsignificant, then so must be any conjunction $N \cdot S$ and any disjunction $N v S$, no matter whether S is significant under the given criterion or not.

We now turn to the initial attempts made in recent empiricism to establish general criteria of cognitive significance. Those attempts were governed by the consideration that a sentence, to make an empirical assertion must be capable of being borne out by, or conflicting with, phenomena which are potentially capable of being directly observed. Sentences describing such potentially observable phenomena—no matter whether the latter do actually occur or not—may be called observation sentences. More specifically, an *observation sentence* might be construed as a sentence—no matter whether true or false—which asserts or denies that a specified object, or group of objects, of macroscopic size has a particular *observable characteristic*, i.e., a characteristic whose presence or absence can, under favorable circumstances, be ascertained by direct observation.

The task of setting up criteria of empirical significance is thus transformed into the problem of characterizing in a precise manner the relationship which obtains between a hypothesis and one or more observation sentences whenever the phenomena described by the latter either confirm or disconfirm the hypothesis in question. The ability of a given sentence to enter into that relationship to some set of observation sentences would then characterize its testability-in-principle, and thus its empirical significance. Let us now briefly examine the major attempts that have been made to obtain criteria of significance in this manner.

One of the earliest criteria is expressed in the so-called *verifiability requirement*. According to it, a sentence is empirically significant if and only if it is not analytic and is capable, at least in principle, of complete verification by observational evidence; i.e., if observational evidence can be described which, if actually obtained, would conclusively establish the truth of the sentence. With the help of the concept of observation sentence, we can restate this requirement as follows: A sentence S has empirical meaning if and only if it is possible to indicate a finite set of observation sentences, $O_1, O_2, \ldots, O_n$, such that if these are true, then S is necessarily true, too. As stated, however, this condition is satisfied also if S is an analytic sentence or if the given observation sentences are logically incompatible with each other. By the following formulation, we rule these cases out and at the same time express the intended criterion more precisely:

(2.1) REQUIREMENT OF COMPLETE VERIFIABILITY IN PRINCIPLE. A sentence has empirical meaning if and only if it is not analytic and follows logically from some finite and logically consistent class of observation sentences. These observation sentences need not be true, for what the criterion is to explicate is testability by "potentially observable phenomena," or testability "in principle."

In accordance with the general conception of cognitive significance outlined earlier, a sentence will now be classified as cognitively significant if either it is analytic or contradictory, or it satisfies the verifiability requirement.

This criterion, however, has several serious defects. One of them has been noted by several writers:

a. Let us assume that the properties of being a stork and of being red-legged are both observable characteristics, and that the former does not logically entail the latter. Then the sentence

(S1) All storks are red-legged

is neither analytic nor contradictory; and clearly, it is not deducible from a finite set of observation sentences. Hence, under the contemplated criterion, S1 is devoid of empirical significance; and so are all other sentences purporting to express universal regularities or general laws. And since sentences of this type constitute an integral part of scientific theories, the verifiability requirement must be regarded as overly restrictive in this respect.

Similarly, the criterion disqualifies all sentences such as 'For any substance there exists some solvent', which contain both universal and existential quantifiers (i.e., occurrences of the terms 'all' and 'some' or their equivalents); for no sentences of this kind can be logically deduced from any finite set of observation sentences.

Two further defects of the verifiability requirement do not seem to have been widely noticed:

b. As is readily seen, the negation of S1

($\sim$S1) There exists at least one stork that is not red-legged

is deducible from any two observation sentences of the type 'a is a stork' and 'a is not red-legged'. Hence, $\sim$S1 is cognitively significant under our criterion, but S1 is not, and this constitutes a violation of condition (A1).

c. Let S be a sentence which does, and N a sentence which does not satisfy the verifiability requirement. Then S is deducible from some set of observation sentences; hence, by a familiar rule of logic, SvN is deducible from the same set, and therefore cognitively significant according to our criterion. This violates condition (A2) above.

Strictly analogous considerations apply to an alternative criterion, which makes complete falsifiability in principle the defining characteristic of empirical significance. Let us formulate this criterion as follows:

(2.2) REQUIREMENT OF COMPLETE FALSIFIABILITY IN PRINCIPLE.   A sentence has empirical meaning if and only if its negation is not analytic and follows logically from some finite logically consistent class of observation sentences.

This criterion qualifies a sentence as empirically meaningful if its negation satisfies the requirements of complete verifiability; as it is to be expected, it is therefore inadequate on similar grounds as the latter:

(a) It denies cognitive significance to purely existential hypotheses, such as 'There exists at least one unicorn', and all sentences whose formulation calls for mixed—i.e., universal and existential—quantification, such as 'For every compound there exists some solvent', for none of these can possibly be conclusively falsified by a finite number of observation sentences.

(b) If 'P' is an observation predicate, then the assertion that all things have the property P is qualified as significant, but its negation, being equivalent to a purely existential hypothesis, is disqualified [cf. (a)]. Hence, criterion (2.2) gives rise to the same dilemma as (2.1).

(c) If a sentence S is completely falsifiable whereas N is a sentence which is not, then their conjunction, S·N (i.e., the expression obtained by connecting the two sentences by the word 'and') is completely falsifiable; for if the negation of S is entailed by a class of observation sentences, then the negation of S·N is, *a fortiori* [inescapably—Ed.], entailed by the same class. Thus, the criterion allows empirical significance to many sentences which an adequate empiricist criterion should rule out, such as 'All swans are white and the absolute is perfect.'

In sum, then, interpretations of the testability criterion in terms of complete verifiability or of complete falsifiability are inadequate because they are overly restrictive in one direction and overly inclusive in another, and because both of them violate the fundamental requirement A.

Several attempts have been made to avoid these difficulties by construing the testability criterion as demanding merely a partial and possibly indirect confirmability of empirical hypotheses by observational evidence.

A formulation suggested by [A. J.—Ed.] Ayer is characteristic of these attempts to set up a clear and sufficiently comprehensive criterion of confirmability. It states, in effect, that a sentence S has empirical import if from S in conjunction with suitable subsidiary hypotheses it is possible to derive observation sentences which are not derivable from the subsidiary hypotheses alone.

This condition is suggested by a closer consideration of the logical structure of scientific testing; but it is much too liberal as it stands. Indeed, as Ayer himself has pointed out in the second edition of his book, *Language, Truth, and Logic*, his criterion allows empirical import to any sentence whatever. Thus, e.g., if S is the sentence 'The absolute is perfect', it suffices to choose as a subsidiary hypothesis the sentence 'If the absolute is perfect then this apple is red' in order to make possible the deduction of the observation sentence 'This apple is red', which clearly does not follow from the subsidiary hypothesis alone.

To meet this objection, Ayer proposed a modified version of his testability criterion. In effect, the modification restricts the subsidiary hypotheses mentioned in the previous version to sentences which either are analytic or can independently be shown to be testable in the sense of the modified criterion.

But it can readily be shown that this new criterion, like the requirement of complete falsifiability, allows empirical significance to any conjunction $S \cdot N$, where S satisfies Ayer's criterion while N is a sentence such as 'The absolute is perfect', which is to be disqualified by that criterion. Indeed, whatever consequences can be deduced from S with the help of permissible subsidiary hypotheses can also be deduced from $S \cdot N$ by means of the same subsidiary hypotheses; and as Ayer's new criterion is formulated essentially in terms of the deducibility of a certain type of consequence from the given sentence, it countenances $S \cdot N$ together with S. Another difficulty has been pointed out by [Alonzo—Ed.] Church, who has shown that if there are any three observation sentences none of which alone entails any of the others, then it follows for any sentence S whatsoever that either it or its denial has empirical import according to Ayer's revised criterion.

All the criteria considered so far attempt to explicate the concept of empirical significance by specifying certain logical connections which must obtain between a significant sentence and suitable observation sentences. It seems now that this type of approach offers little hope for the attainment of precise criteria of meaningfulness: this conclusion is suggested by the preceding survey of some representative attempts, and it receives additional support from certain further considerations, some of which will be presented in the following sections.

3. Characterization of Significant Sentences by Criteria for Their Constituent Terms

An alternative procedure suggests itself which again seems to reflect well the general viewpoint of empiricism: It might be possible to characterize cognitively significant sentences by certain conditions which their constituent terms have to satisfy. Specifically, it would seem reasonable to say that all extralogical terms in a significant sentence must have experiential reference, and that therefore their meanings must be capable of explication by reference to observables exclusively. In order to exhibit certain analogies between this approach and the previous one, we adopt the following terminological conventions:

Any term that may occur in a cognitively significant sentence will be called a *cognitively significant term*. Furthermore, we shall understand by an *observation term* any term which either (a) is an *observation predicate*, i.e., signifies some observable characteristic (as do the terms 'blue', 'warm', 'soft', 'coincident with', 'of greater apparent brightness than') or (b) names some physical object of macroscopic size (as do the terms 'the needle of this instrument', 'the Moon', 'Krakatoa Volcano', 'Greenwich, England', 'Julius Caesar').

Now while the testability criteria of meaning aimed at characterizing the cognitively significant sentences by means of certain inferential connections in which they must stand to some observation sentences, the alternative approach under consideration would instead try to specify the vocabulary that may be used in forming significant sentences. This vocabulary, the class of significant terms, would be characterized by the condition that each of its elements is either a logical term or else a term with empirical significance; in the latter case, it has to stand in certain definitional or explicative connections to some observation terms. This approach certainly avoids any violations of our earlier conditions of adequacy. Thus, e.g., if S is a significant sentence, i.e., contains cognitively significant terms only, then so is its denial, since the denial sign, and its verbal equivalents, belong to the vocabulary of logic and are thus significant. Again, if N is a sentence containing a non-significant term, then so is any compound sentence which contains N.

But this is not sufficient, of course. Rather, we shall now have to consider a crucial question analogous to that raised by the previous approach: Precisely how are the logical connections between empirically significant terms and observation terms to be construed if an adequate criterion of cognitive significance is to result? Let us consider some possibilities.

(3.1) THE SIMPLEST CRITERION THAT SUGGESTS ITSELF MIGHT BE CALLED THE REQUIREMENT OF DEFINABILITY. It would demand that any term with empirical significance must be explicitly definable by means of observation terms.

This criterion would seem to accord well with the maxim of operationism that all significant terms of empirical science must be introduced by operational definitions. However, the requirement of definability is vastly too restrictive, for many important terms of scientific and even pre-scientific discourse cannot be explicitly defined by means of observation terms.

In fact, as [Rudolf—Ed.] Carnap has pointed out, an attempt to provide explicit definitions in terms of observables encounters serious difficulties as soon as disposition terms, such as 'soluble', 'malleable', 'electric conductor', etc., have to be accounted for; and many of these occur even on the pre-scientific level of discourse.

Consider, for example, the word 'fragile'. One might try to define it by saying that an object x is fragile if and only if it satisfies the following condition: If at any time t the object is sharply struck, then it breaks at that time. But if the statement connectives in this phrasing are construed truth-functionally, so that the definition can be symbolized by

(D) $Fx \equiv (t) (Sxt \supset Bxt)$

then the predicate 'F' thus defined does not have the intended meaning. For let a be any object which is not fragile (e.g., a raindrop or a rubber band), but which happens not to be sharply struck at any time throughout its existence. Then 'Sat' is false and hence '$Sat \supset Bat$' is true for all values of 't'; consequently, 'Fa' is true though a is not fragile.

To remedy this defect, one might construe the phrase 'if . . . then . . .' in the original definiens as having a more restrictive meaning than the truth-functional conditional. This meaning might be suggested by the subjunctive phrasing 'If x were to be sharply struck at any time t, then x would break at t.' But a satisfactory elaboration of this construal would require a clarification of the meaning and the logic of counterfactual and subjunctive conditional, which is a thorny problem.

An alternative procedure was suggested by Carnap in his theory of reduction sentences. These are sentences which, unlike definitions, specify the meaning of a term only conditionally or partially. The term 'fragile', for example, might be introduced by the following reduction sentence:

(R) $(x) (t) [Sxt \supset (Fx \equiv Bxt)]$

which specifies that if x is sharply struck at any time t, then x is fragile if and only if x breaks at t.

Our earlier difficulty is now avoided, for if a is a nonfragile object that is never sharply struck, then that expression in R which follows the quantifiers is true of a; but this does not imply that 'Fa' is true. But the reduction sentence R specifies the meaning of 'F' only for application to those objects which meet the "test condition" of being sharply struck at some time; for these it states that fragility then amounts to breaking. For objects that fail to meet the test condition, the meaning of 'F' is left undetermined. In this sense, reduction sentences have the character of partial or conditional definitions.

Reduction sentences provide a satisfactory interpretation of the experiential import of a large class of disposition terms and permit a more adequate formulation of so-called operational definitions, which, in general, are not complete definitions at all. These considerations suggest a greatly liberalized alternative to the requirement of definability:

(3.2) THE REQUIREMENT OF REDUCIBILITY. Every term with empirical significance must be capable of introduction, on the basis of observation terms, through chains of reduction sentences.

This requirement is characteristic of the liberalized versions of positivism and physicalism which, since about 1936, have superseded the older, overly narrow conception of a full definability of all terms of empirical science by means of observables, and it avoids many of the shortcomings of the latter. Yet, reduction sentences do not seem to offer an adequate means for the introduction of the central terms of advanced scientific theories, often referred to as theoretical constructs. This is indicated by the following considerations: A chain of reduction sentences provides a necessary and a sufficient condition for the applicability of the term it introduces. (When the two conditions coincide, the chain is tantamount to an explicit definition.) But now take, for example, the concept of length as used in classical physical theory. Here, the length in centimeters of the distance between two points may assume any positive real number as its value; yet it is clearly impossible to formulate, by means of observation terms, a sufficient condition for the applicability of such expressions as 'having a length of $\sqrt{2}$ cm' and 'having a length of $\sqrt{2} + 10^{-100}$ cm'; for such conditions would provide a possibility for discrimination, in observational terms, between two lengths which differ by only 10^{-100} cm.

It would be ill-advised to argue that for this reason, we ought to permit only such values of the magnitude, length, as permit the statement of sufficient conditions in terms of observables. For this would rule out, among others, all irrational numbers and would prevent us from assigning to the diagonal of a square with sides of length 1, the length $\sqrt{2}$, which is required by Euclidean geometry. Hence, the principles of Euclidean geometry would not be universally applicable in physics. Similarly, the principles of the calculus would become inapplicable, and the system of scientific theory as we know it today would be reduced to a clumsy, unmanageable torso. This, then, is no way of meeting the difficulty. Rather, we shall have to analyze more closely the function of constructs in scientific theories, with a view to obtaining through such an anlysis a more adequate characterization of cognitively significant terms.

Theoretical constructs occur in the formulation of scientific theories. These may be conceived of, in their advanced stages, as being stated in the form of deductively developed axiomatized systems. Classical mechanics, or Euclidean or some Non-Euclidean form of geometry in physical interpretation, present examples of such systems. The extralogical terms used in a theory of this kind may be divided, in familiar manner, into primitive or basic terms, which are not defined within the theory, and defined terms, which are explicitly defined by means of the primitives. Thus, e.g., in [David—Ed.] Hilbert's axiomatization of Euclidean geometry, the terms 'point', 'straight line', 'between' are among the primitives, while 'line segment', 'angle', 'triangle', 'length' are among the defined terms. The basic and the defined terms together with the terms of logic constitute the vocabulary out of which all the sentences of the theory are constructed. The latter are divided, in an axiomatic presentation, into primitive statements (also called postulates or basic statements) which, in the theory, are not derived from any other statements, and derived ones, which are obtained by logical deduction from the primitive statements.

From its primitive terms and sentences, an axiomatized theory can be developed by means of purely formal principles of definition and deduction, without any consideration of the empirical significance of its extralogical terms. Indeed, this is the standard procedure employed in the axiomatic development of uninterpreted mathematical theories such as those of abstract groups or rings or lattices, or any form of pure (i.e., noninterpreted) geometry.

However, a deductively developed system of this sort can constitute a scientific theory only if it has received an empirical interpretation which renders it relevant to the phenomena of our experience. Such interpretation is given by assigning a meaning, in terms of observables, to certain terms or sentences of the formalized theory. Frequently, an interpretation is given not for the primitive terms or statements but rather for some of the terms definable by means of the primitives, or for some of the sentences deducible from the postulates. Furthermore, interpretation may amount to only a partial assignment of meaning. Thus, e.g., the rules for the measurement of length by means of a standard rod may be considered as providing a *partial* empirical interpretation for the term 'the length, in centimeters, of interval *i*', or alternatively, for some sentences of the form 'the length of interval *i* is *r* centimeters'. For the method is applicable only to intervals of a certain medium size, and even for the latter it does not constitute a full interpretation since the use of a standard rod does not constitute the only way of determining length: various alternative procedures are available involving the measurement of other magnitudes which are connected, by general laws, with the length that is to be determined.

This last observation, concerning the possibility of an indirect measurement of length by virtue of certain laws, suggests an important reminder. It is not correct to speak, as is often done, of "the experiential meaning" of a term or a sentence in isolation. In the language of science, and for similar reasons even in pre-scientific discourse, a single statement usually has no experiential implications. A single sentence in a scientific theory does not, as a rule, entail any observation sentences; consequences asserting the occurrence of certain observable phenomena can be derived from it only by conjoining it with a set of other, subsidiary, hypotheses. Of the latter, some will usually be observation sentences, others will be previously accepted theoretical statements. Thus, e.g., the relativistic theory of the deflection of light rays in the gravitational field of the sun entails assertions about observable phenomena only if it is conjoined with a considerable body of astronomical and optical theory as well as a large number of specific statements about the instruments used in those observations of solar eclipses which serve to test the hypothesis in question.

Hence, the phrase 'the experiential meaning of expression *E*' is elliptical: What a given expression "means" in regard to potential empirical data is relative to two factors, namely:

I. *the linguistic framework L* to which the expression belongs. Its rules determine, in particular, what sentences—observational or otherwise—may be inferred from a given statement or class of statements;

II. the theoretical context in which the expression occurs, i.e., the class of those statements in *L* which are available as subsidiary hypotheses.

Thus, the sentence formulating [Isaac—Ed.] Newton's law of gravitation has no experiential meaning by itself; but when used in a language whose logical apparatus permits the development of the calculus, and when combined with a suitable system of other hypotheses—including sentences which connect some of the theoretical terms with observation terms and thus establish a partial interpretation—then it has a bearing on observable phenomena in a large variety of fields. Analogous considerations are applicable to the term 'gravitational field', for example. It can be considered as having experiential meaning only within the context of a theory, which must be at least partially interpreted; and the experiential meaning of the term—as expressed, say, in the form of operational criteria for its application—will depend again on the theoretical system at hand, and on the logical characteristics of the language within which it is formulated.

4. Cognitive Significance as a Characteristic of Interpreted Systems

The preceding considerations point to the conclusion that a satisfactory criterion of cognitive significance cannot be reached through the second avenue of approach here considered, namely by means of specific requirements for the terms which make up significant sentences. This result accords with a general characteristic of scientific (and, in principle, even pre-scientific) theorizing: Theory formation and concept formation go hand in hand; neither can be carried on successfully in isolation from the other.

If, therefore, cognitive significance can be attributed to anything, then only to entire theoretical systems formulated in a language with a well-determined structure. And the decisive mark of cognitive significance in such a system appears to be the existence of an interpretation for it in terms of observables. Such an interpretation might be formulated, for example, by means of conditional or biconditional sentences connecting nonobservational terms of the system with observation terms in the given language; the latter as well as the connecting sentences may or may not belong to the theoretical system.

But the requirement of partial interpretation is extremely liberal; it is satisfied, for example, by the system consisting of contemporary physical theory combined with some set of principles of speculative metaphysics, even if the latter have no empirical interpretation at all. Within the total system, these metaphysical principles play the role of what K. Reach and also O. Neurath liked to call *isolated sentences:* They are neither purely formal truths or falsehoods, demonstrable or refutable by means of the logical rules of the given language system; nor do they have any experiential bearings; i.e., their omission from the theoretical system would have no effect on its explanatory and predictive power in regard to potentially observable phenomena (i.e., the kind of phenomena described by observation sentences). Should we not, therefore, require that a cognitively significant system contain no isolated sentences? The following criterion suggests itself:

(4.1) A THEORETICAL SYSTEM IS COGNITIVELY SIGNIFICANT IF AND ONLY IF IT IS PARTIALLY INTERPRETED TO AT LEAST SUCH AN EXTENT THAT NONE OF ITS PRIMITIVE SENTENCES IS ISOLATED.

But this requirement may bar from a theoretical system certain sentences which might well be viewed as permissible and indeed desirable. By way of a simple illustration, let us assume that our theoretical system T contains the primitive sentence

(S1) $(x) [P_1 x \supset (Qx \equiv P_2 x)]$

where 'P_1' and 'P_2' are observation predicates in the given language L, while 'Q' functions in T somewhat in the manner of a theoretical construct and occurs in only one primitive sentence of T, namely S1. Now S1 is not a truth or falsehood of formal logic; and furthermore, if S1 is omitted from the set of primitive sentences of T, then the resulting system, T', possesses exactly the same systematic, i.e., explanatory and predictive, power as T. Our contemplated criterion would therefore qualify S1 as an isolated sentence which has to be eliminated—excised by means of Occam's razor, as it were—if the theoretical system at hand is to be cognitively significant.

But it is possible to take a much more liberal view of S1 by treating it as a partial definition for the theoretical term 'Q'. Thus conceived, S1 specifies that in all cases where the observable characteristic P_1 is present, 'Q' is applicable if and only if the observable characteristic P_2 is present as well. In fact, S1 is an instance of those partial, or conditional, definitions which Carnap calls bilateral reduction sentences. These sentences are explicitly qualified by Carnap as analytic (though not, of course, as truths of formal logic), essentially on the ground that all their consequences which are expressible by means of observation predicates (and logical terms) alone are truths of formal logic.

Let us pursue this line of thought a little further. This will lead us to some observations on analytic sentences and then back to the question of the adequacy of (4.1).

Suppose that we add to our system T the further sentence

(S2) $(x) [P_3x \supset (Qx \equiv P_4x)]$

where 'P_3', 'P_4' are additional observation predicates. Then, on the view that "every bilateral reduction sentence is analytic", S2 would be analytic as well as S1. Yet, the two sentences jointly entail non-analytic consequences which are expressible in terms of observation predicates alone, such as

(O) $(x) [\sim (P_1x \cdot P_2x \cdot P_3x \cdot \sim P_4x) \cdot \sim (P_1x \cdot \sim P_2x \cdot P_3x \cdot P_4x)]$

But one would hardly want to admit the consequence that the conjunction of two analytic sentences may be synthetic. Hence if the concept of analyticity can be applied at all to the sentences of interpreted deductive systems, then it will have to be relativized with respect to the theoretical context at hand. Thus, e.g., S1 might be qualified as analytic relative to the system T, whose remaining postulates do not contain the term 'Q', but as synthetic relative to the system T enriched by S2. Strictly speaking, the concept of analyticity has to be relativized also in regard to the rules of the language at hand, for the latter determine what observational or other consequences are entailed by a given sentence. This need for at least a twofold relativization of the concept of analyticity was almost to be expected in view of those considerations which required the same twofold relativization for the concept of experiential meaning of a sentence.

If, on the other hand, we decide not to permit S1 in the role of a partial definition and instead reject it as an isolated sentence, then we are led to an analogous conclusion: Whether a sentence is isolated or not will depend on the linguistic frame and on the theoretical context at hand: While S1 is isolated relative to T (and the language in which both are formulated), it acquires definite experiential implications when T is enlarged by $S2$.

Thus we find, on the level of interpreted theoretical systems, a peculiar rapprochement, and partial fusion, of some of the problems pertaining to the concepts of cognitive significance and of analyticity: Both concepts need to be relativized; and a large class of sentences may be viewed, apparently with equal right, as analytic in a given context, or as isolated, or nonsignificant, in respect to it.

In addition to barring, as isolated in a given context, certain sentences which could just as well be construed as partial definitions, the criterion (4.1) has another serious defect. Of two logically equivalent formulations of a theoretical system it may qualify one as significant while barring the other as containing an isolated sentence among its primitives. For assume that a certain theoretical system $T1$ contains among its primitive sentences $S',S'', \ldots$ exactly one, S', which is isolated. Then $T1$ is not significant under (4.1). But now consider the theoretical system $T2$ obtained from $T1$ by replacing the two first primitive sentences, S', S'', by one, namely their conjunction. Then, under our assumptions, none of the primitive sentences of $T2$ is isolated, and $T2$, though equivalent to $T1$, is qualified as significant by (4.1). In order to do justice to the intent of (4.1), we would therefore have to lay down the following stricter requirement:

(4.2) A THEORETICAL SYSTEM IS COGNITIVELY SIGNIFICANT IF AND ONLY IF IT IS PARTIALLY INTERPRETED TO SUCH AN EXTENT THAT IN NO SYSTEM EQUIVALENT TO IT AT LEAST ONE PRIMITIVE SENTENCE IS ISOLATED.

Let us apply this requirement to some theoretical system whose postulates include the two sentences $S1$ and $S2$ considered before, and whose other postulates do not contain 'Q' at all. Since the sentences $S1$ and $S2$ together entail the sentence O, the set consisting of $S1$ and $S2$ is logically equivalent to the set consisting of $S1$, $S2$ and O. Hence, if we replace the former set by the latter, we obtain a theoretical system equivalent to the given one. In this new system, both $S1$ and $S2$ are isolated since, as can be shown, their removal does not affect the explanatory and predictive power of the system in reference to observable phenomena. To put it intuitively, the systematic power of $S1$ and $S2$ is the same as that of O. Hence, the original system is disqualified by (4.2). From the viewpoint of a strictly sensationalist positivism as perhaps envisaged by [Ernst— Ed.] Mach, this result might be hailed as a sound repudiation of theories making reference to fictitious entities, and as a strict insistence on theories couched exclusively in terms of observables. But from a contemporary vantage point, we shall have to say that such a procedure overlooks or misjudges the important function of constructs in scientific theory: The history of scientific endeavor shows that if we wish to arrive at precise, comprehensive, and well-confirmed general laws, we have to rise above the level of direct observation. The phenomena directly accessible to our experience are not connected by general laws of great scope and rigor. Theoretical constructs are needed for the formulation of such higher-level laws. One of the most important functions of a well-chosen construct is its potential ability to serve as a constituent in ever new general connections that may be discovered; and to such connections we would blind ourselves if we insisted on banning from scientific theories all those terms and sentences which could be "dispensed with" in the sense indicated in (4.2). In following such a narrowly phenomenalistic or positivistic course, we would deprive ourselves of the tremendous fertility of theoretical constructs, and we would often render the formal structure of the expurgated theory clumsy and inefficient.

Criterion (4.2), then, must be abandoned, and considerations such as those outlined in this paper seem to lend strong support to the conjecture that no adequate alternative to it can be found; i.e., that it is not possible to formulate general and precise criteria which would separate those partially interpreted systems whose isolated sentences might be said to have a significant function from those in which the isolated sentences are, so to speak, mere useless appendages.

We concluded earlier that cognitive significance in the sense intended by recent empiricism and operationism can at best be attributed to sentences forming a theoretical system, and perhaps rather to such systems as wholes. Now, rather than try to replace (4.2) by some alternative, we will have to recognize further that cognitive significance in a system is a matter of degree: Significant systems range from those whose entire extralogical vocabulary consists of observation terms, through theories whose formulation relies heavily on theoretical constructs, on to systems with hardly any bearing on potential empirical findings. Instead of dichotomizing this array into significant and nonsignificant systems it would seem less arbitrary and more promising to appraise or compare different theoretical systems in regard to such characteristics as these:

a. the clarity and precision with which the theories are formulated, and with which the logical relationships of their elements to each other and to expressions couched in observational terms have been made explicit;
b. the systematic, i.e., explanatory and predictive, power of the systems in regard to observable phenomena;
c. the formal simplicity of the theoretical system with which a certain systematic power is attained:
d. the extent to which the theories have been confirmed by experiential evidence.

Many of the speculative philosophical approaches to cosmology, biology, or history, for example, would make a poor showing on practically all of these counts and would thus prove no matches to available rival theories, or would be recognized as so unpromising as not to warrant further study or development.

If the procedure here suggested is to be carried out in detail, so as to become applicable also in less obvious cases, then it will be necessary, of course, to develop general standards, and theories pertaining to them, for the appraisal and comparison of theoretical systems in the various respects just mentioned. To what extent this can be done with rigor and precision cannot well be judged in advance. In recent years, a considerable amount of work has been done towards a definition and theory of the concept of degree of confirmation, or logical probability, of a theoretical system; and several contributions have been made towards the clarification of some of the other ideas referred to above. The continuation of this research represents a challenge for further constructive work in the logical and methodological analysis of scientific knowledge.

4

Hilary Putnam

Is Semantics Possible?

In the last decade enormous progress seems to have been made in the syntactic theory of natural languages, largely as a result of the work of linguists influenced by Noam Chomsky and Zellig Harris. Comparable progress seems *not* to have been made in the semantic theory of natural languages, and perhaps it is time to ask why this should be the case. Why is the theory of meaning so *hard?*

The Meaning of Common Nouns

To get some idea of the difficulties, let us look at some of the problems that come up in connection with general names. General names are of many kinds. Some, like *bachelor,* admit of an explicit definition straight off ("man who has never been married"); but the overwhelming majority do not. Some are derived by transformations from verbal forms, e.g., *hunter = one who hunts.* An important class, philosophically as well as linguistically, is the class of general names associated with *natural kinds*—that is, with classes of things that we regard as of explanatory importance; classes whose normal distinguishing characteristics are "held together" or even explained by deep-lying mechanisms. *Gold, lemon, tiger, acid,* are examples of such nouns. I want to begin this paper by suggesting that (1) *traditional* theories of meaning radically falsify the properties of such words; (2) logicians like [Rudolf—Ed.] Carnap do little more than formalize these traditional theories, inadequacies and all; (3) such semantic theories as that produced by Jerrold Katz and his co-workers likewise share all the defects of the traditional theory. In [J. L.—Ed.] Austin's happy phrase, what we have been given by philosophers, logicians, and "semantic theorists" alike, is a "myth-eaten description."

On the traditional view, the meaning of, say, "lemon," is given by specifying a conjunction of *properties.* For each of these properties, the statement "lemons have the property P" is an analytic truth; and if $P_1, P_2, \ldots, P_n$ are all of the properties in the conjunction, then "anything with all of the properties $P_1, \ldots, P_n$ is a lemon" is likewise an analytic truth.

In one sense, this is trivially correct. If we are allowed to invent unanalyzable properties *ad hoc,* then we can find a single property—not even a

Reprinted from Hilary Putnam, "Is Semantics Possible?" in M. K. Munitz and H. K. Kiefer (eds.), *Language, Belief and Metaphysics,* Vol. 1 of *Contemporary Philosophical Thought: The International Philosophy Year Conferences at Brockport* (Albany: State University of New York Press, 1970), pp. 50–63, by permission of the State University of New York Press. Copyright © 1970, State University of New York. Reprinted also by permission of the author.

conjunction—the possession of which is a necessary and sufficient condition for being a lemon, or being gold, or whatever. Namely, we just postulate *the property of being a lemon,* or *the property of being gold,* or whatever may be needed. If we require that the properties $P_1, P_2, \ldots, P_n$ *not* be of this *ad hoc* character, however, then the situation is very different. Indeed, with any natural understanding of the term "property," it is just *false* that to say that something belongs to a natural kind is just to ascribe to it a conjunction of properties.

To see why it is false, let us look at the term "lemon." The supposed "defining characteristics" of lemons are: yellow color, tart taste, a certain kind of peel, etc. Why is the term "lemon" *not* definable by simply conjoining these "defining characteristics"?

The most obvious difficulty is that a natural kind may have *abnormal members.* A green lemon is still a lemon—even if, owing to some abnormality, it *never* turns yellow. A three-legged tiger is still a tiger. Gold in the gaseous state is still gold. It is only normal lemons that are yellow, tart, etc.; only normal tigers that are four-legged; only gold under normal conditions that is hard, white or yellow, etc.

To meet this difficulty, let us try the following definition: X is a *lemon =df;* X belongs to a natural kind whose normal members have yellow peel, tart taste, etc.

There is, of course, a problem with the "etc." There is also a problem with "tart taste"—shouldn't it be a *lemon* taste? But let us waive these difficulties, at least for the time being. Let us instead focus on the two notions that have come up with this attempted definition: the notions *natural kind* and *normal member.*

A natural kind *term* (to shift attention, for the moment, from natural kinds to their preferred designations) is a term that plays a special kind of role. If I describe something as a *lemon,* or as an *acid,* I indicate that it is likely to have certain characteristics (yellow peel, or sour taste in dilute water solution, as the case may be); but I also indicate that the presence of those characteristics, if they are present, is likely to be accounted for by some "essential nature" which the thing shares with other members of the natural kind. What the essential nature is is not a matter of language analysis but of scientific theory construction; today we would say it was chromosome structure, in the case of lemons, and being a proton-donor, in the case of acids. Thus it is tempting to say that a natural kind term is simply a term that plays a certain kind of role in scientific or pre-scientific theory: the role, roughly, of pointing to common "essential features" or "mechanisms" beyond and below the obvious "distinguishing characteristics." But this is vague, and likely to remain so. Meta-science is today in its infancy: and terms like "natural kind," and "normal member," are in the same boat as the more familiar meta-scientific terms "theory" and "explanation," as far as resisting a speedy and definitive analysis is concerned.

Even if we *could* define "natural kind"—say, "a natural kind is a class which is the extension of a term P which plays such-and-such a methodological role in some well-confirmed theory"—the definition would obviously embody a theory of the world, at least in part. It is not *analytic* that natural kinds are classes which play certain kinds of roles in theories; what *really* distinguishes the classes we count as natural kinds is itself a matter of (high level and very abstract) scientific investigation and not just meaning analysis.

That the proposed definition of "lemon" uses terms which themselves resist definition is not a fatal objection however. Let us pause to note, therefore, that if it is correct (and we shall soon show that even it is radically oversimplified), then the traditional idea of the force of general terms is badly mistaken. To say that something is a lemon is, on the above definition, to say that it belongs to a natural kind whose normal members have certain properties; but not to say that it necessarily has those properties itself. There are no *analytic* truths of the form *every lemon has* P. What has happened is this: the traditional theory has taken an account which is correct for the "one-criterion" concepts (i.e., for such concepts as "bachelor" and "vixen"), and made it a general account of the meaning of general names. A theory which correctly describes the behavior of perhaps three hundred words has been asserted to correctly describe the behavior of the tens of thousands of general names.

It is also important to note the following: if the above definition is correct, then knowledge of the properties that a thing has (in any natural and non "ad hoc" sense of property) is not enough to determine, in any mechanical or algorithmic way, whether or not it is a lemon (or an acid, or whatever). For even if I have a description in, say, the language of particle physics, of what are in fact the chromosomal properties of a fruit, I may not be able to tell that it is a lemon because I have not developed the theory according to which (1) those physical-chemical characteristics are the chromosomal structure features (I may not even have the notion "chromosome"); and (2) I may not have discovered that chromosomal structure is the *essential* property of lemons. Meaning does not determine extension, in the sense that given the meaning and a list of all the "properties" of a thing (in any particular sense of "property"), one can simply *read off* whether the thing is a lemon (or acid, or whatever). Even given the meaning, whether something is a lemon or not is, or at least sometimes is, or at least may sometimes be, a matter of what is the best conceptual scheme, the best theory, the best scheme of "natural kinds." (This is, of course, one reason for the failure of phenomenalistic translation schemes.)

These consequences of the proposed definition are, I believe, correct, even though the proposed definition is itself still badly oversimplified. Is it a necessary truth that the "normal" lemons, as we think of them (the tart yellow ones) are really normal members of their species? Is it logically impossible that we should have mistaken what are really very atypical lemons (perhaps diseased ones) for normal lemons? On the above definition, if there is no natural kind whose normal members are yellow, tart, etc., then even these tart, yellow, thick-peeled fruits that I make lemonade from are *not literally lemons*. But this is absurd. It is clear that they are lemons, although it is not analytic that they are *normal* lemons. Moreover, if the color of lemons changed—say, as the result of some gasses getting into the earth's atmosphere and reacting with the pigment in the peel of lemons—we would not say that lemons had ceased to exist, although a natural kind whose normal members were *yellow* and had the other characteristics of lemons *would* have ceased to exist. Thus the above definition is correct to the extent that what it says *isn't* analytic indeed isn't; but it is incorrect in that what would be analytic if it were correct isn't. We have loosened up the logic of the natural kind terms, in comparison with the "conjunction of properties" model; but we have still not loosened it up enough.

Two cases have just been considered: (1) the normal members of the natural kind in question may not really be the ones we *think* are normal; (2) the characteristics of the natural kind may change with time, possibly owing to a change in the conditions, without the "essence" changing so much that we want to stop using the same word. In the first case (normal lemons are blue, but we haven't seen any normal lemons), our theory of the natural kind is false; but at least there is a natural kind about which we have a false theory, and that is why we can still apply the term. In the second case, our theory was at least once true; but it has ceased to be true, although the natural kind has not ceased to exist, which is why we can still apply the term.

Let us attempt to cover both these kinds of cases by modifying our definition as follows:

> X is a *lemon* = df X belongs to a natural kind whose . . . (as before) OR X belongs to a natural kind whose normal members used to . . . (as before) OR X belongs to a natural kind whose normal members were formerly believed to, or are now incorrectly believed to . . . (as before).

Nontechnically, the trouble with this "definition" is that it is slightly crazy. Even if we waive the requirement of sanity (and, indeed, it is all too customary in philosophy to waive any such requirement), it still doesn't work. Suppose, for example, that some tens of thousands of years ago lemons were unknown, but a few atypical oranges were known. Suppose these atypical oranges had exactly the properties of peel, color, etc., that lemons have: indeed, we may suppose that only a biologist could tell that they were really queer oranges and not normal lemons. Suppose that the people living at that time took them to be normal members of a species, and thus thought that oranges have exactly the properties that lemons in fact do have. Then all now existing oranges would be lemons, according to the above definition, since they belong to a species (a natural kind) of which it was once believed that the normal members have the characteristics of yellow peel, lemon taste, etc.

Rather than try to complicate the definition still further, in the fashion of system-building philosophers, let us simply observe what has gone wrong. It is true—and this is what the new definition tries to reflect—that one possible use of a natural kind term is the following: to refer to a thing which belongs to a natural kind which does *not* fit the "theory" associated with the natural kind term, but which was believed to fit that theory (and, in fact, to be *the* natural kind which fit the theory) when the theory had not yet been falsified. Even if cats turn out to be robots remotely controlled from Mars we will still call them "cats"; even if it turns out that the stripes on tigers are painted on to deceive us, we will still call them "tigers"; even if normal lemons are blue (we have been buying and raising very atypical lemons, but don't know it), they are still lemons (and so are the yellow ones.) Not only will we still *call* them "cats," they are cats; not only will we still call them "tigers," they are tigers; not only will we still call them "lemons," they are lemons. But the fact that a term has several possible uses does not make it a disjunctive term; the mistake is in trying to represent the complex behavior of a natural kind word in something as simple as an analytic definition.

To say that an analytic definition is too simple a means of representation is not to say that no representation is possible. Indeed, a very simple representation is possible, *viz.*:

lemon: natural kind word   associated characteristics:
                                yellow peel, tart taste, etc.

To fill this out, a lot more should be said about the linguistic behavior of natural kind words; but no more need be said about *lemon*.

Katz's Theory of Meaning

Carnap's view of meaning in natural language is this: we divide up logical space into "logically possible worlds." (That this may be highly language-relative, and that it may presuppose the very analytic-synthetic distinction he hopes to find by his quasi-operational procedure are objections he does not discuss.) The informant is asked whether or not he would say that something is the case in each logically possible world: the assumption being that (1) each logically possible world can be described clearly enough for the informant to tell; and (2) that the informant can say that the sentence in question is *true/false/not clearly either* just on the basis of the description of the logically possible world and the meaning (or "intension") he assigns to the sentence in question. The latter assumption is false, as we have just seen, for just the reason that the traditional theory of meaning is false: even if I know the "logically possible world" you have in mind, deciding whether or not something is, for example, a lemon, may require deciding what the best *theory* is; and this is not something to be determined by asking an informant yes/no questions in a rented office. This is not to say that "lemon" has no meaning, of course: it is to say that meaning is not *that* simply connected with extension, even with "extension in logically possible worlds."

Carnap is not my main stalking horse, however. The theory I want to focus on is the "semantic theory" recently propounded by Jerrold Katz and his co-workers. In main outlines this theory is as follows:

(1) Each word has its meaning characterized by a string of "semantic markers."

(2) These markers stand for "concepts" ("concepts" are themselves brain processes in Katz's philosophy of language; but I shall ignore this *jeu d'esprit* here.) Examples of such concepts are: *unmarried, animate, seal.*

(3) Each such concept (concept for which a semantic marker is introduced) is a "linguistic universal," and stands for an *innate* notion—one in some sense or other "built into" the human brain.

(4) There are recursive rules—and this is the "scientific" core of Katz's "semantic theory"—whereby the "readings" of whole sentences (these being likewise strings of markers) are derived from the meanings of the individual words

and the deep structure (in the sense of transformational grammar) of the sentence.

(5) The scheme as a whole is said to be justified in what is said to be the manner of a scientific theory—by its ability to explain such things as our intuitions that certain sentences have more than one meaning, or that certain sentences are queer.

(6) Analyticity relations are also supposed to be able to be read off from the theory: for example, from the fact that the markers associated with "unmarried" occur in connection with "bachelor," one can see that "all bachelors are unmarried" is analytic; and from the fact that the markers associated with "animal" occur in connection with "cat," one can see (allegedly) that "all cats are animals" is analytic.

There are internal inconsistencies in this scheme which are apparent at once. For example, "seal" is given as an example of a "linguistic universal" (at least, "seal" occurs as part of the "distinguisher" in one reading for "bachelor"— the variant reading: *young male fur seal*, in one of Katz's examples); but in no theory of human evolution is contact with seals universal. Indeed, even contact with *clothing*, or with *furniture*, or with *agriculture* is by no means universal. Thus we must take it that Katz means that whenever such terms occur they could be further analyzed into concepts which really are so primitive that a case could be made for their universality. Needless to say, this program has never been carried out, and he himself constantly ignores it in giving examples. But the point of greatest interest to us is that this scheme is an unsophisticated translation into "mathematical" language of precisely the traditional theory that it has been our concern to criticize! Indeed, as far as general names are concerned, the only change is that whereas in the traditional account each general name was associated with a list of properties, in Katz's account each general name is associated with a list of *concepts*. It follows that each counterexample to the traditional theory is at once a counterexample also to Katz's theory. For example, if Katz lists the concept "yellow" under the noun "lemon," then he will be committed to "all lemons are yellow"; if he lists the concept "striped" under the noun "tiger," then he will be committed to the analyticity of "all tigers are striped"; and so on. Indeed, although Katz denies that his "semantic markers" are themselves *words*, it is clear that they can be regarded as a kind of artificial language. Therefore, what Katz is saying is that:

(1) A mechanical scheme can be given for translating any natural language into this artificial "marker language" (and this scheme is just what Katz's "semantic theory" is).

(2) The string of markers associated with a word has exactly the meaning of the word.

If (1) and (2) were true, we would at once deduce that there exists a possible language—a "marker language"—with the property that every word that human beings have invented or could invent has an analytic definition in that language. But this is something that we have every reason to disbelieve! In fact: (1) We have just seen that if our account of "natural kind" words is correct, then none of these words has an analytic definition. In particular, a natural kind word will be analytically translatable into marker language only in the special case in which a marker happens to have been introduced with that exact meaning. (2) There are many words for which we haven't the foggiest notion what an analytic definition would even look like. What would an analytic definition of "mammoth" look like? (Would Katz say that it is analytic that mammoths are extinct? Or that they have a certain kind of molar? These are the items mentioned in the dictionary!) To say that a word is the name of an extinct species of elephant is to exactly communicate the use of that word; but it certainly isn't an analytic definition (i.e., an analytically necessary and sufficient condition). (3) *Theoretical terms* in science have no analytic definitions, for reasons familiar to every reader of recent philosophy of science; yet these are surely items (and not atypical items) in the vocabulary of natural languages.

We have now seen, I believe, one reason for the recent lack of progress in semantic theory: you may dress up traditional mistakes in modern dress by talking of "recursive rules" and "linguistic universals," but they remain the traditional mistakes. The problem in semantic theory is to get away from the picture of the meaning of a word as something like a *list of concepts*; not to formalize that misguided picture.

Quine's Pessimism

[W. V.—Ed.] Quine has long expressed a profound pessimism about the very possibility of such a subject as "semantic theory." Certainly we cannot assume that *there is* a scientific subject to be constructed here just because ordinary people have occasion to use the word "meaning" from time to time; that would be like concluding that there must be a scientific subject to be constructed which will deal with "causation" just because ordinary people have occasion to use the word "cause" from time to time. In one sense, *all* of science is a theory of causation; but not in the sense that it uses the word *cause*. Similarly, any successful and developed theory of language-use will in one sense be a theory of meaning; but not necessarily in the sense that it will employ any such notion as the "meaning" of a word or of an utterance. Elementary as this point is, it seems to be constantly overlooked in the social sciences, and people seem constantly to expect that psychology, for example, must talk of "dislike," "attraction," "belief," etc., simply because ordinary men use these words in psychological description.

Quine's pessimism cannot, then, be simply dismissed; and as far as the utility of the traditional notion of "meaning" is concerned, Quine may well turn out to be right. But we are still left with the task of trying to say what are the real problems in the area of language-use, and of trying to erect a conceptual framework within which we can begin to try to solve them.

Let us return to our example of the natural-kind words. It is a fact, and one whose importance to this subject I want to bring out, that the use of words can be taught. If someone does not know the meaning of "lemon," I can somehow convey it to him. I am going to suggest that in this simple phenomenon lies the problem, and hence the *raison d'être*, of "semantic theory."

How do I convey the meaning of the word "lemon"? Very likely, I show the man a lemon. Very well, let us change the example. How do I convey the meaning of the word "tiger"? *I tell him what a tiger is.*

It is easy to see that Quine's own theoretical scheme (in *Word and Object*) will not handle this case very well. Quine's basic notion is the notion of *stimulus meaning* (roughly this is the set of nerve-ending stimulations which will "prompt assent" to *tiger*). But: (1) it is very unlikely that I convey exactly the stimulus-meaning that "tiger" has in my idiolect; and (2) in any case I don't convey it directly, i.e., by describing it. In fact, I couldn't describe it. Quine also works with the idea of *accepted sentences*; thus he might try to handle this case somewhat as follows: "the hearer, in your example, already shares a great deal of language with you; otherwise you couldn't tell him what a tiger is. When you 'tell him what a tiger is,' you simply tell him certain sentences that you accept. Once he knows what sentences you accept, naturally he is able to use the word, at least observation words."

Let us, however, refine this last counter somewhat. If conveying the meaning of the word "tiger" involved conveying the totality of accepted scientific theory about tigers, or even the totality of what I believe about tigers, then it would be an impossible task. It is true that when I tell someone what a tiger is I "simply tell him certain sentences"—though not necessarily sentences I *accept*, except as descriptions of linguistically stereotypical tigers. But the point is, *which* sentences?

In the special case of such words as "tiger" and "lemon," we proposed an answer earlier in this paper. The answer runs as follows: there is somehow associated with the word "tiger" a *theory*; not the actual theory we believe about tigers, which is very complex, but an oversimplified theory which describes a, so to speak, tiger *stereotype*. It describes, in the language we used earlier, a *normal member* of the natural kind. It is not necessary that we believe this theory, though in the case of "tiger" we do. But it is necessary that we be aware that *this* theory is associated with the word: if our stereotype of a tiger ever changes, then the word "tiger" will have changed its meaning. If, to change the example, lemons all turn blue, the word "lemon" will not immediately change its meaning. When I first say, with surprise, "lemons have all turned blue," lemon will still mean what it means now—which is to say that "lemon" will still be associated with the stereotype *yellow lemon*, even though I will be using the word to deny that lemons (even normal lemons) are in fact yellow. I can refer to a natural kind by a term which is "loaded" with a theory which is known not to be any longer true of that natural kind, just because it will be clear to everyone that what I intend is to refer to *that* kind, and not to assert the theory. But, of course, if lemons really did turn blue (and stayed that way) then in time "lemon" would come to have a meaning with the following representation:

lemon: natural kind word   associated characteristics:
                                    blue peel, tart taste, etc.

Then "lemon" would have changed its meaning.

To sum this up: there are a few facts about "lemon" or "tiger" (I shall refer to them as *core facts*) such that one can convey the use of "lemon" or "tiger" by simply conveying those facts. More precisely, one can frequently convey the approximate use; and still more precisely, one cannot convey the approximate use *unless* one gets the core facts across.

Let me emphasize that this has the status of an empirical hypothesis. The hypothesis is that there are, in connection with almost any word (not just "natural kind" words), certain core facts such that (1) one cannot convey the normal use of the word (to the satisfaction of native speakers) without conveying those core facts, and (2) in the case of many words and many speakers, conveying those core facts is sufficient to convey at least an approximation to the normal use. In the case of a natural kind word, the core facts are that a normal member of the kind has certain characteristics, or that this idea is at least the stereotype associated with the word.

If this hypothesis is false, then I think that Quine's pessimism is probably justified. But if this hypothesis is right, then I think it is clear what the problem of the theory of meaning is, regardless of whether or not one chooses to call it "theory of *meaning*": the question is to explore and explain this empirical phenomenon. Questions which naturally arise are: What different kinds of words are associated with what different kinds of core facts? and By what mechanism does it happen that just conveying a small set of core facts brings it about that the hearer is able to imitate the normal use of a word?

Wittgensteinians, whose fondness for the expression "form of life" appears to be directly proportional to its degree of preposterousness in a given context, say that acquiring the customary use of such a word as "tiger" is coming to share a form of life. What they miss, or at any rate fail to emphasize, is that while the acquired disposition may be sufficiently complex and sufficiently inter-linked with other complex dispositions to warrant special mention (though hardly the overblown phrase "form of life"), what *triggers* the disposition is often highly discrete—e.g., a simple lexical definition frequently succeeds in conveying a pretty good idea of how a word is used. To be sure, as Wittgenstein emphasizes, this is only possible because we have a shared human nature, and because we have shared an acculturation process—there has to be a great deal of stage-setting before one can read a lexical definition and guess how a word is used. But in the process of "debunking" this fact—the fact that something as simple as a lexical definition *can* convey the use of a word—they forget to be impressed by it. To be sure there is a great deal of stage-setting, but it is rarely stage-setting specifically designed to enable one to learn the use of *this* word. The fact that one *can* acquire the use of an indefinite number of new words, and on the basis of simple "statements of what they mean," is an amazing fact: it is *the* fact, I repeat, on which semantic theory rests.

Sometimes it is said that the key problem in semantics is: how do we come to understand a new sentence? I would suggest that this is a far simpler (though not unimportant) problem. How logical words, for example, can be used to build up complex sentences out of simpler ones is easy to describe, at least in principle (of course, natural language analogues of logical words are far less tidy than the logical words of the mathematical logician), and it is also easy to say how the truth-conditions, etc., of the complex sentences are related to the truth-conditions of the sentences from which they were derived. This much *is* a matter of finding a structure of recursive rules with a suitable relation to the transformational grammar of the language in question. I would suggest that the question, How do we come to understand a new *word?*, has far more to do with the whole phenomenon of giving definitions and writing dictionaries than the former question. And it is this phenomenon—the phenomenon of writing (and needing) dictionaries—that gives rise to the whole idea of "semantic theory."

Kinds of Core Facts

Let us now look a little more closely at the kind of information that one conveys when one conveys the meaning of a word. I have said that in the case of a "natural kind" word one conveys the associated *stereotype:* the associated idea of the characteristics of a normal member of the kind. But this is not, in general, enough; one must also convey the extension, one must indicate *which* kind the stereotype is supposed to "fit."

From the point of view of any traditional meaning theory, be it Plato's or [Gottlob—Ed.] Frege's or Carnap's or Katz's, this is just nonsense. How can I "convey" the extension of, say, "tiger"? Am I supposed to give you all the tigers in the world (heaven forfend!). I can convey the extension of a term only by giving a description of that extension; and then that description must be a "part of the meaning," or else my definition will not be a meaning statement at all. To say: "I gave him certain conditions associated with the word, *and* I gave him the extension" (as if that weren't just giving *further* conditions) can only be nonsense.

The mistake of the traditional theorist lies in his attachment to the word "meaning." If giving the meaning is *giving* the *meaning*, then it is giving a definite thing; but giving the meaning isn't, as we shall see in a moment, giving some one definite thing. To drop the word "meaning," which is here extremely misleading: there is no *one* set of facts which has to be conveyed to convey the normal use of a word; and taking account of this requires a complication in our notion of "core facts."

That the same stereotype might be associated with different kinds seems odd if the kind word one has in mind is "tiger"; but change the example to, say, "aluminum" and it will not seem odd at all. About all *I* know about aluminum is that it is a light metal, that it makes durable pots and pans, and that it doesn't appear to rust (although it does occasionally discolor). For all I know, every one of these characteristics may also fit molybdenum.

Suppose now that a colony of English-speaking Earthlings is leaving in a spaceship for a distant planet. When they arrive on their distant planet, they discover that no one remembers the atomic weight (or any other defining characteristic) of aluminum, nor the atomic weight (or other characteristic) of molybdenum. There is some aluminum in the spacecraft, and some molybdenum. Let us suppose that they guess which is which, and they guess wrong.

Henceforth, they use "aluminum" as the name for molybdenum, and "molybdenum" as the name for aluminum. It is clear that "aluminum" has a different meaning in this community than in ours: in fact, it means *molybdenum*. Yet how can this be? Didn't they possess the normal "linguistic competence"? Didn't they all "know the meaning of the word 'aluminum' "?

Let us duck this question for a moment. If I want to make sure that the word "aluminum" will continue to be used in what counts as a "normal" way by the colonists in my example, it will suffice to give them some test for aluminum (or just to give them a carefully labelled sample, and let them discover a test, if they are clever enough). Once they know how to *tell* aluminum from other metals, they will go on using the word with the correct extension as well as the correct "intension" (i.e., the correct stereotype). But notice: it does not matter *which* test we give the colonists. The test isn't part of the meaning; but that there be some test or other (or something, e.g., a sample, from which one might be derived), is necessary to preservation of "the normal usage." Meaning indeed determines extension; but only because extension (fixed by *some* test or other) is, in some cases, "part of the meaning."

There are two further refinements here: if we give them a test, they mustn't make it part of the stereotype—that would be a change of meaning. (Thus it's better if they don't all *know* the test; as long as only experts do, and the average speaker "asks an expert" in case of doubt, the criteria mentioned in the test can't infect the stereotype.) Asking an expert is enough of a test for the normal speaker; that's why we don't give a test in an ordinary context.

We can now modify our account of the "core facts" in the case of a natural kind word as follows: (1) The core facts are the stereotype *and the extension*. (2) Nothing normally need be said about the extension, however, since the hearer knows that he can always consult an expert if any question comes up. (3) In special cases—such as the case of colonists—there may be danger that the word will get attached to the wrong natural kind, even though the right stereotype is associated with it. In such cases, one must give some way of getting the extension right, but no one *particular* way is necessary.

In the case of "lemon" or "tiger" a similar problem comes up. It is logically possible (although empirically unlikely, perhaps) that a species of fruit biologically unrelated to lemons might be indistinguishable from lemons in taste and appearance. In such a case, there would be two possibilities: (1) to call them *lemons*, and thus let "lemon" be a word for any one of a number of natural kinds; or (2) to say that they are not lemons (which is what, I suspect, biologists would decide to do.) In the latter case, the problems are exactly the same as with *aluminum*: to be sure one has the "normal usage" or "customary meaning" or whatever, one has to be sure one has the right extension.

The problem: that giving the extension is part of giving the meaning arises also in the case of names of sensible qualities, e.g., colors. Here, however, it is normal to give the extension by giving a sample, so that the person learning the word learns to recognize the quality in the normal way. Frequently it has been regarded as a defect of *dictionaries* that they are "cluttered up" with color samples, and with stray pieces of empirical information (e.g., the atomic weight of aluminum), not sharply distinguished from "purely linguistic" information.

The burden of the present discussion is that this is no defect at all, but essential to the function of conveying the core facts in each case.

Still other kinds of words may be mentioned in passing. In the case of "one-criterion" words (words which possess an analytical necessary and sufficient condition) it is obvious why the core fact is just the analytical necessary and sufficient condition (e.g. "man who has never been married," in the case of "bachelor"). In the case of "cluster" words (e.g., the name of a disease which is known not to have any one underlying cause), it is obvious why the core facts are just the typical symptoms or elements of the cluster; and so on. Given the *function* of a kind of word, it is not difficult to explain why certain facts function as core facts for conveying the use of words of that kind.

The Possibility of Semantics

Why, then, is semantics so hard? In terms of the foregoing, I want to suggest that semantics is a typical social science. The sloppiness, the lack of precise theories and laws, the lack of mathematical rigor, are all characteristic of the social sciences today. A general and precise theory which answers the questions (1) why do words have the different sorts of functions they do? and (2) exactly how does conveying core facts enable one to learn the use of a word? is not to be expected until one has a general and precise model of a language-user; and that is still a long way off. But the fact that Utopia is a long way off does not mean that daily life should come to a screeching halt. There is plenty for us to investigate, in our sloppy and impressionistic fashion, and there are plenty of real results to be obtained. The first step is to free ourselves from the over-simplifications foisted upon us by the tradition, and to see where the real problems lie. I hope this paper has been a contribution to that first step.

Reference and Speech Acts

5

Gottlob Frege

On Sense and Nominatum

Gottlob Frege (1848–1925), perhaps the founder of modern mathematical logic, was comparatively unknown and largely misunderstood through his entire career in the mathematics department of the University of Jena. His work notably influenced Edmund Husserl, Bertrand Russell, and Ludwig Wittgenstein, through whose mediation it was gradually recovered if substantially challenged and in critical respects rejected. His philosophical orientation regarding mathematics is restricted by his adherence to logicism (favoring the derivability of the concepts and theorems of mathematics from logical concepts, definitions, and axioms) and platonism.

Logicism is of considerable importance, since, in the attempt to derive all the concepts and theorems of mathematics (apparently excluding geometry), Frege relied on the unanalyzed concept of a class—which he treats as the "extension of a concept." But the discovery of the paradoxes of set theory undermined the notion of a class, and the extraordinarily promising logicist program eventually began to lose interest.

Frege's platonism, the thesis that mathematical objects exist independently of the mind, failed to provide a sufficient basis for the objectivity of mathematics itself. Of more general philosophical interest is his attack on what he called psychologism, the tendency to confuse the origin of an idea for its definition or to confuse the conditions through which we become conscious of a proposition for a proof of it (Die Grundlagen der Arithmetik: The Foundations of Arithmetic, 1884). *The distinction marks the beginning of a strong effort to link the theory of meaning to truth-conditions and to separate it from its traditional association with mental images.*

It is in his work known as the Begriffsschrift (1879: Begriffsschrift, eine der arithmetischen nachgebildete Formelsprache des reinen Denkens) *that the modern use of quantifiers and variables first appeared and was explored in the construction of an axiomatized system of great power.*

In general philosophical circles less concerned with mathematics and logic, Frege is best known for his distinction between sense and reference. By this he explained how identity statements could be informative: The referent of an expression or bearer of a name may be singled out by the use of another expression or name having a significance different from that of the first. He is also known for his pioneer views regarding the dependence of the meaning of words on their function within the context of sentences actually used—as we should now say, in the performance of a linguistic act. Here he seems to have anticipated Wittgenstein.

The idea of Sameness[1] challenges reflection. It raises questions which are not quite easily answered. Is Sameness a relation? A relation between objects? Or between names or signs of objects? I assumed the latter alternative in my *Begriffsschrift* [roughly: a formulae language for managing concepts; usually referred to by the German title—Ed.]. The reasons that speak in its favor are the following: "a = a" and "a = b" are sentences of obviously different cognitive significance: "a = a" is valid *a priori* and according to Kant is to be called analytic, whereas sentences of the form "a = b" often contain very valuable extensions of our knowledge and cannot always be justified in an *a priori* manner. The discovery that it is not a different and novel sun which rises every morning, but that it is the very same, certainly was one of the most consequential ones in astronomy. Even nowadays the re-cognition (identification) of a planetoid or a comet is not always a matter of self-evidence. If we wish to view identity as a relation between the objects designated by the names 'a' and 'b' then "a = b" and "a = a" would not seem different if "a = b" is true. This would express a relation of a thing to itself, namely, a relation such that it holds between everything and itself but never between one thing and another. What one wishes to express with "a = b" seems to be that the signs or names 'a' and 'b' name the same thing; and in that case we would be dealing with those signs: a relation between them would be asserted. But this relation could hold only inasmuch as they name or designate something. The relation, as it were, is mediated through the connection of each sign with the same nominatum. This connection, however, is arbitrary. You cannot forbid the use of an arbitrarily produced process or object as a sign for something else. Hence, a sentence like "a = b" would no longer refer to a matter of fact but rather to our manner of designation; no genuine knowledge would be expressed by it. But this is just what we do want to express in many cases. If the sign 'a' differs from the sign 'b' only as an object (here by its shape) but not by its rôle as a sign, that is to say, not in the manner in which it designates anything, then the cognitive significance of "a = a" would be essentially the same as that of "a = b", if "a = b" is true. A difference could arise only if the difference of the signs corresponds to a difference in the way in which the designated objects are given. Let a, b, c be

---

[1] I use this word in the sense of identity and understand "a = b" in the sense of "a is the same as b" or "a and b coincide".

straight lines which connect the corners of a triangle with the midpoints of the opposite sides. The point of intersection of a and b is then the same as that of b and c. Thus we have different designations of the same point and these' names ('intersection of a and b', 'intersection of b and c') indicate also the manner in which these points are presented. Therefore the sentence expresses a genuine cognition.

Now it is plausible to connect with a sign (name, word combination, expression) not only the designated object, which may be called the nominatum of the sign, but also the sense (connotation, meaning) of the sign in which is contained the manner and context of presentation. Accordingly, in our examples the *nominata* of the expressions 'the point of intersection of a and b' and 'the point of intersection of b and c' would be the same;—not their senses. The nominata of 'evening star' and 'morning star' are the same but not their senses.

From what has been said it is clear that I here understand by 'sign' or 'name' any expression which functions as a proper name, whose nominatum accordingly is a definite object (in the widest sense of this word). But no concept or relation is under consideration here. These matters are to be dealt with in another essay. The designation of a single object may consist of several words or various signs. For brevity's sake, any such designation will be considered as a proper name.

The sense of a proper name is grasped by everyone who knows the language or the totality of designations of which the proper name is a part;[2] this, however, illuminates the nominatum, if there is any, in a very one-sided fashion. A complete knowledge of the nominatum would require that we could tell immediately in the case of any given sense whether it belongs to the nominatum. This we shall never be able to do.

The regular connection between a sign, its sense and its nominatum is such that there corresponds a definite sense to the sign and to this sense there corresponds again a definite nominatum; whereas not one sign only belongs to one nominatum (object). In different languages, and even in one language, the same sense is represented by different expressions. It is true, there are exceptions to this rule. Certainly there should be a definite sense to each expression in a complete configuration of signs, but the natural languages in many ways fall short of this requirement. We must be satisfied if the same word, at least in the same context, has the same sense. It can perhaps be granted that an expression has a sense if it is formed in a grammatically correct manner and stands for a proper name. But as to whether there is a denotation corresponding to the connotation is hereby not decided. The words 'the heavenly body which has the greatest distance from the earth'

---

[2] In the case of genuinely proper names like 'Aristotle' opinions as regards their sense may diverge. As such may, e.g., be suggested: Plato's disciple and the teacher of Alexander the Great. Whoever accepts this sense will interpret the meaning of the statement "Aristotle was born in Stagira" differently from one who interpreted the sense of 'Aristotle' as the Stagirite teacher of Alexander the Great. As long as the nominatum remains the same, these fluctuations in sense are tolerable. But they should be avoided in the system of a demonstrative science and should not appear in a perfect language.

have a sense; but it is very doubtful as to whether they have a nominatum. The expression 'the series with the least convergence' has a sense; but it can be proved that it has no nominatum, since for any given convergent series, one can find another one that is less convergent. Therefore the grasping of a sense does not with certainty warrant a corresponding nominatum.

When words are used in the customary manner then what is talked about are their nominata. But it may happen that one wishes to speak about the words themselves or about their senses. The first case occurs when one quotes some-one else's words in direct (ordinary) discourse. In this case one's own words immediately name (denote) the words of the other person and only the latter words have the usual nominata. We thus have signs of signs. In writing we make use of quotes enclosing the word-icons. A word-icon in quotes must therefore not be taken in the customary manner.

If we wish to speak of the sense of an expression 'A' we can do this simply through the locution 'the sense of the expression 'A''. In indirect (oblique) discourse we speak of the sense, e.g., of the words of someone else. From this it becomes clear that also in indirect discourse words do not have their cus-tomary nominata; they here name what customarily would be their sense. In order to formulate this succinctly we shall say: words in indirect discourse are used *indirectly*, or have *indirect* nominata. Thus we distinguish the *customary* from the *indirect* nominatum of a word; and similarly, its *customary* sense from its *indirect* sense. The indirect nominatum of a word is therefore its customary sense. Such exceptions must be kept in mind if one wishes correctly to comprehend the manner of connection between signs, senses and nominata in any given case.

· · ·

The nominatum of a proper name is the object itself which is designated thereby; the image which we may have along with it is quite subjective; the sense lies in between, not subjective as is the image, but not the object either. . . .

We can now recognize three levels of differences of words, expressions and complete sentences. The difference may concern at most the imagery, or else the sense but not the nominatum, or finally also the nominatum. In regard to the first level, we must note that, owing to the uncertain correlation of images with words, a difference may exist for one person that another does not dis-cover. The difference of a translation from the original should properly not go beyond the first level. Among the differences possible in this connection we mention the shadings and colorings which poetry seeks to impart to the senses. These shadings and colorings are not objective. Every listener or reader has to add them in accordance with the hints of the poet or speaker. Surely, art would be impossible without some kinship among human imageries; but just how far the intentions of the poet are realized can never be exactly ascertained.

We shall henceforth no longer refer to the images and picturizations; they were discussed only lest the image evoked by a word be confused with its sense or its nominatum.

In order to facilitate brief and precise expression we may lay down the following formulations:

A proper name (word, sign, sign-compound, expression) expresses its sense, and designates or signifies its nominatum. We let a *sign express* its sense and *designate* its nominatum.

.   .   .

Thus far we have considered sense and nominatum only of such expressions, words and signs which we called proper names. We are now going to inquire into the sense and the nominatum of a whole declarative sentence. Such a sentence contains a proposition.[3] Is this thought to be regarded as the sense or the nominatum of the sentence? Let us for the moment assume that the sentence has a nominatum! If we then substitute a word in it by another word with the same nominatum but with a different sense, then this substitution cannot affect the nominatum of the sentence. But we realize that in such cases the proposition is changed; e.g., the proposition of the sentence "the morning star is a body illuminated by the sun" is different from that of "the evening star is a body illuminated by the sun". Someone who did not know that the evening star is the same as the morning star could consider the one proposition true and the other false. The proposition can therefore not be the nominatum of the sentence; it will instead have to be regarded as its sense. But what about the nominatum? Can we even ask this question? A sentence as a whole has perhaps only sense and no nominatum? It may in any case be expected that there are such sentences, just as there are constituents of sentences which do have sense but no nominatum. Certainly, sentences containing proper names without nominata must be of this type. The sentence "Odysseus deeply asleep was disembarked at Ithaca" obviously has a sense. But since it is doubtful as to whether the name 'Odysseus' occurring in this sentence has a nominatum, so it is also doubtful that the whole sentence has one. However, it is certain that whoever seriously regards the sentence either as true or as false also attributes to the name 'Odysseus' a nominatum, not only a sense; for it is obviously the nominatum of this name to which the predicate is either ascribed or denied. He who does not acknowledge the nominatum cannot ascribe or deny a predicate to it. It might be urged that the consideration of the nominatum of the name is going farther than is necessary; one could be satisfied with the sense, if one stayed with the proposition. If all that mattered were only the sense of the sentence (i.e., the proposition) then it would be unnecessary to be concerned with the nominata of the sentence-components, for only the sense of the components can be relevant for the sense of the sentence. The proposition remains the same, no matter whether or not the name 'Odysseus' has a nominatum. The fact that we are at all concerned about the nominatum of a sentence-component indicates that we generally acknowledge or postulate a nominatum for the sentence itself. The proposition loses in interest as soon as we recognize that one of its parts is lacking a nominatum. We may therefore be justified to ask for a nominatum of a sentence, in addition to its sense. But why do we wish that every proper name have not only a sense but also a nominatum? Why is

---

[3] By 'proposition' I do not refer to the subjective activity of thinking but rather to its objective content which is capable of being the common property of many.

the proposition alone not sufficient? We answer: because what matters to us is the truth-value. This, however, is not always the case. In listening to an epic, for example, we are fascinated by the euphony of the language and also by the sense of the sentences and by the images and emotions evoked. In turning to the question of truth we disregard the artistic appreciation and pursue scientific considerations. Whether the name 'Odysseus' has a nominatum is therefore immaterial to us as long as we accept the poem as a work of art.[4] Thus, it is the striving for truth which urges us to penetrate beyond the sense to the nominatum.

We have realized that we are to look for the nominatum of a sentence whenever the nominata of the sentence-components are the thing that matters; and that is the case whenever and only when we ask for the truth-value.

Thus we find ourselves persuaded to accept the *truth-value* of a sentence as its nominatum. By the truth-value of a sentence I mean the circumstance of its being true or false. There are no other truth-values. For brevity's sake I shall call the one the True and the other the False. Every declarative sentence, in which what matters are the nominata of the words, is therefore to be considered as a proper name; and its nominatum, if there is any, is either the True or the False. These two objects are recognized, even if only tacitly by everyone who at all makes judgments, holds anything as true, thus even by the skeptic. To designate truth-values as objects may thus far appear as a capricious idea or as a mere play on words, from which no important conclusion should be drawn. What I call an object can be discussed only in connection with the nature of concepts and relations. That I will reserve for another essay. But this might be clear even here: in every judgment[5]—no matter how obvious—a step is made from the level of propositions to the level of the nominata (the objective facts).

It may be tempting to regard the relation of a proposition to the True not as that of sense to nominatum but as that of the subject to the predicate. One could virtually say: "the proposition that 5 is a prime number is true". But on closer examination one notices that this does not say any more than is said in the simple sentence "5 is a prime number". This makes clear that the relation of a proposition to the True must not be compared with the relation of subject and predicate. Subject and predicate (interpreted logically) are, after all, components of a proposition; they are on the same level as regards cognition. By joining subject and predicate we always arrive only at a proposition; in this way we never move from a sense to a nominatum or from a proposition to its truth-value. We remain on the same level and never proceed from it to the next one. Just as the sun cannot be part of a proposition, so the truth-value, because it is not the sense, but an object, cannot be either.

If our conjecture (that the nominatum of a sentence is its truth-value) is

---

[4] It would be desirable to have an expression for signs which have sense only. If we call them 'icons' then the words of an actor on the stage would be icons; even the actor himself would be an icon.

[5] A judgment is not merely the apprehension of a thought or proposition but the acknowledgment of its truth.

correct, then the truth-value must remain unchanged if a sentence-component is replaced by an expression with the same nominatum but with a different sense. Indeed, [G. W.—Ed.] Leibnitz declares: "*Eadem sunt, quae sibi mutuo substitui possunt, salva veritate*" ["Terms that are mutually replaceable, preserving truth, are the same"—Ed.]. What else, except the truth-value, could be found, which quite generally belongs to every sentence and regarding which the nominata of the components are relevant and which would remain invariant for substitutions of the type indicated?

Now if the truth-value of a sentence is its nominatum, then all true sentences have the same nominatum, and likewise all false ones. This implies that all detail has been blurred in the nominatum of a sentence. What interests us can therefore never be merely the nominatum; but the proposition alone does not give knowledge; only the proposition together with its nominatum, i.e., its truth-value, does. Judging may be viewed as a movement from a proposition to its nominatum, i.e., its truth-value. Of course this is not intended as a definition. Judging is indeed something peculiar and unique. One might say that judging consists in the discerning of parts within the truth-value. This discernment occurs through recourse to the proposition. Every sense that belongs to a truth-value would correspond in its own manner to the analysis. I have, however, used the word 'part' in a particular manner here: I have transferred the relation of whole and part from the sentence to its nominatum. This I did by viewing the nominatum of a word as part of the nominatum of a sentence, when the word itself is part of the sentence. True enough, this way of putting things is objectionable since as regards the nominatum the whole and one part of it does not determine the other part; and also because the word 'part' in reference to bodies has a different customary usage. A special expression should be coined for what has been suggested above.

We shall now further examine the conjecture that the truth-value of a sentence is its nominatum. We have found that the truth-value of a sentence remains unaltered if an expression within the sentence is replaced by a synonymous one. But we have as yet not considered the case in which the expression-to-be-replaced is itself a sentence. If our view is correct, then the truth-value of a sentence, which contains another sentence as a part, must remain unaltered when we substitute for the part another of the same truth-value. Exceptions are to be expected if the whole or the part are either in direct or indirect discourse; for as we have seen, in that case the nominata of the words are not the usual ones. A sentence in direct discourse nominates again a sentence but in indirect discourse it nominates a proposition.

Our attention is thus directed to subordinate sentences (i.e., dependent clauses). These present themselves of course as parts of a sentence-structure which from a logical point of view appears also as a sentence, and indeed as if it were a main clause. But here we face the question whether in the case of dependent clauses it also holds that their nominata are truth-values. We know already that this is not the case with sentences in indirect discourse. The grammarians view clauses as representatives of sentence-parts and divide them accordingly into subjective, relative, and adverbial clauses. This might suggest that the nominatum of a clause is not a truth-value but rather that it is of similar nature as that of a noun or of an adjective or of an adverb; in short, of a sentence-part whose sense is not a proposition but only part thereof. Only a thorough investigation can provide clarity in this matter. We shall herein not follow strictly along grammatical lines, but rather group together what is logically of comparable type. Let us first seek out such instances in which, as we just surmised, the sense of a clause is not a self-sufficient proposition.

Among the abstract clauses beginning with 'that' there is also the indirect discourse, of which we have seen that in it the words have their indirect (oblique) nominata which coincide with what are ordinarily their senses. In this case then the clause has as its nominatum a proposition, not a truth-value; its sense is not a proposition but it is the sense of the words 'the proposition that . . .', which is only a part of the proposition corresponding to the total sentence-structure. This occurs in connection with 'to say', 'to hear', 'to opine', 'to be convinced', 'to infer' and similar words.[6] The situation is different, and rather complicated in connection with such words as 'to recognize', 'to know', 'to believe', a matter to be considered later.

One can see that in these cases the nominatum of the clause indeed consists in the proposition, because whether that proposition is true or false is immaterial for the truth of the whole sentence. Compare, e.g., the following two sentences: "Copernicus believed that the planetary orbits are circles" and "Copernicus believed that the appearance of the sun's motion is produced by the real motion of the earth". Here the one clause can be substituted for the other without affecting the truth. The sense of the principal sentence together with the clause is the single proposition; and the truth of the whole implies neither the truth nor the falsity of the clause. In cases of this type it is not permissible to replace in the clause one expression by another of the same nominatum. Such replacement may be made only by expressions of the same indirect nominatum, i.e., of the same customary sense. If one were to infer: the nominatum of a sentence is not its truth-value ("because then a sentence could always be replaced by another with the same truth-value"), he would prove too much; one could just as well maintain that the nominatum of the word 'morning star' is not Venus, for one cannot always substitute 'Venus' for 'morning star'. The only correct conclusion is that the nominatum of a sentence is *not always* its truth-value, and that 'morning star' does not always nominate the planet Venus; for this is indeed not the case when the word is used with its indirect nominatum. Such an exceptional case is before us in the clauses just considered, whose nominatum is a proposition.

When we say "it seems that . . ." then we mean to say "it seems to me that . . ." or "I opine that . . ." This is the same case over again. Similarly with expressions such as: 'to be glad', 'to regret', 'to approve', 'to disapprove', 'to hope', 'to fear'. When Wellington, toward the end of the battle of Belle-Alliance was glad that the Prussians were coming, the ground of his rejoicing was a conviction. Had he actually been deceived, he would not have been less

---

[6] In "A lied, that he had seen B" the clause denotes a proposition of which it is said, firstly, that A asserted it as true, and, secondly, that A was convinced of its falsity.

glad, as long as his belief persisted; and before he arrived at the conviction that the Prussians were coming he could not have been glad about it, even if in fact they were already approaching.

Just as a conviction or a belief may be the ground of a sentiment, so it can also be the ground of another conviction such as in inference. In the sentence "Columbus inferred from the roundness of the earth that he could, traveling westward, reach India" we have, as nominata of its parts two propositions: that the earth is round, and that Columbus traveling westward could reach India. What matters here is only that Columbus was convinced of the one as well as of the other and that the one conviction furnishes the ground for the other. It is irrelevant for the truth of our sentence whether the earth is really round and whether Columbus could have reached India in the manner he fancied. But it is not irrelevant whether for 'the earth' we substitute 'the planet accompanied by one satellite whose diameter is larger than one-fourth of its own diameter'. Here also we deal with the indirect nominata of the words.

Adverbial clauses of purpose with 'so that', likewise belong here; obviously the purpose is a proposition; therefore: indirect nominata of the words, expressed in subjunctive form.

The clause with 'that' after 'to command', 'to request', 'to forbid' would appear in imperative form in direct discourse. Imperatives have no nominata; they have only sense. It is true, commands or requests are not propositions, but they are of the same type as propositions. Therefore the words in the dependent clauses after 'to command', 'to request', etc. have indirect nominata. The nominatum of such a sentence is thus not a truth-value but a command, a request, and the like.

We meet a similar situation in the case of dependent questions in phrases like 'to doubt if', 'not to know what'. It is easy to see that the words, here too, have to be interpreted in terms of their indirect nominata. The dependent interrogatory clauses containing 'who', 'what', 'where', 'when', 'how', 'whereby', etc. often apparently approximate closely adverbial clauses in which the words have their ordinary nominata. These cases are linguistically distinguished through the mode of the verb. In the subjunctive we have a dependent question and the indirect nominata of the words, so that a proper name cannot generally be replaced by another of the same object.

In the instances thus far considered the words in the clause had indirect nominata; this made it intelligible that the nominatum of the clause itself is indirect, i.e., not a truth-value, but a proposition, a command, a request, a question. The clause could be taken as a noun; one might even say, as a proper name of that proposition, command, etc., in whose rôle it functions in the context of the sentence-structure.

We are now going to consider clauses of another type, in which the words do have their customary nominata although there does not appear a proposition as the sense or a truth-value as the nominatum. How this is possible will best be elucidated by examples.

"He who discovered the elliptical shape of the planetary orbits died in misery".

If, in this example, the sense of the clause were a proposition, it would have to be expressible also in a principal sentence. But this cannot be done because the grammatical subject 'he who' has no independent sense. It merely mediates the relations to the second part of the sentence: 'died in misery'. Therefore the sense of the clause is not a complete proposition and its nominatum is not a truth-value, but Kepler. It might be objected that the sense of the whole does include a proposition as its part; namely, that there was someone who first recognized the elliptical shape of the planetary orbits; for if we accept the whole as true we cannot deny this part. Indubitably so; but only because otherwise the clause "he who discovered the elliptical shape, etc." would have no nominatum. Whenever something is asserted then the presupposition taken for granted is that the employed proper names, simple or compound, have nominata. Thus, if we assert "Kepler died in misery" it is presupposed that the name 'Kepler' designates something. However, the proposition that the name 'Kepler' designates something is, the foregoing notwithstanding, not contained in the sense of the sentence "Kepler died in misery". If that were the case the denial would not read "Kepler did not die in misery" but "Kepler did not die in misery, or the name 'Kepler' is without nominatum". That the name 'Kepler' designates something is rather the presupposition of the assertion "Kepler died in misery" as well as of its denial. Now, it is a defect of languages that expressions are possible within them, which, in their grammatical form, seemingly determined to designate an object, nevertheless do not fulfill this condition in special cases; because this depends on the truth of the sentence. Thus it depends upon the truth of the sentence "there was someone who discovered the ellipticity of the orbits" whether the clause 'he who discovered the ellipticity of the orbits' really designates an object, or else merely evokes the appearance thereof, while indeed being without nominatum. Thus it may seem as if our clause, as part of its sense, contained the proposition that there existed someone who discovered the ellipticity of the orbits. If this were so, then the denial would have to read "he who first recognized the ellipticity of the orbits did not die in misery, or there was no one who discovered the ellipticity of the orbits." This, it is obvious, hinges upon an imperfection of language of which, by the way, even the symbolic language of analysis is not entirely free; there, also, sign compounds may occur which appear as if they designated something, but what at least hitherto are without nominatum, e.g., divergent infinite series. This can be avoided, e.g., through the special convention that the nominatum of divergent infinite series be the number 0. It is to be demanded that in a logically perfect language (logical symbolism) every expression constructed as a proper name in a grammatically correct manner out of already introduced symbols, in fact designate an object; and that no symbol be introduced as a proper name without assurance that it have a nominatum. It is customary in logic texts to warn against the ambiguity of expressions as a source of fallacies. I deem it at least as appropriate to issue a warning against apparent proper names that have no nominata. The history of mathematics has many a tale to tell of errors which originated from this source. The demagogic misuse is close (perhaps closer) at hand as in the case of ambiguous expressions. 'The will of the people' may serve as an example in this regard; for it is easily established that there is no generally accepted nominatum of that expression. Thus it is obviously not without importance to obstruct once for all the source of these errors, at least as regards their occurrence in science. Then such objections as the one discussed above will become impossible, for then it will be seen that whether a proper name has a nominatum can never depend upon the truth of a proposition.

Our considerations may be extended from these subjective clauses to the logically related relative and adverbial clauses.

Relative clauses, too, are employed in the formation of compound proper names—even if, in contradistinction to subjective clauses, they are not sufficient by themselves for this purpose. These relative clauses may be regarded as equivalent to appositions. Instead of 'the square root of 4 which is smaller than 0' we can also say 'the negative square root of 4'. We have here a case in which out of a conceptual expression a compound proper name is formed, with the help of the definite article in the singular. This is at any rate permissible when one and only one object is comprised by the concept.[7] Conceptual expressions can be formed in such a fashion that their characteristics are indicated through relative clauses as in our example through the clause 'which is smaller than 0'. Obviously, such relative clauses, just as the subjective clauses above, do not refer to a proposition as their sense nor to a truth-value as their nominatum. Their sense is only a part of a proposition, which in many cases, can be expressed by a simple apposition. As in the subjective clauses an independent subject is missing and it is therefore impossible to represent the sense of the clause in an independent principal sentence.

.   .   .

The sense of a subordinate clause is usually not a proposition but only part of one. Its nominatum is therefore not a truth-value. The reason for this is *either*: that the words in the subordinate clause have only indirect nominata, so that the nominatum, not the sense, of the clause is a proposition, *or*, that the clause, because of a contained indeterminately indicating constituent, is incomplete, such that only together with the principal clause does it express a proposition. However, there are also instances in which the sense of the dependent clause is a complete proposition, and in this case it can be replaced by another clause of the same truth-value without altering the truth-value of the whole; that is, inasmuch as there are no grammatical obstacles in the way.

.   .   .

It is difficult to exhaust all possibilities that present themselves in language; but I hope, in essence at least, to have disclosed the reasons why, in view of the invariance of the truth of a whole sentence, a clause cannot always be replaced by another of the same truth-value. These reasons are:

---

[7] According to our previous remarks such an expression should always be assured of a nominatum, e.g., through the special convention that the nominatum be the number 0 if there is no object or more than one object denoted by the expression.

1. that the clause does not denote a truth-value in that it expresses only a part of a proposition;
2. that the clause, while it does denote a truth-value, is not restricted to this function in that its sense comprises, beside one proposition, also a part of another.

The first case holds

a. with the indirect nominata of the words;
b. if a part of the sentence indicates only indirectly without being a proper name.

In the second case the clause is to be interpreted in a twofold manner; namely, once with its usual nominatum; the other time with its indirect nominatum; or else, the sense of a part of the clause may simultaneously be a constituent of another proposition which, together with the sense expressed in the dependent clause, amounts to the total sense of the main and the dependent clause.

This makes it sufficiently plausible that instances in which a clause is not replaceable by another of the same truth-value do not disprove our view that the nominatum of a sentence is its truth-value and its sense a proposition.

Let us return to our point of departure now.

When we discerned generally a difference in cognitive significance between "$a = a$" and "$a = b$" then this is now explained by the fact that for the cognitive significance of a sentence the sense (the proposition expressed) is no less relevant than its nominatum (the truth-value). If $a = b$, then the nominatum of 'a' and of 'b' is indeed the same and therefore also the truth-value of "$a = b$" is the same as that of "$a = a$". Nevertheless, the sense of 'b' may differ from the sense of 'a'; and therefore the proposition expressed by "$a = b$" may differ from the proposition expressed by "$a = a$"; in that case the two sentences do not have the same cognitive significance. Thus, if, as above, we mean by 'judgment' the transition from a proposition to its truth-value, then we can also say that the judgments differ from one another.

6

Bertrand Russell
On Denoting

By a "denoting phrase" I mean a phrase such as any one of the following: a man, some man, any man, every man, all men, the present King of England, the present King of France, the centre of mass of the Solar System at the first instant of the twentieth century, the revolution of the earth round the sun, the revolution of the sun round the earth. Thus a phrase is denoting solely in virtue of its *form*. We may distinguish three cases: (1) A phrase may be denoting, and yet not denote anything; *e.g.*, "the present King of France". (2) A phrase may denote one definite object; *e.g.*, "the present King of England" denotes a certain man. (3) A phrase may denote ambiguously; *e.g.*, "a man" denotes not many men, but an ambiguous man. The interpretation of such phrases is a matter of considerable difficulty; indeed, it is very hard to frame any theory not susceptible of formal refutation. All the difficulties with which I am acquainted are met, so far as I can discover, by the theory which I am about to explain.

The subject of denoting is of very great importance, not only in logic and mathematics, but also in theory of knowledge. For example, we know that the centre of mass of the Solar System at a definite instant is some definite point, and we can affirm a number of propositions about it; but we have no immediate *acquaintance* with this point, which is only known to us by description. The distinction between *acquaintance* and *knowledge about* is the distinction between the things we have presentations of, and the things we only reach by means of denoting phrases. It often happens that we know that a certain phrase denotes unambiguously, although we have no acquaintance with what it denotes; this occurs in the above case of the centre of mass. In perception we have acquaintance with the objects of perception, and in thought we have acquaintance with objects of a more abstract logical character; but we do not necessarily have acquaintance with the objects denoted by phrases composed of words with whose meanings we are acquainted. To take a very important instance: There seems no reason to believe that we are ever acquainted with other people's minds, seeing that these are not directly perceived; hence what we know about them is obtained through denoting. All thinking has to start from acquaintance; but it succeeds in thinking *about* many things with which we have no acquaintance.

The course of my argument will be as follows. I shall begin by stating the theory I intend to advocate;[1] I shall then discuss the theories of [Gottlob—Ed.]

Bertrand Russell, "On Denoting," *Logic and Knowledge*, R. C. Marsh, ed., © 1956. Reprinted by permission of George Allen & Unwin Ltd.

[1] I have discussed this subject in *Principles of Mathematics*, chapter v., and § 476. The theory there advocated is very nearly the same as Frege's, and is quite different from the theory to be advocated in what follows.

Frege and [Alexius—Ed.] Meinong, showing why neither of them satisfies me; then I shall give the grounds in favour of my theory; and finally I shall briefly indicate the philosophical consequences of my theory.

My theory, briefly, is as follows. I take the notion of the *variable* as fundamental; I use "C (x)" to mean a proposition[2] in which x is a constituent, where x, the variable, is essentially and wholly undetermined. Then we can consider the two notions "C (x) is always true" and "C (x) is sometimes true".[3] Then *everything* and *nothing* and *something* (which are the most primitive of denoting phrases) are to be interpreted as follows:—

C (everything) means "C (x) is always true";
C (nothing) means " 'C (x) is false' is always true";
C (something) means "It is false that 'C (x) is false' is always true".[4]

Here the notion "C (x) is always true" is taken as ultimate and indefinable, and the others are defined by means of it. *Everything, nothing,* and *something,* are not assumed to have any meaning in isolation, but a meaning is assigned to *every* proposition in which they occur. This is the principle of the theory of denoting I wish to advocate: that denoting phrases never have any meaning in themselves, but that every proposition in whose verbal expression they occur has a meaning. The difficulties concerning denoting are, I believe, all the result of a wrong analysis of propositions whose verbal expressions contain denoting phrases. The proper analysis, if I am not mistaken, may be further set forth as follows.

Suppose now we wish to interpret the proposition, "I met a man". If this is true, I met some definite man; but that is not what I affirm. What I affirm is, according to the theory I advocate:—

" 'I met x, and x is human' is not always false".

Generally, defining the class of men as the class of objects having the predicate *human,* we say that:—

"C (a man)" means " 'C (x) and x is human' is not always false".

This leaves "a man," by itself, wholly destitute of meaning, but gives a meaning to every proposition in whose verbal expression "a man" occurs.

Consider next the proposition "all men are mortal". This proposition[5] is really hypothetical and states that *if* anything is a man, it is mortal. That is, it states that if x is a man, x is mortal, whatever x may be. Hence, substituting 'x is human' for 'x is a man,' we find:—

"All men are mortal" means " 'If x is human, x is mortal' is always true".

---

[2] More exactly, a propositional function.

[3] The second of these can be defined by means of the first, if we take it to mean, "It is not true that 'C (x) is false' is always true".

[4] I shall sometimes use, instead of this complicated phrase, the phrase "C (x) is not always false," or "C (x) is sometimes true," supposed *defined* to mean the same as the complicated phrase.

[5] As has been ably argued in Mr. [F. H.—Ed.] Bradley's *Logic,* book i., chap. ii.

This is what is expressed in symbolic logic by saying that "all men are mortal" means " 'x is human' implies 'x is mortal' for all values of x". More generally, we say:—

"C (all men)" means " 'If x is human, then C (x) is true' is always true".

Similarly

"C (no men)" means " 'If x is human, then C (x) is false' is always true".
"C (some men)" will mean the same as "C (a man),"[6] and
"C (a man)" means "It is false that 'C (x) and x is human' is always false".
"C (every man)" will mean the same as "C (all men)".

It remains to interpret phrases containing *the*. These are by far the most interesting and difficult of denoting phrases. Take as an instance "the father of Charles II. was executed". This asserts that there was an x who was the father of Charles II. and was executed. Now *the*, when it is strictly used, involves uniqueness; we do, it is true, speak of "*the* son of So-and-so" even when So-and-so has several sons, but it would be more correct to say "*a* son of So-and-so". Thus for our purposes we take *the* as involving uniqueness. Thus when we say "x was *the* father of Charles II." we not only assert that x had a certain relation to Charles II., but also that nothing else had this relation. The relation in question, without any denoting phrases, is expressed by "x begat Charles II.". To get an equivalent of "x was the father of Charles II.," we must add, "If y is other than x, y did not beget Charles II.," or, what is equivalent, "If y begat Charles II., y is identical with x". Hence "x is the father of Charles II." becomes "x begat Charles II.; and 'if y begat Charles II., y is identical with x' is always true of y".
Thus "the father of Charles II. was executed" becomes:—

"It is not always false of x that x begat Charles II. and that x was executed and that 'if y begat Charles II., y is identical with x' is always true of y".

This may seem a somewhat incredible interpretation; but I am not at present giving reasons, I am merely *stating* the theory.
To interpret "C (the father of Charles II.)," where C stands for any statement about him, we have only to substitute C (x) for "x was executed" in the above. Observe that, according to the above interpretation, whatever statement C may be, "C (the father of Charles II.)" implies:—

"It is not always false of x that 'if y begat Charles II., y is identical with x' is always true of y,"

which is what is expressed in common language by "Charles II. had one father and no more". Consequently if this condition fails, *every* proposition of the form "C (the father of Charles II.)" is false. Thus *e.g.* every proposition of the form "C (the present King of France)" is false. This is a great advantage in the present theory. I shall show later that it is not contrary to the law of contradiction, as might be at first supposed.

---

[6] Psychologically "C (a man)" has a suggestion of *only one*, and "C (some men)" has a suggestion of *more than one*; but we may neglect these suggestions in a preliminary sketch.

The above gives a reduction of all propositions in which denoting phrases occur to forms in which no such phrases occur. Why it is imperative to effect such a reduction, the subsequent discussion will endeavour to show.

The evidence for the above theory is derived from the difficulties which seem unavoidable if we regard denoting phrases as standing for genuine constituents of the propositions in whose verbal expressions they occur. Of the possible theories which admit such constituents the simplest is that of Meinong.[7] This theory regards any grammatically correct denoting phrase as standing for an *object*. Thus "the present King of France," "the round square," etc., are supposed to be genuine objects. It is admitted that such objects do not *subsist*, but nevertheless they are supposed to be objects. This is in itself a difficult view; but the chief objection is that such objects, admittedly, are apt to infringe the law of contradiction. It is contended, for example, that the existent present King of France exists, and also does not exist; that the round square is round, and also not round; etc. But this is intolerable; and if any theory can be found to avoid this result, it is surely to be preferred.

The above breach of the law of contradiction is avoided by Frege's theory. He distinguishes, in a denoting phrase, two elements, which we may call the *meaning* and the *denotation*.[8] Thus "the centre of mass of the Solar System at the beginning of the twentieth century" is highly complex in *meaning*, but its *denotation* is a certain point, which is simple. The Solar System, the twentieth century, etc., are constituents of the *meaning*; but the *denotation* has no constituents at all.[9] One advantage of this distinction is that it shows why it is often worth while to assert identity. If we say "Scott is the author of *Waverley*," we assert an identity of denotation with a difference of meaning. I shall, however, not repeat the grounds in favour of this theory, as I have urged its claims elsewhere (*loc. cit.*), and am now concerned to dispute those claims.

One of the first difficulties that confront us, when we adopt the view that denoting phrases *express* a meaning and *denote* a denotation,[10] concerns the cases in which the denotation appears to be absent. If we say "the King of England is bald," that is, it would seem, not a statement about the complex *meaning* "the King of England," but about the actual man denoted by the meaning. But now consider "the King of France is bald". By parity of form, this also ought to be about the denotation of the phrase "the King of France". But this phrase, though it has a *meaning* provided "the King of England" has a meaning, has certainly no denotation, at least in any obvious sense. Hence one

---

[7] See *Untersuchungen zur Gegenstandstheorie und Psychologie*, Leipzig, 1904, the first three articles (by Meinong, Ameseder and Mally respectively).

[8] See his "Ueber Sinn und Bedeutung," *Zeitschrift für Phil. und Phil. Kritik*, vol. 100.

[9] Frege distinguishes the two elements of meaning and denotation everywhere, and not only in complex denoting phrases. Thus it is the *meanings* of the constituents of a denoting complex that enter into its *meaning*, not their *denotation*. In the proposition "Mont Blanc is over 1,000 metres high," it is, according to him, the *meaning* of "Mont Blanc", not the actual mountain, that is a constituent of the *meaning* of the proposition.

[10] In this theory, we shall say that the denoting phrase *expresses* a meaning; and we shall say both of the phrase and of the meaning that they *denote* a denotation. In the other theory, which I advocate, there is no *meaning*, and only sometimes a *denotation*.

would suppose that "the King of France is bald" ought to be nonsense; but it is not nonsense, since it is plainly false. Or again consider such a proposition as the following: "If u is a class which has only one member, then that one member is a member of u," or, as we may state it, "If u is a unit class, *the u* is a *u*". This proposition ought to be *always* true, since the conclusion is true whenever the hypothesis is true. But "the u" is a denoting phrase, and it is the denotation, not the meaning, that is said to be a u. Now if u is *not* a unit class, "the u" seems to denote nothing; hence our proposition would seem to become nonsense as soon as u is not a unit class.

Now it is plain that such propositions do *not* become nonsense merely because their hypotheses are false. The King in "The Tempest" might say, "If Ferdinand is not drowned, Ferdinand is my only son". Now "my only son" is a denoting phrase, which, on the face of it, has a denotation when, and only when, I have exactly one son. But the above statement would nevertheless have remained true if Ferdinand had been in fact drowned. Thus we must either provide a denotation in cases in which it is at first sight absent, or we must abandon the view that the denotation is what is concerned in propositions which contain denoting phrases. The latter is the course that I advocate. The former course may be taken, as by Meinong, by admitting objects which do not subsist, and denying that they obey the law of contradiction; this, however, is to be avoided if possible. Another way of taking the same course (so far as our present alternative is concerned) is adopted by Frege, who provides by definition some purely conventional denotation for the cases in which otherwise there would be none. Thus "the King of France," is to denote the null-class; "the only son of Mr. So-and-so" (who has a fine family of ten), is to denote the class of all his sons; and so on. But this procedure, though it may not lead to actual logical error, is plainly artificial, and does not give an exact analysis of the matter. Thus if we allow that denoting phrases, in general, have the two sides of meaning and denotation, the cases where there seems to be no denotation cause difficulties both on the assumption that there really is a denotation and on the assumption that there really is none.

A logical theory may be tested by its capacity for dealing with puzzles, and it is a wholesome plan, in thinking about logic, to stock the mind with as many puzzles as possible, since these serve much the same purpose as is served by experiments in physical science. I shall therefore state three puzzles which a theory as to denoting ought to be able to solve; and I shall show later that my theory solves them.

(1) If a is identical with b, whatever is true of the one is true of the other, and either may be substituted for the other in any proposition without altering the truth or falsehood of that proposition. Now George IV. wished to know whether Scott was the author of *Waverley*; and in fact Scott *was* the author of *Waverley*. Hence we may substitute *Scott* for *the author of "Waverley*," and thereby prove that George IV. wished to know whether Scott was Scott. Yet an interest in the law of identity can hardly be attributed to the first gentleman of Europe.

(2) By the law of excluded middle, either "A is B" or "A is not B" must be true. Hence either "the present King of France is bald" or "the present King of

France is not bald" must be true. Yet if we enumerated the things that are bald, and then the things that are not bald, we should not find the present King of France in either list. Hegelians, who love a synthesis, will probably conclude that he wears a wig.

(3) Consider the proposition "A differs from B". If this is true, there is a difference between A and B, which fact may be expressed in the form "the difference between A and B subsists". But if it is false that A differs from B, then there is no difference between A and B, which fact may be expressed in the form "the difference between A and B does not subsist". But how can a non-entity be the subject of a proposition? "I think, therefore I am" is no more evident than "I am the subject of a proposition, therefore I am," provided "I am" is taken to assert subsistence or being,[11] not existence. Hence, it would appear, it must always be self-contradictory to deny the being of anything; but we have seen, in connexion with Meinong, that to admit being also sometimes leads to contradictions. Thus if A and B do not differ, to suppose either that there is, or that there is not, such an object as "the difference between A and B" seems equally impossible.

The relation of the meaning to the denotation involves certain rather curious difficulties, which seem in themselves sufficient to prove that the theory which leads to such difficulties must be wrong.

When we wish to speak about the *meaning* of a denoting phrase, as opposed to its *denotation*, the natural mode of doing so is by inverted commas. Thus we say:—

The centre of mass of the Solar System is a point, not a denoting complex;
"The centre of mass of the Solar System" is a denoting complex, not a point.

Or again,

The first line of Gray's Elegy states a proposition.
"The first line of Gray's Elegy" does not state a proposition.

Thus taking any denoting phrase, say C, we wish to consider the relation between C and "C," where the difference of the two is of the kind exemplified in the above two instances.

We say, to begin with, that when C occurs it is the *denotation* that we are speaking about; but when "C" occurs, it is the *meaning*. Now the relation of meaning and denotation is not merely linguistic through the phrase: there must be a logical relation involved, which we express by saying that the meaning denotes the denotation. But the difficulty which confronts us is that we cannot succeed in *both* preserving the connexion of meaning and denotation *and* preventing them from being one and the same; also that the meaning cannot be got at except by means of denoting phrases. This happens as follows.

The one phrase C was to have both meaning and denotation. But if we speak of "the meaning of C," that gives us the meaning (if any) of the denotation. "The meaning of the first line of Gray's Elegy" is the same as "The mean-

---

[11] I use these as synonyms.

ing of 'The curfew tolls the knell of parting day,' " and is not the same as "The meaning of 'the first line of Gray's Elegy' ". Thus in order to get the meaning we want, we must speak not of "the meaning of C," but of "the meaning of 'C,' " which is the same as "C" by itself. Similarly "the denotation of C" does not mean the denotation we want, but means something which, if it denotes at all, denotes what is denoted by the denotation we want. For example, let "C" be "the denoting complex occurring in the second of the above instances". Then

C = "the first line of Gray's Elegy,"

and the denotation of C = The curfew tolls the knell of parting day. But what we *meant* to have as the denotation was "the first line of Gray's Elegy". Thus we have failed to get what we wanted.

The difficulty in speaking of the meaning of a denoting complex may be stated thus: The moment we put the complex in a proposition, the proposition is about the denotation; and if we make a proposition in which the subject is "the meaning of C," then the subject is the meaning (if any) of the denotation, which was not intended. This leads us to say that, when we distinguish meaning and denotation, we must be dealing with the meaning: the meaning has denotation and is a complex, and there is not something other than the meaning, which can be called the complex, and be said to *have* both meaning and denotation. The right phrase, on the view in question, is that some meanings have denotations.

But this only makes our difficulty in speaking of meanings more evident. For suppose C is our complex; then we are to say that C *is* the meaning of the complex. Nevertheless, whenever C occurs without inverted commas, what is said is not true of the meaning, but only of the denotation, as when we say: The centre of mass of the Solar System is a point. Thus to speak of C itself, *i.e.*, to make a proposition about the meaning, our subject must not be C, but something which denotes C. Thus "C," which is what we use when we want to speak of the meaning, must be not the meaning, but something which denotes the meaning. And C must not be a constituent of this complex (as it is of "the meaning of C"); for if C occurs in the complex, it will be its denotation, not its meaning, that will occur, and there is no backward road from denotations to meanings, because every object can be denoted by an infinite number of different denoting phrases.

Thus it would seem that "C" and C are different entities, such that "C" denotes C; but this cannot be an explanation, because the relation of "C" to C remains wholly mysterious; and where are we to find the denoting complex "C" which is to denote C? Moreover, when C occurs in a proposition, it is not *only* the denotation that occurs (as we shall see in the next paragraph); yet, on the view in question, C is only the denotation, the meaning being wholly relegated to "C". This is an inextricable tangle, and seems to prove that the whole distinction of meaning and denotation has been wrongly conceived.

That the meaning is relevant when a denoting phrase occurs in a proposition is formally proved by the puzzle about the author of *Waverley*. The proposition "Scott was the author of *Waverley*" has a property not possessed by "Scott was Scott," namely the property that George IV. wished to know whether it was true. Thus the two are not identical propositions; hence the meaning of "the author of *Waverley*" must be relevant as well as the denotation, if we adhere to the point of view to which this distinction belongs. Yet, as we have just seen, so long as we adhere to this point of view, we are compelled to hold that only the denotation can be relevant. Thus the point of view in question must be abandoned.

It remains to show how all the puzzles we have been considering are solved by the theory explained at the beginning of this article.

According to the view which I advocate, a denoting phrase is essentially *part* of a sentence, and does not, like most single words, have any significance on its own account. If I say "Scott was a man," that is a statement of the form "*x* was a man," and it has "Scott" for its subject. But if I say "the author of *Waverley* was a man," that is not a statement of the form "*x* was a man," and does not have "the author of *Waverley*" for its subject. Abbreviating the statement made at the beginning of this article, we may put, in place of "the author of *Waverley* was a man," the following: "One and only one entity wrote *Waverley*, and that one was a man". (This is not so strictly what is meant as what was said earlier; but it is easier to follow.) And speaking generally, suppose we wish to say that the author of *Waverley* had the property ∅, what we wish to say is equivalent to "One and only one entity wrote *Waverley*, and that one had the property ∅".

The explanation of *denotation* is now as follows. Every proposition in which "the author of *Waverley*" occurs being explained as above, the proposition "Scott was the author of *Waverley*" (*i.e.* "Scott was identical with the author of *Waverley*") becomes "One and only one entity wrote *Waverley*, and Scott was identical with that one"; or, reverting to the wholly explicit form: "It is not always false of *x* that *x* wrote *Waverley*, that it is always true of *y* that if *y* wrote *Waverley* *y* is identical with *x*, and that Scott is identical with *x*". Thus if "C" is a denoting phrase, it may happen that there is one entity *x* (there cannot be more than one) for which the proposition "*x* is identical with C" is true, this proposition being interpreted as above. We may then say that the entity *x* is the denotation of the phrase "C". Thus Scott is the denotation of "the author of *Waverley*". The "C" in inverted commas will be merely the *phrase*, not anything that can be called the *meaning*. The phrase *per se* [by itself—Ed.] has no meaning, because in any proposition in which it occurs the proposition, fully expressed, does not contain the phrase, which has been broken up.

The puzzle about George IV.'s curiosity is now seen to have a very simple solution. The proposition "Scott was the author of *Waverley*," which was written out in its unabbreviated form in the preceding paragraph, does not contain any constituent "the author of *Waverley*" for which we could substitute "Scott". This does not interfere with the truth of inferences resulting from making what is *verbally* the substitution of "Scott" for "the author of *Waverley*," so long as "the author of *Waverley*" has what I call a *primary* occurrence in the proposition considered. The difference of primary and secondary occurrences of denoting phrases is as follows:—

When we say: "George IV. wished to know whether so-and-so," or when we say "So-and-so is surprising" or "So-and-so is true," etc., the "so-and-so" must be a proposition. Suppose now that "so-and-so" contains a denoting phrase. We may either eliminate this denoting phrase from the subordinate proposition "so-and-so," or from the whole proposition in which "so-and-so" is a mere constituent. Different propositions result according to which we do. I have heard of a touchy owner of a yacht to whom a guest, on first seeing it, remarked, "I thought your yacht was larger than it is"; and the owner replied, "No, my yacht is not larger than it is". What the guest meant was, "The size that I thought your yacht was is greater than the size your yacht is"; the meaning attributed to him is, "I thought the size of your yacht was greater than the size of your yacht". To return to George IV. and Waverley, when we say, "George IV. wished to know whether Scott was the author of Waverley," we normally mean "George IV. wished to know whether one and only one man wrote Waverley and Scott was that man"; but we *may* also mean: "One and only one man wrote Waverley, and George IV. wished to know whether Scott was that man". In the latter, "the author of Waverley" has a *primary* occurrence; in the former, a *secondary*. The latter might be expressed by "George IV. wished to know, concerning the man who in fact wrote Waverley, whether he was Scott". This would be true, for example, if George IV. had seen Scott at a distance, and had asked "Is that Scott?" A *secondary* occurrence of a denoting phrase may be defined as one in which the phrase occurs in a proposition p which is a mere constituent of the proposition we are considering, and the substitution for the denoting phrase is to be effected in p, not in the whole proposition concerned. The ambiguity as between primary and secondary occurrences is hard to avoid in language; but it does no harm if we are on our guard against it. In symbolic logic it is of course easily avoided.

The distinction of primary and secondary occurrences also enables us to deal with the question whether the present King of France is bald or not bald, and generally with the logical status of denoting phrases that denote nothing. If "C" is a denoting phrase, say "the term having the property F," then

"C has the property ϕ" means "one and only one term has the property F, and that one has the property ϕ".[12]

If now the property F belongs to no terms, or to several, it follows that "C has the property ϕ" is false for *all* values of ϕ. Thus "the present King of France is bald" is certainly false; and "the present King of France is not bald" is false if it means

"There is an entity which is now King of France and is not bald,"

but is true if it means

"It is false that there is an entity which is now King of France and is bald".

That is, "the King of France is not bald" is false if the occurrence of "the King of France" is *primary*, and true if it is *secondary*. Thus all propositions in which

---

[12] This is the abbreviated, not the stricter, interpretation.

"the King of France" has a primary occurrence are false; the denials of such propositions are true, but in them "the King of France" has a secondary occurrence. Thus we escape the conclusion that the King of France has a wig.

We can now see also how to deny that there is such an object as the difference between A and B in the case when A and B do not differ. If A and B do differ, there is one and only one entity *x* such that "*x* is the difference between A and B" is a true proposition; if A and B do not differ, there is no such entity *x*. Thus according to the meaning of denotation lately explained, "the difference between A and B" has a denotation when A and B differ, but not otherwise. This difference applies to true and false propositions generally. If "*a* R *b*" stands for "*a* has the relation R to *b*," then when *a* R *b* is true, there is such an entity as the relation R between *a* and *b*; when *a* R *b* is false, there is no such entity. Thus out of any proposition we can make a denoting phrase, which denotes an entity if the proposition is true, but does not denote an entity if the proposition is false. E.g., it is true (at least we will suppose so) that the earth revolves round the sun, and false that the sun revolves round the earth; hence "the revolution of the earth round the sun" denotes an entity, while "the revolution of the sun round the earth" does not denote an entity.[13]

The whole realm of non-entities, such as "the round square," "the even prime other than 2," "Apollo," "Hamlet," etc., can now be satisfactorily dealt with. All these are denoting phrases which do not denote anything. A proposition about Apollo means what we get by substituting what the classical dictionary tells us is meant by Apollo, say "the sun-god." All propositions in which Apollo occurs are to be interpreted by the above rules for denoting phrases. If "Apollo" has a primary occurrence, the proposition containing the occurrence is false; if the occurrence is secondary, the proposition may be true. So again "the round square is round" means "there is one and only one entity *x* which is round and square, and that entity is round," which is a false proposition, not, as Meinong maintains, a true one. "The most perfect Being has all perfections; existence is a perfection; therefore the most perfect Being exists" becomes:—

"There is one and only one entity *x* which is most perfect; that one has all perfections; existence is a perfection; therefore that one exists".

As a proof, this fails for want of a proof of the premiss "there is one and only one entity *x* which is most perfect".[14]

Mr. [H.—Ed.] MacColl (MIND, N.S., No. 54, and again No. 55, p. 401) regards individuals as of two sorts, real and unreal; hence he defines the null-class as the class consisting of all unreal individuals. This assumes that such phrases as "the present King of France," which do not denote a real individual, do,

---

[13] The propositions from which such entities are derived are not identical either with these entities or with the propositions that these entities have being.

[14] The argument can be made to prove validly that all members of the class of most perfect Beings exist; it can also be proved formally that this class cannot have *more* than one member; but, taking the definition of perfection as possession of all positive predicates, it can be proved almost equally formally that the class does not have even one member.

nevertheless, denote an individual, but an unreal one. This is essentially Meinong's theory, which we have seen reason to reject because it conflicts with the law of contradiction. With our theory of denoting, we are able to hold that there are no unreal individuals; so that the null-class is the class containing no members, not the class containing as members all unreal individuals.

It is important to observe the effect of our theory on the interpretation of definitions which proceed by means of denoting phrases. Most mathematical definitions are of this sort: for example, "$m—n$ means the number which, added to n, gives m". Thus $m—n$ is defined as meaning the same as a certain denoting phrase; but we agreed that denoting phrases have no meaning in isolation. Thus what the definition really ought to be is: "Any proposition containing $m—n$ is to mean the proposition which results from substituting for '$m—n$' 'the number which, added to n, gives m' ". The resulting proposition is interpreted according to the rules already given for interpreting propositions whose verbal expression contains a denoting phrase. In the case where m and n are such that there is one and only one number x which, added to n, gives m, there is a number x which can be substituted for $m—n$ in any proposition containing $m—n$ without altering the truth or falsehood of the proposition. But in other cases, all propositions in which "$m—n$" has a primary occurrence are false.

The usefulness of *identity* is explained by the above theory. No one outside a logic-book ever wishes to say "x is x," and yet assertions of identity are often made in such forms as "Scott was the author of W*averley*" or "thou art the man". The meaning of such propositions cannot be stated without the notion of identity, although they are not simply statements that Scott is identical with another term, the author of W*averley*, or that thou art identical with another term, the man. The shortest statement of "Scott is the author of W*averley*" seems to be: "Scott wrote W*averley*; and it is always true of y that if y wrote W*averley*, y is identical with Scott". It is in this way that identity enters into "Scott is the author of W*averley*"; and it is owing to such uses that identity is worth affirming.

One interesting result of the above theory of denoting is this: when there is anything with which we do not have immediate acquaintance, but only definition by denoting phrases, then the propositions in which this thing is introduced by means of a denoting phrase do not really contain this thing as a constituent, but contain instead the constituents expressed by the several words of the denoting phrase. Thus in every proposition that we can apprehend (*i.e.* not only in those whose truth or falsehood we can judge of, but in all that we can think about), all the constituents are really entities with which we have immediate acquaintance. Now such things as matter (in the sense in which matter occurs in physics) and the minds of other people are known to us only by denoting phrases, *i.e.*, we are not *acquainted* with them, but we know them as what has such and such properties. Hence, although we can form propositional functions C (x) which must hold of such and such a material particle, or of So-and-So's mind, yet we are not acquainted with the propositions which affirm these things that we know must be true, because we cannot apprehend the actual entities concerned. What we know is "So-and-so has a mind which has such and such properties" but we do not know "A has such and such properties," where A *is* the mind in question. In such a case, we know the properties of a thing without having acquaintance with the thing itself, and without, consequently, knowing any single proposition of which the thing itself is a constituent.

Of the many other consequences of the view I have been advocating, I will say nothing. I will only beg the reader not to make up his mind against the view—as he might be tempted to do, on account of its apparently excessive complication—until he has attempted to construct a theory of his own on the subject of denotation. This attempt, I believe, will convince him that, whatever the true theory may be, it cannot have such a simplicity as one might have expected beforehand.

7

P. F. Strawson
On Referring

I

We very commonly use expressions of certain kinds to mention or refer to some individual person or single object or particular event or place or process, in the course of doing what we should normally describe as making a statement about that person, object, place, event, or process. I shall call this way of using expressions the "uniquely referring use". The classes of expressions which are most commonly used in this way are: singular demonstrative pronouns ("this" and "that"); proper names (*e.g.* "Venice", "Napoleon", "John"); singular personal and impersonal pronouns ("he", "she", "I", "you", "it"); and phrases beginning with the definite article followed by a noun, qualified or unqualified, in the singular (*e.g.* "the table", "the old man", "the king of France"). Any expression of any of these classes can occur as the subject of what would traditionally be regarded as a singular subject-predicate sentence; and would, so occurring, exemplify the use I wish to discuss.

I do not want to say that expressions belonging to these classes never have any other use than the one I want to discuss. On the contrary, it is obvious that

From P. F. Strawson, "On Referring," *Mind*, LIX (1950), Secs. 1–3, 320–335. Reprinted by permission of the publisher.

they do. It is obvious that anyone who uttered the sentence, "The whale is a mammal", would be using the expression "the whale" in a way quite different from the way it would be used by anyone who had occasion seriously to utter the sentence, "The whale struck the ship". In the first sentence one is obviously *not* mentioning, and in the second sentence one obviously *is* mentioning, a particular whale. Again if I said, "Napoleon was the greatest French soldier", I should be using the word "Napoleon" to mention a certain individual, but I should not be using the phrase, "the greatest French soldier", to mention an individual, but to say something about an individual I had already mentioned. It would be natural to say that in using this sentence I was talking *about* Napoleon and that what I was *saying* about him was that he was the greatest French soldier. But of course I *could* use the expression, "the greatest French soldier", to mention an individual; for example, by saying: "The greatest French soldier died in exile". So it is obvious that at least some expressions belonging to the classes I mentioned *can* have uses other than the use I am anxious to discuss. Another thing I do not want to say is that in any given sentence there is never more than one expression used in the way I propose to discuss. On the contrary, it is obvious that there may be more than one. For example, it would be natural to say that, in seriously using the sentence, "The whale struck the ship", I was saying something about both a certain whale and a certain ship, that I was using each of the expressions "the whale" and "the ship" to mention a particular object; or, in other words, that I was using each of these expressions in the uniquely referring way. In general, however, I shall confine my attention to cases where an expression used in this way occurs as the grammatical subject of a sentence.

I think it is true to say that [Bertrand—Ed.] Russell's Theory of Descriptions, which is concerned with the last of the four classes of expressions I mentioned above (*i.e.* with expressions of the form "the so-and-so") is still widely accepted among logicians as giving a correct account of the use of such expressions in ordinary language. I want to show, in the first place, that this theory, so regarded, embodies some fundamental mistakes.

What question or questions about phrases of the form "the so-and-so" was the Theory of Descriptions designed to answer? I think that at least one of the questions may be illustrated as follows. Suppose some one were now to utter the sentence, "The king of France is wise". No one would say that the sentence which had been uttered was meaningless. Everyone would agree that it was significant. But everyone knows that there is not at present a king of France. One of the questions the Theory of Descriptions was designed to answer was the question: how can such a sentence as "The king of France is wise" be significant even when there is nothing which answers to the description it contains, *i.e.*, in this case, nothing which answers to the description "The king of France"? And one of the reasons why Russell thought it important to give a correct answer to this question was that he thought it important to show that another answer which might be given was wrong. The answer that he thought was wrong, and to which he was anxious to supply an alternative, might be exhibited as the conclusion of either of the following two fallacious arguments. Let us call the sentence "The king of France is wise" the sentence S. Then the first argument is as follows:

(1) The phrase, "the king of France", is the subject of the sentence S.

Therefore (2) if S is a significant sentence, S is a sentence *about* the king of France.

But (3) if there in no sense exists a king of France, the sentence is not about anything, and hence not about the king of France.

Therefore (4) since S is significant, there must in some sense (in some world) exist (or subsist) the king of France.

And the second argument is as follows:

(1) If S is significant, it is either true or false.

(2) S is true if the king of France is wise and false if the king of France is not wise.

(3) But the statement that the king of France is wise and the statement that the king of France is not wise are alike true only if there is (in some sense, in some world) something which is the king of France.

Hence (4) since S is significant, there follows the same conclusion as before.

These are fairly obviously bad arguments, and, as we should expect, Russell rejects them. The postulation of a world of strange entities, to which the king of France belongs, offends, he says, against "that feeling for reality which ought to be preserved even in the most abstract studies". The fact that Russell rejects these arguments is, however, less interesting than the extent to which, in rejecting their conclusion, he concedes the more important of their principles. Let me refer to the phrase, "the king of France", as the phrase D. Then I think Russell's reasons for rejecting these two arguments can be summarised as follows. The mistake arises, he says, from thinking that D, which is certainly the *grammatical* subject of S, is also the *logical* subject of S. But D is not the logical subject of S. In fact S, although grammatically it has a singular subject and a predicate, is not logically a subject-predicate sentence at all. The proposition it expresses is a complex kind of *existential* proposition, part of which might be described as a "uniquely existential" proposition. To exhibit the logical form of the proposition, we should re-write the sentence in a logically appropriate grammatical form; in such a way that the deceptive similarity of S to a sentence expressing a subject-predicate proposition would disappear, and we should be safeguarded against arguments such as the bad ones I outlined above. Before recalling the details of Russell's analysis of S, let us notice what his answer, as I have so far given it, seems to imply. His answer seems to imply that in the case of a sentence which is similar to S in that (1) it is grammatically of the subject-predicate form and (2) its grammatical subject does not refer to anything, then the only alternative to its being meaningless is that it should not really (*i.e.* logically) be of the subject-predicate form at all, but of some quite different form. And this in its turn seems to imply that if there are any sentences which are genuinely of the subject-predicate form, then the very fact of their being significant, having a meaning, guarantees that there *is* something referred to by the logical (and grammatical) subject. Moreover, Russell's answer seems to imply that there are such sentences. For if it is true that one may be misled by the grammatical similarity of S to other sentences into thinking that it is logically of the subject-predicate form, then surely there must be other sentences grammatically similar to S, which *are* of the subject-predicate form. To show not only that Russell's answer seems to imply these conclusions, but that he accepted at least the first two of them, it is enough to consider what he says about a class of expressions which he·calls "logically proper names" and contrasts with expressions, like D, which he calls "definite descriptions". Of logically proper names Russell says or implies the following things:

(1) That they and they alone can occur as subjects of sentences which are genuinely of the subject-predicate form;

(2) that an expression intended to be a logically proper name is *meaningless* unless there is some single object for which it stands: for the *meaning* of such an expression just is the individual object which the expression designates. To be a name at all, therefore, it *must* designate something.

It is easy to see that if anyone believes these two propositions, then the only way for him to save the significance of the sentence S is to deny that it is a logically subject-predicate sentence. Generally, we may say that Russell recognises only two ways in which sentences which seem, from their grammatical structure, to be about some particular person or individual object or event, can be significant:

(1) The first is that their grammatical form should be misleading as to their logical form, and that they should be analysable, like S, as a special kind of existential sentence;

(2) The second is that their grammatical subject should be a logically proper name, of which the meaning is the individual thing it designates.

I think that Russell is unquestionably wrong in this, and that sentences which are significant, and which begin with an expression used in the uniquely referring way fall into neither of these two classes. Expressions used in the uniquely referring way are never either logically proper names or descriptions, if what is meant by calling them "descriptions" is that they are to be analysed in accordance with the model provided by Russell's Theory of Descriptions.

There are no logically proper names and there are no descriptions (in this sense).

Let us now consider the details of Russell's analysis. According to Russell, anyone who asserted S would be asserting that:

(1) There is a king of France.
(2) There is not more than one king of France.
(3) There is nothing which is king of France and is not wise.

It is easy to see both how Russell arrived at this analysis, and how it enables him to answer the question with which we began, *viz.* the question: How can the sentence S be significant when there is no king of France? The way in which he arrived at the analysis was clearly by asking himself what would be the circumstances in which we would say that anyone who uttered the sentence S had made a true assertion. And it does seem pretty clear, and I have no wish to dispute, that the sentences (1)–(3) above do describe circumstances which are at least *necessary* conditions of anyone making a true assertion by uttering the sentence S. But, as I hope to show, to say this is not at all the same thing as to say that

Russell has given a correct account of the use of the sentence S or even that he has given an account which, though incomplete, is correct as far as it goes; and is certainly not at all the same thing as to say that the model translation provided is a correct model for all (or for any) singular sentences beginning with a phrase of the form "the so-and-so".

It is also easy to see how this analysis enables Russell to answer the question of how the sentence S can be significant, even when there is no king of France. For, if this analysis is correct, anyone who utters the sentence S to-day would be jointly asserting three propositions, one of which (*viz.* that there is a king of France) would be false; and since the conjunction of three propositions, of which one is false, is itself false, the assertion as a whole would be significant, but false. So neither of the bad arguments for subsistent entities would apply to such an assertion.

II

As a step towards showing that Russell's solution of his problem is mistaken, and towards providing the correct solution, I want now to draw certain distinctions. For this purpose I shall, for the remainder of this section, refer to an expression which has a uniquely referring use as "an expression" for short; and to a sentence beginning with such an expression as "a sentence" for short. The distinctions I shall draw are rather rough and ready, and, no doubt, difficult cases could be produced which would call for their refinement. But I think they will serve my purpose. The distinctions are between:

(A1) a sentence,
(A2) a use of a sentence,
(A3) an utterance of a sentence,

and, correspondingly, between:

(B1) an expression,
(B2) a use of an expression,
(B3) an utterance of an expression.

Consider again the sentence, "The king of France is wise". It is easy to imagine that this sentence was uttered at various times from, say, the beginning of the seventeenth century onwards, during the reigns of each successive French monarch; and easy to imagine that it was also uttered during the subsequent periods in which France was not a monarchy. Notice that it was natural for me to speak of "the sentence" or "this sentence" being uttered at various times during this period or, in other words, that it would be natural and correct to speak of *one and the same* sentence being uttered on all these various occasions. It is in the sense in which it would be correct to speak of one and the same sentence being uttered on all these various occasions that I want to use the expression (A1) "a sentence". There are, however, obvious differences between different *occasions of the use* of this sentence. For instance, if one man uttered it in the reign of Louis XIV and another man uttered it in the reign of Louis

XV, it would be natural to say (to assume) that they were respectively talking about different people; and it might be held that the first man, in using the sentence, made a true assertion, while the second man, in using the same sentence, made a false assertion. If on the other hand two different men simultaneously uttered the sentence (*e.g.* if one wrote it and the other spoke it) during the reign of Louis XIV, it would be natural to say (assume) that they were both talking about the same person, and, in that case, in using the sentence, they *must* either both have made a true assertion or both have made a false assertion. And this illustrates what I mean by *a use* of a sentence. The two men who uttered the sentence, one in the reign of Louis XV and one in the reign of Louis XIV, each made a different use of the same sentence; whereas the two men who uttered the sentence simultaneously in the reign of Louis XIV, made the same use[1] of the same sentence. Obviously in the case of this sentence, and equally obviously in the case of many others, we cannot talk of *the sentence* being true or false, but only of its being used to make a true or false assertion, or (if this is preferred) to express a true or a false proposition. And equally obviously we cannot talk of *the sentence* being *about* a particular person, for the same sentence may be used at different times to talk about quite different particular persons, but only of *a use* of the sentence to talk about a particular person. Finally it will make sufficiently clear what I mean by an utterance of a sentence if I say that the two men who simultaneously uttered the sentence in the reign of Louis XIV made two different utterances of the same sentence, though they made the same *use* of the sentence.

If we now consider not the whole sentence, "The king of France is wise", but that part of it which is the expression, "the king of France", it is obvious that we can make analogous, though not identical distinctions between (1) the expression, (2) a use of the expression and (3) an utterance of the expression alone, that you can talk about a particular person. Instead, we correctly talk of the expression "the king of France" being used to express a true or false proposition, since in general only sentences can be used truly or falsely; and similarly it is only by using a sentence and not by using an expression alone, that you can talk about a particular person. Instead, we shall say in this case that you *use* the expression to *mention* or *refer to* a particular person in the course of using the sentence to talk about him. But obviously in this case, and a great many others, the *expression* (B1) cannot be said to mention, or refer to, anything, any more than the *sentence* can be said to be true or false. The same expression can have different mentioning-uses, as the same sentence can be used to make statements with different truth-values. "Mentioning", or "referring", is not something an expression does; it is something that some one can use an expression to do. Mentioning, or referring to, something is a characteristic of *a use* of an expression, just as "being about" something, and truth-or-falsity, are characteristics of a *use* of a sentence.

---

[1] This usage of 'use' is, of course, different from (*a*) the current usage in which 'use' (of a particular word, phrase, sentence) = (roughly) 'rules for using' = (roughly) 'meaning'; and from (*b*) my own usage in the phrase "uniquely referring use of expressions" in which 'use' = (roughly) 'way of using'.

A very different example may help to make these distinctions clearer. Consider another case of an expression which has a uniquely referring use, *viz.* the expression "I"; and consider the sentence, "I am hot". Countless people may use this same sentence; but it is logically impossible for two different people to make *the same use* of this sentence: or, if this is preferred, to use it to express the same proposition. The expression "I" may correctly be used by (and only by) any one of innumerable people to refer to himself. To say this is to say something about the expression "I": it is, in a sense, to give its meaning. This is the sort of thing that can be said about *expressions*. But it makes no sense to say of the *expression* "I" that it refers to a particular person. This is the sort of thing that can be said only of a particular use of the expression.

Let me use "type" as an abbreviation for "sentence or expression". Then I am not saying that there are sentences and expressions (types), *and* uses of them, *and* utterances of them, as there are ships *and* shoes *and* sealing-wax. I am saying that we cannot say *the same things* about types, uses of types, and utterances of types. And the fact is that we do talk about types; and that confusion is apt to result from the failure to notice the differences between what we can say about these and what we can say only about the *uses* of types. We are apt to fancy we are talking about sentences and expressions when we are talking about the uses of sentences and expressions.

This is what Russell does. Generally, as against Russell, I shall say this. Meaning (in at least one important sense) is a function of the sentence or expression; mentioning and referring and truth or falsity, are functions of the use of the sentence or expression. To give the meaning of an expression (in the sense in which I am using the word) is to give *general directions* for its use to refer to or mention particular objects or persons; to give the meaning of a sentence is to give *general directions* for its use in making true or false assertions. It is not to talk about any particular occasion of the use of the sentence or expression. The meaning of an expression cannot be identified with the object it is used, on a particular occasion, to refer to. The meaning of a sentence cannot be identified with the assertion it is used, on a particular occasion, to make. For to talk about the meaning of an expression or sentence is not to talk about its use on a particular occasion, but about the rules, habits, conventions governing its correct use, on all occasions, to refer or to assert. So the question of whether a sentence or expression *is significant or not* has nothing whatever to do with the question of whether the sentence, *uttered on a particular occasion*, is, on that occasion, being used to make a true-or-false assertion or not, or of whether the expression is, on that occasion, being used to refer to, or mention, anything at all.

The source of Russell's mistake was that he thought that referring or mentioning, if it occurred at all, must be meaning. He did not distinguish B1 from B2; he confused expressions with their use in a particular context; and so confused meaning with mentioning, with referring. If I talk about my handkerchief, I can, perhaps, produce the object I am referring to out of my pocket. I can't produce the meaning of the expression, "my handkerchief", out of my pocket. Because Russell confused meaning with mentioning, he thought that if there were any expressions having a uniquely referring use, which were what they seemed (*i.e.* logical subjects) and not something else in disguise, their meaning must *be* the particular object which they were used to refer to. Hence the troublesome mythology of the logically proper name. But if some one asks me the meaning of the expression "this"—once Russell's favorite candidate for this status—I do not hand him the object I have just used the expression to refer to, adding at the same time that the meaning of the word changes every time it is used. Nor do I hand him all the objects it ever has been, or might be, used to refer to. I explain and illustrate the conventions governing the use of the expression. This *is* giving the meaning of the expression. It is quite different from giving (in any sense of giving) the object to which it refers; for the expression itself does not refer to anything; though it can be used, on different occasions, to refer to innumerable things. Now as a matter of fact there is, in English, a sense of the word "mean" in which this word does approximate to "indicate, mention or refer to"; *e.g.* when somebody (unpleasantly) says, "I mean you"; or when I point and say, "That's the one I mean." But *the one I meant* is quite different from *the meaning of the expression* I used to talk of it. In this special sense of "mean", it is people who mean, not expressions. People use expressions to refer to particular things. But the meaning of an expression is not the set of things or the single thing it may correctly be used to refer to: the meaning is the set of rules, habits, conventions for its use in referring.

It is the same with sentences: even more obviously so. Every one knows that the sentence, "The table is covered with books", is significant, and every one knows what it means. But if I ask, "What object is that sentence about?" I am asking an absurd question—a question which cannot be asked about the sentence, but only about some use of the sentence: and in this case the sentence hasn't been used, it has only been taken as an example. In knowing what it means, you are knowing how it could correctly be used to talk about things: so knowing the meaning hasn't anything to do with knowing about any particular use of the sentence to talk about anything. Similarly, if I ask: "Is the sentence true or false?" I am asking an absurd question, which becomes no less absurd if I add, "It must be one or the other since it's significant". The question is absurd, because the *sentence* is neither true nor false any more than it's *about* some object. Of course the fact that it's significant is the same as the fact that it *can* correctly be used to talk about something and that, in so using it, some one will be making a true or false assertion. And I will add that it will be used to make a true or false assertion *only* if the person using it *is* talking about something. If, when he utters it, he is not talking about anything, then his use is not a genuine one, but a spurious or pseudo-use: he is not making either a true or a false assertion, though he may think he is. And this points the way to the correct answer to the puzzle to which the Theory of Descriptions gives a fatally incorrect answer. The important point is that the question of whether the sentence is significant or not is quite independent of the question that can be raised about a particular use of it, *viz.* the question whether it is a genuine or a spurious use, whether it is being used to talk about something, or in make-believe, or as an example in philosophy. The question whether the sentence is significant or not is the question whether there exist such language habits, conventions or rules that the sentence logically could be used to talk about something; and is hence quite independent of the question whether it is being so used on a particular occasion.

III

Consider again the sentence, "The king of France is wise", and the true and false things Russell says about it.

There are at least two true things which Russell would say about the sentence:

(1) The first is that it is significant; that if anyone were now to utter it, he would be uttering a significant sentence.
(2) The second is that anyone now uttering the sentence would be making a true assertion only if there in fact at present existed one and only one king of France, and if he were wise.

What are the false things which Russell would say about the sentence? They are:

(1) That anyone now uttering it would be making a true assertion or a false assertion;
(2) That part of what he would be asserting would be that there at present existed one and only one king of France.

I have already given some reasons for thinking that these two statements are incorrect. Now suppose some one were in fact to say to you with a perfectly serious air: "The king of France is wise". Would you say, "That's untrue"? I think it's quite certain that you wouldn't. But suppose he went on to *ask* you whether you thought that what he had just said was true, or was false; whether you agreed or disagreed with what he had just said. I think you would be inclined, with some hesitation, to say that you didn't do either; that the question of whether his statement was true or false simply *didn't arise*, because there was no such person as the king of France.[2] You might, if he were obviously serious (had a dazed astray-in-the-centuries look), say something like: "I'm afraid you must be under a misapprehension. France is not a monarchy. There is no king of France." And this brings out the point that if a man seriously uttered the sentence, his uttering it would in some sense be *evidence* that he *believed* that there was a king of France. It would not be evidence for his believing this simply in the way in which a man's reaching for his raincoat is evidence for his believing that it is raining. But nor would it be evidence for his believing this in the way in which a man's saying, "It's raining" is evidence for his believing that it is raining. We might put it as follows. To say, "The king of France is wise" is, in some sense of "imply", to *imply* that there is a

---

[2] Since this article was written, there has appeared a clear statement of this point by Mr. [P. T.—Ed.] Geach in *Analysis*, Vol. 10, No. 4, March, 1950.

king of France. But this is a very special and odd sense of "imply". "Implies" in this sense is certainly not equivalent to "entails" (or "logically implies"). And this comes out from the fact that when, in response to his statement, we say (as we should) "There is no king of France", we should certainly *not* say we were *contradicting* the statement that the king of France is wise. We are certainly not saying that it's false. We are, rather, giving a reason for saying that the question of whether it's true or false simply doesn't arise.

And this is where the distinction I drew earlier can help us. The sentence, "The king of France is wise", is certainly significant; but this does not mean that any particular use of it is true or false. We use it truly or falsely when we use it to talk about some one; when, in using the expression, "The king of France", we are in fact mentioning some one. The fact that the sentence and the expression, respectively, are significant just is the fact that the sentence *could* be used, in certain circumstances, to say something true or false, that the expression *could* be used, in certain circumstances to mention a particular person; and to know their meaning is to know what sort of circumstances these are. So when we utter the sentence without in fact mentioning anybody by the use of the phrase, "The king of France", the sentence doesn't cease to be significant: we simply *fail* to say anything true or false because we simply fail to mention anybody by this particular use of that perfectly significant phrase. It is, if you like, a spurious use of the sentence, and a spurious use of the expression; though we may (or may not) mistakenly think it a genuine use.

And such spurious uses are very familiar. Sophisticated romancing, sophisticated fiction,[3] depend upon them. If I began, "The king of France is wise", and went on, "and he lives in a golden castle and has a hundred wives", and so on, a hearer would understand me perfectly well, without supposing *either* that I was talking about a particular person, *or* that I was making a false statement to the effect that there existed such a person as my words described. (It is worth adding that where the use of sentences and expressions is overtly fictional, the sense of the word "about" may change. As [G. E.—Ed.] Moore said, it is perfectly natural and correct to say that some of the statements in *Pickwick Papers* are *about* Mr. Pickwick. But where the use of sentences and expressions is not overtly fictional, this use of "about" seems less correct; *i.e.* it would not *in general* be correct to say that a statement was about Mr. X or the so-and-so, unless there were such a person or thing. So it is where the romancing is in danger of being taken seriously that we might answer the question, "Who is he talking about?" with "He's not talking about anybody"; but, in saying this, we are not saying that what he is saying is either false or nonsense.)

Overtly fictional uses apart, however, I said just now that to use such an expression as "The king of France" at the beginning of a sentence was, in some sense of "imply", to imply that there was a king of France. When a man uses such an expression, he does not *assert*, nor does what he says *entail*, a uniquely

---

[3] The unsophisticated kind begins: "Once upon a time there was . . .".

existential proposition. But one of the conventional functions of the definite article is to act as a *signal* that a unique reference is being made—a signal, not a disguised assertion. When we begin a sentence with "the such-and-such" the use of "the" shows, but does not state, that we are, or intend to be, referring to one particular individual of the species "such-and-such". *Which* particular individual is a matter to be determined from context, time, place and any other features of the situation of utterance. Now, whenever a man uses any expression, the presumption is that he thinks he is using it correctly: so when he uses the expression, "the such-and-such", in a uniquely referring way, the presumption is that he thinks both that there is *some* individual of that species, and that the context of use will sufficiently determine which one he has in mind. To use the word "the" in this way is then to imply (in the relevant sense of "imply") that the existential conditions described by Russell are fulfilled. But to use "the" in this way is not to *state* that those conditions are fulfilled. If I begin a sentence with an expression of the form, "the so-and-so", and then am prevented from saying more, I have made no statement of any kind; but I may have succeeded in mentioning some one or something.

The uniquely existential assertion supposed by Russell to be part of any assertion in which a uniquely referring use is made of an expression of the form "the so-and-so" is, he observes, a compound of two assertions. To say that there is a ϕ is to say something compatible with there being several ϕs; to say there is not more than one ϕ is to say something compatible with there being none. To say there is one ϕ and one only is to compound these two assertions. I have so far been concerned mostly with the alleged assertion of existence and less with the alleged assertion of uniqueness. An example which throws the emphasis on to the latter will serve to bring out more clearly the sense of "implied" in which a uniquely existential assertion is implied, but not entailed, by the use of expressions in the uniquely referring way. Consider the sentence, "The table is covered with books". It is quite certain that in any normal use of this sentence, the expression "the table" would be used to make a unique reference, *i.e.* to refer to some one table. It is a quite strict use of the definite article, in the sense in which Russell talks on p. 30 of *Principia Mathematica*, of using the article "*strictly*, so as to imply uniqueness". On the same page Russell says that a phrase of the form "the so-and-so", used strictly, "will only have an application in the event of there being one so-and-so and no more". Now it is obviously quite false that the phrase "the table" in the sentence "the table is covered with books", used normally, will "only have an application in the event of there being one table and no more". It is indeed tautologically true that, in such a use, the phrase will have an application only in the event of there being one table and no more *which is being referred to*, and that it will be understood to have an application only in the event of there being one table and no more which it is understood as being used to refer to. To use the sentence is not to assert, but it is (in the special sense discussed) to imply, that there is only one thing which is *both* of the kind specified (*i.e.* a table) *and is being referred to* by the speaker. It is obviously not to assert this. To refer is not to say you are referring. To say there is *some table or other* to which you are referring is not the same as referring to a particular table. We should have no use for such phrases as "the individual I referred to" unless there were something which counted as referring. (It would make no sense to say you had pointed if there were nothing which counted as pointing.) So once more I draw the conclusion that referring to or mentioning a particular thing cannot be dissolved into any kind of assertion. To refer is not to assert, though you refer in order to go on to assert.

Let me now take an example of the uniquely referring use of an expression not of the form, "the so-and-so". Suppose I advance my hands, cautiously cupped, towards someone, saying, as I do so, "This is a fine red one". He, looking into my hands and seeing nothing there, may say: "What is? What are you talking about?" Or perhaps, "But there's nothing in your hands". Of course it would be absurd to say that in saying "But you've got nothing in your hands", he was *denying* or *contradicting* what I said. So "this" is not a disguised description in Russell's sense. Nor is it a logically proper name. For one must know what the sentence means in order to react in that way to the utterance of it. It is precisely because the significance of the word "this" is independent of any particular reference it may be used to make, though not independent of the way it may be used to refer, that I can, as in this example, use it to *pretend* to be referring to something.

The general moral of all this is that communication is much less a matter of explicit or disguised assertion than logicians used to suppose. The particular application of this general moral in which I am interested is its application to the case of making a unique reference. It is a part of the significance of expressions of the kind I am discussing that they can be used, in an immense variety of contexts, to make unique references. It is no part of their significance to assert that they are being so used or that the conditions of their being so used are fulfilled. So the wholly important distinction we are required to draw is between:

(1) using an expression to make a unique reference; and
(2) asserting that there is one and only one individual which has certain characteristics (*e.g.* is of a certain kind, or stands in a certain relation to the speaker, or both).

This is, in other words, the distinction between:

(1) sentences containing an expression used to indicate or mention or refer to a particular person or thing; and
(2) uniquely existential sentences.

What Russell does is progressively to assimilate more and more sentences of class (1) to sentences of class (2), and consequently to involve himself in insuperable difficulties about logical subjects, and about values for individual variables generally: difficulties which have led him finally to the logically disastrous theory of names developed in the *Enquiry* and in *Human Knowledge*. That view of the meaning of logical-subject-expressions which provides the whole incentive to the Theory of Descriptions at the same time precludes the possibility of Russell's ever finding any satisfactory substitutes for those expressions which, beginning with substantival phrases, he progressively degrades from the status of logical subjects.[4] It is not simply, as is sometimes said, the fascination of the relation between a name and its bearer, that is the root of the trouble. Not even names come up to the impossible standard set. It is rather the combination of two more radical misconceptions: first, the failure to grasp the importance of the distinction (section II above) between what may be said of an expression and what may be said of a particular use of it; second, a failure to recognise the uniquely referring use of expressions for the harmless, necessary thing it is, distinct from, but complementary to, the predicative or ascriptive use of expressions. The expressions which can in fact occur as singular logical sub-jects are expressions of the class I listed at the outset (demonstratives, sub-stantival phrases, proper names, pronouns): to say this is to say that these expressions, together with context (in the widest sense) are what one uses to make unique references. The point of the conventions governing the uses of such expressions is, along with the situation of utterance, to secure uniqueness of reference. But to do this, enough is enough. We do not, and we cannot, while referring, attain the point of complete explicitness at which the referring func-tion is no longer performed. The actual unique reference made, if any, is a matter of the particular use in the particular context; the significance of the expression used is the set of rules or conventions which permit such references to be made. Hence we can, using significant expressions, pretend to refer, in make-believe or in fiction, or mistakenly think we are referring when we are not referring to anything.

This shows the need for distinguishing two kinds (among many others) of linguistic conventions or rules: rules for referring, and rules for attributing and ascribing; and for an investigation of the former. If we recognise this distinction of use for what it is, we are on the way to solving a number of ancient logical and metaphysical puzzles.

.   .   .

---

[4] And this in spite of the danger-signal of that phrase, *"misleading* grammatical form".

8

J. L. Austin

Performative-Constative

Translator's Note: "Performative-Constative" is a straightforward translation of Austin's paper "Performatif-Constatif," which he wrote in French and presented at a (predominantly) Anglo-French conference held at Royaumont in March 1958. The case of the discussion which follows it is somewhat more complex. The actual discussion at Royaumont was carried on in both French and English. What appears in the published volume after Austin's text (*Cahiers de Royaumont, Philosophie* No. IV, *La Philosophie Analytique:* Les Editions de Minuit, 1962, pp. 271–304) is a version of this, based on a transcript but substantially cut and edited, in which the contributions originally made in English were translated into French by M. Béra. It might have been possible, for the present publication, to procure copies at least of those portions of the original transcript that were in English. However, it seemed to me preferable simply to translate into English the entire French text, mainly for the reason that it is this edited version, and this only, that all those taking part are known to have seen and approved for publication.

G. J. WARNOCK

One can quite easily get the idea of the performative utterance—though the expression, as I am well aware, does not exist in the French language, or anywhere else. This idea was brought in to mark a contrast with that of the declarative utterance, or rather, as I am going to call it, the constative utterance. And there we have straight off what I want to call in question. Ought we to accept this Performative-Constative antithesis?

The constative utterance, under the name, so dear to philosophers, of *statement*,[1] has the property of being true or false. The performative utterance, by contrast, can never be either: it has its own special job, it is used to perform an action. To issue such an utterance[2] *is* to perform the action—an action, perhaps, which one scarcely could perform, at least with so much precision, in any other way. Here are some examples:

I name this ship 'Liberté'.
I apologise.
I welcome you.
I advise you to do it.

J. L. Austin, "Performative-Constative," trans. G. J. Warnock, in *La Philosophie Analytique* (Paris: Les Editions de Minuit, 1962), pp. 171–181. Reprinted by permission of the publisher.

---

[1] The French term is 'assertion'. I am sure that 'statement' is the English term Austin would have used here, and I have so translated 'assertion' throughout.

[2] 'Formuler un tel énoncé'. The translation is supplied in a footnote by Austin himself.

Utterances of this kind are common enough: we find them, for instance, everywhere in what are called in English the 'operative' clauses of a legal instrument.* Plainly, many of them are not without interest for philosophers: to say 'I promise to . . .'—to issue, as we say, this performative utterance—just *is* the act of making a promise; not, as we see, at all a mysterious act. And it may seem at once quite obvious that an utterance of this kind can't be true or false—notice that I say it can't *be* true or false, because it may very well *imply* that some *other* propositions are true or are false, but that, if I'm not mistaken, is a quite different matter.

However, the performative utterance is not exempt from all criticism: it may very well be criticized, but in a quite different dimension from that of truth and falsity. The performative must be issued in a situation appropriate in all respects for the act in question: if the speaker is not in the conditions required for its performance (and there are many such conditions), then his utterance will be, as we call it in general, 'unhappy'.[3]

First, our performative, like any other ritual or ceremony, may be, as the lawyers say, 'null and void'. If, for example, the speaker is not in a position to perform an act of that kind, or if the object with respect to which he purports to perform it is not suitable for the purpose, then he doesn't manage, simply by issuing his utterance, to carry out the purported act. Thus a bigamist doesn't get married a second time, he only 'goes through the form' of a second marriage; I can't name the ship if I am not the person properly authorized to name it; and I can't quite bring off the baptism of penguins, those creatures being scarcely susceptible of that exploit.

Second, a performative utterance may be, though not void, 'unhappy' in a different way—if, that is, it is issued *insincerely*. If I say 'I promise to . . .' without in the least intending to carry out the promised action, perhaps even not believing that it is in my power to carry it out, the promise is hollow. It is made, certainly; but still, there is an 'unhappiness': I have *abused* the formula.

Let us now suppose that our act has been performed: everything has gone off quite normally, and also, if you like, sincerely. In that case, the performative utterance will characteristically 'take effect'. We do not mean by that that such-and-such a future event is or will be brought about as an effect of this action functioning as a cause. We mean rather that, in consequence of the performance of this act, such-and-such a future event, *if* it happens, will be *in order*, and such-and-such other events, *if* they happen, will not be in order. If I have said 'I promise', I shall not be in order if I break my word; if I have said 'I welcome you', I shall not be in order if I proceed to treat you as an enemy or an intruder. Thus we say that, even when the performative has taken effect, there may always crop up a third kind of unhappiness, which we call 'breach of commit-

---

* The clauses, that is to say, in which the legal act is actually performed, as opposed to those—the 'preamble'—which set out the circumstances of the transaction.

[3] 'Unhappy' is a term Austin regularly used in this connection, and he supplies it himself in brackets after the French 'malheureux'.

ment'.[4] We may note also that commitments can be more or less vague, and can bind us in very different degrees.

There we have, then, three kinds of unhappiness associated with the performative utterance. It is possible to make a complete classification of these unhappinesses; but it must be admitted that, as practically goes without saying, the different kinds may not always be sharply distinguishable and may even coincide.[5] Then we must add that our performative is both an *action* and an *utterance*: so that, poor thing, it can't help being liable to be substandard in all the ways in which actions in general can be, as well as those in which utterances in general can be. For example, the performative may be issued under duress, or by accident; it may suffer from defective grammar, or from misunderstanding; it may figure in a context not wholly 'serious', in a play, perhaps, or in a poem. We leave all that on one side—let us simply bear in mind the more specific unhappinesses of the performative, that is, nullity, abuse (insincerity), and breach of commitment.

Well, now that we have before us this idea of the performative, it is very natural to hope that we could proceed to find some criterion, whether of grammar or of vocabulary, which would make it possible for us to answer in every case the question whether a particular utterance is performative or not. But this hope is, alas, exaggerated and, in large measure, vain.

It is true that there exist two 'normal forms', so to speak, in which the performative finds expression. At first sight both of them, curiously enough, have a thoroughly constative look. One of these normal forms is that which I have already made use of in producing my examples: the utterance leads off with a verb in the first person singular of the present indicative active, as in 'I promise you that . . .'. The other form, which comes to exactly the same but is more common in utterances issued in writing, employs by contrast a verb in the *passive* voice and in the *second* or *third* person of the present indicative, as in 'Passengers are requested to cross the line by the footbridge only'. If we ask ourselves, as sometimes we may, whether a given utterance of this form is performative or constative, we may settle the question by asking whether it would be possible to insert in it the word 'hereby' or some equivalent—as, in French, the phrase 'par ces mots-ci'.

By way of putting to the test utterances which one might take to be performative, we make use of a well-known asymmetry, in the case of what we call an 'explicit performative' verb, between the first person singular of the present indicative, and other persons and tenses of the same verb. Thus, 'I promise' is a formula which is used to perform the act of promising; 'I promised', on the other hand, or 'he promises', are expressions which serve simply to describe or report an act of promising, not to perform one.

However, it is not in the least necessary that an utterance, if it is to be

---

4 'Rupture d'engagement'. Austin himself supplies the translation.

5 That is to say, a particular case of unhappiness might arguably, or even quite properly, be classifiable under more than one heading.

performative, should be expressed in one of these so-called normal forms. To say 'Shut the door', plainly enough, is every bit as performative, every bit as much the performance of an act, as to say 'I order you to shut the door'. Even the word 'Dog' by itself can sometimes (at any rate in England, a country more practical than ceremonious) stand in place of an explicit and formal performative; one performs, by this little word, the very same act as by the utterance 'I warn you that the dog is about to attack us', or by 'Strangers are warned that here there is a vicious dog'. To make our utterance performative, and quite unambiguously so, we can make use, in place of the explicit formula, of a whole lot of more primitive devices such as intonation, for instance, or gesture; further, and above all, the very context in which the words are uttered can make it entirely certain how they are to be taken—as a description, for example, or again as a warning. Does this word 'Dog' just give us a bit of detail about the local fauna? In the context—when confronted, that is, with the notice on the gate—we just don't need to ask ourselves that question at all.

All we can really say is that our explicit performative formula ('I promise . . .', 'I order you . . .', etc.) serves to make explicit, and at the same time more precise, what act it is that the speaker purports to perform in issuing his utterance. I say 'to make explicit', and that is not at all the same thing as to *state*.[6] Bending low before you, I remove my hat, or perhaps I say 'Salaam'; then, certainly, I am doing obeisance to you, not just engaging in gymnastics; but the word 'Salaam' does not, any more than does the act of removing my hat, in any way *state* that I am doing obeisance to you. It is in this way that our formula *makes* the issuing of the utterance that action which it is, but does not *state* that it is that action.

The other forms of expression, those that have no explicit performative formula, will be more primitive and less precise, one might almost say more vague. If I say simply 'I will be there', there will be no telling, just by considering the words, whether I am taking on a commitment, or declaring an intention, or making perhaps a fatalistic prediction. One may think of the precise formulae as a relatively recent phenomenon in the evolution of language, and as going together with the evolution of more complex forms of society and science.

We can't, then, expect any purely verbal criterion of the performative. We may hope, all the same, that any utterance which is in fact performative will be reducible (in some sense of that word) to an utterance in one or the other of our normal forms. Then, going on from there, we should be able, with the help of a dictionary, to make a list of all the verbs which can figure in one of our explicit formulae. Thus we will achieve a useful classification of all the varieties of acts that we perform in saying something (in one sense, at least, of that ambiguous phrase).

We have now brought in, then, the ideas of the performative utterance, of its unhappinesses, and of its explicit formulae. But we have been talking

---

[6] 'Affirmer'. I have translated this verb by 'state' throughout.

all along as if every utterance had to be *either* constative *or* performative, and as if the idea of the constative at any rate was as clear as it is familiar. But it is not.

Let us note in the first place that an utterance which is undoubtedly a statement of fact, therefore constative, can fail to get by[7] in more than one way. It can be untrue, to be sure; but it can also be absurd, and that not necessarily in some gross fashion (by being, for instance, ungrammatical). I would like to take a closer look at three rather more subtle ways of being absurd, two of which have only recently come to light.

(1) Someone says 'All John's children are bald, but [or 'and'] John has no children'; or perhaps he says 'All John's children are bald', when, as a matter of fact, John has no children.

(2) Someone says 'The cat is on the mat, but [or 'and'] I don't believe it is'; or perhaps he says 'The cat is on the mat', when, as a matter of fact, he does not believe it is.

(3) Someone says 'All the guests are French, and some of them aren't'; or perhaps he says 'All the guests are French', and then afterwards says 'Some of the guests are not French'.

In each of these cases one experiences a feeling of outrage, and it's possible each time for us to try to express it in terms of the same word—'implication', or perhaps that word that we always find so handy, 'contradiction'. But there are more ways of killing the cat than drowning it in butter;* and equally, to do violence to language one does not always need a contradiction.

Let us use the three terms 'presuppose', 'imply', and 'entail'[8] for our three cases respectively. Then:

1. Not only 'John's children are bald', but equally 'John's children are not bald', presupposes that John has children. To talk about those children, or to refer to them, presupposes that they exist. By contrast, 'The cat is not on the mat' does *not*, equally with 'The cat is on the mat', imply that I believe it is; and similarly, 'None of the guests is French' does *not*, equally with 'All the guests are French', entail that it is false that some of the guests are not French.

2. We can quite well say 'It could be the case both that the cat is on the mat and that I do not believe it is'. That is to say, those two propositions are not in the least incompatible: both can be true together. What is impossible is to state both at the same time: his *stating* that the cat is on the mat is what implies that the speaker believes it is. By contrast, we couldn't say 'It could be the case both that John has no children and that his children are bald'; just as we couldn't say 'It could be the case both that all the guests are French and that some of them are not French'.

---

[7] The French phrase is 'peut ne pas jouer'. Austin himself sometimes used in English the coined term 'non-play' (see, e.g., *How to Do Things with Words*, pp. 18n. and 31), but in a more restricted sense than would be appropriate here.

* English proverb. I am told that this rather refined way of disposing of cats is not found in France.

[8] These three English terms are supplied in a footnote by Austin himself.

3. If 'All the guests are French' entails 'It is not the case that some of the guests are not French', then 'Some of the guests are not French' entails 'It is not the case that all the guests are French'. It's a question here of the compatibility and incompatibility of propositions. By contrast, it isn't like this with presupposition: if 'John's children are bald' presupposes that John has children, it isn't true at all that 'John has no children' presupposes that John's children are not bald. Similarly, if 'The cat is on the mat' implies that I believe it is, it isn't true at all that to say 'I don't believe that the cat is on the mat' implies that the cat is not on the mat (not, at any rate, in the same sense of 'implies'; besides, we have already seen that 'implication', for us, is not a matter of the incompatibility of propositions).

Here then are three ways in which a statement can fail to get by without being untrue, and without being a sheer rigmarole either. I would like to call attention to the fact that these three ways of failing to get by correspond to three of the ways in which a performative utterance may be unhappy. To bring out the comparison, let's first take two performative utterances:

4. 'I bequeath my watch to you, but [or 'and'] I haven't got a watch'; or perhaps someone says 'I bequeath my watch to you' when he hasn't got a watch.

5. 'I promise to be there, but [or 'and'] I have no intention of being there'; or perhaps someone says 'I promise to be there' when he doesn't intend to be there.

We compare case 4 with case 1, the case, that is, of presupposition. For to say either 'I bequeath my watch to you' or 'I don't bequeath my watch to you' presupposes equally that I have a watch; that the watch exists is presupposed by the fact that it is spoken of or referred to, in the performative utterance just as much as in the constative utterance. And just as we can make use here of the term 'presupposition' as employed in the doctrine of the constative, equally we can take over for that doctrine the term 'void' as employed in the doctrine of the unhappinesses of the performative. The statement on the subject of John's children is, we may say, 'void for lack of reference', which is exactly what lawyers would say about the purported bequest of the watch. So here is a first instance in which a trouble that afflicts statements turns out to be identical with one of the unhappinesses typical of the performative utterance.

We compare case 5 with case 2, that is, the case where something is 'implied'. Just as my saying that the cat is on the mat implies that I believe it is, so my saying I promise to be there implies that I intend to be there. The procedure of stating is designed for those who honestly believe what they say, exactly as the procedure of promising is designed for those who have a certain intention, namely, the intention to do whatever it may be that they promise. If we don't hold the belief, or again don't have the intention, appropriate to the content of our utterance, then in each case there is lack of sincerity and abuse of the procedure. If, at the same time as we make the statement or the promise, we announce in the same breath that we don't believe it or we don't intend to, then the utterance is 'self-voiding', as we might call it; and hence our feeling of outrage on hearing it. Another instance, then, where a trouble which afflicts statements is identical with one of the unhappinesses which afflict performative utterances.

Let us look back, next, to case 3, the case of entailment among statements. Can we find, in the case of performatives, some analogue for this as well? When I make the statement, for instance, 'All the guests are French', do I not commit myself in a more or less rigorous fashion to behaving in future in such-and-such a way, in particular with respect to the statements I will make? If, in the sequel, I state things incompatible with my utterance (namely, that all the guests are French), there will be a breach of commitment that one might well compare with that of the case in which I say 'I welcome you', and then proceed to treat you as an enemy or an intruder—and perhaps even better, with that of which one is guilty when one says 'I define the word thus' (a performative utterance) and then proceeds to use the word with a different meaning.

So then, it seems to me that the constative utterance is every bit as liable to unhappinesses as the performative utterance, and indeed to pretty much the same unhappinesses. Furthermore, making use of the key provided by our list of unhappinesses noted for the case of performatives, we can ask ourselves whether there are not still more unhappinesses in the case of statements, besides the three we have just mentioned. For example, it often happens that a performative is void because the utterer is not in a state, or not in a position, to perform the act which he purports to perform; thus, it's no good my saying 'I order you' if I have no authority over you: I can't order you, my utterance is void, my act is only purported. Now people have, I know, the impression that where a statement, a constative utterance, is in question, the case is quite different: anybody at all can state anything at all. What if he's ill-informed? Well then, one can be mistaken, that's all. It's a free country, isn't it? To state what isn't true is one of the Rights of Man. However, this impression can lead us into error. In reality nothing is more common than to find that one can state absolutely nothing on some subject, because one is simply not in a position to state whatever it may be—and this may come about, too, for more than one reason. I *cannot* state at this moment how many people there are in the next room: I haven't been to see, I haven't found out the facts. What if I say, nevertheless, 'At this moment there are fifty people in the next room'? You will allow, perhaps, that in saying that I have made a guess,[9] but you will not allow that I have made a statement, not at any rate without adding 'but he had no right whatever to do so'; and in this case my 'I state . . .' is exactly on a par with our 'I order . . .', said, we remember, without any right to give an order. Here's another example. You confide to me 'I'm bored', and I quite coolly reply 'You're not'. You say 'What do you mean, I'm not? What right have you to say how I feel?' I say 'But what do *you* mean, what right have I? I'm just stating what your feelings are, that's all. I may be mistaken, certainly, but what of that? I suppose one can always make a simple statement, can't one?' But no, one can't always: usually, I can't state what your feelings are, unless you have disclosed them to me.

So far I have called attention to two things: that there is no purely verbal

---

[9] The French text has 'conjoncture' here, but this must surely be a misprint for 'conjecture'.

criterion by which to distinguish the performative from the constative utterance, and that the constative is liable to the same unhappinesses as the performative. Now we must ask ourselves whether issuing a constative utterance is not, after all, the performance of an act, the act, namely, of stating. Is stating an act in the same sense as marrying, apologising, betting, etc.? I can't plumb this mystery any further at present. But it is already pretty evident that the formula 'I state that . . .' is closely similar to the formula 'I warn you that . . .'—a formula which, as we put it, serves to make explicit what speech-act[10] it is that we are performing; and also, that one can't issue any utterance whatever without performing some speech-act of this kind.

What we need, perhaps, is a more general theory of these speech-acts, and in this theory our Constative-Performative antithesis will scarcely survive.

Here and now it remains for us to examine, quite briefly, this craze for being true or false, something which people think is peculiar to statements alone and ought to be set up on a pedestal of its own, above the battle. And this time let's begin with the performative utterance: is it the case that there is nothing here in the least analogous with truth?

To begin with, it is clear that if we establish that a performative utterance is not unhappy, that is, that its author has performed his act happily and in all sincerity, that still does not suffice to set it beyond the reach of all criticism. It may always be criticised in a different dimension.

Let us suppose that I say to you 'I advise you to do it'; and let us allow that all the circumstances are appropriate, the conditions for success are fulfilled. In saying that, I actually do advise you to do it—it is not that I *state*, truely or falsely, *that* I advise you. It is, then, a performative utterance. There does still arise, all the same, a little question: was the advice good or bad? Agreed, I spoke in all sincerity, I believed that to do it would be in your interest; but was I right? Was my belief, in these circumstances, justified? Or again—though perhaps this matters less—was it in fact, or as things turned out, in your interest? There is confrontation of my utterance with the situation in, and the situation with respect to which, it was issued. I was fully justified perhaps, but was I right?

Many other utterances which have an incontestably performative flavour are exposed to this second kind of criticism. Allowing that, in declaring the accused guilty, you have reached your verdict properly and in good faith, it still remains to ask whether the verdict was just, or fair. Allowing that you had the right to reprimand him as you did, and that you have acted without malice, one can still ask whether your reprimand was deserved. Here again we have confrontation with the facts, including the circumstances of the occasion of utterance.

That not all performative utterances without exception are liable to this quasi-objective evaluation—which for that matter must here be left pretty vague and multifarious—may very well be true.

There is one thing that people will be particularly tempted to bring up as

---

[10] Austin supplies this English term himself. It is in any case the term he regularly used.

an objection against any comparison between this second kind of criticism and the kind appropriate to statements, and that is this: aren't these questions about something's being good, or just, or fair, or deserved entirely distinct from questions of truth and falsehood? That, surely, is a very simple black-and-white business: either the utterance corresponds to the facts or it doesn't, and that's that.

Well, I for my part don't think it is. Even if there exists a well-defined class of statements and we can restrict ourselves to that, this class will always be pretty wide. In this class we shall have the following statements:

> France is hexagonal.
> Lord Raglan won the battle of Alma.
> Oxford is 60 miles from London.

It's quite true that for each of these statements we can raise the question 'true or false'. But it is only in quite favourable cases that we ought to expect an answer yes or no, once and for all. When the question is raised one understands that the utterance is to be confronted in one way or another with the facts. Very well. So let's confront 'France is hexagonal' with France. What are we to say, is it true or not? The question, plainly, oversimplifies things. Oh well, up to a point if you like, I see what you mean, true perhaps for some purposes or in some contexts, that would do for the man in the street but not for geographers. And so on. It's a rough statement, no denying that, but one can't just say straight out that it's false. Then Alma, a soldier's battle if ever there was one; it's true that Lord Raglan was in command of the allied army, and that this army to some extent won a confused sort of victory; yes, that would be a fair enough judgment, even well deserved, for schoolchildren anyway, though really it's a bit of an exaggeration. And Oxford, well, yes, it's true that that city is 60 miles from London, so long as you want only a certain degree of precision.

Under the heading 'truth' what we in fact have is, not a simple quality nor a relation, not indeed *one* anything, but rather a whole dimension of criticism. We can get some idea, perhaps not a very clear one, of this criticism; what *is* clear is that there is a whole lot of things to be considered and weighed up in this dimension alone—the facts, yes, but also the situation of the speaker, his purpose in speaking, his hearer, questions of precision, etc. If we are content to restrict ourselves to statements of an idiotic or ideal simplicity, we shall never succeed in disentangling the true from the just, fair, deserved, precise, exaggerated, etc., the summary and the detail, the full and the concise, and so on.

From this side also, then, from the side of truth and falsehood, we feel ourselves driven to think about the Performative-Constative antithesis. What we need, it seems to me, is a new doctrine, both complete and general, of *what one is doing in saying something,* in all the senses of that ambiguous phrase, and of what I call the speech-act, not just in this or that aspect abstracting from all the rest, but taken in its totality.

9

W. V. Quine

On What There Is

A curious thing about the ontological problem is its simplicity. It can be put in three Anglo-Saxon monosyllables: 'What is there?' It can be answered, moreover, in a word—'Everything'—and everyone will accept this answer as true. However, this is merely to say that there is what there is. There remains room for disagreement over cases; and so the issue has stayed alive down the centuries.

Suppose now that two philosophers, McX and I, differ over ontology. Suppose McX maintains there is something which I maintain there is not. McX can, quite consistently with his own point of view, describe our difference of opinion by saying that I refuse to recognize certain entities. I should protest, of course, that he is wrong in his formulation of our disagreement, for I maintain that there are no entities, of the kind which he alleges, for me to recognize; but my finding him wrong in his formulation of our disagreement is unimportant, for I am committed to considering him wrong in his ontology anyway.

When *I* try to formulate our difference of opinion, on the other hand, I seem to be in a predicament. I cannot admit that there are some things which McX countenances and I do not, for in admitting that there are such things I should be contradicting my own rejection of them.

It would appear, if this reasoning were sound, that in any ontological dispute the proponent of the negative side suffers the disadvantage of not being able to admit that his opponent disagrees with him.

This is the old Platonic riddle of nonbeing. Nonbeing must in some sense be, otherwise what is it that there is not? This tangled doctrine might be nicknamed *Plato's beard*; historically it has proved tough, frequently dulling the edge of Occam's razor.

It is some such line of thought that leads philosophers like McX to impute being where they might otherwise be quite content to recognize that there is nothing. Thus, take Pegasus. If Pegasus *were* not, McX argues, we should not be talking about anything when we use the word; therefore it would be nonsense to say even that Pegasus is not. Thinking to show thus that the denial of Pegasus cannot be coherently maintained, he concludes that Pegasus is.

McX cannot, indeed, quite persuade himself that any region of space-time, near or remote, contains a flying horse of flesh and blood. Pressed for further details on Pegasus, then, he says that Pegasus is an idea in men's minds. Here, however, a confusion begins to be apparent. We may for the sake of argument concede that there is an entity, and even a unique entity (though this is rather implausible), which is the mental Pegasus-idea; but this mental entity is not what people are talking about when they deny Pegasus.

McX never confuses the Parthenon with the Parthenon-idea. The Parthenon is physical; the Parthenon-idea is mental (according anyway to McX's version of ideas, and I have no better to offer). The Parthenon is visible; the Parthenon-idea is invisible. We cannot easily imagine two things more unlike, and less liable to confusion, than the Parthenon and the Parthenon-idea. But when we shift from the Parthenon to Pegasus, the confusion sets in—for no other reason than that McX would sooner be deceived by the crudest and most flagrant counterfeit than grant the nonbeing of Pegasus.

The notion that Pegasus must be, because it would otherwise be nonsense to say even that Pegasus is not, has been seen to lead McX into an elementary confusion. Subtler minds, taking the same precept as their starting point, come out with theories of Pegasus which are less patently misguided than McX's, and correspondingly more difficult to eradicate. One of these subtler minds is named, let us say, Wyman. Pegasus, Wyman maintains, has his being as an unactualized possible. When we say of Pegasus that there is no such thing, we are saying, more precisely, that Pegasus does not have the special attribute of actuality. Saying that Pegasus is not actual is on a par, logically, with saying that the Parthenon is not red; in either case we are saying something about an entity whose being is unquestioned.

Wyman, by the way, is one of those philosophers who have united in ruining the good old word 'exist'. Despite his espousal of unactualized possibles, he limits the word 'existence' to actuality—thus preserving an illusion of ontological agreement between himself and us who repudiate the rest of his bloated universe. We have all been prone to say, in our common-sense usage of 'exist', that Pegasus does not exist, meaning simply that there is no such entity at all. If Pegasus existed he would indeed be in space and time, but only because the word 'Pegasus' has spatio-temporal connotations, and not because 'exists' has spatio-temporal connotations. If spatio-temporal reference is lacking when we affirm the existence of the cube root of 27, this is simply because a cube root is not a spatio-temporal kind of thing, and not because we are being ambiguous in our use of 'exist'.[1] However, Wyman, in an ill-conceived effort to appear agreeable, genially grants us the nonexistence of Pegasus and then, contrary to what *we* meant by nonexistence of Pegasus, insists that Pegasus *is*. Existence is one thing, he says, and subsistence is another.

---

[1] The impulse to distinguish terminologically between existence as applied to objects actualized somewhere in space-time and existence (or subsistence or being) as applied to other entities arises in part, perhaps, from an idea that the observation of nature is relevant only to questions of existence of the first kind. But this idea is readily refuted by counter-instances such as 'the ratio of the number of centaurs to the number of unicorns'. If there were such a ratio, it would be an abstract entity, viz. a number. Yet it is only by studying nature that we conclude that the number of centaurs and the number of unicorns are both 0 and hence that there is no such ratio.

The only way I know of coping with this obfuscation of issues is to *give* Wyman the word 'exist'. I'll try not to use it again; I still have 'is'. So much for lexicography; let's get back to Wyman's ontology.

Wyman's overpopulated universe is in many ways unlovely. It offends the aesthetic sense of us who have a taste for desert landscapes, but this is not the worst of it. Wyman's slum of possibles is a breeding ground for disorderly elements. Take, for instance, the possible fat man in that doorway; and, again, the possible bald man in that doorway. Are they the same possible man, or two possible men? How do we decide? How many possible men are there in that doorway? Are there more possible thin ones than fat ones? How many of them are alike? Or would their being alike make them one? Are no *two* possible things alike? Is this the same as saying that it is impossible for two things to be alike? Or, finally, is the concept of identity simply inapplicable to unactualized possibles? But what sense can be found in talking of entities which cannot meaningfully be said to be identical with themselves and distinct from one another? These elements are well-nigh incorrigible. By a Fregean therapy of individual concepts, some effort might be made at rehabilitation; but I feel we'd do better simply to clear Wyman's slum and be done with it.

Possibility, along with the other modalities of necessity and impossibility and contingency, raises problems upon which I do not mean to imply that we should turn our backs. But we can at least limit modalities to whole statements. We may impose the adverb 'possibly' upon a statement as a whole, and we may well worry about the semantical analysis of such usage; but little real advance in such analysis is to be hoped for in expanding our universe to include so-called *possible entities*. I suspect that the main motive for this expansion is simply the old notion that Pegasus, for example, must be because otherwise it would be nonsense to say even that he is not.

Still, all the rank luxuriance of Wyman's universe of possibles would seem to come to naught when we make a slight change in the example and speak not of Pegasus but of the round square cupola on Berkeley College. If, unless Pegasus were, it would be nonsense to say that he is not, then by the same token, unless the round square cupola on Berkeley College were, it would be nonsense to say that it is not. But, unlike Pegasus, the round square cupola on Berkeley College cannot be admitted even as an unactualized *possible*. Can we drive Wyman now to admitting also a realm of unactualizable impossibles? If so, a good many embarrassing questions could be asked about them. We might hope even to trap Wyman in contradictions, by getting him to admit that certain of these entities are at once round and square. But the wily Wyman chooses the other horn of the dilemma and concedes that it is nonsense to say that the round square cupola on Berkeley College is not. He says that the phrase 'round square cupola' is meaningless.

Wyman was not the first to embrace this alternative. The doctrine of the meaninglessness of contradictions runs away back. The tradition survives, moreover, in writers who seem to share none of Wyman's motivations. Still, I wonder whether the first temptation to such a doctrine may not have been substantially the motivation which we have observed in Wyman. Certainly the doctrine has no intrinsic appeal; and it has led its devotees to such quixotic extremes as that of challenging the method of proof by *reductio ad absurdum* [the technique of deriving absurd consequences—Ed.]—a challenge in which I sense a *reductio ad absurdum* of the doctrine itself.

Moreover, the doctrine of meaninglessness of contradictions has the severe methodological drawback that it makes it impossible, in principle, ever to devise an effective test of what is meaningful and what is not. It would be forever impossible for us to devise systematic ways of deciding whether a string of signs made sense—even to us individually, let alone other people—or not. For it follows from a discovery in mathematical logic, due to [Alonzo—Ed.] Church, that there can be no generally applicable test of contradictoriness.

I have spoken disparagingly of Plato's beard, and hinted that it is tangled. I have dwelt at length on the inconveniences of putting up with it. It is time to think about taking steps.

[Bertrand—Ed.] Russell, in his theory of so-called singular descriptions, showed clearly how we might meaningfully use seeming names without supposing that there be the entities allegedly named. The names to which Russell's theory directly applies are complex descriptive names such as 'the author of *Waverley*', 'the present King of France', 'the round square cupola on Berkeley College'. Russell analyzes such phrases systematically as fragments of the whole sentences in which they occur. The sentence 'The author of *Waverley* was a poet', for example, is explained as a whole as meaning 'Someone (better: something) wrote *Waverley* and was a poet, and nothing else wrote *Waverley*'. (The point of this added clause is to affirm the uniqueness which is implicit in the word 'the', in '*the* author of *Waverley*'.) The sentence 'The round square cupola on Berkeley College is pink' is explained as 'Something is round and square and is a cupola on Berkeley College and is pink, and nothing else is round and square and a cupola on Berkeley College'.

The virtue of this analysis is that the seeming name, a descriptive phrase, is paraphrased *in context* as a so-called incomplete symbol. No unified expression is offered as an analysis of the descriptive phrase, but the statement as a whole which was the context of that phrase still gets its full quota of meaning—whether true or false.

The unanalyzed statement 'The author of *Waverley* was a poet' contains a part, 'the author of *Waverley*', which is wrongly supposed by McX and Wyman to demand objective reference in order to be meaningful at all. But in Russell's translation, 'Something wrote *Waverley* and was a poet and nothing else wrote *Waverley*', the burden of objective reference which had been put upon the descriptive phrase is now taken over by words of the kind that logicians call bound variables, variables of quantification, namely, words like 'something', 'nothing', 'everything'. These words, far from purporting to be names specifically of the author of *Waverley*, do not purport to be names at all; they refer to entities generally, with a kind of studied ambiguity peculiar to themselves. These quantificational words or bound variables are, of course, a basic part of language, and their meaningfulness, at least in context, is not to be challenged. But their meaningfulness in no way presupposes there being either the author of *Waverley* or the round square cupola on Berkeley College or any other specifically preassigned objects.

Where descriptions are concerned, there is no longer any difficulty in affirming or denying being. 'There *is* the author of *Waverley*' is explained by Russell as meaning 'Someone (or, more strictly, something) wrote *Waverley* and nothing else wrote *Waverley*'. 'The author of *Waverley* is not' is explained, correspondingly, as the alternation 'Either each thing failed to write *Waverley* or two or more things wrote *Waverley*'. This alternation is false, but meaningful; and it contains no expression purporting to name the author of *Waverley*. The statement 'The round square cupola on Berkeley College is not' is analyzed in similar fashion. So the old notion that statements of nonbeing defeat themselves goes by the board. When a statement of being or nonbeing is analyzed by Russell's theory of descriptions, it ceases to contain any expression which even purports to name the alleged entity whose being is in question, so that the meaningfulness of the statement no longer can be thought to presuppose that there be such an entity.

Now what of 'Pegasus'? This being a word rather than a descriptive phrase, Russell's argument does not immediately apply to it. However, it can easily be made to apply. We have only to rephrase 'Pegasus' as a description, in any way that seems adequately to single out our idea; say, 'the winged horse that was captured by Bellerophon'. Substituting such a phrase for 'Pegasus', we can then proceed to analyze the statement 'Pegasus is', or 'Pegasus is not', precisely on the analogy of Russell's analysis of 'The author of *Waverley* is' and 'The author of *Waverley* is not'.

In order thus to subsume a one-word name or alleged name such as 'Pegasus' under Russell's theory of description, we must, of course, be able first to translate the word into a description. But this is no real restriction. If the notion of Pegasus had been so obscure or so basic a one that no pat translation into a descriptive phrase had offered itself along familiar lines, we could still have availed ourselves of the following artificial and trivial-seeming device: we could have appealed to the *ex hypothesi* unanalyzable, irreducible attribute of *being Pegasus*, adopting, for its expression, the verb 'is-Pegasus', or 'pegasizes'. The noun 'Pegasus' itself could then be treated as derivative, and identified after all with a description: 'the thing that is-Pegasus', 'the thing that pegasizes'.

If the importing of such a predicate as 'pegasizes' seems to commit us to recognizing that there is a corresponding attribute, pegasizing, in Plato's heaven or in the minds of men, well and good. Neither we nor Wyman nor McX have been contending, thus far, about the being or nonbeing of universals, but rather about that of Pegasus. If in terms of pegasizing we can interpret the noun 'Pegasus' as a description subject to Russell's theory of descriptions, then we have disposed of the old notion that Pegasus cannot be said not to be without presupposing that in some sense Pegasus is.

Our argument is now quite general. McX and Wyman supposed that we could not meaningfully affirm a statement of the form 'So-and-so is not', with a simple or descriptive singular noun in place of 'so-and-so', unless so-and-so is. This supposition is now seen to be quite generally groundless, since the singular noun in question can always be expanded into a singular description, trivially or otherwise, and then analyzed out *à la* Russell.

We commit ourselves to an ontology containing numbers when we say there are prime numbers larger than a million; we commit ourselves to an ontology containing centaurs when we say there are centaurs; and we commit ourselves to an ontology containing Pegasus when we say Pegasus is. But we do not commit ourselves to an ontology containing Pegasus or the author of *Waverley* or the round square cupola on Berkeley College when we say that Pegasus or the author of *Waverley* or the cupola in question is *not*. We need no longer labor under the delusion that the meaningfulness of a statement containing a singular term presupposes an entity named by the term. A singular term need not name to be significant.

An inkling of this might have dawned on Wyman and McX even without benefit of Russell if they had only noticed—as so few of us do—that there is a gulf between *meaning* and *naming* even in the case of a singular term which is genuinely a name of an object. The following example from [Gottlob— Ed.] Frege will serve. The phrase 'Evening Star' names a certain large physical object of spherical form, which is hurtling through space some scores of millions of miles from here. The phrase 'Morning Star' names the same thing, as was probably first established by some observant Babylonian. But the two phrases cannot be regarded as having the same meaning; otherwise that Babylonian could have dispensed with his observations and contented himself with reflecting on the meanings of his words. The meanings, then, being different from one another, must be other than the named object, which is one and the same in both cases.

Confusion of meaning with naming not only made McX think he could not meaningfully repudiate Pegasus; a continuing confusion of meaning with naming no doubt helped engender his absurd notion that Pegasus is an idea, a mental entity. The structure of his confusion is as follows. He confused the alleged *named object* Pegasus with the *meaning* of the word 'Pegasus', therefore concluding that Pegasus must be in order that the word have meaning. But what sorts of things are meanings? This is a moot point; however, one might quite plausibly explain meanings as ideas in the mind, supposing we can make clear sense in turn of the idea of ideas in the mind. Therefore Pegasus, initially confused with a meaning, ends up as an idea in the mind. It is the more remarkable that Wyman, subject to the same initial motivation as McX, should have avoided this particular blunder and wound up with unactualized possibles instead.

Now let us turn to the ontological problem of universals: the question whether there are such entities as attributes, relations, classes, numbers, functions. McX, characteristically enough, thinks there are. Speaking of attributes, he says: "There are red houses, red roses, red sunsets; this much is prephilosophical common sense in which we must all agree. These houses, roses, and sunsets, then, have something in common; and this which they have in common is all I mean by the attribute of redness." For McX, thus, there being attributes is even more obvious and trivial than the obvious and trivial fact of there being red houses, roses, and sunsets. This, I think, is characteristic of metaphysics, or at least of that part of metaphysics called ontology: one who regards a statement on this subject as true at all must regard it as trivially true. One's ontology is basic to the conceptual scheme by which he interprets all experiences, even the most commonplace ones. Judged within some particular conceptual scheme —and how else is judgment possible?—an ontological statement goes without saying, standing in need of no separate justification at all. Ontological statements follow immediately from all manner of casual statements of commonplace fact, just as—from the point of view, anyway, of McX's conceptual scheme— 'There is an attribute' follows from 'There are red houses, red roses, red sunsets'.

Judged in another conceptual scheme, an ontological statement which is axiomatic to McX's mind may, with equal immediacy and triviality, be adjudged false. One may admit that there are red houses, roses, and sunsets, but deny, except as a popular and misleading manner of speaking, that they have anything in common. The words 'houses', 'roses', and 'sunsets' are true of sundry individual entities which are houses and roses and sunsets, and the word 'red' or 'red object' is true of each of sundry individual entities which are red houses, red roses, red sunsets; but there is not, in addition, any entity whatever, individual or otherwise, which is named by the word 'redness', nor, for that matter, by the word 'househood', 'rosehood', 'sunsethood'. That the houses and roses and sunsets are all of them red may be taken as ultimate and irreducible, and it may be held that McX is no better off, in point of real explanatory power, for all the occult entities which he posits under such names as 'redness.'

One means by which McX might naturally have tried to impose his ontology of universals on us was already removed before we turned to the problem of universals. McX cannot argue that predicates such as 'red' or 'is-red', which we all concur in using, must be regarded as names each of a single universal entity in order that they be meaningful at all. For we have seen that being a name of something is a much more special feature than being meaningful. He cannot even charge us—at least not by *that* argument—with having posited an attribute of pegasizing by our adoption of the predicate 'pegasizes'.

However, McX hits upon a different stratagem. "Let us grant," he says, "this distinction between meaning and naming of which you make so much. Let us even grant that 'is red', 'pegasizes', etc., are not names of attributes. Still, you admit they have meanings. But these *meanings*, whether they are *named* or not, are still universals, and I venture to say that some of them might even be the very things that I call attributes, or something to much the same purpose in the end."

For McX, this is an unusually penetrating speech; and the only way I know to counter it is by refusing to admit meanings. However, I feel no reluctance toward refusing to admit meanings, for I do not thereby deny that words and statements are meaningful. McX and I may agree to the letter in our classification of linguistic forms into the meaningful and the meaningless, even though McX construes meaningfulness as the *having* (in some sense of 'having') of some abstract entity which he calls a meaning, whereas I do not. I remain free to maintain that the fact that a given linguistic utterance is meaningful (or *significant*, as I prefer to say so as not to invite hypostasis of meanings as entities) is an ultimate and irreducible matter of fact; or, I may undertake to analyze it in terms directly of what people do in the presence of the linguistic utterance in question and other utterances similar to it.

The useful ways in which people ordinarily talk or seem to talk about meanings boil down to two: the *having* of meanings, which is significance, and *sameness* of meaning, or synonomy. What is called *giving* the meaning of an utterance is simply the uttering of a synonym, couched, ordinarily, in clearer language than the original. If we are allergic to meanings as such, we can speak directly of utterances as significant or insignificant, and as synonymous or heteronymous one with another. The problem of explaining these adjectives 'significant' and 'synonymous' with some degree of clarity and rigor—preferably, as I see it, in terms of behavior—is as difficult as it is important. But the explanatory value of special and irreducible intermediary entities called meanings is surely illusory.

Up to now I have argued that we can use singular terms significantly in sentences without presupposing that there are the entities which those terms purport to name. I have argued further that we can use general terms, for example, predicates, without conceding them to be names of abstract entities. I have argued further that we can view utterances as significant, and as synonymous or heteronymous with one another, without countenancing a realm of entities called meanings. At this point McX begins to wonder whether there is any limit at all to our ontological immunity. Does *nothing* we may say commit us to the assumption of universals or other entities which we may find unwelcome?

I have already suggested a negative answer to this question, in speaking of bound variables, or variables of quantification, in connection with Russell's theory of descriptions. We can very easily involve ourselves in ontological commitments by saying, for example, that *there is something* (bound variable) which red houses and sunsets have in common or that *there is something* which is a prime number larger than a million. But this is, essentially, the *only* way we can involve ourselves in ontological commitments: by our use of bound variables. The use of alleged names is no criterion, for we can repudiate their namehood at the drop of a hat unless the assumption of a corresponding entity can be spotted in the things we affirm in terms of bound variables. Names are, in fact, altogether immaterial to the ontological issue, for I have shown, in connection with 'Pegasus' and 'pegasize', that names can be converted to descriptions, and Russell has shown that descriptions can be eliminated. Whatever we say with the help of names can be said in a language which shuns names altogether. To be assumed as an entity is, purely and simply, to be reckoned as the value of a variable. In terms of the categories of traditional grammar, this amounts roughly to saying that to be is to be in the range of reference of a pronoun. Pronouns are the basic media of reference; nouns might better have been named propronouns. The variables of quantification, 'something', 'nothing', 'everything', range over our whole ontology, whatever it may be; and we are convicted of a particular ontological presupposition if, and only if, the alleged presuppositum has to be reckoned among the entities over which our variables range in order to render one of our affirmations true.

We may say, for example, that some dogs are white and not thereby commit ourselves to recognizing either doghood or whiteness as entities. 'Some dogs are white' says that some things that are dogs are white; and, in order that this statement be true, the things over which the bound variable 'something' ranges must include some white dogs, but need not include doghood or whiteness. On the other hand, when we say that some zoölogical species are cross-fertile we are committing ourselves to recognizing as entities the several species themselves, abstract though they are. We remain so committed at least until we devise some way of so paraphrasing the statement as to show that the seeming reference to species on the part of our bound variable was an avoidable manner of speaking.

Classical mathematics, as the example of primes larger than a million clearly illustrates, is up to its neck in commitments to an ontology of abstract entities. Thus it is that the great mediaeval controversy over universals has flared up anew in the modern philosophy of mathematics. The issue is clearer now than of old, because we now have a more explicit standard whereby to decide what ontology a given theory or form of discourse is committed to: a theory is committed to those and only those entities to which the bound variables of the theory must be capable of referring in order that the affirmations made in the theory be true.

Because this standard of ontological presupposition did not emerge clearly in the philosophical tradition, the modern philosophical mathematicians have not on the whole recognized that they were debating the same old problem of universals in a newly clarified form. But the fundamental cleavages among modern points of view on foundations of mathematics do come down pretty explicitly to disagreements as to the range of entities to which the bound variables should be permitted to refer.

The three main mediaeval points of view regarding universals are designated by historians as *realism, conceptualism,* and *nominalism.* Essentially these same three doctrines reappear in twentieth-century surveys of the philosophy of mathematics under the new names *logicism, intuitionism,* and *formalism.*

Realism, as the word is used in connection with the mediaeval controversy over universals, is the Platonic doctrine that universals or abstract entities have being independently of the mind; the mind may discover them but cannot create them. *Logicism,* represented by Frege, Russell, [A. N.—Ed.] Whitehead, Church, and [Rudolf—Ed.] Carnap, condones the use of bound variables to refer to abstract entities known and unknown, specifiable and unspecifiable, indiscriminately.

Conceptualism holds that there are universals but they are mind-made. *Intuitionism,* espoused in modern times in one form or another by [Henri—Ed.] Poincaré, [L. E. J.—Ed.] Brouwer, [Hermann—Ed.] Weyl, and others, countenances the use of bound variables to refer to abstract entities only when those entities are capable of being cooked up individually from ingredients specified in advance. As [A. A.—Ed.] Fraenkel has put it, logicism holds that classes are discovered while intuitionism holds that they are invented—a fair statement indeed of the old opposition between realism and conceptualism. This opposition is no mere quibble; it makes an essential difference in the amount of classical mathematics to which one is willing to subscribe. Logicists, or realists, are able on their assumptions to get [Georg—Ed.] Cantor's ascending orders of infinity; intuitionists are compelled to stop with the lowest order of infinity, and, as an indirect consequence, to abandon even some of the classical laws of real numbers. The modern controversy between logicism and intuitionism arose, in fact, from disagreements over infinity.

Formalism, associated with the name of [David—Ed.] Hilbert, echoes intuitionism in deploring the logicist's unbridled recourse to universals. But formalism also finds intuitionism unsatisfactory. This could happen for either of two opposite reasons. The formalist might, like the logicist, object to the crippling of classical mathematics; or he might, like the *nominalists* of old, object to admitting abstract entities at all, even in the restrained sense of mind-made entities. The upshot is the same: the formalist keeps classical mathematics as a play of insignificant notations. This play of notations can still be of utility—whatever utility it has already shown itself to have as a crutch for physicists and technologists. But utility need not imply significance, in any literal linguistic sense. Nor need the marked success of mathematicians in spinning out theorems, and in finding objective bases for agreement with one another's results, imply significance. For an adequate basis for agreement among mathematicians can be found simply in the rules which govern the manipulation of the notations—these syntactical rules being, unlike the notations themselves, quite significant and intelligible.

I have argued that the sort of ontology we adopt can be consequential—notably in connection with mathematics, although this is only an example. Now how are we to adjudicate among rival ontologies? Certainly the answer is not provided by the semantical formula "To be is to be the value of a variable"; this formula serves rather, conversely, in testing the conformity of a given remark or doctrine to a prior ontological standard. We look to bound variables in connection with ontology not in order to know what there is, but in order to know what a given remark or doctrine, ours or someone else's, *says* there is; and this much is quite properly a problem involving language. But what there is is another question.

In debating over what there is, there are still reasons for operating on a semantical plane. One reason is to escape from the predicament noted at the beginning of this essay: the predicament of my not being able to admit that there are things which McX countenances and I do not. So long as I adhere to my ontology, as opposed to McX's, I cannot allow my bound variables to refer to entities which belong to McX's ontology and not to mine. I can, however, consistently describe our disagreement by characterizing the statements which McX affirms. Provided merely that my ontology countenances linguistic forms, or at least concrete inscriptions and utterances, I can talk about McX's sentences.

Another reason for withdrawing to a semantical plane is to find common ground on which to argue. Disagreement in ontology involves basic disagreement in conceptual schemes; yet McX and I, despite these basic disagreements, find that our conceptual schemes converge sufficiently in their intermediate and upper ramifications to enable us to communicate successfully on such topics as politics, weather, and, in particular, language. In so far as our basic controversy over ontology can be translated upward into a semantical controversy about words and what to do with them, the collapse of the controversy into question-begging may be delayed.

It is no wonder, then, that ontological controversy should tend into controversy over language. But we must not jump to the conclusion that what there is depends on words. Translatability of a question into semantical terms is no indication that the question is linguistic. To see Naples is to bear a name which, when prefixed to the words 'sees Naples', yields a true sentence; still there is nothing linguistic about seeing Naples.

Our acceptance of ontology is, I think, similar in principle to our acceptance of a scientific theory, say a system of physics: we adopt, at least in so far as we are reasonable, the simplest conceptual scheme into which the disordered fragments of raw experience can be fitted and arranged. Our ontology is determined once we have fixed upon the over-all conceptual scheme which is to accommodate science in the broadest sense; and the considerations which determine a reasonable construction of any part of that conceptual scheme, for example, the biological or the physical part, are not different in kind from the considerations which determine a reasonable construction of the whole. To whatever extent the adoption of any system of scientific theory may be said to be a matter of language, the same—but no more—may be said of the adoption of an ontology.

But simplicity, as a guiding principle in constructing conceptual schemes, is not a clear and unambiguous idea; and it is quite capable of presenting a double or multiple standard. Imagine, for example, that we have devised the most economical set of concepts adequate to the play-by-play reporting of immediate experience. The entities under this scheme—the values of bound variables—are, let us suppose, individual subjective events of sensation or reflection. We should still find, no doubt, that a physicalistic conceptual scheme, purporting to talk about external objects, offers great advantages in simplifying our over-all reports. By bringing together scattered sense events and treating them as perceptions of one object, we reduce the complexity of our stream of experience to a manageable conceptual simplicity. The rule of simplicity is indeed our guiding maxim in assigning sense data to objects: we associate an earlier and a later round sensum with the same so-called penny, or with two different so-called pennies, in obedience to the demands of maximum simplicity in our total world-picture.

Here we have two competing conceptual schemes, a phenomenalistic one and a physicalistic one. Which should prevail? Each has its advantages; each has its special simplicity in its own way. Each, I suggest, deserves to be developed. Each may be said, indeed, to be the more fundamental, though in different senses: the one is epistemologically, the other physically, fundamental.

The physical conceptual scheme simplifies our account of experience because of the way myriad scattered sense events come to be associated with single so-called objects; still there is no likelihood that each sentence about physical objects can actually be translated, however deviously and complexly, into the phenomenalistic language. Physical objects are postulated entities which round out and simplify our account of the flux of experience, just as the introduction of irrational numbers simplifies laws of arithmetic. From the point of view of the conceptual scheme of the elementary arithmetic of rational numbers alone, the broader arithmetic of rational and irrational numbers would have the status of a convenient myth, simpler than the literal truth (namely, the arithmetic of rationals) and yet containing that literal truth as a scattered part. Similarly, from a phenomenalistic point of view, the conceptual scheme of physical objects is a convenient myth, simpler than the literal truth and yet containing that literal truth as a scattered part.

Now what of classes or attributes of physical objects, in turn? A platonistic ontology of this sort is, from the point of view of a strictly physicalistic conceptual scheme, as much a myth as that physicalistic conceptual scheme itself is for phenomenalism. This higher myth is a good and useful one, in turn, in so far as it simplifies our account of physics. Since mathematics is an integral part of this higher myth, the utility of this myth for physical science is evident enough. In speaking of it nevertheless as a myth, I echo that philosophy of mathematics to which I alluded earlier under the name of formalism. But an attitude of formalism may with equal justice be adopted toward the physical conceptual scheme, in turn, by the pure aesthete or phenomenalist.

The analogy between the myth of mathematics and the myth of physics is, in some additional and perhaps fortuitous ways, strikingly close. Consider, for example, the crisis which was precipitated in the foundations of mathematics, at the turn of the century, by the discovery of Russell's paradox and other antinomies of set theory. These contradictions had to be obviated by unintuitive, *ad hoc* devices; our mathematical myth-making became deliberate and evident to all. But what of physics? An antinomy arose between the undular and the corpuscular accounts of light; and if this was not as out-and-out a contradiction as Russell's paradox, I suspect that the reason is that physics is not as out-and-out as mathematics. Again, the second great modern crisis in the foundations of mathematics—precipitated in 1931 by Gödel's proof that there are bound to be undecidable statements in arithmetic—has its companion piece in physics in Heisenberg's indeterminacy principle.

In earlier pages I undertook to show that some common arguments in favor of certain ontologies are fallacious. Further, I advanced an explicit standard whereby to decide what the ontological commitments of a theory are. But the question what ontology actually to adopt still stands open, and the obvious counsel is tolerance and an experimental spirit. Let us by all means see how much of the physicalistic conceptual scheme can be reduced to a phenomenalistic one; still, physics also naturally demands pursuing, irreducible *in toto* [entirely—Ed.] though it be. Let us see how, or to what degree, natural science may be rendered independent of platonistic mathematics; but let us also pursue mathematics and delve into its platonistic foundations.

From among the various conceptual schemes best suited to these various pursuits, one—the phenomenalistic—claims epistemological priority. Viewed from within the phenomenalistic conceptual scheme, the ontologies of physical objects and mathematical objects are myths. The quality of myth, however, is relative, in this case, to the epistemological point of view. This point of view is one among various, corresponding to one among our various interests and purposes.

10

John R. Searle

What Is a Speech Act?

John R. Searle is Professor of Philosophy at the University of California. He was Special Assistant to the Chancellor, University of California at Berkeley, during the period of strong antiwar sentiment that developed on the West Coast against the Vietnam War. He is best known for his book Speech Acts (1969). *He has written extensively on language; edited* The Philosophy of Language (1971); *and has served as host and discussion leader for the series "World Press" on educational television.*

Speech Acts is an original development of themes drawn from J. L. Austin and P. F. Strawson. It was the first comprehensive effort to construe the entire range of problems concerning the analysis of language in terms of a speech-act model. It attempts to formulate the necessary and sufficient conditions for performing a speech act, which noticeably involve nonlinguistic commitments and assumptions.

In general, Searle treats language as a rule-governed activity. Reference is viewed as a dependent speech act. One salient feature of the book is its adherence to the so-called axiom of existence, the thesis that whatever is referred to must exist; but Searle is not entirely clear about the import of reference to fiction. Searle has also sketched a method for deriving an "ought" from an "is" ("How to Derive 'Ought' from 'Is,' " 1964), which has generated a good deal of controversy.

I. Introduction

In a typical speech situation involving a speaker, a hearer, and an utterance by the speaker, there are many kinds of acts associated with the speaker's utterance. The speaker will characteristically have moved his jaw and tongue and made noises. In addition, he will characteristically have performed some acts within the class which includes informing or irritating or boring his hearers; he will further characteristically have performed acts within the class which includes referring to Kennedy or Khrushchev or the North Pole; and he will also have performed acts within the class which includes making statements, asking questions, issuing commands, giving reports, greeting, and warning. The members of this last class are what Austin[1] called illocutionary acts and it is with this class that I shall be concerned in this paper, so the paper might have been

Reprinted from Max Black (Ed.): *Philosophy in America.* © under the Berne Convention by George Allen & Unwin, Ltd. Used by permission of Cornell University Press and George Allen & Unwin, Ltd.

---

[1] J. L. Austin, *How To Do Things With Words,* Oxford 1962.

called 'What is an Illocutionary Act?' I do not attempt to define the expression 'illocutionary act', although if my analysis of a particular illocutionary act succeeds it may provide the basis for a definition. Some of the English verbs and verb phrases associated with illocutionary acts are: state, assert, describe, warn, remark, comment, command, order, request, criticize, apologize, censure, approve, welcome, promise, express approval, and express regret. Austin claimed that there were over a thousand such expressions in English.

By way of introduction, perhaps I can say why I think it is of interest and importance in the philosophy of language to study speech acts, or, as they are sometimes called, language acts or linguistic acts. I think it is essential to any specimen of linguistic communication that it involve a linguistic act. It is not, as has generally been supposed, the symbol or word or sentence, or even the token of the symbol or word or sentence, which is the unit of linguistic communication, but rather it is the *production* of the token in the performance of the speech act that constitutes the basic unit of linguistic communication. To put this point more precisely, the production of the sentence token under certain conditions is the illocutionary act, and the illocutionary act is the minimal unit of linguistic communication.

I do not know how to *prove* that linguistic communication essentially involves acts but I can think of arguments with which one might attempt to convince someone who was sceptical. One argument would be to call the sceptic's attention to the fact that when he takes a noise or a mark on paper to be an instance of linguistic communication, as a message, one of the things that is involved in his so taking that noise or mark is that he should regard it as having been produced by a being with certain intentions. He cannot just regard it as a natural phenomenon, like a stone, a waterfall, or a tree. In order to regard it as an instance of linguistic communication one must suppose that its production is what I am calling a speech act. It is a logical presupposition, for example, of current attempts to decipher the Mayan hieroglyphs that we at least hypothesize that the marks we see on the stones were produced by beings more or less like ourselves and produced with certain kinds of intentions. If we were certain the marks were a consequence of, say, water erosion, then the question of deciphering them or even calling them hieroglyphs could not arise. To construe them under the category of linguistic communication necessarily involves construing their production as speech acts.

To perform illocutionary acts is to engage in a rule-governed form of behaviour. I shall argue that such things as asking questions or making statements are rule-governed in ways quite similar to those in which getting a base hit in baseball or moving a knight in chess are rule-governed forms of acts. I intend therefore to explicate the notion of an illocutionary act by stating a set of necessary and sufficient conditions for the performance of a particular kind of illocutionary act, and extracting from it a set of semantical rules for the use of the expression (or syntactic device) which marks the utterance as an illocutionary act of that kind. If I am successful in stating the conditions and the corresponding rules for even one kind of illocutionary act, that will provide us with a pattern for analysing other kinds of acts and consequently for explicating the notion in general. But in order to set the stage for actually stating conditions and extracting rules for performing an illocutionary act I have to discuss three other preliminary notions: *rules, propositions,* and *meaning.* I shall confine my discussion of these notions to those aspects which are essential to my main purposes in this paper, but, even so, what I wish to say concerning each of these notions, if it were to be at all complete, would require a paper for each; however, sometimes it may be worth sacrificing thoroughness for the sake of scope and I shall therefore be very brief.

II. Rules

In recent years there has been in the philosophy of language considerable discussion involving the notion of rules for the use of expressions. Some philosophers have even said that knowing the meaning of a word is simply a matter of knowing the rules for its use or employment. One disquieting feature of such discussions is that no philosopher, to my knowledge at least, has ever given anything like an adequate formulation of the rules for the use of even one expression. If meaning is a matter of rules of use, surely we ought to be able to state the rules for the use of expressions in a way which would explicate the meaning of those expressions. Certain other philosophers, dismayed perhaps by the failure of their colleagues to produce any rules, have denied the fashionable view that meaning is a matter of rules and have asserted that there are no semantical rules of the proposed kind at all. I am inclined to think that this scepticism is premature and stems from a failure to distinguish different sorts of rules, in a way which I shall now attempt to explain.

I distinguish between two sorts of rules: Some regulate antecedently existing forms of behaviour; for example, the rules of etiquette regulate interpersonal relationships, but these relationships exist independently of the rules of etiquette. Some rules on the other hand do not merely regulate but create or define new forms of behaviour. The rules of football, for example, do not merely regulate the game of football but as it were create the possibility of or define that activity. The activity of playing football is constituted by acting in accordance with these rules; football has no existence apart from these rules. I call the latter kind of rules constitutive rules and the former kind regulative rules. Regulative rules regulate a pre-existing activity, an activity whose existence is logically independent of the existence of the rules. Constitutive rules constitute (and also regulate) an activity the existence of which is logically dependent on the rules.[2]

Regulative rules characteristically take the form of or can be paraphrased as imperatives, e.g. 'When cutting food hold the knife in the right hand', or 'Officers are to wear ties at dinner'. Some constitutive rules take quite a

---

[2] This distinction occurs in J. Rawls, 'Two Concepts of Rules', *Philosophical Review,* 1955, and J. R. Searle, 'How to Derive "Ought" from "Is" ', *Philosophical Review,* 1964.

different form, e.g. a checkmate is made if the king is attacked in such a way that no move will leave it unattacked; a touchdown is scored when a player crosses the opponents' goal line in possession of the ball while a play is in progress. If our paradigms of rules are imperative regulative rules, such non-imperative constitutive rules are likely to strike us as extremely curious and hardly even as rules at all. Notice that they are almost tautological in character, for what the 'rule' seems to offer is a partial definition of 'checkmate' or 'touchdown'. But, of course, this quasi-tautological character is a necessary consequence of their being constitutive rules: the rules concerning touchdowns must define the notion of 'touchdown' in the same way that the rules concerning football define 'football'. That, for example, a touchdown can be scored in such and such ways and counts six points can appear sometimes as a rule, sometimes as an analytic truth; and that it can be construed as a tautology is a clue to the fact that the rule in question is a constitutive one. Regulative rules generally have the form 'Do X' or 'If Y do X'. Some members of the set of constitutive rules have this form but some also have the form 'X counts as Y'.[3]

The failure to perceive this is of some importance in philosophy. Thus, for example, some philosophers ask 'How can a promise create an obligation?' A similar question would be 'How can a touchdown create six points?' And as they stand both questions can only be answered by stating a rule of the form 'X counts as Y'.

I am inclined to think that both the failure of some philosophers to state rules for the use of expressions and the scepticism of other philosophers concerning the existence of any such rules stem at least in part from a failure to recognize the distinctions between constitutive and regulative rules. The model or paradigm of a rule which most philosophers have is that of a regulative rule, and if one looks in semantics for purely regulative rules one is not likely to find anything interesting from the point of view of logical analysis. There are no doubt social rules of the form 'One ought not to utter obscenities at formal gatherings', but that hardly seems a rule of the sort that is crucial in explicating the semantics of a language. The hypothesis that lies behind the present paper is that the semantics of a language can be regarded as a series of systems of constitutive rules and that illocutionary acts are acts performed in accordance with these sets of constitutive rules. One of the aims of this paper is to formulate a set of constitutive rules for a certain kind of speech act. And if what I have said concerning constitutive rules is correct, we should not be surprised if not all these rules take the form of imperative rules. Indeed we shall see that the rules fall into several different categories, none of which is quite like the rules of etiquette. The effort to state the rules for an illocutionary act can also be regarded as a kind of test of the hypothesis that there are constitutive rules underlying speech acts. If we are unable to give any satisfactory rule formulations, our failure could be construed as partially disconfirming evidence against the hypothesis.

---

[3] The formulation 'X counts as Y' was originally suggested to me by Max Black.

III. Propositions

Different illocutionary acts often have features in common with each other. Consider utterances of the following sentences:

    (1) Will John leave the room?
    (2) John will leave the room.
    (3) John, leave the room!
    (4) Would that John left the room.
    (5) If John will leave the room, I will leave also.

Utterances of each of these on a given occasion would characteristically be performances of different illocutionary acts. The first would, characteristically, be a question, the second an assertion about the future, that is, a prediction, the third a request or order, the fourth an expression of a wish, and the fifth a hypothetical expression of intention. Yet in the performance of each the speaker would characteristically perform some subsidiary acts which are common to all five illocutionary acts. In the utterance of each the speaker *refers* to a particular person John and *predicates* the act of leaving the room of that person. In no case is that all he does, but in every case it is part of what he does. I shall say, therefore, that in each of these cases, although the illocutionary acts are different, at least some of the non-illocutionary acts of reference and predication are the same.

The reference to some person John and predication of the same thing of him in each of these illocutionary acts inclines me to say that there is a common *content* in each of them. Something expressible by the clause 'that John will leave the room' seems to be a common feature of all. We could, with not too much distortion, write each of these sentences in a way which would isolate this common feature: 'I assert that John will leave the room', 'I ask whether John will leave the room', etc.

For lack of a better word I propose to call this common content a proposition, and I shall describe this feature of these illocutionary acts by saying that in the utterance of each of (1)–(5) the speaker expresses the proposition that John will leave the room. Notice that I do not say that the sentence expresses the proposition; I do not know how sentences could perform acts of that kind. But I shall say that in the utterance of the sentence the speaker expresses a proposition. Notice also that I am distinguishing between a proposition and an assertion or statement of that proposition. The proposition that John will leave the room is expressed in the utterance of all of (1)–(5) but only in (2) is that proposition asserted. An assertion is an illocutionary act, but a proposition is not an act at all, although the act of expressing a proposition is a part of performing certain illocutionary acts.

I might summarise this by saying that I am distinguishing between the illocutionary act and the propositional content of an illocutionary act. Of course, not all illocutionary acts have a propositional content, for example, an utterance of 'Hurrah!' or 'Ouch!' does not. In one version or another this distinction is an old one and has been marked in different ways by authors as diverse as Frege, Sheffer, Lewis, Reichenbach and Hare, to mention only a few.

From a semantical point of view we can distinguish between the propositional indicator in the sentence and the indicator of illocutionary force. That is, for a large class of sentences used to perform illocutionary acts, we can say for the purpose of our analysis that the sentence has two (not necessarily separate) parts, the proposition indicating element and the function indicating device.[4] The function indicating device shows how the proposition is to be taken, or, to put it in another way, what illocutionary force the utterance is to have, that is, what illocutionary act the speaker is performing in the utterance of the sentence. Function indicating devices in English include word order, stress, intonation contour, punctuation, the mood of the verb, and finally a set of so-called performative verbs: I may indicate the kind of illocutionary act I am performing by beginning the sentence with 'I apologize', 'I warn', 'I state', etc. Often in actual speech situations the context will make it clear what the illocutionary force of the utterance is, without its being necessary to invoke the appropriate function indicating device.

If this semantical distinction is of any real importance, it seems likely that it should have some syntactical analogue, and certain recent developments in transformational grammar tend to support the view that it does. In the underlying phrase marker of a sentence there is a distinction between those elements which correspond to the function indicating device and those which correspond to the propositional content.

The distinction between the function indicating device and the proposition indicating device will prove very useful to us in giving an analysis of an illocutionary act. Since the same proposition can be common to all sorts of illocutionary acts, we can separate our analysis of the proposition from our analysis of kinds of illocutionary acts. I think there are rules for expressing propositions, rules for such things as reference and prediction, but those rules can be discussed independently of the rules for function indicating. In this paper I shall not attempt to discuss propositional rules but shall concentrate on rules for using certain kinds of function indicating devices.

IV. Meaning

Speech acts are characteristically performed in the utterance of sounds or the making of marks. What is the difference between *just* uttering sounds or making marks and performing a speech act? One difference is that the sounds or marks one makes in the performance of a speech act are characteristically said to *have meaning,* and a second related difference is that one is characteristically said to *mean something* by those sounds or marks. Characteristically when one speaks one means something by what one says, and what one says,

---

[4] In the sentence 'I promise that I will come' the function indicating device and the propositional element are separate. In the sentence 'I promise to come', which means the same as the first and is derived from it by certain transformations, the two elements are not separate.

the string of morphemes that one emits, is characteristically said to have a meaning. Here, incidentally, is another point at which our analogy between performing speech acts and playing games breaks down. The pieces in a game like chess are not characteristically said to have a meaning, and furthermore when one makes a move one is not characteristically said to mean anything by that move.

But what is it for one to mean something by what one says, and what is it for something to have a meaning? To answer the first of these questions I propose to borrow and revise some ideas of Paul Grice. In an article entitled 'Meaning',[5] Grice gives the following analysis of one sense of the notion of 'meaning'. To say that A meant something by x is to say that 'A intended the utterance of x to produce some effect in an audience by means of the recognition of this intention'. This seems to me a useful start on an analysis of meaning, first because it shows the close relationship between the notion of meaning and the notion of intention, and secondly because it captures something which is, I think, essential to speaking a language: In speaking a language I attempt to communicate things to my hearer by means of getting him to recognize my intention to communicate just those things. For example, characteristically, when I make an assertion, I attempt to communicate to and convince my hearer of the truth of a certain proposition; and the means I employ to do this are to utter certain sounds, which utterance I intend to produce in him the desired effect by means of his recognition of my intention to produce just that effect. I shall illustrate this with an example. I might on the one hand attempt to get you to believe that I am French by speaking French all the time, dressing in the French manner, showing wild enthusiasm for de Gaulle, and cultivating French acquaintances. But I might on the other hand attempt to get you to believe that I am French by simply telling you that I am French. Now, what is the difference between these two ways of my attempting to get you to believe that I am French? One crucial difference is that in the second case I attempt to get you to believe that I am French by getting you to recognize that it is my purported intention to get you to believe just that. That is one of the things involved in telling you that I am French. But of course if I try to get you to believe that I am French by putting on the act I described, then your recognition of my intention to produce in you the belief that I am French is not the means I am employing. Indeed in this case you would, I think, become rather suspicious if you recognized my intention.

However valuable this analysis of meaning is, it seems to me to be in certain respects defective. First of all, it fails to distinguish the different kinds of effects—perlocutionary versus illocutionary—that one may intend to produce in one's hearers, and it further fails to show the way in which these different kinds of effects are related to the notion of meaning. A second defect is that it fails to account for the extent to which meaning is a matter of rules or conventions. That is, this account of meaning does not show the connection between one's meaning something by what one says and what that which one says

---

[5] *Philosophical Review*, 1957.

actually means in the language. In order to illustrate this point I now wish to present a counter-example to this analysis of meaning. The point of the counter-example will be to illustrate the connection between what a speaker means and what the words he utters mean.

Suppose that I am an American soldier in the Second World War and that I am captured by Italian troops. And suppose also that I wish to get these troops to believe that I am a German officer in order to get them to release me. What I would like to do is to tell them in German or Italian that I am a German officer. But let us suppose I don't know enough German or Italian to do that. So I, as it were, attempt to put on a show of telling them that I am a German officer by reciting those few bits of German that I know, trusting that they don't know enough German to see through my plan. Let us suppose I know only one line of German, which I remember from a poem I had to memorize in a high school German course. Therefore I, a captured American, address my Italian captors with the following sentence: 'Kennst du das Land, wo die Zitronen blühen?' Now, let us describe the situation in Gricean terms. I intend to produce a certain effect in them, namely, the effect of believing that I am a German officer; and I intend to produce this effect by means of their recognition of my intention. I intend that they should think that what I am trying to tell them is that I am a German officer. But does it follow from this account that when I say 'Kennst du das Land . . .' etc., what I mean is, 'I am a German officer'? Not only does it not follow, but in this case it seems plainly false that when I utter the German sentence what I mean is 'I am a German officer', or even 'Ich bin ein deutscher Offizier', because what the words mean is, 'Knowest thou the land where the lemon trees bloom?' Of course, I want my captors to be deceived into thinking that what I mean is 'I am a German officer', but part of what is involved in the deception is getting them to think that that is what the words which I utter mean in German. At one point in the *Philosophical Investigations* Wittgenstein says 'Say "it's cold here" and mean "it's warm here" '.[6] The reason we are unable to do this is that what we can mean is a function of what we are saying. Meaning is more than a matter of intention, it is also a matter of convention.

Grice's account can be amended to deal with counter-examples of this kind. We have here a case where I am trying to produce a certain effect by means of the recognition of my intention to produce that effect, but the device I use to produce this effect is one which is conventionally, by the rules governing the use of that device, used as a means of producing quite different illocutionary effects. We must therefore reformulate the Gricean account of meaning in such a way as to make it clear that one's meaning something when one says something is more than just contingently related to what the sentence means in the language one is speaking. In our analysis of illocutionary acts, we must capture both the intentional and the conventional aspects and especially the relationship between them. In the performance of an illocutionary act the

---

[6] *Philosophical Investigations*, Oxford 1953, para. 510.

speaker intends to produce a certain effect by means of getting the hearer to recognize his intention to produce that effect, and furthermore, if he is using words literally, he intends this recognition to be achieved in virtue of the fact that the rules for using the expressions he utters associate the expressions with the production of that effect. It is this *combination* of elements which we shall need to express in our analysis of the illocutionary act.

V. How to Promise

I shall now attempt to give an analysis of the illocutionary act of promising. In order to do this I shall ask what conditions are necessary and sufficient for the act of promising to have been performed in the utterance of a given sentence. I shall attempt to answer this question by stating these conditions as a set of propositions such that the conjunction of the members of the set entails the proposition that a speaker made a promise, and the proposition that the speaker made a promise entails this conjunction. Thus each condition will be a necessary condition for the performance of the act of promising, and taken collectively the set of conditions will be a sufficient condition for the act to have been performed.

If we get such a set of conditions we can extract from them a set of rules for the use of the function indicating device. The method here is analogous to discovering the rules of chess by asking oneself what are the necessary and sufficient conditions under which one can be said to have correctly moved a knight or castled or checkmated a player, etc. We are in the position of someone who has learned to play chess without ever having the rules formulated and who wants such a formulation. We learned how to play the game of illocutionary acts, but in general it was done without an explicit formulation of the rules, and the first step in getting such a formulation is to set out the conditions for the performance of a particular illocutionary act. Our inquiry will therefore serve a double philosophical purpose. By stating a set of conditions for the performance of a particular illocutionary act we shall have offered a partial explication of that notion and shall also have paved the way for the second step, the formulation of the rules.

I find the statement of the conditions very difficult to do, and I am not entirely satisfied with the list I am about to present. One reason for the difficulty is that the notion of a promise, like most notions in ordinary language, does not have absolutely strict rules. There are all sorts of odd, deviant, and borderline promises; and counter-examples, more or less bizarre, can be produced against my analysis. I am inclined to think we shall not be able to get a set of knock down necessary and sufficient conditions that will exactly mirror the ordinary use of the word 'promise'. I am confining my discussion, therefore, to the centre of the concept of promising and ignoring the fringe, borderline, and partially defective cases. I also confine my discussion to full-blown explicit promises and ignore promises made by elliptical turns of phrase, hints, metaphors, etc.

Another difficulty arises from my desire to state the conditions without certain forms of circularity. I want to give a list of conditions for the performance of a certain illocutionary act, which do not themselves mention the performance of any illocutionary acts. I need to satisfy this condition in order to offer an explication of the notion of an illocutionary act in general, otherwise I should simply be showing the relation between different illocutionary acts. However, although there will be no reference to illocutionary *acts*, certain illocutionary *concepts* will appear in the analysans as well as in the analysandum; and I think this form of circularity is unavoidable because of the nature of constitutive rules.

In the presentation of the conditions I shall first consider the case of a sincere promise and then show how to modify the conditions to allow for insincere promises. As our inquiry is semantical rather than syntactical, I shall simply assume the existence of grammatically well-formed sentences.

Given that a speaker S utters a sentence T in the presence of a hearer H, then, in the utterance of T, S sincerely (and non-defectively) promises that p to H if and only if:

(1) *Normal input and output conditions obtain.*

I use the terms 'input' and 'output' to cover the large and indefinite range of conditions under which any kind of serious linguistic communication is possible. 'Output' covers the conditions for intelligible speaking and 'input' covers the conditions for understanding. Together they include such things as that the speaker and hearer both know how to speak the language; both are conscious of what they are doing; the speaker is not acting under duress or threats; they have no physical impediments to communication, such as deafness, aphasia, or laryngitis; they are not acting in a play or telling jokes, etc.

(2) *S expresses that p in the utterance of T.*

This condition isolates the propositional content from the rest of the speech act and enables us to concentrate on the peculiarities of promising in the rest of the analysis.

(3) *In expressing that p, S predicates a future act A of S.*

In the case of promising the function indicating device is an expression whose scope includes certain features of the proposition. In a promise an act must be predicated of the speaker and it cannot be a past act. I cannot promise to have done something, and I cannot promise that someone else will do something. (Although I can promise to see that he will do it.) The notion of an act, as I am construing it for present purposes, includes refraining from acts, performing series of acts, and may also include states and conditions: I may promise not to do something, I may promise to do something repeatedly, and I may promise to be or remain in a certain state or condition. I call conditions (2) and (3) the *propositional content conditions.*

(4) *H would prefer S's doing A to his not doing A, and S believes H would prefer his doing A to his not doing A.*

One crucial distinction between promises on the one hand and threats on the other is that a promise is a pledge to do something for you, not to you, but a threat is a pledge to do something to you, not for you. A promise is defective if the thing promised is something the promisee does not want done; and it is further defective if the promisor does not believe the promisee wants it done, since a non-defective promise must be intended as a promise and not as a threat or warning. I think both halves of this double condition are necessary in order to avoid fairly obvious counter-examples.

One can, however, think of apparent counter-examples to this condition as stated. Suppose I say to a lazy student 'If you don't hand in your paper on time I promise you I will give you a failing grade in the course'. Is this utterance a promise? I am inclined to think not; we would more naturally describe it as a warning or possibly even a threat. But why then is it possible to use the locution 'I promise' in such a case? I think we use it here because 'I promise' and 'I hereby promise' are among the strongest function indicating devices for *commitment* provided by the English language. For that reason we often use these expressions in the performance of speech acts which are not strictly speaking promises but in which we wish to emphasize our commitment. To illustrate this, consider another apparent counter-example to the analysis along different lines. Sometimes, more commonly I think in the United States than in England, one hears people say 'I promise' when making an emphatic assertion. Suppose, for example, I accuse you of having stolen the money. I say, 'You stole that money, didn't you?' You reply 'No, I didn't, I promise you I didn't'. Did you make a promise in this case? I find it very unnatural to describe your utterance as a promise. This utterance would be more aptly described as an emphatic denial, and we can explain the occurrence of the function indicating device 'I promise' as derivative from genuine promises and serving here as an expression adding emphasis to your denial.

In general the point stated in condition (4) is that if a purported promise is to be non-defective the thing promised must be something the hearer wants done, or considers to be in his interest, or would prefer being done to not being done, etc.; and the speaker must be aware of or believe or know, etc. that this is the case. I think a more elegant and exact formulation of this condition would require the introduction of technical terminology.

(5) *It is not obvious to both S and H that S will do A in the normal course of events.*

This condition is an instance of a general condition on many different kinds of illocutionary acts to the effect that the act must have a point. For example, if I make a request to someone to do something which it is obvious that he is already doing or is about to do, then my request is pointless and to that extent defective. In an actual speech situation, listeners, knowing the rules for performing illocutionary acts, will assume that this condition is satisfied. Suppose, for example, that in the course of a public speech I say to a member of my audience 'Look here, Smith, pay attention to what I am saying'. In order to make sense of this utterance the audience will have to assume that Smith has not been paying attention, that the question of his paying attention has arisen in some way; because a condition for making a request is that it is not obvious that the hearer is doing or about to do the thing requested.

Similarly with promises. It is out of order for me to promise to do something that it is obvious I am going to do anyway. If I do seem to be making such a promise, the only way my audience can make sense of my utterance is to assume that I believe that it is not obvious that I am going to do the thing promised. A happily married man who promises his wife he will not desert her in the next week is likely to provide more anxiety than comfort.

Parenthetically I think this condition is an instance of the sort of phenomenon stated in Zipf's law. I think there is operating in our language, as in most forms of human behaviour, a principle of least effort, in this case a principle of maximum illocutionary ends with minimum phonetic effort; and I think condition (5) is an instance of it.

I call conditions such as (4) and (5) *preparatory conditions*. They are *sine quibus non* [necessary conditions—Ed.] of happy promising, but they do not yet state the essential feature.

(6) *S intends to do A.*

The most important distinction between sincere and insincere promises is that in the case of the insincere promise the speaker intends to do the act promised; in the case of the insincere promise he does not intend to do the act. Also in sincere promises the speaker believes it is possible for him to do the act (or to refrain from doing it), but I think the proposition that he intends to do it entails that he thinks it is possible to do (or refrain from doing) it, so I am not stating that as an extra condition. I call this condition the *sincerity condition*.

(7) *S intends that the utterance of T will place him under an obligation to do A.*

The essential feature of a promise is that it is the undertaking of an obligation to perform a certain act. I think that this condition distinguishes promises (and other members of the same family such as vows) from other kinds of speech acts. Notice that in the statement of the condition we only specify the speaker's intention; further conditions will make clear how that intention is realized. It is clear, however, that having this intention is a necessary condition of making a promise; for if a speaker can demonstrate that he did not have this intention in a given utterance, he can prove that the utterance was not a promise. We know, for example, that Mr Pickwick did not promise to marry the woman because we know he did not have the appropriate intention.

I call this the *essential condition*.

(8) *S intends that the utterance of T will produce in H a belief that conditions (6) and (7) obtain by means of the recognition of the intention to produce that belief, and he intends this recognition to be achieved by means of the recognition of the sentence as one conventionally used to produce such beliefs.*

This captures our amended Gricean analysis of what it is for the speaker to mean to make a promise. The speaker intends to produce a certain illocutionary effect by means of getting the hearer to recognize his intention to produce that effect, and he also intends this recognition to be achieved in virtue of the fact that the lexical and syntactical character of the item he utters conventionally associates it with producing that effect.

Strictly speaking this condition could be formulated as part of condition (1), but it is of enough philosophical interest to be worth stating separately. I find it troublesome for the following reason. If my original objection to Grice is really valid, then surely, one might say, all these iterated intentions are superfluous; all that is necessary is that the speaker should seriously utter a sentence. The production of all these effects is simply a consequence of the hearer's knowledge of what the sentence means, which in turn is a consequence of his knowledge of the language, which is assumed by the speaker at the outset. I think the correct reply to this objection is that condition (8) explicates what it is for the speaker to 'seriously' utter the sentence, i.e. to utter it and mean it, but I am not completely confident about either the force of the objection or of the reply.

(9) *The semantical rules of the dialect spoken by S and H are such that T is correctly and sincerely uttered if and only if conditions (1)–(8) obtain.*

This condition is intended to make clear that the sentence uttered is one which by the semantical rules of the language is used to make a promise. Taken together with condition (8), it eliminates counter-examples like the captured soldier example considered earlier. Exactly what the formulation of the rules is, we shall soon see.

So far we have considered only the case of a sincere promise. But insincere promises are promises nonetheless, and we now need to show how to modify the conditions to allow for them. In making an insincere promise the speaker does not have all the intentions and beliefs he has when making a sincere promise. However, he purports to have them. Indeed it is because he purports to have intentions and beliefs which he does not have that we describe his act as insincere. So to allow for insincere promises we need only to revise our conditions to state that the speaker takes responsibility for having the beliefs and intentions rather than stating that he actually has them. A clue that the speaker does take such responsibility is the fact that he could not say without absurdity, e.g. 'I promise to do A but I do not intend to do A'. To say 'I promise to do A' is to take responsibility for intending to do A, and this condition holds whether the utterance was sincere or insincere. To allow for the possibility of an insincere promise then we have only to revise condition (6) so that it states not that the speaker intends to do A, but that he takes responsibility for intending to do A, and to avoid the charge of circularity I shall phrase this as follows:

(6*) *S intends that the utterance of T will make him responsible for intending to do A.*

Thus amended (and with 'sincerely' dropped from our analysandum and from condition (9)), our analysis is neutral on the question whether the promise was sincere or insincere.

VI. *Rules for the Use of the Function Indicating Device*

Our next task is to extract from our set of conditions a set of rules for the use of the function indicating device. Obviously not all of our conditions are equally relevant to this task. Condition (1) and conditions of the forms (8) and (9) apply generally to all kinds of normal illocutionary acts and are not peculiar to promising. Rules for the function indicating device for promising are to be found corresponding to conditions (2)–(7).

The semantical rules for the use of any function indicating device P for promising are:

Rule 1. P is to be uttered only in the context of a sentence (or larger stretch of discourse) the utterance of which predicates some future act A of the speaker S.

I call this the *propositional content rule*. It is derived from the propositional content conditions (2) and (3).

Rule 2. P is to be uttered only if the hearer H would prefer S's doing A to his not doing A, and S believes H would prefer S's doing A to his not doing A.

Rule 3. P is to be uttered only if it is not obvious to both S and H that S will do A in the normal course of events.

I call rules (2) and (3) *preparatory rules*. They are derived from the preparatory conditions (4) and (5).

Rule 4. P is to be uttered only if S intends to do A.

I call this the *sincerity rule*. It is derived from the sincerity condition (6).

Rule 5. The utterance of P counts as the undertaking of an obligation to do A.

I call this the *essential rule*.

These rules are ordered: Rules 2–5 apply only if Rule 1 is satisfied, and Rule 5 applies only if Rules 2 and 3 are satisfied as well.

Notice that whereas rules 1–4 take the form of quasi-imperatives, i.e. they are of the form: utter P only if x, rule 5 is of the form: the utterance of P counts as Y. Thus rule 5 is of the kind peculiar to systems of constitutive rules which I discussed in section II.

Notice also that the rather tiresome analogy with games is holding up remarkably well. If we ask ourselves under what conditions a player could be said to move a knight correctly, we would find preparatory conditions, such as that it must be his turn to move, as well as the essential condition stating the actual positions the knight can move to. I think that there is even a sincerity rule for competitive games, the rule that each side tries to win. I suggest that the team which 'throws' the game is behaving in a way closely analogous to the speaker who lies or makes false promises. Of course, there usually are no propositional content rules for games, because games do not, by and large, represent states of affairs.

If this analysis is of any general interest beyond the case of promising then it would seem that these distinctions should carry over into other types of speech act, and I think a little reflection will show that they do. Consider, e.g., giving an order. The preparatory conditions include that the speaker should be in a position of authority over the hearer, the sincerity condition is that the speaker wants the ordered act done, and the essential condition has to do with the fact that the utterance is an attempt to get the hearer to do it. For assertions, the preparatory conditions include the fact that the hearer must have some basis for supposing the asserted proposition is true, the sincerity condition is that he must believe it to be true, and the essential condition has to do with the fact that the utterance is an attempt to inform the hearer and convince him of its truth. Greetings are a much simpler kind of speech act, but even here some of the distinctions apply. In the utterance of 'Hello' there is no propositional content and no sincerity condition. The preparatory condition is that the speaker must have just encountered the hearer, and the essential rule is that the utterance indicates courteous recognition of the hearer.

A proposal for further research then is to carry out a similar analysis of other types of speech acts. Not only would this give us an analysis of concepts interesting in themselves, but the comparison of different analyses would deepen our understanding of the whole subject and incidentally provide a basis for a more serious taxonomy than any of the usual facile categories such as evaluative versus descriptive, or cognitive versus emotive.

Bibliography

ALSTON, WILLIAM P. *Philosophy of Language.* Englewood Cliffs, N.J.: Prentice-Hall, 1964.*

AUSTIN, J. L. *Philosophical Papers.* Oxford: Clarendon, 1961.

———. *How to Do Things with Words.* J. O. Urmson (ed.). London: Oxford University Press, 1962.

AYER, A. J. *The Foundations of Empirical Knowledge.* London: Macmillan, 1940.*

——— (ed.). *Logical Positivism.* New York: Free Press, 1959.†

BLACK, MAX. *Language and Philosophy.* Ithaca, N.Y.: Cornell University Press, 1949.

———. *Models and Metaphors.* Ithaca, N.Y.: Cornell University Press, 1962.

——— (ed.). *The Importance of Language.* Englewood Cliffs, N.J.: Prentice-Hall, 1962.*

CARNAP, RUDOLF. *Meaning and Necessity.* Chicago: Chicago University Press, 1956.†

CATON, CHARLES E. (ed.). *Philosophy and Ordinary Language.* Urbana: University of Illinois Press, 1963.*

CHAPPELL, V. C. (ed.). *Ordinary Language.* Englewood Cliffs, N.J.: Prentice-Hall, 1964.*

CHOMSKY, NOAM. *Aspects of the Theory of Syntax.* Cambridge: MIT Press, 1965.†

FEIGL, HERBERT, and WILFRID SELLARS (eds.). *Readings in Philosophical Analysis.* New York: Appleton-Century-Crofts, 1949.

FLEW, A. G. N. (ed.). *Logic and Language.* Oxford: Blackwell, First Series 1951; Second Series 1953.†

FODOR, JERRY A., and JERROLD J. KATZ (eds.). *The Structure of Language.* Englewood Cliffs, N.J.: Prentice-Hall, 1964.

FREGE, G. *Philosophical Writings,* trans. P. T. GEACH and M. BLACK. Oxford: Blackwell, 1952.

HACKING, IAN. *Why Does Language Matter to Philosophy?* Cambridge: Cambridge University Press, 1975.+

HOOK, SIDNEY (ed.). *Language and Philosophy.* New York: New York University Press, 1969.†

KATZ, JERROLD J. *Philosophy of Language.* New York: Harper & Row, 1966.

LINSKY, LEONARD (ed.). *Semantics and the Philosophy of Language.* Urbana: University of Illinois Press, 1952.

———. *Referring.* London: Routledge & Kegan Paul, 1967.

——— (ed.). *Reference and Modality.* London: Oxford University Press, 1971.*

MACDONALD, MARGARET (ed.). *Philosophy and Analysis.* Oxford: Blackwell, 1954.

PAP, ARTHUR. *Elements of Analytic Philosophy.* New York: Macmillan, 1949.

———. *Semantics and Necessary Truth.* New Haven: Yale University Press, 1958.†

PARKINSON, G. H. R. (ed.). *The Theory of Meaning.* London: Oxford University Press, 1968.*

PUTNAM, HILARY. *Mind, Language and Reality* (Philosophical Papers, Vol. 2). Cambridge: Cambridge University Press, 1975.

———. *Philosophy of Logic.* New York: Harper Torchbooks, 1971.

QUINE, W. V. *From a Logical Point of View.* Cambridge: Harvard University Press, 1953.†

———. *Word and Object.* Cambridge: MIT Press, 1960.†

———. *The Ways of Paradox.* New York: Random House, 1966.*

---

* Paperback edition.   † Also available in paperback edition.

————. *The Roots of Reference.* LaSalle, Ill.: Open Court, 1972.

RORTY, RICHARD (ed.). *The Linguistic Turn.* Chicago: University of Chicago Press, 1967.

ROSENBERG, JAY F., and CHARLES TRAVIS (eds.). *Readings in the Philosophy of Language.* Englewood Cliffs, N.J.: Prentice-Hall, 1971.

ROSENBERG, JAY F. *Linguistic Representation.* Dordrecht: D. Reidel, 1974.

RUSSELL, BERTRAND. *An Inquiry into Meaning and Truth.* London: Allen & Unwin, 1940.†

————. *Logic and Knowledge,* ed. R. C. Marsh. London: Allen & Unwin, 1956.

SEARLE, JOHN. *Speech Acts.* Cambridge: Cambridge University Press, 1969.†

———— (ed.). *The Philosophy of Language.* London: Oxford University Press, 1971.†

STEINBERG, D., and L. A. JAKOBOVITS (eds.). *Semantics. An Interdisciplinary Reader in Philosophy, Linguistics and Psychology.* Cambridge: Cambridge University Press, 1971.†

STRAWSON, P. F. *Individuals.* London: Methuen, 1959.†

———— (ed.). *Philosophical Logic.* London: Oxford University Press, 1967.*

URMSON, J. O. *Philosophical Analysis.* London: Oxford University Press, 1956.

WAISMANN, FRIEDRICH. *The Principles of Linguistic Philosophy.* London: Macmillan, 1965.

WEINBERG, J. R. *An Examination of Logical Positivism.* London: Routledge & Kegan Paul, 1936.†

WITTGENSTEIN, LUDWIG. *The Blue & Brown Books.* Oxford: Blackwell, 1958.†

————. *Philosophical Investigations,* trans. G. E. M. Anscombe. Oxford: Blackwell, 1953.

ZIFF, PAUL. *Semantic Analysis.* Ithaca, N.Y.: Cornell University Press, 1960.

V

EXPLANATORY CONTEXTS: HUMAN BEHAVIOR AND PHYSICAL PHENOMENA

To consider the behavior of human beings and of physical objects together is to pose one of the most effective organizing questions of philosophy: whether and in what respect the conceptual categories appropriate to discourse about physical phenomena can apply to discourse about human behavior. Are the explanations of phenomena of the two sorts similar or different, and in what respects? When we speak in social science contexts, we speak primarily of *persons* and their *actions*. When we speak in natural science contexts, we speak primarily of physical *objects* and *physical events*.

The difficulty of explaining the difference has occupied us already to some extent in Part I. There remains, however, an entire set of issues that concern the compatibility and common ground of our discourse about human beings and physical events. These issues have taken certain classic forms: the analysis of causality, laws of nature, agency, explanation, induction, and confirmation.

The appeal of such concepts lies with the prospect of formulating a method common to all disciplined inquiry, regardless of subject matter, that could result in the prediction and explanation of a range of phenomena. In fact, the very idea of a scientific method presupposes that the public world can be known and understood by human agents pursuing a rational strategy. But even this is not beyond dispute.

There is consequently at least a tripartite focus in the puzzles of methodology, illustrated in the alternative themes for investigating the nature of causal relationships. First, one may inquire whether whatever occurs in the real world could not but have occurred; whether whatever is actual is necessary (given the forces of nature); whether physical or natural possibilities could have obtained at any moment of time but did not (apart from being merely conceivable or consistent).

These issues pose the question of natural necessity or *determinism*, characteristically debated in terms of its compatibility with freedom.

Second, it seems possible to hit on a way of predicting complex phenomena without understanding why they occur as they do. To understand such phenomena, one may need a grasp of the lawlike connections among certain ingredients in the world, and one's predictions may have to be suitably linked to such connections. Yet an experienced hostess might predict the behavior of the guests she has brought together, without knowing the dynamics of human behavior.

Issues of this sort generate questions regarding the nature of causal knowledge itself—in particular, the nature of causal laws, the structure of a *scientific explanation*, and the relationship of explanations to laws. Closely linked to these is the question whether the laws and models in the physical and behavioral sciences are of precisely the same sort or of fundamentally different sorts.

Finally, one may inquire how, given the sample phenomena and incomplete data on which we base our predictions and explanations, we are able to proceed in a way that science can apparently confirm. Here, the issue is the process of inquiry itself, the rational linkage between what we require for an understanding of natural phenomena and the evidence on which that understanding depends—especially since the salient elements of the phenomena to be explained cannot be deduced merely from the evidence.

In short, the issue here is the nature of *induction*, the nature of arguments in which affirming the premises and denying the conclusion is not self-contradictory. It is normally explored in terms of confirming the laws of nature as well as of a strategy for linking propositions that are not logically entailed by one another. In that sense, it is not an alternative to deduction (arguments in which affirming the premises and denying the conclusion is self-contradictory), since one cannot formulate a rational procedure that precludes attention to logical entailments.

The classic beginnings of the modern discussion of induction are to be found in the writings of David Hume (V:1). Hume did not propose a solution to the puzzle of induction so much as formulate the problem effectively. He cast the problem in causal terms, observing (at least in this selection) that there is no necessary connection between cause and effect and that causal relations are discoverable, as he put it, by experience and not by reason.

In asking such questions as how we know that the sun will rise tomorrow, he did not stress what reasons might be given to support the claim (the reasons would depend on accumulated experience of the sun's regularity). Instead he stressed what might justify arguments of the inductive type at all—arguments from the past to the future or from one instance to another or from observed regularities to universal laws of nature.

Hume's conclusion is ultimately skeptical. Having found no principle of demonstration under which inductive arguments can be justified, he argues that to adhere to the principle of relying on experience would be circular, and he suggests that the matter must be considered psychologically rather than logically.

The heart of Hume's thesis rests with his insistence that the uniformity of nature is itself an *inference* from the data of experience. So construed, circularity seems impossible to avoid. Intellectual scandal looms, however, since the charge appears to undermine the rational pretensions of science.

The Humean issue has been revived in our own time by Bertrand Russell (V:2). Russell emphasized the radical difference between demonstrative arguments and inductive arguments (he subsequently modified his view of induction). But his solution to the puzzle of induction is difficult to accept, for it lies in assigning a dubious *a priori* status (see Part II) to the principle of the uniformity of nature. This principle is expected to serve as the justification for all particular inductions.

That the organization of empirical prediction and explanation is itself not significantly based on an examination of empirical nature has been conceptually troublesome. Nevertheless, Russell makes it clear that the principle of the uniformity of nature cannot be an inference by an inductive argument. It is rather a principle on which particular inductive arguments are taken to be valid. The principle had been thought (for example, by John Stuart Mill

[V:7]) to be a suppressed major premise that converted inductive arguments into deductive ones, yet was established by induction by simple enumeration. (In fact, for Mill the necessity of all deductive arguments was derivative from some more fundamental inquiry.)

An alternative conception is offered by Hans Reichenbach (V:3). He interprets the *aim* of induction in terms of determining the limits of the relative frequency of events and then argues that the inductive principle provides the least risky method for achieving that aim. So seen, Reichenbach construes the defense of induction to be essentially the same as the defense of probability statements. In a word, he understands the problem as that of determining the best *assumption* regarding the future in the light of our present knowledge. The principle therefore takes the form of a rational bet. Hence it is neither a simple inference nor a principle that is not based on an inspection of empirical frequencies.

More recently still, Nelson Goodman (V:4) has reinterpreted the problem of induction as the problem of distinguishing between accidental and lawlike generalizations. This returns us to the more general problems of the theory of knowledge (see Part II), but in the context of the relative explanatory power of selected regularities. For example, the observed uniformities among emeralds seem to favor mention of such colors as green and blue. But the choice between "green" and "blue" rather than "grue" (an invented predicate: "green before time *t*, otherwise blue") and "bleen" ("blue before time *t*, otherwise green") in the formulation of familiar lawlike hypotheses has to do with the fruitfulness of selected predicates in explanatory contexts more than with any syntactical differences between accidental and lawlike universals. The question remains, then, what we are to make of the apparent explanatory power of formulations in terms of "grue" (regarding "emeroses"—again, an invented term signifying emeralds examined before time *t* and roses examined later) and of our preference for formulations in terms of green (regarding emeralds). Something more regarding the structure of the world seems suggested.

The analysis of causality and lawfulness has its own disputatious history. Both notions have an anthropomorphic aspect, which the career of the physical sciences has tended to eliminate. In the first case, the dependence of the concept of causality on agency is denied. In the second case, the "oughtness" of the lawlike is interpreted in terms of natural necessity. Both tendencies have met with some difficulty, in the sense that natural laws may be viewed as idealizations of some sort and that causal connections may be construed in terms of the counterfactual. For example, to say that sugar is sweet is to say, in effect, that if one were to taste a sample of sugar under certain relevant, specifiable conditions, it would taste sweet. This is akin to speaking of in-compatible but alternatively possible options available at a time to a competent agent.

The classic account of causality in the ancient world is provided in Aristotle's doctrine of the four causes or explanatory principles (V:5). The most striking feature of Aristotle's view is its joint emphasis on efficient causes and on teleological causes. The concept of teleological causation is linked with the doctrine of natural species and with the causal analysis of human action and art.

Broadly speaking, an efficient cause is a physical or natural event that, on occurring, entails the occurrence of some other physical or natural event. A teleological cause is a seemingly inherent condition in natural things which so orders their careers through time that their early phases lead to a characteristic development or state of maturation. With the advent of Renaissance science and the modern age, causality was made to apply to inanimate physical events.

The turning point in modern views of causality may be linked with David Hume's account (V:6), which was written in the full flowering of eighteenth-century reflection on Newtonian science. Here we find what has since become the standard restriction of the concept to questions of efficient causation, the rejection of any necessary connection between cause and effect in particular causal sequences, and the elimination of anthropomorphic interpretations of efficient causes.

On its positive side, Hume's account of causality was bound to be seen as relatively naive and incomplete. The reason probably lies in the coupling of the overzealous empiricism of the eighteenth century (see Part III) with the recency of the Newtonian synthesis. Although causal connections were construed as lawlike regularities, physical laws were related little if at all to an analysis of scientific theories.

Subsequent science (along with philosophy of science) has been increasingly obliged to consider the relationship between sensory perception and the effect of holding a theory on what is perceived. It has also sought to distinguish between accidental regularities (regularities that are not lawlike) and regularities that genuinely manifest the laws of nature.

The standard account of the laws of nature is delineated by Ernest Nagel (V:8). On the inductive side, it is just the issue that Nelson Goodman presents as a methodological riddle. Metaphysically, the issue concerns the implication of its being possible to discern lawlike connections in specimen regularities that appear to bind future events as well. The issue effectively challenges Hume's account.

Both causality and lawfulness (in the sense proper to the sciences) exhibit a dual face. We are bound to consider them with regard to the structure of the world and with regard to the structure of models that help us understand the way the world behaves. The world and our explanatory models are clearly connected. Still, the analysis of causality and of causal explanations, on the one hand, or of natural necessity and scientific laws, on the other, need not be at all similar.

In general, questions of ontology or metaphysics (the ultimate nature of the real world) are not quite the same as questions of epistemology (the nature of knowledge), though we cannot separate them altogether (see Part II). To appreciate the distinction, however, is to appreciate that when Hume discusses causality from the side of induction, he does not consider the matter of necessity. But when he discusses causality from the side of what takes place in the real world, he emphasizes the relevance of necessity.

Again, Aristotle's conception of causality stresses both the relevance and the compatibility of efficient and teleological factors. The early triumph of the model of efficient causes tended to encourage the movement toward physical reductionism (see Part I). But in our own time the question of the adequacy of that model—particularly when only inanimate forces are postulated—has been seriously challenged.

Charles Taylor's recovery of the teleological model of explanation (V:11) marks the sense that there may not be any single model of adequate explanation in the context of science—certainly not purely mechanical explanations. It also marks the sense that the explanation of human behavior, in requiring teleological explanation, precludes the usual forms of reductionism. Taylor's account is unabashedly committed to the Aristotelian thesis that we understand events in terms of the things for whose sake the events are said to occur. Accompanying this thesis is an exposure of the inadequacies of radical behaviorism, the attempt to explain animal behavior in terms of stimuli and responses, described and correlated in terms of a mechanical model devoid of purposive or teleological features.

Donald Davidson (V:10), on the other hand, has attempted to show that explanations in terms of reasons, intentions, and the like may be classified as explanation in terms of efficient causes. There are anomalies, however, that Davidson has not satisfactorily resolved. In particular, why is it that causes operate as they do regardless of the descriptions under which they are identified, but reasons cannot function as reasons except under preferred descriptions?

To take Davidson's own example, one may be said to cause the light to go on regardless of how we describe one's intention. But one cannot be said to have a reason for turning on the light regardless of how we describe one's intention. Even if having a reason for doing something may function causally, that one *has* a reason for doing what one does is specifiable only in terms of some relationship between intention and action.

Consequently, although Davidson shows the compatibility of explanation by reasons and by causes, his own model of efficient causes incorporates elements that appear to belong to a teleological model. Whether these can be eliminated he does not discuss here. But the issue does show that we must distinguish between causal contexts and contexts of causal explanation, quite apart from whether teleological explanations can be replaced by explanations in terms of efficient causes only.

Classically, the distinction has been drawn between two interpretations of the rubric, "A because B": (1) The event A occurs because the event B occurs; and (2) the fact A is explained by the fact B. To put it another way, interest oscillates between the structure of causal relations in the world (emphasis on events) and the structure of explanations of what occurs in the world (emphasis on facts).

Finally, in this connection, the appraisal of teleological and nonteleological explanations challenges the pretensions of the unity of science—the conviction that the physical and behavioral (or social or historical) sciences exhibit a common methodology. It has been held, for instance, not only that the historical sciences are concerned with characterizing and interpreting unique events rather than with formulating general laws, but that such laws cannot be formulated for the historical disciplines. Carl Hempel's discussion of the question (V:9) is perhaps the best-known reply offered in the spirit of the unity of science.

The most famous issue arising from the intersection of causal and teleological considerations may be the compatibility of human freedom and causality. This question is not entirely tangential to the issue of scientific methodology, for it obliges us to clarify the concepts of freedom and causality. And, as we have seen, the very notion of scientific inquiry seems to entail a measure of human freedom.

Neither freedom nor causality can be a simple notion, of course. Furthermore, the proper analysis of both is a matter of considerable dispute. But apart from that, there remains a persistent intuition that what is caused is so determined that human freedom is not compatible with it, and that freedom is therefore a mere illusion.

The focus of the issue is itself dual. (1) It embraces the perennially intriguing question of the relationship between moral responsibility and science. (2) It raises the even more comprehensive question of the place of human beings in a world that science explains and that scientists comprehend precisely because they are scientists rather than merely scientific specimens. Thus if a man is responsible for what he does, how can it be that what he does is caused? On the other hand, if what he does is caused, how can he act of his own volition, and how can he be held morally responsible for what he does? Further, what account can be given for the causal explanation of a man's conduct and for his freedom?

The problem of reconciling these considerations appears, classically, in Mill's account (V:7). There, liberty or free will designates a distinction within the causal order itself. The elaboration of this conception leads to a model much like Davidson's, in which efficient causality is viewed as adequate for explanations in science but accommodates human freedom as well. Nevertheless, the resolution makes no sense unless a congruent theory of real possibility is provided—a theory in which an agent can pursue either of two alternative lines of action, incompatible with one another but compatible with the state of affairs at the moment of choice.

Freedom entails the capacity of such choice, according to this thesis, and the world must be able to sustain such choice. If whatever is actual exhausts or is coextensive with what is possible in the world, then freedom cannot be anything but an illusion.

But if the world includes possibilities in the sense suggested, then genuine freedom obtains, and freedom and causality can be reconciled. Also, if causality itself presupposes the concept of agency and the counterfactual, then the reconciliation of freedom and causality can hardly be ad hoc.

Thus the apparently remote question of causality in physical science returns us once again to the distinction of human persons (see Part I).

The Problem of Induction

1

David Hume

On Matters of Fact

I

All the objects of human reason or enquiry may naturally be divided into two kinds, to wit, *Relations of Ideas,* and *Matters of Fact.* Of the first kind are the sciences of Geometry, Algebra, and Arithmetic; and in short, every affirmation which is either intuitively or demonstratively certain. *That the square of the hypothenuse is equal to the square of the two sides,* is a proposition which expresses a relation between these figures. *That three times five is equal to the half of thirty,* expresses a relation between these numbers. Propositions of this kind are discoverable by the mere operation of thought, without dependence on what is anywhere existent in the universe. Though there never were a circle or triangle in nature, the truths demonstrated by Euclid would for ever retain their certainty and evidence.

Matters of fact, which are the second objects of human reason, are not ascertained in the same manner; nor is our evidence of their truth, however great, of a like nature with the foregoing. The contrary of every matter of fact is still possible; because it can never imply a contradiction, and is conceived by the mind with the same facility and distinctness, as if ever so conformable to reality. *That the sun will not rise to-morrow* is no less intelligible a proposition, and implies no more contradiction than the affirmation, *that it will rise.* We should in vain, therefore, attempt to demonstrate its falsehood. Were it demonstratively false, it would imply a contradiction, and could never be distinctly conceived by the mind.

It may, therefore, be a subject worthy of curiosity, to enquire what is the nature of that evidence which assures us of any real existence and matter of fact, beyond the present testimony of our senses, or the records of our memory. This part of philosophy, it is observable, has been little cultivated, either by the ancients or moderns; and therefore our doubts and errors, in the prosecution

From David Hume, *An Enquiry Concerning Human Understanding,* L. A. Selby-Bigge, ed., 2nd ed. (Oxford: The Clarendon Press, 1902), Sec. IV, pp. 25–39.

of so important an enquiry, may be the more excusable; while we march through such difficult paths without any guide or direction. They may even prove useful, by exciting curiosity, and destroying that implicit faith and security, which is the bane of all reasoning and free enquiry. The discovery of defects in the common philosophy, if any such there be, will not, I presume, be a discouragement, but rather an incitement, as is usual, to attempt something more full and satisfactory than has yet been proposed to the public.

All reasonings concerning matter of fact seem to be founded on the relation of *Cause and Effect*. By means of that relation alone we can go beyond the evidence of our memory and senses. If you were to ask a man, why he believes any matter of fact, which is absent; for instance, that his friend is in the country, or in France; he would give you a reason; and this reason would be some other fact; as a letter received from him, or the knowledge of his former resolutions and promises. A man finding a watch or any other machine in a desert island, would conclude that there had once been men in that island. All our reasonings concerning fact are of the same nature. And here it is constantly supposed that there is a connexion between the present fact and that which is inferred from it. Were there nothing to bind them together, the inference would be entirely precarious. The hearing of an articulate voice and rational discourse in the dark assures us of the presence of some person: Why? because these are the effects of the human make and fabric, and closely connected with it. If we anatomize all the other reasonings of this nature, we shall find that they are founded on the relation of cause and effect, and that this relation is either near or remote, direct or collateral. Heat and light are collateral effects of fire, and the one effect may justly be inferred from the other.

If we would satisfy ourselves, therefore, concerning the nature of that evidence, which assures us of matters of fact, we must enquire how we arrive at the knowledge of cause and effect.

I shall venture to affirm, as a general proposition, which admits of no exception, that the knowledge of this relation is not, in any instance, attained by reasonings *a priori*; but arises entirely from experience, when we find that any particular objects are constantly conjoined with each other. Let an object be presented to a man of ever so strong natural reason and abilities; if that object be entirely new to him, he will not be able, by the most accurate examination of its sensible qualities, to discover any of its causes or effects. Adam, though his rational faculties be supposed, at the very first, entirely perfect, could not have inferred from the fluidity and transparency of water that it would suffocate him, or from the light and warmth of fire that it would consume him. No object ever discovers, by the qualities which appear to the senses, either the causes which produced it, or the effects which will arise from it; nor can our reason, unassisted by experience, ever draw any inference concerning real existence and matter of fact.

This proposition, *that causes and effects are discoverable, not by reason but by experience*, will readily be admitted with regard to such objects, as we remember to have once been altogether unknown to us; since we must be conscious of the utter inability, which we then lay under, of foretelling what would arise from them. Present two smooth pieces of marble to a man who has no tincture of natural philosophy; he will never discover that they will adhere together in such a manner as to require great force to separate them in a direct line, while they make so small a resistance to a lateral pressure. Such events, as bear little analogy to the common course of nature, are also readily confessed to be known only by experience; nor does any man imagine that the explosion of gunpowder, or the attraction of a lode-stone, could ever be discovered by arguments *a priori*. In like manner, when an effect is supposed to depend upon an intricate machinery or secret structure of parts, we make no difficulty in attributing all our knowledge of it to experience. Who will assert that he can give the ultimate reason, why milk or bread is proper nourishment for a man, not for a lion or a tiger?

But the same truth may not appear, at first sight, to have the same evidence with regard to events, which have become familiar to us from our first appearance in the world, which bear a close analogy to the whole course of nature, and which are supposed to depend on the simple qualities of objects, without any secret structure of parts. We are apt to imagine that we could discover these effects by the mere operation of our reason, without experience. We fancy, that were we brought on a sudden into this world, we could at first have inferred that one Billiard-ball would communicate motion to another upon impulse; and that we need not to have waited for the event, in order to pronounce with certainty concerning it. Such is the influence of custom, that, where it is strongest, it not only covers our natural ignorance, but even conceals itself, and seems not to take place, merely because it is found in the highest degree.

But to convince us that all the laws of nature, and all the operations of bodies without exception, are known only by experience, the following reflections may, perhaps, suffice. Were any object presented to us, and were we required to pronounce concerning the effect, which will result from it, without consulting past observation; after what manner, I beseech you, must the mind proceed in this operation? It must invent or imagine some event, which it ascribes to the object as its effect; and it is plain that this invention must be entirely arbitrary. The mind can never possibly find the effect in the supposed cause, by the most accurate scrutiny and examination. For the effect is totally different from the cause, and consequently can never be discovered in it. Motion in the second Billiard-ball is a quite distinct event from motion in the first; nor is there anything in the one to suggest the smallest hint of the other. A stone or piece of metal raised into the air, and left without any support, immediately falls: but to consider the matter *a priori*, is there anything we discover in this situation which can beget the idea of a downward, rather than an upward, or any other motion, in the stone or metal?

And as the first imagination or invention of a particular effect, in all natural operations, is arbitrary, where we consult not experience; so must we also esteem the supposed tie or connexion between the cause and effect, which binds them together, and renders it impossible that any other effect could result from the operation of that cause. When I see, for instance, a Billiard-ball moving in a straight line towards another; even suppose motion in the second ball should by accident be suggested to me, as the result of their contact or impulse; may I not conceive, that a hundred different events might as well follow from that cause? May not both these balls remain at absolute rest? May not the first ball return in a straight line, or leap off from the second in any line or direction? All these suppositions are consistent and conceivable. Why then should we give the preference to one, which is no more consistent or conceivable than the rest? All our reasonings *a priori* will never be able to show us any foundation for this preference.

In a word, then, every effect is a distinct event from its cause. It could not, therefore, be discovered in the cause, and the first invention or conception of it, *a priori*, must be entirely arbitrary. And even after it is suggested, the conjunction of it with the cause must appear equally arbitrary; since there are always many other effects, which, to reason, must seem fully as consistent and natural. In vain, therefore, should we pretend to determine any single event, or infer any cause or effect, without the assistance of observation and experience.

Hence we may discover the reason why no philosopher, who is rational and modest, has ever pretended to assign the ultimate cause of any natural operation, or to show distinctly the action of that power, which produces any single effect in the universe. It is confessed, that the utmost effort of human reason is to reduce the principles, productive of natural phenomena, to a greater simplicity, and to resolve the many particular effects into a few general causes, by means of reasonings from analogy, experience, and observation. But as to the causes of these general causes, we should in vain attempt their discovery; nor shall we ever be able to satisfy ourselves, by any particular explication of them. These ultimate springs and principles are totally shut up from human curiosity and enquiry. Elasticity, gravity, cohesion of parts, communication of motion by impulse; these are probably the ultimate causes and principles which we shall ever discover in nature; and we may esteem ourselves sufficiently happy, if, by accurate enquiry and reasoning, we can trace up the particular phenomena to, or near to, these general principles. The most perfect philosophy of the natural kind only staves off our ignorance a little longer: as perhaps the most perfect philosophy of the moral or metaphysical kind serves only to discover larger portions of it. Thus the observation of human blindness and weakness is the result of all philosophy, and meets us at every turn, in spite of our endeavours to elude or avoid it.

Nor is geometry, when taken into the assistance of natural philosophy, ever able to remedy this defect, or lead us into the knowledge of ultimate causes, by all that accuracy of reasoning for which it is so justly celebrated. Every part of mixed mathematics proceeds upon the supposition that certain laws are established by nature in her operations; and abstract reasonings are employed, either to assist experience in the discovery of these laws, or to determine their influence in particular instances, where it depends upon any precise degree of distance and quantity. Thus, it is a law of motion, discovered by experience, that the moment or force of any body in motion is in the compound ratio or proportion of its solid contents and its velocity; and consequently, that a small force may remove the greatest obstacle or raise the greatest weight, if, by any contrivance or machinery, we can increase the velocity of that force, so as to make it an overmatch for its antagonist. Geometry assists us in the application of this law, by giving us the just dimensions of all the parts and figures which can enter into any species of machine; but still the discovery of the law itself is owing merely to experience, and all the abstract reasonings in the world could never lead us one step towards the knowledge of it. When we reason *a priori*, and consider merely any object or cause, as it appears to the mind, independent of all observation, it never could suggest to us the notion of any distinct object, such as its effect; much less, show us the inseparable and inviolable connexion between them. A man must be very sagacious who could discover by reasoning that crystal is the effect of heat, and ice of cold, without being previously acquainted with the operation of these qualities.

II

But we have not yet attained any tolerable satisfaction with regard to the question first proposed. Each solution still gives rise to a new question as difficult as the foregoing, and leads us on to further enquiries. When it is asked, *What is the nature of all our reasonings concerning matter of fact?* the proper answer seems to be, that they are founded on the relation of cause and effect. When again it is asked, *What is the foundation of all our reasonings and conclusions concerning that relation?* it may be replied in one word, Experience. But if we still carry on our sifting humour, and ask, *What is the foundation of all conclusions from experience?* this implies a new question, which may be of more difficult solution and explication. Philosophers, that give themselves airs of superior wisdom and sufficiency, have a hard task when they encounter persons of inquisitive dispositions, who push them from every corner to which they retreat, and who are sure at last to bring them to some dangerous dilemma. The best expedient to prevent this confusion, is to be modest in our pretensions; and even to discover the difficulty ourselves before it is objected to us. By this means, we may make a kind of merit of our very ignorance.

I shall content myself, in this section, with an easy task, and shall pretend only to give a negative answer to the question here proposed. I say then, that, even after we have experience of the operations of cause and effect, our conclusions from that experience are *not* founded on reasoning, or any process of the understanding. This answer we must endeavour both to explain and to defend.

It must certainly be allowed, that nature has kept us at a great distance from all her secrets, and has afforded us only the knowledge of a few superficial qualities of objects; while she conceals from us those powers and principles on which the influence of those objects entirely depends. Our senses inform us of the colour, weight, and consistence of bread; but neither sense nor reason can ever inform us of those qualities which fit it for the nourishment and support of a human body. Sight or feeling conveys an idea of the actual motion of bodies; but as to that wonderful force or power, which would carry on a moving body for ever in a continued change of place, and which bodies never lose but by communicating it to others; of this we cannot form the most distant conception. But notwithstanding this ignorance of natural powers and principles, we always presume, when we see like sensible qualities, that they have like secret powers, and expect that effects, similar to those which we have experienced, will follow from them. If a body of like colour and consistence with that bread, which we have formerly eat, be presented to us, we make no scruple of repeating the experiment, and foresee, with certainty, like nourishment and support. Now this is a process of the mind or thought, of which I would willingly know the foundation. It is allowed on all hands that there is no known connexion between the sensible qualities and the secret powers; and consequently, that the mind is not led to form such a conclusion concerning their constant and regular conjunction, by anything which it knows of their nature. As to past *Experience*, it can be allowed to give *direct* and *certain* information of those precise objects only, and that precise period of time, which fell under its cognizance: but why this experience should be extended to future times, and to other objects, which for aught we know, may be only in appearance similar; this is the main question on which I would insist. The bread, which I formerly eat, nourished me; that is, a body of such sensible qualities was, at that time, endued with such secret powers: but does it follow, that other bread must also nourish me at another time, and that like sensible qualities must always be attended with like secret powers? The consequence seems nowise necessary. At least, it must be acknowledged that there is here a consequence drawn by the mind; that there is a certain step taken; a process of thought, and an inference, which wants to be explained. These two propositions are far from being the same, *I have found that such an object has always been attended with such an effect*, and *I foresee, that other objects, which are, in appearance, similar, will be attended with similar effects*. I shall allow, if you please, that the one proposition may justly be inferred from the other: I know, in fact, that it always is inferred. But if you insist that the inference is made by a chain of reasoning, I desire you to produce that reasoning. The connexion between these propositions is not intuitive. There is required a medium, which may enable the mind to draw such an inference, if indeed it be drawn by reasoning and argument. What that medium is, I must confess, passes my comprehension; and it is incumbent on those to produce it, who assert that it really exists, and is the origin of all our conclusions concerning matter of fact.

This negative argument must certainly, in process of time, become altogether convincing, if many penetrating and able philosophers shall turn their enquiries this way and no one be ever able to discover any connecting proposition or intermediate step, which supports the understanding in this conclusion. But as the question is yet new, every reader may not trust so far to his own penetration, as to conclude, because an argument escapes his enquiry, that therefore it does not really exist. For this reason it may be requisite to venture upon a more difficult task; and enumerating all the branches of human knowledge, endeavour to show that none of them can afford such an argument.

All reasonings may be divided into two kinds, namely, demonstrative reasoning, or that concerning relations of ideas, and moral reasoning, or that concerning matter of fact and existence. That there are no demonstrative arguments in the case seems evident; since it implies no contradiction that the course of nature may change, and that an object, seemingly like those which we have experienced, may be attended with different or contrary effects. May I not clearly and distinctly conceive that a body, falling from the clouds, and which, in all other respects, resembles snow, has yet the taste of salt or feeling of fire? Is there any more intelligible proposition than to affirm, that all the trees will flourish in December and January, and decay in May and June? Now whatever is intelligible, and can be distinctly conceived, implies no contradiction, and can never be proved false by any demonstrative argument or abstract reasoning *a priori*.

If we be, therefore, engaged by arguments to put trust in past experience, and make it the standard of our future judgement, these arguments must be probable only, or such as regard matter of fact and real existence, according to the division above mentioned. But that there is no argument of this kind, must appear, if our explication of that species of reasoning be admitted as solid and satisfactory. We have said that all arguments concerning existence are founded on the relation of cause and effect; that our knowledge of that relation is derived entirely from experience; and that all our experimental conclusions proceed upon the supposition that the future will be conformable to the past. To endeavour, therefore, the proof of this last supposition by probable arguments, or arguments regarding existence, must be evidently going in a circle, and taking that for granted, which is the very point in question.

In reality, all arguments from experience are founded on the similarity which we discover among natural objects, and by which we are induced to expect effects similar to those which we have found to follow from such objects. And though none but a fool or madman will ever pretend to dispute the authority of experience, or to reject that great guide of human life, it may surely be allowed a philosopher to have so much curiosity at least as to examine the principle of human nature, which gives this mighty authority to experience, and makes us draw advantage from that similarity which nature has placed among different objects. From causes which appear *similar* we expect similar effects. This is the sum of all our experimental conclusions. Now it seems evident that, if this conclusion were formed by reason, it would be as perfect at first, and upon one instance, as after ever so long a course of experience. But the case is far otherwise. Nothing so like as eggs; yet no one, on account of this appearing similarity, expects the same taste and relish in all of them. It is only after a long course of uniform experiments in any kind, that we attain a firm reliance and security with regard to a particular event. Now where is that process of reasoning which, from one instance, draws a conclusion, so different from that which it infers from a hundred instances that are nowise different from that single one? This question I propose as much for the sake of information, as with an intention of raising difficulties. I cannot find, I cannot imagine any such reasoning. But I keep my mind still open to instruction, if any one will vouchsafe to bestow it on me.

Should it be said that, from a number of uniform experiments, we *infer* a connexion between the sensible qualities and the secret powers; this, I must confess, seems the same difficulty, couched in different terms. The question still recurs, on what process of argument this *inference* is founded? Where is the medium, the interposing ideas, which join propositions so very wide of each other? It is confessed that the colour, consistence, and other sensible qualities of bread appear not, of themselves, to have any connexion with the secret powers of nourishment and support. For otherwise we could infer these secret powers from the first appearance of these sensible qualities, without the aid of experience; contrary to the sentiment of all philosophers, and contrary to plain matter of fact. Here, then, is our natural state of ignorance with regard to the powers and influence of all objects. How is this remedied by experience? It only shows us a number of uniform effects, resulting from certain objects, and teaches us that those particular objects, at that particular time, were endowed with such powers and forces. When a new object, endowed with similar sensible qualities, is produced, we expect similar powers and forces, and look for a like effect. From a body of like colour and consistence with bread we expect like nourishment and support. But this surely is a step or progress of the mind, which wants to be explained. When a man says, *I have found, in all past instances, such sensible qualities conjoined with such secret powers:* And when he says, *Similar sensible qualities will always be conjoined with similar secret powers,* he is not guilty of a tautology, nor are these propositions in any respect the same. You say that the one proposition is an inference from the other. But you must confess that the inference is not intuitive; neither is it demonstrative: Of what nature is it, then? To say it is experimental, is begging the question. For all inferences from experience suppose, as their foundation, that the future will resemble the past, and that similar powers will be conjoined with similar sensible qualities. If there be any suspicion that the course of nature may change, and that the past may be no rule for the future, all experience becomes useless, and can give rise to no inference or conclusion. It is impossible, therefore, that any arguments from experience can prove this resemblance of the past to the future; since all these arguments are founded on the supposition of that resemblance. Let the course of things be allowed hitherto ever so regular; that alone, without some new argument or inference, proves not that, for the future, it will continue so. In vain do you pretend to have learned the nature of bodies from your past experience. Their secret nature, and consequently all their effects and influence, may change, without any change in their sensible qualities. This happens sometimes, and with regard to some objects: Why may it not happen always, and with regard to all objects? What logic, what process of argument secures you against this supposition? My practice, you say, refutes my doubts. But you mistake the purport of my question. As an agent, I am quite satisfied in the point; but as a philosopher, who has some share of curiosity, I will not say scepticism, I want to learn the foundation of this inference. No reading, no enquiry has yet been able to remove my difficulty, or give me satisfaction in a matter of such importance. Can I do better than propose the difficulty to the public, even though, perhaps, I have small hopes of obtaining a solution? We shall at least, by this means, be sensible of our ignorance, if we do not augment our knowledge.

I must confess that a man is guilty of unpardonable arrogance who concludes, because an argument has escaped his own investigation, that therefore it does not really exist. I must also confess that, though all the learned, for several ages, should have employed themselves in fruitless search upon any subject, it may still, perhaps, be rash to conclude positively that the subject must, therefore, pass all human comprehension. Even though we examine all the sources of our knowledge, and conclude them unfit for such a subject, there may still remain a suspicion, that the enumeration is not complete, or the examination not accurate. But with regard to the present subject, there are some considerations which seem to remove all this accusation of arrogance or suspicion of mistake.

It is certain that the most ignorant and stupid peasants—nay infants, nay even brute beasts—improve by experience, and learn the qualities of natural objects, by observing the effects which result from them. When a child has felt the sensation of pain from touching the flame of a candle, he will be careful not to put his hand near any candle; but will expect a similar effect from a cause which is similar in its sensible qualities and appearance. If you assert, therefore, that the understanding of the child is led into this conclusion by any process of argument or ratiocination, I may justly require you to produce that argument; nor have you any pretence to refuse so equitable a demand. You cannot say that the argument is abstruse, and may possibly escape your enquiry; since you confess that it is obvious to the capacity of a mere infant. If you hesitate, therefore, a moment, or if, after reflection, you produce any intricate or profound argument, you, in a manner, give up the question, and confess that it is not reasoning which engages us to suppose the past resembling the future, and to expect similar effects from causes which are, to appearance, similar. This is the proposition which I intended to enforce in the present section. If I be right, I pretend not to have made any mighty discovery. And if I be wrong, I must acknowledge myself to be indeed a very backward scholar; since I cannot now discover an argument which, it seems, was perfectly familiar to me long before I was out of my cradle.

2

Bertrand Russell

On Induction

. . . we have been concerned in the attempt to get clear as to our data in the way of knowledge of existence. What things are there in the universe whose existence is known to us owing to our being acquainted with them? So far, our answer has been that we are acquainted with our sense-data, and, probably, with ourselves. These we know to exist. And past sense-data which are remembered are known to have existed in the past. This knowledge supplies our data.

But if we are to be able to draw inferences from these data—if we are to know of the existence of matter, of other people, of the past before our individual memory begins, or of the future, we must know general principles of some kind by means of which such inferences can be drawn. It must be known to us that the existence of some one sort of thing, A, is a sign of the existence of some other sort of thing, B, either at the same time as A or at some earlier or later time, as, for example, thunder is a sign of the earlier existence of lightning. If this were not known to us, we could never extend our knowledge beyond the sphere of our private experience; and this sphere, as we have seen, is exceedingly limited. The question we have now to consider is whether such an extension is possible, and if so, how it is effected.

Let us take as an illustration a matter about which none of us, in fact, feel the slightest doubt. We are all convinced that the sun will rise to-morrow. Why? Is this belief a mere blind outcome of past experience, or can it be justified as a reasonable belief? It is not easy to find a test by which to judge whether a belief of this kind is reasonable or not, but we can at least ascertain what sort of general beliefs would suffice, if true, to justify the judgment that the sun will rise to-morrow, and the many other similar judgments upon which our actions are based.

It is obvious that if we are asked why we believe that the sun will rise to-morrow, we shall naturally answer, "Because it always has risen every day." We have a firm belief that it will rise in the future, because it has risen in the past. If we are challenged as to why we believe that it will continue to rise as heretofore, we may appeal to the laws of motion: the earth, we shall say, is a freely rotating body, and such bodies do not cease to rotate unless something interferes from outside, and there is nothing outside to interfere with the earth between now and to-morrow. Of course it might be doubted whether we are quite certain that there is nothing outside to interfere, but this is not the

From Bertrand Russell, *The Problems of Philosophy* (London: Oxford University Press, 1912), pp. 60–69. Reprinted by permission of the Oxford University Press.

interesting doubt. The interesting doubt is as to whether the laws of motion will remain in operation until to-morrow. If this doubt is raised, we find ourselves in the same position as when the doubt about the sunrise was first raised.

The *only* reason for believing that the laws of motion will remain in operation is that they have operated hitherto, so far as our knowledge of the past enables us to judge. It is true that we have a greater body of evidence from the past in favour of the laws of motion than we have in favour of the sunrise, because the sunrise is merely a particular case of fulfilment of the laws of motion, and there are countless other particular cases. But the real question is: Do *any* number of cases of a law being fulfilled in the past afford evidence that it will be fulfilled in the future? If not, it becomes plain that we have no ground whatever for expecting the sun to rise to-morrow, or for expecting the bread we shall eat at our next meal not to poison us, or for any of the other scarcely conscious expectations that control our daily lives. It is to be observed that all such expectations are only *probable*; thus we have not to seek for a proof that they *must* be fulfilled, but only for some reason in favour of the view that they are *likely* to be fulfilled.

Now in dealing with this question we must, to begin with, make an important distinction, without which we should soon become involved in hopeless confusions. Experience has shown us that, hitherto, the frequent repetition of some uniform succession or coexistence has been a *cause* of our expecting the same succession or coexistence on the next occasion. Food that has a certain appearance generally has a certain taste, and it is a severe shock to our expectations when the familiar appearance is found to be associated with an unusual taste. Things which we see become associated, by habit, with certain tactile sensations which we expect if we touch them; one of the horrors of a ghost (in many ghost-stories) is that it fails to give us any sensations of touch. Uneducated people who go abroad for the first time are so surprised as to be incredulous when they find their native language not understood.

And this kind of association is not confined to men; in animals also it is very strong. A horse which has been often driven along a certain road resists the attempt to drive him in a different direction. Domestic animals expect food when they see the person who usually feeds them. We know that all these rather crude expectations of uniformity are liable to be misleading. The man who has fed the chicken every day throughout its life at last wrings its neck instead, showing that more refined views as to the uniformity of nature would have been useful to the chicken.

But in spite of the misleadingness of such expectations, they nevertheless exist. The mere fact that something has happened a certain number of times causes animals and men to expect that it will happen again. Thus our instincts certainly cause us to believe that the sun will rise to-morrow, but we may be in no better a position than the chicken which unexpectedly has its neck wrung. We have therefore to distinguish the fact that past uniformities *cause* expectations as to the future, from the question whether there is any reasonable ground for giving weight to such expectations after the question of their validity has been raised.

The problem we have to discuss is whether there is any reason for believing in what is called "the uniformity of nature." The belief in the uniformity of nature is the belief that everything that has happened or will happen is an instance of some general law to which there are *no* exceptions. The crude expectations which we have been considering are all subject to exceptions, and therefore liable to disappoint those who entertain them. But science habitually assumes, at least as a working hypothesis, that general rules which have exceptions can be replaced by general rules which have no exceptions. "Unsupported bodies in air fall" is a general rule to which balloons and aeroplanes are exceptions. But the laws of motion and the law of gravitation, which account for the fact that most bodies fall, also account for the fact that aeroplanes can rise; thus the laws of motion and the law of gravitation are not subject to these exceptions.

The belief that the sun will rise to-morrow might be falsified if the earth came suddenly into contact with a large body which destroyed its rotation; but the laws of motion and the law of gravitation would not be infringed by such an event. The business of science is to find uniformities, such as the laws of motion and the law of gravitation, to which, so far as our experience extends, there are no exceptions. In this search science has been remarkably successful, and it may be conceded that such uniformities have held hitherto. This brings us back to the question: Have we any reason, assuming that they have always held in the past, to suppose that they will hold in the future?

It has been argued that we have reason to know that the future will resemble the past, because what was the future has constantly become the past, and has always been found to resemble the past, so that we really have experience of the future, namely of times which were formerly future, which we may call past futures. But such an argument really begs the very question at issue. We have experience of past futures, but not of future futures, and the question is: Will future futures resemble past futures? This question is not to be answered by an argument which starts from past futures alone. We have therefore still to seek for some principle which shall enable us to know that the future will follow the same laws as the past.

The reference to the future in this question is not essential. The same question arises when we apply the laws that work in our experience to past things of which we have no experience—as, for example, in geology, or in theories as to the origin of the Solar System. The question we really have to ask is: "When two things have been found to be often associated, and no instance is known of the one occurring without the other, does the occurrence of one of the two, in a fresh instance, give any good ground for expecting the other?" On our answer to this question must depend the validity of the whole of our expectations as to the future, the whole of the results obtained by induction, and in fact practically all the beliefs upon which our daily life is based.

It must be conceded, to begin with, that the fact that two things have been found often together and never apart does not, by itself, suffice to *prove* demonstratively that they will be found together in the next case we examine. The most we can hope is that the oftener things are found together, the more probable it becomes that they will be found together another time, and that, if they have been found together often enough, the probability will amount almost to certainty. It can never quite reach certainty, because we know that in spite of frequent repetitions there sometimes is a failure at the last, as in the case of the chicken whose neck is wrung. Thus probability is all we ought to seek.

It might be urged, as against the view we are advocating, that we know all natural phenomena to be subject to the reign of law, and that sometimes, on the basis of observation, we can see that only one law can possibly fit the facts of the case. Now to this view there are two answers. The first is that, even if *some* law which has no exceptions applies to our case, we can never, in practice, be sure that we have discovered that law and not one to which there are exceptions. The second is that the reign of law would seem to be itself only probable, and that our belief that it will hold in the future, or in unexamined cases in the past, is itself based upon the very principle we are examining.

The principle we are examining may be called the *principle of induction,* and its two parts may be stated as follows:

(*a*) When a thing of a certain sort A has been found to be associated with a thing of a certain other sort B, and has never been found dissociated from a thing of the sort B, the greater the number of cases in which A and B have been associated, the greater is the probability that they will be associated in a fresh case in which one of them is known to be present;

(*b*) Under the same circumstances, a sufficient number of cases of association will make the probability of a fresh association nearly a certainty, and will make it approach certainty without limit.

As just stated, the principle applies only to the verification of our expectation in a single fresh instance. But we want also to know that there is a probability in favour of the general law that things of the sort A are *always* associated with things of the sort B, provided a sufficient number of cases of association are known, and no cases of failure of association are known. The probability of the general law is obviously less than the probability of the particular case, since if the general law is true, the particular case must also be true, whereas the particular case may be true without the general law being true. Nevertheless the probability of the general law is increased by repetitions, just as the probability of the particular case is. We may therefore repeat the two parts of our principle as regards the general law, thus:

(*a*) The greater the number of cases in which a thing of the sort A has been found associated with a thing of the sort B, the more probable it is (if no cases of failure of association are known) that A is always associated with B;

(*b*) Under the same circumstances, a sufficient number of cases of the association of A with B will make it nearly certain that A is always associated with B, and will make this general law approach certainty without limit.

It should be noted that probability is always relative to certain data. In our case, the data are merely the known cases of co-existence of A and B. There may be other data, which *might* be taken into account, which would gravely alter the probability. For example, a man who had seen a great many white swans might argue, by our principle, that on the data it was *probable* that all swans were white, and this might be a perfectly sound argument. The argument is not disproved by the fact that some swans are black, because a thing may very well happen in spite of the fact that some data render it improbable. In the case of the swans, a man might know that colour is a very variable characteristic in many species of animals, and that, therefore, an induction as to colour is peculiarly liable to error. But this knowledge would be a fresh datum, by no means proving that the probability relatively to our previous data had been wrongly estimated. The fact, therefore, that things often fail to fulfil our expectations is no evidence that our expectations will not *probably* be fulfilled in a given case or a given class of cases. Thus our inductive principle is at any rate not capable of being *disproved* by an appeal to experience.

The inductive principle, however, is equally incapable of being *proved* by an appeal to experience. Experience might conceivably confirm the inductive principle as regards the cases that have been already examined; but as regards unexamined cases, it is the inductive principle alone that can justify any inference from what has been examined to what has not been examined. All arguments which, on the basis of experience, argue as to the future or the unexperienced parts of the past or present, assume the inductive principle; hence we can never use experience to prove the inductive principle without begging the question. Thus we must either accept the inductive principle on the ground of its intrinsic evidence, or forgo all justification of our expectations about the future. If the principle is unsound, we have no reason to expect the sun to rise to-morrow, to expect bread to be more nourishing than a stone, or to expect that if we throw ourselves off the roof we shall fall. When we see what looks like our best friend approaching us, we shall have no reason to suppose that his body is not inhabited by the mind of our worst enemy or of some total stranger. All our conduct is based upon associations which have worked in the past, and which we therefore regard as likely to work in the future; and this likelihood is dependent for its validity upon the inductive principle.

The general principles of science, such as the belief in the reign of law, and the belief that every event must have a cause, are as completely dependent upon the inductive principle as are the beliefs of daily life. All such general principles are believed because mankind have found innumerable instances of their truth, and no instances of their falsehood. But this affords no evidence for their truth in the future, unless the inductive principle is assumed.

Thus all knowledge which, on a basis of experience, tells us something about what is not experienced, is based upon a belief which experience can neither confirm nor confute, yet which, at least in its more concrete applications, appears to be as firmly rooted in us as many of the facts of experience. . . .

3

Hans Reichenbach
Probability and Induction

Hans Reichenbach (1891–1953) was closely affiliated with the Vienna Circle during the 1920s and 1930s, even sharing with Rudolf Carnap in editing Erkenntnis, *the journal of the positivist movement. But he regarded himself as holding distinct views and identified himself as a logical empiricist. He taught in Germany and in Turkey and, from 1938 until his death, at the University of California. He published widely, for instance on quantum mechanics* (Philosophical Foundations of Quantum Mechanics, 1944), *on probability* (The Theory of Probability, 1939, 1945), *on space and time* (The Philosophy of Space and Time, 1928, 1958; The Direction of Time, 1956), *and on scientific laws* (Nomological Statements and Admissible Operations, 1954). *His best-known books are probably* Experience and Prediction (1938) *and* The Rise of Scientific Philosophy (1951).

Reichenbach's theory of meaning diverged from the verifiability thesis of the positivists. Reichenbach was impressed with the untapped "surplus meaning" of theoretical statements. He also gave a probabilistic interpretation of the sameness of meaning of two statements. And he associated this thesis with the rejection of foundationalism regarding knowledge (see Part II) and the approval of alternative pragmatic constructions facilitating our behavior with respect to the actual world, that, in a sense, we do not actually observe.

Like the positivists, Reichenbach rejected the Kantian a prioristic account of space and time. He also developed a distinctive account of induction. The aim of induction, he believed, is to provide a method that affords the least risky basis for determining the limits of the relative frequencies of events.

§ 38. The Problem of Induction

The frequency interpretation [of probability] has two functions within the theory of probability. First, a frequency is used as a *substantiation* for the probability statement; it furnishes the reason why we believe in the statement. Second, a frequency is used for the *verification* of the probability statement; that is to say, it is to furnish the meaning of the statement. These two functions are not identical. The observed frequency from which we start is only the basis of the probability inference; we intend to state another frequency which concerns *future observations*. The probability inference proceeds from a known frequency to one unknown; it is from this function that its importance

Reprinted from *Experience and Prediction*, Secs. 38–39, pp. 339–342, 346–353, 355–357, by Hans Reichenbach, by permission of The University of Chicago Press. Copyright 1938 by The University of Chicago.

is derived. The probability statement sustains a prediction, and this is why we want it.

It is the problem of induction which appears with this formulation. The theory of probability involves the problem of induction, and a solution of the problem of probability cannot be given without an answer to the question of induction. The connection of both problems is well known; philosophers such as [C. S.—Ed.] Peirce have expressed the idea that a solution of the problem of induction is to be found in the theory of probability. The inverse relation, however, holds as well. Let us say, cautiously, that the solution of both problems is to be given within the same theory.

In uniting the problem of probability with that of induction, we decide unequivocally in favor of that determination of the degree of probability which mathematicians call the *determination a posteriori*. . . .

By "determination a posteriori" we understand a procedure in which the relative frequency observed statistically is assumed to hold approximately for any future prolongation of the series. Let us express this idea in an exact formulation. We assume a series of events A and $\underline{A}$ (non-A); let n be the number of events, m the number of events of the type A among them. We have then the relative frequency

$$h^n = \frac{m}{n}$$

The assumption of the determination a posteriori may now be expressed:

For any further prolongation of the series as far as s events (s > n), *the relative frequency will remain within a small interval around* h^n; *i.e., we assume the relation*

$$h^n - \epsilon \leqq h^s \leqq h^n + \epsilon$$

where ϵ is a small number.

This assumption formulates the *principle of induction*. We may add that our formulation states the principle in a form more general than that customary in traditional philosophy. The usual formulation is as follows: induction is the assumption that an event which occurred n times will occur at all following times. It is obvious that this formulation is a special case of our formulation, corresponding to the case $h^n = 1$. We cannot restrict our investigation to this special case because the general case occurs in a great many problems.

The reason for this is to be found in the fact that the theory of probability needs the definition of probability as the limit of the frequency. Our formulation is a necessary condition for the existence of a limit of the frequency near h^n; what is yet to be added is that there is an h^n of the kind postulated for every ϵ however small. If we include this idea in our assumption, our postulate of induction becomes the hypothesis that there is a limit to the relative frequency which does not differ greatly from the observed value.

If we enter now into a closer analysis of this assumption, one thing needs no further demonstration: the formula given is not a tautology. There is indeed no logical necessity that h^8 remains within the interval $h^n \pm \epsilon$; we may easily imagine that this does not take place.

The nontautological character of induction has been known a long time; Bacon had already emphasized that it is just this character to which the importance of induction is due. If inductive inference can teach us something new, in opposition to deductive inference, this is because it is not a tautology. This useful quality has, however, become the center of the epistemological difficulties of induction. It was David Hume who first attacked the principle from this side; he pointed out that the apparent constraint of the inductive inference, although submitted to by everybody, could not be justified. We believe in induction; we even cannot get rid of the belief when we know the impossibility of a logical demonstration of the validity of inductive inference; but as logicians we must admit that this belief is a deception—such is the result of Hume's criticism. We may summarize his objections in two statements:

1. We have no logical demonstration for the validity of inductive inference.
2. There is no demonstration a posteriori for the inductive inference; any such demonstration would presuppose the very principle which it is to demonstrate.

These two pillars of Hume's criticism of the principle of induction have stood unshaken for two centuries, and I think they will stand as long as there is a scientific philosophy.

. . .

Inductive inference cannot be dispensed with because we need it for the purpose of action. To deem the inductive assumption unworthy of the assent of a philosopher, to keep a distinguished reserve, and to meet with a condescending smile the attempts of other people to bridge the gap between experience and prediction is cheap self-deceit; at the very moment when the apostles of such a higher philosophy leave the field of theoretical discussion and pass to the simplest actions of daily life, they follow the inductive principle as surely as does every earth-bound mind. In any action there are various means to the realization of our aim; we have to make a choice, and we decide in accordance with the inductive principle. Although there is no means which will produce with certainty the desired effect, we do not leave the choice to chance but prefer the means indicated by the principle of induction. If we sit at the wheel of a car and want to turn the car to the right, why do we turn the wheel to the right? There is no certainty that the car will follow the wheel; there are indeed cars which do not always so behave. Such cases are fortunately exceptions. But if we should not regard the inductive prescription and consider the effect of a turn of the wheel as entirely unknown to us, we might turn it to the left as well. I do not say this to suggest such an attempt; the effects of skeptical philosophy applied in motor traffic would be rather unpleasant. But I should say a philosopher who is to put aside his principles any time he steers a motorcar is a bad philosopher.

It is no justification of inductive belief to show that it is a habit. It *is* a habit; but the question is whether it is a good habit, where "good" is to mean "useful for the purpose of actions directed to future events." If a person tells me that Socrates is a man, and that all men are mortal, I have the habit of believing that Socrates is mortal. I know, however, that this is a good habit. If anyone had the habit of believing in such a case that Socrates is not mortal, we could demonstrate to him that this was a bad habit. The analogous question must be raised for inductive inference. If we should not be able to demonstrate that it is a good habit, we should either cease using it or admit frankly that our philosophy is a failure.

Science proceeds by induction and not by tautological transformations of reports. [Francis—Ed.] Bacon is right about Aristotle; but the *novum organon* [i.e., induction as opposed to deduction—Ed.] needs a justification as good as that of the *organon*. Hume's criticism was the heaviest blow against empiricism; if we do not want to dupe our consciousness of this by means of the narcotic drug of aprioristic rationalism, or the soporific of skepticism, we must find a defense for the inductive inference which holds as well as does the formalistic justification of deductive logic.

§ 39. The Justification of the Principle of Induction

We shall now begin to give the justification of induction which Hume thought impossible. In the pursuit of this inquiry, let us ask first what has been proved, strictly, by Hume's objections.

Hume started with the assumption that a justification of inductive inference is only given if we can show that inductive inference must lead to success. In other words, Hume believed that any justified application of the inductive inference presupposes a demonstration that the conclusion is true. It is this assumption on which Hume's criticism is based. His two objections directly concern only the question of the truth of the conclusion; they prove that the truth of the conclusion cannot be demonstrated. The two objections, therefore, are valid only in so far as the Humean assumption is valid. It is this question to which we must turn: Is it necessary, for the justification of inductive inference, to show that its conclusion is true?

A rather simple analysis shows us that this assumption does not hold. Of course, if we were able to prove the truth of the conclusion, inductive inference would be justified; but the converse does not hold: a justification of the inductive inference does not imply a proof of the truth of the conclusion. The proof of the truth of the conclusion is only a sufficient condition for the justification of induction, not a necessary condition.

The inductive inference is a procedure which is to furnish us the best assumption concerning the future. If we do not know the truth about the future, there may be nonetheless a best assumption about it, i.e., a best assumption relative to what we know. We must ask whether such a characterization may be given for the principle of induction. If this turns out to be possible, the principle of induction will be justified.

An example will show the logical structure of our reasoning. A man may be suffering from a grave disease; the physician tells us: "I do not know whether an operation will save the man, but if there *is* any remedy, it is an operation." In such a case, the operation would be justified. Of course, it would be better to know that the operation will save the man; but, if we do not know this, the knowledge formulated in the statement of the physician is a sufficient justification. If we cannot realize the sufficient conditions of success, we shall at least realize the necessary conditions. If we were able to show that the inductive inference is a necessary condition of success, it would be justified; such a proof would satisfy any demands which may be raised about the justification of induction.

Now obviously there is a great difference between our example and induction. The reasoning of the physician presupposes inductions; his knowledge about an operation as the only possible means of saving a life is based on inductive generalizations, just as are all other statements of empirical character. But we wanted only to illustrate the logical structure of our reasoning. If we want to regard such a reasoning as a justification of the principle of induction, the character of induction as a necessary condition of success must be demonstrated in a way which does not presuppose induction. Such a proof, however, can be given.

If we want to construct this proof, we must begin with a determination of the aim of induction. It is usually said that we perform inductions with the aim of foreseeing the future. This determination is vague; let us replace it by a formulation more precise in character:

> The aim of induction is to find series of events whose frequency of occurrence converges toward a limit.

We choose this formulation because we found that we need probabilities and that a probability is to be defined as the limit of a frequency; thus our determination of the aim of induction is given in such a way that it enables us to apply probability methods. If we compare this determination of the aim of induction with determinations usually given, it turns out to be not a confinement to a narrow aim but an expansion. What we usually call "foreseeing the future" is included in our formulation as a special case; the case of knowing with certainty for every event A the event B following it would correspond in our formulation to a case where the limit of the frequency is of the numerical value 1. Hume thought of this case only. Thus our inquiry differs from that of Hume in so far as it conceives the aim of induction in a generalized form. But we do not omit any possible applications if we determine the principle of induction as the means of obtaining the limit of a frequency. If we have limits of frequency, we have all we want, including the case considered by Hume; we have then the laws of nature in their most general form, including both statistical and so-called causal laws—the latter being nothing but a special case of statistical laws, corresponding to the numerical value 1 of the limit of the frequency. We are entitled, therefore, to consider the determination of the limit of a frequency as the aim of the inductive inference.

Now it is obvious that we have no guaranty that this aim is at all attainable. The world may be so disorderly that it is impossible for us to construct series with a limit. Let us introduce the term "predictable" for a world which is sufficiently ordered to enable us to construct series with a limit. We must admit, then, that we do not know whether the world is predictable.

But, if the world is predictable, let us ask what the logical function of the principle of induction will be. For this purpose, we must consider the definition of limit. The frequency h^n has a limit at p, if for any given ϵ there is an n such that h^n is within $p \pm \epsilon$ and remains within this interval for all the rest of the series. Comparing our formulation of the principle of induction (§38) with this, we may infer from the definition of the limit that, if there is a limit, there is an element of the series from which the principle of induction leads to the true value of the limit. In this sense the principle of induction is a necessary condition for the determination of a limit.

It is true that, if we are faced with the value h^n for the frequency furnished by our statistics, we do not know whether this n is sufficiently large to be identical with, or beyond, the n of the "place of convergence" for ϵ. It may be that our n is not yet large enough, that after n there will be a deviation greater than ϵ from p. To this we may answer: We are not bound to stay at h^n; we may continue our procedure and shall always consider the last h^n obtained as our best value. This procedure must at some time lead to the true value p, if there is a limit at all; the applicability of this procedure, as a whole, is a necessary condition of the existence of a limit at p.

To understand this, let us imagine a principle of a contrary sort. Imagine a man who, if h^n is reached, always makes the assumption that the limit of the frequency is at $h^n + a$, where a is a fixed constant. If this man continues his procedure for increasing n, he is sure to miss the limit; this procedure must at some time become false, if there is a limit at all.

We have found now a better formulation of the necessary condition. We must not consider the individual assumption for an individual h^n; we must take account of the procedure of continued assumptions of the inductive type. The applicability of this procedure is the necessary condition sought.

If, however, it is only the whole procedure which constitutes the necessary condition, how may we apply this idea to the individual case which stands before us? We want to know whether the individual h^n observed by us differs less than ϵ from the limit of the convergence; this neither can be guaranteed nor can it be called a necessary condition of the existence of a limit. So what does our idea of the necessary condition imply for the individual case? It seems that for our individual case the idea turns out to be without any application.

This difficulty corresponds in a certain sense to the difficulty we found in the application of the frequency interpretation to the single case. It is to be eliminated by the introduction of a concept already used for the other problem: the concept of posit.

If we observe a frequency h^n and assume it to be the approximate value of the limit, this assumption is not maintained in the form of a true statement; it is a posit such as we perform in a wager. We posit h^n as the value of the limit, i.e., we wager on h^n, just as we wager on the side of a die. We know that h^n is our best wager, therefore we posit it. There is, however, a difference as to the type of posit occurring here and in the throw of the die.

In the case of the die, we know the weight belonging to the posit: it is given by the degree of probability. If we posit the case "side other than that numbered 1," the weight of this posit is 5/6. We speak in this case of a posit with appraised weight, or, in short, of an *appraised posit*.

In the case of our positing h^n, we do not know its weight. We call it, therefore, a *blind posit*. We know it is our best posit, but we do not know how good it is. Perhaps, although our best, it is a rather bad one.

The blind posit, however, may be corrected. By continuing our series, we obtain new values h^n; we always choose the last h^n. Thus the blind posit is of an approximative type; we know that the method of making and correcting such posits must in time lead to success, in case there is a limit of the frequency. It is this idea which furnishes the justification of the blind posit. The procedure described may be called the *method of anticipation*; in choosing h^n as our posit, we anticipate the case where n is the "place of convergence." It may be that by this anticipation we obtain a false value; we know, however, that a continued anticipation must lead to the true value, if there is a limit at all.

.   .   .

These considerations lead, however, to a more precise formulation of the logical structure of the inductive inference. We must say that, if there is any method which leads to the limit of the frequency, the inductive principle will do the same; if there is a limit of the frequency, the inductive principle is a sufficient condition to find it. If we omit now the premise that there is a limit of the frequency, we cannot say that the inductive principle is the necessary condition of finding it because there are other methods using a correction c_n. There is a set of equivalent conditions such that the choice of one of the members of the set is necessary if we want to find the limit; and, if there is a limit, each of the members of the set is an appropriate method for finding it. We may say, therefore, that the *applicability* of the inductive principle is a necessary condition of the existence of a limit of the frequency.

The decision in favor of the inductive principle among the members of the set of equivalent means may be substantiated by pointing out its quality of embodying the smallest risk; after all, this decision is not of a great relevance, as all these methods must lead to the same value of the limit if they are sufficiently continued. It must not be forgotten, however, that the method of clairvoyance is not, without further ado, a member of the set because we do not know whether the correction c_n occurring here is submitted to the condition of convergence to zero. This must be proved first, and it can only be proved by using the inductive principle, viz., a method known to be a member of the set: this is why clairvoyance, in spite of all occult pretensions, is to be submitted to the control of scientific methods, i.e., by the principle of induction.

It is in the analysis expounded that we see the solution of Hume's problem. Hume demanded too much when he wanted for a justification of the inductive inference a proof that its conclusion is true. What his objections demonstrate is only that such a proof cannot be given. We do not perform, however, an inductive inference with the pretension of obtaining a true statement. What we obtain is a wager; and it is the best wager we can lay because it corresponds to a procedure the applicability of which is the necessary condition of the possibility of predictions. To fulfill the conditions sufficient for the attainment of true predictions does not lie in our power; let us be glad that we are able to fulfil at least the conditions necessary for the realization of this intrinsic aim of science.

4

Nelson Goodman
The New Riddle of Induction

Nelson Goodman was Harry Austryn Wolfson Professor of Philosophy at Brandeis University from 1964 until he joined the philosophy department at Harvard University. He is one of the most distinguished contributors to current American philosophy and has been particularly influential in a number of areas. His most recent systematic work, Languages of Art *(1968), develops in an original and powerful way an analysis of the representational aspects of works of art and of notations, among them linguistic notation. But he is best known for his conception of induction and for his strong version of nominalism (that is, for his denial that there are classes or any other "nonindividuals" and his insistence that only "individuals" exist, whether abstract or concrete). These appear particularly in "Steps Toward a Constructive Nominalism" (1947), in collaboration with W. V. Quine;* The Structure of Appearance *(1951);* Fact, Fiction, and Forecast *(1954); and "A World of Individuals" (1956).*

Regarding induction, Goodman stresses the need to formulate rules defining the difference between valid and invalid inferences. The development of what would be required proves to be linked to an analysis of counterfactuals, the definition of scientific laws, and the development of an adequate theory of confirmation. Here, his signal and still unfinished contribution concerns the attribute of hypotheses that he calls "projectibility."

Confirmation of a hypothesis by an instance depends rather heavily upon features of the hypothesis other than its syntactical form. That a given piece of copper conducts electricity increases the credibility of statements asserting that other pieces of copper conduct electricity, and thus confirms the hypothesis that all copper conducts electricity. But the fact that a given man now in this room is a third son does not increase the credibility of statements asserting that other men now in this room are third sons, and so does not confirm the hypothesis that all men now in this room are third sons. Yet in both cases our hypothesis is a generalization of the evidence statement. The difference is that in the former case the hypothesis is a *lawlike* statement; while in the latter case, the hypothesis is a merely contingent or accidental generality. Only a statement that is *lawlike*—regardless of its truth or falsity or its scientific importance—is capable of receiving confirmation from an instance of it; accidental statements are not. Plainly, then, we must look for a way of distinguishing lawlike from accidental statements.

So long as what seems to be needed is merely a way of excluding a few odd and unwanted cases that are inadvertently admitted by our definition of con-

Reprinted by permission of Nelson Goodman from *Fact, Fiction, and Forecast*, Hackett Publishing Company, Indianapolis, Indiana 46205.

firmation, the problem may not seem very hard or very pressing. We fully expect that minor defects will be found in our definition and that the necessary refinements will have to be worked out patiently one after another. But some further examples will show that our present difficulty is of a much graver kind.

Suppose that all emeralds examined before a certain time t are green.[1] At time t, then, our observations support the hypothesis that all emeralds are green; and this is in accord with our definition of confirmation. Our evidence statements assert that emerald a is green, that emerald b is green, and so on; and each confirms the general hypothesis that all emeralds are green. So far, so good.

Now let me introduce another predicate less familiar than "green". It is the predicate "grue" and it applies to all things examined before t just in case they are green but to other things just in case they are blue. Then at time t we have, for each evidence statement asserting that a given emerald is green, a parallel evidence statement asserting that that emerald is grue. And the statements that emerald a is grue, that emerald b is grue, and so on, will each confirm the general hypothesis that all emeralds are grue. Thus according to our definition, the prediction that all emeralds subsequently examined will be green and the prediction that all will be grue are alike confirmed by evidence statements describing the same observations. But if an emerald subsequently examined is grue, it is blue and hence not green. Thus although we are well aware which of the two incompatible predictions is genuinely confirmed, they are equally well confirmed according to our present definition. Moreover, it is clear that if we simply choose an appropriate predicate, then on the basis of these same observations we shall have equal confirmation, by our definition, for any prediction whatever about other emeralds—or indeed about anything else.[2] As in our earlier example, only the predictions subsumed under lawlike hypotheses are genuinely confirmed; but we have no criterion as yet for determining lawlikeness. And now we see that without some such criterion, our definition not merely includes a few unwanted cases, but is so completely ineffectual that it virtually excludes nothing. We are left once again with the intolerable result that anything confirms anything. This difficulty cannot be set aside as an annoying detail to be taken care of in due course. It has to be met before our definition will work at all.

Nevertheless, the difficulty is often slighted because on the surface there seem to be easy ways of dealing with it. Sometimes, for example, the problem is thought to be much like the paradox of the ravens. We are here again, it is

---

[1] Although the example used is different, the argument to follow is substantially the same as that set forth in my note 'A Query on Confirmation' [*Journal of Philosophy*, XLIII (1946), 383–385.]

[2] For instance, we shall have equal confirmation, by our present definition, for the prediction that roses subsequently examined will be blue. Let "emerose" apply just to emeralds examined before time t, and to roses examined later. Then all emeroses so far examined are grue, and this confirms the hypothesis that all emeroses are grue and hence the prediction that roses subsequently examined will be blue. The problem raised by such antecedents has been little noticed, but is no easier to meet than that raised by similarly perverse consequents.

pointed out, making tacit and illegitimate use of information outside the stated evidence: the information, for example, that different samples of one material are usually alike in conductivity, and the information that different men in a lecture audience are usually not alike in the number of their older brothers. But while it is true that such information is being smuggled in, this does not by itself settle the matter as it settles the matter of the ravens. There the point was that when the smuggled information is forthrightly declared, its effect upon the confirmation of the hypothesis in question is immediately and properly registered by the definition we are using. On the other hand, if to our initial evidence we add statements concerning the conductivity of pieces of other materials or concerning the number of older brothers of members of other lecture audiences, this will not in the least affect the confirmation, according to our definition, of the hypothesis concerning copper or of that concerning other lecture audiences. Since our definition is insensitive to the bearing upon hypotheses of evidence so related to them, even when the evidence is fully declared, the difficulty about accidental hypotheses cannot be explained away on the ground that such evidence is being surreptitiously taken into account.

A more promising suggestion is to explain the matter in terms of the effect of this other evidence not directly upon the hypothesis in question but *indirectly* through other hypotheses that *are* confirmed, according to our definition, by such evidence. Our information about other materials does by our definition confirm such hypotheses as that all pieces of iron conduct electricity, that no pieces of rubber do, and so on; and these hypotheses, the explanation runs, impart to the hypothesis that all pieces of copper conduct electricity (and also to the hypothesis that none do) the character of lawlikeness—that is, amenability to confirmation by direct positive instances when found. On the other hand, our information about other lecture audiences *disconfirms* many hypotheses to the effect that all the men in one audience are third sons, or that none are; and this strips any character of lawlikeness from the hypothesis that all (or the hypothesis that none) of the men in *this* audience are third sons. But clearly if this course is to be followed, the circumstances under which hypotheses are thus related to one another will have to be precisely articulated.

The problem, then, is to define the relevant ways in which such hypotheses must be alike. Evidence for the hypothesis that all iron conducts electricity enhances the lawlikeness of the hypothesis that all zirconium conducts electricity, but does not similarly affect the hypothesis that all the objects on my desk conduct electricity. Wherein lies the difference? The first two hypotheses fall under the broader hypothesis—call it "*H*"—that every class of things of the same material is uniform in conductivity; the first and third fall only under some such hypothesis as—call it "*K*"—that every class of things that are either all of the same material or all on a desk is uniform in conductivity. Clearly the important difference here is that evidence for a statement affirming that one of the classes covered by *H* has the property in question increases the credibility of any statement affirming that another such class has this property; while nothing of the sort holds true with respect to *K*. But this is only to say that *H* is lawlike and *K* is not. We are faced anew with the very problem we are trying to solve: the problem of distinguishing between lawlike and accidental hypotheses.

The most popular way of attacking the problem takes its cue from the fact that accidental hypotheses seem typically to involve some spatial or temporal restriction, or reference to some particular individual. They seem to concern the people in some particular room, or the objects on some particular person's desk; while lawlike hypotheses characteristically concern all ravens or all pieces of copper whatsoever. Complete generality is thus very often supposed to be a sufficient condition of lawlikeness; but to define this complete generality is by no means easy. Merely to require that the hypothesis contain no term naming, describing, or indicating a particular thing or location will obviously not be enough. The troublesome hypothesis that all emeralds are grue contains no such term; and where such a term does occur, as in hypotheses about men in *this room*, it can be suppressed in favor of some predicate (short or long, new or old) that contains no such term but applies only to exactly the same things. One might think, then, of excluding not only hypotheses that actually contain terms for specific individuals but also all hypotheses that are equivalent to others that do contain such terms. But, as we have just seen, to exclude only hypotheses of which *all* equivalents contain such terms is to exclude nothing. On the other hand, to exclude all hypotheses that have *some* equivalent containing such a term is to exclude everything; for even the hypothesis

All grass is green

has as an equivalent

All grass in London or elsewhere is green.

The next step, therefore, has been to consider ruling out predicates of certain kinds. A syntactically universal hypothesis is lawlike, the proposal runs, if its predicates are 'purely qualitative' or 'non-positional'.[3] This will obviously accomplish nothing if a purely qualitative predicate is then conceived either as one that is equivalent to some expression free of terms for specific individuals, or as one that is equivalent to no expression that contains such a term; for this only raises again the difficulties just pointed out. The claim appears to be rather that at least in the case of a simple enough predicate we can readily determine by direct inspection of its meaning whether or not it is purely qualitative. But even aside from obscurities in the notion of 'the meaning' of a predicate, this claim seems to me wrong. I simply do not know how to tell whether a predicate is qualitative or positional, except perhaps by completely begging the question at issue and asking whether the predicate is 'well-behaved' —that is, whether simple syntactically universal hypotheses applying it are lawlike.

This statement will not go unprotested. "Consider", it will be argued, "the

---

[3] Carnap took this course in his paper 'On the Application of Inductive Logic', *Philosophy and Phenomenological Research*, vol. 8 (1947), pp. 133–47, which is in part a reply to my 'A Query on Confirmation'. The discussion was continued in my note 'On Infirmities of Confirmation Theory', *Philosophy and Phenomenological Research*, vol. 8 (1947), pp. 149–51; and in Carnap's 'Reply to Nelson Goodman', same journal, same volume, pp. 461–2.

predicates 'blue' and 'green' and the predicate 'grue' introduced earlier, and also the predicate 'bleen' that applies to emeralds examined before time t just in case they are blue and to other emeralds just in case they are green. Surely it is clear", the argument runs, "that the first two are purely qualitative and the second two are not; for the meaning of each of the latter two plainly involves reference to a specific temporal position." To this I reply that indeed I do recognize the first two as well-behaved predicates admissible in lawlike hypotheses, and the second two as ill-behaved predicates. But the argument that the former but not the latter are purely qualitative seems to me quite unsound. True enough, if we start with "blue" and "green", then "grue" and "bleen" will be explained in terms of "blue" and "green" and a temporal term. But equally truly, if we start with "grue" and "bleen," then "blue" and "green" will be explained in terms of "grue" and "bleen" and a temporal term; "green", for example, applies to emeralds examined before time t just in case they are grue, and to other emeralds just in case they are bleen. Thus qualitativeness is an entirely relative matter and does not by itself establish any dichotomy of predicates. This relativity seems to be completely overlooked by those who contend that the qualitative character of a predicate is a criterion for its good behavior.

Of course, one may ask why we need worry about such unfamiliar predicates as "grue" or about accidental hypotheses in general, since we are unlikely to use them in making predictions. If our definition works for such hypotheses as are normally employed, isn't that all we need? In a sense, yes; but only in the sense that we need no definition, no theory of induction, and no philosophy of knowledge at all. We get along well enough without them in daily life and in scientific research. But if we seek a theory at all, we cannot excuse gross anomalies resulting from a proposed theory by pleading that we can avoid them in practice. The odd cases we have been considering are clinically pure cases that, though seldom encountered in practice, nevertheless display to best advantage the symptoms of a widespread and destructive malady.

We have so far neither any answer nor any promising clue to an answer to the question what distinguishes lawlike or confirmable hypotheses from accidental or non-confirmable ones; and what may at first have seemed a minor technical difficulty has taken on the stature of a major obstacle to the development of a satisfactory theory of confirmation. It is this problem that I call the new riddle of induction.

Causality and Laws

5

Aristotle
Causes

Aristotle (b. 4th century B.C.) was (with Plato) one of the two greatest, most productive, and most influential of the ancient Greek philosophers. He studied in Plato's Academy in Athens, served as tutor to Alexander the Great when the latter was a boy, and founded his own school, called the Lyceum. His theories have had a remarkably explicit and detailed interest for philosophers of every age and continue to be debated almost like those of a contemporary. Also, his philosophical work spans very nearly every area of professional concern.

The titles of his works were said to number more than two hundred. Certainly, more than a dozen of what remain are among the most important contributions to their fields.

Whatever the difficulties in interpreting Aristotle's writings, he is most noted for the strong sense of a unified system informing his distinctly original contributions in so many areas. His work on the syllogism Aristotle himself seems to have regarded as novel. It formed the basis for traditional logic until our own century.

The Organon's treatises on the organization of discourse on any and every branch of knowledge, including logic (Prior and Posterior Analytics), are closely linked to Aristotle's conception of reality, in particular to his criticism of Plato. His work on what we would call the physical world, biology, and psychology (in particular, Physics, De Anima) is distinguished by its strong emphasis on a teleological order in nature, natural species, resistance to Plato's theory of Forms, and a functional account of biological species, particularly man.

The so-called Metaphysics, or "first philosophy," the capstone of Aristotle's system, constitutes the science of being as being and is focused on the analysis of substance. In the order of the relative dependence and independence of things, in the order of discourse, and in the order of knowledge, substance is prior to whatever is designated by other terms. It is here that Aristotle integrates his views about the independence of particular things, their essence, and their production (in terms that are at once causal and teleological).

From *Physics*, R. P .Hardie and R. K. Gaye, trans., in *The Works of Aristotle* (Oxford: 1938), Book II, Secs. 1, 3–9, pp. 116–119, 122–138. Reprinted by permission of The Oxford University Press.

Of things that exist, some exist by nature, some from other causes. 'By nature' the animals and their parts exist, and the plants and the simple bodies (earth, fire, air, water)—for we say that these and the like exist 'by nature'.

All the things mentioned present a feature in which they differ from things which are *not* constituted by nature. Each of them has *within itself* a principle of motion and of stationariness (in respect of place, or of growth and decrease, or by way of alteration). On the other hand, a bed and a coat and anything else of that sort, *qua* receiving these designations—i.e. in so far as they are products of art—have no innate impulse to change. But in so far as they happen to be composed of stone or of earth or of a mixture of the two, they *do* have such an impulse, and just to that extent—which seems to indicate that *nature is a source or cause of being moved and of being at rest in that to which it belongs primarily*, in virtue of itself and not in virtue of a concomitant attribute.

I say 'not in virtue of a concomitant attribute', because (for instance) a man who is a doctor might cure himself. Nevertheless it is not in so far as he is a patient that he possesses the art of medicine: it merely has happened that the same man is doctor and patient—and that is why these attributes are not always found together. So it is with all other artificial products. None of them has in itself the source of its own production. But while in some cases (for instance houses and the other products of manual labour) that principle is in something else external to the thing, in others—those which may cause a change in themselves in virtue of a concomitant attribute—it lies in the things themselves (but not in virtue of what they are).

'Nature' then is what has been stated. Things 'have a nature' which have a principle of this kind. Each of them is a substance; for it is a subject, and nature always implies a subject in which it inheres.

The term 'according to nature' is applied to all these things and also to the attributes which belong to them in virtue of what they are, for instance the property of fire to be carried upwards—which is not a 'nature' nor 'has a nature' but is 'by nature' or 'according to nature'.

What nature is, then, and the meaning of the terms 'by nature' and 'according to nature', has been stated. *That* nature exists, it would be absurd to try to prove; for it is obvious that there are many things of this kind, and to prove what is obvious by what is not is the mark of a man who is unable to distinguish what is self-evident from what is not. (This state of mind is clearly possible. A man blind from birth might reason about colours. Presumably therefore such persons must be talking about words without any thought to correspond.)

Some identify the nature or substance of a natural object with that immediate constituent of it which taken by itself is without arrangement, e.g. the wood is the 'nature' of the bed, and the bronze the 'nature' of the statue.

As an indication of this Antiphon points out that if you planted a bed and the rotting wood acquired the power of sending up a root, it would not be a bed that would come up, but *wood*—which shows that the arrangement in accordance with the rules of the art is merely an incidental attribute, whereas the real nature is the other, which, further, persists continuously through the process of making.

But if the material of each of these objects has itself the same relation to something else, say bronze (or gold) to water, bones (or wood) to earth and so on, *that* (they say) would be their nature and essence. Consequently some assert earth, others fire or air or water or some or all of these, to be the nature of the things that are. For whatever any one of them supposed to have this character—whether one thing or more than one thing—this or these he declared to be the whole of substance, all else being its affections, states, or dispositions. Every such thing they held to be eternal (for it could not pass into anything else), but other things to come into being and cease to be times without number.

This then is one account of 'nature', namely that it is the immediate material substratum of things which have in themselves a principle of motion or change.

Another account is that 'nature' is the shape or form which is specified in the definition of the thing.

For the word 'nature' is applied to what is according to nature and the natural in the same way as 'art' is applied to what is artistic or a work of art. We should not say in the latter case that there is anything artistic about a thing, if it is a bed only potentially, not yet having the form of a bed; nor should we call it a work of art. The same is true of natural compounds. What is potentially flesh or bone has not yet its own 'nature', and does not exist by 'nature', until it receives the form specified in the definition, which we name in defining what flesh or bone is. Thus in the second sense of 'nature' it would be the shape or form (not separable except in statement) of things which have in themselves a source of motion. (The combination of the two, e.g. man, is not 'nature' but 'by nature' or 'natural'.)

The form indeed is 'nature' rather than the matter; for a thing is more properly said to be what it is when it has attained to fulfilment than when it exists potentially. Again man is born from man, but not bed from bed. That is why people say that the figure is not the nature of a bed, but the wood is—if the bed sprouted not a bed but wood would come up. But even if the figure *is* art, then on the same principle the shape of man is his nature. For man is born from man.

We also speak of a thing's nature as being exhibited in the process of growth by which its nature is attained. The 'nature' in this sense is not like 'doctoring', which leads not to the art of doctoring but to health. Doctoring must start from the art, not lead to it. But it is not in this way that nature (in the one sense) is related to nature (in the other). What grows *qua* growing grows from something into something. Into what then does it grow? Not into that from which it arose but into that to which it tends. The shape then is nature.

'Shape' and 'nature', it should be added, are used in two senses. For the privation too is in a way form. But whether in unqualified coming to be there is privation, i.e. a contrary to what comes to be, we must consider later.

.   .   .

. . . we must proceed to consider causes, their character and number. Knowledge is the object of our inquiry, and men do not think they know a thing till they have grasped the 'why' of it (which is to grasp its primary cause). So clearly we too must do this as regards both coming to be and passing away and every kind of physical change, in order that, knowing their principles, we may try to refer to these principles each of our problems.

In one sense, then, (1) that out of which a thing comes to be and which persists, is called 'cause', e.g. the bronze of the statue, the silver of the bowl, and the genera of which the bronze and the silver are species.

In another sense (2) the form or the archetype, i.e. the statement of the essence, and its genera, are called 'causes' (e.g. of the octave the relation of 2:1, and generally number), and the parts in the definition.

Again (3) the primary source of the change or coming to rest; e.g. the man who gave advice is a cause, the father is cause of the child, and generally what makes of what is made and what causes change of what is changed.

Again (4) in the sense of end or 'that for the sake of which' a thing is done, e.g. health is the cause of walking about. ('Why is he walking about?' we say. 'To be healthy', and, having said that, we think we have assigned the cause.) The same is true also of all the intermediate steps which are brought about through the action of something else as means towards the end, e.g. reduction of flesh, purging, drugs, or surgical instruments are means towards health. All these things are 'for the sake of' the end, though they differ from one another in that some are activities, others instruments.

This then perhaps exhausts the number of ways in which the term 'cause' is used.

As the word has several senses, it follows that there are several causes of the same thing (not merely in virtue of a concomitant attribute), e.g. both the art of the sculptor and the bronze are causes of the statue. These are causes of the statue *qua* statue, not in virtue of anything else that it may be—only not in the same way, the one being the material cause, the other the cause whence the motion comes. Some things cause each other reciprocally, e.g. hard work causes fitness and *vice versa*, but again not in the same way, but the one as end, the other as the origin of change. Further the same thing is the cause of contrary results. For that which by its presence brings about one result is sometimes blamed for bringing about the contrary by its absence. Thus we ascribe the wreck of a ship to the absence of the pilot whose presence was the cause of its safety.

All the causes now mentioned fall into four familiar divisions. The letters are the causes of syllables, the material of artificial products, fire, &c., of bodies, the parts of the whole, and the premisses of the conclusion, in the sense of 'that from which'. Of these pairs the one set are causes in the sense of substratum, e.g. the parts, the other set in the sense of essence—the whole and the combination and the form. But the seed and the doctor and the adviser, and generally the maker, are all sources whence the change or stationariness originates, while the others are causes in the sense of the end or the good of the rest; for 'that for the sake of which' means what is best and the end of the things that lead up to it. (Whether we say the 'good itself' or the 'apparent good' makes no difference.)

Such then is the number and nature of the kinds of cause.

Now the modes of causation are many, though when brought under heads they too can be reduced in number. For 'cause' is used in many senses and even within the same kind one may be prior to another (e.g. the doctor and the expert are causes of health, the relation 2:1 and number of the octave), and always what is inclusive to what is particular. Another mode of causation is the incidental and its genera, e.g. in one way 'Polyclitus', in another 'sculptor' is the cause of a statue, because 'being Polyclitus' and 'sculptor' are incidentally conjoined. Also the classes in which the incidental attribute is included; thus 'a man' could be said to be the cause of a statue or, generally, 'a living creature'. An incidental attribute too may be more or less remote, e.g. suppose that 'a pale man' or 'a musical man' were said to be the cause of the statue.

All causes, both proper and incidental, may be spoken of either as potential or as actual; e.g. the cause of a house being built is either 'house-builder' or 'house-builder building'.

Similar distinctions can be made in the things of which the causes are causes, e.g. of 'this statue' or of 'statue' or of 'image' generally, of 'this bronze' or of 'bronze' or of 'material' generally. So too with the incidental attributes. Again we may use a complex expression for either and say, e.g., neither 'Polyclitus' nor 'sculptor' but 'Polyclitus, sculptor'.

All these various uses, however, come to six in number, under each of which again the usage is twofold. Cause means either what is particular or a genus, or an incidental attribute or a genus of that, and these either as a complex or each by itself; and all six either as actual or as potential. The difference is this much, that causes which are actually at work and particular exist and cease to exist simultaneously with their effect, e.g. this healing person with this being-healed person and that housebuilding man with that being-built house; but this is not always true of potential causes—the house and the house-builder do not pass away simultaneously.

In investigating the cause of each thing it is always necessary to seek what is most precise (as also in other things): thus man builds because he is a builder, and a builder builds in virtue of his art of building. This last cause then is prior: and so generally.

Further, generic effects should be assigned to generic causes, particular effects to particular causes, e.g. statue to sculptor, this statue to this sculptor; and powers are relative to possible effects, actually operating causes to things which are actually being effected.

This must suffice for our account of the number of causes and the modes of causation.

But chance also and spontaneity are reckoned among causes: many things are said both to be and to come to be as a result of chance and spontaneity. We must inquire therefore in what manner chance and spontaneity are present among the causes enumerated, and whether they are the same or different, and generally what chance and spontaneity are.

Some people[1] even question whether they are real or not. They say that nothing happens by chance, but that everything which we ascribe to chance or spontaneity has some definite cause, e.g. coming 'by chance' into the market and finding there a man whom one wanted but did not expect to meet is due to one's wish to go and buy in the market. Similarly in other cases of chance it is always possible, they maintain, to find something which is the cause; but not chance, for if chance were real, it would seem strange indeed, and the question might be raised, why on earth none of the wise men of old in speaking of the causes of generation and decay took account of chance; whence it would seem that they too did not believe that anything is by chance. But there is a further circumstance that is surprising. Many things both come to be and are by chance and spontaneity, and although all know that each of them can be ascribed to some cause (as the old argument said which denied chance), nevertheless they speak of some of these things as happening by chance and others not. For this reason also they ought to have at least referred to the matter in some way or other.

Certainly the early physicists found no place for chance among the causes which they recognize—love, strife, mind, fire, or the like. This is strange, whether they supposed that there is no such thing as chance or whether they thought there is but omitted to mention it—and that too when they sometimes used it, as Empedocles does when he says that the air is not always separated into the highest region, but 'as it may chance'. At any rate he says in his cosmogony that 'it happened to run that way at that time, but it often ran otherwise.' He tells us also that most of the parts of animals came to be by chance.

There are some[2] too who ascribe this heavenly sphere and all the worlds to spontaneity. They say that the vortex arose spontaneously, i.e. the motion that separated and arranged in its present order all that exists. This statement might well cause surprise. For they are asserting that chance is not responsible for the existence or generation of animals and plants, nature or mind or something of the kind being the cause of them (for it is not any chance thing that comes from a given seed but an olive from one kind and a man from another); and yet at the same time they assert that the heavenly sphere and the divinest of visible things arose spontaneously, having no such cause as is assigned to animals and plants. Yet if this is so, it is a fact which deserves to be dwelt upon, and something might well have been said about it. For besides the other absurdities of the statement, it is the more absurd that people should make it when they see nothing coming to be spontaneously in the heavens, but much happening by chance among the things which as they say are not due to chance; whereas we should have expected exactly the opposite.

Others[3] there are who, indeed, believe that chance is a cause, but that it is inscrutable to human intelligence, as being a divine thing and full of mystery.

---

[1] Apparently Democritus is meant.
[2] Apparently Democritus is meant.
[3] Democritus.

Thus we must inquire what chance and spontaneity are, whether they are the same or different, and how they fit into our division of causes.

First then we observe that some things always come to pass in the same way, and others for the most part. It is clearly of neither of these that chance is said to be the cause, nor can the 'effect of chance' be identified with any of the things that come to pass by necessity and always, or for the most part. But as there is a third class of events besides these two—events which all say are 'by chance'—it is plain that there is such a thing as chance and spontaneity; for we know that things of this kind are due to chance and that things due to chance are of this kind.

But, secondly, some events are for the sake of something, others not. Again, some of the former class are in accordance with deliberate intention, others not, but both are in the class of things which are for the sake of something. Hence it is clear that even among the things which are outside the necessary and the normal, there are some in connexion with which the phrase 'for the sake of something' is applicable. (Events that are for the sake of something include whatever may be done as a result of thought or of nature.) Things of this kind, then, when they come to pass incidentally are said to be 'by chance'. For just as a thing is something either in virtue of itself or incidentally, so may it be a cause. For instance, the housebuilding faculty is in virtue of itself the cause of a house, whereas the pale or the musical[4] is the incidental cause. That which is *per se* [in virtue of itself—Ed.] cause of the effect is determinate, but the incidental cause is indeterminable, for the possible attributes of an individual are innumerable. To resume then; when a thing of this kind comes to pass among events which are for the sake of something, it is said to be spontaneous or by chance. (The distinction between the two must be made later—for the present it is sufficient if it is plain that both are in the sphere of things done for the sake of something.)

Example: A man is engaged in collecting subscriptions for a feast. He would have gone to such and such a place for the purpose of getting the money, if he had known. He actually went there for another purpose, and it was only incidentally that he got his money by going there; and this was not due to the fact that he went there as a rule or necessarily, nor is the end effected (getting the money) a cause present in himself—it belongs to the class of things that are intentional and the result of intelligent deliberation. It is when these conditions are satisfied that the man is said to have gone 'by chance'. If he had gone of deliberate purpose and for the sake of this—if he always or normally went there when he was collecting payments—he would not be said to have gone 'by chance'.

It is clear that chance is an incidental cause in the sphere of those actions for the sake of something which involve purpose. Intelligent reflection, then, and chance are in the same sphere, for purpose implies intelligent reflection.

It is necessary, no doubt, that the causes of what comes to pass by chance

---

[4] Incidental attributes of the housebuilder.

be indefinite; and that is why chance is supposed to belong to the class of the indefinite and to be inscrutable to man, and why it might be thought that, in a way, nothing occurs by chance. For all these statements are correct, because they are well grounded. Things *do*, in a way, occur by chance, for they occur incidentally and chance is an *incidental cause*. But strictly it is not the *cause*—without qualification—of anything; for instance, a housebuilder is the cause of a house; incidentally, a flute-player may be so.

And the causes of the man's coming and getting the money (when he did not come for the sake of that) are innumerable. He may have wished to see somebody or been following somebody or avoiding somebody, or may have gone to see a spectacle. Thus to say that chance is a thing contrary to rule is correct. For 'rule' applies to what is always true or true for the most part, whereas chance belongs to a third type of event. Hence, to conclude, since causes of this kind are indefinite, chance too is indefinite. (Yet in some cases one might raise the question whether *any* incidental fact might be the cause of the chance occurrence, e.g. of health the fresh air or the sun's heat may be the cause, but having had one's hair cut *cannot*; for some incidental causes are more relevant to the effect than others.)

Chance or fortune is called 'good' when the result is good, 'evil' when it is evil. The terms 'good fortune' and 'ill fortune' are used when either result is of considerable magnitude. Thus one who comes within an ace of some great evil or great good is said to be fortunate or unfortunate. The mind affirms the presence of the attribute, ignoring the hair's breadth of difference. Further, it is with reason that good fortune is regarded as unstable; for chance is unstable, as none of the things which result from it can be invariable or normal.

Both are then, as I have said, incidental causes—both chance and spontaneity—in the sphere of things which are capable of coming to pass not necessarily, nor normally, and with reference to such of these as might come to pass for the sake of something.

They differ in that 'spontaneity' is the wider term. Every result of chance is from what is spontaneous, but not everything that is from what is spontaneous is from chance.

Chance and what results from chance are appropriate to agents that are capable of good fortune and of moral action generally. Therefore necessarily chance is in the sphere of moral actions. This is indicated by the fact that good fortune is thought to be the same, or nearly the same, as happiness, and happiness to be a kind of moral action, since it is well-doing. Hence what is not capable of moral action cannot do anything by chance. Thus an inanimate thing or a lower animal or a child cannot do anything by chance, because it is incapable of deliberate intention; nor can 'good fortune' or 'ill fortune' be ascribed to them, except metaphorically, as Protarchus, for example, said that the stones of which altars are made are fortunate because they are held in honour, while their fellows are trodden under foot. Even these things, however, can in a way be affected by chance, when one who is dealing with them does something to them by chance, but not otherwise.

The spontaneous on the other hand is found both in the lower animals and in many inanimate objects. We say, for example, that the horse came 'spon-

taneously', because, though his coming saved him, he did not come for the sake
of safety. Again, the tripod fell 'of itself', because, though when it fell it stood
on its feet so as to serve for a seat, it did not fall for the sake of that.

Hence it is clear that events which (1) belong to the general class of
things that may come to pass for the sake of something, (2) do not come to
pass for the sake of what actually results, and (3) have an external cause, may
be described by the phrase 'from spontaneity'. These 'spontaneous' events are
said to be 'from chance' if they have the further characteristics of being the
objects of deliberate intention and due to agents capable of that mode of
action. This is indicated by the phrase 'in vain', which is used when A, which
is for the sake of B, does not result in B. For instance, taking a walk is for the
sake of evacuation of the bowels; if this does not follow after walking, we say
that we have walked 'in vain' and that the walking was 'vain'. This implies that
what is naturally the means to an end is 'in vain', when it does not effect the
end towards which it was the natural means—for it would be absurd for a man
to say that he had bathed in vain because the sun was not eclipsed, since the
one was not done with a view to the other. Thus the spontaneous is even
according to its derivation the case in which the thing itself happens in vain.
The stone that struck the man did not fall for the purpose of striking him;
therefore it fell spontaneously, because it might have fallen by the action of an
agent and for the purpose of striking. The difference between spontaneity and
what results by chance is greatest in things that come to be by nature; for when
anything comes to be contrary to nature, we do not say that it came to be by
chance, but by spontaneity. Yet strictly this too is different from the spontaneous proper; for the cause of the latter is external, that of the former internal.

We have now explained what chance is and what spontaneity is, and in
what they differ from each other. Both belong to the mode of causation 'source
of change', for either some natural or some intelligent agent is always the cause;
but in this sort of causation the number of possible causes is infinite.

Spontaneity and chance are causes of effects which, though they might
result from intelligence or nature, have in fact been caused by something
incidentally. Now since nothing which is incidental is prior to what is *per se*, it
is clear that no incidental cause can be prior to a cause *per se*. Spontaneity and
chance, therefore, are posterior to intelligence and nature. Hence, however true
it may be that the heavens are due to spontaneity, it will still be true that
intelligence and nature will be prior causes of this All and of many things in it
besides.

It is clear then that there are causes, and that the number of them is what
we have stated. The number is the same as that of the things comprehended
under the question 'why'. The 'why' is referred ultimately either (1), in things
which do not involve motion, e.g. in mathematics, to the 'what' (to the
definition of 'straight line' or 'commensurable', &c.), or (2) to what initiated a
motion, e.g. 'why did they go to war?—because there had been a raid'; or (3) we
are inquiring 'for the sake of what?'—'that they may rule'; or (4), in the case of
things that come into being, we are looking for the matter. The causes, therefore, are these and so many in number.

Now, the causes being four, it is the business of the physicist to know about them all, and if he refers his problems back to all of them, he will assign the 'why' in the way proper to his science—the matter, the form, the mover, 'that for the sake of which'. The last three often coincide; for the 'what' and 'that for the sake of which' are one, while the primary source of motion is the same in species as these (for man generates man), and so too, in general, are all things which cause movement by being themselves moved; and such as are not of this kind are no longer inside the province of physics, for they cause motion not by possessing motion or a source of motion in themselves, but being themselves incapable of motion. Hence there are three branches of study, one of things which are incapable of motion, the second of things in motion, but indestructible, the third of destructible things.

The question 'why', then, is answered by reference to the matter, to the form, and to the primary moving cause. For in respect of coming to be it is mostly in this last way that causes are investigated—'what comes to be after what? what was the primary agent or patient?' and so at each step of the series.

Now the principles which cause motion in a physical way are two, of which one is not physical, as it has no principle of motion in itself. Of this kind is whatever causes movement, not being itself moved, such as (1) that which is completely unchangeable, the primary reality, and (2) the essence of that which is coming to be, i.e. the form; for this is the end or 'that for the sake of which'. Hence since nature is for the sake of something, we must know this cause also. We must explain the 'why' in all the senses of the term, namely, (1) that from this that will necessarily result ('from this' either without qualification or in most cases); (2) that 'this must be so if that is to be so' (as the conclusion presupposes the premises); (3) that this was the essence of the thing; and (4) because it is better thus (not without qualification, but with reference to the essential nature in each case).

We must explain then (1) that Nature belongs to the class of causes which act for the sake of something; (2) about the necessary and its place in physical problems, for all writers ascribe things to this cause, arguing that since the hot and the cold, &c., are of such and such a kind, therefore certain things *necessarily* are and come to be—and if they mention any other cause (one[5] his 'friendship and strife', another[6] his 'mind'), it is only to touch on it, and then good-bye to it.

A difficulty presents itself: why should not nature work, not for the sake of something, nor because it is better so, but just as the sky rains, not in order to make the corn grow, but of necessity? What is drawn up must cool, and what has been cooled must become water and descend, the result of this being that the corn grows. Similarly if a man's crop is spoiled on the threshing-floor, the rain did not fall for the sake of this—in order that the crop might be spoiled —but that result just followed. Why then should it not be the same with the parts in nature, e.g. that our teeth should come up *of necessity*—the front teeth

---

5 Empedocles.
6 Anaxagoras.

sharp, fitted for tearing, the molars broad and useful for grinding down the food—since they did not arise for this end, but it was merely a coincident result; and so with all other parts in which we suppose that there is purpose? Wherever then all the parts came about just what they would have been if they had come to be for an end, such things survived, being organized spontaneously in a fitting way; whereas those which grew otherwise perished and continue to perish, as Empedocles says his 'man-faced ox-progeny' did.

Such are the arguments (and others of the kind) which may cause difficulty on this point. Yet it is impossible that this should be the true view. For teeth and all other natural things either invariably or normally come about in a given way; but of not one of the results of chance or spontaneity is this true. We do not ascribe to chance or mere coincidence the frequency of rain in winter, but frequent rain in summer we do; nor heat in the dog-days, but only if we have it in winter. If then, it is agreed that things are either the result of coincidence or for an end, and these cannot be the result of coincidence or spontaneity, it follows that they must be for an end; and that such things are all due to nature even the champions of the theory which is before us would agree. Therefore action for an end is present in things which come to be and are by nature.

Further, where a series has a completion, all the proceding steps are for the sake of that. Now surely as in intelligent action, so in nature; and as in nature, so it is in each action, if nothing interferes. Now intelligent action is for the sake of an end; therefore the nature of things also is so. Thus if a house, e.g., had been a thing made by nature, it would have been made in the same way as it is now by art; and if things made by nature were made also by art, they would come to be in the same way as by nature. Each step then in the series is for the sake of the next; and generally art partly completes what nature cannot bring to a finish, and partly imitates her. If, therefore, artificial products are for the sake of an end, so clearly also are natural products. The relation of the later to the earlier terms of the series is the same in both.

This is most obvious in the animals other than man: they make things neither by art nor after inquiry or deliberation. Wherefore people discuss whether it is by intelligence or by some other faculty that these creatures work, spiders, ants, and the like. By gradual advance in this direction we come to see clearly that in plants too that is produced which is conducive to the end—leaves, e.g. grow to provide shade for the fruit. If then it is both by nature and for an end that the swallow makes its nest and the spider its web, and plants grow leaves for the sake of the fruit and send their roots down (not up) for the sake of nourishment, it is plain that this kind of cause is operative in things which come to be and are by nature. And since 'nature' means two things, the matter and the form, of which the latter is the end, and since all the rest is for the sake of the end, the form must be the cause in the sense of 'that for the sake of which'.

Now mistakes come to pass even in the operations of art: the grammarian makes a mistake in writing and the doctor pours out the wrong dose. Hence clearly mistakes are possible in the operations of nature also. If then in art there are cases in which what is rightly produced serves a purpose, and if where mistakes occur there was a purpose in what was attempted, only it was not attained, so must it be also in natural products, and monstrosities will be failures in the purposive effort. Thus in the original combinations the 'ox-progeny' if they failed to reach a determinate end must have arisen through the corruption of some principle corresponding to what is now the seed.

Further, seed must have come into being first, and not straightway the animals: the words 'whole-natured first . . .'[7] must have meant seed.

Again, in plants too we find the relation of means to end, though the degree of organization is less. Were there then in plants also 'olive-headed vine-progeny', like the 'man-headed ox-progeny', or not? An absurd suggestion; yet there must have been, if there were such things among animals.

Moreover, among the seeds anything must have come to be at random. But the person who asserts this entirely does away with 'nature' and what exists 'by nature'. For those things are natural which, by a continuous movement originated from an internal principle, arrive at some completion: the same completion is not reached from every principle; nor any chance completion, but always the tendency in each is towards the same end, if there is no impediment.

The end and the means towards it may come about by chance. We say, for instance, that a stranger has come by chance, paid the ransom, and gone away, when he does so as if he had come for that purpose, though it was not for that that he came. This is incidental, for chance is an incidental cause. . . . But when an event takes place always or for the most part, it is not incidental or by chance. In natural products the sequence is invariable, if there is no impediment.

It is absurd to suppose that purpose is not present because we do not observe the agent deliberating. Art does not deliberate. If the ship-building art were in the wood, it would produce the same results *by nature*. If, therefore, purpose is present in art, it is present also in nature. The best illustration is a doctor doctoring himself: nature is like that.

It is plain then that nature is a cause, a cause that operates for a purpose.

As regards what is 'of necessity', we must ask whether the necessity is 'hypothetical', or 'simple' as well. The current view places what is of necessity in the process of production, just as if one were to suppose that the wall of a house necessarily comes to be because what is heavy is naturally carried downwards and what is light to the top, wherefore the stones and foundations take the lowest place, with earth above because it is lighter, and wood at the top of all as being the lightest. Whereas, though the wall does not come to be *without* these, it is not *due* to these, except as its material cause: it comes to be for the sake of sheltering and guarding certain things. Similarly in all other things which involve production for an end; the product cannot come to be without things which have a necessary nature, but it is not due to these (except as its material); it comes to be for an end. For instance, why is a saw such as it is? To effect so-and-so and for the sake of so-and-so. This end, however, cannot be realized unless the saw is made of iron. It is, therefore, necessary for it to be of

___
[7] Empedocles.

iron, *if* we are to have a saw and perform the operation of sawing. What is necessary then, is necessary *on a hypothesis*; it is not a result necessarily determined by antecedents. Necessity is in the matter, while 'that for the sake of which' is in the definition.

Necessity in mathematics is in a way similar to necessity in things which come to be through the operation of nature. Since a straight line is what it is, it is necessary that the angles of a triangle should equal two right angles. But not conversely; though if the angles are *not* equal to two right angles, then the straight line is not what it is either. But in things which come to be for an end, the reverse is true. If the end is to exist or does exist, that also which precedes it will exist or does exist; otherwise just as there, if the conclusion is not true, the premiss will not be true, so here the end or 'that for the sake of which' will not exist. For this too is itself a starting-point, but of the reasoning, not of the action; while in mathematics the starting-point is the starting point of the reasoning only, as there is no action. If then there is to be a house, such-and-such things must be made or be there already or exist, or generally the matter relative to the end, bricks and stones if it is a house. But the end is not due to these except as the matter, nor will it come to exist because of them. Yet if they do not exist at all, neither will the house, or the saw—the former in the absence of stones, the latter in the absence of iron—just as in the other case the premisses will not be true, if the angles of the triangle are not equal to two right angles.

The necessary in nature, then, is plainly what we call by the name of matter, and the changes in it. Both causes must be stated by the physicist, but especially the end; for that is the cause of the matter, not *vice versa*; and the end is 'that for the sake of which', and the beginning starts from the definition or essence; as in artificial products, since a house is of such-and-such a kind, certain things must *necessarily* come to be or be there already, or since health is this, these things must necessarily come to be or be there already. Similarly if man is this, then these; if these, then those. Perhaps the necessary is present also in the definition. For if one defines the operation of sawing as being a certain kind of dividing, then this cannot come about unless the saw has teeth of a certain kind; and these cannot be unless it is of iron. For in the definition too there are some parts that are, as it were, its matter.

6

David Hume
Cause and Effect

. . .

Of Probability; and of the Idea of Cause and Effect

. . .

All kinds of reasoning consist in nothing but a *comparison*, and a discovery of those relations, either constant or inconstant, which two or more objects bear to each other. This comparison we may make, either when both the objects are present to the senses, or when neither of them is present, or when only one. When both the objects are present to the senses along with the relation, we call *this* perception rather than reasoning; nor is there in this case any exercise of the thought, or any action, properly speaking, but a mere passive admission of the impressions thro' the organs of sensation. According to this way of thinking, we ought not to receive as reasoning any of the observations we may make concerning *identity*, and the *relations* of *time* and *place*; since in none of them the mind can go beyond what is immediately present to the senses, either to discover the real existence or the relations of objects. 'Tis only *causation*, which produces such a connexion, as to give us assurance from the existence or action of one object, that 'twas follow'd or preceded by any other existence or action; nor can the other two relations be ever made use of in reasoning, except so far as they either affect or are affected by it. There is nothing in any objects to persuade us, that they are either always *remote* or always *contiguous*; and when from experience and observation we discover, that their relation in this particular is invariable, we always conclude there is some secret *cause*, which separates or unites them. The same reasoning extends to *identity*. We readily suppose an object may continue individually the same, tho' several times absent from and present to the senses; and ascribe to it an identity, notwithstanding the interruption of the perception, whenever we conclude, that if we had kept our eye or hand constantly upon it, it wou'd have convey'd an invariable and un-interrupted perception. But this conclusion beyond the impressions of our senses can be founded only on the connexion of *cause and effect*; nor can we otherwise have any security, that the object is not chang'd upon us, however much the new object may resemble that which was formerly present to the senses. When-ever we discover such a perfect resemblance, we consider, whether it be common in that species of objects; whether possibly or probably any cause cou'd operate in producing the change and resemblance; and according as we determine

From David Hume, A *Treatise of Human Nature*, L. A. Selby-Bigge, ed. (Oxford: The Clarendon Press, 1888), Book I, Part III, Secs. 2–3, pp. 73–82, by permission of The Oxford University Press.

concerning these causes and effects, we form our judgment concerning the identity of the object.

Here then it appears, that of those three relations, which depend not upon the mere ideas, the only one, that can be trac'd beyond our senses, and informs us of existences and objects, which we do not see or feel, is *causation*. This relation, therefore, we shall endeavour to explain fully before we leave the subject of the understanding.

To begin regularly, we must consider the idea of *causation*, and see from what origin it is deriv'd. 'Tis impossible to reason justly, without understanding perfectly the idea concerning which we reason; and 'tis impossible perfectly to understand any idea, without tracing it up to its origin, and examining that primary impression, from which it arises. The examination of the impression bestows a clearness on the idea; and the examination of the idea bestows a like clearness on all our reasoning.

Let us therefore cast our eye on any two objects, which we call cause and effect, and turn them on all sides, in order to find that impression, which produces an idea of such prodigious consequence. At first sight I perceive, that I must not search for it in any of the particular *qualities* of the objects; since, which-ever of these qualities I pitch on, I find some object, that is not possest of it, and yet falls under the denomination of cause or effect. And indeed there is nothing existent, either externally or internally, which is not to be consider'd either as a cause or an effect; tho' 'tis plain there is no one quality, which universally belongs to all beings, and gives them a title to that denomination.

The idea, then, of causation must be deriv'd from some *relation* among objects; and that relation we must now endeavour to discover. I find in the first place, that whatever objects are consider'd as causes or effects, are *contiguous*; and that nothing can operate in a time or place, which is ever so little remov'd from those of its existence. Tho' distant objects may sometimes seem productive of each other, they are commonly found upon examination to be link'd by a chain of causes, which are contiguous among themselves, and to the distant objects; and when in any particular instance we cannot discover this connexion, we still presume it to exist. We may therefore consider the relation of CON-TIGUITY as essential to that of causation; at least may suppose it such, according to the general opinion, till we can find a more proper occasion to clear up this matter, by examining what objects are or are not susceptible of juxtaposition and conjunction.

The second relation I shall observe as essential to causes and effects is not so universally acknowledg'd, but is liable to some controversy. 'Tis that of PRIORITY of time in the cause before the effect. Some pretend that 'tis not absolutely necessary a cause shou'd precede its effect; but that any object or action, in the very first moment of its existence, may exert its productive quality, and give rise to another object or action, perfectly co-temporary with itself. But beside that experience in most instances seems to contradict this opinion, we may establish the relation of priority by a kind of inference or reasoning. 'Tis an establish'd maxim both in natural and moral philosophy, that an object, which exists for any time in its full perfection without producing another, is not its sole cause; but is assisted by some other principle, which pushes it from its state of inactivity, and makes it exert that energy, of which it was secretly possest. Now if any cause may be perfectly co-temporary with its effect, 'tis certain, according to this maxim, that they must all of them be so; since any one of them, which retards its operation for a single moment, exerts not itself at that very individual time, in which it might have operated; and therefore is no proper cause. The consequence of this wou'd be no less than the destruction of that succession of causes, which we observe in the world; and indeed, the utter annihilation of time. For if one cause were co-temporary with its effect, and this effect with *its* effect, and so on, 'tis plain there wou'd be no such thing as succession, and all objects must be co-existent.

If this argument appear satisfactory, 'tis well. If not, I beg the reader to allow me the same liberty, which I have us'd in the preceding case, of supposing it such. For he shall find, that the affair is of no great importance.

Having thus discover'd or suppos'd the two relations of *contiguity* and *succession* to be essential to causes and effects, I find I am stopt short, and can proceed no farther in considering any single instance of cause and effect. Motion in one body is regarded upon impulse as the cause of motion in another. When we consider these objects with the utmost attention, we find only that the one body approaches the other; and that the motion of it precedes that of the other, but without any sensible interval. 'Tis in vain to rack ourselves with *farther* thought and reflexion upon this subject. We can go no *farther* in considering this particular instance.

Shou'd any one leave this instance, and pretend to define a cause, by saying it is something productive of another, 'tis evident he wou'd say nothing. For what does he mean by *production?* Can he give any definition of it, that will not be the same with that of causation? If he can; I desire it may be produc'd. If he cannot; he here runs in a circle, and gives a synonymous term instead of a definition.

Shall we then rest contented with these two relations of contiguity and succession, as affording a compleat idea of causation? By no means. An object may be contiguous and prior to another, without being consider'd as its cause. There is a NECESSARY CONNEXION to be taken into consideration; and that relation is of much greater importance, than any of the other two above-mention'd.

Here again I turn the object on all sides, in order to discover the nature of this necessary connexion, and find the impression, or impressions, from which its idea may be deriv'd. When I cast my eye on the *known qualities* of objects, I immediately discover that the relation of cause and effect depends not in the least on *them*. When I consider their *relations*, I can find none but those of contiguity and succession; which I have already regarded as imperfect and unsatisfactory. Shall the despair of success make me assert, that I am here possest of an idea, which is not preceded by any similar impression? This wou'd be too strong a proof of levity and inconstancy; since the contrary principle has been already so firmly establish'd, as to admit of no farther doubt; at least, till we have more fully examin'd the present difficulty.

We must, therefore, proceed like those, who being in search of any thing that lies conceal'd from them, and not finding it in the place they expected, beat about all the neighbouring fields, without any certain view or design, in hopes their good fortune will at last guide them to what they search for. 'Tis necessary for us to leave the direct survey of this question concerning the nature of that *necessary connexion,* which enters into our idea of cause and effect; and endeavour to find some other questions, the examination of which will perhaps afford a hint, that may serve to clear up the present difficulty. Of these questions there occur two, which I shall proceed to examine, *viz.*

First, For what reason we pronounce it *necessary,* that every thing whose existence has a beginning, shou'd also have a cause?

Secondly, Why we conclude, that such particular causes must *necessarily* have such particular effects; and what is the nature of that *inference* we draw from the one to the other, and to the *belief* we repose in it?

I shall only observe before I proceed any farther, that tho' the ideas of cause and effect be deriv'd from the impressions of reflexion as well as from those of sensation, yet for brevity's sake, I commonly mention only the latter as the origin of these ideas; tho' I desire that whatever I say of them may also extend to the former. Passions are connected with their objects and with one another; no less than external bodies are connected together. The same relation, then, of cause and effect, which belongs to one, must be common to all of them.

Why a Cause Is Always Necessary

To begin with the first question concerning the necessity of a cause: 'Tis a general maxim in philosophy, that *whatever begins to exist, must have a cause of existence.* This is commonly taken for granted in all reasonings, without any proof given or demanded. 'Tis suppos'd to be founded on intuition, and to be one of those maxims, which tho' they may be deny'd with the lips, 'tis impossible for men in their hearts really to doubt of. But if we examine this maxim by the idea of knowledge above-explain'd, we shall discover in it no mark of any such intuitive certainty; but on the contrary shall find, that 'tis of a nature quite foreign to that species of conviction.

All certainty arises from the comparison of ideas, and from the discovery of such relations as are unalterable, so long as the ideas continue the same. These relations are *resemblance, proportions in quantity and number, degrees of any quality, and contrariety;* none of which are imply'd in this proposition, *Whatever has a beginning has also a cause of existence.* That proposition therefore is not intuitively certain. At least any one, who wou'd assert it to be intuitively certain, must deny these to be the only infallible relations, and must find some other relation of that kind to be imply'd in it; which it will then be time enough to examine.

But here is an argument, which proves at once, that the foregoing proposition is neither intuitively nor demonstrably certain. We can never demonstrate the necessity of a cause to every new existence, or new modification of existence, without shewing at the same time the impossibility there is, that any thing can ever begin to exist without some productive principle; and where the latter proposition cannot be prov'd, we must despair of ever being able to prove the former. Now that the latter proposition is utterly incapable of a demonstrative proof, we may satisfy ourselves by considering, that as all distinct ideas are separable from each other, and as the ideas of cause and effect are evidently distinct, 'twill be easy for us to conceive any object to be non-existent this moment, and existent the next, without conjoining to it the distinct idea of a cause or productive principle. The separation, therefore, of the idea of a cause from that of a beginning of existence, is plainly possible for the imagination; and consequently the actual separation of these objects is so far possible, that it implies no contradiction nor absurdity; and is therefore incapable of being refuted by any reasoning from mere ideas; without which 'tis impossible to demonstrate the necessity of a cause.

Accordingly we shall find upon examination, that every demonstration, which has been produc'd for the necessity of a cause, is fallacious and sophistical. All the points of time and place, say some philosophers [Mr. (Thomas—Ed.) Hobbes], in which we can suppose any object to begin to exist, are in themselves equal; and unless there be some cause, which is peculiar to one time and to one place, and which by that means determines and fixes the existence, it must remain in eternal suspense; and the object can never begin to be, for want of something to fix its beginning. But I ask; Is there any more difficulty in supposing the time and place to be fix'd without a cause, than to suppose the existence to be determin'd in that manner? The first question that occurs on this subject is always, *whether* the object shall exist or not: The next, *when* and *where* it shall begin to exist. If the removal of a cause be intuitively absurd in the one case, it must be so in the other: And if that absurdity be not clear without a proof in the one case, it will equally require one in the other. The absurdity, then, of the one supposition can never be a proof of that of the other; since they are both upon the same footing, and must stand or fall by the same reasoning.

The second argument [Dr. (Samuel—Ed.) Clarke and others], which I find us'd on this head, labours under an equal difficulty. Every thing, 'tis said, must have a cause; for if any thing wanted a cause, *it* wou'd produce *itself*; that is, exist before it existed; which is impossible. But this reasoning is plainly unconclusive; because it supposes, that in our denial of a cause we still grant what we expressly deny, *viz.* that there must be a cause; which therefore is taken to be the object itself; and *that*, no doubt, is an evident contradiction. But to say that any thing is produc'd, or to express myself more properly, comes into existence, without a cause, is not to affirm, that 'tis itself its own cause; but on the contrary in excluding all external causes, excludes *a fortiori* [in effect—Ed.] the thing itself which is created. An object, that exists absolutely without any cause, certainly is not its own cause; and when you assert, that the one follows from the other, you suppose the very point in question, and take it for granted, that 'tis utterly impossible any thing can ever begin to exist without a cause, but that upon the exclusion of one productive principle, we must still have recourse to another.

'Tis exactly the same case with the third argument [Mr. (John—Ed.) Locke], which has been employ'd to demonstrate the necessity of a cause. Whatever is produc'd without any cause, is produc'd by *nothing*; or in other words, has nothing for its cause. But nothing can never be a cause, no more than it can be something, or equal to two right angles. By the same intuition, that we perceive nothing not to be equal to two right angles, or not to be something, we perceive, that it can never be a cause; and consequently must perceive, that every object has a real cause of its existence.

I believe it will not be necessary to employ many words in shewing the weakness of this argument, after what I have said of the foregoing. They are all of them founded on the same fallacy, and are deriv'd from the same turn of thought. 'Tis sufficient only to observe, that when we exclude all causes we really do exclude them, and neither suppose nothing nor the object itself to be the causes of the existence; and consequently can draw no argument from the absurdity of these suppositions to prove the absurdity of that exclusion. If every thing must have a cause, it follows, that upon the exclusion of other causes we must accept of the object itself or of nothing as causes. But 'tis the very point in question, whether every thing must have a cause or not; and therefore, according to all just reasoning, it ought never to be taken for granted.

They are still more frivolous, who say, that every effect must have a cause; because 'tis imply'd in the very idea of effect. Every effect necessarily pre-supposes a cause; effect being a relative term, of which cause is the correlative. But this does not prove, that every being must be preceded by a cause; no more than it follows, because every husband must have a wife, that therefore every man must be marry'd. The true state of the question is, whether every object, which begins to exist, must owe its existence to a cause; and this I assert neither to be intuitively nor demonstratively certain, and hope to have prov'd it sufficiently by the foregoing arguments.

.   .   .

7

John Stuart Mill
Of Liberty and Necessity

The question, whether the law of causality applies in the same strict sense to human actions as to other phenomena, is the celebrated controversy concerning the freedom of the will; which, from at least as far back as the time of Pelagius, has divided both the philosophical and the religious world. The affirmative opinion is commonly called the doctrine of Necessity, as asserting human volitions and actions to be necessary and inevitable. The negative maintains that the will is not determined, like other phenomena, by antecedents, but determines itself; that our volitions are not, properly speaking, the effects of causes, or at least have no causes which they uniformly and implicitly obey.

I have already made it sufficiently apparent that the former of these opinions is that which I consider the true one; but the misleading terms in which it is often expressed, and the indistinct manner in which it is usually apprehended, have both obstructed its reception, and perverted its influence when received. The metaphysical theory of free-will, as held by philosophers (for the practical feeling of it, common in a greater or less degree to all mankind, is in no way inconsistent with the contrary theory), was invented because the supposed alternative of admitting human actions to be *necessary* was deemed inconsistent with every one's instinctive consciousness, as well as humiliating to the pride and even degrading to the moral nature of man. Nor do I deny that the doctrine, as sometimes held, is open to these imputations; for the misapprehension in which I shall be able to show that they originate, unfortunately is not confined to the opponents of the doctrine, but is participated in by many, perhaps we might say by most, of its supporters.

Correctly conceived, the doctrine called Philosophical Necessity is simply this: that, given the motives which are present to an individual's mind, and given likewise the character and disposition of the individual, the manner in which he will act might be unerringly inferred; that if we knew the person thoroughly, and knew all the inducements which are acting upon him, we could foretell his conduct with as much certainty as we can predict any physical event. This proposition I take to be a mere interpretation of universal experience, a statement in words of what every one is internally convinced of. No one who believed that he knew thoroughly the circumstances of any case, and the characters of the different persons concerned, would hesitate to foretell how all of them would act. Whatever degree of doubt he may in fact feel,

From John Stuart Mill, A *System of Logic*, 8th ed. (New York: Harper & Bros., 1874), Book VI, Chap. II, pp. 581–586.

arises from the uncertainty whether he really knows the circumstances, or the character of some one or other of the persons, with the degree of accuracy required; but by no means from thinking that if he did know these things, there could be any uncertainty what the conduct would be. Nor does this full assurance conflict in the smallest degree with what is called our feeling of freedom. We do not feel ourselves the less free, because those to whom we are intimately known are well assured how we shall will to act in a particular case. We often, on the contrary, regard the doubt what our conduct will be, as a mark of ignorance of our character, and sometimes even resent it as an imputation. The religious metaphysicians who have asserted the freedom of the will, have always maintained it to be consistent with divine foreknowledge of our actions: and if with divine, then with any other foreknowledge. We may be free, and yet another may have reason to be perfectly certain what use we shall make of our freedom. It is not, therefore, the doctrine that our volitions and actions are invariable consequents of our antecedent states of mind, that is either contradicted by our consciousness, or felt to be degrading.

But the doctrine of causation, when considered as obtaining between our volitions and their antecedents, is almost universally conceived as involving more than this. Many do not believe, and very few practically feel, that there is nothing in causation but invariable, certain, and unconditional sequence. There are few to whom mere constancy of succession appears a sufficiently stringent bond of union for so peculiar a relation as that of cause and effect. Even if the reason repudiates, the imagination retains, the feeling of some more intimate connection, of some peculiar tie, or mysterious constraint exercised by the antecedent over the consequent. Now this it is which, considered as applying to the human will, conflicts with our consciousness, and revolts our feelings. We are certain that, in the case of our volitions, there is not this mysterious constraint. We know that we are not compelled, as by a magical spell, to obey any particular motive. We feel, that if we wished to prove that we have the power of resisting the motive, we could do so (that wish being, it needs scarcely be observed, a *new antecedent*); and it would be humiliating to our pride, and (what is of more importance) paralyzing to our desire of excellence, if we thought otherwise. But neither is any such mysterious compulsion now supposed, by the best philosophical authorities, to be exercised by any other cause over its effect. Those who think that causes draw their effects after them by a mystical tie, are right in believing that the relation between volitions and their antecedents is of another nature. But they could go farther, and admit that this is also true of all other effects and their antecedents. If such a tie is considered to be involved in the word Necessity, the doctrine is not true of human actions; but neither is it then true of inanimate objects. It would be more correct to say that matter is not bound by necessity, than that mind is so.

That the free-will metaphysicians, being mostly of the school which rejects [David—Ed.] Hume's and [Thomas—Ed.] Brown's analysis of Cause and Effect, should miss their way for want of the light which that analysis affords, can not surprise us. The wonder is, that the necessitarians, who usually admit that philosophical theory, should in practice equally lose sight of it. The very same misconception of the doctrine called Philosophical Necessity, which prevents the opposite party from recognizing its truth, I believe to exist more or less obscurely in the minds of most necessitarians, however they may in words disavow it. I am much mistaken if they habitually feel that the necessity which they recognize in actions is but uniformity of order, and capability of being predicted. They have a feeling as if there were at bottom a stronger tie between the volitions and their causes; as if, when they asserted that the will is governed by the balance of motives, they meant something more cogent than if they had only said, that whoever knew the motives, and our habitual susceptibilities to them, could predict how we should will to act. They commit, in opposition to their own scientific system, the very same mistake which their adversaries commit in obedience to theirs; and in consequence do really in some instances suffer those depressing consequences which their opponents erroneously impute to the doctrine itself.

I am inclined to think that this error is almost wholly an effect of the associations with a word, and that it would be prevented, by forbearing to employ, for the expression of the simple fact of causation, so extremely inappropriate a term as Necessity. That word, in its other acceptations, involves much more than mere uniformity of sequence: it implies irresistibleness. Applied to the will, it only means that the given cause will be followed by the effect, subject to all possibilities of counter-action by other causes; but in common use it stands for the operation of those causes exclusively which are supposed too powerful to be counter-acted at all. When we say that all human actions take place of necessity, we only mean that they will certainly happen if nothing prevents; when we say that dying of want, to those who can not get food, is a necessity, we mean that it will certainly happen whatever may be done to prevent it. The application of the same term to the agencies on which human actions depend, as is used to express those agencies of nature which are really uncontrollable, can not fail, when habitual, to create a feeling of uncontrollableness in the former also. This, however, is a mere illusion. There are physical sequences which we call necessary, as death for want of food or air; there are others which, though as much cases of causation as the former, are not said to be necessary, as death from poison, which an antidote, or the use of the stomach-pump, will sometimes avert. It is apt to be forgotten by people's feelings, even if remembered by their understandings, that human actions are in this last predicament: they are never (except in some cases of mania) ruled by any one motive with such absolute sway that there is no room for the influence of any other. The causes, therefore, on which action depends, are never uncontrollable; and any given effect is only necessary provided that the causes tending to produce it are not controlled. That whatever happens, could not have happened otherwise, unless something had taken place which was capable of preventing it, no one surely needs hesitate to admit. But to call this by the name Necessity is to use the term in a sense so different from its primitive and familiar meaning, from that which it bears in the common occasions of life, as to amount almost to a play upon words. The associations derived from the ordinary sense of the term will adhere to it in spite of all we can do; and though the doctrine of Necessity, as stated by most who hold it, is very remote from fatalism, it is probable that most necessitarians are fatalists, more or less, in their feelings.

A fatalist believes, or half believes (for nobody is a consistent fatalist), not only that whatever is about to happen will be the infallible result of the causes which produce it (which is the true necessitarian doctrine), but moreover that there is no use in struggling against it; that it will happen, however we may strive to prevent it. Now, a necessitarian, believing that our actions follow from our characters, and that our characters follow from our organization, our education, and our circumstances, is apt to be, with more or less of consciousness on his part, a fatalist as to his own actions, and to believe that his nature is such, or that his education and circumstances have so moulded his character, that nothing can now prevent him from feeling and acting in a particular way, or at least that no effort of his own can hinder it. In the words of the sect which in our own day has most perseveringly inculcated and most perversely misunderstood this great doctrine, his character is formed *for* him, and not *by* him; therefore his wishing that it had been formed differently is of no use; he has no power to alter it. But this is a grand error. He has, to a certain extent, a power to alter his character. Its being, in the ultimate resort, formed for him, is not inconsistent with its being, in part, formed *by* him as one of the intermediate agents. His character is formed by his circumstances (including among these his particular organization); but his own desire to mould it in a particular way, is one of those circumstances, and by no means one of the least influential. We can not, indeed, directly will to be different from what we are. But neither did those who are supposed to have formed our characters directly will that we should be what we are. Their will had no direct power except over their own actions. They made us what they did make us, by willing, not the end, but the requisite means; and we, when our habits are not too inveterate, can, by similarly willing the requisite means, make ourselves different. If they could place us under the influence of certain circumstances, we, in like manner, can place ourselves under the influence of other circumstances. We are exactly as capable of making our own character, *if we will*, as others are of making it for us.

Yes (answers the Owenite), but these words, "if we will," surrender the whole point: since the will to alter our own character is given us, not by any effort of ours, but by circumstances which we can not help, it comes to us either from external causes, or not at all. Most true: if the Owenite stops here, he is in a position from which nothing can expel him. Our character is formed by us as well as for us; but the wish which induces us to attempt to form it is formed for us; and how? Not, in general, by our organization, nor wholly by our education, but by our experience; experience of the painful consequences of the character we previously had; or by some strong feeling of admiration or aspiration, accidentally aroused. But to think that we have no power of altering our character, and to think that we shall not use our power unless we desire to use it, are very different things, and have a very different effect on the mind. A person who does not wish to alter his character, can not be the person who is supposed to feel discouraged or paralyzed by thinking himself unable to do it. The depressing effect of the fatalist doctrine can only be felt where there *is* a wish to do what that doctrine represents as impossible. It is of no consequence what we think forms our character, when we have no desire of our own about forming it; but it is of great consequence that we should not be prevented from forming such a desire by thinking the attainment impracticable, and that if we have the desire, we should know that the work is not so irrevocably done as to be incapable of being altered.

And indeed, if we examine closely, we shall find that this feeling, of our being able to modify our own character *if we wish*, is itself the feeling of moral freedom which we are conscious of. A person feels morally free who feels that his habits or his temptations are not his masters, but he theirs; who, even in yielding to them, knows that he could resist; that were he desirous of altogether throwing them off, there would not be required for that purpose a stronger desire than he knows himself to be capable of feeling. It is of course necessary, to render our consciousness of freedom complete, that we should have succeeded in making our character all we have hitherto attempted to make it; for if we have wished and not attained, we have, to that extent, not power over our own character; we are not free. Or at least, we must feel that our wish, if not strong enough to alter our character, is strong enough to conquer our character when the two are brought into conflict in any particular case of conduct. And hence it is said with truth, that none but a person of confirmed virtue is completely free.

The application of so improper a term as Necessity to the doctrine of cause and effect in the matter of human character, seems to me one of the most signal instances in philosophy of the abuse of terms, and its practical consequences one of the most striking examples of the power of language over our associations. The subject will never be generally understood until that objectionable term is dropped. The free-will doctrine, by keeping in view precisely that portion of the truth which the word Necessity puts out of sight, namely the power of the mind to co-operate in the formation of its own character, has given to its adherents a practical feeling much nearer to the truth than has generally (I believe) existed in the minds of necessitarians. The latter may have had a stronger sense of the importance of what human beings can do to shape the characters of one another; but the free-will doctrine has, I believe, fostered in its supporters a much stronger spirit of self-culture.

There is still one fact which requires to be noticed (in addition to the existence of a power of self-formation) before the doctrine of the causation of human actions can be freed from the confusion and misapprehensions which surround it in many minds. When the will is said to be determined by motives, a motive does not mean always, or solely, the anticipation of a pleasure or of a pain. I shall not here inquire whether it be true that, in the commencement, all our voluntary actions are mere means consciously employed to obtain some pleasure or avoid some pain. It is at least certain that we gradually, through the influence of association, come to desire the means without thinking of the end; the action itself becomes an object of desire, and is performed without reference to any motive beyond itself. Thus far, it may still be objected that, the action having through association become pleasurable, we are, as much as before, moved to act by the anticipation of a pleasure, namely, the pleasure of the action itself. But granting this, the matter does not end here. As we proceed in the formation of habits, and become accustomed to will a particular act or a particular course of conduct because it is pleasurable, we at last continue to will it without any reference to its being pleasurable. Although, from some change in us or in our circumstances, we have ceased to find any pleasure in the action, or perhaps to anticipate any pleasure as the consequence of it, we still continue to desire the action, and consequently to do it. In this manner it is that habits of hurtful excess continue to be practiced although they have ceased to be pleasurable; and in this manner also it is that the habit of willing to persevere in the course which he has chosen, does not desert the moral hero, even when the reward, however real, which he doubtless receives from the consciousness of well-doing, is any thing but an equivalent for the sufferings he undergoes, or the wishes which he may have to renounce.

A habit of willing is commonly called a purpose; and among the causes of our volitions, and of the actions which flow from them, must be reckoned not only likings and aversions, but also purposes. It is only when our purposes have become independent of the feelings of pain or pleasure from which they originally took their rise, that we are said to have a confirmed character. "A character," says Novalis, "is a completely fashioned will:" and the will, once so fashioned, may be steady and constant, when the passive susceptibilities of pleasure and pain are greatly weakened or materially changed.

With the corrections and explanations now given, the doctrine of the causation of our volitions by motives, and of motives by the desirable objects offered to us, combined with our particular susceptibilities of desire, may be considered, I hope, as sufficiently established for the purposes of this treatise.

8

Ernest Nagel

The Logical Character of Scientific Laws

Ernest Nagel was until his recent retirement Professor of Philosophy at Columbia University. He is an extraordinarily gifted lecturer, known for his detailed and dialectically skillful presentation of the systematic views of the principal contributors to the development of logic and the philosophy of science. He was a student and later a colleague of Morris Raphael Cohen's, and he was co-author with Cohen of the influential text An Introduction to Logic and Scientific Method *(1934). The realism of this he later repudiated in "Logic Without Ontology" (1944), influenced by the developments of logical empiricism.*

Nagel is primarily occupied with the nature and methods of science, which he construes generously. He was particularly active in examining the methodology of the social sciences, the nature and defensibility of teleological explanation, the coherence of Marxism as a scientific methodology, and the logic of historical explanation. His principal work is The Structure of Science *(1961), but he also contributed an early essay on measurement, another on probability, and a later well-known piece (written with James R. Newman),* Gödel's Proof *(1958).*

Nagel characteristically avoided speculation on matters that he saw as not germane to his principal concerns. This tended to make his account of the nature of science, particularly his picture of scientific laws and explanatory theories, best adapted to the smoother, more conventional periods of scientific development. He was inclined to avoid theorizing about the nature and conditions of meaning and changes in meaning and about the theory-laden nature of our observation language. Thus he did not bring his theories into explicit exchange with those who stressed changes through time in our conceptual system. He regarded himself as a naturalist in the tradition of John Dewey, confident about the comprehensive explanatory power of the laws of nature. But he is also regarded as a commonsense philosopher of science.

Accidental and Nomic Universality

The label 'law of nature' (or similar labels such as 'scientific law,' 'natural law,' or simply 'law') is not a technical term defined in any empirical science; and it is often used, especially in common discourse, with a strong honorific intent but without a precise import. There undoubtedly are many statements that are unhesitatingly characterized as 'laws' by most members of the scientific community, just as there is an even larger class of statements to which the label is rarely if ever applied. On the other hand, scientists disagree about the eligibility of many statements for the title of 'law of nature,' and the opinion of even one individual will often fluctuate on whether a given statement is to count as a law. This is patently the case for various theoretical statements . . . which are sometimes construed to be at bottom only procedural rules and therefore neither true nor false, although viewed by others as examples par excellence of laws of nature. Divergent opinions also exist as to whether statements of regularities containing any reference to particular individuals (or groups of such individuals) deserve the label of 'law.' For example, some writers have disputed the propriety of the designation for the statement that the planets move on elliptic orbits around the sun, since the statement mentions a particular body. Similar disagreements occur over the use of the label for statements of statistical regularities; and doubts have been expressed whether any formulation of uniformities in human social behavior (e.g., those studied in economics or linguistics) can properly be called 'laws.' The term 'law of nature' is undoubtedly vague. In consequence, any explication of its meaning which proposes a sharp demarcation between lawlike and non-lawlike statements is bound to be arbitrary.

There is therefore more than an appearance of futility in the recurring attempts to define with great logical precision what is a law of nature—attempts often based on the tacit premise that a statement is a law in virtue of its possessing an inherent "essence" which the definition must articulate. For not only is the term 'law' vague in its current usage, but its historical meaning has undergone many changes. We are certainly free to designate as a law of nature any statement we please. There is often little consistency in the way we apply the label, and whether or not a statement is *called* a law makes little difference in the way in which the statement may be used in scientific inquiry. Nevertheless, members of the scientific community agree fairly well on the applicability of the term for a considerable though vaguely delimited class of universal statements. Accordingly, there is some basis for the conjecture that the predication of the label, at least in those cases where the consensus is unmistakable, is controlled by a felt difference in the "objective" status and function of that class of statements. It would indeed be futile to attempt an ironclad and rigorously exclusive definition of 'natural law.' It is not unreasonable to indicate some of the more prominent grounds upon which a numerous class of statements is commonly assigned a special status.

The *prima facie* difference between lawlike and non-lawlike universal conditionals can be brought out in several ways. One effective way depends on first recalling in what manner modern formal logic construes statements that have the form of universal conditionals. Two points must be noted in this connection. Such statements are interpreted in modern logic to assert merely this: any individual fulfilling the conditions described in the antecedent clause of the conditional also fulfills, *as a matter of contingent fact*, the conditions described in the consequent clause. For example, in this interpretation the statement 'All crows are black' (which is usually transcribed to read 'For any *x*, if *x* is a crow then *x* is black') merely says that any individual thing which happens to exist whether in the past, present, or future and which satisfies the conditions for being a crow is in point of fact also black. Accordingly, the sense assigned to the statement by this interpretation is also conveyed by the equivalent assertions that there never was a crow that was not black, there is no such crow at present, and there never will be such a crow. Universal conditionals construed in this way, so that they assert only matter-of-fact connections, are sometimes said to formulate only a "constant conjunction" of traits and to express "accidental" or *de facto* universality.

The second point to be noted in this interpretation is an immediate consequence of the first. On this interpretation a universal conditional is true, provided that there are no things (in the omnitemporal sense of 'are') which satisfy the conditions stated in the antecedent clause. Thus, if there are no unicorns, then all unicorns are black; but also, if there are no unicorns, then all unicorns are red.[1] Accordingly, on the construction placed upon it in formal logic, a *de facto* [accidental—Ed.] universal conditional is true, irrespective of the content of its consequent clause, if in point of fact there happens to be nothing which satisfies its antecedent clause. Such a universal conditional is said to be "vacuously" true (or "vacuously satisfied").

Does a law of nature assert no more than accidental universality? The answer commonly given is in the negative. For a law is often held to express a "stronger" connection between antecedent and consequent conditions than just a matter-of-fact concomitance. Indeed, the connection is frequently said to involve some element of "necessity," though this alleged necessity is variously conceived and is described by such qualifying adjectives as 'logical,' 'causal,' 'physical,' or 'real.'[2] The contention is that to say that 'Copper always expands on heating' is a law of nature is to claim more than that there never has been and never will be a piece of heated copper that does not expand. To claim for that statement the status of a law is to assert, for example, not merely that there does not happen to exist such a piece of copper, but that it is "physically impossible" for such a piece of copper to exist. When the statement is assumed to be a law of nature, it is thus construed to assert that heating any piece of copper "physically necessitates" its expansion. Universal conditionals understood in this way are frequently described as "universals of law" or "nomological universals," and as expressing a "nomic" universality.

The distinction between accidental and nomic universality can be brought out in another way. Suppose that a piece of copper *c* which has never been heated is called to our attention, and is then destroyed so that it will never be heated. Suppose, further, that after the work of destruction is over we are

---

[1] This will be evident from the following: If there is no *x* such that *x* is a unicorn, then clearly there is no *x* such that *x* is a unicorn that is not black. But on the standard interpretation of the universal conditional, this latter statement immediately yields the conclusion that for any *x*, if *x* is a unicorn then *x* is black. Accordingly, if there are no unicorns then all unicorns are black.

It can also be shown that a universal conditional is true no matter what its antecedent clause may be, provided that everything of which the consequent clause can be significantly predicated satisfies the consequent clause. But we shall ignore any difficulties generated by this feature of universal conditionals.

[2] Cf. A. C. Ewing, *Idealism*, London, 1934, p. 167; C. I. Lewis, *An Analysis of Knowledge and Valuation*, La Salle, Ill., 1946, p. 228; Arthur W. Burks, "The Logic of Causal Propositions," *Mind*, Vol. 60 (1951), pp. 363–82.

asked whether c would have expanded had it been heated, and that we reply in the affirmative. And suppose, finally, that we are pressed for a reason for this answer. What reason can be advanced? A reason that would generally be accepted as cogent is that the natural law 'All copper when heated expands' warrants the contrary-to-fact conditional 'If c had been heated, it would have expanded.' Indeed, most people are likely to go further, and maintain that the nomological universal warrants the subjunctive conditional 'for any x, if x were copper and were heated, then x would expand.'

Laws of nature are in fact commonly used to justify subjunctive and contrary-to-fact conditionals, and such use is characteristic of all nomological universals. Moreover, this function of universals of law also suggests that the mere fact that nothing happens to exist (in the omnitemporal sense) which satisfies the antecedent clause of a nomological conditional is not sufficient to establish its truth. Thus, the assumption that the universe contains no bodies which are under the action of no external forces suffices to establish neither the subjunctive conditional that if there were such bodies their velocities would remain constant, nor the nomological universal that every body which is under the action of no external forces does not maintain a constant velocity.

On the other hand, the patently accidental universal 'All the screws in Smith's current car are rusty' does not justify the subjunctive conditional 'For any x, if x were a screw in Smith's current car x would be rusty.'[3] Certainly no one is likely to maintain on the strength of this *de facto* universal that, if a particular brass screw now resting on a dealer's shelf were inserted into Smith's car, that screw would be rusty. This *prima facie* difference between accidental and nomic universality can be briefly summarized by the formula: A universal of law "supports" a subjunctive conditional, while an accidental universal does not.

· · ·

Causal Laws

Something must finally be said about causal laws. It would be an ungrateful and pointless task to canvass even partially the variety of senses that have been attached to the word 'cause'—varying from the ancient legal associations of the word, through the popular conception of causes as efficient agents, to the more sophisticated modern notions of cause as invariable functional dependence. The fact that the term has this wide spectrum of uses immediately rules out the possibility that there is just one correct and privileged explication for it. It is nevertheless both possible and useful to identify one fairly definite meaning

---

[3] This subjunctive conditional is not to be construed as saying that if any screw were *identical with* one of the screws in Smith's car it would be rusty. The latter subjunctive conditional is clearly true if indeed all the screws in Smith's current car are rusty. The subjunctive conditional in the text is to be understood as saying that for any object x—whether or not it is identical with one of the screws now in Smith's car—if x were a screw in that car it would be rusty.

associated with the word in many areas of science as well as in ordinary discourse, with a view to obtaining from this perspective a rough classification of laws that serve as premises in explanations. On the other hand, it would be a mistake to suppose that, because in one meaning of the word the notion of cause plays an important role in some field of inquiry, the notion is indispensable in all other fields—just as it would be an error to maintain that, because this notion is useless in certain parts of science, it cannot have a legitimate role in other divisions of scientific study.

The sense of 'cause' we wish to identify is illustrated by the following example. An electric spark is passed through a mixture of hydrogen and oxygen gas; the explosion that follows the passage of the spark is accompanied by the disappearance of the gases and the condensation of water vapor. The disappearance of the gases and the formation of water in this experiment are commonly said to be the effects that are caused by the spark. Moreover, the generalization based on such experiments (e.g., 'Whenever a spark passes through a mixture of hydrogen and oxygen gas, the gases disappear and water is formed') is called a "causal law."

The law is said to be a causal one apparently because the relation it formulates between the events mentioned supposedly satisfies four conditions. In the first place, the relation is an invariable or uniform one, in the sense that whenever the alleged cause occurs so does the alleged effect. There is, moreover, the common tacit assumption that the cause constitutes both a necessary and a sufficient condition for the occurrence of the effect. In point of fact, however, most of the causal imputations made in everyday affairs, as well as most of the causal laws frequently mentioned, do not state the sufficient conditions for the occurrence of the effect. Thus, we often say that striking a match is the cause of its bursting into flame, and tacitly assume that other conditions without which the effect would not occur (e.g., presence of oxygen, a dry match) are also present. The event frequently picked out as the cause is normally an event that completes the set of sufficient conditions for the occurrence of the effect, and that is regarded for various reasons as being "important." In the second place, the relation holds between events that are spatially contiguous, in the sense that the spark and the formation of water occur in approximately the same spatial region. Accordingly, when events spatially remote from each other are alleged to be causally related, it is tacitly assumed that these events are but termini in a cause-and-effect chain of events, where the linking events are spatially contiguous. In the third place, the relation has a temporal character, in the sense that the event said to be the cause precedes the effect and is also "continuous" with the latter. In consequence, when events separated by a temporal interval are said to be causally related, they are also assumed to be connected by a series of temporally adjacent and causally related events. And finally, the relation is asymmetrical, in the sense that the passage of the spark through the mixture of gases is the cause of their transformation into water, but the formation of the water is not the cause of the passage of the spark.

The ideas in terms of which this notion of cause are stated have been frequently criticized as being vague, and telling objections have been made in particular against the common-sense conceptions of spatial and temporal continuity, on the ground that they contain a nest of confusions. It is undoubtedly true, moreover, that in some of the advanced sciences such as mathematical physics this notion is quite superfluous; and it is even debatable whether the four conditions just mentioned are in fact fulfilled in alleged illustrations of this notion of cause (such as the above example), when the illustrations are analyzed in terms of modern physical theories. Nevertheless, however inadequate this notion of cause may be for the purposes of theoretical physics, it continues to play a role in many other branches of inquiry. It is a notion that is firmly embodied in the language we employ, even when abstract physical theories are used in the laboratory as well as in practical affairs for obtaining various results through the manipulation of appropriate instrumentalities. Indeed, it is because some things can be manipulated so as to yield other things, but not conversely, that causal language is a legitimate and convenient way of describing the relations of many events.

On the other hand, not all laws of nature are causal in the indicated sense of this term. A brief survey of types of laws that are used as explanatory premises in various sciences will make this evident.

1. As has already been mentioned, a basic and pervasive type of law is involved in the assumption that there are "natural kinds" or "substances." Let us understand by a "determinable" a property such as color or density, which has a number of specific or "determinate" forms. Thus, among the determinate forms of the determinable color are red, blue, green, yellow, etc.; among the determinate forms of the determinable density are the density with magnitude 0.06 (when measured in some standard fashion), the density with magnitude 2, the density with magnitude 12, etc. The determinate forms of a given determinable thus constitute a "related family" of properties such that every individual of which the determinable property can be significantly predicated must, of logical necessity, have one and only one of the determinate forms of the determinable.[4] A law of the type under consideration (e.g., 'There is the substance rock salt') then asserts that there are objects of various kinds, such that every object of a given kind is characterized by determinate forms of a set of determinable properties, and such that objects belonging to different kinds will differ in at least one (but usually more than one) determinate form of a common determinable. For example, to say that a given object a is rock salt is to say that there is a set of determinable properties (crystalline structure, color, melting point, hardness, etc.) such that under standard conditions a has a determinate form of each of the determinables (a has cubical crystals, it is colorless, it has a density of 2.163, a melting point of 804° C, the degree of hardness 2 on Mohs' scale, etc.). Moreover, a differs from an object belonging to a different kind, for example talc, in at least one (and in fact in a great many) determinate forms of these determinables. Accordingly, laws of this type assert that there is an invariable concomitance of determinate properties in every

---

[4] For this terminology, cf. W. E. Johnson, *Logic*, Vol. 1, Cambridge, England, 1921, Chapter 11; and Rudolf Carnap, *Logical Foundations of Probability*, Chicago, 1950, Vol. 1, p. 75.

object that is of a certain kind. It will be clear, however, that laws of this type are not causal laws—they do not assert, for example, that the density of rock salt precedes (or follows) its degree of hardness.

2. A second type of law asserts an invariable sequential order of dependence among events or properties. Two subordinate types can be distinguished. One of these is the class of causal laws, such as the law about the effect of a spark in a mixture of hydrogen and oxygen, or the law that stones thrown into water produce a series of expanding concentric ripples. A second subordinate type is the class of "developmental" (or "historical") laws, such as the law 'The formation of lungs in the human embryo never precedes the formation of the circulatory system' or the law 'Consumption of alcohol is always followed by a dilation of the blood vessels.' Both subordinate types are frequent in areas of study in which quantitative methods have not been extensively introduced, although as the examples indicate such laws are encountered elsewhere as well. Developmental laws can be construed to have the form 'If x has the property P at time t, then x has the property Q at time t' later than t.' They are commonly not regarded as causal laws, apparently for two reasons. In the first place, though developmental laws may state a necessary condition for the occurrence of some event (or complex of events), they do not state the sufficient conditions. Indeed, we usually have only the vaguest sort of knowledge as to what these sufficient conditions are. In the second place, developmental laws generally state relations of sequential order between events separated by a temporal interval of some duration. In consequence, such laws are sometimes regarded as representing only an incomplete analysis of the facts, on the ground that, since something may intervene after the earlier event to prevent the realization of the later one, the sequential order of events is not likely to be invariable. Nevertheless, whatever may be the limitations of developmental laws and however desirable it may be to supplement them by laws of another sort, both causal and developmental laws are extensively used in the explanatory systems of current science.

3. A third type of law, common in the biological and social sciences as well as in physics, asserts invariable statistical (or probabilistic) relations between events or properties. One example of such a law is: 'If a geometrically and physically symmetrical cube is repeatedly tossed, the probability (or relative frequency) that the cube will come to rest with a given face uppermost is ⅙'; other examples have been previously mentioned. Statistical laws do not assert that the occurrence of one event is *invariably* accompanied by the occurrence of some other event. They assert only that, in a sufficiently long series of trials, the occurrence of one event is accompanied by the occurrence of a second event with an *invariable relative frequency*. Such laws are manifestly not causal, though they are not incompatible with a causal account of the facts they formulate. Indeed, the above statistical law about the behavior of a cube can be deduced from laws that are sometimes said to be causal ones, if suitable assumptions are made about the statistical distribution of initial conditions for the application of those causal laws. On the other hand, there are statistical laws even in physics for which at present no causal explanations are known. Moreover, even if one assumes that "in principle" all statistical laws are the

consequences of some underlying "causal order," there are areas of inquiry—in physics as well as in the biological and social sciences—in which the explanation of many phenomena in terms of strictly universal causal laws is not likely to be feasible practically. It is a reasonable presumption that however much our knowledge may increase, statistical laws will continue to be used as the proximate premises for the explanation and prediction of many phenomena.

4. A fourth type of law, characteristic of modern physical science, asserts a relation of functional dependence (in the mathematical sense of "function") between two or more variable magnitudes associated with stated properties or processes. Two subtypes can be distinguished.

a. In the first place, there are numerical laws stating an interdependence between magnitudes such that a variation in any of them is concurrent with variations in the others. An example of such a law is the Boyle-Charles' law for ideal gases, that $pV = aT$, where p is the pressure of the gas, V its volume, T its absolute temperature, and a a constant that depends on the mass and the nature of the gas under consideration. This is not a causal law. It does not assert, for example, that a change in the temperature is followed (or preceded) by some change in the volume or in the pressure; it asserts only that a change in T is concurrent with changes in p or V or in both. Accordingly, the relation stated by the law must be distinguished from the sequential order of the events that may occur when the law is being tested or used for making predictions. For example, in testing the law in a laboratory, one may diminish the volume of an ideal gas in such a way that its temperature remains constant, and then note that its pressure increases. But the law says nothing about the order in which these magnitudes may be varied, nor about the temporal sequence in which the changes may be observed. Laws of this subtype can nevertheless be used for predictive as well as explanatory purposes. For example, if in the case of a suitably "isolated" system the magnitudes mentioned in such a law satisfy the indicated relation between them at one instant, they will satisfy this relation at some future instant, even though the magnitudes may have undergone some change in the interim.

b. A second subtype consists of numerical laws asserting in what manner a magnitude varies with the time, and more generally how a change in a magnitude per unit of time is related to other magnitudes (in some cases, though not always, to temporal durations). Galileo's law for freely falling bodies in a vacuum is one illustration of such a law. It says that the distance d traversed by a freely falling body is equal to $gt^2/2$, where g is constant and t is the duration of the fall. An equivalent way of stating Galileo's law is to say that the change in the distance per unit time of a freely falling body is equal to gt. In this formulation, it is evident that a time-rate of change in one magnitude is related to a temporal interval. Another example of a law belonging to this subtype is the law for the velocity of the bob of a simple pendulum along the path of its motion. The law says that, if v_0 is the velocity of the bob at the lowest point of its motion, h the height of the bob above the horizontal line through this point, and k a constant, then at any point along the arc of its motion the bob has a velocity v such that $v^2 = v_0^2 - kh^2$. Since the velocity v is the change in distance per unit of time, the law thus says that the change in the distance of the bob along its path per unit of time is a certain mathematical function of its velocity at the lowest point of its swing and of its altitude. In this case, the time-rate of change in one magnitude is not given as a function of the time. Laws that belong to this subtype are often called "dynamical laws" because they formulate the structure of a temporal process and are generally explained on the assumption that a "force" is acting on the system under consideration. Such laws are sometimes assimilated in causal laws, although in fact they are not causal in the specific sense distinguished earlier in this section. For the relation of dependence between the variables mentioned in the law is symmetrical, so that a state of the system at a given time is determined as completely by a later state as by an earlier one. Thus, if we know the velocity of the bob of a simple pendulum at any given instant, then provided there is no external interference with the system, the above law enables us to calculate the velocity at any other time, whether it is earlier or later than the given instant.

The preceding classification of laws is not proposed as an exhaustive one . . . The classification does indicate, however, that not all the laws recognized in the sciences are of one type, and that a scientific explanation is often regarded as satisfactory even though the laws cited in the premises are not "causal" in any customary sense.

Forms of Explanation

———◆———

9

Carl G. Hempel

Explanation in Science and in History

1. Introduction

Among the divers factors that have encouraged and sustained scientific inquiry through its long history are two pervasive human concerns which provide, I think, the basic motivation for all scientific research. One of these is man's persistent desire to improve his strategic position in the world by means of dependable methods for predicting and, whenever possible, controlling the events that occur in it. The extent to which science has been able to satisfy this urge is reflected impressively in the vast and steadily widening range of its technological applications. But besides this practical concern, there is a second basic motivation for the scientific quest, namely, man's insatiable intellectual curiosity, his deep concern to *know* the world he lives in, and to *explain*, and thus to *understand*, the unending flow of phenomena it presents to him.

In times past questions as to the *what* and the *why* of the empirical world were often answered by myths; and to some extent, this is so even in our time. But gradually, the myths are displaced by the concepts, hypotheses, and theories developed in the various branches of empirical science, including the natural sciences, psychology, and sociological as well as historical inquiry. What is the general character of the understanding attainable by these means, and what is its potential scope? In this paper I will try to shed some light on these questions by examining what seem to me the two basic types of explanation offered by the natural sciences, and then comparing them with some modes of explanation and understanding that are found in historical studies.

First, then, a look at explanation in the natural sciences.

Reprinted from *Frontiers of Science and Philosophy*, R. G. Colodny, editor, by permission of the University of Pittsburgh Press. © 1962 by the University of Pittsburgh Press.

2. Two Basic Types of Scientific Explanation

2.1 Deductive-Nomological Explanation

In his book, *How We Think*, John Dewey describes an observation he made one day when, washing dishes, he took some glass tumblers out of the hot soap suds and put them upside down on a plate: he noticed that soap bubbles emerged from under the tumblers' rims, grew for a while, came to a standstill, and finally receded inside the tumblers. Why did this happen? The explanation Dewey outlines comes to this: In transferring a tumbler to the plate, cool air is caught in it; this air is gradually warmed by the glass, which initially has the temperature of the hot suds. The warming of the air is accompanied by an increase in its pressure, which in turn produces an expansion of the soap film between the plate and the rim. Gradually, the glass cools off, and so does the air inside, with the result that the soap bubbles recede.

This explanatory account may be regarded as an argument to the effect that the event to be explained (let me call it the explanandum-event) was to be expected by reason of certain explanatory facts. These may be divided into two groups: (i) particular facts and (ii) uniformities expressed by general laws. The first group includes facts such as these: the tumblers had been immersed, for some time, in soap suds of a temperature considerably higher than that of the surrounding air; they were put, upside down, on a plate on which a puddle of soapy water had formed, providing a connecting soap film, etc. The second group of items presupposed in the argument includes the gas laws and various other laws that have not been explicitly suggested concerning the exchange of heat between bodies of different temperature, the elastic behavior of soap bubbles, etc. If we imagine these various presuppositions explicitly spelled out, the idea suggests itself of construing the explanation as a deductive argument of this form:

$$\text{(D)} \quad \frac{C_1, C_2, \ldots, C_k}{E} \\ L_1, L_2, \ldots, L_r$$

Here, $C_1, C_2, \ldots, C_k$ are statements describing the particular facts invoked; $L_1, L_2, \ldots, L_r$ are general laws: jointly, these statements will be said to form the explanans. The conclusion E is a statement describing the explanandum-event; let me call it the explanandum-statement, and let me use the word "explanandum" to refer to either E or to the event described by it.

The kind of explanation thus characterized I will call *deductive-nomological explanation*; for it amounts to a deductive subsumption of the explanandum under principles which have the character of general laws: it answers the question "Why did the explanandum event occur?" by showing that the event resulted from the particular circumstances specified in $C_1, C_2, \ldots, C_k$ in accordance with the laws $L_1, L_2, \ldots, L_r$. This conception of explanation, as exhibited in schema (D), has therefore been referred to as the covering law model, or as the deductive model, of explanation.

A good many scientific explanations can be regarded as deductive-nomological in character. Consider, for example, the explanation of mirror-images, of rainbows, or of the appearance that a spoon handle is bent at the point where it emerges from a glass of water: in all these cases, the explanandum is deductively subsumed under the laws of reflection and refraction. Similarly, certain aspects of free fall and of planetary motion can be accounted for by deductive subsumption under Galileo's or [Johann—Ed.] Kepler's laws.

In the illustrations given so far the explanatory laws had, by and large, the character of empirical generalizations connecting different observable aspects of the phenomena under scrutiny: angle of incidence with angle of reflection or refraction, distance covered with falling time, etc. But science raises the question "why?" also with respect to the uniformities expressed by such laws, and often answers it in basically the same manner, namely, by subsuming the uniformities under more inclusive laws, and eventually under comprehensive theories. For example, the question, "Why do Galileo's and Kepler's laws hold?" is answered by showing that these laws are but special consequences of the Newtonian laws of motion and of gravitation; and these, in turn, may be explained by subsumption under the more comprehensive general theory of relativity. Such subsumption under broader laws or theories usually increases both the breadth and the depth of our scientific understanding. There is an increase in breadth, or scope, because the new explanatory principles cover a broader range of phenomena; for example, [Isaac—Ed.] Newton's principles govern free fall on the earth and on other celestial bodies, as well as the motions of planets, comets, and artificial satellites, the movements of pendulums, tidal changes, and various other phenomena. And the increase thus effected in the depth of our understanding is strikingly reflected in the fact that, in the light of more advanced explanatory principles, the original empirical laws are usually seen to hold only approximately, or within certain limits. For example, Newton's theory implies that the factor g in Galileo's law, $s = \frac{1}{2}gt^2$, is not strictly a constant for free fall near the surface of the earth; and that, since every planet undergoes gravitational attraction not only from the sun, but also from the other planets, the planetary orbits are not strictly ellipses, as stated in Kepler's laws.

One further point deserves brief mention here. An explanation of a particular event is often conceived as specifying its *cause*, or causes. Thus, the account outlined in our first illustration might be held to explain the growth and the recession of the soap bubbles by showing that the phenomenon was *caused* by a rise and a subsequent drop of the temperature of the air trapped in the tumblers. Clearly, however, these temperature changes provide the requisite explanation only in conjunction with certain other conditions, such as the presence of a soap film, practically constant pressure of the air surrounding the glasses, etc. Accordingly, in the context of explanation, a cause must be allowed to consist in a more or less complex set of particular circumstances; these might be described by a set of sentences: $C_1, C_2, \ldots, C_k$. And, as suggested by the principle "Same cause, same effect," the assertion that those circumstances jointly caused a given event—described, let us say, by a sentence E—implies that whenever and wherever circumstances of the kind in question occur, an event of the kind to be explained comes about. Hence, the given causal explanation implicitly claims that there are general laws—such as L_1, L_2, . . . , L_r in schema (D)—by virtue of which the occurrence of the causal antecedents mentioned in C_1, C_2, . . . , C_k is a sufficient condition for the occurrence of the event to be explained. Thus, the relation between causal factors and effect is reflected in schema (D): causal explanation is deductive-nomological in character. (However, the customary formulations of causal and other explanations often do not explicitly specify all the relevant laws and particular facts: to this point, we will return later.)

The converse does not hold: there are deductive-nomological explanations which would not normally be counted as causal. For one thing, the subsumption of laws, such as Galileo's or Kepler's laws, under more comprehensive principles is clearly not causal in character: we speak of causes only in reference to *particular* facts or events, and not in reference to *universal* facts as expressed by general laws. But not even all deductive-nomological explanations of particular facts or events will qualify as causal; for in a causal explanation some of the explanatory circumstances will temporally precede the effect to be explained: and there are explanations of type (D) which lack this characteristic. For example, the pressure which a gas of specified mass possesses at a given time might be explained by reference to its temperature and its volume at the same time, in conjunction with the gas law which connects simultaneous values of the three parameters.

In conclusion, let me stress once more the important role of laws in deductive-nomological explanation: the laws connect the explanandum-event with the particular conditions cited in the explanans, and this is what confers upon the latter the status of explanatory (and, in some cases, causal) factors in regard to the phenomenon to be explained.

2.2 Probabilistic Explanation

In deductive-nomological explanation as schematized in (D), the laws and theoretical principles involved are of *strictly universal form:* they assert that in *all* cases in which certain specified conditions are realized an occurrence of such and such a kind will result; the law that any metal, when heated under constant pressure, will increase in volume, is a typical example; Galileo's, Kepler's, Newton's, Boyle's, and Snell's laws, and many others, are of the same character.

Now let me turn next to a second basic type of scientific explanation. This kind of explanation, too, is nomological, i.e., it accounts for a given phenomenon by reference to general laws or theoretical principles; but some or all of these are of *probabilistic-statistical form*, i.e., they are, generally speaking, assertions to the effect that if certain specified conditions are realized, then an occurrence of such and such a kind will come about with such and such a statistical probability.

For example, the subsiding of a violent attack of hay fever in a given case might well be attributed to, and thus explained by reference to, the administration of 8 milligrams of chlor-trimeton. But if we wish to connect this antecedent event with the explanandum, and thus to establish its explanatory significance for the latter, we cannot invoke a universal law to the effect that the administration of 8 milligrams of that antihistamine will invariably terminate a hay fever attack: this simply is not so. What can be asserted is only a generalization to the effect that administration of the drug will be followed by relief with high statistical probability, i.e., roughly speaking, with a high relative frequency in the long run. The resulting explanans will thus be of the following type:

John Doe had a hay fever attack and took 8 milligrams of chlor-trimeton.
The probability for subsidence of a hay fever attack upon administration of 8 milligrams of chlor-trimeton is high.

Clearly, this explanans does not deductively imply the explanandum, "John Doe's hay fever attack subsided"; the truth of the explanans makes the truth of the explanandum not certain (as it does in a deductive-nomological explanation) but only more or less likely or, perhaps "practically" certain.

Reduced to its simplest essentials, a probabilistic explanation thus takes the following form:

$$(P) \qquad \left. \begin{array}{c} Fi \\ \hline p(O, F) \text{ is very high} \\ \hline\hline Oi \end{array} \right\} \text{makes very likely}$$

The explanandum, expressed by the statement "Oi," consists in the fact that in the particular instance under consideration, here called i (e.g., John Doe's allergic attack), an outcome of kind O (subsidence) occurred. This is explained by means of two explanans-statements. The first of these, "Fi," corresponds to $C_1, C_2, \ldots, C_k$ in (D); it states that in case i, the factors F (which may be more or less complex) were realized. The second expresses a law of probabilistic form, to the effect that the statistical probability for outcome O to occur in cases where F is realized is very high (close to 1). The double line separating explanandum from explanans is to indicate that, in contrast to the case of deductive-nomological explanation, the explanans does not logically imply the explanandum, but only confers a high likelihood upon it. The concept of likelihood here referred to must be clearly distinguished from that of statistical probability, symbolized by "p" in our schema. A statistical probability is, roughly speaking, the long-run relative frequency with which an occurrence of a given kind (say, F) is accompanied by an "outcome" of a specified kind (say, O). Our likelihood, on the other hand, is a relation (capable of gradations) not between kinds of occurrences, but between statements. The likelihood referred to in (P) may be characterized as the strength of the inductive support, or the degree of rational credibility, which the explanans confers upon the explanandum; or, in [Rudolf—Ed.] Carnap's terminology, as the *logical*, or *inductive*, (in contrast to statistical) *probability* which the explanandum possesses relative to the explanans.

Thus, probabilistic explanation, just like explanation in the manner of schema (D), is nomological in that it presupposes general laws; but because these laws are of statistical rather than of strictly universal form, the resulting explanatory arguments are inductive rather than deductive in character. An inductive argument of this kind *explains* a given phenomenon by showing that, in view of certain particular events and certain statistical laws, its occurrence was to be expected with high logical, or inductive, probability.

By reason of its inductive character, probabilistic explanation differs from its deductive-nomological counterpart in several other important respects; for example, its explanans may confer upon the explanandum a more or less high degree of inductive support; in this sense, probabilistic explanation admits of degrees, whereas deductive-nomological explanation appears as an either-or affair: a given set of universal laws and particular statements either does or does not imply a given explanandum statement. A fuller examination of these differences, however, would lead us far afield and is not required for the purposes of this paper.

One final point: the distinction here suggested between deductive-nomological and probabilistic explanation might be questioned on the ground that, after all, the universal laws invoked in a deductive explanation can have been established only on the basis of a finite body of evidence, which surely affords no exhaustive verification, but only more or less strong probability for it; and that, therefore, all scientific laws have to be regarded as probabilistic. This argument, however, confounds a logical issue with an epistemological one: it fails to distinguish properly between the *claim* made by a given law-statement and the *degree of confirmation*, or *probability*, which it possesses on the available evidence. It is quite true that statements expressing laws of either kind can be only incompletely confirmed by any given finite set—however large—of data about particular facts; but law-statements of the two different types make claims of different kinds, which are reflected in their logical forms: roughly, a universal law-statement of the simplest kind asserts that *all* elements of an indefinitely large reference class (e.g., copper objects) have a certain characteristic (e.g., that of being good conductors of electricity); while statistical law-statements assert that in the long run, a specified proportion of the members of the reference class have some specified property. And our distinction of two types of law and, concomitantly, of two types of scientific explanation, is based on this difference in claim as reflected in the difference of form.

The great scientific importance of probabilistic explanation is eloquently attested to by the extensive and highly successful explanatory use that has been made of fundamental laws of statistical form in genetics, statistical mechanics, and quantum theory.

3. Elliptic and Partial Explanations: Explanation Sketches

As I mentioned earlier, the conception of deductive-nomological explanation reflected in our schema (D) is often referred to as the covering law model, or the deductive model, of explanation: similarly, the conception underlying schema (P) might be called the probabilistic or the inductive-statistical, model of explanation. The term "model" can serve as a useful reminder that the two types of explanation as characterized above constitute ideal types or theoretical idealizations and are not intended to reflect the manner in which working scientists actually formulate their explanatory accounts. Rather, they are meant to provide explications, or rational reconstructions, or theoretical models, of certain modes of scientific explanation.

In this respect our model might be compared to the concept of mathematical proof (within a given theory) as constructed in meta-mathematics. This concept, too, may be regarded as a theoretical model: it is not intended to provide a descriptive account of how proofs are formulated in the writings of mathematicians: most of these actual formulations fall short of rigorous and, as it were, ideal, meta-mathematical standards. But the theoretical model has certain other functions: it exhibits the rationale of mathematical proofs by revealing the logical connections underlying the successive steps; it provides standards for a critical appraisal of any proposed proof constructed within the mathematical system to which the model refers; and it affords a basis for a precise and far-reaching theory of proof, provability, decidability, and related concepts. I think the two models of explanation can fulfill the same functions, if only on a much more modest scale. For example, the arguments presented in constructing the models give an indication of the sense in which the models exhibit the rationale and the logical structure of the explanations they are intended to represent.

I now want to add a few words concerning the second of the functions just mentioned; but I will have to forgo a discussion of the third.

When a mathematician proves a theorem, he will often omit mention of certain propositions which he presupposes in his argument and which he is in fact entitled to presuppose because, for example, they follow readily from the postulates of his system or from previously established theorems or perhaps from the hypothesis of his theorem, if the latter is in hypothetical form; he then simply assumes that his readers or listeners will be able to supply the missing items if they so desire. If judged by ideal standards, the given formulation of the proof is elliptic or incomplete; but the departure from the ideal is harmless: the gaps can readily be filled in. Similarly, explanations put forward in everyday discourse and also in scientific contexts are often *elliptically formulated*. When we explain, for example, that a lump of butter melted because it was put into a hot frying pan, or that a small rainbow appeared in the spray of the lawn sprinkler because the sunlight was reflected and refracted by the water droplets, we may be said to offer elliptic formulations of deductive-nomological explanations; an account of this kind omits mention of certain laws or particular facts which it tacitly takes for granted, and whose explicit citation would yield a complete deductive-nomological argument.

In addition to elliptic formulation, there is another, quite important, respect in which many explanatory arguments deviate from the theoretical model. It often happens that the statement actually included in the explanans, together with those which may reasonably be assumed to have been taken for granted in the context at hand, explain the given explanandum only *partially*, in a sense which I will try to indicate by an example. In his *Psychopathology of Everyday Life*, [Sigmund—Ed.] Freud offers the following explanation of a slip of the pen that occurred to him: "On a sheet of paper containing principally short daily notes of business interest, I found, to my surprise, the incorrect date, 'Thursday, October 20th,' bracketed under the correct date of the month of September. It was not difficult to explain this anticipation as the expression of a wish. A few days before I had returned fresh from my vacation and felt ready for any amount of professional work, but as yet there were few patients. On my arrival I had found a letter from a patient announcing her arrival on the 20th of October. As I wrote the same date in September I may certainly have thought 'X. ought to be here already; what a pity about that whole month!,' and with this thought I pushed the current date a month ahead."

Clearly, the formulation of the intended explanation is *at least incomplete* in the sense considered a moment ago. In particular, it fails to mention any laws or theoretical principles in virtue of which the subconscious wish, and the other antecedent circumstances referred to, could be held to explain Freud's slip of the pen. However, the general theoretical considerations Freud presents here and elsewhere in his writings suggest strongly that his explanatory account relies on a hypothesis to the effect that when a person has a strong, though perhaps unconscious, desire, then if he commits a slip of pen, tongue, memory, or the like, the slip will take a form in which it expresses, and perhaps symbolically fulfills, the given desire.

Even this rather vague hypothesis is probably more definite than what Freud would have been willing to assert. But for the sake of the argument let us accept it and include it in the explanans, together with the particular statements that Freud did have the subconscious wish he mentions, and that he was going to commit a slip of the pen. Even then, the resulting explanans permits us to deduce only that the slip made by Freud would, *in some way or other*, express and perhaps symbolically fulfill Freud's subconscious wish. But clearly, such expression and fulfillment might have been achieved by many other kinds of slip of the pen than the one actually committed.

In other words, the explanans does not imply, and thus fully explains, that the particular slip, say s, which Freud committed on this occasion, would fall within the narrow class, say W, of acts which consist in writing the words "Thursday, October 20th"; rather, the explanans implies only that s would fall into a wider class, say F, which includes W as a proper subclass, and which consists of all acts which would express and symbolically fulfill Freud's subconscious wish *in some way or other*.

The argument under consideration might be called a *partial explanation*: it provides complete, or conclusive, grounds for expecting s to be a member of F, and since W is a subclass of F, it thus shows that the explanandum, i.e., s falling within W, accords with, or bears out, what is to be expected in consideration of the explanans. By contrast, a deductive-nomological explanation of the form (D) might then be called *complete* since the explanans here does imply the explanandum.

Clearly, the question whether a given explanatory argument is complete or partial can be significantly raised only if the explanandum sentence is fully specified; only then can we ask whether the explanandum does or does not follow from the explanans. Completeness of explanation, in this sense, is relative to our explanandum sentence. Now, it might seem much more important and interesting to consider instead the notion of a complete explanation of some *concrete event,* such as the destruction of Pompeii, or the death of Adolf Hitler, or the launching of the first artificial sattellite: we might want to regard a particular event as completely explained only if an explanatory account of deductive or of inductive form had been provided for all of its aspects. This notion, however, is self-defeating; for any particular event may be regarded as having infinitely many different aspects or characteristics, which cannot all be accounted for by a finite set, however large, of explanatory statements.

In some cases, what is intended as an explanatory account will depart even further from the standards reflected in the model schemata (D) and (P) above. An explanatory account, for example, which is not explicit and specific enough to be reasonably qualified as an elliptically formulated explanation or as a partial one, can often be viewed as an *explanation sketch:* it may suggest, perhaps quite vividly and persuasively, the general outlines of what, it is hoped, can eventually be supplemented so as to yield a more closely reasoned argument based on explanatory hypotheses which are indicated more fully, and which more readily permit of critical appraisal by reference to empirical evidence.

The decision whether a proposed explanatory account is to be qualified as an elliptically formulated deductive or probabilistic explanation, as a partial explanation, as an explanation sketch, or perhaps as none of these is a matter of judicious interpretation; it calls for an appraisal of the intent of the given argument and of the background assumptions that may be assumed to have been tacitly taken for granted, or at least to be available, in the given context. Unequivocal decision rules cannot be set down for this purpose any more than for determining whether a given informally stated inference which is not deductively valid by reasonably strict standards is to count nevertheless as valid but enthymematically formulated, or as fallacious, or as an instance of sound inductive reasoning, or perhaps, for lack of clarity, as none of these.

4. Nomological Explanation in History

So far, we have examined nomological explanation, both deductive and inductive, as found in the natural sciences; and we have considered certain characteristic ways in which actual explanatory accounts often depart from the ideal standards of our two basic models. Now it is time to ask what light the preceding inquiries can shed on the explanatory procedures used in historical research.

In examining this question, we will consider a number of specific explanatory arguments offered by a variety of writers. It should be understood from the beginning that we are here concerned, not to appraise the factual adequacy of these explanations, but only to attempt an explication of the claims they make and of the assumptions they presuppose.

Let us note first, then, that some historical explanations are surely nomological in character: they aim to show that the explanadum phenomenon resulted from certain antecedent, and perhaps, concomitant, conditions; and in arguing these, they rely more or less explicitly on relevant generalizations. These may concern, for example, psychological or sociological tendencies and may best be conceived as broadly probabilistic in character. This point is illustrated by the following argument, which might be called an attempt to explain Parkinson's Law by subsumption under broader psychological principles:

"As the activities of the government are enlarged, more people develop a vested interest in the continuation and expansion of governmental functions. People who have jobs do not like to lose them; those who are habituated to certain skills do not welcome change; those who have become accustomed to the exercise of a certain kind of power do not like to relinquish their control— if anything, they want to develop greater power and correspondingly greater prestige. . . . Thus, government offices and bureaus, once created, in turn institute drives, not only to fortify themselves against assault, but to enlarge the scope of their operations."

The psychological generalizations here explicitly adduced will reasonably have to be understood as expressing, not strict uniformities, but strong *tendencies*, which might be formulated by means of rough probability statements; so that the explanation here suggested is probabilistic in character.

As a rule, however, the generalizations underlying a proposed historical explanation are largely left unspecified; and most concrete explanatory accounts have to be qualified as partial explanations or as explanation sketches. Consider, for example, F. J. Turner's essay "The Significance of the Frontier in American History," which amplifies and defends the view that "Up to our own day American history has been in a large degree the history of the colonization of the Great West. The existence of an area of free land, its continuous recession, and the advance of American settlement westward explain American development. . . . The peculiarity of American institutions is the fact that they have been compelled to adapt themselves . . . to the changes involved in crossing a continent, in winning a wilderness, and in developing at each area of this progress, out of the primitive economic and political conditions of the frontier, the complexity of city life." One of the phenomena Turner considers in developing his thesis is the rapid westward advance of what he calls the Indian trader's frontier. "Why was it," Turner asks, "that the Indian trader passed so rapidly across the continent?"; and he answers, "The explanation of the rapidity of this advance is bound up with the effects of the trader on the Indian. The trading post left the unarmed tribes at the mercy of those that had purchased firearms—a truth which the Iroquois Indians wrote in blood, and so the remote and unvisited tribes gave eager welcome to the trader. . . . This accounts for the trader's power and the rapidity of his advance." There is no explicit mention here of any laws, but it is clear that this sketch of an explanation presupposes, first of all, various particular facts, such as that the remote and unvisited tribes had heard of the efficacy and availability of firearms, and that there were no culture patterns or institutions precluding their use by those tribes; but in addition, the account clearly rests also on certain assumptions as to how human beings will tend to behave in situations presenting the kinds of danger and of opportunity that Turner refers to.

Similar comments apply to Turner's account of the westward advance of what he calls the farmer's frontier: "Omitting those of the pioneer farmers who move from the love of adventure, the advance of the more steady farmer is easy to understand. Obviously the immigrant was attracted by the cheap lands of the frontier, and even the native farmer felt their influence strongly. Year by year the farmers who lived on soil, whose returns were diminished by un-rotated crops, were offered the virgin soil of the frontier at nominal prices. Their growing families demanded more lands, and these were dear. The competition of the unexhausted, cheap, and easily tilled prairie lands compelled the farmer either to go West . . . or to adopt intensive culture." This passage is clearly intended to do more than describe a sequence of particular events: it is meant to afford an understanding of the farmers' westward advance by pointing to their interests and needs and by calling attention to the facts and the opportunities facing them. Again, this explanation takes it for granted that under such conditions normal human beings will tend to seize new opportunities in the manner in which the pioneer farmers did.

Examining the various consequences of this moving-frontier history, Turner states that "the most important effect of the frontier has been in the promotion of democracy here and in Europe," and he begins his elaboration of this theme with the remark that "the frontier is productive of individualism. . . . The tendency is anti-social. It produces antipathy to control, and particularly to any direct control": and this is, of course, a sociological generalization in a nutshell.

Similarly, any explanation that accounts for a historical phenomenon by reference to economic factors or by means of general principles of social or cultural change are nomological in import, even if not in explicit formulation.

But if this be granted there still remains another question, to which we must now turn, namely, whether, in addition to explanations of a broadly nomological character, the historian also employs certain other distinctly historical ways of explaining and understanding whose import cannot be adequately characterized by means of our two models. The question has often been answered in the affirmative, and several kinds of historical explanation have been adduced in support of this affirmation. I will now consider what seem to me two especially interesting candidates for the role of specifically historical explanation; namely first, genetic explanation, and secondly, explanation of an action in terms of its underlying rationale.

5. Genetic Explanation in History

In order to make the occurrence of a historical phenomenon intelligible, a historian will frequently offer a "genetic explanation" aimed at exhibiting the principal stages in a sequence of events which led up to the given phenomenon.

Consider, for example, the practice of selling indulgences as it existed in Luther's time. H. Boehmer, in his work, *Luther and the Reformation*, points out that until about the end of the 19th century, "the indulgence was in fact still a great unknown quantity, at sight of which the scholar would ask himself with a sigh: 'Where did it come from?' " An answer was provided by Adolf Gottlob, who tackled the problem by asking himself what led the Popes and

Bishops to offer indulgences. As a result, ". . . origin and development of the unknown quantity appeared clearly in the light, and doubts as to its original meaning came to an end. It revealed itself as a true descendant of the time of the great struggle between Christianity and Islam, and at the same time a highly characteristic product of Germanic Christianity."

In brief outline, the origins of the indulgence appear to go back to the 9th century, when the popes were strongly concerned with the fight against Islam. The Mohammedan fighter was assured by the teachings of his religion that if he were to be killed in battle his soul would immediately go to heaven; but the defender of the Christian faith had to fear that he might still be lost if he had not done the regular penance for his sins. To allay these doubts, John VII, in 877, promised absolution for their sins to crusaders who should be killed in battle. "Once the crusade was so highly thought of, it was an easy transition to regard participation in a crusade as equivalent to the performance of atonement . . . and to promise remission of these penances in return for expeditions against the Church's enemies." Thus, there was introduced the indulgence of the Cross, which granted complete remission of the penitential punishment to all those who participated in a religious war. "If it is remembered what inconveniences, what ecclesiastical and civil disadvantages the ecclesiastical penances entailed, it is easy to understand that the penitents flocked to obtain this indulgence." A further strong incentive came from the belief that whoever obtained an indulgence secured liberation not only from the ecclesiastical penances, but also from the corresponding suffering in purgatory after death. The benefits of these indulgences were next extended to those who, being physically unfit to participate in a religious war, contributed the funds required to send a soldier on a crusade: in 1199, Pope Innocent III recognized the payment of money as adequate qualification for the benefits of a crusading indulgence.

When the crusades were on the decline, new ways were explored of raising funds through indulgences. Thus, there was instituted a "jubilee indulgence," to be celebrated every hundred years, for the benefit of pilgrims coming to Rome on that occasion. The first of these indulgences, in 1300, brought in huge sums of money; and the time interval between successive jubilee indulgences was therefore reduced to 50, 33 and even 25 years. And from 1393 on the jubilee indulgence was made available, not only in Rome, for the benefit of pilgrims, but everywhere in Europe, through special agents who were empowered to absolve the penitent of their sins upon payment of an appropriate amount. The development went even further: in 1477, a dogmatic declaration by Sixtus IV attributed to the indulgence the power of delivering even the dead from purgatory.

Undeniably, a genetic account of this kind can enhance our understanding of a historical phenomenon. But its explanatory role, far from being *sui generis*, [unique—Ed.] seems to me basically nomological in character. For the successive stages singled out for consideration surely must be qualified for their function by more than the fact that they form a temporal sequence and that they all precede the final stage, which is to be explained: the mere enumeration in a yearbook of "the year's important events" in the order of their occurrence clearly is not a genetic explanation of the final event or of anything else. In a genetic explanation each stage must be shown to "lead to" the next, and thus to be linked to its successor by virtue of some general principle which makes the occurrence of the latter at least reasonably probable, given the former. But in this sense, even successive stages in a physical phenomenon such as the free fall of a stone may be regarded as forming a genetic sequence whose different stages—characterized, let us say, by the position and the velocity of the stone at different times—are interconnected by strictly universal laws; and the successive stages in the movement of a steel ball bouncing its zigzaggy way down a Galton pegboard may be regarded as forming a genetic sequence with probabilistic connections.

The genetic accounts given by historians are not, of course, of the purely nomological kind suggested by these examples from physics. Rather, they combine a certain measure of nomological interconnecting with more or less large amounts of straight description. For consider an intermediate stage mentioned in a genetic account: some aspects of it will be presented as having evolved from the preceding stages (in virtue of connecting laws, which often will be no more than hinted at); while other aspects, which are not accounted for by information about the preceding development, will be descriptively added because they are relevant to an understanding of subsequent stages in the genetic sequence. Thus, schematically speaking, a genetic explanation will begin with a pure description of an initial stage; thence, it will proceed to an account of a second stage, part of which is nomologically linked to, and explained by, the characteristic features of the initial stage; while the balance is simply described as relevant for a nomological account of some aspects of the third stage; and so forth.

In our illustration the connecting laws are hinted at in the mention made of motivating factors: the explanatory claims made for the interest of the popes in securing a fighting force and in amassing ever larger funds clearly presuppose suitable psychological generalizations as to the manner in which an intelligent individual will act, in the light of his factual beliefs, when he seeks to attain a certain objective. Similarly, general assumptions underlie the reference to the fear of purgatory in explaining the eagerness with which indulgences were bought. And when, referring to the huge financial returns of the first jubilee indulgence, [E. G.—Ed.] Schwiebert says "This success only whetted the insatiable appetite of the popes. The intervening period of time was variously reduced from 100 to 50 to 33 to 25 years . . . ," the explanatory force here implied might be said to rest on some principle of reinforcement by rewards. As need hardly be added, even if such a principle were explicitly introduced, the resulting account would provide at most a partial explanation; it could not be expected to show, for example, why the intervening intervals should have the particular lengths here mentioned.

In the genetic account of the indulgences, those factors which are simply described (or tacitly presupposed) rather than explained include, for example, the doctrines, the organization, and the power of the Church; the occurrence of the crusades and their eventual decline; and innumerable other factors which are not even explicitly mentioned, but which have to be understood as background conditions if the genetic survey is to serve its explanatory purpose.

The general conception here outlined of the logic of genetic explanation could also be illustrated by reference to Turner's studies of the American frontier; this will be clear even from the brief remarks made earlier on Turner's ideas.

Some analysts of historical development put special emphasis on the importance of the laws underlying a historical explanation; thus, e.g., A. Gerschenkron maintains, "Historical research consists essentially in application to empirical material of various sets of empirically derived hypothetical generalizations and in testing the closeness of the resulting fit, in the hope that in this way certain uniformities, certain typical situations, and certain typical relationships among individual factors in these situations can be ascertained," and his subsequent substantive observations include a brief genetic survey of patterns of industrial development in 19th century Europe, in which some of the presumably relevant uniformities are made reasonably explicit.

6. Explanation by Motivating Reasons

Let us now turn to another kind of historical explanation that is often considered as *sui generis*, namely, the explanation of an action in terms of the underlying *rationale*, which will include, in particular, the ends the agents sought to attain, and the alternative courses of action he believed to be open to him. The following passage explaining the transition from the indulgence of the Cross to the institution of the jubilee indulgence illustrates this procedure: ". . . in the course of the thirteenth century the idea of a crusade more and more lost its power over men's spirits. If the Popes would keep open the important source of income which the indulgence represented, they must invent new motives to attract people to the purchase of indulgences. It is the merit of Boniface VIII to have recognized this clearly. By creating the jubilee indulgence in 1300 he assured the species a further long development most welcome to the Papal finances." This passage clearly seeks to explain the establishment of the first jubilee indulgence by suggesting the reasons for which Boniface VIII took this step. If properly spelled out, these reasons would include not only Boniface's objective of ensuring a continuation of the income so far derived from the indulgence of the Cross, but also his estimate of the relevant empirical circumstances, including the different courses of action open to him, and their probable efficacy as well as potential difficulties in pursuing them and adverse consequences to which they might lead.

The kind of explanation achieved by specifying the rationale underlying a given action is widely held to be fundamentally different from nomological explanation as found in the natural sciences. Various reasons have been adduced in support of this view; but I will limit my discussion largely to the stimulating ideas on the subjects that have been set forth by [William—Ed.] Dray. According to Dray, there is an important type of historical explanation whose features "make the covering law model peculiarly inept"; he calls it "rational explanation," i.e., "explanation which displays the *rationale* of what was done," or, more fully, "a reconstruction of the agent's *calculation* of means to be adopted toward his chosen end in the light of the circumstances in which he found himself." The object of rational explanation is not to subsume the explanandum under general laws, but "to show that what was done was the thing to have done for the reasons given, rather than merely the thing that is done on such occasions, perhaps in accordance with certain laws." Hence, a rational explanation has "an element of *appraisal*" in it: it "must exhibit what was done as appropriate or justified." Accordingly, Dray conceives a rational explanation as being based on a standard of appropriateness or of rationality of a special kind which he calls a "*principle of action*," i.e., "a judgment of the form 'When in a situation of type C_1, C_2, . . . C_n the thing to do is X.' "

Dray does not give a full account of the kind of "situation" here referred to; but to do justice to his intentions, these situations must evidently be taken to include, at least, items of the following three types: (i) the end the agent was seeking to attain; (ii) the empirical circumstances, as seen by the agent, in which he had to act; (iii) the moral standards or principles of conduct to which the agent was committed. For while this brief list requires considerable further scrutiny and elaboration, it seems clear that only if at least those items are specified does it make sense to raise the question of the appropriateness of what the agent did in the given "situation."

It seems fair to say, then, that according to Dray's conception a rational explanation answers a question of the form "Why did agent A do X?" by offering an explanans of the following type (our formulation replaces the notation "C_1, C_2, . . . C_n" by the simpler "C," without, of course, precluding that the kind of situation thus referred to may be extremely complex):

(R)
    A was in a situation of type C
    In a situation of type C, the appropriate thing to do is X

But can an explanans of this type possibly serve to explain A's having in fact done X? It seems to me beyond dispute that in any adequate explanation of an empirical phenomenon the explanans must provide good grounds for believing or asserting that the explanandum phenomenon did in fact occur. Yet this requirement, which is necessary though not sufficient for an adequate explanation, is not met by a rational explanation as conceived by Dray. For the two statements included in the contemplated explanans (R) provide good reasons for believing that the appropriate thing for A to do was X, but not for believing that A did in fact do X. Thus, a rational explanation in the sense in which Dray appears to understand it does not explain what it is meant to explain. Indeed, the expression "the thing to do" in the standard formulation of a principle of action, "functions as a value term," as Dray himself points out: but then, it is unclear, on purely logical grounds, how the valuational principle expressed by the second sentence in (R), in conjunction with the plainly empirical, non-valuational first sentence, should permit any inferences concerning empirical matters such as A's action, which could not be drawn from the first sentence alone.

To explain, in the general vein here under discussion, why A did in fact do X, we have to refer to the underlying rationale not by means of a normative principle of action, but by descriptive statements to the effect that, at the time in question A was a rational agent, or had the disposition to act rationally; and that a rational agent, when in circumstances of kind, will always (or: with high probability) do X. Thus construed, the explanans takes on the following form:

(R′)
    (a) A was in a situation of type C
    (b) A was disposed to act rationally
    (c) Any person who is disposed to act rationally will, when in a situation of type C, invariably (with high probability) do X

But by this explanans A's having done X is accounted for in the manner of a deductive or of a probabilistic nomological explanation. Thus, in so far as reference to the rationale of an agent does explain his action, the explanation conforms to one of our nomological models.

An analogous diagnosis applies, incidentally, also to explanations which attribute an agent's behavior in a given situation not to rationality and more or less explicit deliberation on his part, but to other dispositional features, such as his character and emotional make-up. The following comment on Luther illustrates this point: "Even stranger to him than the sense of anxiety was the allied sense of fear. In 1527 and 1535, when the plague broke out in Wittenberg, he was the only professor besides Bugenhagen who remained calmly at his post to comfort and care for the sick and dying. . . . He had, indeed, so little sense as to take victims of the plague into his house and touch them with his own hand. Death, martyrdom, dishonor, contempt . . . he feared just as little as infectious disease." It may well be said that these observations give more than a description: that they shed some explanatory light on the particular occurrences mentioned. But in so far as they explain, they do so by presenting Luther's actions as manifestations of certain personality traits, such as fearlessness; thus, the particular acts are again subsumed under generalizations as to how a fearless person is likely to behave under certain circumstances.

It might seem that both in this case and in rational explanation as construed in (R′), the statements which we took to express general laws—namely, (c) in (R′), and the statement about the probable behavior of a fearless person in our last illustration—do not have the character of empirical laws at all, but rather that of analytic statements which simply express part of what is *meant* by a rational agent, a fearless person, or the like. Thus, in contrast to nomological explanations, these accounts in terms of certain dispositional characteristics of the agent appear to presuppose no general laws at all. Now, the idea of analyticity gives rise to considerable philosophical difficulties; but let us disregard these here and take the division of statements into analytic and synthetic to be reasonably clear. Even then, the objection just outlined cannot be upheld. For dispositional concepts of the kind invoked in our explanations have to be regarded as governed by entire clusters of general statements—we might call them symptom statements—which connect the given disposition with various specific manifestations, or symptoms, of its presence (each symptom will be a particular mode of "responding," or acting, under specified "stimulus" conditions); and the whole cluster of these symptom statements for a given disposition will have implications which are plainly not analytic (in the intuitive sense here assumed). Under these circumstances it would be arbitrary to attribute to some of the symptom statements the analytic character of partial definitions.

The logic of this situation has a precise representation in Carnap's theory of reduction sentences. Here, the connections between a given disposition and its various manifest symptoms are assumed to be expressed by a set of so-called reduction sentences (these are characterized by their logical form). Some of these state, in terms of manifest characteristics, sufficient conditions for the presence of the given disposition; others similarly state necessary conditions. The reduction sentences for a given dispositional concept cannot, as a rule, all be qualified as analytic; for jointly they imply certain non-analytic consequences which have the status of general laws connecting exclusively the manifest characteristics; the strongest of the laws so implied is the so-called representative sentence, which "represents, so to speak, the factual content of the set" of all the reduction sentences for the given disposition concept. This representative sentence asserts, in effect, that whenever at least one of the sufficient conditions specified by the given reduction sentences is satisfied, then so are all the necessary conditions laid down by the reduction sentences. And when A is one of the manifest criteria sufficient for the presence of a given disposition, and B is a necessary one, then the statement that whenever A is present so is B will normally turn out to be synthetic.

So far then, I have argued that Dray's construal of explanation by motivating reasons is untenable; that the normative principles of action envisaged by him have to be replaced by statements of a dispositional kind; and that, when this is done, explanations in terms of a motivating rationale, as well as those referring to other psychological factors, are seen to be basically nomological.

Let me add a few further remarks on the idea of rational explanation. First: in many cases of so-called purposive action, there is no conscious deliberation, no rational calculation that leads the agent to his decision. Dray is quite aware of this; but he holds that a rational explanation in his sense is still possible; for "in so far as we say an action is purposive at all, no matter at what level of conscious deliberation, there is a calculation which could be constructed for it: the one the agent would have gone through if he had had time, if he had not seen what to do in a flash, if he had been called upon to account for what he did after the event, etc. And it is by eliciting some such calculations that we explain the action." But the explanatory significance of reasons or "calculations" which are "reconstructed" in this manner is certainly puzzling. If, to take Dray's example, an agent arrives at his decision "in a flash" rather than by deliberation, then it would seem to be simply false to say that the decision can be accounted for by some argument which the agent might have gone through under more propitious circumstances, or which he might produce later if called upon to account for his action; for, by hypothesis, no such argument was in fact gone through by the agent at the crucial time; considerations of appropriateness or rationality played no part in shaping his decision; the rationale that Dray assumes to be adduced and appraised in the corresponding rational explanation is simply fictitious.

But, in fairness to Dray, these remarks call for a qualifying observation: in at least some of the cases Dray has in mind it might not be fictitious to ascribe the action under study to a disposition which the agent acquired through a learning process whose initial stages did involve conscious ratiocination. Consider, for example, the various complex maneuvers of accelerating, braking, signaling, dodging jaywalkers and animals, swerving into and out of traffic lanes, estimating the changes of traffic lights, etc., which are involved in driving a car through city traffic. A beginning driver will often perform these only upon some sort of conscious deliberation or even calculation; but gradually, he learns to do the appropriate thing automatically, "in a flash," without giving them any conscious thought. The habit pattern he has thus acquired may be viewed as consisting in a set of dispositions to react in certain appropriate ways in various situations; and a particular performance of such an appropriate action would then be explained, not by a "constructed" calculation which actually the agent did not perform but by reference to the disposition just mentioned and thus, again, in a nomological fashion.

The method of explaining a given action by "constructing," in Dray's sense, the agent's calculation of means faces yet another, though less fundamental, difficulty: it will frequently yield a rationalization rather than an explanation, especially when the reconstruction relies on the reasons the agent might produce when called upon to account for his action. As G. Watson remarks, "Motivation, as presented in the perspective of history, is often too simple and straightforward, reflecting the psychology of the Age of Reason. . . . Psychology has come . . . to recognize the enormous weight of irrational and intimately personal impulses in conduct. In history, biography, and in autobiography, especially of public characters, the tendency is strong to present 'good' reasons instead of 'real' reasons." Accordingly, as Watson goes on to point out, it is important, in examining the motivation of historical figures, to take into account the significance of such psychological mechanisms as reaction formation, "the dialectic dynamic by which stinginess cloaks itself in generosity, or rabid pacifism arises from the attempt to repress strong aggressive impulses."

These remarks have a bearing also on an idea set forth by P. Gardiner in his illuminating book on historical explanation. Commenting on the notion of the "real reason" for a man's action, Gardiner says: "In general, it appears safe to say that by a man's 'real reasons' we mean those reasons he would be prepared to give under circumstances where his confession would not entail adverse consequences to himself." And he adds "An exception to this is the psychoanalyst's usage of the expression where different criteria are adopted." This observation might be taken to imply that the explanation of human actions in terms of underlying motives is properly aimed at exhibiting the agent's "real reasons" in the ordinary sense of the phrase, as just described; and that, by implication, reasons in the psychoanalyst's sense require less or no consideration. But such a construal of explanation would give undue importance to considerations of ordinary language. Gardiner is entirely right when he reminds us that the "language in which history is written is for the most part the language of ordinary speech"; but the historian in search of reasons that will correctly explain human actions will obviously have to give up his reliance on the everyday conception of "real reasons" if psychological or other investigations show that real reasons, thus understood, do not yield as adequate an account of human actions as an analysis in terms of less familiar conceptions such as, perhaps, the idea of motivating factors which are kept out of the agent's normal awareness by processes of repression and reaction formation.

I would say, then, first of all, that historical explanation cannot be bound by conceptions that might be implicit in the way in which ordinary language deals with motivating reasons. But secondly, I would doubt that Gardiner's expressly tentative characterization does justice even to what we ordinarily mean when we speak of a man's "real reasons." For considerations of the kind that support the idea of subconscious motives are quite familiar in our time, and we are therefore prepared to say in ordinary, non-technical discourse that the reasons given by an agent may not be the "real reasons" behind his action, even if his statement was subjectively honest, and he had no grounds to expect that it would lead to any adverse consequences for him. For no matter whether an explanation of human actions is attempted in the language of ordinary speech or in the technical terms of some theory, the overriding criterion for what-if-anything should count as a "real," and thus explanatory, reason for a given action is surely not to be found by examining the way in which the term "real reason" has thus far been used, but by investigating what conception of real reason would yield the most satisfactory explanation of human conduct; and ordinary usage gradually changes accordingly.

7. Concluding Remarks

We have surveyed some of the most prominent candidates for the role of characteristically historical mode of explanation; and we have found that they conform essentially to one or the other of our two basic types of scientific explanation.

This result and the arguments that led to it do not in any way imply a mechanistic view of man, of society, and of historical processes; nor, of course, do they deny the importance of ideas and ideals for human decision and action. What the preceding considerations do suggest is, rather, that the nature of understanding, in the sense in which explanation is meant to give us an understanding of empirical phenomena, is basically the same in all areas of scientific inquiry; and that the deductive and the probabilistic models of nomological explanation accommodate vastly more than just the explanatory arguments of, say, classical mechanics: in particular, they accord well also with the character of explanations that deal with the influence of rational deliberation, of conscious and subconscious motives, and of ideas and ideals on the shaping of historical events. In so doing, our schemata exhibit, I think, one important aspect of the methodological unity of all empirical science.

10

Donald Davidson

Actions, Reasons, and Causes

Donald Davidson, currently Professor of Philosophy at the University of Chicago, has taught in recent years at Princeton and Rockefeller Universities. He is the author of a number of strategic papers on issues central to the work of W. V. Quine and Alfred Tarski. For instance, in such papers as "In Defense of Convention T" (1973), "Truth and Meaning" (1967), and "Thought and Talk" (1974), Davidson undertakes to treat sameness of meaning in terms of Tarski's semantic conception of truth, thereby permitting "meanings" to be eliminated; and to link the analysis of mental states to constraints on our analysis of speech. His best-known paper is "Actions, Reasons and Causes" (1963), which, together with "Events as Particulars" (1970) and "The Logical Form of Action Sentences" (1967), constitutes his most sustained effort to introduce an ontology of events and to reconcile discourse about human action with our causal accounts of physical events.

What is the relation between a reason and an action when the reason explains the action by giving the agent's reason for doing what he did? We may call such explanations *rationalizations*, and say that the reason *rationalizes* the action.

In this paper I want to defend the ancient—and common-sense—position that rationalization is a species of ordinary causal explanation. The defense no doubt requires some redeployment, but not more or less complete abandonment of the position, as urged by many recent writers.[1]

I

A reason rationalizes an action only if it leads us to see something the agent saw, or thought he saw, in his action—some feature, consequence, or aspect of the action the agent wanted, desired, prized, held dear, thought dutiful, beneficial, obligatory, or agreeable. We cannot explain why someone did what he did simply by saying the particular action appealed to him; we must indicate

Donald Davidson, "Actions, Reasons, and Causes," *The Journal of Philosophy*, LX (1963), 685–700. Reprinted by permission of the publisher and the author.

---

[1] Some examples: G. E. M. Anscombe, *Intention*, Oxford, 1959; Stuart Hampshire, *Thought and Action*, London, 1959; H. L. A. Hart and A. M. Honoré, *Causation in the Law*, Oxford, 1959; William Dray, *Laws and Explanation in History*, Oxford, 1957; and most of the books in the series edited by R. F. Holland, *Studies in Philosophical Psychology*, including Anthony Kenny, *Action, Emotion and Will*, London, 1963, and A. I. Melden, *Free Action*, London, 1961. Page references in parentheses will all be to these works.

what it was about the action that appealed. Whenever someone does something for a reason, therefore, he can be characterized as (*a*) having some sort of pro attitude toward actions of a certain kind, and (*b*) believing (or knowing, perceiving, noticing, remembering) that his action is of that kind. Under (*a*) are to be included desires, wantings, urges, promptings, and a great variety of moral views, aesthetic principles, economic prejudices, social conventions, and public and private goals and values in so far as these can be interpreted as attitudes of an agent directed toward actions of a certain kind. The word 'attitude' does yeoman service here, for it must cover not only permanent character traits that show themselves in a lifetime of behavior, like love of children or a taste for loud company, but also the most passing fancy that prompts a unique action, like a sudden desire to touch a woman's elbow. In general, pro attitudes must not be taken for convictions, however temporary, that every action of a certain kind ought to be performed, is worth performing, or is, all things considered, desirable. On the contrary, a man may all his life have a yen, say, to drink a can of paint, without ever, even at the moment he yields, believing it would be worth doing.

Giving the reason why an agent did something is often a matter of naming the pro attitude (*a*) or the related belief (*b*) or both; let me call this pair the *primary reason* why the agent performed the action. Now it is possible to reformulate the claim that rationalizations are causal explanations, and give structure to the argument as well, by stating two theses about primary reasons:

1. For us to understand how a reason of any kind rationalizes an action it is necessary and sufficient that we see, at least in essential outline, how to construct a primary reason.
2. The primary reason for an action is its cause.

I shall argue for these points in turn.

II

I flip the switch, turn on the light, and illuminate the room. Unbeknownst to me I also alert a prowler to the fact that I am home. Here I do not do four things, but only one, of which four descriptions have been given.[2] I flipped

---

[2] We would not call my unintentional alerting of the prowler an action, but it should not be inferred from this that alerting the prowler is therefore something different from flipping the switch, say just its consequence. Actions, performances, and events not involving intention are alike in that they are often referred to or defined partly in terms of some terminal stage, outcome, or consequence.

The word 'action' does not very often occur in ordinary speech, and when it does it is usually reserved for fairly portentous occasions. I follow a useful philosophical practice in calling anything an agent does intentionally an action, including intentional omissions. What is really needed is some suitably generic term to bridge the following gap: suppose 'A' is a description of an action, 'B' is a description of something done voluntarily, though not intentionally, and 'C' is a description of something done involuntarily and unintentionally; finally, suppose A = B = C. Then A, B, and C are the same—what? 'Action', 'event',

the switch because I wanted to turn on the light, and by saying I wanted to turn on the light I explain (give my reason for, rationalize) the flipping. But I do not, by giving this reason, rationalize my alerting of the prowler nor my illuminating of the room. Since reasons may rationalize what someone does when it is described in one way and not when it is described in another, we cannot treat what was done simply as a term in sentences like 'My reason for flipping the switch was that I wanted to turn on the light'; otherwise we would be forced to conclude, from the fact that flipping the switch was identical with alerting the prowler, that my reason for alerting the prowler was that I wanted to turn on the light. Let us mark this quasi-intensional[3] character of action descriptions in rationalizations by stating a bit more precisely a necessary condition for primary reasons:

> C1. R is a primary reason why an agent performed the action A under the description d only if R consists of a pro attitude of the agent toward actions with a certain property, and a belief of the agent that A, under the description d, has that property.

How can my wanting to turn on the light be (part of) a primary reason, since it appears to lack the required element of generality? We may be taken in by the verbal parallel between 'I turned on the light' and 'I wanted to turn on the light'. The first clearly refers to a particular event, so we conclude that the second has this same event as its object. Of course it is obvious that the event of my turning on the light can't be referred to in the same way by both sentences, since the existence of the event is required by the truth of 'I turned on the light' but not by the truth of 'I wanted to turn on the light'. If the reference were the same in both cases, the second sentence would entail the first; but in fact the sentences are logically independent. What is less obvious, at least until we attend to it, is that the event whose occurrence makes 'I turned on the light' true cannot be called the object, however intensional, of 'I wanted to turn on the light'. If I turned on the light, then I must have done it at a precise moment, in a particular way—every detail is fixed. But it makes no sense to demand that my want be directed at an action performed at any one moment or done in some unique manner. Any one of an indefinitely large number of actions would satisfy the want, and can be considered equally eligible as its object. Wants and desires often are trained on physical objects. However, 'I want that gold watch in the window' is not a primary reason, and explains why I went into the store only because it suggests a primary reason— for example, that I wanted to buy the watch.

'thing done', each have, at least in some contexts, a strange ring when coupled with the wrong sort of description. Only the question "Why did you (he) do A?" has the true generality required. Obviously, the problem is greatly aggravated if we assume, as Melden does (*Free Action*, 85), that an action ("raising one's arm") can be identical with a bodily movement ("one's arm going up").

[3] "Quasi-intensional" because, besides its intensional aspect, the description of the action must also refer in rationalizations; otherwise it could be true that an action was done for a certain reason and yet the action not have been performed. Compare 'the author of *Waverley*' in 'George IV knew the author of *Waverley* wrote *Waverley*'.

Because 'I wanted to turn on the light' and 'I turned on the light' are logically independent, the first can be used to give a reason why the second is true. Such a reason gives minimal information: it implies that the action was intentional, and wanting tends to exclude some other pro attitudes, such as a sense of duty or obligation. But the exclusion depends very much on the action and the context of explanation. Wanting seems pallid beside lusting, but it would be odd to deny that someone who lusted after a woman or a cup of coffee wanted her or it. It is not unnatural, in fact, to treat wanting as a genus including all pro attitudes as species. When we do this and when we know some action is intentional, it is empty to add that the agent wanted to do it. In such cases, it is easy to answer the question 'Why did you do it?' with 'For no reason', meaning not that there is no reason but that there is no *further* reason, no reason that cannot be inferred from the fact that the action was done intentionally; no reason, in other words, besides wanting to do it. This last point is not essential to the present argument, but it is of interest because it defends the possibility of defining an intentional action as one done for a reason.

A primary reason consists of a belief and an attitude, but it is generally otiose to mention both. If you tell me you are easing the jib because you think that will stop the main from backing, I don't need to be told that you want to stop the main from backing; and if you say you are biting your thumb at me because you want to insult me, there is no point in adding that you think that by biting your thumb at me you will insult me. Similarly, many explanations of actions in terms of reasons that are not primary do not require mention of the primary reason to complete the story. If I say I am pulling weeds because I want a beautiful lawn, it would be fatuous to eke out the account with 'And so I see something desirable in any action that does, or has a good chance of, making the lawn beautiful'. Why insist that there is any *step*, logical or psychological, in the transfer of desire from an end that is not an action to the actions one conceives as means? It serves the argument as well that the desired end explains the action only if what are believed by the agent to be means are desired.

Fortunately, it is not necessary to classify and analyze the many varieties of emotions, sentiments, moods, motives, passions, and hungers whose mention may answer the question 'Why did you do it?' in order to see how, when such mention rationalizes the action, a primary reason is involved. Claustrophobia gives a man's reason for leaving a cocktail party because we know people want to avoid, escape from, be safe from, put distance between themselves and what they fear. Jealousy is the motive in a poisoning because, among other things, the poisoner believes his action will harm his rival, remove the cause of his agony, or redress an injustice, and these are the sorts of things a jealous man wants to do. When we learn a man cheated his son out of greed, we do not necessarily know what the primary reason was, but we know there was one, and its general nature. [Gilbert—Ed.] Ryle analyzes 'he boasted from vanity' into "he boasted on meeting the stranger and his doing so satisfies the lawlike proposition that whenever he finds a chance of securing the admiration and envy of others, he does whatever he thinks will produce this admiration and envy" (*The Concept of Mind*, 89). This analysis is often, and perhaps justly, criticized on the ground that a man may boast from vanity just once. But if Ryle's boaster did what he did from vanity, then something entailed by Ryle's analysis is true: the boaster wanted to secure the admiration and envy of others, and he believed that his action would produce this admiration and envy; true or false, Ryle's analysis does not dispense with primary reasons, but depends upon them.

To know a primary reason why someone acted as he did is to know an intention with which the action was done. If I turn left at the fork because I want to get to Katmandu, my intention in turning left is to get to Katmandu. But to know the intention is not necessarily to know the primary reason in full detail. If James goes to church with the intention of pleasing his mother, then he must have some pro attitude toward pleasing his mother, but it needs more information to tell whether his reason is that he enjoys pleasing his mother, or thinks it right, his duty, or an obligation. The expression 'the intention with which James went to church' has the outward form of a description, but in fact it is syncategorematic and cannot be taken to refer to an entity, state, disposition, or event. Its function in context is to generate new descriptions of actions in terms of their reasons; thus 'James went to church with the intention of pleasing his mother' yields a new, and fuller, description of the action described in 'James went to church'. Essentially the same process goes on when I answer the question 'Why are you bobbing around that way?' with 'I'm knitting, weaving, exercising, sculling, cuddling, training fleas'.

Straight description of an intended result often explains an action better than stating that the result was intended or desired. 'It will soothe your nerves' explains why I pour you a shot as efficiently as 'I want to do something to soothe your nerves', since the first in the context of explanation implies the second; but the first does better, because, if it is true, the facts will justify my choice of action. Because justifying and explaining an action so often go hand in hand, we frequently indicate the primary reason for an action by making a claim which, if true, would also verify, vindicate, or support the relevant belief or attitude of the agent. 'I knew I ought to return it', 'The paper said it was going to snow', 'You stepped on *my* toes', all, in appropriate reason-giving contexts, perform this familiar dual function.

The justifying role of a reason, given this interpretation, depends upon the explanatory role, but the converse does not hold. Your stepping on my toes neither explains nor justifies my stepping on your toes unless I believe you stepped on my toes, but the belief alone, true or false, explains my action.

III

In the light of a primary reason, an action is revealed as coherent with certain traits, long- or short-termed, characteristic or not, of the agent, and the agent is shown in his role of Rational Animal. Corresponding to the belief and attitude of a primary reason for an action, we can always construct (with a little ingenuity) the premises of a syllogism from which it follows that the action has some (as Miss [G. E. M.—Ed.] Anscombe calls it) "desirability characteristic."[4] Thus there is a certain irreducible—though somewhat anemic—sense in which every rationalization justifies: from the agent's point of view there was, when he acted, something to be said for the action.

Noting that nonteleological causal explanations do not display the element of justification provided by reasons, some philosophers have concluded that the concept of cause that applies elsewhere cannot apply to the relation between reasons and actions, and that the pattern of justification provides, in the case of reasons, the required explanation. But suppose we grant that reasons alone justify in explaining actions; it does not follow that the explanation is not also—and necessarily—causal. Indeed our first condition for primary reasons (C1) is designed to help set rationalizations apart from other sorts of explanation. If rationalization is, as I want to argue, a species of causal explanation, then justification, in the sense given by C1, is at least one differentiating property. How about the other claim: that justifying is a kind of explaining, so that the ordinary notion of cause need not be brought in? Here it is necessary to decide what is being included under justification. Perhaps it means only what is given by C1: that the agent has certain beliefs and attitudes in the light of which the action is reasonable. But then something essential has certainly been left out, for a person can have a reason for an action, and perform the action, and yet this reason not be the reason why he did it. Central to the relation between a reason and an action it explains is the idea that the agent performed the action *because* he had the reason. Of course, we can include this idea too in justification; but then the notion of justification becomes as dark as the notion of reason until we can account for the force of that 'because'.

When we ask why someone acted as he did, we want to be provided with an interpretation. His behavior seems strange, alien, outré, pointless, out of character, disconnected; or perhaps we cannot even recognize an action in it. When we learn his reason, we have an interpretation, a new description of what he did which fits it into a familiar picture. The picture certainly includes some of the agent's beliefs and attitudes; perhaps also goals, ends, principles, general character traits, virtues or vices. Beyond this, the redescription of an action afforded by a reason may place the action in a wider social, economic, linguistic, or evaluative context. To learn, through learning the reason, that the agent conceived his action as a lie, a repayment of a debt, an insult, the fulfillment of an avuncular obligation, or a knight's gambit is to grasp the point of the action in its setting of rules, practices, conventions, and expectations.

---

[4] Miss Anscombe denies that the practical syllogism is deductive. This she does partly because she thinks of the practical syllogism, as Aristotle does, as corresponding to a piece of practical reasoning (whereas for me it is only part of the analysis of the concept of a reason with which someone acted), and therefore she is bound, again following Aristotle, to think of the conclusion of a practical syllogism as corresponding to a judgment, not merely that the action has a desirable characteristic, but that the action is desirable (reasonable, worth doing, etc.).

Remarks like these, inspired by the later [Ludwig—Ed.] Wittgenstein, have been elaborated with subtlety and insight by a number of philosophers. And there is no denying that this is true: when we explain an action, by giving the reason, we do redescribe the action; redescribing the action gives the action a place in a pattern, and in this way the action is explained. Here it is tempting to draw two conclusions that do not follow. First, we can't infer, from the fact that giving reasons merely redescribes the action and that causes are separate from effects, that therefore reasons are not causes. Reasons, being beliefs and attitudes, are certainly not identical with actions; but, more important, events are often redescribed in terms of their causes. (Suppose someone was injured. We could redescribe this event "in terms of a cause" by saying he was burned.) Second, it is an error to think that, because placing the action in a larger pattern explains it, therefore we now understand the sort of explanation involved. Talk of patterns and contexts does not answer the question of how reasons explain actions, since the relevant pattern or context contains both reason and action. One way we can explain an event is by placing it in the context of its cause; cause and effect form the sort of pattern that explains the effect, in a sense of 'explain' that we understand as well as any. If reason and action illustrate a different pattern of explanation, that pattern must be identified.

Let me urge the point in connection with an example of [A. I.—Ed.] Melden's. A man driving an automobile raises his arm in order to signal. His intention, to signal, explains his action, raising his arm, by redescribing it as signaling. What is the pattern that explains the action? Is it the familiar pattern of an action done for a reason? Then it does indeed explain the action, but only because it assumes the relation of reason and action that we want to analyze. Or is the pattern rather this: the man is driving, he is approaching a turn; he knows he ought to signal; he knows how to signal, by raising his arm. And now, in this context, he raises his arm. Perhaps, as Melden suggests, if all this happens, he does signal. And the explanation would then be this: if, under these conditions, a man raises his arm, then he signals. The difficulty is, of course, that this explanation does not touch the question of why he raised his arm. He had a reason to raise his arm, but this has not been shown to be the reason why he did it. If the description 'signaling' explains his action by giving his reason, then the signaling must be intentional; but, on the account just given, it may not be.

If, as Melden claims, causal explanations are "wholly irrelevant to the understanding we seek" of human actions (184) then we are without an analysis of the 'because' in 'He did it because . . .', where we go on to name a reason. [Stuart—Ed.] Hampshire remarks, of the relation between reasons and action, "In philosophy one ought surely to find this . . . connection altogether mysterious" (166). Hampshire rejects Aristotle's attempt to solve the mystery by introducing the concept of wanting as a causal factor, on the grounds that the resulting theory is too clear and definite to fit all cases and that "There is still no compelling ground for insisting that the word 'want' *must* enter into every full statement of reasons for acting" (168). I agree that the concept of wanting is too narrow, but I have argued that, at least in a vast number of typical cases, some pro attitude must be assumed to be present if a statement of an agent's reasons in acting is to be intelligible. Hampshire does not see how Aristotle's scheme can be appraised as true or false, "for it is not clear what could be the basis of assessment, or what kind of evidence could be decisive" (167). Failing a satisfactory alternative, the best argument for a scheme like Aristotle's is that it alone promises to give an account of the "mysterious connection" between reasons and actions.

IV

In order to turn the first 'and' to 'because' in 'He exercised *and* he wanted to reduce and thought exercise would do it', we must, as the basic move,[5] augment condition C1 with:

C2. A primary reason for an action is its cause.

The considerations in favor of C2 are by now, I hope, obvious; in the remainder of this paper I wish to defend C2 against various lines of attack and, in the process, to clarify the notion of causal explanation involved.

A. The first line of attack is this. Primary reasons consist of attitudes and beliefs, which are states or dispositions, not events; therefore they cannot be causes.

It is easy to reply that states, dispositions, and conditions are frequently named as the causes of events: the bridge collapsed because of a structural defect; the plane crashed on takeoff because the air temperature was abnormally high; the plate broke because it had a crack. This reply does not, however, meet a closely related point. Mention of a causal condition for an event gives a cause only on the assumption that there was also a preceding event. But what is the preceding event that causes an action?

In many cases it is not difficult at all to find events very closely associated with the primary reason. States and dispositions are not events, but the onslaught of a state or disposition is. A desire to hurt your feelings may spring up at the moment you anger me; I may start wanting to eat a melon just when I see one; and beliefs may begin at the moment we notice, perceive, learn, or remember something. Those who have argued that there are no mental events to qualify as causes of actions have often missed the obvious because they have insisted that a mental event be observed or noticed (rather than an observing or a noticing) or that it be like a stab, a qualm, a prick or a quiver, a mysterious prod of conscience or act of the will. Melden, in discussing the driver who signals a turn by raising his arm, challenges those who want to explain actions causally to identify "an event which is common and peculiar to all such cases"

---

[5] I say "as the basic move" to cancel the suggestion that C1 and C2 are jointly *sufficient* to define the relation of reasons to the actions they explain. I believe C2 can be strengthened to make C1 and C2 sufficient as well as necessary conditions, but here I am concerned only with the claim that both are, as they stand, necessary.

(87), perhaps a motive or an intention, anyway "some particular feeling or experience" (95). But of course there is a mental event; at some moment the driver noticed (or thought he noticed) his turn coming up, and that is the moment he signaled. During any continuing activity, like driving or elaborate performance, like swimming the Hellespont, there are more or less fixed purposes, standards, desires, and habits that give direction and form to the entire enterprise, and there is the continuing input of information about what we are doing, about changes in the environment, in terms of which we regulate and adjust our actions. To dignify a driver's awareness that his turn has come by calling it an experience, much less a feeling, is no doubt exaggerated, but whether it deserves a name or not, it had better be the reason why he raises his arm. In this case, and typically, there may not be anything we would call a motive, but if we mention such a general purpose as wanting to get to one's destination safely, it is clear that the motive is not an event. The intention with which the driver raises his arm is also not an event, for it is no thing at all, neither event, attitude, disposition, nor object. Finally, Melden asks the causal theorist to find an event that is common and peculiar to all cases where a man intentionally raises his arm, and this, it must be admitted, cannot be produced. But then neither can a common and unique cause of bridge failures, plane crashes, or plate breakings be produced.

The signaling driver can answer the question 'Why did you raise your arm when you did?', and from the answer we learn the event that caused the action. But can an actor always answer such a question? Sometimes the answer will mention a mental event that does not give a reason: 'Finally I made up my mind'. However, there also seem to be cases of intentional action where we cannot explain at all why we acted when we did. In such cases, explanation in terms of primary reasons parallels the explanation of the collapse of the bridge from a structural defect: we are ignorant of the event or sequence of events that led up to (caused) the collapse, but we are sure there was such an event or sequence of events.

B. According to Melden, a cause must be "logically distinct from the alleged effect" (52); but a reason for an action is not logically distinct from the action; therefore, reasons are not causes of actions.[6]

One possible form of this argument has already been suggested. Since a reason makes an action intelligible by redescribing it, we do not have two events, but only one under different descriptions. Causal relations, however, demand distinct events.

Someone might be tempted into the mistake of thinking that my flipping of the switch caused my turning on of the light (in fact it caused the light to go on). But it does not follow that it is a mistake to take 'My reason for flipping the switch was that I wanted to turn on the light' as entailing, in part,

---

[6] This argument can be found, in one or more versions, in Kenny, Hampshire, and Melden, as well as in P. Winch, *The Idea of a Social Science*, London, 1958, and R. S. Peters, *The Concept of Motivation*, London, 1958. In one of its forms, the argument was of course inspired by Ryle's treatment of motives in *The Concept of Mind*.

'I flipped the switch, and this action is further describable as having been caused by my wanting to turn on the light'. To describe an event in terms of its cause is not to identify the event with its cause, nor does explanation by redescription exclude causal explanation.

The example serves also to refute the claim that we cannot describe the action without using words that link it to the alleged cause. Here the action is to be explained under the description: 'my flipping the switch', and the alleged cause is 'my wanting to turn on the light'. What possible logical relation is supposed to hold between these phrases? It seems more plausible to urge a logical link between 'my turning on the light' and 'my wanting to turn on the light', but even here the link turned out, on inspection, to be grammatical rather than logical.

In any case there is something very odd in the idea that causal relations are empirical rather than logical. What can this mean? Surely not that every true causal statement is empirical. For suppose 'A caused B' is true. Then the cause of $B = A$; so, substituting, we have 'The cause of B caused B', which is analytic. The truth of a causal statement depends on *what* events are described; its status as analytic or synthetic depends on *how* the events are described. Still, it may be maintained that a reason rationalizes an action only when the descriptions are appropriately fixed, and the appropriate descriptions are not logically independent.

Suppose that to say a man wanted to turn on the light *meant* that he would perform any action he believed would accomplish his end. Then the statement of his primary reason for flipping the switch would entail that he flipped the switch—"straightaway he acts," as Aristotle says. In this case there would certainly be a logical connection between reason and action, the same sort of connection as that between 'It's water-soluble and was placed in water' and 'It dissolved'. Since the implication runs from description of cause to description of effect but not conversely, naming the cause still gives information. And, though the point is often overlooked, 'Placing it in water caused it to dissolve' does not entail 'It's water-soluble'; so the latter has additional explanatory force. Nevertheless, the explanation would be far more interesting if, in place of solubility, with its obvious definitional connection with the event to be explained, we could refer to some property, say a particular crystalline structure, whose connection with dissolution in water was known only through experiment. Now it is clear why primary reasons like desires and wants do not explain actions in the relatively trivial way solubility explains dissolvings. Solubility, we are assuming, is a pure disposition property: it is defined in terms of a single test. But desires cannot be defined in terms of the actions they may rationalize, even though the relation between desire and action is not simply empirical; there are other, equally essential criteria for desires—their expression in feelings and in actions that they do not rationalize, for example. The person who has a desire (or want or belief) does not normally need criteria at all—he generally knows, even in the absence of any clues available to others, what he wants, desires, and believes. These logical features of primary reasons show that it is not just lack of ingenuity that keeps us from defining them as dispositions to act for these reasons.

C. According to [David—Ed.] Hume, "we may define a cause to be an object, followed by another, and where all the objects similar to the first are followed by objects similar to the second." But, [H. L. A.—Ed.] Hart and [A. M.—Ed.] Honoré claim, "The statement that one person did something because, for example, another threatened him, carries no implication or covert assertion that if the circumstances were repeated the same action would follow" (52). Hart and Honoré allow that Hume is right in saying that ordinary singular causal statements imply generalizations, but wrong for this very reason in supposing that motives and desires are ordinary causes of actions. In brief, laws are involved essentially in ordinary causal explanations, but not in rationalizations.

It is common to try to meet this argument by suggesting that we do have rough laws connecting reasons and actions, and these can, in theory, be improved. True, threatened people do not always respond in the same way; but we may distinguish between threats and also between agents, in terms of their beliefs and attitudes.

The suggestion is delusive, however, because generalizations connecting reasons and actions are not—and cannot be sharpened into—the kind of law on the basis of which accurate predictions can reliably be made. If we reflect on the way in which reasons determine choice, decision, and behavior, it is easy to see why this is so. What emerges, in the *ex post facto* atmosphere of explanation and justification, as *the* reason frequently was, to the agent at the time of action, one consideration among many, *a* reason. Any serious theory for predicting action on the basis of reasons must find a way of evaluating the relative force of various desires and beliefs in the matrix of decision; it cannot take as its starting point the refinement of what is to be expected from a single desire. The practical syllogism exhausts its role in displaying an action as falling under one reason; so it cannot be subtilized into a reconstruction of practical reasoning, which involves the weighing of competing reasons. The practical syllogism provides a model neither for a predictive science of action nor for a normative account of evaluative reasoning.

Ignorance of competent predictive laws does not inhibit valid causal explanation, or few causal explanations could be made. I am certain the window broke because it was struck by a rock—I saw it all happen; but I am not (is anyone?) in command of laws on the basis of which I can predict what blows will break which windows. A generalization like 'Windows are fragile, and fragile things tend to break when struck hard enough, other conditions being right' is not a predictive law in the rough—the predictive law, if we had it, would be quantitative and would use very different concepts. The generalization, like our generalizations about behavior, serves a different function: it provides evidence for the existence of a causal law covering the case at hand.

We are usually far more certain of a singular causal connection than we are of any causal law governing the case; does this show that Hume was wrong in claiming that singular causal statements entail laws? Not necessarily, for Hume's claim, as quoted above, is ambiguous. It may mean that 'A caused B' entails some particular law involving the predicates used in the descriptions 'A' and 'B', or it may mean that 'A caused B' entails that there exists a causal law instantiated by some true descriptions of A and B.[7] Obviously, both versions of Hume's doctrine give a sense to the claim that singular causal statements entail laws, and both sustain the view that causal explanations "involve laws." But the second version is far weaker, in that no particular law is entailed by a singular causal claim, and a singular causal claim can be defended, if it needs defense, without defending any law. Only the second version of Hume's doctrine can be made to fit with most causal explanations; it suits rationalizations equally well.

The most primitive explanation of an event gives its cause; more elaborate explanations may tell more of the story, or defend the singular causal claim by producing a relevant law or by giving reasons for believing such exists. But it is an error to think no explanation has been given until a law has been produced. Linked with these errors is the idea that singular causal statements necessarily indicate, by the concepts they employ, the concepts that will occur in the entailed law. Suppose a hurricane, which is reported on page 5 of Tuesday's *Times*, causes a catastrophe, which is reported on page 13 of Wednesday's *Tribune*. Then the event reported on page 5 of Tuesday's *Times* caused the event reported on page 13 of Wednesday's *Tribune*. Should we look for a law relating events of these *kinds?* It is only slightly less ridiculous to look for a law relating hurricanes and catastrophes. The laws needed to predict the catastrophe with precision would, of course, have no use for concepts like hurricane and catastrophe. The trouble with predicting the weather is that the descriptions under which events interest us—'a cool, cloudy day with rain in the afternoon'—have only remote connections with the concepts employed by the more precise known laws.

The laws whose existence is required if reasons are causes of actions do not, we may be sure, deal in the concepts in which rationalizations must deal. If the causes of a class of events (actions) fall in a certain class (reasons) and there is a law to back each singular causal statement, it does not follow that there is any law connecting events classified as reasons with events classified as actions—the classifications may even be neurological, chemical, or physical.

D. It is said that the kind of knowledge one has of one's own reasons in acting is not compatible with the existence of a causal relation between reasons and actions: a person knows his own intentions in acting infallibly, without induction or observation, and no ordinary causal relation can be known in this way. No doubt our knowledge of our own intentions in acting will show many of the oddities peculiar to first-person knowledge of one's own pains, beliefs, desires, and so on; the only question is whether these oddities prove that reasons do not cause, in any ordinary sense at least, the actions that they rationalize.

---

[7] We could roughly characterize the analysis of singular causal statments hinted at here as follows: 'A caused B' is true if and only if there are descriptions of A and B such that the sentence obtained by putting these descriptions for 'A' and 'B' in 'A caused B' follows from a true causal law. This analysis is saved from triviality by the fact that not all true generalizations are causal laws; causal laws are distinguished (though of course this is no analysis) by the fact that they are inductively confirmed by their instances and by the fact that they support counterfactual and subjunctive singular causal statements.

You may easily be wrong about the truth of a statement of the form 'I am poisoning Charles because I want to save him pain', because you may be wrong about whether you are poisoning Charles—you may yourself be drinking the poisoned cup by mistake. But it also seems that you may err about your reasons, particularly when you have two reasons for an action, one of which pleases you and one which does not. For example, you do want to save Charles pain; you also want him out of the way. You may be wrong about which motive made you do it.

The fact that you may be wrong does not show that in general it makes sense to ask you how you know what your reasons were or to ask for your evidence. Though you may, on rare occasions, accept public or private evidence as showing you are wrong about your reasons, you usually have no evidence and make no observations. Then your knowledge of your own reasons for your actions is not generally inductive, for where there is induction, there is evidence. Does this show the knowledge is not causal? I cannot see that it does.

Causal laws differ from true but nonlawlike generalizations in that their instances confirm them; induction is, therefore, certainly a good way to learn the truth of a law. It does not follow that it is the only way to learn the truth of a law. In any case, in order to know that a singular causal statement is true, it is not necessary to know the truth of a law; it is necessary only to know that some law covering the events at hand exists. And it is far from evident that induction, and induction alone, yields the knowledge that a causal law satisfying certain conditions exists. Or, to put it differently, one case is often enough, as Hume admitted, to persuade us that a law exists, and this amounts to saying that we are persuaded, without direct inductive evidence, that a causal relation exists.

E. Finally I should like to say something about a certain uneasiness some philosophers feel in speaking of causes of actions at all. Melden, for example, says that actions are often identical with bodily movements, and that bodily movements have causes; yet he denies that the causes are causes of the actions. This is, I think, a contradiction. He is led to it by the following sort of consideration: "It is futile to attempt to explain conduct through the causal efficacy of desire—all *that* can explain is further happenings, not actions performed by agents. The agent confronting the causal nexus in which such happenings occur is a helpless victim of all that occurs in and to him" (128, 129). Unless I am mistaken, this argument, if it were valid, would show that actions cannot have causes at all. I shall not point out the obvious difficulties in removing actions from the realm of causality entirely. But perhaps it is worth trying to uncover the source of the trouble. Why on earth should a cause turn an action into a mere happening and a person into a helpless victim? Is it because we tend to assume, at least in the arena of action, that a cause demands a causer, agency an agent? So we press the question; if my action is caused, what caused it? If I did, then there is the absurdity of infinite regress; if I did not, I am a victim. But of course the alternatives are not exhaustive. Some causes have no agents. Primary among these are those states and changes of state in persons which, because they are reasons as well as causes, make persons voluntary agents.

11

Charles Taylor
Purpose and Teleology

Charles Taylor has taught bilingually, in political science and philosophy, at McGill University and the University of Montreal. He has also been active in Canadian politics. He is known chiefly for The Explanation of Behavior (1964), *which not only undertakes a full-scale attack on behaviorism but also formulates the distinction between mechanical and teleological explanation. The distinction of the second, in the context of Taylor's argument, is that "the most basic laws" of a system may be such that the explanation of an event may not be given except in terms of that event's being required for a certain goal.*

Taylor argues that the present state of empirical science does not permit us to decide the comparative adequacy of the two sorts of explanation. In his view, the issue will have to be decided by empirical rather than merely logical considerations. There is a question, however, whether teleological explanations are favored in the absence of empirical evidence to support mechanical or at least nonteleological explanations expressed in terms of efficient causes. Teleology and deterministic accounts appear to preclude one another. Regardless of the solution, this consideration shows that a conceptual question remains as to the phenomena that would require a teleological account rather than a mechanical one. Taylor has also recently written a compendious study of Hegelian philosophy (Hegel, 1975).

It is often said that human behavior, or for that matter the behaviour of animals or even living organisms in general, is in some way fundamentally different from the processes in nature which are studied by the natural sciences. This opposition is variously expressed. It is sometimes said that the behaviour of human beings and animals shows a purposiveness which is not found elsewhere in nature, or that it has an intrinsic 'meaning' which natural processes do not. Or it is said that the behaviour of animate organisms exhibits an order which cannot be accounted for by the 'blind accident' of processes in nature. Or again, to draw the circle somewhat narrower, it is said of human beings and some animals that they are conscious of and direct their behaviour in a way which finds no analogue in inanimate nature, or that, specifically in an account of human affairs, concepts like 'significance' and 'value' play a uniquely important part which is denied them in natural science.

Against this view stands the opinion of many others, in particular of many students of the sciences of human behaviour, that there is no difference in principle between the behaviour of animate organisms and any other processes in nature, that the former can be accounted for in the same way as the latter, by

From Charles Taylor, *The Explanation of Behaviour* (London: Routledge and Kegan Paul, 1964). Reprinted also by permission of Humanities Press Inc., New Jersey.

laws relating physical events, and that the introduction of such notions as 'purpose' and 'mind' can only serve to obscure and confuse. This is in particular the point of view of the widely spread school of thought in psychology known as 'behaviourist'.

Now the issue between these two views is one of fundamental and perennial importance for what is often called philosophical anthropology, the study of the basic categories in which man and his behaviour is to be described and explained. That this question is central to any science of human behaviour—if such a science is possible—needs no showing. But this does not by any means exhaust its importance. For it is also central to ethics. Thus there is a type of ethical reflexion, exemplified for instance in the work of Aristotle, which attempts to discover what men should do and how they should behave by a study of human nature and its fundamental goals. This is the attempt to elaborate what is often called a 'humanism'. The premiss underlying this reflexion, which is by no means confined to philosophers, is that there is a form of life which is higher or more properly human than others, and that the dim intuition of the ordinary man to this effect can be vindicated in its substance or else corrected in its content by a deeper understanding of human nature. But this premiss collapses once it is shown, if it ever is, that human behaviour cannot be accounted for in terms of goals or purposes but must be explained on mechanistic principles; for then the concept of fundamental human goals or of a way of life more consonant with the purposes of human nature—or even the existentialist notion that our basic goals are chosen by ourselves—will be shown to have no application.

A similar premiss, that a purpose or set of purposes which are intrinsically human can be identified, underlies all philosophical and other reflexion concerning the 'meaning' of human existence, and this, too, would collapse if the mechanistic thesis were shown to hold.

These brief remarks, which still do not exhaust the ramifications of this question, are enough to show why it has been of perennial interest to philosophers and laymen. And yet in spite of, or perhaps because of this, it still awaits resolution. We might try to explain this simply by pleading lack of evidence. In fact the sciences of man are in their infancy. But this cannot be the whole explanation. In fact, it seems simply to put us before the same question in another form. For we might just as truly say that the sciences of man, and particularly psychology, are in their infancy because this question remains unresolved. It is not enough, therefore, simply to invoke research. In fact the trouble is deeper: we have first to know where to look. And when we ask ourselves *this* question, we find ourselves well and truly at sea.

In fact there has never been agreement among philosophers or other students as to what is at stake here, that is, on the meaning of the claim that human behaviour is purposive, or, what is the same thing, on what the relevant evidence is which would decide it. As a matter of fact, it is not even generally agreed that it is a matter of finding evidence in the first place, for some thinkers hold that the issue is not in any sense an empirical one, but rather that it can be decided simply by logical argument.

This confusion might tempt us to say that the question is insoluble, or even that it is a pseudo-question. But this radical 'solution' would itself have to be established by some argument about the nature of the putative issue involved. Before finally turning our backs on the matter in this way, therefore, it is worth trying once more to define what is at stake. . . .

1. Teleological Explanation

What, then, does it mean to say that human, or animal, behaviour is purposive? Central to this claim would seem to be the view that the order or pattern which is visible in animate behaviour is radically different from that visible elsewhere in nature in that it is in some sense self-imposed; the order is itself in some way a factor in its own production. This seems to be the force of the rejection of 'blind accident': the prevalence of order cannot be accounted for on principles which are only contingently or 'accidentally' connected with it, by laws whose operation only contingently results in it, but must be accounted for in terms of the order itself.

The point, then, could perhaps be put in this way: the events productive of order in animate beings are to be explained not in terms of other unconnected antecedent conditions, but in terms of the very order which they produce. These events are held to occur because of what results from them, or, to put it in a more traditional way, they occur 'for the sake of' the state of affairs which follows. And this of course is part of what is meant by the term 'purpose' when it is invoked in explanation. For to explain by purpose is to explain by the goal or result aimed at, 'for the sake of' which the event is said to occur.

Explanation which invokes the goal for the sake of which the explicandum occurs is generally called teleological explanation, and thus at least part of what we mean by saying that human or animal behaviour is purposive is that it is to be accounted for by a teleological form of explanation.[1]

But does this take us any further ahead? What is meant by teleological explanation and how can we establish whether it holds or not of a given range of phenomena? The remainder of this chapter will be devoted to an attempt to answer this question, and to cut through the skein of confusions which usually makes it difficult to bring this question into focus.

2. An Empirical Question?

Now a first difficulty arises straight off with the objection that this question, whether or not a teleological explanation holds, is not an empirical one at all. In fact many theorists, and particularly students of what can roughly be called

---

[1] That this is not all that is meant by 'purposive' will be made clear in [later chapters—Ed.]. But it will help as a simplifying assumption for the discussion in this chapter if we forget this and treat 'explanation by purpose' and 'teleological explanation' as interchangeable.

the behavioural sciences, would hold that the claim that animate behaviour must be explained teleologically or in terms of purpose is a meaningless one, empirically empty or 'metaphysical', that the whole question is a 'pseudo-question'. This is especially true of many theorists in the field of experimental psychology, those of the behaviourist school, on which the discussion later . . . will mainly centre. These thinkers, extremely hostile to the claims of teleo-logical explanation, make short work of it by purporting to expose, in summary fashion, its non-empirical character.

If this objection is a valid one, then our whole enquiry is stopped before it starts. But, as a matter of fact, it is not. In fact, it reposes on an interpretation of the notions of purpose and teleological explanation which is arbitrary and by no means imposed on us.

Thus the claim that we must explain the behaviour of a given system in terms of purpose is often taken to mean that we must explain it by laws of the form $x = f(P)$, where 'x' is the behaviour and 'P' is the Purpose considered as a separate entity which is the cause or antecedent of x. Of course the view that an explanation in terms of purpose involves the postulating of a special entity is by no means confined to those who are hostile to the idea. Many who were on the 'vitalist' side of the controversy in biology made use of a hypothetical entity of this kind. (Cf. [H.—Ed.] Driesch's 'entelechy.') But there is no doubt that the end result of this is to create a handy Aunt Sally for the mechanists. For a theory of this kind can neither be confirmed nor add in any way to our power of predicting and controlling the phenomena.

This can be readily seen. In fact, the only empirical evidence for the operation of the purpose is the behaviour which its operation is used to explain. There is thus no conceivable evidence which could falsify a hypothesis of this kind because whenever the behaviour is emitted, the purpose responsible is *ex hypothesi* assumed to have been operating. And at the same time we would never be able to predict behaviour with the aid of such a hypothesis. For if x having a value of x_1 is due to P having the value P_1, and if the only evidence for P_1 is the occurrence of x_1, then we have no way of knowing beforehand what the value of x will be.

Now, of course, we might find some antecedent conditions for P, such that we could determine the value of P *ex ante* [from those conditions—Ed.] by means of a function such as $P = f(a)$. But then we would be turning P into what is often called an 'intervening variable',[2] that is, a term useful in calculation which is nevertheless without empirical content, which is not itself an empirical descriptive term. For in this case the entire empirical content of the two functions $P = f(a)$ and $x = f(P)$ could be expressed in one more complex function linking a and x directly, $x = F(a)$. What is meant by saying that 'P' is not an empirical descriptive term is that no single proposition about P is open to empirical confirmation or infirmation. Thus, in the case above,

---

[2] Cf. K. MacCorquodale and P. E. Meehl, 'On a Distinction Between Hypothetical Constructs and Intervening Variables', *Psychological Review*, 1948, although the sense of the term here differs slightly from their interpretation.

neither of these functions can be verified singly. We have seen above that this is true of $x = f(P)$, but it is equally so of $P = f(a)$. The proposition formed by the conjunction of both is open to empirical confirmation, but then the evidence for this is the same as the evidence for $x = F(a)$ which makes no mention of P. That is, no empirical sense can be given to the supposition that $x = F(a)$ be true and the conjunction of the two functions false. Thus the question whether or not the functions containing 'P' are to be accepted is not an empirical but purely a stipulative question, to be determined by the convenience in the calculation. 'P' is therefore not an empirical descriptive term.

Thus those who hold that 'purpose' is essential to the explanation of the behaviour of animate organisms are left with the unattractive choice either of making an unverifiable claim of no explanatory utility in science or of winning their point at the expense of making the laws true by stipulation. This view of the matter is very common among behaviour psychologists who are unsympathetic to this claim. Their view seems to be that their opponents adopt the first position, that of positing an unobservable entity, propositions about which cannot be verified. Thus [D. O.—Ed.] Hebb in the first chapter of his *The Organization of Behaviour* speaks interchangeably of 'animism' (the view that animate behaviour must be explained in terms of 'purpose') and 'interactionism' (the view that behaviour is the result of the interaction of observable physical and unobservable 'inner' or mental processes) and of course 'mysticism' (which doesn't seem to have a very clear sense in Hebb's usage but which means something counter-empirical, unscientific and generally nasty). Similarly, [K.—Ed.] Spence[3] speaks of animistic theories as those in which the relation of the (unobservable) constructs to the empirical (observable) variables is left entirely unspecified (and hence they are unverifiable as in the first alternative above).

The upshot of this view, then, is that the claim that animate organisms have a special status is undecidable, or rather that even to make it is to say something which cannot be verified. If the question is not to be closed here we shall have to examine explanation by purpose more closely in order to determine whether it must involve the postulating of an unobservable entity which is the cause or the antecedent condition of behaviour.

Now, as we have said, explanation by purpose involves the use of a teleological form of explanation, of explanation in terms of the result for the sake of which the events concerned occur. Now when we say that an event occurs for the sake of an end, we are saying that it occurs because it is the type of event which brings about this end. This means that the condition of the event's occurring is that a state of affairs obtain such that it will bring about the end in question, or such that this event is required to bring about that end.[4] To offer

---

[3] 'The Nature of Theory Construction in Contemporary Psychology,' *Psychological Review*, 1944.

[4] The difference is small between these two formulae. To say that an event is required for an end is to say more than that it will bring it about; for it adds that no other event, or none other in the system concerned can bring it about. A sufficient condition of a teleological kind can only be found for an event if it is in this unique position; if there are several possibilities we cannot account for the selection between them unless we add another

a teleological explanation of some event or class of events, e.g., the behaviour of some being, is, then, to account for it by laws in terms of which an event's occurring is held to be dependent on that event's being required for some end.

To say that the behaviour of a given system should be explained in terms of purpose, then, is, in part, to make an assertion about the form of the laws, or the type of laws which hold of the system. But *qua* teleological these laws will not be of the kind which makes behaviour a function of the state of some unobservable entity; rather the behaviour is a function of the state of the system and (in the case of animate organisms) its environment; but the relevant feature of system and environment on which behaviour depends will be what the condition of both makes necessary if the end concerned is to be realized. Thus for instance, we can say that the conditions for a given action, say a predator stalking his prey, are (1) that the animal be hungry, and (2) that this be the 'required' action, i.e., the action in his repertoire which will achieve the result—catching his next meal. The condition of an event B occurring, is, then, not a certain state of P, but that the state of the system S and the environment E be such that B is required for the end G_2 by which the system's purpose is defined.

Now the fact that the state of a system and its environment is such as to require a given event if a certain result is to accrue can be perfectly observable, and the fact that this antecedent condition holds can be established independently of the evidence provided by the occurrence of the event itself. This type of law, therefore, does not suffer from the disabilities of functions of the type $x = f(P)$. On the contrary, whether laws of this kind hold can be verified or falsified, and, if true, they can be used to predict and control the phenomena like any others. To say that a system can only be explained in terms of purpose, then—at least insofar as this is an assertion about the form of the laws— does not involve making an unverifiable claim any more than it involves postulating an unobservable entity. The element of 'purposiveness' in a given system, the inherent tendency towards a certain end, which is conveyed by saying that the events happen 'for the sake of' the end, cannot be identified as a special entity which directs the behaviour from within, but consists rather in the fact that in beings with a purpose an event's being required for a given end is a sufficient condition of its occurrence. It is not a separable feature, but a property of the whole system, that by which it tends 'naturally' towards a certain result or end. It is this notion of a 'natural tendency' towards a certain result or end—which we shall discuss at greater length in the next section— which lies behind the notion that, in systems whose behaviour must be accounted for by laws of this kind, the order which results cannot be attributed to 'blind accident', that is, to principles which are only contingently connected

---

teleological principle, e.g., of least effort. Since the putative teleological systems [in question— Ed.], i.e., organisms, seem to manifest some such principle, or else to select between alternatives when these are available in the repertoire on some other teleological principle, e.g., by certain standards which are norms to be observed, we shall generally assume the selection as made, and speak elliptically of 'the event required for' the goal or end.

with the bringing about and maintenance of this order; for the principle underlying the laws by which the behaviour is explained is itself a tendency to produce
this order.

3. Assumptions of Atomism

What considerations, then, led to the belief held by mechanists and vitalists
alike that the claim to some special status involved the postulating of some
special entity? The background to this belief is very complex and exploring
it would involve unravelling a skein of connected questions which surround this
subject, some of which we hope to return to [later.—Ed.]. But at this stage one
of the causes can perhaps be laid bare.

We can readily see that, in any explanatory functional law, the antecedent
and the consequent must be separately identifiable. Thus it cannot be a logical
condition for the occurrence of the antecedent that the consequent occur.
Something like this was what was the matter with our $x = f(P)$. True, it was
not a condition (logically) of P having a certain value that x have the corresponding value demanded by the function, but since the latter was the only
evidence for the former, it came to much the same thing. Similarly, the
antecedent's occurring cannot be a logical condition of the consequent's being
held to occur. Now teleological laws meet this requirement. For the antecedent
may occur independently of the consequent, and vice versa.

But there is a stronger requirement which teleological laws cannot meet.
This not only demands that the two terms which are linked in a law be identifiable separately from each other, that is, that it not be a condition for identification of either term that it be linked to the other term in the law,[5] but also that
each term be identified separately from *any* law in which it may figure, i.e., that
it not be a condition for the identification of any term that it be linked to any
other. Now this more stringent requirement arises from the atomism which is
part of the tradition of empiricism, and is ultimately founded on epistemological
grounds. The notion is that the ultimate evidence for any laws we frame about
the world is in the form of discrete units of information,[6] each of which could
be as it is even if all others were different, i.e., each of which is separably
identifiable from its connexions with any of the others. Our knowledge of the
world is built up from the empirical connexions which are found to hold (contingently) in experience between these units. Thus the evidence for any law
can ultimately be given, although perhaps with great tedium, in terms of
connexions between such discrete units. Thus if a given chemical C, with
defining properties x, y and z, is held to produce a certain result R in some

---

[5] We can, of course, decide to make this a condition of identification, but then we
cease to have an empirical law which can figure in explanation. This may, however, be more
convenient. Thus, e.g., we can consider it to be among the defining properties of a chemical
that it melt at a certain temperature.

[6] E.g., [David—Ed.] Hume's 'impressions' to which all 'ideas' must be ultimately referred.

conditions, although we may usually for convenience sake speak of this law as $C - R$, the ultimate evidence for it is the concomitance of x, y, z and R, each of which is identifiable separably from the others.

Now teleological laws cannot meet this stringent requirement of reduction to the basic type of evidence required by atomism. In this way, teleological explanation is, as has often been remarked, connected with some form of holism, or anti-atomistic doctrine. The first term of a teleological correlation violates the stringent requirement since it identifies the antecedent condition of the event to be accounted for, B, as a state of affairs in which B will lead to G. Thus the antecedent is identified in terms of its law-like connexions with two other events, B and G, i.e., as that state of affairs in which, when B occurs, G will follow. This law, therefore, is elliptical as it stands, and, on atomist assumptions, we should be able to restate it in a more satisfactory way. But this cannot be done, or at least it cannot be done without transforming the law into a non-teleological one.

This might seem odd. Surely that state of affairs which is such that B will lead to $G(B - G)$ can also be identified intrinsically, that is, without reference to its relation to other states of affairs. Thus to return to the examples above of the predator stalking his prey: instead of describing the environment in which the animal is now beginning to stalk as one which requires this action for the goal of getting food, we could characterize it intrinsically, without making any reference to his goals, e.g., by simply enumerating the components, or by mentioning certain key stimuli which are impinging on his receptors. Let us call this intrinsic type of characterization E. Then for any teleological law we can state a new law $E - B$ and this, together with a law to the effect that E and B together produce G will convey the content of the original teleological law. We will assume that E, B and G are all separably identifiable from each other (and either that they are separably identifiable from all other terms or that they could be further broken down). But now a startling result has occurred. We no longer have a teleological law, but instead two laws of a non-teleological kind, $E - B$ and $E + B - G$, from which can be deduced a third, also non-teleological law $E - G$; for none of these characterizes the antecedent as requiring the consequent if some result is to accrue. The teleological explanation has disappeared like the morning dew.

It is commonly assumed among empiricist philosophers that such a translation-out-of-existence can always be effected. Thus [Ernest—Ed.] Nagel[7] assumes that a non-teleological account can always be given of a system which, like the living organism, shows 'goal-directedness'. He imagines a system S which maintains state G and has three components A, B and C, which operate in such a way that if A undergoes a change which will carry the system out of G, B and C will compensate so as to maintain the system in this condition. Such a system is recognizably like living organisms in their 'homeostatic' functions, e.g., if the

---

[7] 'Teleological Explanations and Teleological Systems' in Feigl and Brodbeck, (Eds), *Readings in the Philosophy of Science*.

temperature of the air falls, the body will 'compensate' to maintain 'G', in this case the body temperature normal for the species. Of course, as I have stated it, the account is still teleological in form, for the changes in B and C were characterized as 'compensating' so as to maintain the G-state. But there is no reason, thinks Nagel, why we should not characterize the functions linking changes in B and C to those in A in a non-teleological way, by laws of the form, whenever A changes from Am to An, then B changes from Bx to By and C . . . , etc.[8] Thus, for instance, we would be able to express the antecedent for a given change in B, say, which in fact produces G, in terms other than that this change is required by the system for G, namely in terms of the states of A and C. This would correspond, in our above example, to the E-term.

But we have no right to make this assumption. Of course, any given antecedent condition of B which fulfilled the conditions for the description 'requiring B for G' (let us call this T) would also fulfil some other 'intrinsic' description, E. But this is not to say that B's occurring is a function of E's occurring, i.e. that B depends on E. For it may be that in other circumstances a situation which fulfils the description E is not followed by B, the circumstances being precisely those in which the situation does not also fulfil the conditions for the description T; whereas all cases of T may be followed by B. Thus in our above example, it may be that the key stimuli we isolate in one case may impinge on the receptors of our predator in other contexts without inducing stalking behaviour; and this may happen in just those contexts where such an action would not bring about the goal of getting food. Now in such circumstances we would not say that B depended on E, but rather on T. The correlation $E - B$ would be explained by means of $T - B$, and could be derived from this law together with a statement of the conditions in which $E - B$ holds, $E = T$. When the antecedent in a teleological type law T is replaced by a non-teleological antecedent E, the assumption is that all cases of T which are followed by B are cases of E. But whether this is so or not is an empirical matter. We have no guarantee *a priori* that we shall discover an 'intrinsic' characterization E which will apply to all cases of T (assuming for the sake of simplicity that $T - B$ holds invariably[9]), and which will never apply to a case which is not followed by B. Of course, we might be able to discover a disjunction of such descriptions, E, F, G, etc., but there is no reason *a priori* why this list should be finite. A similar objection applies to Nagel's proposed translations. There is no guarantee that a finite list of laws of the form, $An - By - Cq$, etc., which will cover the phenomena, i.e., enable us to make the predictions which we now make with teleological laws, can be found. Whether this is so or not must be discovered empirically. But if it is not, we cannot be held to have replaced the teleological law. On the contrary we will have to explain the fact that these rules of thumb hold when they do in terms of this law.

---

[8] I have paraphrased and greatly compressed Nagel's account, but I hope done no violence to it.

[9] By 'invariably' is meant here not necessarily every time, but such that the exceptions can be cogently explained by interfering factors.

The belief that the regularities cited in teleological type explanations must also be accountable for in terms of non-teleological laws is a manifestation of the tendency on the part of those who are opposed to the view that organisms have a special status to assume the problems away and to close an empirical question with a logical clasp.[10] And once we see that this assumption is an empirical one, we can see what is wrong with the atomist position. For the proposed translation using only intrinsic terms is not another, epistemologically sounder, way of stating the evidence for the teleological law; it is a rival account of the matter; it differs in meaning and in the evidence required to substantiate it. For what is claimed by the teleological explanation is that what occurs is a function of what is required for the system's end, G, that an event's being required for G is a sufficient condition of its happening, whereas the proposed 'translation' offers us a quite different sufficient condition. And which claim is correct is an empirical question, that is to say, the evidence required for the one is not the same as that required for the other. Whether the stringent atomist requirement can be met by all valid laws, then, is itself an empirical question, which hinges partly on the question whether all teleological explanation—or any other type of explanation which involves holistic assumptions—can be done away with. It cannot be decided by epistemological fiat, by a rule to the effect that the evidence for teleological laws must be such that it can be stated by means of non-teleological laws.

But we have perhaps discovered part of the answer to our question. It would seem plausible to conclude that one of the reasons for the widespread belief that explanations involving 'purpose' required the postulation of some special entity is the hold of atomist assumptions. For atomism in effect rules out teleological explanation and thus also the possibility of construing purposiveness as a feature of the whole system and its manner of operation. On the contrary, since all laws hold between discrete entities intrinsically characterized, then to invoke a purpose must be to postulate some new discrete entity as a causal antecedent. This seems the only interpretation of explanation by purpose which can fit the epistemological requirements. But, of course, it violates these requirements in another way, for this entity is unobservable, and so the whole enterprise is doomed from the start. But once we examine the assumptions on which this rests we can see that this interpretation is not forced on us.

The influence of atomism can also be seen in the common misinterpretation of teleological explanation as explanation in terms of a correlation between intrinsically characterized terms which has the peculiarity that the antecedent comes after the consequent. Thus while an ordinary type law is of the form $A - B$, where A, the antecedent, comes before B, the consequent, a teleological

---

[10] Something of the same features may perhaps be observed in [R. B.—Ed.] Braithwaite's account, *Scientific Explanation*, Chapter X. Braithwaite, too, speaks of a variety of chains which, starting from different points, all end in the same final state. But the point of teleological explanation is not the co-incidence of different antecedents having the same consequent, but the type of antecedent involved.

law is of the form $G — B$, where the occurrence of B is explained by the result G which follows from it. Thus [C. L.—Ed.] Hull, in his *Principles of Behaviour*, holds that:

> In its extreme form teleology is the name of the belief that the *terminal* stage of certain environmental-organismic interaction cycles somehow is at the same time one of the antecedents determining conditions which bring the behaviour cycle about.[11]

And, thus interpreted, teleological explanations can be shown to be of no value because we cannot determine whether the antecedent conditions of behaviour obtain until after it has happened. Thus:

> In effect this means that the task of deduction cannot begin until after it is completed! Naturally this leaves the theorist completely helpless.[12]

Thus once again the whole enterprise can be shown to be misguided. And once again this demonstration is based on an arbitrary interpretation. For this is, of course, a travesty of teleological explanation. In a teleological law the antecedent of an event is not the result which follows but the state of affairs obtaining prior to it in which this event is what must happen if the result is to ensue. The whole idea that teleological explanation is like causal explanation in that it uses correlations between separate events but unlike it in that the time order is reversed, i.e., the antecedent comes after the consequent,[13] is mistaken. Because it is not necessarily a counter-example to a teleological correlation if the event first in time (the B-event) does not occur, while that second in time, G, does; that is, comes about by accident or through some cause outside the system. And a case where the first (B) occurs without the second (G) may still be taken as evidence for the correlation if, say, some factor interferes to prevent G at the last moment; whereas this case would have no relevance to a correlation of the form $G — B$. This misrepresentation of teleological explanation seems to be based on atomist assumptions which involve the rejection of what is in fact the antecedent term in teleological laws, and the construction of these as holding between discrete entities, i.e., entities which meet the stringent requirement for independent specifiability. The peculiarity of teleological explanation, that it accounts for the events by final causes, by that for the sake of which they happen, is then construed as a reversal of the usual time order. The goal or final cause is cast as an ordinary antecedent causal condition which happens to come after what it brings about. The whole thing has a most bizarre air, and the temptation to reject it out of hand becomes overwhelming.

Both here and in the interpretation above of purpose as an 'unobservable entity', atomism has stacked the cards against those who maintain that animate beings show a type of behaviour radically different from other processes in nature. The only way to make any progress in this question is to reject its assumptions and start afresh.

---

[11] P. 26. Hull's emphasis.
[12] Loc. cit.
[13] Cf. Braithwaite, *Scientific Explanation*, p. 337.

4. The Asymmetry of Explanation

Some progress has, perhaps, already been made. The claim is that animate beings are special in that the order visible in their behaviour must itself enter into an explanation of how this order comes about. This can in part be expressed by the claim that the events which bring about or constitute this order are to be accounted for in terms of final causes, as occurring 'for the sake of' the order which ensues. Now this claim is not inherently 'mystical' or non-empirical in nature, and nor does it entail postulating any unobservable entities. It involves, in part, the thesis that the laws by which we explain the behavior of these organisms are teleological in form, and whether the laws which hold of a system are or are not of this kind is an empirical question.

But although not inherently 'mystical', this claim does involve some features which are *prima facie* at variance with certain common views about scientific procedure. Thus an explanation of a teleological type does involve the assumption that the system concerned 'naturally' or inherently tends towards a certain result, condition or end; for the principle of laws of this kind is that an event's being required for this end is a sufficient condition of its occurring. But in this we seem to be reverting (some would say, regressing) to a pre-Galilean form of explanation in terms of 'powers'. Much discredit, not to say ridicule, has been cast on this form of explanation. One has only to think of the merciless attack by Molière on the medical profession of his day in *Le Malade Imaginaire* [*The Imaginary Invalid*—Ed.]. On being asked for the

> 'causam et rationem quare
> opium facit dormire',
> [reason opium puts one to sleep—Ed.]

the protagonist replies:

> 'quia est in eo
> virtus dormitiva,
> cujus est natura
> sensus assoupire';
> [Because of its dormative power—Ed.]

this to the applause of the assembled doctors'.

But these very just strictures on verbal non-empirical explanations do not show that this way of talking is always absurd. It is so, as we have seen, if the reference to 'powers' is meant as the identification of a causal antecedent. And this was the kind of case which Molière chose. For the supposed antecedent, like Purpose or Entelechy, can never be observed. But, as we mentioned above, the appeal to 'powers' or 'natural tendencies' can be a way of attributing certain properties to the system as a whole and its manner of operation, and this can be empirically verified.

But the appeal to 'natural' or 'inherent' tendencies, although not empty, does involve some of the other traditional features of pre-Galilean explanation which have been no less frowned on. It involves, for instance, the assumption that the basic level of explanation has been reached. For the claim that a system is purposive is a claim about the laws holding at the most basic level of explanation.

The distinction between levels of explanation can be made in the following way: If explanation is conceived here as explanation in terms of a functional law, then an explanation can be considered as less basic than another when the regularities which the laws cited in the first describe are themselves explained in terms of the laws cited in the second. Thus if the behaviour of a system can be explained by the laws $y = f_1(z)$ and laws $y = f_2(x)$, where 'x' and 'z' range over different domains, we can call the second explanation more basic if the fact that laws $y = f_1(z)$ hold of the system can be explained in terms of $y = f_2(x)$. Thus the behaviour of gas in a container can be explained by Boyle's Law, and also in terms of the Kinetic Theory of Gases, but it is the second explanation which is the more basic.

Why we should be concerned with explanation at the more basic level is clear once we see what it is for the regularities described in one set of laws to be explained by another. This is sometimes interpreted as meaning that the first set of laws can be deduced from the second which are at the same time more general in their application.[14] But this interpretation obviously cannot apply here because a set of laws which are purposive in character, i.e., describe the behaviour as tending towards a certain condition, cannot be *deduced* from a set of laws which are non-purposive. We are dealing here with 'explanation' in a stronger sense, in which the less basic laws $y = f_1(z)$ can be derived not from the more basic $y = f_2(x)$ alone, but from these together with some other contingent statement of 'initial conditions' which ensure that z is related in some way to x. What this strong type of explanation gives us which the weaker one did not is the set of conditions on which the behaviour of the system depends, and this increases our ability to exercise control over it or, at least, if our technology is inadequate, to predict changes in it.[15] Thus we can say that the set of laws $y = f_2(x)$ is more basic than $y = f_1(z)$, for the former provides us with the conditions in which the latter will apply or not apply, so that we know how to construct systems exemplifying it, or at least when to predict of any system that it will exemplify it.

---

[14] I.e., other laws can be deduced from them or other evidence is relevant to them. Cf. Braithwaite; *Scientific Explanation*, pp. 300–3.

[15] This feature of explanation seems to be ignored by many philosophers of the empiricist school, who tend to confine their account to the weaker sense of the term. Thus Braithwaite: *Scientific Explanation*, pp. 302–3, accepts the proposition 'all animals are mortal' as an explanation of 'all men are mortal,' because the second can be deduced from the first, and at the same time the evidence for the first is not confined to the second; for we also know that horses, dogs, etc., are mortal. But this is only an explanation in the weaker sense, for it adds nothing to our knowledge of the conditions for men dying. For the statement of 'initial conditions' which permits the derivation of explicandum from explicans is itself a necessary proposition, 'all men are animals.' But this is surely a caricature of explanation in science where the type of discovery implied in the stronger form has been so much in evidence with such amazing results in control over our environment. (If all scientific explanation had been of the form suggested by Braithwaite's example we would still be living in a pre-technological age.)

Now it is clear that the claim that the behaviour of a system must be accounted for in terms of purpose or 'natural' or 'inherent' tendencies concerns the laws which hold at the most basic level of explanation. For a more basic explanation can be said to set out the regularities on which those cited in the less basic depend. $y = f_1(z)$ is true because $y = f_2(x)$ is true of the system, that is, the former can come to apply or not to apply to the system because the latter constantly applies to it. But if $y = f_1(z)$ is teleological in character and $y = f_2(x)$ is not, then the tendency towards a certain condition or state described in the first set could itself be shown to depend on the fact that the behaviour of the system is a function of those factors set out in $y = f_2(x)$. Thus we could construct a mechanical dog, programmed to behave like a real one. In this case the laws descriptive of his external behaviour $[y = f(_1z)]$ would be teleological like those of his real counterpart, they would characterize the behaviour as 'goal-directed', but the more basic explanation $[y = f_2(x)]$ would not. With systems of this kind we can hardly speak of an account in terms of 'natural' or 'inherent' tendencies. What we have in effect is the fact of the convergence of events towards a certain result which in turn is accounted for on quite different principles. We could account for the behaviour of such a system without using anything like the notion of purpose or tendency and without losing at all, but on the contrary gaining, in explanatory or predictive power or the capacity to control it. Those who claim a special status for animate organisms on the grounds that the order evident in their behaviour must be accounted for in terms of a tendency or 'purpose' of the events to realize this order could hardly hold that their claim had been vindicated by an explanation of this kind, where the tendency to realize the given order could itself be accounted for by other factors.[16]

Thus the claim that 'the purposes' of a system are of such and such a kind affects the laws which hold at the most basic level. In other words, it is incompatible with the view that the natural tendency towards a certain condition

---

[16] The issue is confused in this way by some thinkers in the field of cybernetics research who adopt a usage of 'purposive' and 'teleological' such that it can be applied without change of sense to animate beings and to machines which have been designed to imitate them. Thus [Arturo—Ed.] Rosenblueth and [Norbert—Ed.] Wiener, in their discussion with Taylor, *Philosophy of Science*, 1950: 'if the notion of purpose is applicable to living organisms, it is also applicable to non-living entities when they show the same observable traits of behaviour." But if this is the only sense given to 'purpose' then the claim that animate organisms are radically different cannot be stated, or else it must be interpreted as the obviously untrue claim that machines cannot be devised which show the same 'observable traits'. And this is not part of what is meant when people say that humans and animals are different from non-living entities. The distinction concerns not certain features of the observable behaviour but rather the laws which account for the behaviour at a more basic level. There is a widespread belief that just this distinction holds between animals and machines imitating them. Whether this is so or not is, of course, the point at issue. But this question is prejudged if we apply the notion 'purposive' to either case indiscriminately. This redefinition of 'purposive' would be permissible only if it were true that the class of systems of which the notion in its ordinary sense, that in which it refers to the most basic laws, holds was the null class, which, of course, is exactly what Rosenblueth and Wiener assume. In fact our usual notion of purpose cannot properly be applied except in a metaphorical way to machines. . . .

can itself be accounted for by other laws. Thus the function of an explanation invoking powers or natural tendencies can be precisely to shut off further enquiry. And this is why it is absurd when it is taken as an attempt to state some antecedent. For the fact that a tendency towards a given condition results in this condition neither requires nor admits of further explanation. It is, rather, the break-down of such a 'correlation' which stands in need of explanation. And this logical feature of an account in terms of powers which makes it a block to further enquiry is also the one which unfits it to serve itself as an empirical law linking two terms. On the contrary, it can serve only to characterize the type of laws which hold of the system.

Now this claim to have reached the rock bottom of explanation is not one which is usually made in scientific theory, the possibility always being left open, however unlikely it may seem, that another set of laws will be discovered which are more basic. In this way, therefore, teleological explanation represents a deviation from the modern norm and a throw-back to an earlier type of explanation.

The block to further enquiry is connected with another feature of pre-Galilean forms, viz., their assumption of an asymmetry of explanation. This is implicit in what has been said above. In holding that the most basic laws are such that a sufficient condition of an event's happening is that it be required for a certain goal, that the tendency towards this result cannot be accounted for by other, more basic, laws, teleological explanation places one result among those which are ideally possible for the system in a special position. For that the system achieves this result-condition neither calls for nor admits of explanation; but should it achieve any other condition, we are bound to give an account. For the second type of result, being at odds with the tendency of the system, must, if the theory is correct, be accounted for by some special interfering factor. Thus we usually explain abnormal behaviour by invoking fatigue, sickness, alcohol, nervous strain, or some such special condition. The adducing of an interfering factor here differs from the ordinary cases, not involving teleological laws, where this is done. If we explain a breakdown in the correlation $A — B$, by adducing the interfering factor I, both the correlations $A — B$ and $A + I$—not-B can be accounted for by the same set of laws. But in this case, the fact that the system brings about the result towards which it tends cannot be further accounted for, and *a fortiori* not by the same set of laws by which we account for the link between the interfering factor and some other result. Thus, if we were dealing with some non-teleological system, say, a machine designed to imitate animal behaviour, then the difference between normal and non-normal operation could be explained by the same set of laws in terms of different programming of the mechanism. But if we are dealing with a species of live animals (according to the usual hypothesis) then there is no set of more basic laws by which we can explain their tendency to emit the behaviour in question. In other words, granted the existence of animals of this species, there are no antecedent conditions for their normal behaviour—unless one wants to count the absence of all lesions, drugs, and any other factors producing abnormality as an antecedent—but any abnormal result has some special factor to which it is traceable. And thus the normal operation of the system, i.e., the occurrence of events which result in the normal condition is accounted for by teleological laws, while any abnormal functioning must bring in a set of laws linking interfering factors and non-normal conditions which are not teleological.[17] And this is the basis for the distinction between 'normal' and 'abnormal' itself, between the 'natural' result and the 'unnatural' ones, that the two must be accounted for in quite different ways; that there exists, in other words, an asymmetry of explanation.

Now this is recognizably a pre-Galilean feature; one has only to think of the distinction between 'natural' and 'violent' movement in pre-Galilean physics.[18] And this is often enough to discredit this form of explanation with many thinkers, for whom the principles laid down by Galileo are binding on all scientific thought. And, indeed, the gap between teleological explanation and that in vogue in modern physical science can be seen if we compare principles of asymmetry with their modern analogues. The term 'principle' is apposite here because asymmetry plays something of the kind of role in a teleological science of behaviour that Inertia does, for instance, in Newtonian physics. In both cases the principles serve to make clear the kinds of event for which an antecedent must be adduced and the kinds of event for which this is not the case. For Newton's first Law, the continuation of a body at rest or in uniform rectilinear motion did not admit of explanation in this sense, only changes in velocity were to be accounted for. Continued rest or rectilinear motion could be spoken of in this sense as 'natural'. This represented, of course, a radical change from Aristotelian science which held that continued motion must always be accounted for by a mover.

But this analogy serves to show the importance of the dis-analogy. For the Principle of Inertia is 'neutral' in an important sense in which a principle of asymmetry is not. That is, it is not part of what is asserted by the Principle of Inertia that, for any system, one particular condition or set of results is natural. The Principle of Inertia does not single out any particular direction in which bodies 'naturally' tend to move or any constellation which they tend to move towards. And thus it can be said to be neutral between the different states of any system of which it may be invoked to explain the behaviour (that is, where the theory of which it is one of the foundations is invoked). But this cannot be said of a principle of asymmetry, whose function is precisely to distinguish a privileged state or result.

The point could be put in this way: The analogy between the Principle of Inertia and the various principles of asymmetry which preceded it, specifying the 'natural kinds' and their natural tendencies, lies in the fact that both are used to define the type of event which requires an explanation; for the latter

---

[17] For the specification of an intervening factor would be different from that of an antecedent in a teleological law, i.e., the factor would not be characterized as a state of affairs requiring B for G.

[18] Perhaps we should say here 'pre-Newtonian', for Galileo did not entirely free himself from the language of his predecessors. His reputation as a pioneer, however, has taken on such a symbolic importance among those who discuss these questions as to justify the use of his name in this context.

motion, and for the former only changes in velocity. But there is another sense of 'requiring an explanation,' that is, an explanation in terms of external forces, in which a principle of asymmetry distinguishes between the type of movement a given body can make, so that only movement in certain *directions* requires an explanation. And this is the disanalogy: That a principle of asymmetry does distinguish between different states of a system where it is invoked in explanation, that it is not neutral between different results.

'Natural' movements are only a sub-class of those requiring explanation. In this sense the natural course of events is reversible. And yet it is the 'natural' course, that is, that this goal or condition is reached does not admit of further explanation, but on the contrary, the tendency towards it must be itself invoked in explaining the system's behaviour. Thus teleological explanation gives us a notion of 'tendency towards' a given condition which involves more than simply the universal and exceptionless movement of events in that direction. For, like Inertia, it concerns not so much how the events move as how they must be accounted for however they move. And yet unlike Inertia it holds that a particular result in a given system is privileged, that, in other words, this result will be brought about unless countervailing factors arise. And thus the notion arises not just of an empirically discovered direction of events, but of a bent or pressure of events towards a certain consummation, one which can only be checked by some countervailing force. This, then, is the force of the notion of 'power' or 'natural tendency', not the *de facto* trend of events, but rather a press of events, which lies behind the view that order exhibited in the behaviour of living organisms does not come about by 'accident', but is somehow part of their 'essential nature'.[19]

We can see, then, why this view is resisted, for the result of the Galilean

---

[19] The principle of asymmetry seems to be invoked in a doctrine held by some thinkers: e.g., R. S. Peters, *The Concept of Motivation*, pp. 9–16; cf. also D. W. Hamlyn, *The Psychology of Perception*, about the role of causal explanations in terms of the physiological substratum in accounting for behaviour. These causal factors are held to be *necessary* but not *sufficient* conditions of behaviour. They do provide, however, 'sufficient conditions for breakdowns in performance, as in the case of brain lesions, by indicating a necessary condition which was absent'. Peters, op. cit., p. 16. This might be interpreted as the thesis that the normal operation of the organism follows teleological laws. We can therefore never give sufficient conditions for normal behaviour in terms of 'causal' (i.e., non-teleological) antecedent conditions, whether these be physiological or of any other kind. But we can so account for breakdowns or non-natural functioning. The negations of these causal conditions for breakdown, then, are conditions for the normal functioning. But these being 'causal' (i.e., non-teleological) are not sufficient conditions, but only conditions *sine qua non*.

Thus the existence and freedom from damage of certain organs may be a necessary condition for certain behaviour. But a sufficient condition would be a state of these organs together with states of others and the environment which constituted together an antecedent of a teleological type. Without the existence and capacity to function of these organs such a global state couldn't exist, but the existence of the organ is not the cause of the state (its sufficient condition) and therefore not the cause (the sufficient condition) of the behaviour either. The widespread assumption that, because certain physiological states are *necessary* conditions of behaviour, behaviour must be accounted for by non-teleological physiological laws involves an illegitimate inference.

revolution was precisely to sweep away all the asymmetries of Aristotelian science, between 'natural' and 'violent' movement, between sub- and supra-lunar events, and so on, and to replace them by a homogeneous science of nature in which all the differences could be accounted for in terms of the same set of antecedent variables. But, although understandable, the resistance is not thereby necessarily justified. For whether or not an explanation of a teleological sort holds is plainly an empirical matter. And therefore whether the principle of asymmetry is valid and whether the most basic laws are of this sort are also empirical questions. The inadequacy of Aristotelian physics lay not in any inherent absurdity, but in its gross inadequacy in accounting for natural events. But to assume from the superiority of Galilean principles in the sciences of inanimate nature that they *must* provide the model for the sciences of animate behaviour is to make a speculative leap, not to enunciate a necessary conclusion.

Bibliography

ACHINSTEIN, PETER. *Concepts of Science.* Baltimore: Johns Hopkins University Press, 1968.

——. *Law and Explanation.* New York: Oxford University Press, 1971.

——, and STEPHEN F. BARKER (eds.). *The Legacy of Logical Positivism.* Baltimore: Johns Hopkins University Press, 1969.

BARKER, S. F. *Induction and Hypothesis.* Ithaca, N.Y.: Cornell University Press, 1957.

BAUMRIN, BERNARD (ed.). *Philosophy of Science* (The Delaware Seminar, II, 1962–1963). New York: Interscience, 1963.

BEAUCHAMP, TOM L. (ed.). *Philosophical Problems of Causation.* Encino, Calif.: Dickenson, 1974.*

BERGMANN, GUSTAV. *Philosophy of Science.* Madison: University of Wisconsin Press, 1957.

BEROFSKY, BERNARD. *Determinism.* Princeton: Princeton University Press, 1971.

BORGER, R., and F. CIOFFI (eds.). *Explanation in the Behavioural Sciences.* Cambridge: Cambridge University Press, 1970.†

BRAITHWAITE, R. B. *Scientific Explanation.* Cambridge: Cambridge University Press, 1963.

BUNGE, MARIO. *Causality.* Cambridge: Harvard University Press, 1959.

CAMPBELL, NORMAN R. *What Is Science?* New York: Dover, 1952.*

DANTO, ARTHUR, and SIDNEY MORGEN-BESSER (eds.). *Philosophy of Science.* New York: Meridian Books, 1960.*

DRAY, WILLIAM. *Laws and Explanation in History.* New York: Oxford University Press, 1957.

FEIGL, HERBERT, and MAY BRODBECK (eds.). *Readings in the Philosophy of Science.* New York: Appleton-Century-Crofts, 1953.

——, and MICHAEL SCRIVEN (eds.). *Minnesota Studies in the Philosophy of Science,* I. Minneapolis: University of Minnesota Press, 1956.

——, ——, and GROVER MAXWELL (eds.). *Minnesota Studies in the Philosophy of Science,* II. Minneapolis: University of Minnesota Press, 1958.

——, and GROVER MAXWELL (eds.). *Minnesota Studies in the Philosophy of Science,* III. Minneapolis: University of Minnesota Press, 1962.

FEYERABEND, PAUL. *Against Method.* London: NLB, 1975.

——, and GROVER MAXWELL (eds.). *Mind, Matter, and Method.* Minneapolis: University of Minnesota Press, 1966.

FRANK, PHILIPP. *Philosophy of Science.* Englewood Cliffs, N.J.: Prentice-Hall, 1962.

GARDINER, PATRICK (ed.). *The Philosophy of History.* London: Oxford University Press, 1974.

GOODMAN, NELSON. *Fact, Fiction, and Forecast* (2nd ed.). Indianapolis: Bobbs-Merrill, 1965.*

HANSON, NORWOOD RUSSELL. *Patterns of Discovery.* Cambridge: Cambridge University Press, 1958.*

——. *Observation and Explanation.* New York: Harper Torchbooks, 1971.*

HARRÉ, R. *The Principles of Scientific Thinking.* Chicago: University of Chicago Press, 1970.

HART, H. L. A., and A. M. HONORÉ. *Causation and the Law.* Oxford: Clarendon, 1959.

HEMPEL, CARL G. *Philosophy of Natural Science.* Englewood Cliffs, N.J.: Prentice-Hall, 1966.*

---

* Paperback edition.   † Also available in paperback edition.

————. *Aspects of Scientific Explanation and Other Essays in the Philosophy of Science*. New York: Free Press, 1965.

HESSE, MARY B. *Models and Analogies in Science*. London: Sheed & Ward, 1963.†

KAHN, RUSSELL (ed.). *Studies in Explanation*. Englewood Cliffs, N.J.: Prentice-Hall, 1963.

KNEALE, WILLIAM. *Probability and Induction*. Oxford: Clarendon, 1949.

KUHN, THOMAS S. *The Structure of Scientific Revolutions* (2nd ed., enl.). Chicago: University of Chicago Press, 1963, 1970.*

KYBURG, HENRY E., JR. "Recent Work in Inductive Logic," *American Philosophical Quarterly*, I (1964), 249–287.

KYBURG, HENRY E., JR., and ERNEST NAGEL (eds.). *Induction: Some Current Issues*. Middletown, Conn.: Wesleyan University Press, 1963.

MACKIE, J. L. *The Cement of the Universe*. Oxford: Clarendon, 1974.

NAGEL, ERNEST. "Principles of the Theory of Probability." *International Encyclopedia of Unified Science*. Vol. I, No. 6. Chicago: University of Chicago Press, 1939.*

————. *The Structure of Science*. New York: Harcourt Brace Jovanovich, 1961.

————, PATRICK SUPPES, and ALFRED TARSKI (eds.). *Logic, Methodology and Philosophy of Science*. Stanford, Calif.: Stanford University Press, 1962.

NEURATH, OTTO, et al. (eds.). *Foundations of the Unity of Science* (Vols. I–II, International Encyclopedia of Unified Science). Chicago: University of Chicago Press, 1938.*

NIDDITCH, P. H. (ed.). *The Philosophy of Science*. London: Oxford University Press, 1968.*

PAP, ARTHUR. *An Introduction to the Philosophy of Science*. New York: Free Press, 1962.

POPPER, KARL. *The Logic of Scientific Discovery*. London: Hutchinson, 1959.†

REICHENBACH, H. *Experience and Prediction*. Chicago: University of Chicago Press, 1938.

RESCHER, NICHOLAS. *Scientific Explanation*. New York: Free Press, 1970.

RUDNER, RICHARD S. *Philosophy of Social Science*. Englewood Cliffs, N.J.: Prentice-Hall, 1966.*

RYAN, ALAN (ed.). *The Philosophy of Social Explanation*. London: Oxford University Press, 1973.*

SCHEFFLER, ISRAEL. *The Anatomy of Inquiry*. New York: Knopf, 1963.

————. *Science and Subjectivity*. Indianapolis: Bobbs-Merrill, 1967.*

SKYRMS, BRIAN. *Choice and Chance*. Belmont, Calif.: Dickenson, 1966.*

SOSA, ERNEST (ed.). *Causation and Conditionals*. London: Oxford University Press, 1975.*

SUPPÉ, FREDERICK (ed.). *The Structure of Scientific Theory*. Urbana, Ill.: University of Illinois Press, 1974.

SWINBURNE, RICHARD (ed.). *The Justification of Induction*. London: Oxford University Press, 1973.*

VON WRIGHT, G. H. *Explanation and Understanding*. Ithaca, N.Y.: Cornell University Press, 1971.

WALLACE, WILLIAM A. *Causality and Scientific Explanation*, Vols. 1–2. Ann Arbor: University of Michigan Press, 1972.

INDEX

References to entire selections are given in italics.

Abduction, 434
Aboutness, 14
Accidental property, 250–251
Acquaintance, 486
Actions, 550, *635–647* passim
Agnoiology, 204
"Agreement" with reality, 263, 264, 270–271
Analytic, 234, 236, 237, 240–248 passim
Analytic-for-L, 242–243
Analytic/synthetic, 158–159, 160, 234, 245, 429
  Kant on, *215–223*
Analyticity, 234, 236–237, 240–245 passim, 459
Animals
  language of, 417, 420
  languageless, 314, 406–407, 417
Animation, 29, 31
Anscombe, G. E. M., 640
Antiphon, 583
a posteriori, 159, 246, 248, 571
  Kant on, *215–223* passim
a priori, 159, 227–230 passim, 246–249 passim, 475, 551, *557–562* passim
  Kant on, *215–223* passim
Aprioricity, 246, 255
Aquinas, St. Thomas, 13, 14
Argument from analogy
  Malcolm on, *134–141* passim
  Russell on, *117–121*
Argument from illusion, 375–381
Aristotle, 3, 7, 13, 14, 235, 266, 315, 383, *552–553*, *582–594*, 641, 642, 644
Art, 584, 585
Artificial language, 242, 244
Assertion, 279, 535
Atomism, 117, 118, *654–658*
Attributes, 12–16 passim, 118
  functional, 13
Augustine, St., 196, 412–413
Austin, J. L., 3, 158, 276–277, *277–288*, 312, *375–381*, 428, 462, *510–518*, 531
  Strawson on, *289–306*
Automata, 119
Axiom of existence, 531

Axioms, 227–228
Ayer, A. J., 109, 176, *176–180*, 192, 312, *355–361*, 453

Bacon, Francis, 572
Bacon's Prerogative Instances, 231
Bain, A., 123, 124, 127–128
Basic particulars, 256
Behaviorism, 33–34, 107–108, 404
Belief, 156, 161, 434–436
  Chisholm on, *194–203* passim
  Malcolm on, *181–191* passim
Bentham, Jeremy, 224
Berkeley, George, 123, 311, 319, 330, *330–345*
Berlin Group, 449
Black, Max, 68, 71, 72
Body
  Descartes on, *18–27* passim
  Ryle on, *33–42* passim
  Strawson on, *84–102* passim
Boyle, Robert, 386
Bradley, F. H., 117, 118
Brentano, Franz, 13–14, 122, *122–133*, 194
Bridgman, P., 444
British Hegelianism, 117
Broad, C. D., 12, 28, *28–33*
Brouwer, L. E. J., 527
Brown, Roger, 417, 420
Brown, Thomas, 602
"Bundle of ideas," 76, 131

Cantor, Georg, 528
Cardaillac, J. J., 130
Carnap, Rudolf, 56, 67, 144, 236, 237, 242, 244, 432, 441, 445, 454–455, 459, 462, 471, 527, 570, 620, 632
Cartesian problem, 12–13
Cartesianism, 33, 95
Category mistake, 33, 34, 37–42
Causal interaction, 12
  Broad on, *28–33*
Causal laws, 550, *610–615*
Causality, 552, 553, 555, *595–600* passim, 602–603

671

About the Author

Joseph Margolis is Professor of Philosophy, Temple University. He has taught widely in the United States and Canada. He is the author of some twelve books and numerous articles. His most recent book is *Persons and Minds* (1977); *Art and Philosophy* is forthcoming. Professor Margolis has also initiated a publishing venture, PHILOSOPHICAL MONOGRAPHS, addressed to the needs of the philosophical profession.

A Note on the Type

This book is set in Electra, a Linotype face designed by W. A. Dwiggins. This face cannot be classified as either modern or old-style. It is not based on any historical model, nor does it echo any particular period or style. It avoids the extreme contrasts between thick and thin elements that mark most modern faces, and attempts to give a feeling of fluidity, power, and speed.

Book design by Brenda Kamen
Cover design by Carole Lowenstein